Poverty, Inequality, and Inclusive Growth in Asia

Measurement, Policy Issues, and Country Studies

Poverty, Inequality, and Inclusive Growth in Asia

Measurement, Policy Issues, and Country Studies

Edited by

Juzhong Zhuang

A copublication of the Asian Development Bank and Anthem Press

Anthem Press
www.anthempress.com

Asian Development Bank
www.adb.org

This edition first published in 2011 by

ANTHEM PRESS
75–76 Blackfriars Road
London SE1 8HA, UK
or PO Box 9779, London SW19 7ZG, UK
and 244 Madison Ave. #116, New York,
NY 10016, USA

and
Asian Development Bank
6 ADB Avenue, Mandaluyong City, 1550
Metro Manila, Philippines

British Library Cataloguing-in-Publication Data
A catalogue record for this book is available from the British Library.

Library Congress Cataloging-in-Publication Data
Poverty, inequality, and inclusive growth in Asia : measurement,
policy issues, and country studies / edited by Juzhong Zhuang.
p. cm.
Includes bibliographical references and index.
ISBN 978-0-85728-414-3 (pbk. : alk. paper)
1. Poverty–Asia. 2. Equality–Asia. 3. Income distribution–Asia.
4. Economic development–Social aspects–Asia. 5. Asia–Economic
policy. 6. Asia–Social policy. 7. Asia–Economic conditions–1945-
I. Zhuang, Juzhong. II. Asian Development Bank.
HC415.P6P6854 2010
338.95–dc23
2011030266

ISBN-13: 978 0 85728 414 3 (Pbk)
ISBN-10: 0 85728 414 2 (Pbk)

Contents

1 Poverty, Inequality, and Inclusive Growth in Asia

Juzhong Zhuang and Ifzal Ali

Part A. Measuring Inequality and Poverty   33

2 Inequality and Poverty in Asia

J. Salcedo Cain, Rana Hasan, and Rhoda Magsombol

3 Non-Income Poverty and Inequality in Asia

Ajay Tandon and Susan Sparkes

Foreword

T he single biggest policy challenge facing Asia is how to sustain rapid economic growth that reduces poverty and is socially inclusive and environmentally sustainable. The challenges—and opportunities—are all the greater given rapid population growth in much of the region, the need to rebalance growth in light of the global financial crisis, and the multiple challenges of responding to climate change. This timely book brings together some of the latest research and findings on poverty reduction, inequality, and conceptual and policy issues of inclusive growth in Asia.

The book highlights Asia's remarkable economic achievements. Between 1990 and 2008, the region's per capita gross domestic product (GDP) increased almost three-fold, expanding 5.7% a year.[1] Growth was most pronounced in East Asia, at over 8% a year, driven largely by the People's Republic of China (PRC). It was also solid in many countries in Southeast Asia—where the shock of the 1997/98 financial crisis was particularly strong—and, more recently, in India. But per capita GDP growth was nowhere near as robust elsewhere. The economy of Central and West Asia grew just 1.3% annually over 1990–2008, and the Pacific only 0.3%.

In much of Asia, rapid growth has improved the livelihoods of vast numbers of people. The percentage of people living below the $1.25-a-day poverty line[2] fell from 52.3% in 1990 to 27.1% in 2005. The poverty reduction was the largest in the PRC, where it fell from 60.2% in 1990 to 15.9% in 2005, but it was also significant in many other countries.

But the region still faces tremendous challenges in eradicating poverty. It remains home to two-thirds of the world's poor: 1.8 billion people living on less than $2 a day, with 903 million struggling on less than $1.25 a day. Analysis of the Asian Development Bank (ADB) suggests that the fallout from recent crises—first, soaring energy and food crises, followed by the slump in the global economy and financial markets—may have prevented tens of millions of Asians from escaping poverty. Moreover, many Asians live just above the poverty line and are therefore highly vulnerable to economic and other shocks that could easily tip them back into poverty.

Equally disturbing is the fact that, despite decades of strong growth, suffering remains high on other planes too, as shown by a number of key social indicators. Malnutrition among children under five years of age is worse in Asia than in sub-Saharan Africa. More than half of Asians live without basic sanitation and the region is still home to the largest number of people infected with tuberculosis. Women and children—already disproportionately represented among the poor and vulnerable—bear the brunt: 41% of all deaths of children under five years, 44% of maternal deaths, and 56% of newborn baby deaths occur in this region.

---

1   Measured in 2005 purchasing power parity and weighted by population.
2   Based on 2005 purchasing power parity.

Rising inequality, in both income and non-income dimensions, is an emerging and important concern. The book shows that a large number of developing Asian countries have seen their Gini coefficient—a measure of income inequality—increase in recent decades. Unequal access to basic social services such as education and health is also persistently high, exacerbated by income inequality. In part, as the book explains, rising inequality could reflect the fact that economic development and structural transformation are likely to entail processes that increase inequality. But much of it is due to market and policy failures, governance and institutional weaknesses, and social exclusion.

All these suggest that the benefits of Asia's rapid economic growth need to be shared more widely. More and more developing Asian countries are therefore embracing the concept of inclusive growth, and exploring ways and policy options to distribute more equitably the fruits of economic expansion. ADB, in its recently adopted long-term strategic framework, Strategy 2020, vowed to focus on inclusive economic growth, environmentally sustainable growth, and regional integration as three critical strategic agendas in supporting its developing member countries in Asia and the Pacific in the coming decade.

This book brings together the findings of recent research on inclusive growth carried out by ADB staff and their collaborators. It presents a conceptual framework for inclusive growth, provides measures of poverty and inequality in Asia, examines policy options, and looks at country experiences. In this book, inclusive growth is defined as "growth coupled with equality of opportunity", with three policy pillars: creating productive employment and economic opportunities through high, efficient, and sustained economic growth; promoting equal access to the opportunities by investing in human capacity and leveling the playing field; and improving social safety nets to mitigate risks and vulnerability and prevent extreme poverty. Hence, inclusive growth is about creating economic opportunity and making it accessible to all men and women.

It is hoped that the ideas and findings presented in this volume will provide a useful way forward for operationalizing an inclusive growth agenda. Such an agenda will enable developing Asian countries not only to ultimately eradicate extreme poverty, but also allow all members of society to participate in, contribute to, and benefit from economic growth on an equitable basis, regardless of individual circumstances. It is also hoped that this book will lead to more research on the critical subject of inclusive growth.

Ursula Schaefer-Preuss
Vice President
Knowledge Management and Sustainable Development
Asian Development Bank

Preface and Acknowledgments

The Asian Development Bank (ADB) has adopted a long-term strategic framework for 2008–2020 (Strategy 2020) in response to the evolving needs of and emerging development challenges facing the Asia and Pacific region. Strategy 2020 sets out three strategic agendas to help ADB turn its vision—an Asia and Pacific region free of poverty—into reality: inclusive economic growth, environmentally sustainable growth, and regional integration.

To support the deliberation and implementation of Strategy 2020, ADB staff and their collaborators in recent years carried out a series of studies under the inclusive growth research program of the Economics and Research Department (ERD). These aim to improve understanding of the concept of inclusive growth, its policy ingredients, and its importance in helping the region achieve the Millennium Development Goals and eradicate extreme poverty.

This volume presents a selection of papers arising from these studies in three parts. The first focuses on recent trends of income and non-income inequality and poverty in the region, and their underlying driving forces; the second examines selected policy issues concerning inclusive growth, including employment, access to public services, social protection, and governance and institutions. The third comprises six country studies with rich information on growth, poverty, and inequality dynamics and policy challenges.

The completion of this volume would not have been possible without contributions from numerous people. A total of 21 ADB staff and their research collaborators were involved in writing various chapters. The volume was copy-edited by Cherry Zafaralla, Eric Van Zant, and Anneli Lagman-Martin. The design, layout, and typesetting were carried out by Echie Cabañeros and Joe Mark Ganaban. Lilibeth Poot, Fatima de Ramos-Blanco, and Rina Sibal provided proofreading and administrative assistance at various stages.

Deep appreciation goes to Ifzal Ali, the former Chief Economist of ADB, who started and led ADB's research program on inclusive growth during his time in ERD. Special thanks go to Jong-Wha Lee, Chief Economist of ADB, for his strong support and encouragement in preparing this volume. Thanks also go to Rana Hasan, Xianbin Yao, Jesus Felipe, Tun Lin, Hyun Son, Armin Bauer, and other ADB colleagues for useful discussions on conceptual issues related to inclusive growth.

It is hoped that the ideas and findings presented in the book will enrich the policy-making discourse in developing countries, and contribute to making the Asia and Pacific region more inclusive and free of poverty.

Finally, the views and opinions expressed in the book are those of the authors and do not necessarily reflect those of ADB or its Board of Governors or the governments they represent.

Juzhong Zhuang
Editor

March 2010

Contributors

Ifzal Ali, former Chief Economist, Asian Development Bank (ADB)

J. Salcedo Cain, former Assistant Economics and Statistics Analyst, Economics and Research Department (ERD), ADB

Emmanuel de Dios, Dean, School of Economics, University of the Philippines

Jesus Felipe, Principal Economist, Central and West Asia Department, ADB

Ruth Francisco, Consultant, ADB

Rana Hasan, Principal Economist, ERD, ADB

Shikha Jha, Senior Economist, ERD, ADB

Niny Khor, Economist, ERD, ADB

Fen Lin, Assistant Professor, City University of Hong Kong

Tun Lin, Natural Resource Specialist, East Asia Department, ADB

Rhoda Magsombol, former Associate Economics Analyst, ERD, ADB

Anneli Lagman-Martin, Senior Economics Officer, ERD, ADB

Aashish Mehta, Assistant Professor of Global and International Studies, University of California-Santa Barbara; former Economist, ERD, ADB

Yoko Niimi, Economist, ERD, ADB

Donghyun Park, Senior Economist, ERD, ADB

John Pencavel, Pauline K. Levin–Robert L. Levin and Pauline C. Levin–Abraham Levin Professor, School of Humanities and Sciences and Department of Economics, Stanford University; and Senior Fellow, Stanford Institute for Economic Policy Research.

Hyun Son, Economist, ERD, ADB

Susan Sparkes, Junior Professional Associate, Health, Nutrition, and Population Anchor Unit, World Bank

Ajay Tandon, Senior Economist, Health, Nutrition, and Population Anchor Unit, World Bank; former Economist, ERD, ADB

Guanghua Wan, Senior Economist, Regional and Sustainable Development Department, ADB

Damaris Yarcia, Consultant, ADB

Juzhong Zhuang, Assistant Chief Economist, ERD, ADB

Abbreviations, Acronyms, and Symbols

ADB	Asian Development Bank
CHIP	Chinese Household Income Project
COL	cost of living
FIES	Family Income and Expenditure Survey, Philippines
GDI	gender-related development index
GDP	gross domestic product
GE	general entropy index
GEM	gender empowerment measure
GNI	gross national income
GNP	gross national product
Lao PDR	Lao People's Democratic Republic
MDGs	Millennium Development Goals
MDG3	third Millennium Development Goal
NAIRU	non-accelerating inflation rate of unemployment
NBSC	National Bureau of Statistics of China
NFA	National Food Authority, Philippines
NGO	nongovernment organization
NIE	new institutional economics
NLSS	Nepal Living Standards Survey
NSO	National Statistics Office, Philippines
OECD	Organisation for Economic Co-operation and Development
PPP	purchasing power parity
PRC	People's Republic of China
SBA	skilled birth attendant
SPCOV	social protection coverage
SPDIST	social protection distribution/poverty targeting
SPEXP	social protection expenditure
SPIMP	social protection impact on incomes of the poor
SPSI	social protection summary indicator
TBA	traditional birth attendant

Symbols

CNY	Chinese yuan
$	United States dollar
₱	Philippine peso

Tables, Figures, and Boxes

Tables

Figures

Boxes

1

Poverty, Inequality, and Inclusive Growth in Asia

Juzhong Zhuang and Ifzal Ali

1.1   Introduction

Developing Asia's stellar growth rates have masked rising inequality, leading to "two faces of Asia"—one "shining" and the other "suffering". Competing internationally and benefiting from the forces of globalization, technological change, and economies of scale, the shining Asia has grabbed the attention of the media and the world. In the suffering Asia—not as well publicized—unacceptably high numbers of people are vulnerable and live in poverty. These two faces present both a beacon of hope and a symbol of despair. Merging them will be a development challenge for many years to come.

Inclusive growth, with its focus on creating economic opportunity and ensuring equal access, will play a pivotal role. More and more countries in developing Asia are adopting inclusive growth as the goal of development policy. India recently switched to a development strategy focusing on two objectives: raising economic growth and making growth more inclusive (Planning Commission of India 2006). In the People's Republic of China (PRC), the government made the creation of a "harmonious society", a concept very closely related to inclusive growth, the top priority in its 11th Five Year Plan (State Council of China 2006). In Thailand, growth with equity is one of the elements of its "sufficiency philosophy", underpinning the government's development efforts (UNDP 2007). A similar theme can be found in Viet Nam's socioeconomic development strategy, which advocates "quick and sustainable development, economic growth in parallel with implementation of initiatives, social equity, and environment protection" (Central Committee of the Communist Party of Viet Nam 2001).

This chapter asks why developing Asia[1] is embracing inclusive growth, discusses the concept of inclusive growth and its policy ingredients, and highlights key findings of the entire volume.

---

[1]   See Appendix for the list of developing Asian economies.

1.2 Why is developing Asia embracing inclusive growth?

The recognition of the relevance and importance of inclusive growth in developing Asia has been triggered by rising concern that the benefits of spectacular economic growth have not been equitably shared (Ali 2007).

Economic growth in the region has been rapid in recent decades, with gross domestic product (GDP) per capita in 2005 purchasing power parity (PPP) terms increasing from $1,631 to $4,430 during 1990–2008. The region's annual growth rate of 5.7% has few parallels in history (Table 1.1). Across the region, growth was most pronounced in East Asia, at 8.1% per year on average, driven largely by the PRC. Southeast Asia grew at 3.4% per year, despite the interruption of the 1997/1998 financial crisis. South Asia grew at 4.5% per year, which, although low, represents a significant improvement, particularly given the recent acceleration of growth in Bhutan, India, and Sri Lanka. Central and West Asia and the Pacific have lagged all subregions, growing at only 1.3% and 0.3% per year, respectively.

The region's rapid growth has led to a dramatic reduction in the level of extreme poverty. Using the $1.25-a-day poverty line (based on 2005 PPP), the incidence of income poverty declined from 52.3% to 27.1% during 1990–2005 (Table 1.1).[2] The decline in percentage-point terms was most pronounced in the PRC (44.3), followed by Cambodia (37.1), Pakistan (35.9), Indonesia (32.8), Lao People's Democratic Republic (30.2), Bhutan (24.2), Nepal (22.3), Azerbaijan (16.1), Mongolia (12.5), Viet Nam (11.4), India (9.6), Thailand (9.0), Philippines (7.1), Sri Lanka (4.7), Armenia (1.6), and Malaysia (1.4). In Georgia, Kyrgyz Republic, Tajikistan, and Uzbekistan, however, the $1.25-a-day poverty incidence increased significantly and, in Bangladesh, remained more or less unchanged. Using the $2-a-day poverty line, the decline in poverty incidence for developing Asia, from 79.4% to 54%, was equally significant, although with similarly large cross-country variation.

Nevertheless, poverty reduction remains a significant challenge. As of 2005, 903 million Asians still lived below $1.25 a day. In 14 out of the 22 countries listed in Table 1.1, poverty incidence measured by this poverty line was above 20% and, in four, was above 40%. Using the $2-a-day poverty line, 1.803 billion Asians lived in poverty, with 17 out of the 22 countries having a poverty incidence at above 30% and 12 countries at above 50%. Even in high-growth countries such as the PRC and Viet Nam, as of 2005, poverty incidence remained at 36% and 51%, respectively.

---

2   The year 2005 is the latest year when internationally comparable poverty data are available for a broad cross-section of countries.

Table 1.1   Income per capita and poverty incidence in selected developing Asian economies

Economy	GDP per capita (2005 PPP $)		Average annual growth rate	Headcount ratio (%) $1.25 a day (in 2005 PPP)			Headcount ratio (%) $2 a day (in 2005 PPP)		
	1990	2008	(%)	1990	2005	Change	1990	2005	Change
Central and West Asia	2,598	3,292	1.3	38.6	21.5	−17.1	58.5	53.8	−4.7
Armenia	2,936	5,611	3.7	6.3	4.7	−1.6	20.9	29.2	8.3
Azerbaijan	4,754	8,102	3.0	16.1	0.0	−16.1	40.3	0.3	−40.0
Georgia	5,398	4,526	−1.0	2.9	13.4	10.6	8.3	30.4	22.1
Kazakhstan	7,089	10,458	2.2	0.5	1.2	0.6	4.8	10.4	5.6
Kyrgyz Republic	2,505	2,023	−1.2	4.8	21.8	17.0	7.8	51.9	44.2
Pakistan	1,678	2,444	2.1	58.5	22.6	−35.9	85.4	60.3	−25.1
Tajikistan	3,064	1,761	−3.0	1.5	21.5	20.0	6.8	50.9	44.1
Turkmenistan	3,749	6,138	2.8	...	...	...	...	...	...
Uzbekistan	2,002	2,455	1.1	4.9	38.8	33.9	8.7	69.7	61.1
East Asia	1,582	6,385	8.1	60.1	15.9	−44.2	84.6	36.3	−48.3
PRC	1,099	5,511	9.4	60.2	15.9	−44.3	84.6	36.3	−48.3
Hong Kong, China	23,697	40,599	3.0	−	−	−	−	−	−
Korea, Rep. of	11,383	25,498	4.6	−	−	−	−	−	−
Mongolia	2,332	3,297	1.9	34.9	22.4	−12.5	65.0	49.1	−15.9
Pacific	2,062	2,192	0.3						
Fiji Islands	3,406	4,051	1.0	...	...	...	...	...	...
Kiribati	1,686	2,296	1.7	...	...	...	...	...	...
Micronesia	2,867	2,616	−0.5	...	...	...	...	...	...
Papua New Guinea	1,712	2,041	1.0	43.0	29.7	−13.3	64.3	51.0	−13.3
Samoa	2,719	4,145	2.4	...	...	...	...	...	...
Solomon Islands	2,252	2,413	0.4	...	...	...	...	...	...
Timor-Leste	...	740	...	71.3	43.6	−27.7	64.3	51.0	−13.3
Tonga	2,666	3,535	1.6	...	...	...	...	...	...
Vanuatu	3,399	3,677	0.4	...	...	...	...	...	...
South Asia	1,151	2,555	4.5	51.0	42.5	−8.5	82.4	75.6	−6.8
Bangladesh	680	1,233	3.4	49.9	50.5	0.6	84.0	80.3	−3.7
Bhutan	1,669	4,395	5.5	51.0	26.8	−24.2	72.9	50.1	−22.8
India	1,208	2,747	4.7	51.3	41.6	−9.6	82.6	75.6	−7.0
Maldives	...	5,087	...	...	...	...	...	...	...
Nepal	710	1,028	2.1	77.0	54.7	−22.3	91.8	77.3	−14.5
Sri Lanka	2,018	4,215	4.2	15.0	10.3	−4.7	49.5	34.4	−15.1
Southeast Asia	2,575	4,661	3.4	39.1	18.8	−20.3	66.0	44.6	−21.4
Brunei Darussalam	49,438	...	...	−	−	−	−	−	−
Cambodia	...	1,760	...	77.3	40.2	−37.1	91.8	68.2	−23.6
Indonesia	2,077	3,674	3.2	54.3	21.4	−32.8	84.6	53.8	−30.8
Lao PDR	947	1,986	4.2	65.9	35.7	−30.2	89.2	70.4	−18.8
Malaysia	6,646	13,139	3.9	1.9	0.5	−1.4	11.1	7.8	−3.3
Philippines	2,385	3,244	1.7	29.7	22.6	−7.1	54.9	45.0	−9.9
Singapore	23,855	45,553	3.7	−	−	−	−	−	−
Thailand	3,769	7,120	3.6	9.4	0.4	−9.0	30.5	11.5	−19.0
Viet Nam	902	2,574	6.0	34.2	22.8	−11.4	65.3	50.5	−14.8
Total	1,631	4,430	5.7	52.3	27.1	−25.2	79.4	54.0	−25.3
Poor (million)				1,416.0	903.4	−512.6	2,149.1	1,802.6	−346.6

... = data not available, − = data not available and poverty likely negligible, GDP = gross domestic product, Lao PDR = Lao People's Democratic Republic, PPP = purchasing power parity, PRC = People's Republic of China.

Source: World Bank, World Development Indicators Online and PovcalNet Database.

It is also true that large proportions of populations live just above the poverty lines, and could easily slip into poverty given economic shocks. A recent study on the impact of the global economic crisis on poverty reduction efforts in developing Asia indicates that, under the baseline scenario of no economic slowdown, 586 million Asians would live below $1.25 a day and 1.43 billion below $2 a day in 2010 (ADB 2009). Assuming a mild slowdown due to the global economic crisis —with per capita GDP growth in 2008, 2009 and 2010 at 1 percentage point lower than the 2007 level—an additional 33.5 million would live below the $1.25-a-day poverty line and an additional 41.9 million below the $2-a-day line in 2010. Much slower growth would lead to a higher number of additional poor (Table 1.2).

Table 1.2   Projected impact of the global economic crisis on poverty incidence and the number of poor in developing Asia, 2009–2010[a]

Scenario	Headcount ratio (%)		Number of poor (million)		Additional poor [b] (million)	
	2009	2010	2009	2010	2009	2010
$1.25, baseline growth	19.1	16.7	665.9	585.9	–	–
1 pp below baseline	19.7	17.6	686.5	619.0	20.7	33.5
2 pp below baseline	20.3	18.5	706.6	651.5	40.8	65.9
3 pp below baseline	20.9	19.4	726.5	683.3	60.7	97.7
$2.00, baseline growth	43.9	40.7	1526.8	1431.0	–	–
1 pp below baseline	44.6	41.9	1552.6	1472.5	25.8	41.9
2 pp below baseline	45.4	43.0	1577.7	1513.2	50.9	82.6
3 pp below baseline	46.1	44.2	1602.6	1553.1	75.8	122.5

– = not applicable, pp = percentage point.
a   Based on 24 developing Asian economies where sufficient data are available for both growth and poverty.
b   Relative to the baseline scenario.
Source: ADB (2009).

An emerging issue for developing Asia is rising inequality, which has raised concern that the benefits of spectacular growth have not been equitably shared. Chapter 2 shows that a large number of developing Asian economies (14 out of the 20 where data are available) saw Gini coefficients—a commonly used measure of income inequality—increasing during 1990–2005, with large increases in Bangladesh, Cambodia, PRC, Nepal, and Sri Lanka (see Figure 1.1). Also disturbing—though not necessarily for economists who pay more attention to measures of relative inequality—is the increase in absolute inequality as measured by differences in the mean consumption of the top quintile relative to the bottom quintile. The ratio of expenditure growth of the top to the bottom quintile was 2.1 for PRC, 2.4 for India, 3.8 for Nepal, and 6.5 for Sri Lanka between the 1990s and 2000s. The widening of the absolute gap between rich and poor, and very visible changes in consumption patterns and lifestyles among the rich that this implies could lead to perceptibly higher social and political tension, undermining social cohesiveness.

Figure 1.1   Recent trends in income/expenditure inequality in developing Asia: Changes in Gini coefficients between the early 1990s and early 2000s (%)

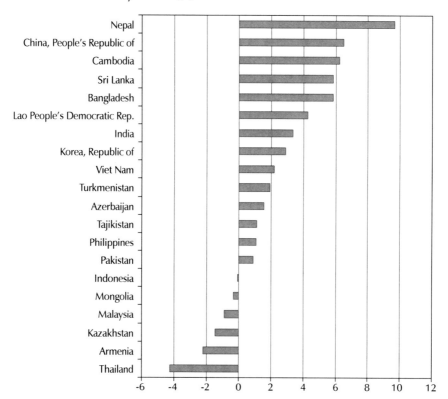

Source: See Figure 2.3, Chapter 2 of this volume.

Persistently high and growing inequality in access to basic social services such as education and health, exacerbated by income inequality, is also a significant concern (see Chapters 3 and 6). In many countries, primary school-age children from households of the poorest quintile are almost 3 times more likely to be out of school than those from the richest quintile; and the child mortality rate for the poorest quintile is 2–3 times higher than for the richest quintile.

In the Philippines, for example, primary enrolment and measles immunization—the latter with significant impact on child mortality—are worse today than in 1990 (Ali 2007). Even in the rapidly growing PRC, rising disparities in health between urban and rural populations have slowed the improvement of population health in the last 2 decades (Tandon and Zhuang 2007). For many countries in Asia and the Pacific, it is widely believed that even though they are on track to meet the Millennium Development Goal (MDG) of halving the proportion of people living on less than $1.25 a day, they are unlikely to meet several non-income MDG targets (Table 1.3). ESCAP, ADB, and UNDP (2010) also report that while the region has made good progress in a number of indicators, considerable variations exist between urban and rural areas and across subregions, and that the 2008 global financial crisis has revealed the region's vulnerability to setbacks.

Table 1.3   Developing Asia's progress in achieving selected MDG targets by 2015

Goal	1		2			3			4		5		6			7	
	$1/day poverty	Underweight children	Primary enrolment	Reaching grade 5	Primary completion rate	Gender primary	Gender secondary	Gender tertiary	Under-5 mortality	Infant mortality	Antenatal care, at least once	Births by skilled professional	HIV prevalence	TBC prevalence	TBC death rate	Water, total	Sanitation, total
Central and West Asia																	
Afghanistan		■				■	▼		■	■	▼	■		▲	●	■	▼
Armenia	▲	▼	■	●	●	●	●	●	▲	▲	▲	■	▲	●	●	●	■
Azerbaijan	●	■	●	●	●	●	●	▲	▲	▲	■	▲	▼	●	●	■	▼
Georgia	▼	▲	▲	●	▼	●	●	●	■	■	▼	▲	▲	●	●	●	▼
Kazakhstan	■	●	●	●	●	●	●	●	■	■	●	■		▼	▼	■	▼
Kyrgyz Republic	▼	●	▼	●	▲	●	●	●	■	■	●	▼	▲	●	●	●	■
Pakistan	●	▼	■			▲	▲	▲	■	■	■	■	▲	▲	●	■	▲
Tajikistan	●		●	●	▲	●	▼	■	■	■	■	■	▼	▼	▼	■	●
Turkmenistan	●	■							■	■	●	●		▼	●		
Uzbekistan	▼	●	▲	●	●	●	●	▼	■	■	●	●	▲	▼	▼	▼	▲
East Asia																	
China, People's Rep. of	●	●			●	●	●	●	■	■	■	▲	▲	●	●	●	■
Hong Kong, China			▼		●	●	●	●							●	●	
Korea, Republic of			●	●	●	●	▼	■	■	■			▲	▼	▼	■	
Mongolia	■	▲	●	▼	●	●	●	●	▲	■	●	●	▲	▲	●	■	■
Pacific																	
Cook Islands		▼		▼	●	●			■	■		■		▼	▼	■	●
Fiji Islands		▼	▼	▼	●	●			■	■			▲	●	●	▼	■

continued.

Table 1.3 continued.

Goal	1	2				3			4		5		6			7	
	$1/day poverty	Underweight children	Primary enrolment	Reaching grade 5	Primary completion rate	Gender primary	Gender secondary	Gender tertiary	Under-5 mortality	Infant mortality	Antenatal care, at least once	Births by skilled professional	HIV prevalence	TBC prevalence	TBC death rate	Water, total	Sanitation, total
Kiribati		●			●	●	●		■	■		▲		●	●	▲	■
Marshall Islands		▼		▼	●	●			■	■				●	●	▼	▲
Micronesia, Fed. States of					●				■	■				●	●	●	▼
Nauru				▼	●	●		▼	▼					●	●		
Palau					●	●	●		■	■	●			●	●	▼	■
Papua New Guinea					▼				■	■	▼	▼	▲	●		■	■
Samoa		●			●	●	●		■	■	●			●	●	▼	●
Solomon Islands					●	▲			■	■		▼		●	●	■	■
Timor-Leste	▼					▲			■	■	▼	▼	▲	●		■	■
Tonga		●	▼	●	●	●	●	●	■	■		▲		●	●	●	■
Tuvalu					●	●			■	■		●		●	●	■	●
Vanuatu		▼		▲	●	▲			■	■		■		●	●	▼	■
South Asia																	
Bangladesh	■	▲			▼	●	■		▲	▲	■	■	▲	●	●	■	■
Bhutan			■	■	■	●	▲	▼	■	■	▲	▲	▲	●	●	▼	▼
India	■	■	▲	■	■	●	▲		■	■	■	■	●	▲	●	●	■
Maldives		▲	●		●	●	●		●	●		▼	▲	●	●	▼	●
Nepal	■	■	■	■	■	●	▲	■	▲	▲	■	■	▲	●	●	●	■
Sri Lanka	■	▲	●		●	●	●		■	■	●	▲	▲	▲	●	▲	●
Southeast Asia																	
Brunei Darussalam			●	●	●	●	●	●	■	■		▲		▼	●		
Cambodia	■	■	■	■	▲	▲	▲	■	■		■	■	●	●	●	●	▲
Indonesia		■	●	▲	●	●	●	●	▲	▲	▲	▲	▼	●	●	■	■
Lao PDR	■	■	■	■	■	▲	■	▲	▲	▲	■	■	●	●	●	▲	▲
Malaysia	●	●	●	▼	●	●	●	●	■	■		▲	▼	●	●	●	▼
Myanmar		■		■					■	■	▼	■	●	▲	●	●	●
Philippines	■	■	▼	▼	▼	●	●	●	▲	■	■	■	▲	●	●	●	▲
Singapore							▲	●					▼	●	●		
Thailand	●	●		●		●	●	●	●	●	●	▼	●	▲	●	●	●
Viet Nam	●	●	▲	▲		▲			●	●	▲	▲	▼	●	●	●	●

Keys: ● early achiever ▲ on track ■ slow ▼ regressing/no progress

CFC = chlorofluorocarbons, Lao PDR = Lao People's Democratic Republic, MDG = Millennium Development Goal, ODP = ozone-depleting potential, TBC = tuberculosis cases.
Source: ESCAP, ADB, and UNDP (2010).

High poverty and rising inequality could have serious consequences for the region's efforts to narrow still astonishingly high income gaps with the developed world. In 2007, developing Asia's average per capita GDP in 2005 PPP terms was less than 12% of Japan's. Even in the PRC, with about 9% annual growth for more than 20 years, per capita GDP was only 16% of Japan's (Figure 1.2). Assuming that each developing Asian economy will continue to grow at the rate registered in 2007, to reach Singapore's per capita GDP level, it would take 9 years for Azerbaijan, 15 years for Bhutan, 17 years for Armenia, 19 years for Georgia, 20 years for the PRC, 32 years for Malaysia, 40 years for India, 45 years for Thailand, and 82 years for Pakistan. Thus, even within developing Asia, eliminating cross-country income gaps will be a significant development challenge.

Figure 1.2   GDP per capita in 2005 PPP $, as a percent of Japan's, for selected developing Asian economies, 2007

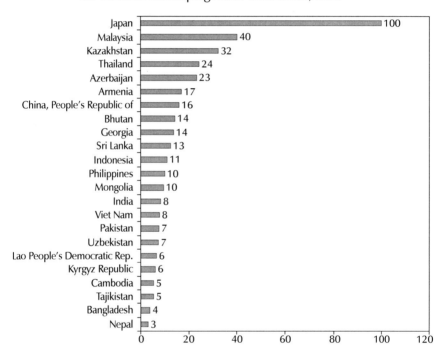

GDP = gross domestic product, PPP = purchasing power parity.
Source: World Bank, World Development Indicators Online.

High levels of poverty and inequality could slow the narrowing and elimination of income gaps by complicating reforms, reducing the quality of institutions and policies, undermining social cohesion, endangering social and political stability, and making growth unsustainable. To prevent these, the development agenda will need to be expanded to include not only the eradication of extreme poverty, but also the improvement of the living standards of a much larger group who feel disenfranchised by the real or perceived disadvantages associated with rising inequality in access to economic opportunity. An inclusive growth strategy will enable developing Asia not only to eradicate extreme poverty, but also to address these legitimate concerns.

1.3   Inclusive growth: Conceptual issues

Ali and Zhuang (2007) argue that there is as yet no widely agreed definition for inclusive growth. But a consensus on what it should entail is emerging from the policy statements of various countries and their development partners, from discussions on development policies at international and regional forums, and from the studies and reports of academic and policy researchers. On the basis of these, they define inclusive growth as "growth coupled with equality of opportunity". Since equality of opportunity will be attained by reducing inequality of opportunity over time, inclusive growth can also mean "growth coupled with declining inequality of opportunity". In either case, inclusive growth focuses on both creating economic opportunity and making opportunity accessible to all. Growth is inclusive when it allows all members of society to participate in, contribute to, and benefit from growth on an equal basis, regardless of individual circumstances.

The importance of equal opportunity for all lies in its intrinsic value as well as its instrumental role. Intrinsically, this is based on the belief that equal opportunity is a basic human right and that it is unethical and immoral to treat individuals differently in access to opportunity. The instrumental role stems from the recognition that equal access to opportunity increases growth potential, while inequality diminishes it and makes growth unsustainable by leading to inefficient use of human resources, lowering the quality of institutions and policies, eroding social cohesion, and increasing social conflict.

Inclusive growth based on equal opportunity differentiates inequality due to individual circumstance from that due to individual effort. According to Roemer (2006), an individual's circumstances such as culture, religious belief, family background and parental education, gender, and (sometimes) geographical location are outside the control of the individual, and he or she should not be held responsible for them. Inequality due to differences in circumstances often reflects market, policy, and institutional and governance failures; and social exclusion. It should be addressed through public policy interventions. By contrast, individual effort is under the individual's control and he or she should be held responsible. Such inequality reflects and reinforces the market-based incentives needed to foster innovation, entrepreneurship, and growth (Chaudhuri and Ravallion 2007).

Distinguishing inequality related to effort from that related to circumstance leads to an important distinction between inequality of outcome and inequality of opportunity (World Bank 2006). Inequality of opportunity arises largely from differences in individual circumstance, while inequality of outcome, such as income, often reflects some combination of differences in effort and in circumstance. If policy interventions succeeded in ensuring full equality of opportunity, inequality in outcome would then only reflect differences in effort, and could be viewed as "good inequality", inherent to any growth process (Chaudhuri and Ravallion 2007). On the other hand, if all individuals exerted the same level of effort while policy interventions could not fully eliminate circumstance-related inequality, the resulting inequality of outcome is "bad inequality". While these two extreme cases are analytically useful, it has been argued that recent rising inequality in many developing Asian countries is likely to consist of "good" and "bad" inequality (Chaudhuri and Ravallion 2007).[3] Equalizing opportunity, which emphasizes eliminating circumstance-related bad inequality to reduce inequality in outcomes, should be at the core of inclusiveness and a major focus of an inclusive growth strategy for developing Asia.

Chaudhuri and Ravallion (2007) argue that "good inequality" can turn to bad if not properly managed; and "bad inequality" can drive out the good. The former could happen if those the market or society rewards with considerable market or political power use the rewards to engage in rent-seeking and to change the "rules of the game." For instance, public investment and expenditure could be skewed to benefit the elite, or even the entire system of property and civil rights could be skewed in their favor (Bourguignon, Ferreira, and Walton 2007; Rajan and Zingales 2007). Bad inequality could drive out the good if its persistence—for example, when certain groups are left behind as a result of residing in a neglected region—reduces the tolerance for even good inequality. The result can be social unrest.

In the real world, sometimes a clear distinction between effort and circumstance may not be straightforward. There could be differences of opinion on what constitutes circumstance and what constitutes effort in a

---

3   Easterly (2007) makes a distinction between "structural inequality" and "market inequality". Structural inequality reflects such historical events as conquest, colonization, slavery, and land distribution by the state or colonial power, with these non-market mechanisms creating an elite; market inequality arises from uneven success in the free market across different individuals, cities, regions, and industries. He argues that structural inequality is unambiguously bad for subsequent development, but market inequality has ambiguous effects. It is obvious that, according to these definitions, structural inequality can be entirely attributed to differences in circumstance; while market inequality could arise either from differences in effort or in circumstance. Uneven success in the free market can be due to individuals exerting different levels of effort, but can also result from unequal access to economic opportunity.

society. Effort could also be partly determined by circumstance (Roemer 1996 and 2006). But even with these complications, in many developing countries it is relatively easy to observe extreme circumstances that severely limit opportunity for a large segment of the population. These circumstances relate, especially among the poor, to lack of access to high-quality basic education, health care, and social protection; lack of access to productive employment and assets such as credit and land; and corruption in managing and allocating public resources. Such circumstances are not only fundamentally unfair, they are also likely to work as serious constraints to poverty reduction, social cohesion, and economic growth. Eliminating these circumstances will go a long way toward inclusive growth.

Figure 1.3   Three policy pillars of inclusive growth

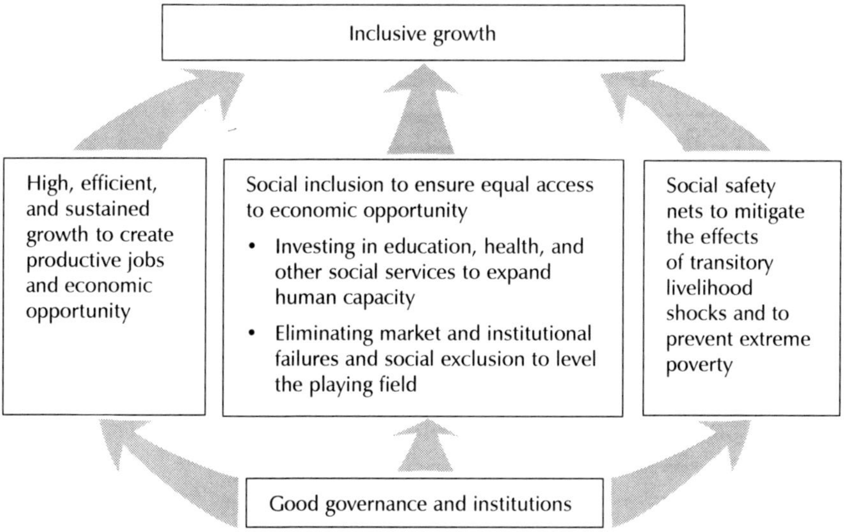

Inclusive growth

| High, efficient, and sustained growth to create productive jobs and economic opportunity | Social inclusion to ensure equal access to economic opportunity

• Investing in education, health, and other social services to expand human capacity

• Eliminating market and institutional failures and social exclusion to level the playing field | Social safety nets to mitigate the effects of transitory livelihood shocks and to prevent extreme poverty |

Good governance and institutions

Ali and Zhuang (2007) argue that given that inclusive growth focuses on both creating economic opportunity and ensuring equal access, an effective inclusive growth strategy should have three policy pillars: (i) high, efficient, and sustained growth to create productive jobs and economic opportunity; (ii) social inclusion to ensure equal access to opportunity; and (iii) social safety nets to prevent extreme poverty (Figure 1.3). While the second pillar is essential to equalizing opportunity, the third pillar is needed to cater to the special needs of people who, for reasons beyond their control, cannot participate in and benefit from the opportunity created by growth, and to alleviate transitory livelihood shocks, risks, and vulnerability. Ali and Zhuang further argue that

11

promoting social inclusion requires public intervention in two areas: (i) investing in education, health, and other social services to expand human capacity, especially of the disadvantaged; and (ii) eliminating various market and institutional failures and social exclusion to level the playing field. Finally, all three policy pillars need to be supported by good governance and institutions.

The concept of inclusive growth as defined above provides a useful framework for operationalizing a development strategy that aims to keep growth high and sustained while ensuring that all members of society benefit from growth. Moreover, a development strategy anchored on inclusive growth—or an inclusive growth strategy—will enhance developing Asia's poverty reduction agenda. This is because, first, the impact of growth on poverty reduction is higher when the initial level of inequality is lower and/or inequality declines over time; and second, inclusive growth makes poverty reduction more effective by focusing on creating productive employment and making it equally accessible to all, while addressing extreme poverty through social safety nets.

Inclusive growth as defined above differs from the concept of "pro-poor growth"[4]—although the two are closely related and share similar concerns. A key difference is that pro-poor growth targets people living below a specific poverty line—whether it is "growth that leads to poverty reduction more than it would have if all incomes had grown at the same rate" (Kakwani and Pernia 2000), or simply "growth that reduces poverty" (Ravallion and Chen 2003). Inclusive growth is concerned with a broader population, including the poor, people living just above the poverty line, and the non-poor but disadvantaged. Inclusive growth is therefore relevant not only for countries where reducing extreme poverty is the overarching task, but also for those where the level of extreme poverty is no longer high and the greater challenge is to ensure that the benefits of growth are more equitably shared. Another difference is that pro-poor growth is defined solely by poverty reduction—a one-dimensional outcome—whether it is in the sense of Kakwani and Pernia (2000), or of Ravallion and Chen (2003). Inclusive growth as defined above focuses on development processes that lead to poverty reduction and more equitable distribution of opportunity and, consequently, income.[5]

To implement an inclusive growth strategy, the government, public sector, and public-private partnerships will play a critical role. Although growth will have to be largely driven by a dynamic private sector, there

---

4   This was also at the heart of development policy discussions not long ago.
5   This also means that measuring progress in inclusive growth will be more challenging than measuring progress in outcome-focused pro-poor growth.

are many instances where the market fails to function efficiently. The central role of the government is to develop and maintain an enabling environment for business investment and private entrepreneurship by eliminating impediments created by market, institutional, or policy failures. This requires the government and public sector to invest in physical infrastructure and human capital, build institutional capacity, maintain macroeconomic stability, adopt market-friendly policy, protect property rights, and maintain rule of law. In setting policy and reform priorities, the government should identify the binding constraints to growth, and target its efforts and resources at relaxing them. Partnerships with the private sector in creating productive jobs should also be part of the policy package (see Chapter 5). The government should pay attention not only to the pace, but also to the pattern of growth, and make it "broad-based" (Ianchovichina and Lundstrom 2009).

The government has an equally important role to play in ensuring equal access to opportunity by investing in education, health, and other basic public services (because of their public goods nature and strong externality) and by levelling the playing field. The government needs to ensure that public services have adequate funding, good physical infrastructure, strong institutional capacity, sound policy frameworks, and good governance. In many countries, the government is often directly involved in public service provision. Although there are instances of effective public provision, more often than not, there is abundant anecdotal evidence of the failure of public services (see Chapter 6). This is often attributed to a host of factors, including budgetary constraints, the corruption and governance problem, weak capacity, and a plethora of other forms of institutional weakness. Equally worrying, countries where public provision fails are often the ones unlikely to effectively regulate and monitor alternatives, such as private provision of health and education services. Therefore, equal access to social services needs to be complemented by supply-side policies to ensure the efficiency and quality of public services and demand-side policies to avoid moral hazard behavior and waste.

To level the playing field, the government needs to address all the market, institutional/governance, and policy failures, and to ensure that people would not be excluded from participating in and benefiting from growth because of individual circumstances, or because they do not belong to certain power groups that control political and economic decision making (Rajan and Zingales 2007).

Promoting social inclusion also requires the government to provide social safety nets to mitigate the effects of transitory livelihood shocks as well as to meet the minimum needs of the chronically poor. Livelihood shocks are often created by ill health, macroeconomic crisis, industrial structuring, and natural disasters. Developing and improving social safety nets through public actions is particularly important for developing Asia as markets for insuring such risks are often rudimentary and, even if they exist, only cover a small segment of the population. Social safety nets typically take the following forms: (i) labor market policies and programs aimed to reduce risks of unemployment, underemployment, or low wages resulting from inappropriate skills or poorly functioning labor markets; (ii) social insurance programs designed to cushion risks associated with unemployment, ill health, disability, work-related injuries, and old age, examples being pensions, health and disability insurance, and unemployment insurance; (iii) social assistance and welfare schemes such as welfare and social services, and cash or in-kind transfers intended for the most vulnerable groups with no other means of adequate support, such as single-parent households, victims of natural disasters or civil conflicts, people with disabilities, or the destitute poor; and (iv) child protection to ensure the healthy and productive development of children, examples being early childhood development programs, school feeding programs, scholarships, free or subsidized health services for mothers and children, and family allowances or credit (Ali and Zhuang 2007).

1.4   Background of this volume and key findings

This volume consists of 13 papers prepared by ADB staff and their collaborators under the Economics and Research Department's research program on inclusive growth. Some papers provided analytical inputs to the deliberation of ADB's newly adopted long-term strategic framework—Strategy 2020—which sets inclusive economic growth, environmentally sustainable growth, and regional integration as three strategic agendas for achieving an Asia and Pacific region free of poverty (ADB 2008). The 13 papers are grouped into three parts: (A) measuring inequality and poverty; (B) selected policy issues for inclusive growth; and (C) country studies.

1.4.1   Measuring inequality and poverty

Part A comprises three chapters and focuses on measuring income and non-income inequality and poverty, and gender equality in developing Asia.

Chapter 2 by Cain, Hasan, and Magsombol examines recent trends in income distribution in developing Asia. They find that expenditure/income distributions in many developing Asian economies have become more unequal over the last 2 decades. Both absolute inequality—in terms of the gap in per capita expenditure/income between the top quintile and bottom quintile—and relative inequality have increased virtually everywhere. However, increasing inequality reflects the fact that "the rich are getting richer faster than the poor", rather than "the rich are getting richer and the poor are getting poorer", as many may think. Therefore, while inequality has increased, expenditures and incomes have increased at all points along the distribution in most countries and, consequently, absolute poverty has also declined. Nevertheless, rising inequality has dampened the extent of poverty reduction associated with rapid income growth in developing Asia. In other words, if the region had been able to generate distribution-neutral economic growth, the reduction in poverty would have been far greater.

The authors then look at reasons for rising inequality, drawing on recent empirical work on its proximate (or immediate) drivers and the broader literature on policy and structural drivers. For the proximate drivers of rising inequality, they highlight the importance of uneven growth across sectors (particularly agricultural vis-à-vis non-agricultural sectors) and regions (among provinces or states, and between urban and rural areas). They find that growth in the agricultural sector has been far more limited than in industry and services in most developing Asian countries, while the agricultural sector in these countries has continued to account for 40% or more of total employment, often at very low levels of productivity. This slower income growth in the agricultural sector than the non-agricultural sectors also leads to a widening of the income gap between urban and rural areas, as in the case of Cambodia, PRC, Nepal, and Viet Nam.

For policy and structural drivers, they emphasize factors such as neglect of agriculture, economic transition, and the impact of market-oriented reforms and integration on the relative returns to labor. They argue that the interplay between market-oriented reforms, globalization, and the introduction of new technology is an important part of the story of unequal income growth across households. The more educated or better placed in society are more likely to gain from the opportunities brought about by market reforms and international integration. Further, a fast-changing economic environment can create substantial economic rents, and how these rents are distributed depends partly on the institutional framework of a country. Where it is strong and progressive, these rents can be taxed for financing public goods without creating distortions. However, where it is weak, economic rents could lead to rent-seeking behavior and rising inequality that are detrimental to the process of economic growth itself.

Cain, Hasan, and Magsombol argue that there is no simple answer to the question of how the rising income inequality in developing Asia should be addressed. On one hand, a higher level of inequality may imply a slower pace of poverty reduction; and increases in inequality could also have adverse consequences for social cohesion and the quality of

15

institutions, which in turn can have negative implications for growth prospects. On the other hand, it has to be acknowledged that economic development is likely to entail processes that increase inequality. They argue that, ultimately, guidance for policy must come from a nuanced analysis of inequality. To the extent that a significant part of these increasing inequalities are related to policy biases and/or disparities in access to opportunity (to accumulate human capital, to access financial services, etc.), they are a serious problem requiring attention. Fighting inequality by focusing public policy on improving delivery of basic health care and education services to the poor, strengthening social protection, and significantly increasing the employment opportunities and incomes of the poor must be a minimum agenda to which developing Asia's policy makers must commit. They argue that, while some redistribution will be inevitable in promoting greater equality of opportunity, the challenge is to design redistributive policies that are well targeted, effective, and funded through mechanisms that do not detract from economic growth.

Chapter 3 by Tandon and Sparkes assesses the inclusiveness of developing Asia's growth by looking at the non-income dimensions of poverty and inequality, focusing on key components of the MDGs and Human Development Index, including life expectancy, infant mortality, under-five mortality, enrollment rates, and literacy rates. Their cross-country comparisons reveal that while, on average, impressive gains have been made in the reduction of non-income poverty, there is a wide degree of disparity in health and education outcomes across the region, with many countries off-track in achieving MDGs such as under-five mortality and universal primary education. A review of the historical trends suggests that over the last 100 years there has been significant catching-up in developing Asia's human development indicators toward the levels of developed countries, but there has been limited change in the relative country ranking. They argue that finding the root causes of such persistent underdevelopment is critical for policy making. At the same time, they also note that a few countries were able to defy their initial conditions and moved up in rank in areas such as education, and argue that understanding how this was achieved is equally important.

Tandon and Sparkes find that large disparities or inequalities in health and education outcomes also exist across different household groups within many developing Asian countries, and that there are indications that the inequalities have been increasing in recent years. They show that in a large number of countries, the under-five mortality rate for the population in the bottom wealth quintile is more than 3 times as high as that for the population in the top wealth quintile, and that children from the households of the poorest quintile are 3–5 times more likely to be out of school than those of the richest quintile. They argue that while income inequality is an important determinant of non-income inequality, other factors could affect non-income inequality, such as the existence or absence of public policies for and of targeted government interventions in human development, as well as other structural factors; so a country with a high degree of income inequality can have a relatively low level of inequality in health or education outcomes, and vice versa.

To further examine the relationship between income and non-income welfare attainments and to make the point that the link from the former to the latter cannot be taken for granted, they show that while, on average, population health and education outcomes tend to be highly correlated with the level of income, there are significant variations around this relationship in developing Asia. In some cases, rapid income growth has not led to corresponding improvement in population health and education outcomes, and in others, non-income poverty declined significantly in the absence of strong income growth. They conclude that making growth more inclusive should not only address income poverty and inequality, but also non-income poverty and inequality; and that economic growth alone would not be sufficient to achieve this, and targeted public sector interventions in human development should play a critical part. They argue that, with human capital a key determinant of economic growth, the imperative of reducing poverty and inequality in health and education outcomes should be looked at not only as a key part of development goals and human well-being, but also preventing them from becoming constraints on growth.

Chapter 4 by Niimi starts with a review of the progress toward gender equality in developing Asia in recent years by examining a number of indicators proposed under the MDG3 plus approach, focusing on gender inequality in education and health outcomes (capability) and in labor market and political participation (access to resources and opportunity). She finds that most countries in the region have made progress toward gender parity. However, the rate of progress varies across different dimensions of gender equality and across countries. While improvement in education, especially primary education, has been significant, progress is far less impressive in health status and even more disappointing in labor market outcomes. In many countries, women's improved capabilities do not seem to have been translated into an equal participation between men and women in economic and political activity. Further, she finds that gender gaps in almost all aspects reviewed remain significant in South Asia, except Maldives and Sri Lanka. Many South Asian countries perform even worse than sub-Saharan Africa as a whole, which has made the least progress toward gender equality in many dimensions.

From her survey of recent empirical literature, Niimi notes that the prevalence and persistence of gender inequality are often caused and reinforced by interlinked cultural, social, and economic factors. For example, gender inequality in capabilities could be partly attributed

17

to gender bias in favor of boys against girls in intrahousehold resource allocation, including spending on education and health. Such gender bias may not only reflect parental preference for sons to daughters embedded in traditions and cultural norms, but also be explained by relatively lower returns to investment in human capital for girls than for boys. The differential returns to investment in human capital could in turn be partly attributed to discrimination against women in the labor market, and partly to the traditional division of labor between men and women in domestic work as well as in the labor market. In the case of gender inequality in labor market outcomes, the literature has emphasized a number of causal factors, including women's relative human capital attainments compared to men; the incompatibility of labor market participation with women's childbearing role and the traditional division of labor between men and women; occupational segregation; and discrimination against women. Empirical evidence also seems to suggest that gender inequality is greater when a country's economic opportunity is more limited or households are in greater economic hardship.

Niimi concludes that removing cultural, social, and institutional obstacles by educating the public and introducing and enforcing anti-gender discrimination legislation, promoting economic development to generate economic opportunity, and improving women's capabilities and access to opportunity are the key ingredients of a policy package for greater progress toward gender equality and inclusive growth.

1.4.2   Selected policy issues for inclusive growth

Part B comprises four chapters and discusses selected policy issues of great relevance for a development strategy anchored on inclusive growth, as outlined in Section 1.3 of this chapter, including employment, access to public services, social protection, and governance and institutions.

Chapter 5 by Felipe argues that to achieve inclusive growth, governments must commit effort and resources to the pursuit of the full employment of the labor force—defined as "zero involuntary unemployment". He provides a number of reasons why full employment is key to inclusive growth. The most important way for a person to participate in society and contribute to its progress as a productive member is through a productive and decent job. Maintaining the economy as close as possible to full employment will also keep overall purchasing power high, leading to more buoyant markets, businesses, and investment. Further, full employment enables an economy to deliver great individual and social benefits by eliminating the misery, poverty, and social injustice associated with unemployment and underemployment; lowers the need for safety net expenditures for disadvantaged groups; and helps maintain social and political stability.

He argues that employment is a basic human right; that persistent unemployment and underemployment act as a form of social exclusion; and that the right to employment, as an objective of economic policy can be found in many international declarations and conventions.

Noting that the elasticity of employment with respect to output has not been particularly high (or has even decreased) in many parts of developing Asia in recent years, Felipe concludes that the region's impressive growth has not led to equally impressive increases in the level of employment; it has not been inclusive. The free market system, he argues, does not guarantee full employment in a developing country, and that the market failure in attaining full employment provides strong justification for government involvement and commitment to it. He notes that the goal of creating a full-employment economy has not been actively pursued by the governments of many countries and international organizations (with the exception of the International Labor Organization) in the past several decades. This is because of the belief that low unemployment and low inflation are incompatible, leading to economic policies that pursue low inflation but often at the cost of sluggish growth, unemployment, and income inequality.

Felipe argues that if developing countries and their development partners are serious about making growth inclusive, they must place full employment at the top of the policy agenda. He argues that unemployment and underemployment of the labor force in developing countries are largely the result of the shortage of capital equipment and productive capacity, and the main policy option to achieve full employment is therefore to step up investment.

However, in reality this is not so simple. The private sector, being the driver of investment and growth, may decide not to invest because of lack of "animal spirits" or due to a poor investment environment and the high costs of doing business. Or it may invest in areas that may be profitable but not necessarily help achieve full employment. Also, the public sector may face obstacles to undertaking public investment required to achieve the level of investment compatible with full employment.

Felipe argues that solving these problems requires improved coordination between the private and public sectors and understanding of each other's role in generating employment and eliminating underemployment. Industrial policy, best understood as a process whereby the state and the private sector jointly arrive at diagnoses about the sources of blockage in new economic activities, he says, has an important role to play in promoting investment to achieve full employment.

Finally, Felipe emphasizes that the successful transformation of developing economies requires embedding private initiative in a framework of public action that encourages restructuring, diversification, and technological dynamism.

19

Chapter 6 by Wan and Francisco focuses on the second policy pillar of an inclusive growth strategy, exploring issues related to the access to basic services in developing Asia, and on primary education, health care, water and sanitation, and electricity. They find that while many countries and development institutions have made significant effort to increase the supply and improve the quality of basic social and infrastructure services and to make them more accessible, outcomes have been mixed. In particular, the poor have not benefited sufficiently from such efforts, as evidenced by sharp differences among different wealth quintiles in children's school attendance, facilities-based birth delivery, access to safe and improved sanitation, and access to electricity.

Wan and Francisco then examine the possible constraints the poor face in accessing these basic services. On the demand side, they argue that the lack of financial resources is the most critical barrier. This could be the case even when the services are provided free or at very low cost, as poor households may face many other costs, such as connection fees for water and electricity services, travel costs for visiting health clinics, and opportunity costs in terms of foregone incomes when children attend schools.

On the supply side, no or inadequate physical access is often a major constraint. Even when physical access is not a problem, the poor quality of services can also constrain the improvement in human development outcomes of the poor. The quality of health and education is often determined by many factors, including the level of competency, effort, attitude, regular availability, and attendance of teachers and health professionals; the availability of adequate material inputs such as instructional materials in schools and medical supplies in hospitals; and the availability of appropriate health and school facilities and infrastructure.

Many studies have shown that absenteeism is often a crucial barrier to access to health care and education for rural communities in developing countries. Apart from demand and supply-side factors, those related to institutional weaknesses, such as the lack of information or awareness, poor governance, and corruption also contribute to the failure of basic services provision to the poor.

In conclusion, Wan and Francisco highlight a number of policy priorities to improve access to basic services, especially for poor communities. These include making services available and affordable to the poor; removing physical barriers; promoting knowledge and awareness about what services to access and where the services could be accessed; making greater effort to improve the quality of services; and enhancing governance and addressing corruption. They also stress the importance of exercising due diligence when designing policy interventions because what works for some communities might not work for others due to different binding constraints.

Chapter 7 by Park focuses on the third policy pillar of providing social safety nets to prevent extreme poverty. He argues that social protection is an essential ingredient of inclusive growth because it is a mechanism for ensuring that the marginalized and vulnerable participate in and benefit from growth. It also stimulates economic activity by encouraging individuals to take risks. The task of strengthening social protection in developing Asia has become more urgent in recent years because of rapid population ageing and the concomitant risk that large numbers of the elderly will fall into old-age poverty. Two additional rationales for stronger social protection are: (i) weakening of informal family-based support mechanisms associated with urbanization, industrialization, and sociocultural changes; and (ii) globalization and competition which accelerate restructuring and reallocation of resources, create the need for greater labor market flexibility, and exacerbate economic insecurity. At the same time, Asians who need social protection most, especially the poor and vulnerable, are beginning to vocally demand it and ask for government assistance in managing the risks they face.

On the basis of a review of the major findings of an ADB study on a social protection index covering 31 Asian countries, Park concludes that, on one hand, developing Asian countries now all have formal social protection systems and are making progress in fortifying them. The fact that some poorer Asian countries have also established relatively well-functioning systems indicates that effective social protection is as much a matter of political will and good governance as resources. On the other hand, he notes that a lot more remains to be done. In many countries the coverage of social protection programs is largely limited to the formal sector, government workers, and urban areas, which means that millions do not have access to any protection at all. Another common problem, clearly seen in the case of pension systems, is that the level of protection provided is often inadequate. A further region-wide problem is that social protection programs have generally failed to effectively target those in greatest need of assistance.

In terms of policy priorities, Park argues that sustained economic growth is the ultimate form of social protection, especially in poor developing countries. Against this, he argues that, while there is no one-size-fits-all solution, Asian policy makers may consider the following measures to help set the direction for reforming and strengthening social protection throughout the region. These include (i) strengthening the institutional and administrative capacity of social protection systems to perform their core functions through better accounting, more rigorous financial controls, human resource development, computerization, and greater disclosure to stakeholders; (ii) separation of social protection programs targeting the entire population from those targeting specific high-risk groups, thereby helping prevent the diversion of scarce social protection resources to less vulnerable groups, and channeling them to those who need them most; and (iii) twinning social protection reform with complementary reform in other areas, such as fiscal management and the labor market, since a social protection system does not exist in a vacuum but within the context of the broader economy and society that defines its objectives and constraints.

Chapters 5, 6, and 7 emphasize the importance of good governance and institutions as a key policy issue for an inclusive growth strategy. Chapter 8 by Zhuang, de Dios, and Lagman-Martin asks where developing Asia stands in governance and institutional quality and how they are linked with the region's growth performance and pattern of income inequality. They note that, while the intrinsic value of good governance and institutions as ends of development in their own right is now universally accepted and underlies the very notion of inclusiveness, their instrumental value as means toward higher growth and lower inequality has not yet been well understood.

Their literature review shows that a long-run positive association between governance and institutional quality, on one hand, and growth and level of income, on the other, is strong and incontrovertible, both conceptually and empirically. There is also wide agreement on two-way causal links between the two. However, consensus on the relative importance of the two links is still lacking. They also show that there are convincing arguments for an association between governance/institutional quality—particularly in the dimensions of political accountability, democracy, and control of corruption—on one hand, and income inequality, on the other, but this association is empirically weaker. There is also wide agreement on two-way causal links between the two, with the link from lower income inequality to better governance/institutional quality arguably stronger than the reverse.

They then ask where developing Asia stands in various attributes of governance and institutional quality. Using the World Bank's widely used six composite governance indicators, they show that, compared with other regions in the world, developing Asia in 2008 scored relatively high in government effectiveness and rule of law, but low in political stability, and voice and accountability. Scores on regulatory quality and control of corruption lay in between. Further, compared with developed countries and Eastern Europe, developing Asia as a whole still has a lot to catch up in all governance dimensions. During 1998–2008, however, a large number of developing Asian economies saw their governance scores improving in various dimensions, although there were also a large number of economies experiencing slippage. But in the areas of rule of law and control of corruption, more economies improved than slipped. Further, there was a significant increase in the proportion of economies with surplus in control of corruption (compared with an international reference line), from 26% to 47%. These results suggest that significant improvements in governance do and can occur within a relatively short period of time.

Zhuang, et al. also ask whether high initial governance scores lead to better subsequent growth performance. They find that developing Asian economies with government effectiveness, regulatory quality, and rule of law in surplus in 1998 grew faster during 1998–2008 by 1.6, 2.0, and 1.2 percentage points per year on average, respectively, than the economies with governance in deficit in these dimensions (oil- and gas-rich countries excluded). These results provide support for a causal link from good governance and institutions to superior growth performance, and dispel the notion that developing Asian economies are "outliers" to this relationship. However, such a causal link cannot be detected in the cases of voice and accountability, political stability, and control of corruption. A number of possible explanations for the paradoxical results are discussed, including measurement problems associated with governance indicators, the reverse causality, the context-specific nature of the governance-growth nexus, and the role of informal institutions.

Applying the same classification framework, they find that levels of income inequality across economies with governance in surplus are not very different from those with governance in deficit in almost all dimensions. Possible explanations for such results range from an imperfect understanding or specification of the underlying causal relationships; measurement problems associated with governance indicators; and the varying nature of rising inequality in the region.

In conclusion, Zhuang et al. argue that given its intrinsic value and positive association with the level of development, good governance should be pursued in all dimensions as a basic development goal. To maximize its instrumental value, the current literature points to the need for recognizing the context-specific nature of the linkages between governance and institutional quality, on one hand, and growth and inequality, on the other, and for focusing on the aspects that are most binding and critical to a country's development in a particular period. There is also a need for cautioning against unguarded expectations that any institutional improvement would lead to better growth performance and more equal income distribution in a relatively short period of time. Taken at face value, the empirical findings in this chapter seem to suggest that strengthening government effectiveness, improving regulatory quality and rule of law, and control of corruption could well be used as potential entry points of development strategies for many countries in the region. There is also a need for more efforts to improve the measurement of governance and institutional quality and more research to better understand the complex relationships between institutional and economic developments.

1.4.3   Country studies

Country studies provide insights into the country-specific dynamics of poverty, inequality, and inclusiveness of growth, and policy challenges in promoting inclusive growth. Part C comprises six chapters, each focusing on a set of issues related to poverty, the labor market, or inequality for particular developing Asian countries.

Chapter 9 by Son examines the relationship between growth and inequality in the Philippines, with a particular focus on the role of the labor market. From the national family income and expenditure survey and the labor force survey for the years 1997, 2000, and 2003, she finds that Philippine households derive their incomes mainly from labor employment, with the poor relying more on earnings from self-employment in the informal sector. Her estimates of inequality elasticity with respect to different income components show that agricultural wage income and earnings from self-employment reduce inequality, while non-agricultural wage income increases it. She also shows that the average per capita real labor income of the households covered by the two surveys declined at an annual rate of 2.73% from 1997 to 2000 and of 1.1% from 2000 to 2003. Decomposing the decline into changes in labor force participation, employment rate, work hours per employed, and real labor productivity (measured in hourly labor earnings), the decline in real labor productivity is found to be the most important contributing factor.

To investigate how labor market conditions impact income inequality, Son estimates inequality in per capita labor income using the Theil index and decomposes the changes in the Theil index over time into various contributions. She finds that inequality was high and caused largely by differences in labor productivity across individuals, similar to the findings on the determinants of labor income growth. On the basis of this finding, Son argues that, to reduce inequality, what matters is not only creating jobs for the poor, but also creating productive or decent jobs.

Son further finds that, while real labor productivity declined, educational attainments of the labor force increased during 1997–2003, as evidenced by the rising proportion of employed household members having secondary and tertiary education and the declining proportion of those having primary education only. She also finds that employability declined for people with primary education only, but increased for those with secondary or tertiary education. She argues that these may not be reflective of rising demand for labor with secondary and tertiary education in the labor market; instead, the analysis of the survey data appears to suggest that a large expansion in the supply of workers with higher education led to them taking over low-productivity jobs from workers with less education and, at the same time, caused the wage rate of skilled labor to fall. She concludes that this could suggest a mismatch between labor demand and supply in terms of the skill mix in the Philippines. Therefore, in addition to creating productive jobs, public policy could also focus on making the education system supply the kinds of skills that are demanded by the labor market.

Chapter 10 by Niimi assesses the inclusiveness of Nepal's recent economic growth and examines what factors help households escape poverty, based on data from the Nepal Living Standards Surveys conducted in 1995–1996 and in 2003–2004. She notes that despite impressive progress in reducing poverty in recent years, the country's poverty incidence remains high. There were also large variations in the rates of poverty reduction geographically as well as by ethnicity/caste. For instance, the poverty headcount ratio was more than halved in urban areas between 1995–1996 and 2003–2004, while it declined by only 20% in rural areas. Hence about 35% of the population in the rural sector was still found to live below the poverty line in 2003–2004. Further, there was a sharp increase in income inequality, implying that the benefits of economic growth have not been shared equally, with relatively well-off households benefiting more than poorer households.

Niimi then looks at what factors help households escape poverty, using a multinomial logit model to analyze the determinants of poverty dynamics. The estimation results suggest that, among other things, educational attainment, land ownership, access to irrigation, employment in the non-agricultural sector, and receipt of domestic remittances are all important in lifting households out of poverty. On the other hand, being Dalits (the lowest caste) seems to prevent households from becoming non-poor, even after controlling for other factors.

In conclusion, Niimi argues that in Nepal, where the inclusiveness of growth was found to be limited, special effort is required to help the poor and excluded catch up and participate in growth on more equal terms. In other words, to ensure that economic opportunity generated by growth is within reach of every segment of society, the government must redress the weak human capabilities of poor and excluded groups as well as the unequal access to productive assets.

Chapter 11 by Lin, Zhuang, Yarcia, and Lin looks at changes in income inequality and their sources in the PRC during 1990–2005. It does so using unit-level data extrapolated from the grouped income data of 23 provinces, covering both rural and urban households and representing more than 85% of the population. They find that, at the national level, the Gini coefficient of per capita nominal income increased from 0.345 in 1990 to 0.456 in 2005. But after adjusting for interprovincial and between-urban-rural cost of living (COL) differences, the Gini coefficient increased from 0.287 in 1990 to 0.387 in 2005. These figures suggest that without adjusting for COL differences, the Gini coefficient could be overestimated by almost 20%. They also find that income inequality increased in both urban and rural areas, but urban inequality increased at a much faster pace, although its level was still lower than that of rural inequality in 2005. Across regions, they find that income inequality in the coastal, central, and western regions increased during 1990–2005.

Their decomposition analysis shows that during 1990–2005 rising inequality between urban and rural areas and that within the urban sector were the major sources of rising national inequality. In 1990, after adjusting for COL differences, the between-urban-rural inequality and within-urban inequality accounted for 12.1% and 15.7%, respectively, of the national inequality; in 2005, their contributions increased to 30.4% and 34%, respectively. While the within-rural inequality also increased, the extent of the increase was smaller and, consequently, its contribution to national inequality declined from more than 70% in 1990 to about 36% in 2005. Decomposing national inequality by province, they find that the within-province inequality was the major source of national inequality. After adjusting for COL differences, the contribution of the within-province inequality to national inequality increased from 86% in 1990 to 89% in 2005, while the contribution of the between-province inequality declined from 14% to 11% during the same period. These figures show that rising regional inequality was not a major driver of the increases in national inequality in the PRC.

On the basis of their findings, Lin et al. argue that the most effective ways of reducing overall inequality in the PRC are to narrow the income gap between urban and rural areas and to reduce income inequality among the urban population. Regional income disparity (between coastal and western regions and among rich and poor provinces) remains large and needs to be reduced; however, because it is not a major source of inequality, the impact of this reduction on inequality at the national level may be limited. But reducing regional income disparity is very important for poverty reduction, because the majority of the poor in the PRC is located in the western region.

Chapter 12 by Khor and Pencavel argues that annual income data may provide a misleading indicator of enduring income inequality in societies where there is considerable year-to-year income mobility. Using panel data on household incomes, they measure income mobility in the PRC between the early 1990s and early 2000s. They find that, in the early 1990s, the increase in income inequality was accompanied by a level of income mobility comparable to other developing countries in transition and higher than that found in developed countries such as the United

States. By the early 2000s, however, while income inequality increased further, income mobility decreased, implying that the probability of being stuck in a relatively lower level of income increased for households.

They also find divergent experiences between urban and rural households as the urban-rural gap widened. In the early 1990s, income mobility was higher among urban households than among rural households; between the early 1990s and early 2000s, income mobility decreased for both urban and rural households, but the decrease was more pronounced for the former; therefore, in the early 2000s, urban and rural households had more or less the same level of income mobility. These findings are found to be robust to alternative ways of defining household income groups and of analyzing income mobility.

An examination of the correlates of income mobility suggests significant differences between urban and rural households as well. In urban areas, several characteristics of heads of households are found to be positively correlated with upward income mobility, including higher levels of schooling, being a woman, and being an ethnic minority, among others. For rural households, on the other hand, the major correlate associated positively with upward income mobility is household size. While the education level of heads of rural households mattered in the 1990s, by the 2000s the only other positive correlate with upward income mobility is Communist Party membership.

Khor and Pencavel also look at the relationship between measures of income inequality based on incomes averaged over 3 years in contrast to those based on incomes for a single year. They find that Gini coefficients for 3-year average incomes are between 90% and 95% of the corresponding Gini coefficients for single-year incomes, suggesting that income mobility could mitigate the levels of income inequality.

Khor and Pencavel contend that all these have implications for policy. In particular, policies targeted toward inclusive growth should take into account longer-term income.

Chapter 13 by Son examines the extent of gender discrimination in labor markets in Thailand and Viet Nam, using data from the 2002 Viet Nam living standards survey and 2004 Thailand labor force survey. She derives a welfare measure based on Atkinson's welfare function that takes into account the sensitivity of earnings inequality within each occupation as well as between male and female workers. The gender welfare disparity in favor of male workers is estimated at 17.9% for Viet Nam and 8.3% for Thailand when the inequality aversion parameter is set at unity. A higher inequality aversion parameter (with less tolerance of inequality) leads to much higher gender welfare disparity, implying that gender disparity is far greater among the ultra-poor than among the not-so-poor in the labor market.

27

Decomposing the gender welfare disparity into three components —gender discrimination, occupational segregation, and earnings inequality—Son finds discrimination against female workers (measured by the earnings differential between males and females within each occupation) to be a dominant factor for both Thailand and Viet Nam. It explains more than 100% of the total disparity in Thailand. In Viet Nam, gender discrimination accounts for 80% of the total disparity with an inequality aversion parameter at unity and about 40% with an inequality aversion parameter at 2.

On the other hand, occupational segregation (measured by the difference in the proportion of male and female workers in each occupation) is found to reduce gender disparity, especially for Thailand. This is because a significant proportion of females work in relatively high-paying professions, such as teaching, life science, and health professions. Earnings inequality is found to increase gender welfare disparity, suggesting that earnings inequality is greater among female workers than among male workers. But its contribution is relatively small, except in the case of Viet Nam when the inequality aversion parameter is set at 2.

When differentials in individual earnings are adjusted for differences in individual characteristics such as hours of work, education, years of work experience, and location in calculating the gender welfare disparity, gender discrimination remains a dominant contributor (although smaller in magnitude) to the total disparity. But the contribution of occupational segregation becomes positive. The contribution of earnings inequality remains positive but smaller for Viet Nam, and becomes negative but negligible for Thailand, implying that controlling for individual characteristics reduces the difference in earnings inequality between male and female workers and, in the case of Thailand, leads to earnings inequality among male workers becoming greater than among female workers.

Son also looks at the impact of workers' individual characteristics on occupational segregation, gender discrimination, and earnings inequality. Education and work experience stand out as important explanatory factors. Education is found to help reduce occupational segregation and gender discrimination, and increase the difference in earnings inequality between male and female workers. But overall, education reduces gender welfare disparity. This suggests that female workers, on average, have higher levels of education than their male counterparts. Female workers are also found to have a higher average level of education than male workers among the ultra-poor in the labor market in Thailand. On the other hand, work experience is found to be an important factor affecting occupational segregation, gender discrimination, and earnings inequality, but overall, it increases gender welfare disparity. This suggests that women work fewer years than men. Apart from individual characteristics, Son highlights other factors that could explain gender welfare disparity, including the difference in the nature and type of jobs engaged in by men and women, employers' preferences and cultural factors, and differences in education and career choices between men and women.

Son concludes that to narrow the gender gap in the labor market, in addition to instituting anti-gender discrimination measures, governments could gear resources toward providing affordable child care to reduce the opportunity cost of working for women and raising their productivity as formal workers. Governments could also pursue programs that enhance girls' subject choices and improve career advice at school to ensure that girls are encouraged to pursue fields such as mathematics and science.

Finally, Chapter 14 by Jha and Mehta focuses on the issues of hunger and food security in the Philippines, noting that the incidence of hunger rose rapidly in the Philippines beginning in 2003, associated with rapidly rising food prices, particularly those of rice in the poorest parts of the country. To understand why this has happened despite good income growth and significant public expenditure on food security programs, they look at the country's main food security agency—the National Food Authority (NFA). They argue that the NFA's effectiveness is hobbled by conflicting and poorly defined objectives to achieve food security in the country, including the provision of price support to consumers and producers and stabilization of market prices. In their analysis of household survey data, Jha and Mehta find that much of the subsidized rice the NFA distributes is consumed by non-poor households. They cite evidence that households report consuming less than half of the total amount of rice the NFA claims to have distributed in 2006. The targeting effectiveness of the program is low as only 25% of the poor benefit from the program while 75% are excluded. Also, leakage is high, and more so for urban areas than in rural areas.

Jha and Mehta argue that a renewal of the upward trend in prices will affect food security in the Philippines. The authorities will need to be prepared to shield the poor from price shocks through well-targeted, reliable, and efficient food safety nets. Institutional reforms at the NFA—including a clarification of its objectives and the rationale for its monopoly on rice imports, better targeting, and greater transparency—are prerequisites for tackling food insecurity. Hunger, which is highly prevalent but localized within the populace, calls for localized policy interventions, not blanket attempts to control prices of staples, especially given that the Philippines has prioritized fiscal prudence as it attempts to reduce its debt burden.

Appendix: Composition of developing Asia

Afghanistan
Armenia
Azerbaijan
Bangladesh
Bhutan
Brunei Darussalam
Cambodia
China, People's Republic of
Cook Islands
Fiji Islands
Georgia
Hong Kong, China
India
Indonesia
Kazakhstan
Kiribati
Korea, Republic of
Kyrgyz Republic
Lao People's Democratic Republic
Malaysia
Maldives
Marshall Islands, Republic of the
Micronesia, Federated States of

Mongolia
Myanmar
Nauru
Nepal
Pakistan
Palau, Republic of
Papua New Guinea
Philippines
Samoa
Singapore
Solomon Islands
Sri Lanka
Taipei,China
Tajikistan
Thailand
Timor-Leste
Tonga
Turkmenistan
Tuvalu
Uzbekistan
Vanuatu
Viet Nam

References

ADB. 2008. *Strategy 2020: The Long-Term Strategic Framework of the Asian Development Bank 2008–2020*. Asian Development Bank, Manila.

_____. 2009. *Asian Development Outlook 2009*. Asian Development Bank, Manila.

Ali, I. 2007. Pro-Poor to Inclusive Growth: Asian Prescriptions. ERD Policy Brief No. 48, Economics and Research Department, Asian Development Bank, Manila.

Ali, I., and J. Zhuang. 2007. Inclusive Growth toward a Prosperous Asia: Policy Implications. ERD Working Paper Series No. 97, Economics and Research Department, Asian Development Bank, Manila.

Bourguignon, F., F. H. G. Ferreira, and M. Walton. 2007. "Equity, Efficiency and Inequality Traps." *Journal of Economic Inequality* 5:235–56.

Central Committee of the Communist Party of Viet Nam. 2001. *Strategy for Socio-Economic Development 2001–2010*. Hanoi.

Chaudhuri, S., and M. Ravallion. 2007. "Partially Awakened Giants: Uncover Growth in China and India." In L. Alan Winters, and S. Yusuf, eds., *Dancing with Giants: China, India, and the Global Economy*. The World Bank, Washington, DC.

Easterly, W. 2007. "Inequality does Cause Underdevelopment: Insights from a New Instrument." *Journal of Development Economics* 64:755–76.

ESCAP, ADB, and UNDP. 2010. *Achieving the Millennium Development Goals in an Era of Global Uncertainty: Asia-Pacific Regional Report 2009/10*. United Nations Economic and Social Commission for Asia and the Pacific.

Ianchovichina, E., and S. Lundstrom. 2009. What is Inclusive Growth? A note requested by donors supporting the Diagnostic Facility for Shared Growth. Available: http://siteresources.worldbank.org/INTDEBTDEPT/Resources/468980-1218567884549/WhatIsInclusiveGrowth20081230.pdf.

Kakwani, N., and E. M. Pernia. 2000. "What is Pro-Poor Growth?" *Asian Development Review* 18(1):1–16.

Planning Commission of India. 2006. *Towards Faster and More Inclusive Growth: An Approach to the 11th Five Year Plan*. New Delhi.

Rajan, R., and L. Zingales. 2007. The Persistence of Underdevelopment: Constituencies and Competitive Rent Preservation. NBER Working Paper Series No. 12093, National Bureau of Economic Research.

Ravallion, M., and S. Chen. 2003. "Measuring Pro-Poor Growth." *Economics Letters* 78(1):93–99.

Roemer, J. E. 1996. *Theories of Distributive Justice*. Cambridge, MA: Harvard University Press.

_____. 2006. Economic Development as Opportunity Equalization. Cowles Foundation Discussion Paper No. 1583, Yale University, New Haven.

State Council of China. 2006. *The 11th Five Year Plan of National Economy and Social Development of People's Republic of China 2006–2010*. Beijing.

Tandon, A., and J. Zhuang. 2007. Inclusiveness of Economic Growth in the People's Republic of China: What Do Population Health Outcomes Tell Us? ERD Policy Brief Series No. 47, Economics and Research Department, Asian Development Bank, Manila.

UNDP. 2007. *Thailand National Human Development Report 2007*. United Nations Development Programme, Bangkok.

World Bank. 2006. "Equity and Development." In *World Development Report 2006*. Washington, DC.

Part A

Measuring Inequality
and Poverty

2

Inequality and Poverty in Asia

J. Salcedo Cain, Rana Hasan, and Rhoda Magsombol

2.1   Introduction

Asian development between the 1960s and the 1980s featured rapid growth in the newly industrializing economies—Hong Kong, China; Republic of Korea (Korea); Singapore; and Taipei,China (later followed by several Southeast Asian economies)—and more sluggish growth in South Asia. Interestingly, though there were exceptions, low income inequality appeared to characterize both groups in comparison with developing countries in other regions, especially Latin America. However, since at least the 1990s, high rates of economic growth have become more common in the region, and it is widely believed that inequality has grown in many countries.

How correct is this perception, and how broadly does it apply to a region as diverse as developing Asia? This chapter brings together recent evidence on inequality in incomes and, especially, consumption expenditures.[1] Clearly, incomes or expenditures are by no means all that goes into determining economic well-being, that is, an individual's access to goods and services.[2] Educational and health status, political power, or access to justice, among others, are all important factors that contribute to economic well-being. Accordingly, the manner in which these other variables are distributed over a population is relevant to a study of inequality. However, this chapter's focus is on the distribution of economic well-being as captured through data on incomes and expenditures. (See Chapter 3 for a detailed examination of issues related to education and health.)

This chapter closely examines whether the distribution of economic well-being has become more or less "equal" in developing Asian countries

---

[1]   As will be explained later, data on consumption expenditures can be viewed as a proxy for households' "permanent" incomes; additionally, data availability and other considerations suggest that consumption expenditure data can capture economic well-being more completely than income data.

[2]   In most of this chapter, the terms consumption and expenditure are used interchangeably. Although the two are not identical concepts, using the two terms interchangeably rarely presents a problem.

over the last 10 years or so. Inequality has increased within countries in much of the region. Indeed, in 15 out of the 21 developing economies for which sufficient data are available, inequality is found to have increased over the last 10 years or so, rather sharply in Bangladesh, Cambodia, People's Republic of China (PRC), Lao People's Democratic Republic (Lao PDR), Nepal, and Sri Lanka.[3] But the rise in inequality has not always been large—indeed, it remains mostly below the high levels of many Latin American and sub-Saharan African countries. Conversely, declining levels of inequality characterize many of the Central Asian republics and the three Southeast Asian countries worst affected by the economic and financial crisis of 1997/1998, namely, Indonesia, Malaysia, and Thailand.

There is no simple answer, however, to how developing Asia's policy makers should view rising income inequality. On one hand, there are several reasons for concern. First, increasing inequality may imply a slower pace of poverty reduction. As is now widely recognized, for a given growth rate, a growth process in which inequality is increasing sharply will be one in which poverty reduction is lower. More generally, increasing inequality suggests that relatively poor individuals and households are not benefiting from, or participating in, economic growth to the same extent as richer individuals and households. Second, there are compelling reasons why high levels of inequality can dampen growth prospects. This is especially important to consider in light of the evidence that distribution is becoming more unequal in Asia. Among other things, high levels of inequality can hold adverse consequences for social cohesion and the quality of institutions and policies. In turn, social divisions and low-quality institutions and policies can hold adverse implications for growth prospects.

On the other hand, it has to be acknowledged that economic development is likely to entail processes that increase inequality. This is not to suggest that policy makers should subscribe to the idea of the "Kuznets curve" (or the "inverted-U hypothesis") in which inequality first rises and then falls with economic growth. As a large number of studies have demonstrated, the evidence for the Kuznets curve is weak (see Fields 2001 for a comprehensive review). Moreover, as can be seen from Figure 2.1, the Gini coefficient of incomes for two newly industrialized economies—Korea and Taipei,China—never touched 40 during their phase of rapid growth between the 1970s and 1990s, and even declined over some periods.

Still, Nobel Laureate Arthur Lewis' point about inequality and the development process is a powerful one:

"Development must be inegalitarian because it does not start in every part of an economy at the same time. Somebody develops a mine, and employs a thousand people. Or farmers in one province start

---

3   Data constraints force the use of a period of less than 10 years for several countries.

planting cocoa, which grows in only 10% of the country. Or the Green Revolution arrives to benefit those farmers who have plenty of rain or access to irrigation, while offering nothing to the other 50% in the drier regions" (Lewis 1983, 443).

Figure 2.1   Trend in inequality: Republic of Korea and Taipei,China
(Gini coefficients, 1970s–2000s)

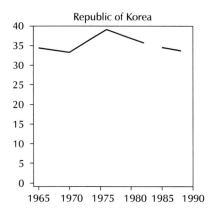
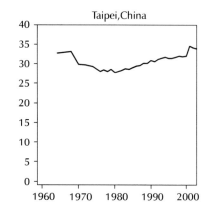

Note: Gini coefficients are based on income surveys.
Source: World Institute for Development Economic Research, *World Income Inequality Database* (Taipei,China); Fields (1989); Korea National Statistical Office.

Ultimately, guidance for policy must come from a nuanced analysis of inequality. In particular, it is important to examine what factors lie behind the increases in inequality that may be found in the data. Some important questions to ask include: To what extent are increases in inequality because of policy biases against the sectors and industries in which the poor are more likely to be engaged? To what extent do the inequalities seen in *outcomes* (such as incomes, expenditures, health status, and educational attainments, etc.) reflect inequalities in *opportunity*? To the extent that a significant part of increasing inequalities are related to policy biases and/or disparities in access to opportunity (to accumulate human capital, to access financial services, etc.) they are a serious problem requiring attention. It is only by examining inequality and its evolution that such issues can begin to be addressed.

Section 2.2 provides a brief discussion of the measurement of inequality, and Section 2.3 examines recent levels of income inequality. The data reveal that inequality over the last 10 years or so has increased in a majority of the countries looked at. But the increase does not reflect the "rich getting richer and the poor poorer", but rather "the rich getting richer faster". Section 2.4 then looks into the causes of changes in inequality and the elements of the policy environment that may explain the observed patterns of inequality. Section 2.5 concludes with some thoughts on how public policy should deal with inequality. In what is clearly a controversial area, it is suggested that fighting inequality by focusing public policy on improving delivery of basic health care and education services to the poor, strengthening social protection, and significantly raising employment opportunity and the incomes of the poor should be a minimum common agenda for Asia's policy makers.

2.2   Measures of inequality

The term inequality has many different meanings. In this chapter, it is used primarily to describe how an indicator of economic well-being is distributed over a particular population. A *measure* of inequality[4] in turn provides a single "numerical representation" of the interpersonal differences in income for a given population (Cowell 1995). More broadly, a measure of inequality quantifies the disparity that allows one individual certain material choices denied to another (Ray 1998). Box 2.1 describes measures of inequality used in the literature.

Box 2.1   Some common measures of inequality

Measures of inequality can differ from one another in the concepts on which they are based and their sensitivity to incomes at different points along the income distribution. Differences in concepts of inequality are discussed in the text. This box describes some popular measures of inequality and the portions of the overall distribution they focus on. The discussion is carried out in terms of income inequality; the treatment of expenditure inequality would be identical.

The **quintile income ratio** compares the income earned by the top 20% of the population with that of the lowest 20%. More generally, income ratios can be computed for different "quantiles", a generic term that refers to any specific population proportion. For example, income ratios may be computed on the basis of deciles (one tenth of the population ranked by income), quartiles (one quarter of the population), etc. As should be clear, income ratios only use specific segments of the complete distribution.

continued.

---

4   Cowell (1995) and Fields (2001) provide excellent and detailed discussions on the measurement of inequality.

Box 2.1 *continued.*

The **Gini coefficient** is one of the most commonly used measures of inequality and ranges from 0 to 1 (or 0–100 when expressed in percentage terms, as is done in this chapter). With perfect equality, the Gini coefficient would be equal to zero. With perfect inequality, it would be equal to one (or 100). Numerically, the Gini coefficient can be computed as follows:

$$Gini = \frac{-(n+1)}{n} + \frac{2}{n^2 \mu_x} \sum_{i=1}^{n} i \cdot x$$

where x_i is the income of recipient/individual i, μ_x is the average income, and n is the total number of recipients/individuals.

Generalized entropy (GE) measures are derived from the notion of entropy in information theory. As discussed in more detail in the text, they satisfy five important properties for comparing inequality across distributions. The formulas for computing these are:

$$GE(\alpha) = \begin{cases} \frac{1}{\alpha(1-\alpha)} \frac{1}{n} \sum_{i=1}^{n} \left[1 - \left(\frac{x_i}{\mu_x} \right)^{\alpha} \right] & for\ \alpha \neq 0 \\ \frac{1}{n} \sum_{i=1}^{n} \frac{x_i}{\mu_x} ln\left(\frac{x_i}{\mu_x} \right) & for\ \alpha = 1 \\ \frac{1}{n} \sum_{i=1}^{n} ln\left(\frac{x_i}{\mu_x} \right) & for\ \alpha = 0 \end{cases}$$

The parameter α represents the weight given to income differences at different points of the income distribution. The GE measure is more sensitive to changes in income at the lower end of the distribution for lower values of α. Higher values of α make the GE measure more sensitive to changes in income at the upper end of the distribution. The parameter α can take any real value. However, the typical values used are 0, 1, and 2. The GE measure places more weight on income differences at the lower end of the distribution with a value of 0, while more weight is placed on income differences at the upper end of the distribution with a value of 2. A value of 1, also known as the Theil index, places equal weights on income differences across the entire distribution.

Source: Fields (2001), ADB (2004).

Which specific measure (or measures) of inequality should one use to compare inequality across distributions? In the first instance, the answer depends crucially on how inequality is conceptualized. An example is useful to illustrate this point. Consider two simple measures of inequality: (i) the difference between the highest and lowest income in a given population (also known as the range), and (ii) the ratio of the highest and lowest income (a variant of the quintile ratio described in Box 2.1). To simplify matters further, suppose that the population consists of only two people whose incomes are observed at two points of time, say, in 1995 and 2005. In 1995, the first person's income is $100 per month while the second person's is $1,000. Suppose that 10 years later both incomes have doubled so that the first person's income becomes $200 and the second's $2,000. Has inequality increased, decreased, or stayed the same? It depends on the perspective of the analyst. In this example, it depends on whether the analyst cares more about *relative* inequality (i.e., proportionate differences in incomes), or *absolute* inequality (i.e., absolute differences in incomes). If it is the former, inequality as measured by the proportionate differences in incomes will reveal inequality to be unchanged ($1,000/$100 = $2,000/$200 = 10). But if the analyst is concerned with the absolute differences in high and low incomes, inequality has clearly increased (the difference between the two incomes in 1995 being $900 and in 2005 being $1,800).

More generally, an important consideration on which inequality measures differ from one another is the extent to which they satisfy five properties[5] (or axioms): (i) income scale independence, (ii) population independence, (iii) anonymity, (iv) the transfer principle, and (v) decomposability.

The first of these properties is one already encountered. Formally, the property of income scale independence requires that inequality be unchanged for proportionate changes in all incomes. Measures of relative inequality satisfy this property; measures of absolute inequality do not.

It is important to note that a measure of inequality that does not satisfy income scale independence is neither "wrong" nor "right". As Fields (2001, 16) points out, "absolute inequality and relative inequality are not alternative measures of the same underlying concept; they measure fundamentally different concepts." While most economists would prefer to analyze inequality using measures that satisfy scale independence (i.e., they prefer measures of relative inequality), the issue is tied to value judgments about distributive justice.

A very practical and real-world context in which the distinctions between absolute and relative concepts of inequality can matter is provided by the debate on how the economic gains from globalization are shared. Ravallion (2004a) argues that a key driver of the debate on how much poor people have shared in the benefits of globalization is the different concepts of inequality adopted—explicitly or implicitly—by the

---

[5]   Even within the context of similar conceptualizations of inequality, different measures can lead to different conclusions about how inequality compares across distributions. As is made clearer below, measures of inequality can differ based on their sensitivity to incomes at different points along the income distribution.

main protagonists of the debate: relative inequality by proponents of globalization and absolute inequality by opponents of globalization.

The second and third properties are less controversial. The population independence axiom enables the comparison of inequality across populations of different sizes by postulating that the inequality of two populations, one of which is simply a scale replica of the other, be identical. The anonymity property enables a focus solely on incomes (or whichever welfare indicator is being analyzed) by requiring that the measure of inequality depend only on incomes and no other characteristic.

The fourth and fifth properties are weightier. According to the transfer principle, transferring some income from a richer person to a poorer person, without changing their ranks in the income distribution, should register as a fall in inequality. The decomposability property of an inequality measure concerns the relationship between inequality in a given population and that in its consequent parts (or among subgroups of the population). For example, consider the relationship between inequality at the national, rural, and urban levels. An inequality measure that satisfies decomposability will allow inequality at the national level to be decomposed into inequality *within* each of the rural and urban sectors and inequality *between* the rural and urban sectors. As can be seen later on, decomposability is a rather attractive property, especially when one analyzes the proximate causes of inequality in a given population.

Drawing on Cowell (1995), Table 2.1 lists how various inequality measures compare in terms of four of the properties, except anonymity, which is satisfied by all. As popular as the Gini coefficient is, it does not satisfy the decomposability property, except in unusual circumstances.[6] Decomposability is, however, satisfied by the GE class of inequality measures. In fact, inequality measures that satisfy all five properties are said to belong to the GE class of measures.

There is a preference among many economists in favor of inequality measures that satisfy the five properties (or at least four of the five—as reflected by the popularity of the Gini coefficient, a measure that does not satisfy decomposability). It is fair to ask why there is a need for alternative measures of inequality that satisfy the given axioms. For example, why are there alternative measures within the GE class? The reason, and one that applies broadly (i.e., not just to measures within the GE class), is that different measures of inequality differ in their sensitivity to income (expenditure) at different points along the distribution of income (expenditure).

---

6   The Gini coefficient is decomposable if the population subgroups being analyzed do not overlap in terms of their incomes or expenditures. While methods have been devised for decomposing the Gini, the component terms of total inequality can lack intuitive appeal.

Table 2.1   Properties of common inequality measures

Inequality measure	Income scale independence	Population independence	Transfer principle	Decomposability
Variance	No[a]	No	Yes[b]	Yes
Logarithmic variance	Yes	Yes	No	No
Gini coefficient	Yes	Yes	Yes	No
Generalized entropy	Yes	Yes	Yes[b]	Yes

a   Increases with income.
b   The transfer principle is satisfied in strong form, i.e., the reduction in inequality arising from a transfer from a richer to a poorer person depends only on the "distance" between two individuals. See Cowell (1995) for details.
Source: Adapted from Cowell (1995, 66).

In particular, and as noted in Box 2.1, the GE measure with parameter zero, i.e., GE(0), is more sensitive to income differences at the lower end of the distribution. Conversely, the GE(2) measure puts more weight on income differences at the upper end, while the GE(1) measure puts equal weights on income differences across the entire distribution. Thus, for example, if incomes at the top of the distribution become more unequal, it is the GE(2) measure that will most clearly pick this up. The GE(1) measure would register a smaller change in inequality, and the GE(0) measure may barely pick it up at all. As for the Gini coefficient, this measure of inequality is more sensitive to income differences in the middle of the distribution.

2.3   Inequality in Asia

This chapter first examines inequality within countries, using available distribution data on consumption expenditures (and in some cases, incomes). It presents estimates of inequality for the most recent year available, as well as approximately 10 years earlier, allowing an examination of the unfolding of inequality in that period. Second, it describes how economic well-being, as opposed to simply inequality, has changed over the last 10 years or so. Finally, the empirical relationship between inequality, poverty, and growth as reflected in the data is described. Technically minded readers may note that the estimates and analysis of inequality in this section are based on Lorenz curves fitted using grouped/tabulated distribution data (see Appendix for details).

2.3.1   Inequality within developing Asian economies

A. Recent estimates

Table 2.2 presents the most recent available estimates of the Gini coefficient and the ratio of per capita expenditures/incomes of the top 20% (fifth quintile) to bottom 20% (i.e., first quintile) of the distribution (henceforth, top to bottom quintile ratio) for 22 developing Asian economies. Most of the underlying distribution data refer to per capita consumption expenditures. Exceptions are given in the notes.

Table 2.2   Gini coefficient and top to bottom quintile ratio: Developing Asia

Economy	Latest year	Gini coefficient (%)	Quintile ratio
Armenia [a]	2003	33.80	5.08
Azerbaijan	2001	36.50	5.96
Bangladesh	2005	34.08	5.03
Cambodia [a]	2004	38.05	7.04
China, People's Rep. of [a,b]	2004	47.25	11.37
India [a,b]	2004	36.22	5.52
Indonesia	2002	34.30	5.13
Kazakhstan	2003	33.85	5.61
Korea, Rep. of [c]	2004	31.55	5.47
Kyrgyz Republic	2003	30.30	4.43
Lao People's Democratic Rep. [a]	2002	34.68	5.40
Malaysia	2004	40.33	7.70
Mongolia	2002	32.84	5.44
Nepal [a]	2003	47.30	9.47
Pakistan	2004	31.18	4.46
Philippines	2003	43.97	9.11
Sri Lanka	2002	40.18	6.83
Taipei,China [c]	2003	33.85	6.05
Tajikistan	2003	32.63	5.14
Thailand	2002	41.96	7.72
Turkmenistan [a]	2003	43.02	8.33
Viet Nam	2004	37.08	6.24

a   Estimates are from the Beta Lorenz parameterization of grouped/tabulated data.
b   Estimates are based on combining separate rural and urban distributions.
c   Distributions for the Republic of Korea and Taipei,China refer to household incomes (urban wage-earning households for the former).
Note: Estimates of the Gini coefficient and expenditure/income share are based on parameterized (generalized quadratic or Beta) Lorenz curves using grouped/tabulated data on per capita expenditure/income distributions.
Source: Authors' estimates using grouped/tabulated data from World Bank, POVCALNET; World Institute for Development Economic Research, *World Income Inequality Database* (Taipei,China); publications of national statistics offices or personal communications (India, Republic of Korea, Turkmenistan, and Viet Nam); and decile-level distributions generated from unit record data (Bangladesh, Malaysia, and Philippines).

Figure 2.2 displays the values of the Gini coefficient and the quintile ratio. Gini coefficients range from a low of 30.30 (Kyrgyz Republic) to a high of 47.30 (Nepal). The median value of the Gini coefficient in developing Asia is around 34.50.

Figure 2.2   Gini coefficient and top to bottom quintile ratio

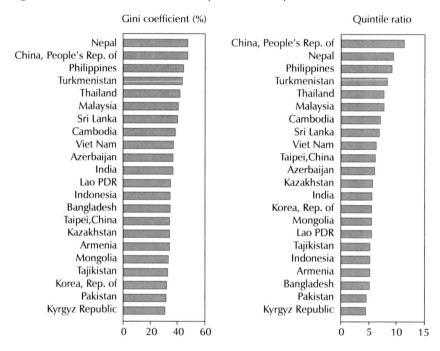

Lao PDR = Lao People's Democratic Republic.
Note: Estimates are for the following years: Armenia (2003); Azerbaijan (2001); Bangladesh (2005); Cambodia (2004); People's Republic of China (2004); India (2004); Indonesia (2002); Kazakhstan (2003); Republic of Korea (2004); Kyrgyz Republic (2003); Lao PDR (2002); Malaysia (2004); Mongolia (2002); Nepal (2003); Pakistan (2004); Philippines (2003); Sri Lanka (2002); Taipei,China (2003); Tajikistan (2003); Thailand (2002); Turkmenistan (2003); and Viet Nam (2004).
Source: Authors' estimates using grouped/tabulated data from World Bank, POVCALNET; World Institute for Development Economic Research, *World Income Inequality Database* (Taipei,China); publications of national statistics offices or personal communications (India, Republic of Korea, Turkmenistan, and Viet Nam); and decile-level distributions generated from unit record data (Bangladesh, Malaysia, and Philippines).

One may be tempted to state that Gini coefficients tend to be lowest in the Central Asian republics. But this is not always the case, as the coefficient for Turkmenistan reveals. As far as the ratio of the top to the bottom 20% is concerned, these range from a low of 4.43 (once again,

Kyrgyz Republic) to a high of 11.37 (PRC). The median value of the ratio in developing Asia is 5.78.[7]

Almost all the inequality estimates shown in Table 2.2 and Figure 2.2 refer to expenditures. Table 2.3 describes some estimates of Gini coefficients from income distributions for selected developing Asian economies. As may be seen, inequality estimates based on income distributions are higher, sometimes considerably so, than those based on expenditure distributions.

Table 2.3   Estimates of Gini coefficient—expenditure versus income surveys: Developing Asia

| Economy | Year | Gini coefficient (%) | |
		Expenditure	Income
Bangladesh[a]	2000	33.4	39.2
Nepal[a]	1996	36.6	51.3
Nepal[b]	2003	47.3	56.4
Philippines[b]	2003	40.0	48.7
Thailand[a]	2000	42.8	52.3
Viet Nam[a]	1998	36.2	48.9

a   Taken from World Bank (2005, 38).
b   Based on unit-level record data.

Table 2.4 presents estimates of the Gini coefficient and the top to bottom quintile ratio from countries outside developing Asia. A comparison with the Gini coefficients for developing Asia presented above reveals some interesting regional dimensions of inequality estimates.

By and large, the highest inequality is in Latin America. Inequality can also be high in Africa. In fact, the highest Gini coefficient reported in Table 2.4 is for South Africa (57.77 from a consumption expenditure survey). Inequality tends to be far lower in industrial countries. The Gini coefficient for income inequality was only 24.90 in Japan. It is similarly low in many European countries (especially Nordic countries) and New Zealand. Among industrial countries, the highest level of inequality, whether in terms of the Gini coefficient or the ratio of the top 20% to the bottom 20% of incomes/expenditures, is found in the United States.

Levels of inequality in developing Asia are generally below those of Latin America. However, their difference somewhat reflects the fact that inequality estimates for Latin America invariably refer to incomes while for many Asian countries they are based on expenditures. More

---

7   The Gini coefficient and the top to bottom quintile ratio are highly correlated. The Spearman rank correlation is 0.90.

importantly, some of the recent estimates of inequality for developing Asia indicate levels approaching those of Latin America.

Table 2.4   International estimates of inequality: Selected economies

Economy	Year	Survey type	Gini coefficient (%)	Quintile ratio
Australia	2002	Income	30.90	–
Argentina (urban)	2003	Income	51.28	18.40
Belarus	1998	Income	27.67	3.97
Brazil	2004	Income	56.99	23.00
Canada	2000	Income	32.45	5.48
Chile	1998	Income	55.77	16.72
Ecuador	1998	Income	53.53	18.70
Egypt	1995	Expenditure	34.42	4.70
El Salvador	1997	Income	50.79	15.20
Ethiopia	1995	Expenditure	28.66	5.09
Finland	2003	Income	25.80	3.58
France	2001	Income	27.00	4.11
Germany	2001	Income	25.00	3.50
Ghana	1998	Expenditure	40.75	8.40
Italy	2002	Income	33.30	5.80
Jamaica	1998	Expenditure	38.45	8.05
Japan	1993	Income	24.90	3.37
Mexico	1998	Income	53.11	16.90
New Zealand	1997	Expenditure	23.65	–
Nigeria	2003	Expenditure	43.60	9.80
Norway	2002	Income	29.60	4.64
Panama	1997	Income	57.19	28.86
South Africa	2000	Expenditure	57.77	20.50
Spain	1998	Income	34.00	5.86
Sweden	2002	Income	25.80	3.58
United Kingdom	2002	Income	34.37	5.59
United States	2000	Income	39.42	8.45

– = data not available.
Source: World Institute for Development Economic Research, *World Income Inequality Database*; World Bank, POVCALNET.

B. Recent trends

Turning to trends in inequality for 21 of the 22 developing Asian countries considered above,[8] Table 2.5 provides estimates of the Gini

---

[8]   The omitted country is Kyrgyz Republic, for which an estimate of the Gini coefficient for an earlier year, 1993, yielded a value of 53.7. Whether this estimate is accurate or reflects serious survey errors is difficult to say.

coefficient and the top to bottom quintile ratio for 2 years. Figure 2.3 depicts changes in the coefficient and the ratio.

Table 2.5   Trends in inequality

Economy	Period	Gini coefficient (%)			Quintile ratio		
		Initial year	Final year	Annualized growth rate	Initial year	Final year	Annualized growth rate
Armenia	1998–2003	36.01	33.80	–1.27	5.87	5.08	–2.90
Azerbaijan	1995–2001	34.96	36.50	0.72	6.09	5.96	–0.36
Bangladesh	1991–2005	28.27	34.08	1.34	4.06	5.03	1.53
Cambodia	1993–2004	31.80	38.05	1.63	5.24	7.04	2.68
PRC	1993–2004	40.74	47.25	1.35	7.57	11.37	3.70
India	1993–2004	32.89	36.22	0.88	4.85	5.52	1.18
Indonesia	1993–2002	34.37	34.30	–0.02	5.20	5.13	–0.15
Kazakhstan	1996–2003	35.32	33.85	–0.61	6.20	5.61	–1.43
Korea, Rep. of	1993–2004	28.68	31.55	0.87	4.38	5.47	2.02
Lao PDR	1992–2002	30.40	34.68	1.32	4.27	5.40	2.35
Malaysia	1993–2004	41.22	40.33	–0.20	7.72	7.70	–0.02
Mongolia	1995–2002	33.20	32.84	–0.16	5.53	5.44	–0.23
Nepal	1995–2003	37.65	47.30	2.85	6.19	9.47	5.31
Pakistan	1992–2004	30.31	31.18	0.24	4.22	4.46	0.46
Philippines	1994–2003	42.89	43.97	0.28	8.34	9.11	0.98
Sri Lanka	1995–2002	34.36	40.18	2.24	5.34	6.83	3.52
Taipei,China	1993–2003	31.32	33.85	0.78	5.41	6.05	1.12
Tajikistan	1999–2003	31.52	32.63	0.87	4.97	5.14	0.84
Thailand	1992–2002	46.22	41.96	–0.97	9.41	7.72	–1.98
Turkmenistan	1998–2003	41.08	43.02	0.92	7.88	8.33	1.11
Viet Nam	1993–2004	34.91	37.08	0.55	5.40	6.24	1.31

Lao PDR = Lao People's Democratic Republic, PRC = People's Republic of China.
Source: Authors' estimates using grouped/tabulated data from World Bank, POVCALNET; World Institute for Development Economic Research, *World Income Inequality Database* (Taipei,China); publications of national statistics offices or personal communications (India, Republic of Korea, Turkmenistan, and Viet Nam); and decile-level distributions generated from unit record data (Bangladesh, Malaysia, and Philippines).

In 15 of 21 cases, Gini coefficients have risen, though the increases are not always very large. In Azerbaijan, for example, the Gini coefficient has increased by only about half a percentage point over a 6-year period. In several cases, however, increases in the Gini coefficient are quite large. This includes Bangladesh, Cambodia, PRC, Lao PDR, Nepal, and Sri Lanka. In all these countries the Gini coefficient has grown by an average of more than 1% a year over the years covered by the data. In contrast, similarly large magnitudes of change in the Gini coefficient in the opposite direction (i.e., declines) have taken place only in Armenia (out of a total of six countries in which it has declined).[9] In all the other cases where the Gini coefficient has declined, the magnitudes of decline tend to be small.

Figure 2.3   Changes in the Gini coefficient and in the quintile ratio

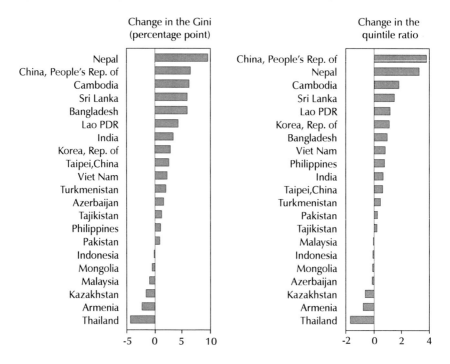

Lao PDR = Lao People's Democratic Republic.
Note: Changes are computed over the following years: Armenia (1998–2003); Azerbaijan (1995–2001); Bangladesh (1991–2005); Cambodia (1993–2004); People's Republic of China (1993–2004); India (1993–2004); Indonesia (1993–2002); Kazakhstan (1996–2003); Republic of Korea (1993–2004); Lao PDR (1992–2002); Malaysia (1993–2004); Mongolia (1995–2002); Nepal (1995–2003); Pakistan (1992–2004); Philippines (1994–2003); Sri Lanka (1995–2002); Taipei,China (1993–2003); Tajikistan (1999–2003); Thailand (1992–2002); Turkmenistan (1998–2003); and Viet Nam (1993–2004).
Source: Authors' estimates using grouped/tabulated data from World Bank, POVCALNET; World Institute for Development Economic Research, *World Income Inequality Database* (Taipei,China); publications of national statistics offices or personal communications (India, Republic of Korea, Turkmenistan, and Viet Nam); and decile-level distributions generated from unit record data (Bangladesh, Malaysia, and Philippines).

---

9   As discussed in footnote (8), the Gini coefficient for Kyrgyz Republic in 1993 is very high. Including this would show Kyrgyz Republic as having had a very dramatic reduction in inequality.

The qualitative behavior of the top to bottom quintile ratio is fairly similar. For example, the direction of change is almost identical across the Gini coefficient and the quintile ratio. Almost always, an increase in the Gini coefficient is accompanied by an increase in the quintile ratio, and vice versa. The only exception is Azerbaijan where, in contrast to a mild increase in the Gini coefficient between 1995 and 2001, the quintile ratio declined.

Interestingly, of the six cases where the Gini coefficient declined, three pertain to transition economies. The other three are Southeast Asian economies that were quite severely affected by the Asian financial crisis of 1997/1998.

An examination of the actual growth in mean per capita consumption expenditures or incomes across the five quintile groups sheds some light on what has been driving the pattern.[10] These growth rates are presented in Table 2.6. In 14 out of 21 economies, the fastest growth of expenditures or incomes has been in the fifth, or top, quintile. This includes Bangladesh; Cambodia; PRC; India; Korea; Lao PDR; Nepal; Sri Lanka; Taipei,China; Turkmenistan; and Viet Nam. In six developing Asian economies, by contrast, the fastest growth has taken place in the bottom quintile. This group of countries is made up of transition economies (Armenia, Azerbaijan, Kazakhstan, and Mongolia) and two Southeast Asian economies (Indonesia and Thailand).

Table 2.6   Annualized growth rate of per capita expenditure/income by quintile

Economy	Period	Annualized growth rate of per capita expenditure/income (%)				
		Quintile 1 (bottom 20%)	Quintile 2	Quintile 3	Quintile 4	Quintile 5 (top 20%)
Armenia	1998–2003	5.05	3.61	2.80	2.19	2.15
Azerbaijan	1995–2001	5.43	3.42	3.16	3.34	5.07
Bangladesh	1991–2005	0.07	–0.24	–0.08	0.27	1.60
Cambodia	1993–2004	0.69	1.27	1.84	2.39	3.38
PRC	1993–2004	3.40	4.46	5.42	6.19	7.10
India	1993–2004	0.85	0.77	0.82	1.04	2.03
Indonesia	1993–2002	2.09	1.97	1.86	1.77	1.93
Kazakhstan	1996–2003	0.81	0.19	–0.20	–0.51	–0.63
Korea, Rep. of	1993–2004	2.00	3.32	3.69	3.91	4.02
Lao PDR	1992–2002	1.47	2.22	2.85	3.40	3.82
Malaysia	1993–2004	2.26	2.65	2.72	2.68	2.23
Mongolia	1995–2002	0.95	0.94	0.86	0.77	0.69

continued.

10 The mean per capita expenditure/income of any quintile group can be easily computed based on knowledge of mean per capita expenditure/income and the quintile shares of expenditure/income.

Table 2.6 *continued.*

Economy	Period	Annualized growth rate of per capita expenditure/income (%)				
		Quintile 1 (bottom 20%)	Quintile 2	Quintile 3	Quintile 4	Quintile 5 (top 20%)
Nepal	1995–2003	1.92	2.04	2.56	3.32	7.23
Pakistan	1992–2004	–0.07	0.19	0.31	0.38	0.39
Philippines	1994–2003	1.28	1.70	2.00	2.25	2.27
Sri Lanka	1995–2002	0.64	0.59	1.08	1.83	4.14
Taipei,China	1993–2003	1.42	1.37	1.60	1.86	2.55
Tajikistan	1999–2003	5.87	4.85	5.36	6.19	6.69
Thailand	1992–2002	2.35	2.27	1.96	1.51	0.38
Turkmenistan	1998–2003	6.79	6.21	5.91	5.91	7.90
Viet Nam	1993–2004	3.37	3.92	4.29	4.61	4.69

Lao PDR = Lao People's Democratic Republic, PRC = People's Republic of China.
Source: Authors' estimates using grouped/tabulated data from World Bank, POVCALNET; World Institute for Development Economic Research, *World Income Inequality Database* (Taipei,China); publications of national statistics offices or personal communications (India, Republic of Korea, Turkmenistan, and Viet Nam); and decile-level distributions generated from unit record data (Bangladesh, Malaysia, and Philippines).

The overall pattern that emerges is one where inequality has increased in a majority of developing Asian economies (at least by the measures discussed above). However, in the main, increases in inequality are not a story of the rich getting richer and the poor getting poorer. Rather, it is the rich getting richer faster than the poor. For the most part, the countries where inequality has declined are either economies in transition or those that went through a financial crisis.

If inequality were measured differently, would results change? The opposite movement in the two inequality measures in the case of Azerbaijan described above (recall the numbers in Table 2.5) raises the issue of whether other measures of inequality could present a different picture of the recent trends in inequality in developing Asia. A quick answer to this can be provided by an examination of Lorenz curves. Measures of relative inequality will reveal different trends only when Lorenz curves cross. Table 2.7 lists the relationship between Lorenz curves for the 21 economies. Figure 2.4 depicts Lorenz curves for selected economies.

Table 2.7   Lorenz curve: Initial and recent years

Status of Lorenz curve	Economy
Recent year below initial year	Bangladesh; Cambodia; People's Republic of China; India; Republic of Korea; Lao PDR; Nepal; Pakistan; Philippines; Sri Lanka; Taipei,China; Tajikistan; Turkmenistan; Viet Nam
Recent year above initial year	Armenia, Kazakhstan, Malaysia, Mongolia, Thailand
Crossing	Azerbaijan, Indonesia

Figure 2.4   Lorenz curves: Selected economies

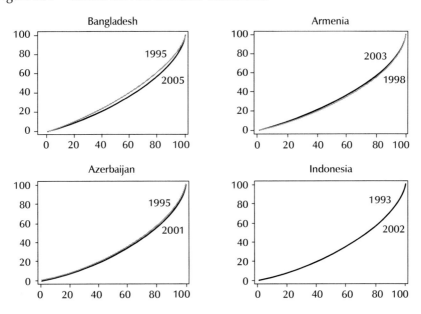

Note: The x-axis refers to cumulative share of population (%); the y-axis refers to cumulative share of per capita expenditure (%).

Source: Authors' estimates using grouped/tabulated data from World Bank, POVCALNET and decile-level distributions generated from unit record data (Bangladesh).

Consider the Lorenz curves for Bangladesh. The 2005 curve lies below the 1991 curve, indicating that all measures of relative inequality would show an unambiguous increase in inequality between 1991 and 2005. This pattern, whereby the more recent Lorenz curve lies completely below the earlier Lorenz curve, is repeated for a majority of economies (not shown).[11] The second set of Lorenz curves is for Armenia. Here the pattern is opposite to Bangladesh in that the more recent Lorenz curve lies entirely above the earlier Lorenz curve. All the measures of relative inequality would therefore be unambiguous in reporting a decline in inequality. The final two Lorenz curves shown are for Azerbaijan and Indonesia. Here, the Lorenz curves for the earlier and later periods appear to have regions of overlapping/crossing. This is confirmed by Figure 2.5, which depicts the difference between the two Lorenz curves for these two countries.

---

11   It is worth emphasizing that the Lorenz curves here are not based on unit-level records but on either the generalized quadratic or beta Lorenz curves based on extrapolation from grouped/tabulated distribution data. These generally do a good job of tracking the actual distribution, except at the upper and lower ends.

Figure 2.5   Difference in Lorenz curves for Azerbaijan and Indonesia

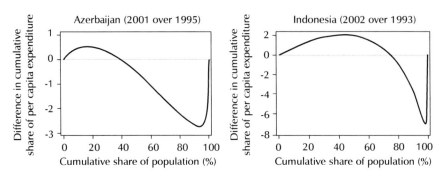

Source: Authors' estimates using grouped data from World Bank, POVCALNET.

2.3.2   Economic well-being in Asia

As seen from the estimates and analysis of the previous subsection, expenditure/income distributions in many Asian economies have become more unequal over the last 10 years or so. This does not imply that economic well-being, which refers to household or individual access to goods and services, has also been reduced. A distribution of income or expenditure that is becoming more unequal over time may yet allow, even those at the bottom of the distribution, greater access to goods and services. By bringing economic well-being into the picture, the question turns to whether or not income/expenditure distributions have become "better."

But clearly "better" involves a value judgment. For example, an observer comparing two distributions may treat as "better" the distribution into which the observer would prefer to be born (Fields 2001).

Consider two approaches to determining whether—and in which countries—the distribution has become better over the last 10 years.[12] One approach is that of the abbreviated social welfare function, in which the economic well-being of society as a whole is expressed in terms of statistics that arise from a given income or expenditure distribution. Fields (2001), for example, considers a specific form of the abbreviated social welfare function in which it is a function of three variables: gross national product (GNP) per capita (a proxy for average incomes), the Gini coefficient as a measure of inequality, and $1-a-day poverty rate as a measure of absolute poverty. The relationship among these three variables and social welfare is taken to be such that the latter increases

---

[12]   Both approaches rely on "outcome-based evaluation criteria." That is, evaluation is based on the consumption or income distributions actually seen in countries and not on the processes by which the specific consumption or income distributions arise (see Fields 2001).

with gains in per capita income, decreases with increases in inequality, and decreases with a rise in absolute poverty.

This approach does not yield an unambiguous answer to the question of how economic well-being has evolved in many Asian countries. Using mean per capita household expenditure/income in place of GNP per capita, Table 2.8 reveals that average "incomes" have increased in almost all developing Asian economies over the time period concerned (the exception being Kazakhstan). Similarly, absolute poverty in terms of either a $1-a-day or $2-a-day poverty line has fallen in virtually all over the period under consideration (the exceptions being $1-a-day poverty in Bangladesh and Pakistan). However, as seen in Section 2.3.1 earlier, inequality has increased in many countries. Thus, an improvement in social welfare due to increasing average incomes and reductions in absolute poverty are countered by the effects of a rise in inequality.

An alternative approach to determining whether one distribution is better than another is that of stochastic dominance analysis, which allows distributions to be ranked in terms of social welfare—a level of welfare for the population in question. A particularly intuitive type of stochastic dominance is "first order dominance." In the current context, it essentially entails checking whether expenditures or incomes have increased at each point of the distribution for the 2 years being compared. For example, whether per capita expenditure at each percentile of the 2004 distribution is higher than the corresponding percentile of the 1993 distribution for a given country can be verified. If the 2004 figure is higher for at least some percentile, and not lower for all other percentiles, it can be said that the 2004 distribution "first order dominates" the 1993 distribution. This means that the 2004 distribution will record higher levels of welfare in terms of any social welfare function that is increasing in incomes (and anonymous).[13]

A first approximation testing for first order dominance can be obtained by comparing the mean per capita expenditures or incomes across quintile groups for the 1990s and 2000s for each of the 21 economies shown in Table 2.8. In the case of the PRC and India, data for rural and urban areas are presented separately. The data for the 21 economies are presented in Table 2.9.

---

13   Given a distribution of income or expenditures for some population, a social welfare function assigns a level of welfare for the population as a whole (i.e., a measure of economic well-being of the population as a whole). There are many different ways of defining a social welfare function, i.e., for mapping a given distribution of incomes or expenditures to a level of welfare for the population in question. Social welfare functions that are increasing in incomes have the property that social welfare increases with an increase in the income of any individual (keeping all other incomes fixed). The anonymity property simply means that the welfare function depends on incomes but does not depend on which individual gets what.

Table 2.8   Assessing abbreviated social welfare over time

Economy	Reference year	Annualized growth rate (%) (log differences divided by number of years elapsed between final and initial years)			
		Mean per capita expenditure/ income from household surveys	Gini coefficient	$1-a-day poverty line	$2-a-day poverty line
Armenia	1998–2003	2.64	−1.27	−26.05	−6.91
Azerbaijan	1995–2001	4.21	0.72	−24.46	−5.29
Bangladesh	1991–2005	0.66	1.34	0.52	−0.31
Cambodia	1993–2004	2.50	1.63	−2.91	−1.96
PRC	1993–2004	6.23	1.35	−8.75	−4.86
India	1993–2004	1.39	0.88	−1.60	−0.61
Indonesia	1993–2002	1.90	−0.02	−9.13	−2.15
Kazakhstan	1996–2003	−0.33	−0.61	–	−1.17
Korea, Rep. of	1993–2004	3.69	0.87	–	–
Lao PDR	1992–2002	3.18	1.32	−5.06	−1.66
Malaysia	1993–2004	2.45	−0.20	–	−6.13
Mongolia	1995–2002	0.79	−0.16	−2.61	−1.23
Nepal	1995–2003	4.78	2.85	−4.13	−2.32
Pakistan	1992–2004	0.31	0.24	0.36	−0.46
Philippines	1994–2003	2.12	0.28	−3.52	−2.11
Sri Lanka	1995–2002	2.52	2.24	−4.93	−1.33
Taipei,China	1993–2003	2.00	0.78	–	–
Tajikistan	1999–2003	6.06	0.87	−16.90	−8.07
Thailand	1992–2002	1.12	−0.97	–	−3.73
Turkmenistan	1998–2003	6.88	0.92	−27.16	−29.60
Viet Nam	1993–2004	4.43	0.55	−10.75	−4.84

– = data not available, Lao PDR = Lao People's Democratic Republic, PRC = People's Republic of China.
Note: Republic of Korea and Taipei,China have very low/negligible estimates of initial poverty. Underlying data and poverty lines are expressed in 1993 purchasing power parity dollars.
Source: Authors' estimates using grouped/tabulated data from World Bank, POVCALNET; World Institute for Development Economic Research, *World Income Inequality Database* (Taipei,China); publications of national statistics offices or personal communications (India, Republic of Korea, Turkmenistan, and Viet Nam); and decile-level distributions generated from unit record data (Bangladesh, Malaysia, and Philippines).

In only a few cases does the more recent distribution fail to first order dominate the earlier distribution. Thus, even in the case of Nepal, which registered an almost 10 percentage-point increase in the Gini coefficient between 1995 and 2003, the per capita expenditure of each quintile group is higher than its earlier corresponding value. Thus, while per capita expenditure of the first quintile group was $20.6 a month (in 1993 purchasing power parity [PPP] consumption dollars) in 1995, this had increased to $23.8 by 2003.

Table 2.9 Mean monthly per capita expenditure/income by quintile (1993 PPP $)

Economy	Period	Quintile 1 Initial	Quintile 1 Final	Quintile 2 Initial	Quintile 2 Final	Quintile 3 Initial	Quintile 3 Final	Quintile 4 Initial	Quintile 4 Final	Quintile 5 Initial	Quintile 5 Final
Armenia	1998–2003	35.65	45.57	54.13	65.27	72.68	83.56	98.02	109.76	207.68	231.60
Azerbaijan	1995–2001	29.45	40.80	50.60	62.13	69.97	84.58	95.00	116.11	179.38	243.16
Bangladesh	1991–2005	21.56	21.78	31.15	30.11	39.74	39.31	50.72	52.66	87.45	109.48
Cambodia	1993–2004	24.88	26.84	34.77	39.97	44.61	54.61	59.13	76.94	130.36	189.09
PRC (rural)	1993–2004	19.70	27.17	28.58	42.03	37.46	58.15	49.65	81.63	91.32	177.68
PRC (urban)	1993–2004	55.85	90.80	83.15	143.47	107.99	194.55	140.12	264.14	233.80	500.93
PRC	1993–2004	21.59	31.38	33.90	55.37	49.06	89.03	76.27	150.68	163.40	356.71
India (rural)	1993–2004	18.83	20.67	26.37	28.57	33.24	35.85	42.57	46.12	75.95	90.26
India (urban)	1993–2004	25.15	27.11	37.53	41.60	50.74	57.87	69.39	81.47	136.25	171.70
India	1993–2004	19.81	21.76	28.21	30.71	36.40	39.85	48.43	54.30	96.03	120.00
Indonesia	1993–2002	28.42	34.31	40.17	47.94	53.44	63.20	72.90	85.49	147.94	175.95
Kazakhstan	1996–2003	50.52	53.47	84.73	85.84	120.43	118.80	169.51	163.61	313.37	299.85
Korea, Rep. of	1993–2004	238.99	297.75	378.42	545.13	493.85	741.23	634.87	975.58	1,046.44	1,629.17
Lao PDR	1992–2002	19.77	22.90	26.75	33.39	33.67	44.79	43.53	61.17	84.39	123.61
Malaysia	1993–2004	51.39	65.87	82.81	110.80	119.51	161.15	174.66	234.52	396.70	507.18
Mongolia	1995–2002	29.40	31.41	48.01	51.28	66.84	71.00	92.14	97.23	162.68	170.76
Nepal	1995–2003	20.57	23.99	30.64	36.07	41.44	50.85	57.37	74.83	127.45	227.26
Pakistan	1992–2004	33.03	32.77	44.45	45.47	56.11	58.22	72.19	75.59	139.28	145.98
Philippines	1994–2003	26.66	29.92	42.60	49.65	62.63	74.95	94.36	115.59	222.35	272.64
Sri Lanka	1995–2002	35.43	37.04	52.19	54.40	69.98	75.46	95.04	108.00	189.23	252.84
Taipei,China	1993–2003	250.59	288.94	456.65	523.86	621.24	728.90	818.14	985.78	1,354.57	1,748.07
Tajikistan	1999–2003	27.76	35.11	44.59	54.13	58.90	72.98	76.75	98.33	138.04	180.43
Thailand	1992–2002	36.45	46.12	56.78	71.22	84.04	102.20	129.64	150.70	342.88	356.13
Turkmenistan	1998–2003	65.55	92.03	109.14	148.87	157.98	212.35	229.47	308.32	516.34	766.41
Viet Nam	1993–2004	23.60	34.19	34.18	52.64	45.72	73.31	62.27	103.42	127.36	213.43

Lao PDR = Lao People's Democratic Republic, PPP = purchasing power parity, PRC = People's Republic of China.

Source: Authors' estimates using grouped/tabulated data from World Bank, POVCALNET; World Institute for Development Economic Research, *World Income Inequality Database* (Taipei,China); publications of national statistics offices or personal communications (India, Republic of Korea, Turkmenistan, and Viet Nam); and decile-level distributions generated from unit record data (Bangladesh, Malaysia, and Philippines).

The exceptions in which the more recent distribution fails to first order dominate the earlier distribution are Bangladesh, Kazakhstan, and Pakistan. As an examination of the per capita consumption expenditure for 1991 and 2005 shows, the second and third quintile groups have declined slightly in expenditure in Bangladesh. Cases in which the more recent distribution comes close to failing to first order dominate the earlier distributions are rural India between 1993 and 2004 and Sri Lanka between 1995 and 2002.

Figure 2.6 presents a graphical means for checking for first order dominance. This entails comparing the relative position of two (or more) distributions' "quantile" functions, i.e., curves that depict income or expenditure at each quantile. The cases presented are those for selected countries including Azerbaijan, for which Lorenz curves for 1995 and 2001 crossed (as seen earlier), as well as rural India and rural PRC, Bangladesh, Nepal, Indonesia, Philippines, and Viet Nam.

Figure 2.6   Quantile function for selected economies,
1990s versus 2000s

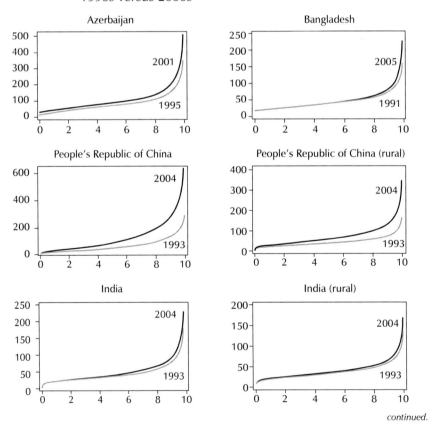

continued.

Figure 2.6 *continued.*

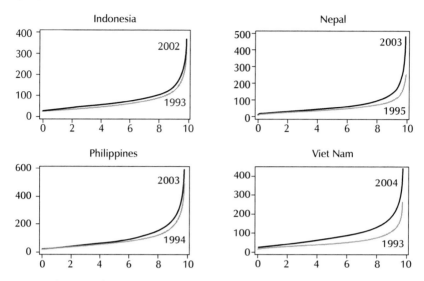

Note: The x-axis refers to quantile of expenditure recipients ordered from lowest to highest; the y-axis depicts per capita expenditures in 1993 PPP dollars.

Source: Authors' estimates using grouped/tabulated data from World Bank, POVCALNET; World Institute for Development Economic Research, *World Income Inequality Database* (Taipei,China); publications of national statistics offices or personal communications (India, Republic of Korea, Turkmenistan, and Viet Nam); and decile-level distributions generated from unit record data (Bangladesh, Malaysia, and Philippines).

While some caution is needed in interpreting the results of these quantile functions,[14] they confirm the two features that other cuts of the data suggest. First, expenditure levels have tended to grow at all points of the distribution so that more recent distributions first order dominate earlier ones in most developing Asian countries. Second, however, the growth in expenditure at the lower end of the distribution has been relatively low in many cases. This suggests that poorer households have benefited from and/or participated in overall growth less than richer households. This is clearly the case in an "absolute" sense—one only needs to compare the larger distance between the quantile functions at the higher end of the distribution; it is also true for many developing Asian economies in a "relative" sense (as already discussed in reference to Table 2.5).

2.3.3   Poverty reduction: Links with inequality and growth

What are the implications of the foregoing for poverty? That expenditure levels have increased in all percentiles and in most developing Asian economies over the approximately 10-year period considered here suggests

---

14   Extrapolations are based on information provided in grouped/tabulated distribution data.

that for a broad class of measures, poverty has declined regardless of which poverty line is used.[15] This indeed seems to be the case as demonstrated in Table 2.10, which lists the initial and final poverty rates at $1-a-day and $2-a-day poverty lines for 19 developing Asian economies.[16]

Table 2.10   Poverty headcount ratio, 1990s versus 2000s

Economy	Reference year	Headcount ratio, $1 a day (%)		Headcount ratio, $2 a day (%)	
		Initial year	Final year	Initial year	Final year
Armenia	1998–2003	6.38	1.73	42.80	30.29
Azerbaijan	1995–2001	12.44	2.87	45.67	33.25
Bangladesh	1991–2005	33.71	36.26	85.30	81.71
Cambodia	1993–2004	25.45	18.47	76.50	61.66
PRC	1993–2004	28.33	10.82	64.45	37.76
India	1993–2004	41.83	35.07	85.11	79.63
Indonesia	1993–2002	17.39	7.65	64.19	52.89
Kazakhstan	1996–2003	0.42	0.00	18.49	17.04
Lao PDR	1992–2002	47.84	28.84	89.94	74.41
Malaysia	1993–2004	0.00	0.00	19.17	9.77
Mongolia	1995–2002	13.24	11.03	48.87	44.83
Nepal	1995–2003	34.42	24.74	77.39	64.27
Pakistan	1992–2004	9.33	9.75	63.36	59.97
Philippines	1994–2003	18.09	13.18	52.72	43.58
Sri Lanka	1995–2002	6.82	4.83	45.51	41.47
Tajikistan	1999–2003	14.77	7.51	58.67	42.49
Thailand	1992–2002	6.02	0.00	37.48	25.81
Turkmenistan	1998–2003	0.35	0.09	9.28	2.11
Viet Nam	1993–2004	27.32	8.38	73.46	43.16

Lao PDR = Lao People's Democratic Republic, PRC = People's Republic of China.
Note: Underlying poverty data are based on 1993 purchasing power parity dollars.
Source: Authors' estimates using grouped/tabulated data from World Bank, POVCALNET; publications of national statistics offices or personal communications (India, Turkmenistan, and Viet Nam); and decile-level distributions generated from unit record data (Bangladesh, Malaysia, and Philippines).

Of course, the degree to which poverty has declined varies across economies. A key factor that explains the different rates of decline is the rate of aggregate growth. Figure 2.7 plots the changes in poverty rates against changes in two alternative measures of aggregate growth

---

[15]   The term "suggests" is used deliberately. Given that the analysis here is based on grouped/tabulated data, the authors' statements regarding expenditures/incomes at the extremes of the distribution need to be viewed with some caution.

[16]   Republic of Korea; Taipei,China, and Kyrgyz Republic are omitted from this analysis. For the first two economies, even $2-a-day poverty data turn out to be nonexistent by 1993, the initial year being considered in this analysis. For Kyrgyz Republic, the initial year's data lack sufficient credibility, as noted earlier.

for selected economies: per capita GDP and mean per capita household consumption expenditure.

Figure 2.7   Growth and poverty reduction: $2-a-day poverty line

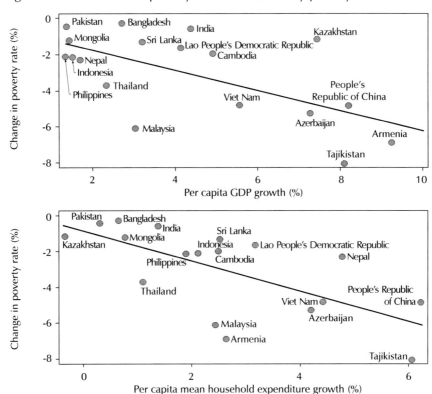

GDP = gross domestic product.
Note: Underlying data used the $2-a-day poverty line, based on 1993 purchasing power parity dollars
            (estimates exclude Republic of Korea; Kyrgyz Republic; Taipei,China; and Turkmenistan). Reference
            years used for each country are as follows: Armenia (1998–2003); Azerbaijan (1995–2001);
            Bangladesh (1991–2005); Cambodia (1993–2004); People's Republic of China (1993–2004); India
            (1993–2004); Indonesia (1993–2002); Kazakhstan (1996–2003); Lao PDR (1992–2002); Malaysia
            (1993–2004); Mongolia (1995–2002); Nepal (1995–2003); Pakistan (1992–2004); Philippines
            (1994–2003); Sri Lanka (1995–2002); Tajikistan (1999–2003); Thailand (1992–2002); and Viet
            Nam (1993–2004).
Source: Authors' estimates using grouped/tabulated data from World Bank, POVCALNET; publications
            of national statistics offices or personal communications (India and Viet Nam); and decile-level
            distributions generated from unit record data (Bangladesh, Malaysia, and Philippines).

In both cases, aggregate growth is strongly associated with poverty reduction. The relationship is stronger, however, for growth measured in terms of mean household expenditure rather than GDP. This reflects the fact that changes in per capita GDP and changes in household expenditure do not track each other perfectly.

But even the same growth rate can be associated with different rates of poverty reduction. Two proximate factors that play a role in explaining this are the initial level of inequality and the increase in inequality over time (Ravallion 2004b). The higher the initial level, or increase, the lower will be the extent of poverty reduction for a given growth rate. As an illustration of how increases in inequality over a period of positive growth can dampen the extent of poverty reduction, Figure 2.8 shows actual $1-a-day and $2-a-day poverty versus that which would have been seen had the growth that was experienced (over the period considered here) occurred without any changes in the distribution for those economies where the Gini coefficient increased.[17] As may be seen, distributional changes adverse to poverty reduction have been relatively high in countries such as Cambodia and Nepal for $1-a-day poverty. Interestingly, this pattern does not exist to the same degree if switched to $2-a-day poverty. This is because the $2-a-day poverty line is high relative to mean expenditure levels in many economies, so that applying current means to earlier, less unequal distribution, in effect, only "redistributes" poverty.

More formally, in many of the cases considered so far, growth over the time period here has not been pro-poor (for $1-a-day poverty) in the sense of Kakwani and Son (2009), because growth benefits the non-poor proportionately more than the poor.

2.4   Looking into the causes of inequality

The discussion in Section 2.3 has highlighted the following about inequality in developing Asia. First, measures of relative inequality in expenditures/incomes have increased in many economies over the last 10 years or so. Absolute inequality—in terms of the gap in per capita expenditure/income between the top and bottom quintiles, in particular —have increased virtually everywhere. Second, in most economies where relative inequality has increased, however, expenditures/incomes have increased at all points along the distribution so that economic well-being has improved. Third, rising inequality is nevertheless of concern since it partly reflects low growth in the expenditures and incomes of the poor—the very group of people whose consumption and incomes are low to begin with.

---

[17]   It should be noted that there is no one-to-one monotonic relationship between changes in the Gini coefficient and changes in poverty, holding mean consumption expenditure/ income fixed. The exact relationship will depend on the position of the poverty line vis-à-vis a given distribution, and the specific manner in which the distribution changes over time. Nevertheless, in most cases it turns out that the actual increases in the Gini coefficient are associated with an increase in the poverty rate for a given increase in mean consumption expenditures per capita.

Figure 2.8   Poverty headcount ratio (%)

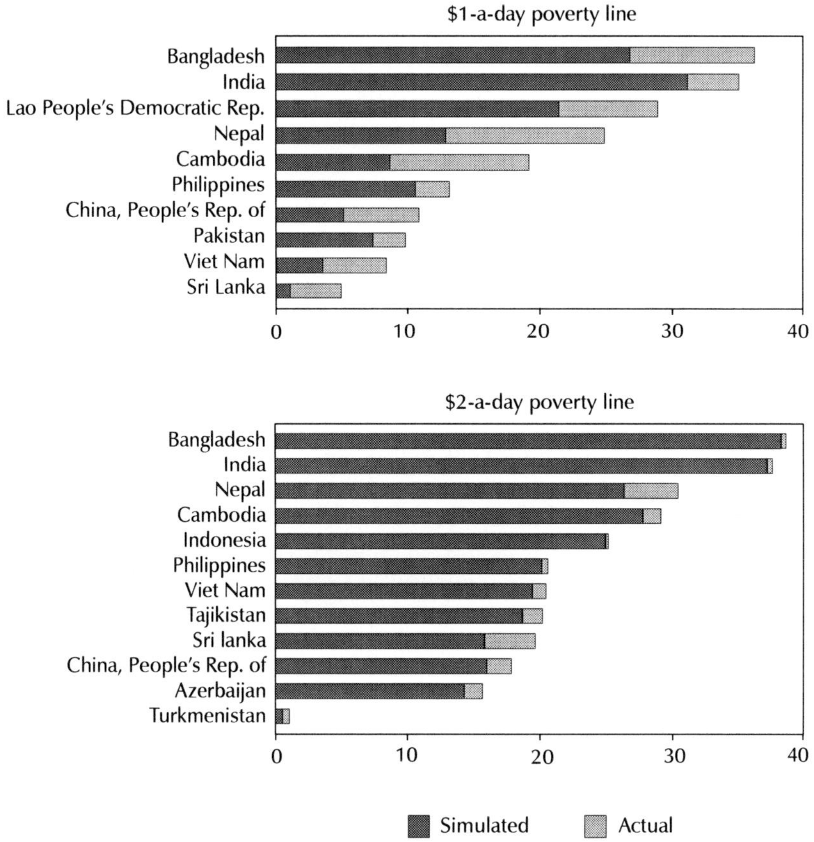

$1-a-day poverty line

Bangladesh
India
Lao People's Democratic Rep.
Nepal
Cambodia
Philippines
China, People's Rep. of
Pakistan
Viet Nam
Sri Lanka

0   10   20   30   40

$2-a-day poverty line

Bangladesh
India
Nepal
Cambodia
Indonesia
Philippines
Viet Nam
Tajikistan
Sri lanka
China, People's Rep. of
Azerbaijan
Turkmenistan

0   10   20   30   40

■ Simulated   ▨ Actual

Note: Underlying poverty data are based on 1993 purchasing power parity dollars. Poverty rates are for
the following years: Azerbaijan (2001); Bangladesh (2005); Cambodia (2004); People's Republic
of China (2004); India (2004); Indonesia (2002); Lao PDR (2002); Nepal (2003); Pakistan (2004);
Philippines (2003); Sri Lanka (2002); Tajikistan (2003); Turkmenistan (2003); and Viet Nam (2004).
Simulated poverty rates are computed using expenditure distributions for the following years:
Azerbaijan (1995); Bangladesh (1991); Cambodia (1993); People's Republic of China (1993); India
(1993); Indonesia (1993); Lao PDR (1992); Nepal (1995); Pakistan (1992); Philippines (1994);
Sri Lanka (1995); Turkmenistan (1998); and Viet Nam (1993).

Source: Authors' estimates using grouped/tabulated data from World Bank, POVCALNET; World Institute for
Development Economic Research, *World Income Inequality Database* (Taipei,China); publications
of national statistics offices or personal communications (India, Republic of Korea, Turkmenistan,
and Viet Nam); and decile-level distributions generated from unit record data (Bangladesh,
Malaysia, and Philippines).

This section looks deeper into the reasons for inequality and changes
in it, drawing upon what recent empirical work says about the proximate
(or immediate) drivers of inequality in developing Asia, and the broader
literature on inequality and its policy and structural drivers. But, it is
useful first to briefly review what international comparisons of inequality
reveal about the correlates of inequality.

2.4.1   Correlates of inequality: International comparisons

Drawing on studies that have examined the correlates of inequality across countries, Fields (2001) points to some patterns. First, inequality tends to be lower in socialist countries than elsewhere. The factors responsible no doubt include the patterns of asset ownership and government spending in socialist countries. By extension, countries with a relatively large share of public sector employment in the total and extensive government intervention (in price setting, industrial and trade regulation, etc.), and large public expenditures on social spending are generally those with lower inequality (all else being equal).

Second, countries with a larger share of agriculture (in output and/ or employment) tend to have lower inequality. Interestingly, countries with a large share of mineral exports in total output tend to be more unequal, a result that is quite likely driven by the unequal ownership of the resource in question and the capital-intensive nature of production.

Third, measures of economic dualism, whereby workers with similar characteristics but employed in different sectors of the economy get very different wages, also appear to be correlated with inequality. For example, a higher ratio of non-agricultural labor productivity to agricultural productivity—i.e., a proxy for the extent of dualism—tends to be associated with higher inequality.

Fourth, countries with high levels of asset inequality tend to have high levels of income inequality. In principle, asset inequality can be of several types—for example, inequality in the distribution of (or access to) land, in financial capital, or in human capital (from education/training and experience). Traditionally, an important correlate of income inequality in the context of developing countries is land inequality.

The effects of human capital as captured through education are more complex. Theoretically, whether inequality increases or decreases as a result of an expansion in education depends on the evolving supply of and demand for different levels of education. Empirically, while studies using data up to the 1980s generally found higher rates of literacy and education to be associated with lower inequality (controlling for other factors), it is unclear what recent data would show. An analysis of labor force survey data from several countries, including India and the Philippines, reveals that earnings differentials between the college educated and those with less education have increased over time—a phenomenon that can be described as increasing "convexity" in returns to education (ADB 2007a and 2007c). This finding is also found for the PRC (Park et al. 2004), Nepal (World Bank/DFID/ADB 2006), Thailand (ADB 2007a), and Viet Nam (Nguyen et al. 2007). Of course, increases in convexity do not necessarily imply that inequality will increase, but all else being equal, they should put upward pressure on inequality.

2.4.2 Inequality in developing Asia: Proximate drivers and policy drivers

A. Proximate drivers: Unevenness in growth

As noted by Chaudhuri and Ravallion (2007), a useful way to think about the increases in inequality in many economies is in terms of whether growth has been uneven, and in which dimensions. Chaudhuri and Ravallion focused on the PRC and India, pointing to three ways in which growth has been uneven: (i) across provinces in the PRC and states in India; (ii) sectorally, as growth in agriculture has lagged growth in the secondary and tertiary sectors, with the result that urban incomes have grown faster than rural incomes; and (iii) at the household level, such that incomes at the top of the distribution have grown faster than those in the middle and/or bottom.

What do the data analyzed in Section 2.3 reveal if examined through the above lens? The aggregated data for the PRC in Section 2.3 are certainly consistent with the above. Although those data cannot distinguish between provincial differences, the differences that are clearly evident are those between average expenditure across rural areas and urban areas, and the high growth of expenditure/income at the top end of the distribution (recall Table 2.5 and the two charts for the PRC in Figure 2.6).

Using grouped data on income distributions in the PRC for 1985–2005, Lin et al. in Chapter 11 suggest that in terms of nominal income, the main contributor to both inequality today, as well as increases in inequality from the period studied, consists of the gap in average incomes between rural and urban households. At the same time, uneven growth in incomes among urban households has become a prominent source of the more recent increases in inequality (i.e., over 2001–2005). These patterns can be seen in Figure 2.9(a), which decomposes national inequality as measured by the Theil index, GE(1), into inequality within each of the rural and urban sectors and inequality between the rural and urban sectors in 1990–2005. While the relative contribution of each sector changed when using real income, a pronounced increase in between-rural-urban inequality and within-urban inequality is still observed in Figure 2.9 (b).

The observations also seem to apply to Viet Nam. Rural-urban gaps in expenditure have increased over time. Data from nationally representative household expenditure surveys reveal that average monthly per capita expenditure in urban areas was almost twice that of rural areas in 1993 (310,500 versus 157,800 dong in 2002 prices). Over the next 9 years, per capita expenditure in urban areas grew 5.6% per year while the corresponding figure for rural areas was two percentage points lower.

Figure 2.9   Decomposing inequality in the People's Republic of China,
1990–2005

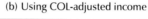

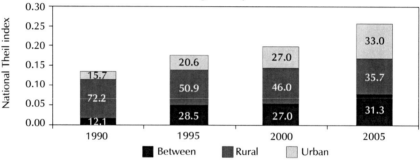

COL = cost of living.
Note: Numbers inside bars add up to 100%.
Source: See Figure 11.8, Chapter 11 of this volume.

Further, together with regional differences, rural-urban differences can explain a large component of the increase in inequality as measured by the Gini coefficient. This can be seen using a regression-based decomposition technique developed by Fields (2003) that allows a determination of what proportion of total inequality can be accounted for by various observable household characteristics.

The first two data columns of Table 2.11 describe the contribution of various observable household characteristics to the Gini coefficient for 1993 and 2002. The R-squared reveals that the household characteristics considered are able to explain 32% and 47% of inequality in 1993 and 2002, respectively. The rural-urban location of a household and the region in which the household resides together account for a little more than 50% of *explained* inequality.

Table 2.11   Contribution of household characteristics to explained inequality in consumption expenditure and changes in Gini coefficient (%): Viet Nam

Household characteristic	1993	2002	Accounting for change in Gini coefficient (1993–2002)
Age[a]	5.8	3.3	–2.1
Gender[a]	3.0	2.2	2.1
Production sector	19.4	15.4	18.8
Rural/urban	26.9	30.5	81.3
Education[a]	19.6	28.2	94.3
Region	25.3	20.4	27.1
Residual			–121.5
R-squared	0.32	0.47	
Log-variance	0.32	0.37	
Gini coefficient	33.25	36.11	
Change in Gini coefficient			2.86

a   Refers to characteristic of household head.
Note: The contribution of categorical variables is cumulative, and is obtained by summing the contributions of constituent variables (i.e., the contribution of education is based on four education categories; that of production sector is based on three industrial categories; age is made up of two terms, age and age squared).
Source: ADB (2007c, Table 5.9).

However, as may be seen from the last column—which describes how the various household characteristics account for the change in the Gini coefficient between 1993 and 2002—the two factors account for 108.4% of the 2.9 percentage-point increase in the Gini coefficient between 1993 and 2002. In other words, had other (largely unobservable) factors not worked to dampen the increase in inequality, the Gini coefficient would have registered an even larger increase than it actually did because of regional and rural-urban differences together. At the same time, the differences in educational attainment across households is the single most important household characteristic associated with the increase in the Gini coefficient.

Studies for other countries are also supportive of the importance of uneven growth across sectors and regions as an important driver of increasing inequality. Thus, in Cambodia, which as seen in Section 2.3 experienced a fairly large increase in the Gini coefficient between 1993 and 2004, a recent study has highlighted uneven growth between the agricultural sector and non-agricultural sector, as well as lower growth in rural areas relative to urban areas, as key drivers of the increases in inequality (World Bank 2006). As the study notes, a majority of Cambodia's labor force is in agriculture; low growth in this sector therefore constrains incomes. A lack of physical infrastructure (especially relating to irrigation and transport), increasing landlessness, and declining availability and accessibility of common property resources contribute to low growth.

The situation in Nepal is similar. Underlying the large increases in inequality documented in Section 2.3 has been very unequal growth across urban and rural areas (World Bank/DFID/ADB 2006). While real per capita expenditures increased by 42% in urban areas between 1995/1996 and 2003/2004, rural areas saw only 27% growth. Given that rural areas start out with lower expenditures/incomes, the lower growth rates only served to dramatically widen the urban-rural gap. Similarly, while real average per capita expenditures rose by about 30% in Kathmandu and the rural Western Hills and Eastern Terai regions, they increased only by about 5% in the rural Eastern Hills region. Finally, an important dimension of widening inequality has been dramatic increases in the returns to higher education as well as employment in professional occupations (along with self-employment in manufacturing and services). That professionals and the self-employed in manufacturing and services represent only a little over 10% of the total population thus helps explain the rapid increase in inequality in Nepal.

More generally, growth in the agricultural sector has been far more limited than in industry and services in developing Asia. Table 2.12 shows that, in 10 developing Asian economies, the average annual growth rate during 1991–2005 declined relative to 1980–1990. In contrast, growth rates for industry and services increased in the more recent period in 50% of the cases.

Table 2.12   Growth rate of gross value added by sector (%), 1980–1990 and 1991–2005

Economy	Agriculture		Industry		Services	
	1980–1990	1991–2005	1980–1990	1991–2005	1980–1990	1991–2005
Bangladesh	2.32	2.98	4.79	7.11	3.74	4.88
PRC	5.54	3.85	10.00	12.67	11.78	10.11
India	4.40	2.74	6.89	6.20	6.39	7.93
Indonesia	3.98	2.42	7.77	5.11	7.28	5.08
Malaysia	3.07	1.63	7.12	7.26	6.81	6.79
Nepal	3.79	2.77	7.40	5.68	3.46	5.35
Pakistan	4.30	3.81	8.03	5.01	6.56	4.79
Philippines	1.44	2.48	1.03	3.08	3.66	4.41
Sri Lanka	2.93	1.43	4.53	5.55	5.23	5.62
Thailand	3.70	1.75	9.82	6.43	7.60	4.06

PRC = People's Republic of China.
Source: World Bank, World Development Indicators Online.

In itself, neither of these two features of growth in developing Asia is a problem. Indeed, faster growth in industry and services is integral to economic development and structural transformation. But a problem arises when a large proportion of total employment is agricultural employment with very low productivity. Thus, in a majority of developing Asian economies, including those with very large populations (such as Bangladesh, PRC, India, Indonesia, and Pakistan), agriculture has continued to account for 40% or more of total employment, with very low levels of productivity relative to the industry and services sectors (Table 2.13).

Table 2.13   Value added per worker by sector and share of agricultural employment: Selected developing Asian economies

Region/Economy	Year	Share of agricultural employment (%)	Value added per worker (constant 2000 $)		
			Agriculture	Industry	Services
Central Asia					
Azerbaijan	2001	39.3	635	5,993	1,098
Kazakhstan	1999	33.5	1,142	5,376	2,198
Kyrgyz Republic	1999	52.7	494	1,676	644
Tajikistan	1997	–	410	1,095	1,031
Uzbekistan	1999	–	1,171	1,585	1,556
East Asia					
PRC	2002	44.1	600	4,961	5,080
Korea, Rep. of	2004	7.9	12,302	38,978	22,775
Mongolia	2003	40.2	516	1,686	1,396
Southeast Asia					
Cambodia	2004	60.3	412	1,685	1,116
Indonesia	2004	44.0	748	5,111	2,153
Malaysia	2004	14.8	6,606	17,317	7,882
Philippines	2004	37.0	1,134	5,728	3,130
Thailand	2004	42.6	1,028	9,163	5,407
Viet Nam	2004	57.9	367	2,251	1,509
South Asia					
Bangladesh	2003	51.7	389	1,772	1,389
India	1999	60.8	432	1,602	2,039
Nepal	1998	76.1	270	1,061	1,292
Pakistan	2002	42.1	929	1,823	2,383
Sri Lanka	2003	34.3	1334	2,714	3,389

– = data not available, PRC = People's Republic of China.
Source: ADB (2005); World Bank, World Development Indicators Online.

B. Policy and structural drivers

What policy and structural factors account for these patterns in which growth in urban areas and incomes accruing to those with high levels of education have outstripped rural incomes, lagging regions, agricultural incomes, and incomes of those with less than a college degree?

The discussion on the cross-country correlates of inequality (Section 2.4.1) focused mainly on what explains levels of inequality. But it also offers clues to the policy changes that may have led to increased inequality. For example, that inequality has been lowest in socialist countries would imply that their transition to more market-based economies and a diminishing role for the public sector would put upward pressure on inequality. Similarly, if inequality is lower when agriculture accounts for a relatively large share of output or employment, rapid growth in other sectors (as seen from Table 2.12) would be associated with some upward tendency in inequality.

The following briefly discusses three dimensions of policy that may be important drivers of the unequal growth just described. The complexity of the issues involved necessarily means that the discussion cannot be definitive.

(i) Neglect of agriculture

The relatively slow growth of agriculture—certainly relative to the growth of industry and services, but also relative to agricultural growth before the 1990s—is one explanation for uneven growth across sectors (rural/urban, agriculture/non-agriculture). Additionally, because most poor in much of developing Asia rely on agriculture for their livelihood, its slow growth can also account for relatively slow growth in their incomes/expenditures.

The specific reasons for this pattern of growth vary by country. However, there appear to be some common features, including a slowdown of public investment in rural infrastructure, stagnation in resources devoted to developing and spreading new agricultural technologies, and rapid depletion of natural resources. In some countries, a policy environment that has kept private investment away from agriculture seems to have exacerbated the lack of public investment.

(ii) Transition

An important feature of the economic landscape of many countries in the region during the 1980s and 1990s was the dramatic move from socialism and strong public sector influence to greater reliance on markets. Privatization of public enterprises, liberalization of trade, deregulation of industrial relations, and dismantling of administrative prices were seen in various countries, including the PRC, Viet Nam, and the Central Asian republics (and even some non-socialist countries, in particular, India).

It should not be surprising that the net effect of all these would be to put upward pressure on inequality in many of the countries undergoing this transition. In the PRC, for example, the Bureau of Labor and Personnel determined the wages of all workers in urban areas from the late 1950s to the late 1970s. There were eight distinct grade levels for factory workers and technicians and 24 levels for administrative and managerial workers. Increases in wages were based on seniority, and wage differentials across levels were quite small (Zhang et al. 2005). A transition from centrally planned to progressively more market-based systems for production, employment, and wage-setting decisions in the PRC's urban sector began in the early to mid-1980s. For example, wages were allowed to respond in accordance with various profit-sharing arrangements, and the creation of special economic zones led to the emergence of a new set of enterprises that received much more freedom in production and labor issues (Tao 2006).

Returns to education, especially college or post-secondary education, seem to have responded to these institutional changes. Using data from six PRC provinces to estimate returns to education via Mincerian earnings regressions, the analysis in Zhang et al. (2005) reveals, for example, that the returns to college education relative to high school increased from 12% in 1988 to 37% in 2001.[18] Why was this gain so dramatic? Reviewing different options (including a possible role for trade and foreign direct investment), Zhang et al. conclude that the transition from centrally planned to market-oriented decision making on production and labor issues was the decisive factor. Overall, a fairly similar process seems to have taken place in Viet Nam with the market-oriented reforms (*doi moi*) ushered in since 1986 (Nguyen et al. 2006).

(iii) Market-oriented reforms and international integration

More broadly, virtually all economies in the region have in recent years undertaken a variety of market-oriented reforms and integrated themselves more closely with the international economy, the main exceptions being the two economies of Hong Kong, China and Singapore— which have been very open and market-oriented for at least the past several decades.

---

[18] Returns to technical school versus high school as well as high school versus junior high school also increased. However, returns to junior high school versus primary school have not displayed a consistent trend.

How may market-oriented reforms and international integration have contributed to uneven growth and affected inequality? The specific channel that was discussed above in the context of the transition economies, where wage setting moved from central planning to being set by market forces, is an obvious contributor to uneven growth in incomes across households. Beyond that, however, the channels become more complicated. Market-oriented reforms entail moving economic decision making away from the public sector to the private sector, and are affected by the deregulation of domestic industrial policies, privatization, etc. Market-oriented reforms can also include trade and investment liberalization as well as financial liberalization.[19] Trade and investment liberalization have been particularly important in integrating developing Asian countries with the global economy.[20] Liberalization of investment regimes has usually accompanied trade liberalization quite closely and, in any case, the overall thrust of these policy changes is quite similar. But one needs to ask how these policy changes have affected inequality and how they are connected to uneven growth.

(iv) Regional inequality

As noted earlier, uneven growth across regions/states within countries has been an important contributor to increases in inequality (in some countries). The interplay between market-oriented reforms; international integration; and structural features such as geography, agglomeration economies (whereby firms derive benefits from locating close to other firms), and history (especially an unequal initial distribution of infrastructure) are probably important drivers of uneven growth across regions/states. In the PRC, there appears to be a general consensus that increased openness contributed to sharpening income disparities between coastal and interior regions. As Lin (2005) notes, an important feature of that country's global integration is the

---

[19]   Trade liberalization essentially involves the substitution of nontariff barriers to trade (for example, quantitative restrictions, performance requirements, and voluntary export restrictions) with tariff barriers and a reduction in these tariff barriers over time. Investment liberalization, in comparison, involves the removal of restrictions on investment decisions by private agents, both domestic and foreign. Finally, financial liberalization involves the movement toward market determination of interest rates and the removal of restrictions on the inflows and outflows of foreign and domestic private capital.

[20]   Liberalization of financial markets, especially in terms of the removal of restrictions on the inflows and outflows of private capital, has been more uneven across countries. Moreover, the experience of the financial crisis of 1997/1998 in several Southeast and East Asian economies has led policy makers and economists alike to reconsider the wisdom of liberalizing financial flows in a context of weak domestic supervision and regulation of the financial sector. In so far as the effects of financial liberalization, especially the liberalization of international capital flows, is concerned, several researchers have linked them to increasing inequality and a tendency toward crisis (Cornia and Court 2001).

depth of concentration of international trade along the east coast. An important reason for this is that east coast provinces have considerably lower transportation costs to the PRC's major markets such as Hong Kong, China; Japan; and the United States.[21]

Similarly in India, the process of industrial deregulation (an important component of market-oriented reforms in the country from the mid-1980s to the early 1990s) has increasingly led commercial considerations rather than government mandates to determine the choice of location in investment decisions (Kumar 2006). Why should this contribute to unevenness in growth across regions? As a plant-level study of industrial location in India finds, new private-sector industrial investments in the country typically take place in existing industrial and coastal districts. Industrial investments by the public sector, however, are less likely to be made in such districts, in line with considerations such as a concern for balanced regional development (Lall and Chakravorty 2005). Since investments by the private sector have outstripped investments by the public sector, overall investments have become more concentrated within the country. This, of course, raises another question: Why does the private sector locate in existing industrial districts and coastal districts? Lall and Chakravorty find that it is profitable for them to do so. In particular, industrial diversity *within* a given district or metropolitan area is associated with lower costs of production for a given plant.

More generally, the interplay between market-oriented reforms and economies of agglomeration appear to have given certain regions within countries an edge when it comes to economic growth. Indeed, this interplay has been recently linked to increasing inequality in Southeast Asia and East Asia's middle-income economies (Gill and Kharas 2007).

(v) The relative returns to labor[22]

Differential returns to education and occupations—a facet of unevenness in growth across households—are among the most important drivers of inequality and changes in it. In addition to the studies and findings cited above, the analysis of labor force survey data from India

---

21 Interestingly, even among coastal provinces, those in which trade is more important tend to have higher wages on average. Indeed, Lin (2005) finds that around 25% of the wage differences in coastal provinces and 15% of the wage differences in interior provinces can be explained by trade-related variables.

22 "Relative" is important. As seen from the data in Section 2.3, average per capita expenditure and income have increased across the board in almost all countries examined. However, some groups of households and earners, typically those at the top end of the distribution, have experienced higher growth in expenditure and income. It is the differentials in growth in expenditure among different segments of the population that matter for inequality—hence the emphasis on "relative."

captures this phenomenon quite clearly. Table 2.14 describes the contribution of urban full-time wage and salaried workers' observable characteristics to changes in the Gini coefficient over weekly earnings during 1993–2004.

The residual reveals that 50% of the 6.63 percentage-point increase in the Gini coefficient from 1993 to 2004 (from 40.53 to 47.16) is driven by unknown factors. Of the remaining, education and occupation together exert dramatic upward pressure on inequality. Indeed, the two together account for a little more than the entire increase in the Gini coefficient actually registered. Had other, mostly unobservable, factors not put downward pressure on inequality in earnings, urban inequality in wages would have increased much more on account of differential returns to education and occupation.

Table 2.14   Contribution of individual characteristics to change in the Gini coefficient: Urban India

Individual characteristic	1993–2004
Age (%)	28.8
Gender (%)	11.9
Social group (%)	1.6
Production sector (%)	–0.9
Occupation (%)	25.4
Education (%)	81.5
Geography[a] (%)	1.8
Residual (%)	–50.0
Change in Gini coefficient	6.63

a   Geographic categories pertain to India's major states.
Source: ADB (2007c, Table 6.6).

What role, if any, have market-oriented reforms and international integration played in increasing these differentials? The literature answers this question in terms of the effects of trade (and investment) liberalization.

The conventional wisdom is that liberalization would benefit a country's abundant factors of production. More specifically, given the abundance of labor in many parts of developing Asia, international integration— or globalization as it is more commonly known—has been expected to increase the relative rewards to labor and thereby lower inequality. The conventional wisdom seems to have played out in this manner in the case of the newly industrialized economies in the mid 1960s–1970s when these economies opened up to foreign trade (Wood 1997).[23]

---

[23]   The *manner* in which these economies opened up to foreign trade is, however, disputed by scholars.

Since the 1980s, however, the evidence has pointed to a contemporaneous increase in measures of globalization and inequality across the developing world. Indeed, as Goldberg and Pavcnik (2007) note in their recent survey of the distributional effects of globalization in developing countries, two clear trends emerge from the available data. First, the exposure of developing countries to international markets—whether in terms of measures of protection, share of trade in GDP, foreign direct investment, and others—has increased dramatically in recent years. Second, the overall movement of the various available measures of inequality is upward. While causality is difficult to establish, the available evidence has "provided little support for the conventional wisdom that trade openness in developing countries would favor the least fortunate (at least in relative terms)" (Goldberg and Pavcnik 2007, 77).

Why might greater openness have led to greater inequality? Two specific factors are worth highlighting, namely the bargaining power of labor, and new technology. With regard to the former, some have argued that greater openness to trade may increase inequality by reducing the bargaining power of labor (see, for example, Rodrik 1997). Since greater openness makes it easier to import all kinds of goods—capital inputs, finished goods, and intermediate goods—it can make it easier to replace the services of domestic workers via the import of capital inputs or the products they were producing. In this way, trade liberalization can erode the bargaining power of workers vis-à-vis the owners of capital in the sharing of profits.[24] Further distinguishing skilled and unskilled workers, it is the latter who may be expected to suffer the brunt of the reduction in bargaining power.

In terms of the second specific factor, links between greater openness and new technology have also received considerable scrutiny in explaining the association between openness and growing inequality. Two channels that rely on these links are based on the following observations. First, closer integration with global markets has led developing countries to experience greater inflows of technology (embodied in imported capital goods, for example) from industrial

---

24　Hasan, Mitra, and Ramaswamy (2007) use industry-level panel data from India's formal manufacturing sector along with industry-specific information on average tariff rates and nontariff barrier (NTB) coverage ratios to examine whether the country's trade liberalization, begun in earnest in 1991, has made the demand for labor more elastic. They find that estimates of labor demand elasticity are larger after 1991 and larger in industries with lower tariff rates or NTB coverage ratios. They also find that the share of the wage bill in either total output or value-added is lower in the more open trading environment after 1991, and is lower in industries that have lower barriers to trade. For example, controlling for industry and location (through the introduction of industry-location fixed effects), their estimates of labor share equations suggest that labor shares would decline by around 4% (as a share of total output) and 5% (as a share of value-added) for a reduction in tariffs from 150% to 40%.

countries. If new technology is designed for use by skilled or highly educated workers (which is entirely plausible given conditions in the industrial countries where new technologies are invariably developed, i.e., conditions of relative abundance of skilled workers), then greater openness could well be associated with increasing returns to skilled or highly educated workers, and hence growing inequality.

Second, a considerable part of trade is made in intermediate products—a phenomenon sometimes referred to as global production sharing or outsourcing. It has been argued that outsourcing also raises returns to skilled labor in *both* industrial and developing countries (Feenstra and Hanson 1996 and 2003). Why should this be so? Prior to any outsourcing, industrial countries generally specialize in products or tasks that are skill-intensive, and developing countries in products or tasks that are less skill-intensive. For an industrial country firm contemplating outsourcing, it will usually make most sense to outsource less skill-intensive products or tasks. It is easy enough therefore to see that outsourcing will raise the relative demand for skilled workers in industrial countries. However, outsourcing will also raise the relative demand for skilled workers in developing countries. This will happen when the product or task that is outsourced is itself more skill-intensive than the average product or task that is produced/carried out in developing countries. Through either channel, greater openness will be associated with increasing inequality.

To the extent that higher educational attainments can proxy for high levels of skills, the finding that returns to higher education (post-secondary or college) have increased in many countries over a period in which trade has also been accounting for a steadily increasing share of GDP is consistent with the trade/technology and inequality linkages just described.

Whether or not it is the trade/technology story as described above that is driving the increasing convexity of returns to education is an issue that needs to be examined more closely. Among other things, definitions and measures of "skills" and "skill-biased technical change" are all somewhat controversial. Moreover, there are other channels that can explain why returns to college education have gone up and that do not need to rely on technical changes, but that may still be linked to market-oriented reforms. In particular, increases in returns to post-secondary or college education can be linked to the increasing returns to specific occupations that also require, or are typically staffed by, people with a college education. In Mexico, for example, the rapid increase in earnings of professionals and administrators was the key driving force behind increases in the returns to post-secondary education over a period of trade reforms, a finding that has been attributed to greater demand for individuals who could respond to the rapid changes introduced by the reforms (Cragg and Epelbaum 1996).

The specific channels through which market-oriented reforms have influenced wage inequality are important to disentangle, however, since the policy implications can differ, depending on which channels are more relevant. For example, to the extent that increasing returns to post-secondary education are driven by the returns to particular occupations (or industries, for that matter), increasing the share of college education in the population will not do much to raise incomes generally or dampen increases in inequality (though it will probably reduce the returns to college education).[25] Put differently, even if it is feasible to raise the educational attainments of a large majority of young adults, it is not possible for everybody to be a manager.

C. Summing Up

Overall, the interplay between market-oriented reforms, globalization, and the introduction of new technology is probably an important part of the story of unequal growth across households—though perhaps not in the same form that many studies have considered. All else being equal, it is the more educated who will most likely be able to make the most of the opportunity that market reforms and international integration bring. This may be because education itself confers special advantages on individuals (e.g., engineering degree holders who can capitalize on the boom in information technology through their computer programming experience). Alternatively, the individuals most able to seize opportunities are the ones most likely to have a college education in the first place (e.g., English-speaking young adults who can capitalize on the boom in information technology-enabled services).

A more general point is that a fast-changing economic environment can create substantial economic rents, the surplus above and beyond the income needed to pay owners of labor and capital. How these rents are distributed depends partly on the institutional framework of a country. Where it is strong and progressive, these rents can be taxed for financing public goods without creating distortions (Gill and Kharas 2007). Where it is weak, economic rents can lead to rent-seeking behavior and become detrimental to the process of economic growth itself.

---

[25] Moreover, rapid expansion of the supply of any given level of education may well be associated with declining quality of that education (on average, at least).

2.5 Concluding remarks: Public policy and inequality

What should be the response of public policy to inequality? As seen from the evidence in this chapter, increasing inequality in developing Asia reflects not so much "the rich getting richer and the poor getting poorer", but the rich getting richer faster than the poor. Moreover, as suggested in Section 2.4, it is quite likely that rapid income growth among the rich has been driven in one way or another by the opportunities unleashed by market-oriented reforms, international integration, and new technologies.

One way to deal with growing inequality would be to significantly roll back reforms and engagement with the international economy. However, this is unlikely to be feasible. It would also be undesirable. Lewis' (1983) view that development is inherently inegalitarian may not be an iron-clad law that applies in all cases—after all Asia's newly industrialized economies seemed to have been able to develop rapidly without significant increases in inequality—but there appears to be considerable force behind his point that the process of development is unlikely to start in every part of an economy at the same time. The gains from market-oriented reforms and international integration may be seen in a similar way.[26]

At the same time, the historical record does not show that declining inequality is an automatic outcome of continued economic development. Given that high levels of inequality and/or rapidly increasing inequality can imply slow improvement in the economic well-being of the poor even in a growing economy—and can also undermine both social cohesion and the quality of policies and institutions—public policy cannot simply ignore inequality.

A pragmatic way forward would be to focus on policies that would significantly lift the incomes of the poor—defined broadly here to include not only those living in extreme poverty but also the $2-a-day poor—by enabling them to access the opportunity that reforms and integration bring, while recognizing and limiting the very real danger that concentrations of income and wealth pose for social cohesion and growth-promoting policies and institutions. In what follows, broad principles for policy making relevant to the issue of inequality are described.[27]

---

[26] For example, while the relationship between trade policies and economic growth remains the subject of much debate among economists, there is significantly wider agreement that autarkic trade policies stifle economic growth. For a review of the evidence on the links between trade and growth, see Rodriguez and Rodrik (2000).

[27] Many of these principles draw on World Bank (2005).

2.5.1   Equalizing opportunity

Not all inequality is undesirable. Much of the data on inequality presented in this chapter refers to inequality in *outcomes*. Differences in outcomes, such as differences in incomes among individuals or expenditures of households, typically reflect some combination of differences in *effort* (the set of actions that are under the control of the individual), and differences in *circumstance* (the factors, including economic, social, or biological, that are outside the control of the individual) (Roemer 2006).[28]

The inequality that results from differences in effort is acceptable and even desirable to the extent that it reflects the incentives that an economy provides to its citizens for working harder, looking out for new opportunity, and taking the risks entailed in seizing it. However, inequality resulting from differences in circumstance is not only ethically unacceptable, it results in wasted productive potential and misallocation of resources.[29] From this perspective, it is circumstance-based inequality that gives rise to *inequality of opportunity* and that must be the target of public policies aimed at reducing inequality.

But making a clear distinction between effort and circumstance is not straightforward. In the real world, there is bound to be a plethora of circumstances leading to inequality of opportunity. There can also be differences of opinion on what constitutes circumstance and what constitutes effort.[30] But even with these difficulties, it is relatively easy to identify the most extreme circumstances that severely limit opportunity for many people. These circumstances relate, especially among the poor, to social exclusion; lack of access to high-quality basic education, health care, and social protection; and lack of access to income- and productivity-enhancing employment opportunity. Such circumstances

---

[28]   Roemer (2006) also considers policy to be a factor influencing a person's income relative to that of others. By only considering effort and circumstances, policy is implicitly treated as part of the circumstances that an individual faces.

[29]   Circumstances are doubly pernicious. In addition to the first-round disadvantages they create—as when access to education, health care, job opportunities, etc., is unevenly distributed—they can create second-round disadvantages by affecting the amount of effort that an individual in unfortunate circumstances is willing to make.

[30]   While race, caste, and gender certainly qualify as circumstances in which individuals find themselves, and as clear and worthy targets of policy to attack when opportunity is limited on account of these, things become murkier as the list of opportunity-affecting circumstances that individuals may find themselves in is broadened. How about being born to parents who do not instill good work ethics in a child? Is the child then responsible for his or her low effort as a working adult? At a different level, are the vastly high sums paid to chief executive officers in many countries truly commensurate with their effort? Yet another layer of complexity enters when effort is a function of circumstance. For example, faced with discrimination in the labor market, an individual may well decide to forgo expending effort.

are not only fundamentally unfair, they are also likely to work as serious constraints to poverty reduction, social cohesion, and economic growth; such circumstances must form a primary target of policy.[31]

2.5.2 Expanding employment for the poor involves policies that expand opportunity for the non-poor as well

It is not the case that only policies with a favorable impact on the distribution of opportunities should be considered. It is the overall policy framework and how the various policies interact and complement one another to promote opportunities for the poor that matter (World Bank 2005). For example, policies that improve productivity and incomes in the rural sector and the urban informal economy are vital for generating better employment for the poor. But policies also need to be combined with policies that generate employment opportunities more generally in the economy, including those for the non-poor. As argued in ADB (2007a), policies that promote structural change are crucial for economic development. It may well be the case that the first beneficiaries of structural change are the non-poor.

Similarly, a policy that improves access to finance may well, in the first round, benefit mainly lower-middle-income groups running small and medium enterprises. But the second-round effects of these policies may be quite beneficial for the poor. In the case of improvements in access to finance, for example, dynamism among small and medium enterprises should turn out to be pro-poor on account of the employment they can generate.

Another illustration of this principle may be seen in the context of trade policy. As noted in Section 2.4, a large body of empirical work suggests that trade liberalization and globalization, more broadly, have increased inequality. It is quite likely that this increase has arisen because the opportunities from globalization are best seized by those with specific

---

31   The distinction between circumstance-based inequality and effort-based inequality is similar to Chaudhuri and Ravallion's (2007) distinction between "good" and "bad" inequality. Good inequality reflects rewards to effort and reinforces market-based incentives needed to foster innovation, entrepreneurship, and growth. Bad inequality stems from circumstances that are outside the control of individuals and that limit a person's access to opportunity. Social exclusion, geographic poverty traps (i.e., a situation whereby residence in a well-endowed area enables a poor household to eventually escape poverty; the same household, were it living in a poor area, would find it very difficult), corruption, lack of access to education and health care, and lack of access to financial services such as credit and insurance all lead to bad inequality. Chaudhuri and Ravallion (2007) argue that: (i) in addition to being intrinsically unfair, bad inequality is a constraint on growth and poverty reduction; (ii) even good inequality can turn bad, however, as those who are rewarded by the market use some of these rewards to engage in rent-seeking activity and/or change the "rules of the game"; and (iii) bad inequality can drive out good because the persistence of bad inequality reduces society's tolerance for even good inequality.

attributes (for example, a college education and the ability to speak fluent English) or those located in specific regions (e.g., coastal). The concern with inequality of opportunity does not imply that policies that liberalize or encourage trade should be avoided. In the first place, the overall benefits from trade can be large. Moreover, trade liberalization may be poverty reducing even if it increases inequality.[32]

Second, in so far as the distributional impacts of trade policy are concerned, well-designed social protection mechanisms and skills and training programs could be useful to mitigate some of the adverse distributional impacts that may accompany an increase in import competition. Similarly, where the export response of trade liberalization is muted—for example, the failure of labor-intensive exports to take off—a careful assessment of factors preventing the export take-off and a resolution are needed.

2.5.3 Some redistribution will be inevitable in promoting greater equality of opportunity

Redistribution can occur at many levels. At one level, it can involve the redistribution of assets, such as land or access to it. At another, it can involve realignment of the recipients of public subsidies and public investments. For example, some amount of switching of public subsidies from tertiary education to basic education, and from urban to rural areas (from current norms and levels) may be critical for improving the access of the poor to basic social and physical infrastructure.

The feasibility and effectiveness of carrying out any such redistribution will depend on various factors including those relating to "voice" and political power.[33] Encouraging accountability and giving voice to the disadvantaged facilitate redistribution, and thus become important goals for public policy as well. Lindert (2004), in his path-breaking study of social spending in the contemporary industrial world, points to the important role of the spread of political voice in driving governments to devote more of their resources to spreading education and health care among the population at large.

---

[32]   For example, Hasan, Mitra, and Ural (2007) find that Indian states and regions that became more open to trade (as captured by having steeper declines in employment-weighted nontariff barriers) saw faster reductions in poverty.

[33]   In the context of equalizing access to land, for example, it is worth noting that the most successful redistributions have taken place in fairly unusual political and historical circumstances. In the Republic of Korea and Taipei,China, for example, these took place against the backdrop of foreign occupation prior to and right after World War II. In the PRC and Viet Nam, egalitarian distribution of land took place in the context of communist revolutions. Is the redistribution of land possible in less extreme circumstances? While the answer to this question may well be "no", recent experience does suggest that a variety of land reforms that improve the access of disadvantaged groups to land is possible.

2.5.4 Getting the design of redistributive policies right is critical

Correct design is crucial for securing the intended effects.[34] Equally, it is vital that redistributive policies do not hurt the growth process. This may happen if redistribution dampens the incentive for investment (say, through an overly steep tax on incomes or assets). It can also happen in other ways. For example, writing in the context of the Indian experience, Panagariya (2006, 11) argues that, "[v]irtually all anti-growth and anti-poor policies India has been struggling to shed for two decades had their origins in the pursuit of equity.... To be sure, equity-orientated policies that improve opportunities for the poor without compromising efficiency and growth do exist. The catch, however, is that once equity becomes central to policy making, self-interested lobbies capture the policies in the name of fairness. The policies then adopted are precisely those that impede growth and poverty alleviation."

The challenge of designing redistributive policies that are well targeted, effective, and funded through mechanisms that do not detract from economic growth is certainly formidable. But the need for redistributive policies will not go away—especially if increasing inequality turns out to be an enduring feature of developing Asia over the next 2 or 3 decades. It is imperative for all concerned stakeholders, including policy makers, to learn from the mistakes and successes of past attempts at redistribution.

Appendix: Distribution data used in Section 2.3

The analysis of Section 2.3 is based on grouped/tabulated distribution of per capita expenditure/income. A key source of information is the World Bank's POVCALNET online database, which provides data on the distribution of per capita expenditure (or income where available). POVCALNET also reports monthly mean per capita expenditure in purchasing power parity (PPP) 1993 (consumption) dollars corresponding to these distributions.

---

34 For example, equity-related concerns have prompted the Indian government to reserve 27% of positions in institutions of higher education managed by the central government for "other backward classes." While it may well be that caste-based discrimination denies educational opportunities to the disadvantaged, a policy of reservations applied to higher education may not be a particularly effective remedy. For example, household survey data reveal that the under-representation of disadvantaged social groups in higher education can mainly be accounted for by their low higher secondary school completion rates (Hasan and Mehta 2006). Thus, the primary distortions creating unequal representation in college appears to lie earlier in education. Attention to the quality of basic education, not college reservation, may well be the economically "first-best" response.

The information on distributions from the POVCALNET database has been augmented/replaced as follows.[35]

Bangladesh: distribution data are based on micro data from the Household Income and Expenditure Survey (2005).

Cambodia: distribution data are from the World Bank "Poverty Assessment 2006" report prepared by the World Bank's East Asia Department.

India: distribution data are from the National Sample Survey consumer expenditure survey of Round 61 (2004/2005) from NSS Report No. 508.

Republic of Korea: distribution data pertain to household income for urban wage-earning households published by the Korea National Statistical Office.[36] Mean household income was divided by average household size to arrive at a proxy for mean per capita income.

Malaysia: distribution data are based on micro data from the Household Expenditure Survey for 1993/1994 and 2004/2005.[37]

Philippines: distribution data are based on micro data from the Family Income and Expenditure Survey 2003.

Taipei,China: distribution data pertain to annual household income reported in the World Institute for Development Economic Research's World Income Inequality 2a database. Mean household income was divided by average household size to arrive at a proxy for mean per capita income.

Turkmenistan: distribution data are from reports of the Turkmenistan Living Standards Surveys of 1998 and 2003.

Viet Nam: distribution data came from the Government Statistics Office.

In all these cases, mean per capita incomes/expenditures are converted from local currency units into 1993 PPP dollars (and expressed in monthly terms) using (i) PPP exchange rates (consumption) from the World Bank and Penn World Tables (Taipei,China); and (ii) consumer price indexes from the World Banks World Development Indicators and national sources (as needed). [38, 39]

---

[35] For consistency purposes, the analysis of Section 2.4 is based entirely on grouped/tabulated distribution data. Thus, even where micro data were available, these were used to generate decile-based distribution data.

[36] Since the share of the urban population was already about 76% in 1993, the limitation to the urban sector may not be that problematic.

[37] The POVCALNET data were relatively out of date. In addition, they were based on per capita incomes.

[38] Mean per capita expenditures for Cambodia, Lao PDR, and Viet Nam were expressed in 1993 PPP dollars using information contained in the World Bank's East Asia Update (various issues) used in conjunction with the World Bank's "Poverty Assessment 2006" for Cambodia.

[39] Separate rural and urban consumer price indexes were used to convert the monthly mean per capita expenditures into 1993 PPP dollars in the case of the Indian data for 2004/05.

References

ADB. 2004. *Development Indicators Reference Manual.* Asian Development Bank, Manila.

_____. 2005. "Labor Markets in Asia: Promoting Full, Productive, and Decent Employment." In *Key Indicators 2005.* Asian Development Bank, Manila.

_____. 2007a. "Education and Structural Change in Four Asian Countries." In *Asian Development Outlook 2007.* Asian Development Bank, Manila.

_____. 2007b. "Growth Amid Change." In *Asian Development Outlook 2007.* Asian Development Bank, Manila.

_____. 2007c. "Inequality in Asia." In *Key Indicators 2007.* Asian Development Bank, Manila.

Bureau of Statistics. 2005. Household Income and Expenditure Survey Dataset. Dhaka.

Chaudhuri, S., and M. Ravallion. 2007. "Partially Awakened Giants: Uneven Growth in China and India." In L. A. Winters, and S. Yusuf, eds., *Dancing With Giants: China, India and the Global Economy.* World Bank, Washington, DC.

Cornia, G. A., and J. Court. 2001. Inequality, Growth and Poverty in the Era of Liberalization and Globalization. UNU-WIDER Policy Brief No. 4, World Institute for Development Economic Research, United Nations University, Helsinki.

Cowell, F. A. 1995. *Measuring Inequality.* 2nd ed. Hemel Hempstead: Harvester Wheatsheaf.

Cragg, M. I., and M. Epelbaum. 1996. "Why has Wage Dispersion Grown in Mexico? Is it the Incidence of Reforms or the Growing Demand for Skills?" *Journal of Development Economics* 51(1):99–116.

Department of Statistics. Various years. Household Expenditure Survey Datasets for 1993/94 and 2004/05. Putrajaya.

Feenstra, R. C., and G. H. Hanson. 1996. "Foreign Investment, Outsourcing and Relative Wages." In R. C. Feenstra, G. M. Grossman, and D. A. Irwin, eds., *The Political Economy of Trade Policy: Papers in Honor of Jagdish Bhagwati.* Cambridge, MA: MIT Press.

_____. 2003. "Global Production Sharing and Rising Inequality: A Survey of Trade and Wages." In E. K. Choi, and J. Harrigan, eds., *Handbook of International Trade.* Malden, MA: Blackwell.

Fields, G. 1989. *A Compendium of Data on Inequality and Poverty for the Developing World.* Ithaca: Cornell University.

_____. 2001. *Distribution and Development: A New Look at the Developing World.* New York: Russell Sage Foundation.

_____. 2003. "Accounting For Income Inequality and Its Changes: A New Method with Application to the Distribution of Earnings in the United States." *Research in Labor Economics* 22:1–38.

General Statistics Office. Various years. Viet Nam Living Standards Survey Datasets. Hanoi.

Gill, I., and H. Kharas. 2007. *An East Asian Renaissance: Ideas for Economic Growth.* World Bank, Washington, DC.

Goldberg, P., and N. Pavcnik. 2007. "Distributional Effects of Globalization in Developing Countries." *Journal of Economic Literature* 45(1):39–82.

Hasan, R., and A. Mehta. 2006. "Under-representation of Disadvantaged Classes in Colleges: What Do the Data Tell Us?" *Economic and Political Weekly* 3791–6.

Hasan, R., D. Mitra, and K. V. Ramaswamy. 2007. "Trade Reforms, Labor Regulations, and Labor-Demand Elasticities: Empirical Evidence from India." *Review of Economics and Statistics* 89(3):466–81.

Hasan, R., D. Mitra, and B. P. Ural. 2007. "Trade Liberalization, Labor Market Institutions, and Poverty Reduction: Evidence from Indian States." *India Policy Forum 2006–07* (3):71–122.

Kakwani, N., and H. H. Son. 2009. "Poverty Equivalent Growth Rate." *Review of Income and Wealth* 54(4):643–55.

Kumar, U. 2006. "Economic Geography, Spatial Inequality and Liberalization: Evidence from India." University of Maryland. Processed.

Lall, S. V., and S. Chakravorty. 2005. "Industrial Location and Spatial Inequality: Theory and Evidence from India." *Review of Development Economics* 9(1):47–68.

Lewis, W. A. 1983. "Development and Distribution." In M. Gersovitz, ed., *Selected Economic Writings of W. Arthur Lewis.* New York: New York University Press.

Lin, S. 2005. "International Trade, Location and Wage Inequality in China." In R. Kanbur, and A. J. Venables, eds., *Spatial Inequality and Development.* Oxford: Oxford University Press.

Lindert, P. H. 2004. *Growing Public: Social Spending and Economic Growth Since the Eighteenth Century.* New York: Cambridge University Press.

National Institute of State Statistics and Information (Turkmenmillihasabat). Various years. "Grouped/Tabulated Expenditure Distribution Data." In Living Standards Survey 1998 and 2003. Turkmenistan.

National Sample Survey Organization. 2007. "National Sample Survey Reports." NSS, Round 61, Schedules 1 and 10. New Delhi.

_____. Various years. Consumer Expenditure Survey Datasets. New Delhi.

_____. Various years. Employment and Unemployment Survey Datasets. New Delhi.

National Statistical Office. 2005. "Grouped/Tabulated Income Distribution Data." *Social Indicators in Korea*. Seoul.

National Statistics Office. Various years. Family Income and Expenditure Survey Datasets. Manila.

_____. Various years. Labor Force Survey Datasets. Manila.

Nguyen, B. T., J. W. Albrecht, S. Vroman, and M. D. Westbrook. 2007. "A Quantile Regression Decomposition of Urban-Rural Inequality in Vietnam." *Journal of Development Economics* 83(2):466–90.

Nguyen, B. T., C. C. Loi, and N. C. Thang. 2006. "A Stocktaking of Viet Nam's Labor Market Policies." In J. Felipe, and R. Hasan, eds., *Labor Markets in Asia: Issues and Perspectives*. London: Palgrave MacMillan for the Asian Development Bank.

Panagariya, A. 2006. "Pursuit of Equity Threatens Poverty Alleviation." *Financial Times*. 31 May, Page 11.

Park, A., X. Song, J. Zhang, and Y. Zhao. 2004. "The Growth of Wage Inequality in Urban China, 1988 to 1999." Department of Economics, University of Michigan, Ann Arbor. Processed.

Ravallion, M. 2004a. Competing Concepts of Inequality in the Globalization Debate. Policy Research Working Paper No. 3243, World Bank, Washington, DC.

_____. 2004b. Pro-Poor Growth: A Primer. Policy Research Working Paper No. 3242, World Bank, Washington, DC.

Ray, D. 1998. *Development Economics*. Princeton: Princeton University Press.

Rodriguez, F., and D. Rodrik. 2000. "Trade Policy and Economic Growth: A Skeptic's Guide to the Cross-National Evidence." *NBER Macroeconomics Annual* 15:261–325.

Rodrik, D. 1997. *Has Globalization Gone Too Far?* Institute of International Economics, Washington, DC.

Roemer, J. 2006. Economic Development as Opportunity Equalization. Discussion Paper No. 1583, Cowles Foundation for Research in Economics, Yale University, New Haven.

Tao, R. 2006. "The Labor Market in the People's Republic of China: Development and Policy Challenges in Economic Transition." In J. Felipe and R. Hasan, eds., *Labor Markets in Asia: Issues and Perspectives*. London: Palgrave MacMillan for the Asian Development Bank.

Wood, A. 1997. "Openness and Wage Inequality in Developing Countries: The Latin American Challenge to East Asian Conventional Wisdom." *The World Bank Economic Review* 11(1):33–57.

World Bank. World Development Indicators Online. Available: http://devdata. worldbank.org/dataonline/.

_____. 2005. *World Development Report 2006: Equity and Development*. New York: Oxford University Press.

_____. 2006. Cambodia: Halving Poverty by 2015? Poverty Assessment 2006. Report No. 35213-KH. Washington, DC.

_____. Various years. "East Asia Updates." Washington, DC. Available: www.worldbank.org/eapupdate/.

World Bank, Department for International Development, and Asian Development Bank. 2006. Nepal: Resilience Amidst Conflict: An Assessment of Poverty in Nepal, 1995–96 and 2003–04. Report No. 34834-NP, World Bank, Washington, DC.

World Institute for Development Economic Research. Various years. World Income Inequality Database. Available: www.wider.unu.edu/wiid/wiid.htm.

Zhang, J., Y. Zhao, A. Park, X. Song. 2005. "Economic Returns to Schooling in Urban China, 1988–2001." *Journal of Comparative Economics* 33:730–52.

3

Non-Income Poverty and Inequality in Asia

Ajay Tandon and Susan Sparkes[1]

3.1   Introduction

This chapter is an overview of non-income poverty and human development in Asia. This focus is justifiable not only from an ethical and moral perspective, but also pragmatically given the importance of these issues to political and social stability. As will be discussed, human development must be viewed as an end in itself and not just a means for attaining economic growth. Nevertheless, the extent to which economic growth has not been inclusive poses a threat to growth prospects in the region. Growing socioeconomic inequality often triggers crime and political and civil unrest. The growth elasticity of poverty also tends to be higher with higher levels of human development and lower levels of income inequality.[2]

Section 3.2 discusses the concepts and measurement of non-income poverty and inequality. Section 3.3 summarizes broad trends in non-income poverty indicators while Section 3.4 examines inequality in non-income poverty indicators, both focusing on developing Asian economies. Section 3.5 explores the relationship between income and non-income poverty, and summarizes some empirical findings. Section 3.6 concludes with a brief discussion.

3.2   Concepts and measurement of non-income poverty and inequality

In broad terms, non-income poverty refers to dimensions that go beyond the traditional monetary and consumption-driven aspects of

---

[1]   The views expressed in this paper are those of the authors and do not represent the views and opinions of their affiliated institutions. Portions of this chapter are derived from ADB (2006).

[2]   The growth elasticity of poverty is the percentage decline in poverty observed for a percentage increment in per capita income.

individual and societal well-being. Whereas it is important to know the level of consumption or income of individuals and countries, it is equally important to assess the attainment of non-income "human development" welfare indicators—such as nutrition, health, and education, among others—at a given level of income or consumption. A key theme underlying this chapter is that, although income and non-income poverty indicators are often correlated, this correlation cannot be taken for granted. The information content in non-income poverty measures can often be far more revealing of individual and societal welfare than income poverty measures alone.

Conceptually, the emergence of non-income poverty as a metric of welfare owes a lot to the work of Amartya Sen and others who have persuasively argued that income in itself is merely an *instrumental* goal in human welfare. Sen (1998) has argued that health and education—unlike income—are of *intrinsic* value because they are critical for capability enhancement: they allow individuals to lead lives they have reason to value. This line of thinking was the motivation behind the development of the United Nations Development Programme's Human Development Index, which ranks countries on income, health, and educational attainment, each having the same weight (UNDP 2007). The importance of health and education as intrinsic welfare outcomes is also very much in evidence in the United Nations' Millennium Development Goals (MDGs), a compact among 189 countries to time-bound improvements in a host of indicators including those related to malnutrition, child mortality, maternal mortality, and the reduction in the prevalence of diseases such as HIV/AIDS, malaria, and tuberculosis (United Nations 2000).

This chapter takes a more holistic view of the conceptualization and measurement of non-income poverty indicators. Non-income poverty is difficult to summarize in a single metric and hence no attempt is made to characterize country performance on a unitary scale. There are several different dimensions of non-income poverty and, for the most part, this chapter discusses the attainment of widely recognized and accepted non-income poverty indicators. These indicators include those that are part of the MDGs and Human Development Index, including life expectancy, infant mortality, under-five mortality, maternal mortality, malnutrition rates, enrollment rates, literacy rates, and the like. Each, on its own, provides an incomplete indication of welfare on non-income poverty dimensions in any given country, and therefore the ensuing discussion of levels and trends in developing Asia focuses on a parsimonious multiplicity of these indicators. The terms "non-income poverty" and "human development" are used interchangeably in the remainder of this chapter and signify attainments in the broad areas of health, nutrition, and education.

In discussing non-income inequality, similar caveats pertain. Again, there is no single metric that can be used to determine if one country is more unequal than another across a range of non-income poverty measures. The most common measure of income inequality is the Gini coefficient, which measures the extent to which incomes are evenly distributed in a population. Using data from 2000 to 2005, the Gini coefficient for developing Asia varied from 0.328 for Mongolia to 0.469 for the People's Republic of China (PRC). This shows a relatively high and varied level of income inequality, which is often highly correlated with indicators of non-income poverty. The dual causality between poverty and ill health and low levels of educational attainment contributes to the level of inequality of both income and non-income indicators. However, not all non-income inequality can be directly attributed to differences in income levels. For instance, the level of educational attainment may differ greatly between men and women in a country for cultural reasons or reasons related to gender discrimination.

Wagstaff (2002) argues that the poor tend to be more disadvantaged in access to health care and health outcomes which, in turn, contributes to their poverty. The poor are unable to access health services, causing their health to deteriorate, leaving them unable to work and increase income levels. This also holds true for education. The poor may be unable to send their children to school, stunting educational attainment, and possibly keeping them from increasing overall income for the next generation. Through this cycle, non-income inequality not only persists, but also feeds into persistent income inequality and an inability to break the cycle of poverty.

While this chapter primarily examines inequalities within countries by focusing on non-income factors, researchers are able to examine intrahousehold inequalities. Ravallion (1996) points to a multilevel analysis of non-income inequality that includes child nutritional status, food consumption, access to public health and education services, infant mortality rates, and primary school enrollment.

This chapter focuses on the inequality of non-income poverty indicators within countries in developing Asia. To measure their relative level, it is important to look at differences between men and women, rural and urban, high income and low income, and age dynamics. This issue is not explored extensively; rather, pertinent examples showing the difference in both health and education indicators within certain countries are provided to highlight this important dimension of poverty. While aggregate numbers are important, it is also crucial to examine the dynamics of poverty and inequality within countries.

3.3   Non-income poverty

Developing Asia's success in reducing income poverty rates has been spectacular. Absolute poverty rates—the proportion of the population living on $1 a day or less—have declined significantly in the region, primarily as a result of robust economic growth in the PRC and India, as well as in some other countries such as Viet Nam. For example, from 1990 to 2004, the $1-a-day poverty rate declined from 32.5% to 10.8% in the PRC; from 43.5% to 35.1% in India; from 50.7% to 8.4% in Viet Nam; and from 47.8% to 9.8% in Pakistan (ADB 2007). This section assesses whether dramatic declines in income poverty in Asia over the past few decades have been matched by improvements in non-income poverty measures.

3.3.1   Current attainment in population health

Figure 3.1 gives a snapshot of infant mortality and life expectancy in Asia relative to the rest of the world for 2007 (the vertical and horizontal lines are the global averages). There remains a notable diversity in health indicators. Countries such as Bangladesh, Cambodia, India, Pakistan, and Papua New Guinea fall in the upper left-hand quadrant for having less than the global average attainment of life expectancy and infant mortality rates—two key population health outcomes. By contrast, countries such as PRC, Indonesia, Philippines, Sri Lanka, and Viet Nam have above-average population health outcomes, in some cases significantly so. In general, as can be seen in Figure 3.1, higher life expectancy is correlated with lower infant mortality, in that both adult mortality and infant mortality tend to move together. However, a couple of countries are somewhat anomalous in this regard: Kazakhstan, for instance, is above average in infant mortality but below average on life expectancy, in some ways reflecting the recent experience of several ex-Soviet republics. Azerbaijan, on the other hand, exhibits the anomaly in the other direction: having relatively high infant mortality but above average life expectancy.

Under-five mortality rates follow a similar pattern as infant mortality in the developing Asian countries. However, as one of the MDGs—the specific goal being the attainment of a two-thirds reduction in under-five mortality rates over the period 1990–2015—the trend is important to track. The under-five mortality MDG is a relative measure in that performance is judged relative to a given country's attainment in 1990 and not on an absolute scale. As can be seen in Figure 3.2, the attainment of this MDG varies widely across countries and regions in

Asia. The Pacific region appears to have had the most countries off-track in 2006, when countries ought to have attained 64% of the targeted two-thirds reduction. India is notable as the only country off-track in South Asia. Azerbaijan, Georgia, and Pakistan are also off-track.

Figure 3.1   Infant mortality versus life expectancy, 2007

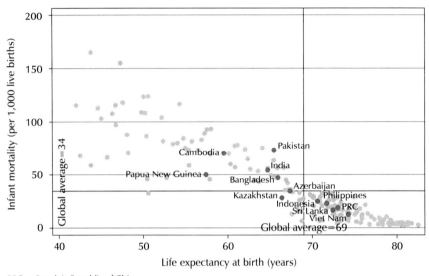

PRC = People's Republic of China.
Note: Averages are population weighted.
Source: World Bank, World Development Indicators Online.

Figure 3.2   Attainment of the under-five mortality MDG in selected Asian countries (% of target attained), 2006

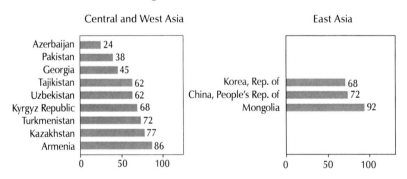

continued.

Figure 3.2 *continued.*

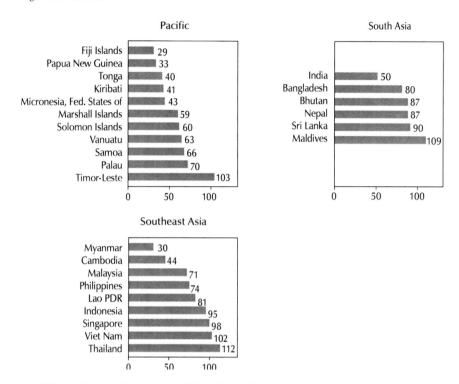

Lao PDR = Lao People's Democratic Republic, MDG = Millennium Development Goal.
Source: World Bank, World Development Indicators Online.

3.3.2   Educational attainment

Figure 3.3 provides a broad overview of educational attainment in Asia relative to the rest of the world. The x-axis plots the expected years of schooling in a country, which is a synthetic measure of the number of years spent in school derived from age-specific enrollment rates in a country in a given year. The y-axis measures net primary enrollment, one of the MDGs. Both measures are averaged over 2000–2007 because data were not available consistently for all countries for the same year. As can be seen, countries such as Azerbaijan, Indonesia, Kazakhstan, and Philippines are in the upper right quadrant, reflecting above average performance in both primary enrollment and education expectancy, the latter implying high secondary and tertiary enrollment as well. Pakistan is notable for its low enrollment and low education expectancy. Bangladesh and Cambodia have relatively high primary enrollment rates, but lag in education expectancy.

Figure 3.3   Education expectancy versus primary enrollment, 2000–2007

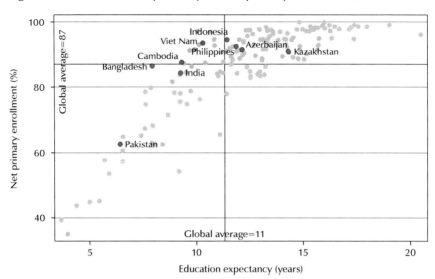

Note: Averages are population weighted.
Source: World Bank, World Development Indicators Online.

Education expectancy and enrollment rates are "flow" measures in that they reflect likely future changes in educational attainment. Table 3.1 summarizes the situation on a more "stock" measure such as adult literacy and adult female literacy rates in selected Asian countries. The disparity in flow measures is reflected in the variance among Asian countries in adult and female adult literacy rates. Seven of the 12 countries in the table have a literacy rate above 90%. On the other hand, countries such as Bangladesh and Pakistan have very low literacy rates (around 40%). Looking at female adult literacy rates, the average for the 12 countries when weighted by the total female population is 68.8%, lower than average in the total population. Bangladesh and Pakistan fare worst, with female literacy of 40.8% and 35.4%, while in Azerbaijan and Kazakhstan, 98.2% and 99.3% of adult women are literate, respectively. The link between education expectancy and primary enrollment and literacy rates is strong, with those countries tending to do better in the current stock of literate populations also expected to do better in indicators that measure future educational attainment.

Table 3.1   Adult and female literacy rates in selected Asian countries

Country	Year	Adult literacy (%)	Female adult literacy (%)
Azerbaijan	1999	98.8	98.2
Bangladesh	2001	47.5	40.8
Cambodia	2004	73.6	64.1
China, People's Rep. of	2000	90.9	86.5
India	2001	61.0	47.8
Indonesia	2004	90.4	86.8
Kazakhstan	1999	99.5	99.3
Pakistan	2005	49.9	35.4
Papua New Guinea	2000	57.3	50.9
Philippines	2003	92.6	93.6
Sri Lanka	2001	90.7	89.1
Viet Nam	1999	90.3	86.9

Note: Latest available data.
Source: World Bank, World Development Indicators Online.

3.3.3   A bit of history

In the early 20th century, human development was extremely low in most of Asia, probably because large parts of the region were under colonial administration; low levels of human capital at the time likely reflected extractive public administrations that were not really geared toward human resource investments.[3] Table 3.2 reports life expectancy in selected Asian countries for 1940 and 2006 as well as for some selected colonizers in the region such as Japan, Netherlands, United Kingdom, and United States. Although the sample of countries for which life expectancy data were available in 1940 is small, there are some interesting trends to note. First, even in 1940, there were differences among Asian countries, with South Asia (except Sri Lanka) generally having lower life expectancy compared to East Asia and Southeast Asia, such as Republic of Korea (Korea), Malaysia, and Philippines. Also remarkable is that, without exception, countries with life expectancy in the 30s in 1940 had rates in the 60s in 2006; and those in the 40s in 1940 had rates in the 70s in 2006. At least in the sample of countries in Table 3.2, there has been little or no change in the relative ranking of life expectancy over the past 65 years.

---

3   For instance, Acemoglu et al. (2001) argue that general institutional development was weak in colonies where settler mortality rates were high.

As can be seen in Figure 3.4, average life expectancy in Asia in 1900 was far below Europe and the Americas, but over the course of the 20th century it almost caught up. At an average of 67.1, life expectancy in Asia—although still below both Europe and the Americas (76.8 and 70.8 years, respectively)—is rapidly approaching levels in the more developed regions.

Table 3.2   Life expectancy in selected countries and colonizers (years)

Country	Life expectancy 1940	Life expectancy 2006
Bangladesh	29.9	63.7
China, People's Rep. of	43.9	72.0
India	30.0	64.5
Indonesia	34.3	68.2
Korea, Republic of	48.7	78.5
Malaysia	42.6	74.0
Myanmar	36.6	61.6
Pakistan	30.0	65.2
Philippines	47.3	71.4
Sri Lanka	42.3	75.0
Thailand	42.6	70.2
Japan	50.0	82.0
Netherlands	67.4	80.0
United Kingdom	65.0	79.1
United States	63.8	77.8

Source: Acemoglu and Johnson (2007); Brody et al. (2000); World Bank, World Development Indicators Online.

Figure 3.4   Comparison of regional average life expectancy, 1900–2001

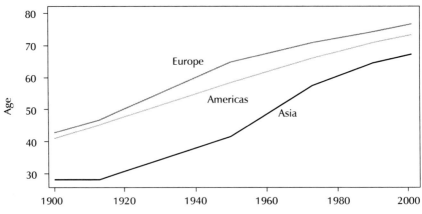

Source: Riley (2005).

Similarly, Figure 3.5 shows the big differences in primary school enrollment in North America and northern Europe relative to Asia and sub-Saharan Africa in the late 19th and early 20th centuries. As far back as 1900, North America and northern Europe had reached primary enrollment rates that several developing Asian countries have yet to achieve. Figure 3.6 shows enrollment rates over the period 1870–1940 disaggregated for selected Asian countries. Some colonial anomalies are in evidence, emphasizing the need to look beyond averages. Sri Lanka, for instance, had a relatively high primary enrollment rate in 1900 (20%) compared to India (<5%) despite the fact that both were British colonies. Some argue that the Colebrook-Cameron Reforms in Sri Lanka in the 19th century, which unified the country and encouraged some degree of local participation, were partly responsible for the differences (see Box 3.1). Similarly, after 1900, the Philippines saw a rapid rise in primary enrollment after the United States took over the former Spanish colony.

Figure 3.5   Primary enrollment in selected regions, 1870–1940

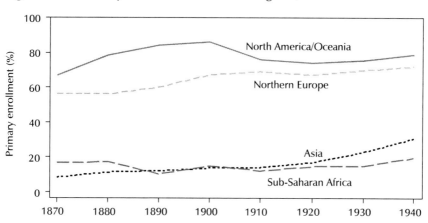

Source: Benavot and Riddle (1988).

Why might it be important to look at health and education from a historical perspective? First, Gallego (2005) points out that there is a startlingly high correlation between past and present. For instance, the correlation coefficient between primary enrollment in 1900 and average years of education in 1985–1995 was 0.79. Banerjee and Iyer (2005) show how historical experiences can influence present-day policy choices. Using data from the 1950s to the 1990s, they find that districts in India—where British colonial authorities handed over land rights and tax revenue collection to land owners in the 19th century—

tended to invest less in health and education even after independence in 1947. They argue that one reason may stem from polarization, which caused differences in preferences across classes and which appears to have persisted over time in these districts. Rajan and Zingales (2006) make a similar point. They argue that, rather than focusing on institutions, it may be more productive to look at historical sources of polarization and "self-perpetuating constituencies" among population subgroups. The latter, they argue, are the root cause of the persistence of underdevelopment. In many instances, it is not so much the issue of what policies to pursue, but more of finding ways of garnering the political consensus to pursue the appropriate policies.

As the above discussion has emphasized, in order to understand some of the institutional weaknesses that may explain current health and education deficiencies, it may be necessary to take a broader view of past trends and "initial conditions." However, even though history can matter, several countries in Asia have defied these initial deficiencies (e.g., Korea and Malaysia in education). Understanding how these countries overcame their disadvantages and deviated from the norm can yield important insights to guide policy makers.

Figure 3.6   Primary enrollment in selected Asian countries, 1860–1940

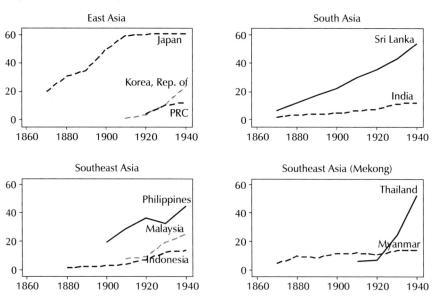

PRC = People's Republic of China.
Note: The y-axis refers to primary enrollment (%).
Source: Benavot and Riddle (1988).

Box 3.1   Colonial origins of Sri Lanka's educational advantage
           over India

Based on the latest available indicators, adult literacy in Sri Lanka was an impressive 90.7%. Net primary enrollment was 97.2% and the average years of education was 6.1. By contrast, Indian adult literacy was an abysmal 61.0%. There have been some signs of improvement in recent years: India's net primary enrollment rate is now a respectable 90%. But the population on average still has only about 4.8 years of education (World Bank 2006, Barro and Lee 2000).[1]

These educational disparities are not new: even as far back as 1900, Sri Lanka enjoyed much higher enrollment rates than India (Figure 3.5). What explains the historical origins of differences in educational attainment between the two countries, especially given that both were British colonies?

Lindert (2003) argues that a key difference relates to the extent of local democratic participation. Britain introduced universal adult suffrage in Sri Lanka in 1931. In contrast, in 1919, suffrage in colonial India was extended only to the relatively privileged classes, namely, the educated and those owning land. This "elite bias"—his argument goes—partly explains historically low primary enrollment in India. This trend continued even after independence, with public funds favoring tertiary education at the expense of mass primary schooling. He argues that imperfections in India's local democratic institutions have made it difficult for the underprivileged to voice and influence their preferences, especially at lower administrative tiers.

But a puzzle remains: Sri Lankan enrollment in 1900 was already more than 4 times higher than that of India, significantly before the introduction of universal adult suffrage in Sri Lanka in 1931 (Gallego 2005). Hence, one needs to look back even further to investigate the roots of the educational attainment differences. Gallego argues that the Colebrook-Cameron Reforms—the recommendations of a committee sent by Britain in 1829–1832 to investigate the colonial government of what was then Ceylon—were instrumental in encouraging social cohesion by centralizing the administration, allowing for the opening up of administrative posts to locals, encouraging political decentralization, and calling for the development of a unified English-medium education system.

---

[1]   Enrollment and literacy data refer to 2003; average years of education are for those aged 25 and above and are estimates for 2000.

Cross-country comparisons reveal the variation in non-income poverty outcomes across Asia. While, on average, impressive gains have been made in the reduction of income and non-income poverty, there is a wide degree of disparity in health and education outcomes. This disparity in results across countries is highlighted in both current outcomes, as well as historically. For instance, in most cases, those countries that were below the average in both education and health outcomes remain so today, despite relative improvements across the board. The next section goes a step beyond the cross-country analysis to examine trends in non-income poverty indicators within countries. In looking beyond country level averages, growing inequality in health and education outcomes is revealed within countries.

3.4   Inequalities in non-income poverty

Levels of attainment in health and education tell one side of the story of development in Asia. However, inequalities in education and health outcomes are of equal importance since they indicate the extent to which the poor and other socio-demographic groups are (or are not) being marginalized in the economic development process. In addition, inequalities tend to have strong geographic dimensions. Understanding these can make it considerably easier to target cost-effective policy interventions to improve educational attainment and improve the health status of indigent populations.[4]

Despite human development progress in developing Asia, inequalities in non-income poverty remain large, and there are indications that these have been increasing. The rise in inequality of human development in Asia has been mirrored as well by increases in income inequality in the region. In ADB (2007), for instance, 15 of 21 Asian economies reviewed experienced increases in income inequality between the 1990s and early 2000s.[5] More specifically, in a sample of 15 Asian countries, the average percentage change in the Gini coefficient from the mid-1990s until the early part of this decade was 5%.[6] While this does not negate the region's impressive gains in poverty reduction, it does highlight the need to focus on more inclusive growth strategies to ensure that poorer segments of the population are not left behind.

---

4   For example, in his analysis of MDG attainment for India, Deolalikar (2005) reports that in malnutrition, only about 10%–20% of all villages and districts in the country accounted for half of all infant deaths.

5   "For whosoever hath, to him shall be given, and he shall have more." See *The Economist* (2007).

6   Data from World Bank, World Development Indicators Online.

3.4.1   Inequality in health

There is evidence that health inequality within countries remains considerable in Asia, despite overall improvement in average population health throughout the region. And evidence shows that in some countries health-related inequality is actually increasing. For instance, Minujin and Delamonica (2003), using data from the Demographic and Health Surveys, show that inequality in child mortality by wealth level increased from the mid-1980s to the mid-1990s in Bangladesh, Indonesia, Kazakhstan, and Philippines. Considerable inequality in under-five mortality between the lowest and highest wealth quintiles using more recent data are reported in Table 3.3. Wealth-related inequality is greater than that between rural and urban populations. Furthermore, there is a large variation among the sample countries. For example, in Indonesia those in the lowest wealth quintile had an under-five mortality rate 3.5 times higher than that for the highest wealth quintile, but only 1.5 times higher in Turkmenistan.

Table 3.3   Inequalities in under-five mortality rate

Region/country	Year	Low/high ratio	Rural/urban ratio
Central and West Asia			
Armenia	2005	2.3	1.6
Kazakhstan	1999	1.8	1.5
Pakistan	1991	1.7	1.4
Kyrgyz Republic	1997	2.0	1.4
Turkmenistan	2000	1.5	1.4
South Asia			
Bangladesh	2004	1.7	1.1
India	2006	3.0	1.6
Nepal	2006	2.1	1.8
Southeast Asia			
Cambodia	2005	3.0	1.5
Indonesia	2003	3.5	1.5
Philippines	2003	3.1	1.7
Viet Nam	2002	3.3	2.2

Note: The low/high ratio shows the ratio of under-five mortality rates for those in the bottom quintile of wealth versus those in the top quintile. The rural/urban ratio shows the ratio of under-five mortality rates for those living in rural areas versus those in urban areas.
Source: WHO (various years), Gwatkin et al. (2007).

Inequality in health outcomes is mirrored in some countries by variations in health outputs. Figure 3.7 shows the disparity in both diptheria, pertussis, and tetanus (DPT3) immunization and skilled birth attendance among districts in Indonesia. Some districts in Indonesia have DPT3 immunization rates similar to Turkey and Viet Nam, while others have rates below those found in Niger and Somalia. A similar variation in outputs is seen in the level of skilled birth attendance within Indonesia.

Figure 3.7   DPT3 immunization and skilled birth attendance:
             Indonesian districts and selected countries, 2005

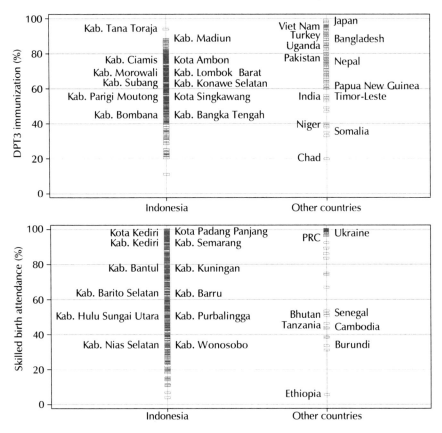

Kab. = *Kabupaten* (district), PRC = People's Republic of China.
Source: SUSENAS (Central Bureau of Statistics 2005) and World Bank, World Development Indicators
           Online.

3.4.2   Inequality in education

Inequality in education is difficult to measure, as the quality dimension of education, in particular, is not easy to capture through survey and census instruments. Taking into account these discrepancies, as with health, measurable inequality in education persists in developing Asia. The most prominent can be seen in the inequality between rich and poor children who are out of school. Globally, it is estimated that almost 20% of all primary school-age children are out of school. However, in many Asian countries the numbers far exceed the average. For example, in the Lao People's Democratic Republic recent estimates show that 60% of primary school-age children in the poorest quintile were out of school, compared to only 12.7% in the richest quintile (Table 3.4).

Table 3.4   Out-of-school primary school-age children (%), 1999–2003

Region/country	Total	Poorest quintile	Richest quintile
Central and West Asia			
Armenia	3.0	2.7	3.9
Azerbaijan	9.1	11.3	6.4
Kazakhstan	1.5	3.0	0.6
Pakistan	19.7	23.0	14.6
Tajikistan	19.3	20.1	17.7
East Asia			
Mongolia	20.8	29.4	9.8
South Asia			
Bangladesh	20.7	35.9	13.6
India	23.1	33.2	9.8
Nepal	33.8	41.4	25.4
Southeast Asia			
Cambodia	34.7	52.4	14.3
Indonesia	5.6	11.2	2.0
Lao People's Democratic Republic	37.9	60.0	12.7
Myanmar	20.5	35.8	10.1
Philippines	18.1	30.0	10.6
Viet Nam	12.4	21.3	7.0

Source: UNESCO (2005).

Table 3.5 examines in greater depth the inequality in education between two large countries: India and Indonesia. Although the two are widely diverse in culture and socio-demographic structures, they show similar trends in the distribution of primary school-age children across various gender, location, and wealth categories. However, there are large differences between them in the out-of-school children groups. In India, there are more primary school-age males than females, but a smaller proportion of the males are out of school than females. This trend is reversed in Indonesia. While there is still a higher percentage of male primary school-age children, there is also a higher percentage of male children out of school (56.6%) than female (43.4%). Out-of-school children from the poorest households in both countries, however, are 9 times the proportion of out-of-school children from the richest households.

Table 3.5   Enrollment inequality among primary school-age children in India and Indonesia, 2000–2003

Category		Children of primary school age			
		Out of total (%)		Out of school (%)	
		India	Indonesia	India	Indonesia
Gender	Female	48.6	47.9	59.0	43.4
	Male	51.4	52.1	41.0	56.6
Location	Rural	76.7	55.3	87.1	70.2
	Urban	23.3	44.7	12.9	29.8
Economic status	Bottom quintile	22.7	23.6	37.3	52.2
	Top quintile	15.2	17.6	3.6	6.0

Note: Total refers to both in-school and out-of-school primary school-age children.
Source: UNESCO (2005).

While income inequality is an important determinant of non-income inequality, disparity in health and education outcomes among income levels differ significantly among countries. A country with a high relative degree of income inequality can also have lower relative inequality in health or education outcomes. For instance, in India about 5% of children in the highest wealth quintile are underweight, compared to 28% in the lowest wealth quintile. However, in Cambodia, which has a higher Gini coefficient and therefore greater income inequality than India, 5.6% of children in the highest wealth quintile are severely underweight, and a relatively low 16.7% of children are underweight in the lowest wealth quintile (Gwatkin et al. 2007, ADB 2007). The variance in school participation rates mirrors this pattern. In Viet Nam, where income inequality is similar to India, 98.1% of girls are in school in the highest income quintile, falling slightly to 90.6% among the lowest income quintile. In India, 94% of girls in the highest income quintile and 58.1% of girls in the lowest income quintile are in school.

Determinants of health inequality can include the lower likelihood that the poor will seek professional medical care, despite their greater likelihood of illness. Furthermore there is evidence that, on average, government subsidies tend to favor the rich, even though they can more readily seek private medical care (Wagstaff 2002). Health inequality is often correlated with rising income levels due to quicker assimilation of new technology by the rich compared to the poor (Wagstaff 2001). The rise in health inequality can also be tied to the rise in income inequality in the region (Kanbur et al. 2006). In general, higher health inequality often indicates declining access to health systems or growing differences in the quality of care received.

Income inequality is strongly correlated with inequality in education and health within countries. Furthermore, given that income poverty is also a determinant of non-income poverty it is important to examine this relationship in greater depth, to better assess growing inequality in non-income poverty in Asia and address it through targeted policy interventions.

3.5 Relationship between income and non-income poverty

As noted earlier, there is a strong correlation between income and non-income poverty indicators. However, as this section underscores, the relationship between income and non-income welfare attainment cannot be taken for granted. A detailed examination of the interrelationship between the two is critical to understanding the underpinnings of inclusive economic growth.

The focus of this section is on the interplay between income and non-income poverty, with a specific focus on developing Asia. As with income poverty, this section assesses the evidence on whether or not economic growth is a key driver of improvements in non-income poverty. In doing so, it emphasizes several critical aspects of the interrelationship between growth and non-income poverty from a policy perspective. First, improvements in non-income welfare are, in themselves, contributors to economic growth. Second, economic growth—unlike in the case of income poverty—is not a necessary condition for improvements in non-income poverty. Furthermore, higher levels of attainment in non-income welfare measures increase the elasticity of the relationship between economic growth and income poverty. In addition, the long-term sustainability of economic growth is dependent on the extent to which it is inclusive and translates into improvements in non-income welfare measures. Some of these issues are addressed below.

By far the biggest determinant of declining income poverty is good, old-fashioned economic growth (Dollar and Kraay 2002). Sustained economic growth and the associated rise in productive employment and capital are endogenous drivers of reductions in absolute poverty. There is no region that has exemplified this more than Asia over the past few decades. Sustained economic growth beginning in the 1960s transformed the original Asian "tigers": Hong Kong, China; Korea; Singapore; and Taipei,China. Subsequently, many other Asian economies have joined the club, including PRC, Indonesia, Malaysia, Thailand and, more recently,

India and Viet Nam. This was associated with often spectacular declines in income poverty. The Commission on Growth and Development (2008) presents a case in point, providing examples and policy options based on the experience of 13 countries that have experienced growth of 7% or greater for at least 25 consecutive years since 1950. Of the 13 high-growth economies highlighted in the Commission's report, nine are Asian: PRC; Hong Kong, China; Indonesia; Japan; Korea; Malaysia; Singapore; Taipei,China; and Thailand. Only four (Botswana, Brazil, Malta, and Oman) were from other regions.

3.5.1 Human development and economic growth

Theoretically, it is easy to see why human capital—education, health, and nutrition—can be important for economic growth. Human capital enhances functional capacity, income-generating potential, and economic productivity, among other things, and hence can be important for economic growth. Empirically—despite some prominent pockets of controversy regarding the significance of estimates—there is evidence suggesting that human capital is indeed a key determinant of economic growth.

For health, there is a clear positive relationship between population health outcomes such as life expectancy, for example, and levels of income across countries at any given point in time (Figure 3.8). While, on average, population health outcomes tend to be highly correlated with income, there is significant variation around this trend. Most developing Asian countries—except for Kazakhstan and Papua New Guinea, for instance—do better than the average given their gross national income (GNI) per capita in 2007. However, this is not the case for under-five mortality. A larger number of developing Asian countries—including Azerbaijan, India, Kazakhstan, and Pakistan—have worse than the average under-five mortality rates for their income levels (Figure 3.8).

Evidence of a positive relationship between health and income across countries, as seen in Figure 3.8, does not necessarily mean that health drives growth (or vice versa). To assess whether or not health has a causal impact on economic growth, one needs to control for the impact that higher income levels might have on health as well as for the impact of other possible confounding variables. One strategy employed in growth regressions is to look at the impact of initial levels of health on subsequent levels of economic growth, controlling for other determinants of the latter or through the use of instrumental variables (Bloom and Canning 2007; see Box 3.2). The literature has generally tended to find a positive link between health and subsequent economic growth; examples can be found in Bloom, Canning, and Sevilla (2004) and Bhargava et al. (2001).

Figure 3.8   Life expectancy and under-five mortality versus income, 2007

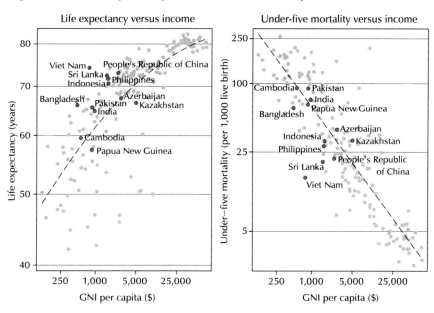

GNI = gross national income.
Note: Axes are in log scale.
Source: World Bank, World Development Indicators Online.

Box 3.2   Economic analysis of the pure growth effect on health
           outcomes

In their paper *Wealthier is Healthier*, Pritchett and Summers (1996) decompose
the idea that higher income countries tend to have better health outcomes.
They use instrumental variables estimation to analyze cross-country data from
1960 to 1990 to show that the relationship between income and health is
causal. They use instruments that are determinants of income growth but
exogenous to health and are not driven by a third variable that could be causing
the relationship. The assumption is that by incorporating these instruments
into the regression analysis, if a change in the coefficient relating income to
infant mortality is observed, gross domestic product (GDP) per capita is driven
by some other variable that also impacts mortality.

    Their analysis is indicative of a causal relationship, with income a key
determinant of health outcomes. The instruments include terms of trade shocks
(which have been shown in large part to explain growth rates); the deviation

continued.

Box 3.2 *continued.*

from the official exchange rate from its income level-adjusted purchasing power parity level (as a proxy for policies that reduce outward orientation); the ratio of investment to GDP (as it is related to economic growth); and the black market premium (which has been shown to have a negative impact on economic growth). As the final instrument, if countries are subjected to similar shocks from the external environment then the correlation between changes in one country's growth rate and the other country's growth rate is used as an indicator of the effect of the external environment on the first country's growth rate. In order to measure this effect, the authors construct an indicator that is a vector of similar growth between countries.

Using this technique, their results show that using any component of income variations related to any of a group of other variables produces estimates of the impact on health better than using income itself. The elasticity of infant mortality to GDP per capita using all instrumental variables is –0.32. Without using any of these indicators, the elasticity is smaller at –0.19, only controlling for years of schooling. These results point to a causal and structural link in the relationship going from income to infant mortality rates.

The report of the Commission on Growth and Development (2008) also underscores the inimical impact of ill health and poor nutrition in early childhood on economic growth and inequality. Poor health and nutrition in early childhood can permanently impair a child's learning potential. Furthermore, in populations suffering disproportionately from malnutrition and poor health, lower learning and physical capacity can lead to a widening gap with those children with access to better health care and nutrition at an early age. The Commission report stresses the vital importance of targeting policy interventions at early childhood health and focusing on the health of neglected populations as part of a country's overall economic growth strategy.

Looking at other non-income poverty indicators, such as those related to education, the same positive relationship with income level is evident across countries at a given point in time. However, at least visually, there appears to be a greater variation across countries in the relationship between education and income than between health and income. Figure 3.9 plots education expectancy and adult literacy versus GNI per capita, along with the predicted line showing the average relationship between the two pairs of indicators. Cambodia, PRC, Indonesia, Philippines, and Sri Lanka all have above-average adult literacy rates given their income levels. Interestingly, those countries that have above average literacy rates do not necessarily also have above-average education expectancy. Only two countries, Indonesia and Philippines, experience both. Kazakhstan and

Viet Nam also have high levels of education expectancy relative to their income. This positive correlation between income and adult literacy rates and education expectancy reveals that non-income and income poverty are linked, although additional analysis is needed to assess causality.

Figure 3.9   Literacy and education results relative to income, 2000–2007

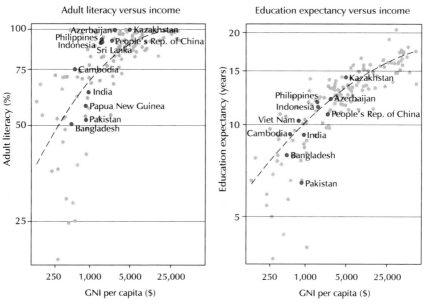

GNI = gross national income.
Note: Axes are in log scale.
Source: World Bank, World Development Indicators Online.

Regarding the impact of education on economic growth, the seminal study of Mankiw, Romer, and Weil (1992) estimate a human-capital augmented Solow model using cross-country data over the period 1960–1985. The study finds a significant, positive impact of education, even after controlling for other traditional determinants of economic growth, such as investment rates. The authors use secondary school enrollment rates as a proxy for their measure of human capital, which has been criticized as not reflective of the stock of education except where a country is in a steady state, although this is an unlikely scenario for many of the developing countries included in their sample. Benhabib and Spiegel (1994) reestimate the Mankiw-Romer-Weil model with an alternate measure of education capital and find no significant relationship between education and economic growth when education is specified as a direct input into the aggregate production function. They find that education capital has an impact on economic growth, but through its influence on technological innovation and not as a direct factor of production. Other studies have underscored the importance not just of the quantity but also the quality of education—as measured by attainment on international aptitude tests, for instance—on economic growth (Jamison, Jamison, and Hanushek 2007).

The Commission on Growth and Development report also stresses the importance of education in fostering economic growth. It notes that each of the 13 economies that experienced periods of sustained high growth invested large amounts of money in education and human capital improvements. Furthermore, the report argues that evidence shows that those developing countries not experiencing high levels of economic growth are also not investing as much in human development relative to high-growth countries. The Commission makes a case for strong public sector involvement in the provision of education due to its high potential economic return and the market failures associated with the sector. Furthermore, the report argues that return to investment in education is not uniform: greater economic returns are associated with early childhood investment.

3.5.2   Delinking human development from economic growth

While the impact of economic growth on income poverty is usually taken for granted, the same is not true for the impact on non-income poverty. In other words, it does not necessarily follow that economic growth will automatically reduce non-income poverty or that economic growth is a precondition for human development. Evidence of this comes from the fact that the income-health relationship seen in cross-section data has itself been shifting over time: the same level of income in 1960 and 2000, for instance, is associated with higher health outcomes in 2000 than in 1960. These secular shifts in health outcomes are likely a result of better public health interventions as well as of health technology improvements and diffusion (Preston 1975). Income by itself cannot account for the dramatic improvements in health in the last century, nor can it be relied upon as the only strategy for making progress on health in the future (Jamison et al. 2006). Furthermore, in decomposing the relationship between income and health, the variation in results points to country-specific intervening variables that have an impact on the translation of economic growth into improvements in health outcomes.

While in many cases those countries that are economically better off also tend to have better health outcomes, there are important outliers that do not follow this trend. Pre-reform PRC, Cuba, Kerala (India), and

Sri Lanka demonstrate that rapid economic growth is not a precondition for health improvements. For instance, during the 1960s and 1970s, the PRC's life expectancy grew rapidly while it was concurrently experiencing relatively low growth. In contrast, India's GDP per capita before 1980 was higher than the PRC's, but its life expectancy rates were far lower. After 1980, in the PRC's post-reform era when the economy was booming, life expectancy improvements slowed markedly, moving away from a trajectory similar to Korea and toward the Philippines (Figure 3.10).

Figure 3.10   Historic evolution of life expectancy in selected economies, 1960–2006

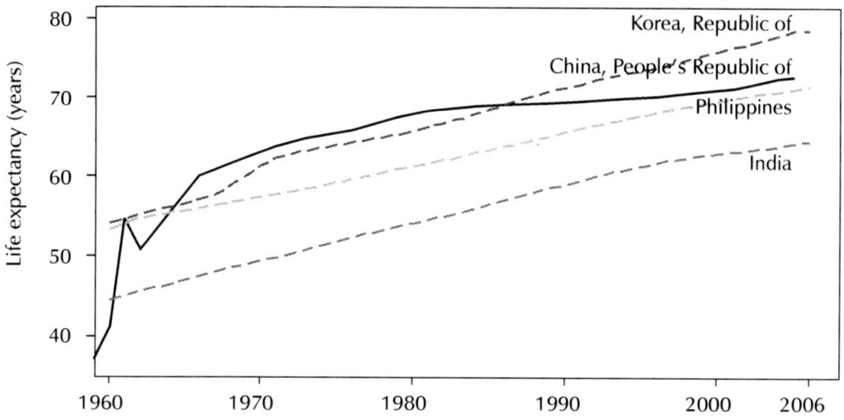

Source: World Bank, World Development Indicators Online.

Improvements in well-being indicators such as life expectancy, infant mortality, under-five mortality, maternal mortality, malnutrition, enrollment rates, and literacy rates can be rationally tied to improvements in water and sanitation, infrastructure, access to health and education facilities, societal and cultural norm adaptation, public information campaigns, industrialization, urbanization, improved technology, and targeted interventions. These determinants can go hand in hand with economic growth, but this is by no means a precondition. It is possible to focus public and private interventions on the reduction of non-income poverty even in the absence of strong economic growth. These interventions can be in the form of investment, public policies, incentives, or enabling environment improvements, to name a few. Within countries, the levels of inequality in health and education can be addressed through targeted policy interventions that adequately address their root causes.

In trying to deconstruct the determinants of non-income poverty, Lambert, Ravallion, and van de Walle (2007) examine the change in school enrollment over time by using data from Living Standards Surveys for Morocco and Viet Nam and decomposing changes in aggregate human development outcomes into four components: (i) pure "growth" effect associated with differences in mean income; (ii) redistribution effect attributed to differences in the distribution of income; (iii) "non-income" factors; and (iv) a structural component, which measures the human development returns to income and non-income characteristics. The authors find that not only does growth play an important role in the observed changes in school enrollment, but that structural factors are the dominant determinants in explaining the changes. While it is not clear exactly what is driving these results, it does suggest that government policies focusing specifically on increasing school enrollment rates have been successful.

Bangladesh and India present further examples. While India's enrollment and child mortality rates were better than those of Bangladesh in 1990 (Figure 3.11), things had reversed by 2004, leaving India worse off on both measures. Economic growth cannot explain this reversal, as India was richer than Bangladesh in 1990 (India's per capita income was $315 versus $274 for Bangladesh in constant 2000 dollars), and over the period 1990–2004, India grew much faster than Bangladesh. By 2004, India's per capita income was $538 versus $402 for Bangladesh. However, while India was growing economically, the rate of growth for social indicators was much faster in Bangladesh. Furthermore, Bangladesh's government spent less on health and education than India's, both in aggregate outlay per capita and as a percentage of GDP. Clearly, as the Bangladesh-India comparison illustrates, if a poorer country is spending less on health and education per capita and can attain better social outcomes, this ought to be a signal that something is not right in the way that the health and education systems are functioning, compared to other countries.

While the link between income and non-income variables is important to highlight, the analysis shows that a pure income poverty focus will not necessarily translate into a large-scale reduction in non-income poverty. Within Asia there is a large degree of variation in how countries have translated impressive economic growth into improvements in health and education. The evidence shows that by targeting policy on improving education and health outcomes and the equity of these indicators within countries, while reducing income poverty levels, Asian countries can benefit most from economic growth.

Figure 3.11   Education and health trends: Bangladesh and India, 1990–2004

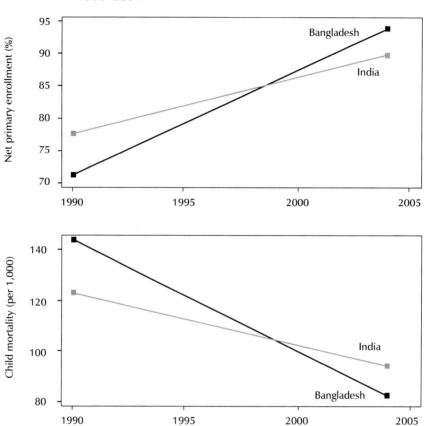

Source: World Bank, World Development Indicators Online.

3.6   Conclusions

Despite Asia's widely reported success in reducing $1-a-day poverty rates, there remains cause for concern about the state of non-income poverty. Large portions of the region are behind on health and education indicators, with some of the biggest deficiencies among poorer segments of the population. Despite recent progress, several economies, including Azerbaijan, Mongolia, Nepal, Pakistan, and Papua New Guinea, are far from reaching the MDG target of universal primary education. India and Bangladesh have significantly improved primary school enrollment rates, but concerns remain about the quality of basic education. India is off-track for the MDG on child mortality, as are Cambodia, Pakistan,

Papua New Guinea, and several Central Asian republics. India's levels of child malnourishment, for example, are almost double those of sub-Saharan Africa (Chaudhury and Devarajan 2006). Levels of child malnourishment also remain high in Indonesia, Philippines, and even in Sri Lanka. And there is evidence that health (and income) inequalities within countries are growing (Minujin and Delamonica 2003, Gwatkin et al. 2007).

The policy imperative for Asia is therefore not just sustaining economic growth but also making it more inclusive. Human capital investment in health and education is often viewed as one mechanism to mainstream marginalized populations: not simply in terms of equipping them with the skills to participate in the economy, but also by protecting them from shocks and improving their general welfare. Evidence from panel data[7] shows that education is one of the most prominent determinants of movement out of chronic poverty, although the levels of education required might vary by country (McKay and Lawson 2002). In India, for example, illiteracy is strongly associated with chronic poverty. In other countries, secondary education has been found to be a key determinant of being non-poor. Health-related shocks, on the other hand, are prominent factors pushing people into poverty. To prevent inequalities in human development from constraining future economic growth, Asia needs to invest more now to level the playing field.

References

ADB. 2006. "Measuring Policy Effectiveness in Health and Education." In *Key Indicators 2006*. Asian Development Bank, Manila.

_____. 2007. "Inequality in Asia." In *Key Indicators 2007*. Asian Development Bank, Manila.

Acemoglu, D., and S. Johnson. 2007. "Disease and Development: The Effect of Life Expectancy on Economic Growth." *Journal of Political Economy* 115(6):925–85.

Acemoglu, D., S. Johnson, and J. A. Robinson. 2001. "Colonial Origins of Comparative Development: An Empirical Investigation." *American Economic Review* 91:1369–401.

Banerjee, A., and L. Iyer. 2005. "History, Institutions, and Economic Performance: The Legacy of Colonial Land Tenure Systems in India." *American Economic Review* 95(4):1190–213.

Barro, R. J., and J-W. Lee. 2000. International Data on Educational Attainment: Updates and Implications. NBER Working Paper No. 7911, National Bureau of Economic Research, Cambridge, MA.

7　Data that are tracked over time for the same unit of observation (e.g., a given household or country).

Benavot, A., and P. Riddle. 1988. "The Expansion of Primary Education, 1870–1940: Trends and Issues." *Sociology of Education* 61(3):191–210.

Benhabib, J., and M. M. Spiegel. 1994. "The Role of Human Capital in Economic Development: Evidence from Aggregate Cross-Country Data." *Journal of Monetary Economics* 34:143–73.

Bhargava, A., D. Jamison, L. Lau, and C. J. L. Murray. 2001. "Modeling the Effects of Health on Economic Growth." *Journal of Health Economics* 20:423–40.

Bloom, D. E., and D. Canning. 2007. Population Health and Economic Growth. Working Paper, Harvard School of Public Health, Boston.

Bloom, D. E., D. Canning, and J. Sevilla. 2004. "The Effect of Health on Economic Growth: A Production Function Approach." *World Development* 32:1–13.

Brody, J. A., M. D. Grant, L. J. Frateschi, S. C. Miller, and H. Zhang. 2000. "Reproductive Longevity and Increased Life Expectancy." *Age and Aging* 29:75–8.

Central Bureau of Statistics. 2005. Survei Sosial Ekonomi Nasional (SUSENAS, National Socioeconomic Survey). Indonesia.

Chaudhury, N., and S. Devarajan. 2006. "Human Development and Service Delivery in Asia." *Development Policy Review* 24(s1):s81–97.

Commission on Growth and Development. 2008. *Growth Report: Strategies for Sustained Growth and Inclusive Development*. World Bank, Washington, DC.

Deolalikar, A. B. 2005. *Attaining the Millennium Development Goals in India*. New Delhi: Oxford University Press.

Dollar, D., and A. Kraay. 2002. "Growth is Good for the Poor." *Journal of Economic Growth* 7:195–225.

Economist, The. 2007. "High Gini is Loosed Upon Asia." 7 August. Available: www.economist.com/displaystory.cfm?story_id=9616888.

Gallego, F. 2005. Historical Origins of School: The Role of Political Decentralization. Massachusetts Institute of Technology, Cambridge, MA. Available: econ-www.mit.edu/graduate/candidates/download_res.php?id=214. Processed.

Gwatkin, D. R., S. Rutstein, K. Johnson, E. A. Suliman, A. Wagstaff, and A. Amouzou. 2007. Socioeconomic Differences in Health, Nutrition and Population within Countries: An Overview. World Bank, Washington, DC.

Jamison, D. T., J. G. Breman, A. R. Measham, G. Alleyne, M. Claeson, D. B. Evans, P. Jha, A. Mills, and P. Musgrove, eds. 2006. *Disease Control Priorities in Developing Countries*. 2nd Ed. World Bank, Washington, DC.

Jamison, E. A., D. T. Jamison, and E. A. Hanushek. 2007. "The Effects of Education Quality on Economic Growth and Mortality Decline." *Economics of Education Review* 26:772–89.

Kanbur, R., A. J. Venables, and G. Wan, eds. 2006. *Spatial Disparities in Human Development: Perspectives from Asia*. New York: United Nations University Press.

Lambert, S., M. Ravallion, and D. Van De Walle. 2007. A Micro-Decomposition Analysis of the Macroeconomic Determinants of Human Development. Policy Research Working Paper No. 4358, World Bank, Washington, DC.

Lindert, P. 2003. "Voice and Growth: Was Churchill Right?" *The Journal of Economic History* 63(2):315–50.

Mankiw, N. G., D. Romer, and D. N. Weil. 1992. "A Contribution to the Empirics of Economic Growth." *Quarterly Journal of Economics* 107(2):407–37.

McKay, A., and D. Lawson. 2002. Chronic Poverty: A Review of Current Quantitative Evidence. CPRC Working Paper No. 15, IDPM, University of Manchester, Manchester.

Minujin, A., and E. Delamonica. 2003. "Mind the Gap! Widening Child Mortality Disparities." *Journal of Human Development* 4(3):397–418.

Preston, S. 1975. "The Changing Relationship between Mortality and Level of Economic Development." *Population Studies* 29(2):231–48.

Pritchett, L., and L. Summers. 1996. "Wealthier is Healthier." *Journal of Human Resources* 31(4):841–68.

Rajan, R. G., and L. Zingales. 2006. The Persistence of Underdevelopment: Institutions, Human Capital, or Constituencies? NBER Working Paper No. 12093, National Bureau of Economic Research, Cambridge, MA.

Ravallion, M. 1996. Issues in Measuring and Modeling Poverty. Policy Research Working Paper No. 1615, World Bank, Washington, DC.

Riley, J. C. 2005. "Estimates of Regional and Global Life Expectancy, 1800–2001." *Population and Development Review* 31(3):537–43.

Sen, A. 1998. "Mortality as an Indicator of Economic Success and Failure." *Economic Journal* 108:1–25.

UNDP. 2007. *Human Development Report*. New York: Oxford University Press.

UNESCO. 2005. *Children Out of School: Measuring Exclusion from Primary Education*. UNESCO Institute of Statistics, Montreal.

United Nations. 2000. "United Nations Millennium Declaration." 55th Session General Assembly, 8 September, New York.

Wagstaff, A. 2001. Inequalities in Health in Developing Countries: Swimming Against the Tide? Policy Research Working Paper No. 2795, World Bank, Washington, DC.

_____. 2002. "Poverty and Health Sector Inequalities." *Bulletin of the World Health Organization* 80(2):97–105.

World Bank. 2006. *World Development Indicators 2006*. Washington, DC.

_____. Various years. World Development Indicators Online. Available: http://devdata. worldbank.org/dataonline/.

4

Gender Equality
and Inclusive Growth in Asia

Yoko Niimi [1]

4.1   Introduction

The importance of pursuing gender equality has long been recognized around the world, including Asia and the Pacific. Virtually all countries in the region are parties to the Convention on the Elimination of All Forms of Discrimination against Women, and gender equality is explicitly guaranteed in many constitutions and statutes (ADB et al. 2006). Indeed the region has made impressive progress in reducing gender inequality over the last few decades. Nevertheless, women remain disadvantaged in access to economic opportunity and resources, basic human rights, and political voice (World Bank 2007). Because gender discrimination directly affects the well-being of women, gender equality is a legitimate policy goal in its own right. At the same time, development organizations increasingly acknowledge the role of gender equality and women's empowerment as a powerful means to foster development and poverty reduction (e.g., ADB 2007 and 2008, World Bank 2008).

Inequality can result from differences in either *effort*, which is under the control of an individual, or *circumstance*—such as gender, religious background, geographical location, and parental education—which is not (Roemer 2006). Gender inequality is a prominent example of the latter. As described elsewhere in this book, inclusive growth is growth that not only generates economic opportunity, but also ensures equal access to opportunity to all segments of society (Ali and Zhuang 2007). Hence, inclusive growth can only be achieved if, among other things, gender disparity is properly addressed.

Inequality due to differences in circumstance often reflect social exclusion, and should be tackled through public policy intervention (Ali 2007). However, gender inequality is the archetypical "inequality trap" (World Bank 2006), caused and reinforced by interlinked cultural,

---

[1]   The author would like to thank A. R. Morrison, S. Sabarwal, and M. Sjöblom from the World Bank for sharing valuable data for the indicators of monitoring progress toward gender equality.

social, and economic factors within and outside the household. There is certainly no single panacea to eliminate gender inequality. To assist policy makers in designing effective policy to reduce gender disparity, this chapter contributes to the understanding of gender inequality in Asia and the Pacific by reviewing its current status and surveying existing empirical studies.

The next section provides a conceptual framework for understanding gender equality and why gender inequality needs to be addressed to achieve economic growth and poverty reduction. It also introduces a set of indicators through which gender inequality can be measured. Through these, section 4.3 asssesses recent progress and highlights significant gender gaps. Section 4.4 reviews the existing literature of empirical studies on the key dimensions of gender inequality. Section 4.5 summarizes the key findings and possible measures to improve gender equality.

4.2   Gender equality and inclusive growth: Concepts and measurement

4.2.1   Conceptual framework

The United Nations Millennium Project Task Force on Education and Gender Equality (UN Millennium Project 2005) conceptualizes gender equality under three dimensions. These are: (i) capabilities domain, (ii) access to resources and opportunities domain, and (iii) security domain (see Figure 4.1). The capabilities domain refers to basic human abilities as measured by education, health, and nutrition, which are all fundamental to individual well-being and are an important means to gaining access to opportunity. The access to resources and opportunities domain refers primarily to equality of opportunity to use or apply basic capabilities through access to economic assets (e.g., land, housing, and infrastructure); resources (e.g., income and employment); and political decision making (e.g., representation in parliament and other political bodies). Finally, the security domain refers to vulnerability to violence and conflict, which can reduce the ability of individuals, households, and communities to fulfill their potential (UN Millennium Project 2005).

These three domains are interrelated. For instance, improvement in capabilities will increase the likelihood that women will gain access to economic and/or political opportunity. Similarly, access to opportunity decreases the likelihood that women will experience violence (UN Millennium Project 2005). It is therefore important to ensure improvement in all three to achieve overall gender equality. Note also that gender equality is not equality of outcomes between men and women, but equality in the determinants of these outcomes (World Bank 2001).

Figure 4.1   Gender equality in three domains

Source: Based on the operational framework developed by the UN Millennium Project Task Force on Education and Gender Equality (UN Millennium Project 2005).

When assessing the important role of gender equality in promoting inclusive growth, its intrinsic value and instrumental value may be distinguished (Klasen 2002). Intrinsic value is based on the belief that equal access to opportunity is a basic human right, and it is unethical and immoral to treat individuals differently in this regard (Ali and Zhuang 2007). Gender equality should thus be considered a development goal in its own right, as evidenced by the Convention on the Elimination of All Forms of Discrimination against Women and by the existence of the Third Millennium Development Goal (MDG3) on gender equality and women's empowerment. Instrumental value comes from the recognition that inequality in access to opportunity diminishes growth potential and its sustainability. Gender inequality can also undermine other development goals which, in turn, affects growth.

A number of empirical studies have examined the impact of gender inequality, particularly in education, on economic growth.[2] The available empirical evidence often suggests a negative relationship between the two, that is, higher gender inequality leads to lower growth (e.g., Klasen 2002, UNESCAP 2007). An important question to ask is what is the underlying mechanism. One of the consequences of gender inequality in access to economic opportunity is the inefficient allocation and/or underutilization of resources. If a woman with appropriate capabilities is excluded from the labor market because of her gender, she cannot maximize her production potential, which can lower societal output and impose costs on economic development. Restrictions on women's access

2   See Klasen (2002) and Morrison et al. (2007) for a review of the existing literature on the effect of gender inequality on economic growth.

to opportunity can also indirectly affect the household power relationship between men and women, potentially resulting in the misallocation of resources. Gender inequality in capabilities also lowers average human capital and productivity, which can subsequently hinder economic growth. Moreover, gender-based violence can have a lasting psychological impact on its victims, lowering women's self-esteem and productivity and destroying marriages, with all the costs that children will eventually have to bear (UNESCAP 2007).

Another important link between gender inequality and economic growth is through its effect on child well-being (Morrison et al. 2007). A mother's health or well-being affects her pregnancy and ability to nurse (e.g., Galloway and Anderson 1994, Thomas and Strauss 1992). Mothers with better educational attainment are also found to be associated with better child development outcomes through, for example, better use of available health care services and programs (e.g., Cebu Study Team 1991). Women with greater control over household resources are also likely to allocate more for children's health and education (e.g., Hoddinott and Haddad 1995, Quisumbing and Maluccio 2003). Through these effects, improvements in gender equality can improve the capabilities and productivity of future generations, and, ultimately, a country's long-term prospects for economic growth and poverty reduction.

4.2.2 Gender inequality indicators

There are many ways to measure gender inequality. Morisson et al. (2008) distinguish between two broad approaches: (i) using composite or aggregate indexes, and (ii) using discrete or individual indicators. The most well-known composite indexes of gender inequality are the gender empowerment measure (GEM) and the gender-related development index (GDI) introduced by the United Nations Development Programme (UNDP). The GEM is principally a measure of female empowerment in three dimensions—political participation, economic participation, and power over economic resources. The GDI is an adjusted Human Development Index according to the degree of aversion to gender inequality and gaps in three dimensions—a long and healthy life, knowledge, and a decent standard of living (UNDP 2007).[3] Such indexes provide a useful summary

---

[3] The GEM is constructed based on four individual indicators: (i) male and female shares of parliamentary seats (for the political participation dimension); (ii) male and female shares of positions as legislators, senior officials, and managers; (iii) male and female shares of professional and technical positions (both [ii] and [iii] are for the economic participation dimension); and (iv) male and female estimated earned income (for the power over economic resources dimension). On the other hand, the GDI adjusts the Human Development Index to reflect the inequalities between men and women using the following four indicators: (i) male

statistic or measure of gender inequality that captures media and policy attention. However, in addition to the problems related to the choice of weights and methods of aggregation, the interpretation of indexes is often not straightforward and they may not provide sufficient information for policy makers to make judgments about policies, programs, and resource allocations (Grown 2008).

The individual indicators most frequently used to assess gender inequality are those defined in the Millennium Declaration to monitor MDG3 on promoting gender equality and empowering women. These include (i) the ratio of girls' to boys' enrollment in primary, secondary, and tertiary education; (ii) the ratio of literate females to males in the 15–25 age group; (iii) the share of women in wage employment in the non-agricultural sector; and (iv) the percentage of seats held by women in national parliaments.

While these individual indicators are useful for monitoring progress toward gender equality, they only give a partial picture (e.g., UN Millennium Project 2005, World Bank 2007). To provide a more complete and nuanced description of gender equality, the World Bank (2007) proposed five additional indicators, chosen on the basis of three criteria: data availability (i.e., wide country coverage), a strong link to poverty reduction and growth, and amenability to policy interventions.[4] These additional indicators include: (i) primary school completion rate of girls and boys; (ii) under-five mortality rate for girls and boys; (iii) percentage of reproductive-age women and their sexual partners using modern contraception; (iv) percentage of 15 to 19 year-old girls who are mothers or pregnant with their first child; and (v) labor force participation rate among women aged 20–24 and 25–49 (World Bank 2007).[5] Morisson et al. (2008) call this set of indicators—including one additional indicator of their own recommendation that measures the ratio of female to male hourly earnings in primary, secondary, and tertiary sectors—an "MDG3 plus approach"; it is summarized in Table 4.1. These indicators cover two of the three domains of gender equality—the capabilities domain and the access to resources and opportunities domain—at different levels of aggregation (household, economy and markets, and society).

---

and female life expectancy at birth (for the long and healthy life dimension); (ii) male and female adult literacy rate; (iii) male and female combined primary, secondary, and tertiary gross enrollment ratio (both [ii] and [iii] are for the knowledge dimension); and (iv) male and female estimated earned income (for the decent standard of living dimension). See *Technical Note 1* of UNDP (2007) for further details.

4   The UN Millennium Project Task Force also suggested a number of indicators to overcome the shortcomings of the official MDG3 indicators (UN Millennium Project 2005). However, data are not widely available for many of their recommended indicators (Morrison et al. 2008).

5   See World Bank (2007) for a detailed discussion on the selection of these additional indicators.

Table 4.1   Indicators of gender equality under the MDG3 plus approach

Domain	Indicators	Level of aggregation
Capabilities		
Education	Ratio of girls' to boys' enrollment in primary, secondary, and tertiary education	Household
	Ratio of literate females to males among 15–24 years old	
	Primary completion rate of girls and boys	
Health	Under-five mortality rate for girls and boys	
	Percentage of reproductive-age women and their sexual partners using modern contraception	
	Percentage of girls aged 15–19 who are mothers or pregnant with their first child	
Access to resources and opportunities		
Employment	Share of women in non-agricultural wage employment	Economy and market
	Labor force participation rates among women aged 20–24 and 25–49	
	Ratio of female to male hourly earnings in primary, secondary, and tertiary sectors	
Political participation	Percentage of seats held by women in national parliaments	Society

MDG3 = Third Millennium Development Goal.
Source: Morrison et al. (2008).

The MDG3 plus approach is certainly not without limitations. It does not, for instance, cover security-related gender equality, a critical aspect of gender equality. Available evidence suggests that women in many parts of the world are often subject to violence by their male partners (Heise et al. 1999). However, due to the unavailability of comparable cross-country data for violence-related indicators, it is not included in this set of indicators (World Bank 2007). In addition, the MDG3 plus approach does not cover other important aspects of gender equality, including access to productive assets (e.g., land and credit) and infrastructure. Such indicators would be particularly useful for identifying constraints to women's economic empowerment. Furthermore, the proposed indicator for measuring gender inequality in accessing political opportunity cannot assess women's actual influence in the political decision-making process or their political representation at local or regional levels (Grown et al. 2005).

Despite these limitations, this set of indicators allows the monitoring of a wider scope of gender equality than the MDG3 official indicators. This chapter uses the MDG3 plus approach to review recent progress.

4.3 Progress toward gender equality in Asia and the Pacific

To the author's best knowledge, Morisson et al. (2008) provide the most recent review of the progress toward gender equality in the world, among recent studies.[6] While Morisson et al. report the progress largely at the regional level, the main contribution of this chapter is to provide evidence on gender equality at the individual country level, with particular attention to developing countries in the region using the MDG3 plus approach. The indicators are provided for all developing countries in Asia and the Pacific, whenever data are available.[7] The corresponding average figures for the world and other regions are also reported for comparison purposes.

4.3.1 Capabilities: Education

Achieving gender equality in capabilities such as education and health is a viable avenue for improving women's access to opportunity and children's well-being, and eventually to economic growth. Figures 4.2 and 4.3 illustrate the progress toward gender equality in primary and secondary enrollment rates between 1991 and 2006. Figure 4.4 shows the ratio of girls' to boys' enrollment rates in tertiary education for 2006.[8] Most countries achieved or almost achieved gender parity in primary education by the latter period (see Figure 4.2). The significant progress in countries that started with a relatively high level of gender inequality in 1991—namely India and Nepal and, to a lesser extent, Cambodia, Lao People's Democratic Republic (Lao PDR), and Solomon Islands—is encouraging. In contrast, further effort is needed in Afghanistan and Papua New Guinea, where there was little or no progress toward gender parity during this period. With the exception of these two, all economies in the region fare better than sub-Saharan Africa, which has achieved the least gender parity among the world's regions.

As for secondary education, while the level of gender equality is less uniform than that for primary education, great progress was also made in many countries in the region (see Figure 4.3). Gender parity has been achieved in East Asia, Central Asia, and most countries in Southeast Asia. But, gender gaps remain large in South Asian countries, except Sri Lanka, and a number of countries in Southeast Asia and the Pacific. While some

---

6   For example, ADB et al. 2006, Morisson et al. 2008, UNESCAP 2007, World Bank 2007.
7   Note that a slightly different indicator was used for measuring adolescent fertility, use of contraception, and gender wage gaps to maintain wide country coverage.
8   Due to the limited data availability on tertiary enrollment rates for the earlier period, the ratio of girls' to boys' enrollment rates in tertiary education is reported only for 2006 or the latest year for which data are available.

of these countries score better than sub-Saharan Africa, they all lag Latin America and the Caribbean as well as the Middle East and North Africa. It is rather worrying to observe a reduction in the ratio of girls' to boys' secondary school enrollment rates in Afghanistan. The underlying data suggest that a relatively large increase in boys' enrollment rates has driven the widening gap. Measures should be undertaken to ensure that girls are not left behind in the improvement of the country's education system.

In tertiary education, it is interesting that in some countries that have already achieved gender parity, girls' enrollment rates exceed boys', notably Maldives and Palau, where girls' rates are more than twice as high (Figure 4.4). Many of these countries also perform better than Latin America and the Caribbean, whose average ratio is higher than the world average. In contrast, the rest of South Asia appears to be far behind other regions (some are even behind sub-Saharan Africa) in achieving gender equality in tertiary education enrollment.

Figure 4.2   Ratio of girls' to boys' gross enrollment in primary education, 1991 and 2006

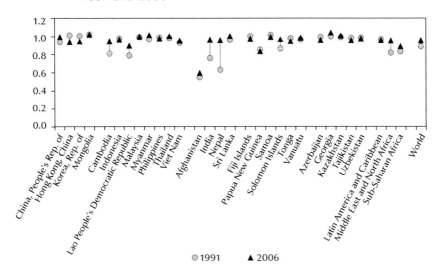

Note: The figure is based on 1991 data and the latest available data between 2000 and 2006 for each country and region.
Source: World Bank, World Development Indicators Online, downloaded 16 October 2008.

Measuring gender equality in education tends to emphasize differences in school enrollment rates, providing only a crude picture of the gender gap in education. Outcome variables, including completion rates or measures of skills, are arguably more relevant for economic development (Morisson et al. 2008). Figure 4.5 provides the ratio of girls' to boys' primary enrollment and completion rates. Although completion rates seem to reflect enrollment rates relatively well, there is a wider gender gap in completion rates than in enrollment rates for a number of countries, most notably Afghanistan. The underlying causes for the higher dropout rates for girls in these countries need to be identified and addressed to ensure that girls are able to complete their primary education.

Figure 4.3   Ratio of girls' to boys' gross enrollment in secondary education, 1991 and 2006

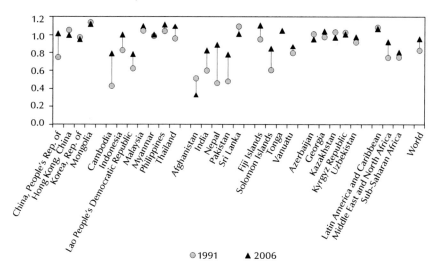

Note: The figure is based on 1991 data and the latest available data between 2000 and 2006 for each country and region.
Source: World Bank, World Development Indicators Online, downloaded 16 October 2008.

Another way of measuring gender gaps in educational outcomes is to compare literacy rates between men and women. The most recent available data on the ratio of literate women to men aged 15–24 are presented in Figure 4.6. The figure clearly shows that South Asian countries, except Maldives and Sri Lanka, lag other parts of the world in eliminating gender gaps in literacy rates. The recent progress in school enrollment in this region will hopefully contribute to narrowing the gap in the near future.

123

Figure 4.4   Ratio of girls' to boys' gross enrollment in tertiary education, 2006

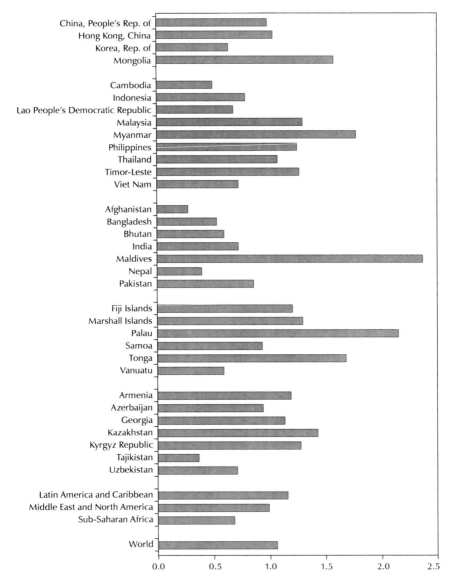

Note: The figure is based on the latest available data between 2000 and 2006 for each country and region.

Source: World Bank, World Development Indicators Online, downloaded 16 October 2008.

124

Figure 4.5   Ratio of girls' to boys' primary enrollment and completion rates, 2006

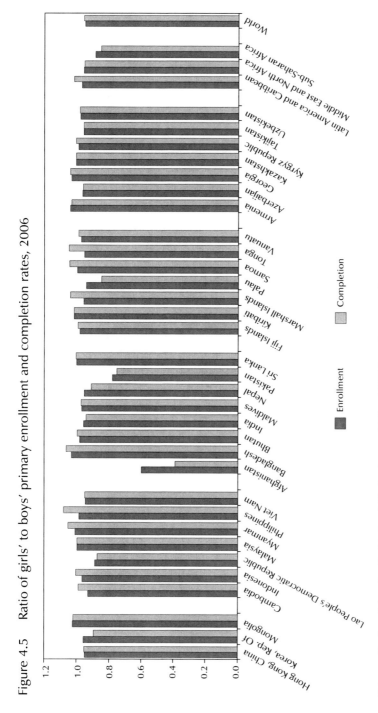

Note: The figure is based on the latest available data between 2000 and 2006 for each country and region.
Source: World Bank, World Development Indicators Online, downloaded 16 October 2008.

Figure 4.6   Ratio of literate females to males aged 15–24, 2006

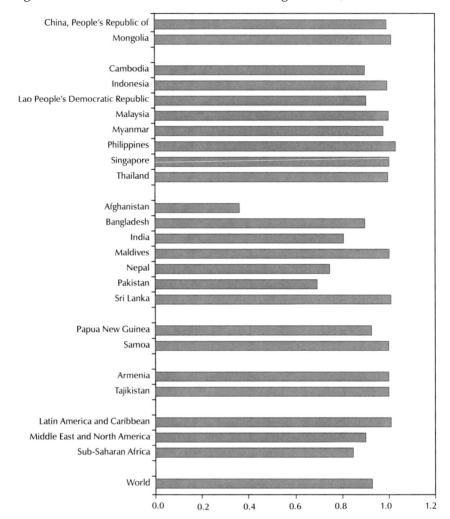

Note: The figure is based on the latest available data between 2000 and 2006 for each country and region.
Source: World Bank, World Development Indicators Online, downloaded 16 October 2008.

4.3.2   Capabilities: Health

Health—an important element of human capability—enables women to access opportunity and to take better care of their children. Indeed, good health is a basic human right. Yet the official MDG3 indicators do not contain any measurement of women's and girls' health conditions. This section applies the MDG3 plus approach and looks at three indicators that measure gender equality in health.

Figure 4.7 plots under-five mortality rates for girls and boys for each country. These rates reflect gender equality in nutrition and health care during early childhood (Morrison et al. 2008). Significantly high mortality rates for both boys and girls in Afghanistan is alarming. A number of countries in Asia and the Pacific also record relatively high under-five mortality rates compared to the world average, though lower than the average rate for sub-Saharan Africa.

While boys' under-five mortality rates are higher than girls' in most countries in the region and in other parts of the world, girls' rates exceed those of boys' in the People's Republic of China (PRC), most of South Asia, and some Pacific islands. It has been argued that the "son preference" in these countries may be a causal factor, making the opportunity to life itself dependent on a predetermined characteristic— gender (World Bank 2006).

Son preference has resulted in what Sen (1992) calls "missing women". The observed greater number of male than female infants in these countries is not only due to the differential care after birth, but also partly due to sex-selective abortion (World Bank 2006), though this cannot be captured by mortality rates.

The second health indicator considered in this chapter is adolescent fertility rates. Morisson et al. (2008) point out three reasons why this indicator is of special interest: (i) adolescent pregnancy tends to have a higher probability of being unplanned and untimely, and hence carries a higher risk of mortality for both mother and child; (ii) early motherhood often results in early departure from school and lower human capital accumulation, which is ultimately likely to undermine women's empowerment; and (iii) adolescent motherhood is associated with poorer development outcomes for children, perpetuating the vicious circle of poverty.

Figure 4.8 reports adolescent fertility rates expressed as the number of births per 1,000 women aged 15–19. It shows that the fertility rate among young girls in Bangladesh and Nepal, and to a lesser extent, Lao PDR and India, is relatively high. The rate for Bangladesh is even higher than the average rate for sub-Saharan Africa. Unlike the other indicators examined so far, adolescent fertility in Latin America and the Caribbean is relatively high; indeed higher than in most Asian and Pacific countries.

Figure 4.7   Under-five mortality rate for girls and boys (deaths per 1,000 births), 2000–2005

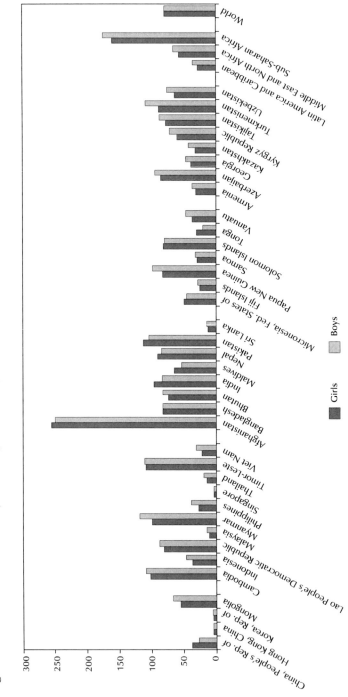

Source: United Nations, World Population Prospects Database, downloaded 16 October 2008.

Figure 4.8   Adolescent fertility rate
              (births per 1,000 women aged 15–19), 2006

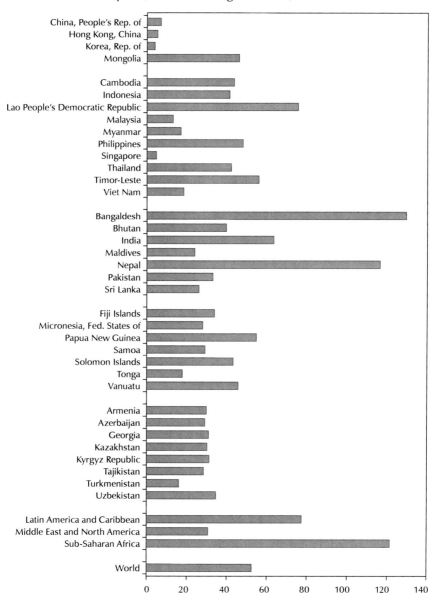

Source: World Bank, World Development Indicators Online, downloaded 16 October 2008.

The third health-related indicator is the prevalence rate of contraceptive use, which is measured as the percentage of married women aged 15—49 who use contraception. The use of contraception increases women's control over fertility decisions (e.g., on the spacing of pregnancies or how many children to bear). It therefore likely enables women to control economic activities. According to Figure 4.9, a relatively large number of countries have made significant progress in increasing the use of contraception since the early 1990s. Nevertheless, the prevalence rate remains below the world average—about 60%—in most countries in Asia and the Pacific, though higher than in sub-Saharan Africa. To guarantee women's reproductive rights, continuous effort is needed to promote the use of contraception in the region.

Figure 4.9   Contraceptive prevalence rate
(% of married women aged 15–49), 1990 and 2006

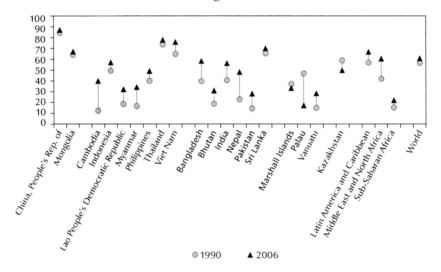

Note: The figure is based on the earliest available data between 1990 and 1995 and the latest available data between 2000 and 2006 for each country and region.
Source: World Bank, World Development Indicators Online, downloaded 16 October 2008.

Before moving on to the discussion on gender inequality in the access to opportunities domain, it is worth noting maternal mortality ratios, even though they are not part of MDG3 or the MDG3 plus approach (they are under MDG5). Maternal mortality is often related to women's access to health services. Figure 4.10 illustrates a disturbing picture of relatively high mortality rates for many countries in Asia and the Pacific, particularly in South Asia. While maternal mortality in the region (except Afghanistan) is below the average rate for sub-Saharan Africa, many countries in Southeast Asia, South Asia, and the Pacific record higher rates than Latin America and the Caribbean as well as Middle East and North Africa. This clearly calls for improvement in women's access to pre- and post-natal care and assisted birth deliveries in countries that lag in reducing maternal mortality.

Figure 4.10   Maternal mortality ratio
(deaths per 100,000 live births), 2005

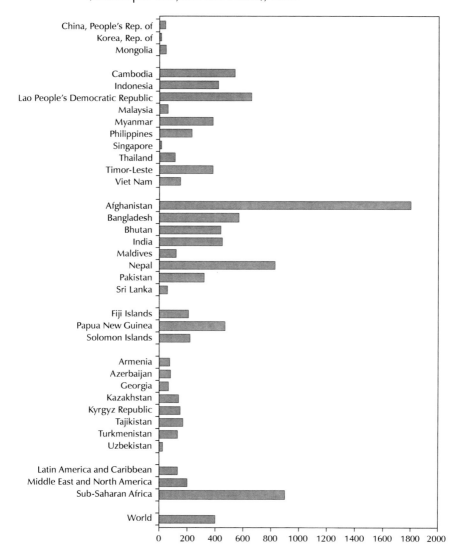

Source: World Bank, World Development Indicators Online, downloaded 16 October 2008.

131

4.3.3   Access to resources and opportunity: Employment

Even if countries advance toward gender parity in basic human capabilities, the instrumental effects of gender equality on economic development would be limited unless women have as much access as men to economic and political opportunities. As the next section illustrates, economic empowerment, in particular, is crucial to reducing gender disparity within and outside the household.

Figure 4.11 shows changes in the percentage of women in non-agricultural wage employment from 1990 to 2006. There seems to be a general upward trend in the share of women in wage employment in the non-agricultural sector. However, women's shares remain low, particularly in South Asia (except Maldives and Sri Lanka), which are well below the world average, even below sub-Saharan Africa. Note that women in the Middle East and North Africa also have very limited engagement in non-agricultural wage employment. This seems to reflect the limited mobility of women, constrained, at least partly, by cultural and social factors as well as limited access to education and health.

One of the main criticisms concerning this official MDG3 indicator is that it does not describe the complete status of women's access to economic opportunity. In many developing countries, the majority of the poor, including women, are employed in the agricultural sector. As a result, the share of women in non-agricultural wage employment is inadequate to measure gender equality in accessing economic opportunity. Additional indicators incorporated in the MDG3 plus approach are thus intended to overcome some of these shortcomings.

Figure 4.12 presents labor force participation rates among women aged 20–24 and 25–49, based on data from various household and labor force surveys, with efforts to broaden and standardize the definitions of female economic activities (Morisson et al. 2008). A number of observations can be made. First, with few exceptions, there was a lack of progress in women's labor force participation between 1991 and 2007. In some countries, including Armenia, Indonesia, Nepal, and Pakistan, female labor force participation actually declined—substantially for the latter two countries—for both age groups. Second, women's participation in the labor market seemed particularly low in South Asia, as in the case of the non-agricultural sector. In contrast, taking into account women's labor force participation in both the agricultural and non-agricultural sectors, the participation rates for sub-Saharan Africa are found to be higher than the world average. This indicates a relatively high representation of women in the agricultural sector in sub-Saharan Africa.

Figure 4.11   Share of women in non-agricultural wage employment (%),
1990 and 2006

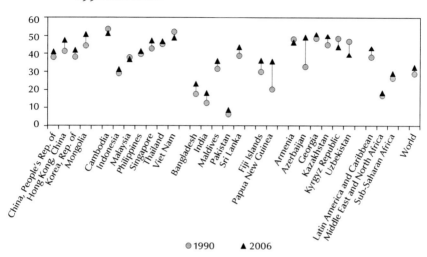

Note: The figure is based on the earliest available data between 1990 and 1995 and the latest available
           data between 2000 and 2006.
Source: Morisson et al. (2008).

Even when women enter the labor market, this does not necessarily mean that the returns to their work, women's opportunity to gain skills, or their working conditions are equal to those of men's. Indeed women, particularly in developing countries, are more likely to be engaged in the informal sector, which offers low wages, no formal social protection, and limited opportunity to gain skills (UNESCAP 2007). Unfortunately, gender-disaggregated wage data are scarce, and to keep relatively wide country coverage, Figure 4.13 presents the wage-related indicator in terms of the ratio of female to male wages for similar work—based on data from the World Economic Forum's Executive Opinion Survey (World Economic Forum 2007). While this ratio only captures a limited group of workers in the formal sector, the figure still illustrates that there is a wide gender wage gap in all regions, particularly in South Asia.

In sum, contrary to significant progress in reducing gender gaps in education enrollment, the overall improvement in women's access to economic opportunity has turned out to be very limited. As the literature review in the following section shows, incompatibility with their childbearing role as well as the traditional division of labor between men and women, reinforced by cultural norms and people's attitudes, seem to be the main obstacles preventing women from participating in the labor market.

Figure 4.12   Labor force participation rates among women aged 20–24
and 25–49 (%), 1991 and 2007

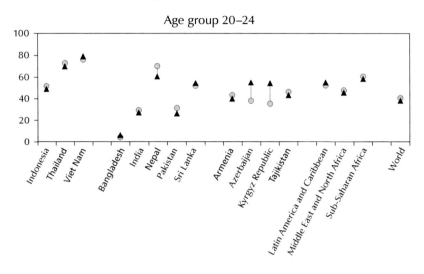

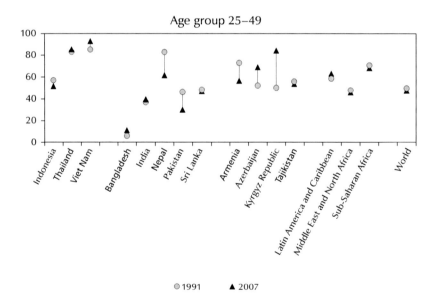

◎ 1991   ▲ 2007

Note: The figure is based on the earliest available data between 1991 and 1998 and the latest available
data between 2000 and 2007.
Source: Morisson et al. (2008).

Figure 4.13   Ratio of female to male wage for similar work, 2007

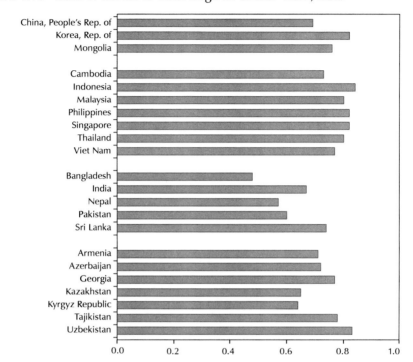

Source: World Economic Forum (2007).

4.3.4   Access to resources and opportunity: Political participation

Women's participation in public decision making is an important indicator of their empowerment. This is often measured in terms of the percentage of seats held by women in national parliaments, as presented in Figure 4.14. In spite of the still low share of women, it is encouraging to observe significant progress between 1990 and 2007 in a great number of countries. In contrast, many countries in the Pacific still have no or very few women in parliament. Other exceptions include Armenia, Mongolia, and Turkmenistan, where women's share of seats fell significantly during this period. Former centrally planned economies in Central Asia used to reserve a certain share of parliamentary seats for women and, as a result, women in these countries had fared much better than women in other parts of the world. With the removal of this reserve, the share of women in parliaments has fallen sharply in some of these countries (UNESCAP 2007).

Figure 4.14   Share of seats held by women in national parliaments (%), 1990 and 2007

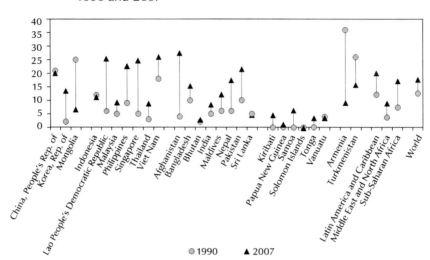

Note: The figure is based on the 1990 data and the latest available data between 2006 and 2007 for each country and region.
Source: World Bank, World Development Indicators Online, downloaded 16 October 2008.

By comparison, representation of women in national parliaments in Southeast Asia and South Asia is relatively high, though most countries in Asia and the Pacific are below the world average. Note that this indicator provides only a partial level of women's political participation as it does not measure women's actual influence in the political decision-making process or their political representation at local or regional levels (Grown et al. 2005). Furthermore, improvements in women's representation in parliaments do not automatically guarantee empowerment or an elimination of gender inequality. Bangladesh, India, and Pakistan had female heads of state in the past, but these countries lag in narrowing gender gaps in many dimensions (UNESCAP 2007).

This section's review of the progress toward gender equality in the capabilities and access to opportunities domains reveals significant progress in achieving gender parity in education, particularly primary education, in Asia and the Pacific as in the rest of the world. But gender gaps in secondary education remain large in a number of countries in Southeast Asia, South Asia, and the Pacific. Some of these countries even report wider gaps than in sub-Saharan Africa, which has made relatively little progress in reducing gender disparity in secondary enrollment rates. In tertiary education, while girls' enrollment rates exceed boys' in some countries that have already achieved gender parity, there remains a significant gender gap, particularly in South Asia.

In health, progress in reducing gender inequality is less impressive. Under-five mortality rates for girls still exceed those for boys in the PRC, most of South Asia, and some Pacific islands, while boys' rates tend to be higher than girls' in the rest of the world. Adolescent fertility rates also remain high for a number of countries, including Bangladesh, India, Lao PDR, and Nepal. Yet most in the region have lower fertility rates than Latin America and the Caribbean or sub-Saharan Africa. In all countries in the region, with the exception of Afghanistan, maternal mortality is below the average figure for sub-Saharan Africa, but a large number in Southeast Asia, South Asia, and the Pacific record higher rates than other regions in the world.

A more alarming issue is that very little progress has been made in achieving gender equality in access to economic opportunity. Women's labor force participation remains limited, particularly in South Asia, where some countries even observed a decline over the years. In addition to continuing efforts at reducing gender inequality in the capabilities domain, measures need to be undertaken to remove the constraints on enhancing women's economic activities.

4.4 Review of empirical studies on gender inequality

Despite progress toward gender equality over the years, gender gaps remain in many parts of women's lives, as illustrated in the previous section. To formulate effective policy to reduce the gaps, it is important to understand the fundamental causes of gender inequality. The main purpose of this section is, therefore, to uncover some of the underlying causal factors by reviewing relevant empirical studies. The section will focus its discussion on the following two areas: (i) intrahousehold resource allocation, and (ii) the labor market. While the former will provide important insights into why girls continue to fare worse than boys in the attainment of basic capabilities, such as education and health, the latter will improve the understanding of the primary factors that constrain women's access to employment.

4.4.1 Gender bias in intrahousehold resource allocation

Intrahousehold resource allocation has been an area of focus in explaining the observed inequality in the attainment of basic capabilities between boys and girls. It has received increasing attention from policy makers and academics since the early 1990s. This is mainly due to the growing recognition of its importance for the design, implementation, and outcomes of development policies, given that many decisions that affect individuals' well-being are undertaken within the household (Quisumbing 2003b). It had been traditionally assumed that individual household members pooled their resources and shared the same preferences for the allocation—the so-called unitary model (Becker 1965 and 1981). Under this model, the household was thus characterized as one and the equal distribution of household resources was assumed.

However, a growing body of literature challenges the key assumptions underlying the unitary model.[9] Alternative models, such as collective models, assume that individual household members have different preferences and view intrahousehold resource allocation as the outcome of a bargaining process among household members (e.g., McElroy and Horney 1981, Manser and Brown 1980) or as Pareto-efficient outcomes reached through a collective decision-making process (e.g., Chiappori 1988). Empirical work has increasingly provided evidence against the assumptions that individual household members share the same preferences for resource allocation in the household and that resources are shared equally among household members. One of the most commonly claimed findings is that when women have greater control over household resources, they tend to allocate a larger share of household resources on nutrition, health, and education of their children than men do.[10] An important implication of such findings is that changes in individual-specific control of resources can translate into changes in the patterns of the way resources are allocated within the household (Chiappori 1992 and 1997).

Control over household resource allocation is said to be determined by the bargaining power of individual household members (e.g., McElroy and Horney 1981, Manser and Brown 1980, Pollak 1994). Researchers often have difficulty measuring relative power empirically because it is derived from multiple sources. There are a number of possible determinants of bargaining power: (i) individual-specific control of resources such as unearned income, premarital assets brought to the marriage, transfer payments, and welfare receipts; (ii) factors influencing the bargaining process including legal rights (e.g., divorce law and laws regarding the disposition of property upon divorce) and education; (iii) personal networks of individuals such as support from family; and (iv) basic attitudinal attributes including self-esteem, self-confidence, and emotional satisfaction (Quisumbing 2003c). Unfortunately, the distribution of power and thus the control over resources within the household tends to favor men (Quisumbing 2003b).

Another important empirical question to ask is how household resources are allocated between sons and daughters within the household,

---

9   See Haddad et al. (1997) for a review of the literature.
10   See Haddad et al. (1997) and Quisumbing (2003a) for a review of the literature.

if the assumption that resources are not allocated equally among household members is rejected. As the previous section has highlighted, there are apparent disparities in the outcomes between boys and girls, such as school enrollment rates and health status. One of the possible explanations for these disparities is that household resources are allocated differently between boys and girls.

There are mainly two approaches for detecting any discrimination in such allocation through expenditure analysis. Given that data on expenditure of individual household members are generally absent in household surveys, the attractiveness of these methodologies is that they can be applied using readily available household-level expenditure data. The first is the Rothbarth approach, which is based on the argument that expenditure on adult goods (e.g., alcohol and tobacco) can be considered a measure of parental welfare (Rothbarth 1943). Given that the household faces a fixed budget, the addition of children can be modeled as a negative income effect, with expenditure on children displacing adult goods consumption, leading to a reduction in adult goods expenditure and welfare (Deaton 1997). Under the Rothbarth approach, if the presence of boys reduces adult goods consumption more than girls, this can indicate greater valuation of boys than girls. This methodology can, however, be applied only when one can identify a set of goods consumed only by adults and for which there are no substitution effects of children.

The second approach, commonly referred to as the Engel method, seeks to detect differential treatment within the household by examining how household expenditure on a particular good, such as schooling and health care, changes with the household age-gender composition (Deaton 1989). The Engel method has been particularly popular for examining gender bias in intrahousehold resource allocation and has been widely applied to data from various countries.

Using these indirect household expenditure methodologies, some studies find gender bias against girls in the allocation of household resources; see for example, Burgess and Zhuang (2002) for the PRC, and Gibson and Rozelle (2004) for Papua New Guinea. Nevertheless, most studies—based on either the Rothbarth approach or the Engel method—have failed to detect discrimination against girls in household consumption patterns. For example, various studies find no systematic gender differential in the allocation of household expenditures on children.[11] This is puzzling given the observed disparities in the outcomes between boys and girls. This issue has also been acknowledged by Deaton who notes "it is a puzzle that expenditure patterns so consistently fail

---

[11]   Deaton (1989) on Côte d'Ivoire and Thailand, Haddad and Hoddinott (1991) on Côte d'Ivoire, Subramanian and Deaton (1991) on India, Ahmad and Morduch (1993) on Bangladesh, Haddad and Reardon (1993) on Burkina Faso, and Bhalotra and Attfield (1998) on Pakistan.

to show strong gender effects even when measures of outcomes show differences between boys and girls" (Deaton 1997, 240).

Several explanations have been put forward to explain the failure to detect a bias.[12] Kingdon (2005), for instance, points out the limitations of the Engel method. Based on individual data[13] on educational outcomes and expenditure of each household member aged 35 or younger, Kingdon (2005) investigates gender bias in the allocation of education expenditure, both by directly examining individual educational spending on boys and girls and by the indirect Engel approach. She finds that while the Engel method fails to find biased resource allocation against girls, the individual-level data on educational expenditures confirm that in the Indian states where there is evidence of significantly worse educational outcomes for girls than boys, household expenditure on girls' education is significantly lower than on boys'.

Kingdon (2005) provides two reasons for the failure of the Engel method. First, in the case of rural Indian households, gender bias mainly occurs through zero educational spending for girls (i.e., no enrollment) rather than lower expenditure for girls than for boys—conditional on both being enrolled in school. However, the Engel method simply estimates a single budget share equation, ignoring the two-stage decision process (i.e., the binary decision of whether to send a child to school and the decision of how much to spend on the child's education—conditional on sending him/her to school). Averaging across the two mechanisms can offset the main discriminatory process of not sending girls to school and lead to the conclusion that there is no pro-boy bias. Second, household-level expenditure data are a poor substitute for individual-level data for measuring the extent of gender discrimination in household resource allocation.

There are also a number of explanations for the failure to detect gender bias in household resource allocation, which are not related to methodological issues. One of them is that girls have been so discriminated against that they have already died, i.e., there exists gender bias in mortality selection instead (Rose 1999, Udry 1997). This can be supported by the observation of "missing women" in certain regions in East Asia and South Asia where both sex ratios at birth and child survival rates are highly skewed toward boys (e.g., Sen 1992). Alternatively, if couples have a strong desire for a male offspring, they will continue childbearing until they have at least one boy. As a result, a situation arises where girls tend to have more siblings and larger households than boys. Given fewer resources for each child in larger households, girls are found to be worse off than boys in their outcomes even when there is

---

12   See Gibson and Rozelle (2004) and Kingdon (2005) for a review.
13   Collected through the 1994 National Council of Applied Economic Research Rural Household Survey of 16 major states in India.

no observed differential treatment by parents in intrahousehold resource allocation (Jensen 2002).

Another possible explanation for the absence of discrimination against girls in the allocation of household resources is that, in certain countries, women are actually economically productive and girls are treated relatively equally by their parents. In the Philippines, no bias against girls in intergenerational transfers of land, investment in schooling, and the allocation of household expenditures is found. Although there is a tendency for daughters to receive less land than sons, they are compensated by more schooling. This may partly reflect the fact that Filipino women have historically enjoyed a position relatively equal to their male counterparts, including in the labor market. The earnings gap between men and women in the Philippines is, in fact, narrower than in the United States, Japan, or many other countries (Estudillo et al. 2001). Hence it may be argued that discrimination against girls is likely to decline as economic opportunities for women increase (Haddad and Reardon 1993).

Similarly, based on data from Pakistan, Mansuri (2007) finds that migration-induced resource flows have a positive and significant impact for girls on height for age and educational attainment, while the effects are much smaller for boys. This suggests that boys may get preference in education, nutrition, and health care when resources are stretched, whereas girls are treated better only when additional resources are available. These findings seem to demonstrate that the son preference is not only due to embedded cultural norms, but also because of economic factors. Some studies do show that medical care or education for girls is more income elastic than for boys—e.g., medical care in Pakistan (Alderman and Gertler 1997), and education in Malaysia (DeTray 1988) and Viet Nam (Behrman and Knowles 1999). By using data from both a rich (Jiangsu) and a poor (Sichuan) province in the PRC, Burgess and Zhuang (2002) also find that biases against girls in health and education spending occur predominantly in poor, rural households that are highly dependent on agriculture. Moreover, Sawada and Lokshin (2001) show, in rural Pakistan, that while there are some gender-specific, birth-order effects on household allocation patterns (i.e., suggesting resource competition among siblings), the schooling progression rates become comparable between boys and girls at a high level of education. These observations indicate that parents might pick the "winners", which would be consistent with the theoretical implications of the optimal educational investment behavior under binding credit constraints.

The findings from studies on gender bias in intrahousehold resource allocation are mixed, perhaps due to one of the reasons outlined above. Nonetheless, this section has also provided empirical evidence that suggests gender inequality in capabilities can, at least partly, be

141

attributed to how parents allocate household resources between sons and daughters. It also suggests that gender bias in the allocation of household resources is caused not only by cultural and social factors, but also by economic hardships. This implies that, in addition to further efforts in improving access to education and health services for girls and women as well as in raising public awareness of gender equality, policy makers can also strengthen the capabilities of girls and women by promoting economic development.

4.4.2　Gender inequality in the labor market

Gender inequality in access to economic opportunity, particularly related to the labor market, is a much-debated issue. The disparity between men and women is generally observed in labor force participation, occupational segregation, and gender wage gaps. Although there have been improvements—such as women's increased educational attainments and the introduction of anti-discrimination and equal opportunity laws—progress toward gender equality in the labor market has not been satisfactory, even in developed countries, as illustrated in Section 4.3.

　　Gender inequality in the labor market not only results in the inefficient use of resources and slower economic growth, but also has repercussions on the power relationship between men and women within the household. It is, therefore, important for policy makers to ensure equal access to economic opportunity for men and women. The purpose of this section is to understand the factors causing the persistence of gender inequality in the labor market. More specifically, it will identify (i) constraints that prevent women from entering labor markets, and (ii) factors that cause gender inequality in the labor market.

A.　Labor force participation

　　Section 4.3 highlighted the significant differences between men and women in labor force participation in many countries in Asia and the Pacific, particularly in South Asia. The available empirical studies suggest a number of important factors that restrict women's entry into the labor market, including: (i) women's limited educational attainment; (ii) lower wage levels for female workers; and (iii) the incompatibility of labor market participation with women's childbearing role and the traditional division of labor between men and women. It should, however, be noted that improvement in education and wage levels does not necessarily increase the female labor force participation rate in developing countries, particularly among poor households, as discussed below.

　　Education is a key determinant of female labor force participation. Although it is commonly assumed that women with better educational

142

attainment are more likely to enter the labor market, this may not necessarily be the case for women in developing countries. By comparing five Asian countries, Cameron et al. (2001) illustrate that in countries where traditional gender roles are rigidly defined, such as the Republic of Korea (Korea) and Sri Lanka (in comparison with the Philippines and Thailand), an increase in women's education is less likely to bolster women's labor force participation rates. These findings seem to underline the important influence of cultural and social norms on female labor force participation.[14] However, based on data from Egypt, El-Hamidi (2004) shows that while social and traditional gender roles govern women's participation in the labor market, economic factors matter in decision making when household income falls below a certain level. In other words, at low income levels or below some threshold, economic hardships are likely to press women to work outside the home to meet household economic needs.

Another important determinant of labor force participation is the wage rate. Women's labor supply has often been found more sensitive to wages than men's.[15] This is mainly due to their responsibility for housework. However, the traditional labor supply model is sometimes criticized for failing to capture the behavior of poor workers who, especially in developing countries, tend to work longer hours to cover their basic needs in response to a fall in wages (e.g., Dessing 2002). Based on data from the Philippines, Dessing (2002) finds negative wage elasticity for women at low wage rates. Similarly, Dasgupta and Goldar (2006) show that for women from households below the poverty line in rural India, women's labor supply is inversely related to the wage rate and the number of earning members in the family. These findings suggest that a positive effect of wage increases on female labor force participation among women from poor households cannot simply be assumed.

While the education and wage levels of women certainly affect their labor force participation, the main underlying causes of women's limited participation are arguably the incompatibility of labor market participation with their childbearing role and the traditional division of labor between men and women reinforced by cultural norms and people's attitudes. While increased economic demands from larger family size could push women into the labor force, the majority of empirical work suggests a negative effect of childbearing on women's labor force

---

14 Fernandez (2007) also examines the possible relationship between culture and women's labor supply based on data for second-generation women in the United States to separate the effect of market and institutional factors from culture. Using both female labor force participation rates and attitudes in the women's country of ancestry as cultural proxies, she finds that these cultural proxies have quantitatively significant effects on women's labor supply.

15 See Blundell and MaCurdy (1999) for a survey of the studies.

participation (e.g., Angrist and Evans 1998, Chevalier and Viitanen 2002, Chun and Oh 2002, Narayan and Smyth 2006). Limited female labor force participation is also closely linked with the traditional role played by men and women within the household. Indeed the traditional division of labor—father goes to work, mother stays at home to look after the children—is still the prevalent domestic arrangement, particularly in developing countries (Cigno 2007). Even in developed countries where there has been a steady increase in female labor force participation, there remains a significant difference in participation rates between men and women. While there has been a more egalitarian trend over the last few decades in people's attitudes toward gender division of labor—including attitudes about women's rights to a career—a couple's actual behavior is much less egalitarian and women continue to be primarily responsible for housework and childcare (Alvarez and Miles 2003).

One of the main explanations for the unequal division of housework between husbands and wives is based on the comparative advantage framework, whereby each spouse performs various tasks in which the spouse has a comparative advantage (Becker 1981). Hence the spouse with the lowest opportunity cost (i.e., the lowest human capital or the highest home productivity) contributes the most to housework. It could, however, also be argued that women's lower bargaining power, mainly due to the lower earnings they could bring to the household, results in the unequal allocation of housework between men and women (McElroy and Horney 1981, Lundberg and Pollak 1993). What is common between these two explanations is that an increase in women's education and earnings could lead to a more equal share of work within the household. Further, a more equal allocation of housework between men and women is likely to have a positive impact on women's living standards as well as on their labor market outcomes (Blau et al. 1998, Hersch and Stratton 1997 and 2002), leading to a potentially self-fulfilling feedback mechanism (Olivetti and Albanesi 2006).

Nevertheless, the available empirical evidence suggests a more complicated picture of the relationship between gender inequality in domestic work and labor market outcomes (e.g., Aguiar and Hurst 2006, Alvarez and Miles 2003, Chen et al. 2007, Fernandez and Sevilla-Sanz 2006). For instance, improvements in women's labor market outcomes do not automatically translate into a more equal allocation of housework between men and women, partly due to social norms. It could, instead, increase women's market efforts without releasing them from their household duties, resulting in a "double burden" on women (Chen et al. 2007).

Although much of the above empirical evidence on the gender division of labor comes from developed countries, there are a number of studies that look at gender differences in time allocation in developing countries (e.g., Ilahi 2001, Khandker 1988, Skoufias 1993). One of the most important issues is whether this is governed by local social norms and customs or whether women also respond to economic incentives and constraints to alter their time use at home. Using data from rural Bangladesh, Khandker (1988) finds that a woman's time-use pattern is not fixed exclusively by society, but is also partially influenced by individual- and household-level economic constraints. Given that women do respond to market opportunities, if economic development proceeds in rural Bangladesh, more women are likely to participate in market-oriented production even if "patriarchy" exists. In other words, there is room for policy intervention to enhance female labor force participation, through, for example, anti-discrimination policy against gender wage differentials, improving access to education for girls, and, above all, modernization programs that will increase market opportunities for women (Khandker 1988).

B. Gender inequality in the labor market

Unfortunately, when women enter the labor market, they are likely to face gender inequality. This has been extensively examined in the last few decades and almost all studies confirm its persistent existence.[16] The most apparent forms of gender disparity are gender wage gap and occupational segregation, though the latter is often considered one of the possible causes of gender pay differentials. In developing countries, in addition to occupational segregation, a relatively large representation of women in the informal sector is another manifestation of gender inequality in the labor market.[17] Hence, in addition to examining the causal factors for the gender wage gaps, the issues related to the informal sector will be discussed here.

Many studies have attempted to explain gender pay differentials by a variety of factors.[18] The main causes of gender wage gaps suggested by the existing literature include (i) women's lower human capital relative to men, (ii) occupational segregation, and (iii) discrimination against women.

---

[16]   See Altonji and Blank (1999) for a review of the literature.

[17]   Note that the term "informal sector" itself is often used to refer to a heterogeneous group of economic arrangements ranging from self-employed producers and traders to wage workers such as casual workers and subcontractors. In addition, unpaid housework is sometimes regarded as one of the categories of the informal sector.

[18]   One of the most popular ways of analyzing gender wage differentials has been to decompose them into two components—differences in observable characteristics including qualifications, and differences in treatment of otherwise equally qualified men and women. The latter is sometimes interpreted as a measure of discrimination. This type of analysis is commonly done through the application of a decomposition methodology proposed by Oaxaca (1973).

One of the most frequently noted explanations for gender pay differentials is that women invest less in their human capital, typically in education and work experience (Becker 1964, Mincer 1974). Many empirical studies support this argument.[19] The weaker human capabilities of women in developing countries, as noted in Section 4.3, are likely to constrain their earnings relative to men.

Given the existence of a significant wage variation across occupations, another strand of the literature suggests the importance of gender occupational segregation in explaining the gender wage gap (e.g., Breunig and Rospabe 2007, Brown et al. 1980, Ilkkaracan and Selim 2007, Meng and Miller 1995). A relatively significant role of occupational segregation in gender pay disparity implies that pay structures within occupations are equitable while women tend to be more concentrated in poorly paid occupations due to reasons including physical constraints, incompatibility with their responsibilities at home, and lower level of education. Yet other studies show that most gender wage gaps are actually found within occupations, for example, in Hong Kong, China (Sung et al. 2001) and Taipei,China (Zveglich and Van der Meulen Rodgers 2004). These findings suggest that women are not receiving equal pay for work of equal value.

Another, and perhaps more prominent, factor contributing to gender wage gaps is the discrimination against women in the labor market. Employers sometimes use observable characteristics of potential workers such as race and gender as a proxy for unobservable ones such as ability, attitudes, or signals of their future productivity (e.g., Arrow 1973, Phelps 1972). Given their greater responsibilities at home, women are sometimes thought to be less productive at work and they tend to be offered lower wages (e.g., Becker 1985, Bryan and Sanz 2007, Hughes and Maurer-Fazio 2002). In the PRC, for instance, married women are found to experience a larger absolute gender wage gap than their unmarried counterparts (Hughes and Maurer-Fazio 2002). The same analysis also shows that the proportion of the gap due to discrimination is higher for married women than single women. An encouraging finding is that education may have a discrimination-reducing effect as it signals women's strong commitment to a job and career (e.g., Monk-Turner and Turner 2001, Montgomery and Powell 2003, Chapter 13 of this book). Monk-Turner and Turner (2001) find that more educated women tend to face a relatively smaller wage disparity in Korea. Son, in Chapter 13, also finds the discrimination-reducing effect of education in Thailand and Viet Nam.

On the other hand, gender pay differentials may also result from the sociocultural habit of employers to discriminate against women despite

---

19   For example, Brown and Corcoran (1997), Ilkkaracan and Selim (2007), Light and Ureta (1995), Loury (1997), Machin and Puhani (2003), Myck and Paull (2004), O'Neill and Polachek (1993).

their capabilities (e.g., Becker 1957, Liu 2004, Antecol 2001). Liu (2004) examines the case of Viet Nam, a transitional economy where—with the abolition of a centrally determined wage system—employers enjoy increased autonomy to reward workers according to their productivity, but also in accordance with their taste for discrimination. Her analysis illustrates the importance of discrimination as an obstacle to gender wage convergence in Viet Nam. She suggests that such discrimination arises from Viet Nam's underlying cultural beliefs and traditions based on Confucianism, which tends to discriminate against women.

It has, however, been argued that discriminating employers may be driven out of the market place if the cost of discrimination becomes too high (e.g., Arrow 1973, Becker 1957, Phelps 1972). In an open economy, for example, trade is likely to increase competition, which makes it more costly for employers to discriminate (e.g., Black and Brainerd 2004, Liu et al. 2000, Weichselbaumer and Winter-Ebmer 2007). In the PRC, while economic liberalization and decentralization have increased gender wage differentials, market competition is found to have reduced the relative magnitude of gender discrimination and its contribution to the overall differential (Liu et al. 2000). But it should be noted that competition can also hurt the bargaining power of women if they are engaged in declining industries due to international competition. Berik et al. (2003) provide findings for Korea and Taipei,China that support this view.

Another important aspect of gender equality in the labor market for developing economies is informal sector employment. In the developing world, a large proportion of economically active people are engaged in the informal sector. Such employment is generally perceived as a survival activity of the very poor (Sudarshan and Unni 2003), and women, in particular, are disproportionately represented in this sector (Beneria and Roldan 1987, Carr et al. 2000, Mitra 2005, Standing 1999). Even in the once rapidly growing economies of East Asia and Southeast Asia which experienced substantial growth of modern sector employment, a significant share of female workers were outside the formal sector (Carr et al. 2000).

The existing literature on women's engagement in the informal sector can be divided broadly into two strands (Gallaway and Bernasek 2002). One takes a relatively positive view of the sector and considers it as a provider of opportunities to earn an income for the poorest and most marginalized people. For women, informal sector employment is thought to be a choice because of its compatibility with their household work. According to this argument, public policy should support women in their choice by improving opportunity in the informal sector and improving working conditions (e.g., Adair et al. 2002, Berger and Buvinic 1989, Dignard and Havet 1995). In contrast, others take a more negative view of the sector, and regard informal sector employment as further marginalizing the poorest and most vulnerable people in society, including women. In order to address this, public policy should make formal sector employment more available to women by removing the constraints that prevent them from entering the formal labor market (Beneria and Roldan 1987, Mitra 2005, Moser 1984).

Despite the opposing views, both perspectives agree that women tend to work in the informal sector, at least partly, as a consequence of their household responsibilities. Moreover, it cannot be denied that the informal sector is an inferior alternative to formal sector employment in terms of earnings, security, and protection from exploitation (Gallaway and Bernasek 2002). In light of these facts, there are a number of important issues that should be noted regarding informal employment. First, a relatively large percentage of women engaged in the informal sector indicates women's vulnerable employment status without any formal social protection. Second, given that the informal economy is not generally accounted for in national account systems, women's contribution to the economy is likely to be underestimated. Finally, gender wage gaps are often measured based on data from the formal sector. Given the lower average earnings in the informal sector than in the formal sector and a relatively large representation of women in the informal sector, reported gender wage differentials are likely to be an underestimation of the overall gender pay disparity. While policy makers should address the constraints that prevent women from acquiring formal sector employment—by enhancing women's educational and vocational skills and implementing and enforcing equal opportunity and anti-discrimination legislation—they should also take measures to improve the working conditions of the informal sector, including the provision of social protection.

This section has reviewed the existing literature on gender bias in intrahousehold resource allocation and in access to economic opportunity to identify the underlying causes of gender inequality in capabilities attainment and in the labor market. While social and cultural norms play an important role in gender disparity in these areas, economic factors also seem to influence the behavior of men and women. The section has also highlighted the significance of women's economic empowerment in achieving gender parity in various aspects of their lives, as it can have a positive effect on the share of domestic work between husbands and wives, women's control over household resources, and the allocation of resources between boys and girls. Improving women's capabilities as well as their access to economic opportunity, therefore, seem to be key to enhancing progress toward gender equality within and outside the household.

4.5   Conclusions

This chapter has reviewed the progress toward gender equality in Asia and the Pacific over the last few decades. By examining a number of indicators proposed under the MDG3 plus approach, it has found that most countries in the region have made some progress in achieving gender parity. However, the rate of progress varies across the different dimensions of gender equality and also across countries. While improvement in the area of education has been notable, advancement has been less impressive in health status and even more disappointing in labor market outcomes. Women's improved capabilities do not seem to have been translated into the equal participation of men and women in economic and political activities. In addition, gender gaps in almost all aspects reviewed remain significant, particularly in South Asia. Often with the exception of Maldives and Sri Lanka, South Asian countries tend to perform worse than sub-Saharan Africa, which made the least progress toward gender parity in many dimensions. Concerted action is thus very much needed to help South Asia catch up with the rest of the world.

More effort is also required to improve the collection of data on indicators to effectively monitor progress toward gender equality. Despite the importance of the security aspect of gender equality, the limited availability of data prevented the examination of the status of gender equality in this dimension. The scarcity of gender-disaggregated data on access to productive assets (e.g., land and credit) as well as to infrastructure should also be overcome. This would not only allow measurement of gender equality in these aspects, but also help identify barriers to women's economic empowerment. Similarly, to get a better picture of women's economic activities, particularly in developing countries, data on the informal sector, including subsistence agricultural and home-based activities, are necessary. Another challenge is to monitor gender inequality at a more disaggregated level within each country. MDG progress reports on several countries in the region show that women in disadvantaged or socially excluded groups (due to their race, ethnicity, caste, income, location, disability, or other factors) tend to lag the national average in achieving gender equality (ADB et al. 2006). To ensure that girls and women from disadvantaged groups are not left behind in the progress toward gender equality, data monitoring must be undertaken at a more disaggregated level so that policy makers can formulate targeted policies.

The chapter also tried to explain the underlying causes of the prevalence and persistence of gender disparity by surveying the relevant literature. Empirical studies show that gender inequality is caused and reinforced by interlinked cultural, social, and economic factors. The importance of cultural and social norms in the prevalence of anti-female bias poses serious challenges to policy makers. These obstacles cannot be removed overnight, but have to be overcome gradually in order to eliminate gender disparity within and outside the household. Policy makers can enhance the process by introducing and enforcing anti-discrimination legislation and educating the public.

Empirical findings also underline the potential role of economic factors in gender disparity. Some studies show that the son preference in certain parts of the region is not only due to embedded cultural norms, but also to economic hardships. Economic growth can, therefore, ease the economic constraints of parents and allow them to treat sons and daughters equally. Such findings suggest room for public policies to play an important role in improving the standing of girls relative to boys by promoting economic growth and modernization. Moreover, relatively lower returns to investment in education and health for girls than for boys (due to limited employment opportunity and lower wage levels for women) are also partly responsible for the observed differences in capabilities attainment between boys and girls. Hence improving women's access to employment opportunities and more equal treatment between men and women in the labor market are likely to reduce gender bias in household resource allocation.

In addition, the existing literature suggests that gender disparity in one aspect can reinforce gender inequality in another, forming a self-fulfilling mechanism. Women's improved labor outcomes can, for example, increase their bargaining power over the share of domestic work as well as intra-household resource allocation. On the other hand, a more equal sharing of domestic work by men and women can allow women to work outside the household, as long as they have the appropriate capabilities and equal access to economic opportunity. However, the available evidence also shows that despite the close links among different dimensions of gender inequality, progress in equality in one aspect does not always translate into progress in others. The most obvious example is that women are often not released from domestic responsibilities even when they work outside the home, doubling their burden.

The chapter has highlighted the importance of women's economic empowerment in achieving gender parity in various aspects of women's lives. Unfortunately, progress toward gender equality in the labor market has been limited so far, and further effort is needed to reduce gender disparities in labor market outcomes. Policy makers should not only introduce anti-discrimination legislation, but also ensure that they are implemented and enforced effectively. Moreover, public effort in improving women's educational attainments must continue so that women can take advantage of available economic opportunity. In sum, along with efforts at removing cultural and social obstacles through public awareness, enhancing economic development and improving women's capabilities as well as their access to economic opportunity appear to be crucial to enhancing progress toward gender equality and, ultimately, to inclusive growth.

References

Adair, L., D. Guilkey, E. Bisgrove, and S. Gultiano. 2002. "Effect of Childbearing on Filipino Women's Work Hours and Earnings." *Journal of Population Economics* 15:625–45.

ADB. 2007. *Gender and Development Plan of Action (2008–2010)*. Asian Development Bank, Manila.

_____. 2008. *Strategy 2020: The Long-Term Strategic Framework of the Asian Development Bank 2008–2020*. Asian Development Bank, Manila.

ADB, United Nations Development Programme, and United Nations Economic and Social Commission of Asia and the Pacific. 2006. *Pursuing Gender Equality through the Millennium Development Goals in Asia and the Pacific*. Asian Development Bank, Manila.

Aguiar, M., and E. Hurst. 2006. Measuring Trends in Leisure: The Allocation of Time Over Five Decades. NBER Working Paper No. 12082, National Bureau of Economic Research, Cambridge, MA.

Ahmad, A., and J. Morduch. 1993. Identifying Sex Bias in the Allocation of Household Resources: Evidence from Linked Household Surveys from Bangladesh. Harvard Institute for Economic Research Discussion Paper No. 1636, Harvard University, Cambridge, MA.

Alderman, H., and P. Gertler. 1997. "Family Resources and Gender Differences in Human Capital Investments: the Demand for Children's Medical Care in Pakistan." In L. Haddad, J. Hoddinott, and H. Alderman, eds. *Intrahousehold Resource Allocation in Developing Countries: Models, Methods, and Policy*. Baltimore, MD: Johns Hopkins University Press.

Ali, I. 2007. "Inequality and the Imperative for Inclusive Growth in Asia." *Asian Development Review* 24(2):1–16.

Ali, I., and J. Zhuang. 2007. Inclusive Growth Toward a Prosperous Asia: Policy Implications. ERD Working Paper Series No. 97, Economics and Research Department, Asian Development Bank, Manila.

Altonji, J. G., and R. M. Blank. 1999. "Race and Gender in the Labor Market." In O. Ashenfelter, and D. Card, eds., *Handbook of Labor Economics* Vol. 3. Amsterdam: North-Holland.

Alvarez, B., and D. Miles. 2003. "Gender Effect on Housework Allocation: Evidence from Spanish Two-Earner Couples." *Journal of Population Economics* 16:227–42.

Angrist, J. D., and W. N. Evans. 1998. "Children and Their Parent's Labor Supply: Evidence from Exogenous Variation in Family Size." *American Economic Review* 88:450–77.

Antecol, H. 2001. "Why is There Interethnic Variation in the Gender Wage Gap? The Role of Cultural Factors." *Journal of Human Resources* 36(1):119–43.

Arrow, K. 1973. "The Theory of Discrimination." In O. Ashenfelter, and A. Rees, eds. *Discrimination in Labor Markets*. Princeton, NJ: Princeton University Press.

Becker, G. 1957. *The Economics of Discrimination*. Chicago: University of Chicago Press.

_____.1964. *Human Capital: A Theoretical and Empirical Analysis with Special Reference to Education*. Chicago: Chicago University Press.

_____.1965. "A Theory of the Allocation of Time." *Economic Journal* 75:493–517.

_____.1981. *A Treatise on the Family*. Cambridge, MA: Harvard University Press.

_____.1985. "Human Capital, Effort, and the Sexual Division of Labor." *Journal of Labor Economics* 3(1):S33–58.

Behrman, J. R., and J. C. Knowles. 1999. "Household Income and Child Schooling in Vietnam." *World Bank Economic Review* 13:211–56.

Beneria, L., and M. Roldan. 1987. *The Crossroads of Class and Gender: Industrial Homework, Sub-Contracting and Household Dynamics in Mexico City*. Chicago: Chicago University Press.

Berger, M., and M. Buvinic, eds. 1989. *Women's Ventures: Assistance to the Informal Sector in Latin America*. Hartford: Kumarian Press.

Berik, G., Y. van der Meulen Rodgers, and J. E. Zveglich, Jr. 2003. International Trade and Wage Discrimination. Policy Research Working Paper No. 3111, World Bank, Washington, DC.

Bhalotra, S., and C. Attfield. 1998. "Intrahousehold Resource Allocation in Rural Pakistan: A Semiparametric Analysis." *Journal of Applied Econometrics* 13:463–80.

Black, S. E., and E. Brainerd. 2004. "Importing Equality? The Impact of Globalization on Gender Discrimination." *Industrial Labor Relations Review* 57(4):540–59.

Blau, F. D., M. A. Ferber, A. E. Winkler. 1998. *The Economics of Women, Men and Work* 3rd ed. Upper Saddle River: Prentice Hall.

Blundell, R., and T. MaCurdy. 1999. "Labor Supply: A Review of Alternative Approaches." In O. Ashenfelter, and D. Card, eds., *Handbook of Labor Economics* Vol. 3A. Amsterdam: Elsevier.

Breunig, R., and S. Rospabe 2007. Parametric vs. Semi-parametric Estimation of the Male-Female Wage Gap: An Application to France. Center for Economic Policy Research Discussion Paper No. 538, Australian National University, Canberra.

Brown, C., and M. Corcoran. 1997. "Sex-Based Difference in School Content and the Male-Female Wage Gap." *Journal of Labor Economics* 15(3):431–65.

Brown, R. S., M. Moon, and B. S. Zoloth. 1980. "Incorporating Occupational Attainment in Studies of Male–Female Earnings Differentials." *Journal of Human Resources* 15(1):3–28.

Bryan, M. L., and A. S. Sanz. 2007. Does Housework Lower Wages and Why? Evidence for Britain. Economic Series Working Papers No. 331, Department of Economics, University of Oxford, Oxford.

Burgess, R., and J. Zhuang. 2002. Modernization and Son Preference in People's Republic of China. ERD Working Paper Series No. 20, Economics and Research Department, Asian Development Bank, Manila.

Cameron, L. A., J. M. Dowling, and C. Worswick. 2001. "Education and Labor Market Participation of Women in Asia: Evidence from Five Countries." *Economic Development and Cultural Change* 49(3):461–77.

Carr, M., M. A. Chen, and J. Tate. 2000. "Globalization and Home-Based Workers." *Feminist Economics* 6(3):123–42.

Cebu Study Team. 1991. "Underlying and Proximate Determinants of Child Health: The CEBU Longitudinal Health and Nutrition Study." *American Journal of Epidemiology* 133(2):185–201.

Chen, N., P. Conconi, and C. Perroni. 2007. Women's Earning Power and the "Double Burden" of Market and Household Work. Warwick Economic Research Paper No. 800, University of Warwick, Coventry.

Chevalier, A., and T. K. Viitanen. 2002. "The Causality between Female Labor Force Participation and the Availability of Childcare." *Applied Economics Letters* 9:915–18.

Chiappori, P. A. 1988. "Rational Household Labor Supply." *Econometrica* 56(1):63–89.

_____. 1992. "Collective Labor Supply and Welfare." *Journal of Political Economy* 100(3):437–67.

_____. 1997. "Introducing Household Production in Collective Models of Labor Supply." *Journal of Political Economy* 105(1):191–209.

Chun, H., and J. Oh. 2002. "An Instrumental Variable Estimate of the Effect on the Labour Force Participation of Married Women." *Applied Economics Letters* 9:631–34.

Cigno, A. 2007. A Theoretical Analysis of the Effects of Legislation on Marriage, Fertility, Domestic Division of Labour, and the Education of Children. CESIFO Working Paper No. 2143, University of Florence, Florence.

Dasgupta, P., and B. Goldar. 2006. "Female Labour Supply in Rural India: An Econometric Analysis." *Indian Journal of Labour Economics* 49(2):293–310.

Deaton, A. 1989. "Looking for Boy-Girl Discrimination in Household Expenditure Data." *World Bank Economic Review* 1(1):1–15.

_____. 1997. *The Analysis of Household Surveys: A Microeconometric Approach to Development Policy.* Baltimore, MD: Johns Hopkins University Press.

Dessing, M. 2002. "Labor Supply, the Family and Poverty: The S-Shaped Labor Supply Curve." *Journal of Economic Behavior and Organization* 49:433–58.

DeTray, D. 1988. "Government Policy, Household Behavior, and the Distribution of Schooling: A Case Study of Malaysia." *Research in Population Economics* 6:303–36.

Dignard, L., and J. Havet. 1995. *Women in Micro and Small Scale Enterprise Development.* Boulder: Westview Press.

El-Hamidi, F. 2004. "Does Wealth Influence Women's Labor Participation Decision?: Evidence from Egypt." Paper presented at the Economic Research Forum Workshop on Gender, Work and Family, 8–10 June, Mahdia City, Tunisia.

Estudillo, J. P., A. R. Quisumbing, and K. Otsuka. 2001. "Gender Differences in Wealth Transfer and Expenditure Allocation: Evidence from the Rural Philippines." *Developing Economies* 39(4):366–94.

Fernandez, R. 2007. Women, Work, and Culture. NBER Working Paper No. 12888, National Bureau of Economic Research, Cambridge, MA.

Fernandez, C., and A. Sevilla-Sanz. 2006. Social Norms and Household Time Allocation. Discussion Paper Series No. 291, Department of Economics, University of Oxford, Oxford.

Gallaway, J. H., and A. Bernasek. 2002. "Gender and Informal Sector Employment in Indonesia." *Journal of Economic Issues* 36(2):313–21.

Galloway, R., and M. A. Anderson. 1994. "Prepregnancy Nutritional Status and Its Impact on Birthweight." *SCN News* 11:6–10.

Gibson, J., and S. Rozelle. 2004. "Is it Better to be a Boy? A Disaggregated Outlay Equivalent Analysis of Gender Bias in Papua New Guinea." *Journal of Development Studies* 40(4):115–36.

Grown, C. 2008. "Indicators and Indices of Gender Equality: What Do They Measure and What Do They Miss?" In M. Buvinic, A. R. Morisson, A. W. Ofosu-Amaah, and M. Sjoblom, eds., *Equality for Women: Where Do We Stand on Millennium Development Goal 3?* World Bank, Washington, DC.

Grown, C., G. Gupta, and A. Kes. 2005. *Taking Action: Achieving Gender Equality and Empowering Women.* London: Earthscan and the Millennium Project.

Haddad, L., and J. Hoddinott. 1991. Gender Aspects of Household Expenditures and Resource Allocation in the Cote d'Ivoire. Economics Series Working Papers, Department of Economics, University of Oxford, Oxford.

Haddad, L., J. Hoddinott, and H. Alderman, eds. 1997. *Intrahousehold Resource Allocation in Developing Countries: Models, Methods, and Policy.* Baltimore, MD: Johns Hopkins University Press.

Haddad, L., and T. Reardon. 1993. "Gender Bias in the Allocation of Resources within Households in Burkina Faso: A Disaggregated Outlay Equivalent Analysis." *Journal of Development Studies* 29(2):260–76.

Heise, L., M. Ellsberg, and M. Gottemoeller. 1999. Ending Violence Against Women. Population Reports Series L No. 11, Johns Hopkins School of Public Health, Baltimore, MD.

Hersch, J., and L. S. Stratton. 1997. "Housework, Fixed Effects, and Wages of Married Workers." *Journal of Human Resources* 32(2):285–307.

_____. 2002. "Housework and Wages." *Journal of Human Resources* 37(1):217–29.

Hoddinott, J., and L. Haddad. 1995. "Does Female Income Share Influence Household Expenditures? Evidence from the Cote d'Ivoire." *Oxford Bulletin of Economics and Statistics* 57(1):77–96.

Hughes, J., and M. Maurer-Fazio. 2002. "Effects of Marriage, Education, and Occupation on the Female/Male Wage Gap in China." *Pacific Economic Review* 7(1):137–56.

Ilahi, N. 2001. Gender and the Allocation of Adult Time: Evidence from the Peru LSMS Panel Data. Policy Research Working Paper No. 2744, World Bank, Washington, DC.

Ilkkaracan, I., and R. Selim. 2007. "The Gender Wage Gap in the Turkish Labor Market." *Labour* 21(3):563–93.

Jensen, R. 2002. Equal Treatment, Unequal Outcomes? Generating Gender Inequality through Fertility Behavior. John F. Kennedy School of Government, Harvard University. Processed.

Khandker, S. R. 1988. "Determinants of Women's Time Allocation in Rural Bangladesh." *Economic Development and Cultural Change* 37:111–26.

Kingdon, G. G. 2005. "Where Has All the Bias Gone? Detecting Gender Bias in the Intrahousehold Allocation of Educational Expenditure." *Economic Development and Cultural Change* 53(2):409–51.

Klasen, S. 2002. "Low Schooling for Girls, Slower Growth for All? Cross-Country Evidence on the Effect of Gender Inequality in Education on Economic Development." *World Bank Economic Review* 16(3):345–73.

Light, A., and M. Ureta. 1995. "Early-Career Work Experience and Gender Wage Differentials." *Journal of Labor Economics* 13(1):121–54.

Liu, A. Y. C. 2004. "Gender Wage Gap in Vietnam: 1993 to 1998." *Journal of Comparative Economics* 32:586–96.

Liu, P. W., X. Meng, and J. Zhang. 2000. "Sectoral Gender Wage Differentials and Discrimination in the Transitional Chinese Economy." *Journal of Population Economics* 13:331–52.

Loury, L. D. 1997. "The Gender Earnings Gap among College-Educated Workers." *Industrial and Labor Relations Review* 50(4):580–93.

Lundberg, S., and R. A. Pollak. 1993. "Separate Spheres Bargaining and the Marriage Market." *Journal of Political Economy* 101(6):988–1010.

Machin, S., and P. Puhani. 2003. "Subject of Degree and the Gender Wage Differential: Evidence from the UK and Germany." *Economics Letters* 79(3):393–400.

Manser, M., and M. Brown. 1980. "Marriage and Household Decision Making: A Bargaining Analysis." *International Economic Review* 21(1):31–44.

Mansuri, G. 2007. "Does Work Migration Spur Investment in Origin Communities? Entrepreneurship, Schooling, and Child Health in Rural Pakistan." In C. Ozden, and M. Schiff, eds., *International Migration, Economic Development, and Policy.* Washington, DC: Palgrave Macmillan for the World Bank.

McElroy, M. B., and M. J. Horney. 1981. "Nash-Bargained Household Decision: Toward a Generalization of the Theory of Demand." *International Economic Review* 22(2):333–49.

Meng, X., and W. P. Miller. 1995. "Occupational Segregation and its Impact on Gender Wage Discrimination in China's Rural Industrial Sector." *Oxford Economic Papers* 47(1):136–55.

Mincer, J. 1974. *Schooling, Experience and Earnings*. National Bureau of Economic Research, Cambridge, MA.

Mitra, A. 2005. "Women in the Urban Informal Sector: Perpetuation of Meager Earnings." *Development and Change* 36(2):291–316.

Monk-Turner, E., and C. G. Turner. 2001. "Sex Differentials in Earnings in the South Korean Labor Market." *Feminist Economics* 7(1):63–78.

Montgomery, M., and I. Powell. 2003. "Does an Advanced Degree Reduce the Gender Wage Gap? Evidence from MBAs." *Industrial Relations* 42(3):396–418.

Morisson, A. R., D. Raju, and N. Sinha. 2007. Gender Equality, Poverty and Economic Growth. Policy Research Working Paper No. 4349, World Bank, Washington, DC.

Morisson, A. R., S. Sabarwal, and M. Sjoblom. 2008. "The State of World Progress: 1990–2007." In M. Buvinic, A. R. Morisson, A. W. Ofosu-Amaah, and M. Sjoblom, eds., *Equality for Women: Where Do We Stand on Millennium Development Goal 3?* World Bank, Washington, DC.

Moser, C. 1984. "The Informal Sector Revisited: Viability and Vulnerability in Urban Development." *Regional Development Dialogue* 5:135–78.

Myck, M., and G. Paull. 2004. The Role of Employment Experience in Explaining the Gender Wage Gap. Working Paper WP04/16, Institute for Fiscal Studies, London.

Narayan, P. K., and R. Smyth. 2006. "Female Labor Force Participation, Fertility and Infant Mortality in Australia: Some Empirical Evidence from Granger Causality Tests." *Applied Economics* 38:563–72.

Niimi, Y. 2009. Gender Equality and Inclusive Growth in Developing Asia. ADB Economics Working Paper Series No. 186, Asian Development Bank, Manila.

Oaxaca, R. 1973. "Male–Female Wage Differentials in Urban Labor Markets." *International Economic Review* 14(3):693–709.

Olivetti, C., and S. Albanesi. 2006. Home Production, Market Production and the Gender Wage Gap: Incentives and Expectations. NBER Working Paper No. 12212, National Bureau of Economic Research, Cambridge, MA.

O'Neill, J., and S. Polachek. 1993. "Why the Gender Gap in Wages Narrowed in the 1980s." *Journal of Labor Economics* 11(1):205–28.

Phelps, E. 1972. "The Statistical Theory of Racism and Sexism." *American Economic Review* 62:659–61.

Pollak, R. 1994. "For Better or Worse: The Roles of Power in Models of Distribution within Marriage." *American Economic Review* 84(2):148–52.

Quisumbing, A. R., ed. 2003a. *Household Decision, Gender, and Development: A Synthesis of Recent Research*. International Food Policy Research Institute, Washington, DC.

_____. 2003b. "What Have We Learned from Research on Intrahousehold Allocation?" In A. R. Quisumbing, ed., *Household Decision, Gender, and Development: A Synthesis of Recent Research*. International Food Policy Research Institute, Washington, DC.

_____. 2003c. "Power and Resources within the Household: Overview." In A. R. Quisumbing, ed., *Household Decision, Gender, and Development: A Synthesis of Recent Research*. International Food Policy Research Institute, Washington, DC.

Quisumbing, A. R., and J. A. Maluccio. 2003. "Intrahousehold Allocation and Gender Relations: New Empirical Evidence from Four Developing Countries." In A. R. Quisumbing, ed., *Household Decision, Gender, and Development: A Synthesis of Recent Research*. International Food Policy Research Institute, Washington, DC.

Roemer, J. E. 2006. Economic Development as Opportunity Equalization. Cowles Foundation Discussion Paper No. 1583, Yale University, New Haven.

Rose, E. 1999. "Consumption Smoothing and Excess Female Mortality in Rural India." *Review of Economics and Statistics* 81(1):41–9.

Rothbarth, E. 1943. "A Note on a Method of Determining Equivalent Income for Families of Different Composition." In C. Madge, *Wartime Pattern of Saving and Spending*. Occasional Paper No. 4, National Institute for Economic and Social Research, London.

Sawada, Y., and M. Lokshin. 2001. Household Schooling Decisions in Rural Pakistan. World Bank Policy Research Working Paper No. 2541, World Bank, Washington, DC.

Sen, A. 1992. "Missing Women." *The British Medical Journal* 304:586–7.

Skoufias, E. 1993. "Labor Market Opportunities and Intrafamily Time Allocation in Rural Households in South Asia." *Journal of Development Economics* 40:227–310.

Standing, G. 1999. *Global Flexible Labour: Seeking Distributive Justice*. London: MacMillan.

Subramanian, S., and A. Deaton. 1991. "Gender Effects in Indian Consumption Patterns." *Sarvekshana* 14:1–12.

Sudarshan, R. M., and J. Unni. 2003. "Measuring the Informal Economy." In R. Jhabvala, R. M. Sudarshan, and J. Unni, eds., *Informal Economy Centrestage: New Structures of Employment*. New Delhi: SAGE Publications.

Sung, Y. W., J. Zhang, and C. S. Chan. 2001. "Gender Wage Differentials and Occupational Segregation in Hong Kong, 1981–1996." *Pacific Economic Review* 6(3):345–59.

Thomas, D., and J. Strauss. 1992. "Prices, Infrastructure, Household Characteristics and Child Height." *Journal of Development Economics* 39(2):301–31.

Udry, C. 1997. "Recent Advances in Empirical Microeconomic Research in Poor Countries: An Annotated Bibliography." *Journal of Economic Education* 28(1):58–75.

UNDP. 2007. *Human Development Report 2007/2008*. United Nations Development Programme, New York.

UNESCAP. 2007. *Economic and Social Survey of Asia and the Pacific 2007: Surging Ahead in Uncertain Times*. New York: United Nations.

United Nations. Various years. World Prospects Population Database. Available: http://esa.un.org/unpp/.

UN Millennium Project. 2005. *Taking Action: Achieving Gender Equality and Empowering Women*. London: Earthscan and the Millennium Project.

Weichselbaumer, D., and R. Winter-Ebmer. 2007. "The Effects of Competition and Equal Treatment Laws on the Gender Wage Differential." *Economic Policy* 50:235–73.

World Bank. 2001. *Engendering Development: Through Gender Equality in Rights, Resources, and Voice*. New York: Oxford University Press.

———. 2006. *World Development Report 2006: Equity and Development*. Washington, DC.

———. 2007. *Global Monitoring Report 2007: Confronting the Challenges of Gender Equality and Fragile States*. Washington, DC.

———. 2008. *Gender Equality as Smart Economics: A World Bank Group Action Plan*. Washington, DC.

———. Various years. World Development Indicators Online. Available: http://devdata.worldbank.org/dataonline/.

World Economic Forum. 2007. *The Global Gender Gap Report 2007*. Geneva.

Zveglich, J. E., Jr., and Y. Van der Meulen Rodgers. 2004. "Occupational Segregation and the Gender Wage Gap in a Dynamic East Asian Economy." *Southern Economic Journal* 70(4):850–75.

Part B

Selected Policy Issues
for Inclusive Growth

5

Inclusive Growth through Full Employment: The Role of Investment and Industrial Policy

Jesus Felipe[1]

5.1   Introduction: What is inclusive growth?

While developing Asia has done remarkably well during the last 4 decades, achieved high growth, and reduced poverty significantly, Felipe and Hasan (2006) estimate that there are still about 500 million people unemployed and/or underemployed in the region. Perhaps for this reason during the last few years, terms such as "harmonious society" in the People's Republic of China (PRC), "sufficiency economy" in Thailand, and the like in other countries, have made their way into policy making discussions across Asia. The Indian government, for example, boasts of having fostered "inclusive growth". By this it means that the budget has increased allocations to school meals or rural road-building (The Economist 2008). The message in all cases is similar: development is more than growth. The high-growth policies implemented across the region since the 1960s were successful and led to increases in per capita income and dramatic reductions in poverty; helping to close the gap with the developed world. But there is a feeling today that these policies have become obsolete and citizens in Asia demand more than growth. Issues such as inequality, the environment, health, or climate change are becoming increasingly important in the agendas of policy makers. Institutions such as the World Bank or the Asian Development Bank also acknowledge the issue and argue that growth and globalization have to be inclusive.

What is inclusive growth? Though the term has not been formally defined, Ali and Zhuang (2007) claim that a consensus is emerging as to what it means and entails, namely, "growth with equal opportunity" (Ali and Zhuang 2007). In a related paper, Ali and Son (2007) further

[1]   The author is grateful to Juzhong Zhuang for useful discussions, comments, and suggestions. This chapter is based on *Inclusive Growth, Full Employment, and Structural Change: Implications and Policies for Developing Asia* (Felipe 2009). The usual disclaimer applies.

argue that inclusive growth is "growth that not only creates new economic opportunities, but also one that ensures equal access to the opportunities created for all segments of society. Growth is inclusive when it allows all members of society to participate in, and contribute to, the growth process on an equal basis regardless of their individual circumstances."

This chapter discusses the implications of inclusive growth for policy making in developing Asia. If the term inclusive growth is a useful concept for developing countries, how should it be interpreted for policy purposes? What sort of policies should policy makers implement to achieve it? Can it be achieved? The central argument is that to achieve inclusive growth, governments must commit effort and resources to the pursuit of the full employment of the labor force. The most important way for a person to participate in society and contribute to its progress as a productive member is through a productive and decent job. Moreover, maintaining the economy as close as possible to full employment will lower the need to develop safety net expenditures for disadvantaged groups. Full employment is the most direct way to achieve the ultimate objective of economic policy, that is, to improve the long-run well-being of all the people in the country, especially the most disadvantaged.

This does not mean that growth is unimportant. It is fundamental for developing countries. For example, there is agreement on the close relationship between growth and structural change (Felipe and Estrada 2008, Felipe et al. 2007), and understanding the dynamics of the latter is essential to comprehending the difficulties in achieving full employment. However, there is evidence that the elasticity of employment with respect to output in many parts of Asia is not particularly high, and in some cases is decreasing (Table 5.1). What does this mean? To cite Felipe and Hasan in discussing the PRC's employment elasticity: "In the 1980s, it took 3 percentage points of growth in output to induce one percentage of increase in employment. By the 1990s, however, it took more than twice as much growth, about 7.8 percentage points, to achieve the same result" (Felipe and Hasan 2006, 113).

The expectation that labor could be released from agriculture and be rapidly absorbed by industry has largely not been realized during the last 15 years. While the share of employment in agriculture has declined in much of developing Asia, labor has found new employment in the services sector (formal or informal) in relatively low-productivity occupations in trade and personal services. In other words, it is not clear today whether a high-growth economy necessarily generates the level and quality of employment that many developing Asian countries need. And without creation of employment it will be very difficult to reduce poverty. If growth is inclusive, it has to reduce poverty; in particular, a faster decline in poverty for a given growth rate should be observed. The empirical evidence (Pasha 2007), however, indicates that, with the exception of East Asia, the degree of inclusiveness of Asian growth is relatively low. This is especially true of South Asia.

Table 5.1   Employment elasticity of growth in Asia

Economy	1980s	1990s
Bangladesh	0.550	0.495
China, People's Republic of	0.330	0.129
Indonesia	0.435	0.379
India	0.384	0.312
Korea, Republic of	0.223	0.225
Malaysia	0.683	0.406
Pakistan	0.406	0.553
Philippines	0.535	0.731
Singapore	0.375	0.711
Thailand	0.315	0.193
Taipei,China	0.242	0.139

Source: Felipe and Hasan (2006, Table 3.6).

The Philippines is a telling example. In 2007, the country registered its highest growth in decades, 7.3%. However, there is a general view that this growth is not benefiting the majority of Filipinos. Obviously, the mere quantity of economic activity—as measured by a common indicator like gross domestic product (GDP) growth—taken alone, "says virtually nothing about whether life for the common Filipino is getting better or worse. It ignores the distribution of income and makes no distinction between workers with top-paying jobs and those who can barely eke out a living. It ignores the fact, for instance, that the record remittances which make economic figures rosy have a heavy social toll in terms of broken families. The booming mining industry which the government touts has environmental costs too which should count for something when you're calculating economic balance" (Herrera 2008).

A preliminary conclusion is that policy makers should, perhaps, reverse the causality between growth and employment, and start thinking that a full employment economy has a lot of virtues, and that this is what will lead to high growth.

Section 5.2 of this chapter frames the full employment problem in the context of the discussion of the main constraint that developing countries face. This is the shortage of capital equipment and productive capacity. Section 5.3 elaborates on the virtues of full employment as an objective of policy making and argues that society makes the government responsible for its achievements. Section 5.4 discusses investment, the most important issue in achieving full employment of the labor force in developing countries. The section also discusses the roles of the public and private sectors. Section 5.5 looks at the role of planning and industrial policy. Section 5.6 concludes.

5.2   What is the main constraint developing countries face?

At the most aggregate level, the fundamental constraint of most developing countries is the unemployment/underemployment of an important segment of the labor force. Caused by the shortage of capital equipment and productive capacity, this is what constrains potential output. This view is consistent with the analyses of the classical authors. According to Kalecki (1944, 43), "if the maximum capacity of equipment is inadequate to absorb the available labor, as will be the case in backward countries, the immediate achievement of full employment is clearly hopeless." It is also in line with modern treatments such as that of Hausmann et al. (2005).

Suppose the quantities produced of two goods are represented by the transformation curve in Figure 5.1. This curve depicts the different combination of goods x and y that the economy can produce using its resources fully. But also suppose that the economy produces the combination of goods represented by point p, inside the curve. It is clear that in this case some of the available resources are not fully utilized (e.g., people are unemployed). Under such circumstances, growth can be achieved through increasing utilization of the country's production capacity. The country has to try to get closer to the transformation curve. This is the typical problem most developing countries suffer from.

This does not mean that developing countries do not suffer from inadequacy of effective demand or from allocative efficiency problems. Indeed they do. Effective demand problems are not entirely absent in developing countries and they can even become binding constraints on production at a fairly advanced stage of industrialization (e.g., PRC, Malaysia, Thailand).[2] Effective demand problems can also be the result of being balance-of-payments-constrained (McCombie and Thirlwall 1994). Certainly, the problem of markets, that is, that due to their small internal demand there will be no outlet for the products of the newly built factories, thus, limiting developing countries' growth rates; or, in other words, it is not just enough to produce a good, but there is need to

---

[2]   Even in these cases one must be careful not to confuse bottlenecks in some markets with a generalized problem of effective demand. The People's Republic of China, for example, still suffers from weak domestic demand, and while there are a few isolated bottlenecks in the economy, in general there are plenty of inputs, mostly labor, available to increase production.

find a market. Hence, industrialization will prove impossible unless it is oriented toward external markets. This problem could also potentially be solved if investment were sufficiently high, as this would generate demand for both investment and consumption goods.[3]

Figure 5.1   Economy with underutilized resources

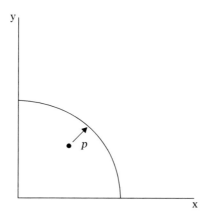

Allocative efficiency problems are also present in developing countries. The combination of goods and services being produced in developing countries is often not the one that maximizes the value of output at the prevailing prices. In Figure 5.2, p is on the transformation curve. The problem is that the combination of goods and services produced may not be the optimal one, in the sense that it may not maximize the value of total output at the prevailing prices. The relative prices of the two goods are shown in line ZZ. Point p' is the combination of the two goods that maximizes the value of goods at these prices. Growth will occur by moving from p to p', thus producing a different combination, even with constant productive capacity. Growth in this case is said to be due to an improvement in allocative efficiency. This is a problem that affects mostly developed countries, and their efforts are directed toward eliminating this inefficiency, e.g., through reforms in product and factor markets. Growth, therefore, might occur, even at a constant productive

---

3   For productive capacity to be fully utilized there must be sufficient effective demand. Classical (and neoclassical) economists believed this to be the case due to their belief in Say's Law (that is, supply creates its own demand) and the neglect of demand factors. Hence, they concluded that the level of production would correspond to productive capacity. The belief in Say's Law ultimately derives from the view that markets function efficiently and competitively so that the prices of all factors and goods speedily adjust to their equilibrium level at which demand equals supply. On these assumptions, all factors of production are fully utilized. Moreover, market forces allocate the resources available at any time in such an optimal manner that the total value of all goods and services produced in an economy is the maximum that can be attained.

capacity, by producing a different combination of goods and services (which, at the prevailing prices, would lead to higher output).[4]

Figure 5.2   Growth due to improvements in allocative efficiency

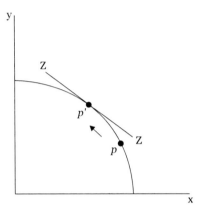

But while this problem is pervasive in most developing countries, it is not as important as the lack of productive capacity that prevents the fuller utilization of resources. Indeed, from the point of view of the national economy as a whole, the major obstacle to the development of many poor countries in developing Asia is the shortage of productive capacity. This is obvious in policy discussions in countries like India, Pakistan, or Philippines, where there are constant references to the "low investment" problem. This constraint prevents the elimination of unemployment and underemployment, even when an increase in demand would make the expansion of output profitable.[5, 6, 7]

---

4   This was the problem of the former Soviet Union, namely, the lack of market signals guiding production decisions (together with the fact that the budget was severely misallocated toward military expenditures).

5   It is important to stress, however, that increasing productive capacity does not guarantee full employment.

6   Certainly, developing countries do have many other candidates for fundamental problems. McCombie and Thirlwall (1994) discuss the importance of the balance of payments constraint. Easterly (2002) emphasizes lack of incentives and argues that good policy must provide the right economic incentives. Rajan and Zingales (2003) stress the importance of financial development. However, especially for purposes of the questions raised in this chapter, the starting point of analysis of developing economies should be their lack of productive capacity.

7   An increase in a country's productive capacity consists of an outward shift in the transformation curve. Many growth theories (e.g., neoclassical model) have concentrated on explanations of growth of this type. These theories assume that the countries efficiently allocate their available resources. The problem is thus how to expand the frontier. The truth is that whether productive capacity is fully utilized or not, for economic growth to be sustained over a long period, there must be an expansion of productive capacity. What will

Developed economies and a number of semi-industrialized economies possess a level of capital equipment that is adequate for the existing labor force. This allows them to generate high labor productivity and, consequently, a high income per capita, provided that capital is fully utilized and is used productively.[8] The problem in many developing countries is different. It is true that their capital equipment, however small, may be underutilized. The issue, however, is that even if equipment were fully utilized, it would not be capable of absorbing the available labor force, leading to low capital-labor ratios—a form of underemployment. In other words, the problem of many developing countries is the deficiency of productive capacity rather than the anomaly of its underutilization (Kalecki 1966). Hence, most developing countries are often below full employment. Most likely, the poorer the country, the more important the problem of lack of productive capacity will be; while the more advanced the country, the more important the problem of lack of effective demand will be. Therefore, for purposes of the discussion here, it is assumed that the binding constraint is the former. From this point of view, the objective of development is to increase productive capacity, and the process of economic development may be described as a generalized process of capital accumulation.

The above analysis implies that the objective of public policy in developing countries should be to increase productive capacity with the purpose of attaining the full employment of the labor force (defined as a situation such that no one who is ready and willing to work for an appropriate wage is without a job). Full employment must be the basic measure of a socially just economic policy. This is not an easy objective and it will be discussed below. But the point to stress is that it will be very difficult (and even almost pointless) for a government that does not place this objective at the top of its agenda and that does not aim at achieving it to set ambitious objectives for reducing poverty and inequality, and for achieving inclusive growth. What this means is that a society must achieve a "…steady expansion of the economy and therewith a steady and reliable increase in the number of workers employed" (Galbraith 1996, 33). This is even more compelling in developing countries. The reason is that the ultimate cause of lack of inclusive growth in developing countries is the nonexistence of adequate employment opportunities (Felipe and

---

make this happen? Most probably this is the result of a dynamic interaction between capital accumulation and technological progress.

[8] One could visualize this chain through the following two identities: (i) income per capita $(Y / P) = (Y / L) \times (L / P)$, where (L / P) is the employment–population ratio; and (ii) labor productivity $(Y / L) = (Y / K) \times (K / K^*) \times (K^* / L)$, where (Y / K) is capital productivity measured in terms of the actual or utilized level of capital (K), (K / K^*) denotes the level of utilization of the existing capital $(K^*$ is the trend of the capital stock), and (K^* / L) is the trend of the capital–labor ratio.

Hasan 2006). It is important to keep in mind that increasing a country's productive capacity is a long-term issue that will take, in most cases, generations (as it took in the developed countries).

5.3 Why full employment and who should be responsible for achieving it?

If achieving full employment should be the main objective of developing countries, it is fair to ask whether policy makers are implementing policies to achieve it. To answer this question it is important to first note that full employment means different things to different people. There are two important issues in this respect. The first one concerns the resource the term refers to. In this chapter, full employment refers to labor. Full employment of plant and equipment is not the problem that developing countries face, as noted above. The second issue regards the level to which "full" refers. During the last 3 decades, the term "full employment", as used in orthodox circles, refers to the "Non-Accelerating Inflation Rate of Unemployment" (NAIRU), one of the most powerful notions in economic policy since the 1970s. This is the level of unemployment that is associated with price stability even if that means that many workers ready and willing to work are unemployed. The basic proposition underlying the NAIRU is that policy makers cannot use deficit spending or an increase in the money supply to reduce unemployment below some "equilibrium" rate, except at the cost of accelerating inflation.[9] This is an important departure from the Keynesian view that inflation poses a problem only when the economy approaches full employment.[10]

Full employment in the framework of the NAIRU obviously places fighting inflation above combating unemployment (as a macroeconomic objective). Indeed, the view that price stability requires maintaining a pool of unemployed means that the fiscal and monetary brakes have to be slammed as soon as economic growth causes unemployment to drop below a certain level. Many policy makers and politicians also seem to

---

[9]   This implies that those who believe that full employment is incompatible with macroeconomic stability (inflation) will be hesitant to implement policies that lead to the full employment of labor.

[10] To be precise, the NAIRU is that level of unemployment where the labor market is said to be in equilibrium. This occurs at the so-called natural rate of unemployment. Here, actual and expected rates of inflation are equal (that is, inflation is fully anticipated). At this point (that is, the natural rate of unemployment), the Phillips curve is vertical and there is no long-run trade-off between unemployment and wage inflation. In the NAIRU view the Phillips curve is only a short-run relationship. Models of inflation targeting, for example, associate full employment with the NAIRU.

have accepted this concept and hold the view that there is a natural rate of unemployment that is invariant to aggregate spending. They argue that this natural rate can only be reduced through supply-side measures, such as deregulation, privatization, welfare reforms (e.g., cutting the minimum wage, eliminating unemployment benefits), or upgrading the skills of workers. For those who view the economy through this lens, supply-side measures are the only way to reduce unemployment. Moreover, when it is close to the level associated with the NAIRU, the monetary authorities must take prompt anti-inflationary action to prevent the economy from overheating. If this is not done, inflation will not only be higher but will accelerate. However, it is also possible to conceive of a situation where low unemployment leads to low inflation (Eisner 1995). Indeed, low unemployment is most likely associated with a more efficient use of resources. Increases in wages derived from low unemployment may encourage the substitution of capital for labor and raise anticipated future productivity, which would lower inflation. With profits high, firms may decide to keep prices low to prevent others from entering the market.

Full employment in the context of the discussion in this chapter, on the other hand, refers to zero involuntary unemployment. It means that no one who is ready and willing to work for an appropriate wage is without a job. This also means zero involuntary part-time employment, a type of underemployment pervasive across the developing world.[11] In the context of a developing country the latter aspect is very important. The reason is that underemployment is a much more serious problem than open unemployment. For this reason, the goal of full employment in developing countries is about reducing unemployment as well as reducing underemployment (Felipe and Hasan 2006).

Felipe and Hasan (2006) distinguish four types of underemployment: (i) time-based, (ii) high-skilled workers forced to take up low-paying jobs, (iii) overstaffing, and (iv) workers carrying out their work with very little capital. Therefore, the objective of full employment must be complemented with that of generating productive employment. Naturally, the question to consider here is the meaning of productive.[12] The objective of policy making must also be to generate decent employment (that is, employment

---

[11]   Ideally, full employment à la Beveridge (1944) comes to mind, that is, full employment holds when there are at least as many unfilled job openings as there are unemployed individuals seeking work. That is, society's responsibility is to create more positions than job seekers, so that firms do the search for workers, not the other way around. Certainly this is very unrealistic given the conditions in developing countries, hence this idea is used simply as a target.

[12]   Is flipping hamburgers (a job created by the private sector) more productive than cleaning streets or taking care of the elderly (jobs created by the public sector)? Does productivity (simply) reflect the technical conditions of production, as in neoclassical economics (that is, a low wage is the reflection of a low marginal productivity)? Or is it socially determined?

that provides living wages, benefits and reasonable job security, and a healthy work environment).

The point of departure of this chapter's arguments is that the free market system does not guarantee full employment in a developing country. Traditional neoclassical theory puts forward a theory of how, under certain conditions, a market economy will tend toward full employment. This occurs through the workings of the price mechanism. However, the assumptions used to derive this result do not apply and the reality, that is, the existence of persistent unemployment and underemployment, is that this theory is not too useful. As Keynes (1936) showed, even with flexible wages an economy has a tendency toward unemployment. To do this, he demolished the classical notion of "supply curve of labor" and showed that there was no reason to expect that an excess of unemployment would drive down real wages. Keynes showed that even with high unemployment, the employed workers would resist reduction of their nominal wages; and even if this opposition failed, the subsequent reduction in nominal wages would bring down prices, leaving real wages unchanged.[13]

The analysis of the "labor market" as if it behaved like the market for oranges is fallacious. For this reason, Galbraith (1997) speaks of a "job structure", that is, "a historically, socially, and politically specific set of status and pay relationships in the economy, within and between firms and across industries" (Galbraith 1997, 15). The elements of a job structure are much more complex than the simple supply and demand characterization of textbook analyses. This means that wages are not determined by the workings of supply and demand, but by a very complex process of comparisons within and across occupations and industries, as well as the qualifications of the worker. Once the notions of supply and demand of labor (as in the market for oranges) are questioned, the idea of the NAIRU crumbles.

Before moving on to the arguments for full employment, two digressions are in order. The first is that inclusive growth is obviously related to inequality. In this sense, inclusive growth essentially means broad-based growth, which implies rising living standards for all socioeconomic levels.[14] There is a wide perception that the more unequal the distribution of income the more dysfunctional a society becomes and the worse its prospects for growth and development in general. Therefore, as excessive inequality is inherently damaging, a society will

---

13   Felipe and McCombie (2008 and 2009) show that empirical estimations of the so-called "labor demand curve", that is, the inverse relationship between the level of employment and the wage rate (used to show since the 1930s that both variables are indeed inversely related) are driven by an accounting identity that forces the inverse relationship. This invalidates the standard interpretation of the labor demand curve and, in particular, renders empirical estimates pointless.

14   For an excellent introduction and review of income distribution in Asia, see Fields (1995).

need to take care of those groups that are left behind.[15] Although from an optimality perspective the acceleration in the incomes of some segments of the population without the rest of the population being worse off would be welfare-enhancing, from a social and moral point of view this is not acceptable (Sen 1999). In chapter 24 of the General Theory, Keynes argued as follows: "...I believe that there is social and psychological justification for significant inequalities of incomes and wealth, but not for such large disparities as exist today" (Keynes 1936, 374). Keynes believed that there are activities that justify the accumulation of wealth. But he clearly argued that "...it is not necessary for the stimulation of these activities and the satisfaction of these proclivities that the game should be played for such high stakes as at the present" (Keynes 1936, 374).

This chapter argues that neither human nature nor the market system is consistent with equality; and that the process of development is inherently not egalitarian. People have different commitments to excelling in the business of making money. This should be acknowledged. And capitalism as an economic system rewards according to one's contribution to the product. Hence, this need not be unfair. However, it can lead to a highly unequal and socially adverse distribution of income, especially when one's talents are unclear or when compensation bears little relationship to the contribution to the product. Excessive inequality can be neither accepted nor intellectually justified; much less argued that it responds to a "moral entitlement" (Galbraith 1996, 61).[16]

If inequality is a fact of life, it is important to understand the forces that drive the distribution of income with a view to designing an adequate policy on income distribution. It is true that some individuals work "harder" than others under the same set of opportunities and they should be rewarded for that. But this is not the main reason underlying the huge income inequalities pervasive in many societies.[17] For example, today, the modern corporate and financial world rewards, in a disproportionate manner, a group of privileged people through astronomical salaries, stock options and, at times, illegal means.

Are the high inequalities observed today across much of developing Asia (ADB 2007a) the result of individual effort (Roemer 2006)? While

---

15 It is somewhat difficult to determine the point at which inequality becomes, technically speaking, "excessive". Rather, it is something that is perceived by the different groups of society. On this see in particular section 2 of ADB (2007a).

16 Akerloff (1982) argued that wage rates that are not a "fair" reflection of a firm's ability to pay will result in poor worker morale and hence, lower productivity.

17 Chapter X in Book I of the Wealth of Nations (Smith 1776) contains a discussion of "inequalities arising from the nature of the employments themselves". Smith discusses five reasons: (i) the agreeableness or disagreeableness of the employments themselves; (ii) the easiness and cheapness, or the difficulty and expence of learning them; (iii) the constancy or inconstancy of employment in them; (iv) the small or great trust which must be reposed in those who exercise them; and (v) the probability or improbability of success in them.

Roemer's arguments do have weight and in some cases effort may be more important than circumstance in explaining inequality (though it is very difficult in general to disentangle both effort and circumstance), it is very difficult to justify inequality in many developing countries as the result of individual effort; much less support the argument with hard empirical evidence. CEOs and highly educated knowledge workers in these countries belong to a narrow aristocracy. Are their high wages and other benefits exclusively the result of returns to education?[18] If this were the case, it would suggest that nobody is to blame for rising inequality as this would be the result of demand and supply at work. The super-high paychecks of some CEOs (whose talent may be dubious) are then easily justified. The way to mitigate inequality would then be to improve the educational system. However, these inequalities, supposedly the result of individual effort, are more the consequence of power relations than of market forces.[19, 20] The point of this discussion is that full employment can be an important tool in the fight against inequality.

The second digression is that diametrically different views about the world, namely those of Karl Marx and Milton Friedman, come to the same conclusion: unemployment is functional to a market (capitalist) economy, the result of class struggle over the distribution of income and political power. Marx called unemployment the reserve army, while Friedman called it the natural rate (Pollin 1998). Both held that high unemployment in capitalist economies occurs when workers have the capacity to use their bargaining power.[21] The difference in their theories lies in how they reached the same conclusion: Friedman (and other orthodox economists) reached it by arguing that workers demand more

---

18   In a recent paper, Dew-Becker and Gordon (2005) have argued that the biggest cause of increased wage inequality in the United States has not been a rise in returns to education and skills, but instead it has been the result of increased payments to superstars such as baseball players, and out-of-control pay rises for chief executives. Think also of how lucky some workers in India are as a result of outsourcing from developed countries. This has automatically increased their salaries.

19   On the other hand, the individual effort and talent of opera singers such as Placido Domingo or Luciano Pavarotti is an exception.

20   For this reason, Galbraith (1996, 63–5) proposes some basic policies to address income inequality: (i) a support system for the poor; (ii) the need to deal with the tendencies of the financial world, e.g., insider trading, speculative behavior; (iii) the need for stockholder and informed public criticism to address the personal income maximization of corporate management; (iv) the removal of tax concessions to the affluent should they exist; and (v) a progressive income tax.

21   Eisner noted that: "I have only half jokingly accused [financial and business circles] of being closet Marxists, wedded to the notion that a "reserve" army of unemployed is necessary for a private-profit economy to function successfully...[E]conomists over the last several decades have most unfortunately offered modern rationalizations in seemingly rigorous theory of this old bit of Marxian dogma. The seeds were planted in the enshrinement of the old Phillips curve" (Eisner 1997).

than they deserve, while for Marx, capitalists use unemployment as a weapon to prevent workers from getting their fair share.[22] But both Marx and Friedman thought that full employment was not attainable.[23]

It is very unfortunate that the goal of creating a full employment economy has been abandoned by many central banks of developed countries, national governments, and international organizations (with the exception of the International Labor Organization), although all of them talk today about the seriousness of the unemployment–underemployment problem.[24] Why have policy makers abandoned this goal? Between World War II and the early 1970s, the so-called Golden Age of Capitalism, governments and central banks in most advanced western nations were committed (in different forms and degrees) to this goal and most central banks were integrated into the government's macroeconomic policy apparatus. For this purpose, they manipulated their spending levels (fiscal policy) and could adjust interest rates and the availability of credit (monetary policy) to maintain a level of aggregate demand close to full employment. Likewise, during this period, there was a tacit accord between the social classes according to which progressive taxation financed an expanding welfare state and a set of social rights, which in turn

---

22   Galbraith has argued that "Unemployment has, in fact, some socially and economically attractive effects: services are well staffed by eager workers forced thereto by the lack of other job opportunity; employed workers, fearing unemployment, may well be more cooperative, even docile, as may their unions. And even more significantly, for most citizens, including those with influential political voice, joblessness is not a threat" (Galbraith 1996).

23   Reminiscent of Marx's ideas concerning the reserve army of labor, Shapiro and Stiglitz (1984) developed a shirking model that stresses the difficulties of monitoring workers' on-the-job effort in order to explain the persistence of involuntary unemployment. In essence, if firms pay more than the going wage, workers will work harder because the cost of being fired for shirking increases. When all firms do this, increased wage levels result in unemployment. On the other hand, employers will not reduce wages to the market clearing level because this will result in lower work effort. Shapiro and Stiglitz conclude that persistent unemployment may actually be required in a market economy as a "worker discipline device." It is worth noting, though, that Shapiro and Stiglitz's (1984) argument is not identical to Marx's. Marx argued that the reserve army is the result of rising labor intensity via mechanization. This exerts downward pressure on the wage rate. However, in Shapiro and Stiglitz's model, unemployment is supposedly generated by the firm's need to raise wage rates above the market clearing level to induce workers not to shirk.

24   Ironically, one of the roles envisaged for the International Monetary Fund at its foundation in 1944 was to help finance the external gap (that is, trade deficit) when the market does not close it, so as to guarantee that full employment policies can be pursued. Developing countries do not have an open commitment to full employment. At most, they acknowledge the employment problem. As an example, Felipe and Hasan (2006, 497, endnote 44) indicate that the main objective of the central bank of the Philippines, as stated by the central bank itself, is to ensure price stability. Objectives such as balanced and sustained growth and employment are secondary to the main objective. And these other objectives have not quantified targets.

translated into a relatively low degree of social confrontation.[25] During a large part of this period, wages increased hand in hand with productivity and full employment and expanding social benefits gave workers the upper hand in wage bargaining, while the rapid pace of investment in new technologies provided a countervailing force that kept inflation in check. This period was marked by the willingness of governments to maintain levels of aggregate demand that would create enough jobs to meet the preferences of the labor force.

Since the late 1960s, this state of affairs started to change and, in the mid-1970s, the failure of the OECD economies to contain inflation following the oil shocks led to the downfall of full employment as an objective, as governments became convinced that low unemployment and low inflation were incompatible. As a consequence, intellectual support for these policies vanished and the use of budget deficits to maintain full employment started being openly opposed. Friedman's notion of the natural rate of unemployment was instrumental in this change of focus. The result was a battle that led to the victory over inflation but at the cost of sluggish growth, high unemployment, and income inequality in many parts of the world.

Despite this state of affairs, there are powerful reasons today to argue the case for full employment, if key institutions in developing countries, as well as multilateral lending institutions, are serious about reducing poverty, making growth inclusive, and achieving the Millennium Development Goals. First and foremost, an economy running at full employment creates a high level of overall purchasing or spending power. This leads to more buoyant markets, businesses, investment, and employment. A full employment economy will provide opportunity for everyone.

Second, an economy operating at full employment has the capacity to deliver great individual and social benefits. The economic and social costs of unemployment and underemployment are huge. It causes not only direct economic costs (e.g., loss of potential output and income, lower tax revenues due to a lower tax base, deterioration of labor skills and productivity) but also poverty, misery, malnutrition, and social injustice

---

25 Kalecki (1943) argued, in the context of the 1930s and 1940s in Europe, that there were two solutions to the unemployment problem. One was the authoritarian solution in the form of fascism, which replaces the discipline of unemployment by the direct repression of the working class by force. The other was the democratic solution (which he favored), in which trade unions cooperate with employers in return for income redistribution and other egalitarian measures. This type of cooperation became widespread in Northern Europe after World War II. Sweden, for example, implemented policies that kept the economy close to full employment with low inflation and provided decent wages between 1951 and 2000. The key to it was the development of a system based on cooperation among different groups. In the absence of this cooperation, employers and the financial sector will turn against full employment policies.

(Rawls 1971, Sen 1999).[26] Persistent unemployment and underemployment act as a form of social exclusion that violates basic concepts of membership and citizenship, and thus they do not allow inclusive growth.

Third, employment is a right, and full employment as an objective of economic policy is found in the International Covenant on Economic, Social and Cultural Rights, the International Covenant on Civil and Political Rights, the International Labor Organization Conventions, the Charter of the United Nations (Article 55 and 56), and in the UN Universal Declaration of Human Rights (Article 23). In the United States, high employment is a mandate of the Federal Reserve. The Humphrey-Hawkins Full Employment and Balanced Growth Act of 1978 makes high employment, balanced growth, and price stability specific policy goals.[27]

Fourth, since 2006, decent work is a target of the first Millennium Development Goal, namely, to eradicate extreme poverty and hunger.

Fifth, full employment in the developing world could play a crucial role, as it would contribute to ensuring a fair degree of political stability as the levels of consumption of large segments of the population would be higher than under conditions of unemployment. Moreover, peace and prosperity in the developed world also depend on the well-being of the people in the developing world. And finally, full employment should be an ethical imperative in today's world.

It is important to stress that even if full employment could never be achieved due to the failure of the market mechanism to attain it, this should not be a justification not to pursue it by other means, e.g., government involvement and commitment to it.[28]

The benefits of full employment outweigh the costs of its achievement. It benefits everyone, including—and contrary to Marx—capitalists. These may end up getting a smaller share (in terms of percentage) of the pie, but the size of the pie will possibly be growing faster than with significant levels of unemployment. Therefore, it is more rational to argue that developing countries cannot afford unemployment and underemployment, rather

---

[26] As Stiglitz et al. (2006, 42) put it vividly: "For conservatives who believe that the unemployed have chosen not to work, the mystery of the unemployed's profound unhappiness is a matter for psychologists more than economists."

[27] The Employment Act of 1946 commits the United States to the goal of "maximum employment, production and purchasing power". Most likely, although the term was not used, it meant "full employment." The Humphrey-Hawkins Act refers, on the other hand, to "high" employment, not to "full". In practice, the United States government has never adopted policies that guarantee the latter outcome. Rather, it has adopted a variety of "supply-side" policies and some "demand-side" policies in the hope that markets would operate at a sufficiently high level to ensure high employment. Since the market has not done this, the government has been forced to supplement these policies with various "welfare" programs.

[28] It is often argued that Keynesian economics has little to offer developing countries in terms of economic policy. This is utterly incorrect. See Thirlwall (1987).

than to suppose that they cannot afford full employment. In the words of Paul Krugman: "An unsold commodity is a nuisance, an unemployed worker a tragedy; it is terribly unjust that such tragedies are created every day by new technologies, changing tastes, and the ever-shifting flows of world trade" (Krugman 1999, 15).[29] Expressing a similar sentiment, Alan Blinder stated that "...high unemployment represents a waste of resources so colossal that no one truly interested in efficiency can be complacent about it. It is both ironic and tragic that, in searching out ways to improve economic efficiency, we seem to have ignored the biggest inefficiency of them all" (Blinder 1987, 33). For this reason, full employment must be the natural point of reference for economic policy and for evaluating a government's performance.[30]

Finally, if full, as well as productive and decent employment is a desirable state of the economy (so that it must be the basic measure of a just society and the goal of economic policy), one has to ask who should be responsible for achieving it and for keeping the economy as close as possible to it. Unemployment and underemployment may be the result of skills mismatch or of problems with the individuals who are unemployed, in which case the solution might be training. This is a widely held view of the causes of unemployment and underemployment. These tend to be viewed as individual problems. Policies to solve them directly target those affected by it. But if the problem is a shortage of jobs because the economy does not generate employment for all those in the labor force and willing to work, that is, a systemic failure of the aggregate economy to create enough jobs, then training will not do much.

In a market economy the private sector must be the generator of wealth and employment. To do this, the private sector must operate in an enabling environment, which the government must provide. However, this role of the private sector is compatible with the existence of significant involuntary unemployment and underemployment.

Who is, therefore, ultimately responsible for the achievement of full, productive and decent employment? Unfortunately, society makes the government responsible. The reality is that if at the end of the year unemployment has increased in a country, it is the government, not the private sector that is blamed for it. And indeed, many governments make promises about reductions in unemployment and employment creation

---

29   The former Soviet republics of Central Asia present a peculiar case. After the collapse of the Soviet Union, most of these republics went into recession and the industrial sector collapsed, causing massive unemployment. One way to cope with it was a shift of many workers to the agricultural and service sectors. The experience of these countries cannot be taken as evidence that the pursuit of full employment is the "wrong" policy. Full employment was not what caused their collapse.

30   Pollin (1998) tells the story of a visit to Bolivia in 1990. There, he was told that the country did not suffer from any employment problem: people begging, shining shoes, or hawking in the streets were indeed employed.

during election campaigns (while they do not create these jobs). For these reasons, it is of paramount importance that private and public sectors coordinate their actions and understand each other's role in employment generation (and elimination of unemployment).

5.4 What is the role of investment in delivering full employment?

Achieving full employment requires the synchronization of policies on many fronts: fiscal, monetary, exchange rate, etc. But following the arguments in Section 5.2, developing countries' main problem is the unemployment of the labor force. This is caused by a shortage of capital equipment. This section discusses the role of investment, while the next, that of planning and industrial policy.

Kalecki (1944) distinguished three ways to achieve and maintain full employment: (i) by government spending on public investment (e.g., schools, hospitals, highways, etc.) or on subsidies to mass consumption (e.g., family allowances, reduction of indirect taxation, subsidies to keep down the prices of necessities, etc.); (ii) by stimulating private investment (e.g., through a reduction in the rate of interest, lowering of income tax, or other measures assisting private investment); and (iii) by redistributing income from higher- to lower-income classes. Kalecki favored the first and third methods.

A dynamic economy will need increases in the growth rate of the capital stock (that is, capital accumulation) in the form of, among others, investment in public transportation and in public utilities. Increases in the growth rate of the capital stock can be achieved in two ways. The first one is to increase the productivity with which capital is used (see Section 5.2). This route, however, is very difficult. In fact, the empirical evidence shows that capital productivity tends to decline in the long run (Foley and Marquetti 1999, Foley and Michl 1999, Marquetti 2003, Felipe et al. 2008). It seems that development entails increases in labor productivity combined with decreases in capital productivity.

The second mechanism to increase the growth rate of the capital stock is to increase the investment-to-output ratio. This is the basis for a policy of industrialization, and is the one followed by the successful East and Southeast Asian economies (see, for example, Lau 1990 on the Republic of Korea [Korea] and Taipei,China), and the PRC (see Wang and Li 1995). The importance of investment for development is crucial. There is no lack of candidate projects: schools, hospitals, transportation, power, and telecommunications, are all underserved in much of developing Asia. This is because investment plays a dual role. On one hand, investment expenditures are a source of demand when they are incurred. On the other, investment increases the productive capacity of the economy in the long run. This second role is the one to be considered here.[31]

How did the successful Asian countries increase their investment-to-GDP ratios? To see this, it is worth considering the relationship between the labor share, real wage rates, and labor productivity.[32] In the context of full employment, if there is a rise in labor productivity, and if the labor share is approximately constant, real wages will have to increase. But it is also possible that the labor share decreases and yet workers see their real wages increase. This will happen if productivity increases quickly but such increases are not passed on to wages one-to-one (but these nevertheless increase quickly too). Under these circumstances wages will increase by a lesser amount than labor productivity and thus the labor share will decrease.[33] Although workers see their share in total income decrease, they will tolerate the situation. This was possible in many Asian countries because there was little militancy in the labor force, because of a substantial labor surplus in the economy, and because of repression by state agencies.[34]

While some Asian countries made huge effort to increase investment (much of it into the manufacturing sector), it is important to also understand that these countries were initially somewhat lucky. In the late 1960s, the developed world started experiencing important internal changes that led them to relocate entire industries or particular industrial processes to the Third World. One important reason was the

---

31   Kalecki (1939, 148–9) in his discussion of "what causes periodical crises?" argued that investment is both an expenditure and an addition to capital accumulation. The tragedy of investment is that it causes crises because it is useful. The basic contradiction underlying investment lies in the different time horizon of the effects of investments on demand and on capacity; that is, the fact that while the impact of the former is exhausted in a short time, the one on capacity lasts longer.

32   Algebraically, the relationship is as follows:
$s^l = \frac{W_n}{Y_n} = \frac{w_n \times L}{Y_n} = \frac{(w_n/P_w) \times L}{(Y_n / P_y)} \times \frac{P_w}{P_y} = \frac{w_r \times L}{Y_r} \times \frac{P_w}{P_y}$, where the subscript n denotes nominal values and the subscript r denotes real values. W is the overall wage bill, Y is output (hence s^l is labor's share), w is the wage rate, L is employment, and (P_w/P_y) is the ratio of the wage-to-output deflators.

33   From the definition of the labor share, the growth rate of the labor share is, $\hat{s}^l = \hat{w}_r - \hat{q} + (\hat{P}_w - \hat{P}_y)$ where the symbol ^ denotes growth rate, and q is labor productivity (i.e., Y_r/L). If $\hat{q} > \hat{w}_r$ (assuming the growth of the deflators is approximately similar), $\hat{s}^l < 0$ and the labor share will decline. In practice, the labor share cannot decline below a certain value. This is because, first, labor unions would not accept a constantly dwindling share in total output. Second, as countries develop and the service sector dominates the economy, productivity increases become smaller, which allows smaller increases in real wages. At this point, workers become much more conscious of their wage rate increases and of shifts in the labor share.

34   For example, in the Republic of Korea, real wages in the manufacturing industry rose rapidly through the 1960s and 1970s (see Hamilton 1986 and Deyo 1987).

increase in wages in the advanced economies, resulting from the fact that the social contract established after World War II favored labor. At the same time, rapid technological progress led to the development of highly standardized manufacturing processes. This made it possible to transfer particular stages of production, namely, the labor-intensive processes that required low-skilled workers. What options did companies in the developed world have? Only two: Latin America and East and Southeast Asia. However, Latin America was ruled out for being much more politically unstable. This left only Asia. Thus, in the late 1960s, a number of electronics firms, including Hewlett-Packard, Texas Instruments and others, built factories in Singapore to assemble components, particularly semiconductors. This process was extended to Malaysia, Philippines, and Thailand.

But, what were the internal conditions that enabled capitalist Southeast Asia to respond to the opportunities created by restructuring in the industrial core? Brown (1997, 262) argues that "one crucial condition... was the presence of a copious supply of cheap, largely unskilled, and essentially docile labour". To this one must add the role of women, whose "dexterous fingers and patient temperament fitted them for such repetitive, minutely detailed tasks as electronic components assembly or garment production" (Brown 1997, 262–3);[35] and weak labor unions. These same factors are today important components of what is referred to as "the PRC's competitiveness".

A second internal condition was that Southeast Asia was resource-rich (except Singapore). This gave it an important advantage in the production of manufactures such as wood products, processed foods, cement, chemical fertilizer, and paper, all of which involve the intensive use of local inputs. Finally, a third condition is that these countries possessed an acceptable level of communication, commercial, and administrative infrastructure.

However, a dose of luck and these internal conditions do not entirely explain East and Southeast Asia's success. The key lies in the social contract implemented in many countries, and in the political pressure derived from the communist threat (Rodriguez 2005). Underlying these, there was a series of complex structures of political, economic, and bureaucratic interests that favored the accumulation of capital.

Naturally, the counterpart of the decrease in the labor share was the increase in the capital share. A good deal of evidence suggests that capital accumulation for industrialization is largely financed by profits in the form of retentions, rather than by household savings (Akyüz and Gore 1996). Indeed, according to Arthur Lewis (1954, 157): "...the major

---

[35] Today, much foreign manufacturing in the PRC is assembly activity and the workforce is disproportionately female and recruited from rural areas. The high female literacy rate has given the PRC a crucial advantage in attracting foreign investment in manufacturing vis-à-vis India.

source of savings is profits, and if we find that savings are increasing as a proportion of the national income, we may take it for granted that this is because the share of profits in the national income is increasing." Over the long run, a high rate of retained profits tends to be associated with a high rate of corporate investment. Using data for 30 developing countries for the 1980s, Ros (2000, 79–83) showed that there is a strong relationship between a high savings rate, a high share of manufacturing output in GDP, and a high profit share in manufacturing value added in East Asia.[36, 37]

It is important to emphasize a key point about this strategy of industrialization (that is, the increase in the investment-output ratio). This is that real wages should not fall in the process. This requires both a high rate of labor productivity and that the prices of essential consumer goods be stable, which implies that their supply must rise in step with their demand. Achieving this will also require that investment in the different sectors of the economy, in particular in the capital and consumer goods sectors, be undertaken in the "right" proportions. And it will also necessitate the adjustment of the rate of growth of employment to the limit set by the increase in food supply and articles of mass consumption in general. Certainly this is not easy.

Moreover, maintaining the purchasing power of wages is also important because declines in real wages limit the expansion of the market for mass consumption articles. However, given the importance of the objective of full employment as the basic measure of a socially equitable economic policy, it may appear that the constraint that real wages do not decrease could pose a problem. For this reason, the lower acceptable limit for society should be that real wages be stable for the better-off workers and that wage rates of the bottom workers increase.

To be more precise, inclusive growth should favor policies that encourage faster wage growth for low-paying jobs than for highly paid work. This means that, at the low end, wage growth will exceed productivity growth, while at the high end, productivity growth will exceed wage growth. This proposal is consistent with the idea of broad-based growth, which should translate into development efforts directed toward raising the standard of living of those at the bottom. This policy implies that, most likely, prices will grow in the low-wage sector as costs rise. Preventing inflation will require some constraint on prices and wages in high-wage sectors (see Kalecki 1966; Minsky 1965, 1968, and 1973).

What is the impact of this development strategy on consumption? Given that workers have a high propensity to consume, the decrease in the labor share will affect overall consumption. How should policy

---

[36]   This is how the successful East Asian countries addressed the savings constraint. The foreign exchange constraint was addressed by following the export-led growth model.

[37]   See Morgan Stanley's surveys on the PRC and India (Ahya et al. 2004 and 2006).

makers proceed, that is, what consumption categories should be reduced? In order to accomplish this in a "fair manner", policy makers would have to restrain the consumption of non-essentials (something that is politically very difficult). For this, appropriate taxes should be imposed. In these circumstances, an acceleration of income (induced by the acceleration of investment) will be accompanied by an increase in the supply of necessities adequate to prevent inflationary pressures. Thus, a higher share of investment in output will be offset by a decline in the share of non-essential consumption via direct and indirect taxation of the upper classes.

At what point is the share of investment too high and that of consumption too low? This is difficult to ascertain, but there will be signals (Felipe et al. 2008). Profitability may decrease precipitously leading the economy into a profitability slump. On the other hand, if authorities are not careful and the share of consumption of essential goods goes down, the problem might be underconsumption.

There are, however, three important potential obstacles to increasing investment (Kalecki 1966). First, as noted above, in a market economy the private sector is the generator of wealth. However, in many developing countries, private investment may not collaborate due to, for example, low profitability, large uncertainty, high cost of investment, or because the full level of firms' savings out of profits is not reinvested.[38]

One possibility is, of course, to identify and relax the binding constraint on private investment. But perhaps doing this is not easy and may not be enough to increase investment to the necessary levels. For this reason, a policy of stimulating exclusively private investment may not be satisfactory. It is clear that, in these circumstances, the government will have to step in to reach the desired level of investment.

The role of government investment is not, it must be stressed, to replace or crowd out private investment, but to complement it due to the latter's insufficiency. Indeed, the most effective and egalitarian way to achieve full employment is through a program of public investments targeted carefully at location-specific high employment activities.

For this reason, it will be the government's responsibility to provide a large volume of public sector investment, e.g., in infrastructure. This, it must be stressed, is not to deprive the private sector of any active role in the economy—quite the opposite. The private sector has to invest in whatever activities it finds profitable. This is the way a market economy will prosper, although this does not guarantee the full employment of the labor force.

---

[38] The reasons underlying this can be analyzed in terms of the growth diagnostics approach (Hausmann et al. 2005).

Indeed, in many developing countries the private sector cannot be relied upon to undertake the required volume, and appropriate structure, of investment (think, for example, of Afghanistan).[39] The reason is that nobody can force this sector to invest the required volume and in the areas that a developing country may need. Moreover, in some developing countries the business class does not play, on a large scale, the role of dynamic entrepreneur that it should (contrary to what occurred in today's developed countries at the time they underwent deep structural changes), driven by "animal spirits" (that is, a spontaneous urge to action and willingness to take risks), using the terminology of Keynes (1936).

In some cases it is due to a poor investment climate (e.g., difficulties in opening a new business), the result of government-imposed constraints; in other cases, the oligopolistic characteristics of some sectors of the economy favor some privileged groups that enjoy rents. These groups lobby to perpetuate this situation. The problem is neither the high cost of investment nor low returns (in the growth diagnostics terminology of Hausmann et al. 2005) but the desire to maintain a situation of privilege. Investment takes place in the areas that these groups control and at the pace that suits them. At some point, and for strategic reasons, they might be unwilling to expand capital expenditures simply because doing so favors their objectives.

In many developing countries, the capacity for entrepreneurship that the private sector has must be nurtured and developed, since the driving force in a capitalist economy is the decision to invest and the rate of capital accumulation (and the demand for labor depends on it). But the objective of the private sector is not the maximization of employment and hence it *cannot* be, and should not be, made responsible for the achievement of full employment. Although some may not like it, this requires some planning (see next section).

Stimulation of private investment (the second of Kalecki's methods to achieve full employment) through, for example, reductions in interest and/or tax rates or through subsidies to private investment, will not deliver full employment. If the economy is already in a boom, measures to stimulate investment further will be pointless. And in a slump some of these measures may not work, e.g., reductions in interest rates may be ineffective due to the existence of excess capacity. Private investment depends, especially in developing countries, on expectations and political stability. Moreover, a "one-time" reduction in interest or tax rates does not eliminate a downturn (business cycle). Policy makers would have to

---

[39]   Of course, the private sector may bring in crucial expertise to countries like Afghanistan. Also, the public sector is poorly run and dysfunctional. This calls for even more planning and coordination between private and public sectors.

lower them successively and continuously to keep the investment rate going. Moreover, Vickrey (1993 and 1997) argued that firms' savings out of profits represent income not spent. These savings cause the income of others to fall (through the multiplier effect). This is because savings not immediately transformed into capital simply "vanish" and lead to reduced income.

Therefore, private sector investment is the mechanism through which the sector's profits are recycled into the income stream (that is, the mechanism through which non-spending is transformed into spending). If a country's total surplus were reinvested, the economy would get closer to the achievement of full employment. But when the total full employment level of firms' savings is not recycled into spending by private investment (in fact, Vickrey believed that the private sector would not recycle the full employment level of its savings), some of the full employment level of output will not be justified by actual sales, that is, part of the product will not be sold and goods will accumulate in stock. This will lead to reductions in production and employment. Unemployment is, therefore, the evidence of this gap (that is, savings that are "kept idle" and not put to productive investment). Income (the equilibrating variable, and not interest rates) will fall and consequently savings will also decline until they are brought back to match the below full employment level of private investment. For Vickrey there is only one solution to closing this gap and bringing the economy to full employment: government deficits.

However, achievement of the full employment of labor through a large volume of public investment faces serious political obstacles. Kalecki (1943, 138) argued that "The assumption that a Government will maintain full employment in a capitalist economy if it only knows how to do it is fallacious". He gave three "reasons for the opposition of the 'industrial leaders' to full employment achieved by Government spending" (Kalecki 1943, 139): (i) the opposition against government spending based on a budget deficit and the dislike of government interference in the problems of employment; (ii) the opposition against this spending being directed toward public investment (or toward subsidizing consumption, for example through subsidies to keep down the prices of necessities), except when it is confined to objectives that do not compete with private investment, that is, for construction of hospitals, schools, highways, etc. It is interesting, however, that even these areas are contested today as domains of the private sector, and some argue that public investment crowds out private investment on the grounds that the former lowers the real rate of return of the latter (e.g., Tatom 2006); and (iii) the opposition against maintaining full employment as this may give workers a very strong and dangerous position at the bargaining table (on this see also Shapiro and Stiglitz

1984). No wonder Kalecki (1943, 138) asked: "...why do not they [businessmen] accept gladly the 'synthetic' boom which the Government is able to offer them?"[40]

Kalecki's (1966) second potential obstacle to increasing investment is that the investment goods sector (e.g., the construction sector) may be already running at close to or full capacity and thus it may not be possible to increase its output.

The third and final obstacle is that the country may run into the problem of how to secure an adequate supply of necessities to cover the demand resulting from the increase in employment. This increased demand will induce inflationary pressures as the supply of necessities (especially food) is limited.[41] This situation has an additional implication. Suppose that the economy is capable of increasing investment. This will lead to more employment and to a higher total nominal wage bill. However, the overall wage bill in real terms will remain unchanged as a result of the increase in the price level. What is the implication? That although the level of employment has increased (certainly a positive outcome), the real wage rate (that is, wage per worker) will have declined, and this is an unfair way of financing the acceleration in growth. The conclusion is that the increase in investment under conditions of an inelastic supply of food will cause both a fall in the real wage and the acceleration in prices. For this reason, it is important to expand food production in parallel to industrial development. Investment in public transportation and public utilities should be accompanied by measures to expand agricultural production, such as land reform and easy credit to farmers.

This discussion means that inclusive growth cannot throw the costs of capital formation on the wage earners and, in general, on the poor. In a command economy investment is funded out of the incomes of state institutions and not out of the savings of private individuals (Dobb 1959); but in countries that have followed the capitalist path of development (that is, where savings and investment decisions are distinct), who bears the cost of capital accumulation is an important political economy question that needs to be answered. In the same way that governments must be accountable for their actions, policies, goals, and ultimately for their performance and capacity to deliver, the domestic upper and business class of developing countries, in many cases a relatively small group

---

[40]   It is worth considering the grounds underlying these arguments, given that higher output and employment benefit both workers and firms, as profits rise. Moreover, a policy of full employment based on loan-financed government spending does not affect profits as it does not require additional taxes. Despite that Kalecki wrote this article more than six decades ago, the argument is still valid and relevant today. One just has to read some newspapers or listen to the business segment of the news.

[41]   Of course, inflation may not show up if entrepreneurs are unwilling to expand their capital expenditures.

of individuals and families, must also be made ethically and politically responsible for the development of the country.[42] Domestic investment often depends on the decisions of a reduced group of businessmen. As long as private investment cannot be "enforced", the public sector will have to cover the gap up to full employment. In many developing countries, however, the tax collection system is not strictly enforceable, tax evasion is rampant, and the implementation of progressive financial reforms is an uphill battle.[43] Under these circumstances, the funds for investment are hard to extract. Both agriculture and manufacturing fail to develop efficiently and growth of total output is swallowed up in growing consumption.

Two final comments on investment are needed. First, Keynes (1936, chapter 24) argued that since it is investment that causes saving (and not the other way around, as in classical theory), and investment is promoted by a low interest rate, it is important to maintain low interest rates. However, he continued, since it is unlikely that banking policy will be sufficient by itself to determine an optimum rate of investment, he argued that a "somewhat comprehensive socialization of investment will prove the only means of securing an approximation to full employment; though this need not exclude all manner of compromises and of devices by which public authority will co-operate with private initiative. But beyond this no obvious case is made out for a system of State Socialism which would embrace most of the economic life of the community" (Keynes 1936, 378).

Second, the role of investment in development is not well understood, and even agreed upon, by economists. While the proposition that investment is a key variable for growth seems obvious, the empirical evidence is not conclusive. See, for example, Easterly (2002, 39–42) or Oulton and O'Mahony (1994), who claim that capital does not play any special role. On the other hand, Prichett (2003, 217–21) claims that "except for the causality issue, the role of physical investment in growth is well understood". On the issue of causality, Blomstrom et al. (1996) used causality tests and found that a faster rate of GDP growth causes a higher investment–output ratio and not vice versa. If this is true, the implication is that investment is not a key determining exogenous variable in the growth process. Once growth is

---

42 Haque (2006) refers to 22 controlling families in Pakistan. See Coronel et al. (2004) for an in-depth analysis of how a group of wealthy families dominates politics in the Philippines.

43 One such case is the Philippines, where collecting direct taxes is a serious problem. In 2005, the Philippine government extended the value-added tax (VAT) to previously exempt energy products. And in 2006 it raised the VAT rate on all taxable products (including energy) from 10% to 12%. Given that most energy is consumed by the wealthier groups, and because the government used part of the proceeds from VAT to reduce taxes on kerosene and to increase spending on infrastructure and social services, the negative effects on the poor were somewhat reduced. Nevertheless, VAT is not a progressive tax and the big loophole is in direct taxation.

under way, the resulting profits will cause the investment rate to increase in a Keynesian fashion. As Kaldor (1970) pointed out, Henry Ford did not build up his automobile business from high initial savings, but from the profits his factory generated. Moreover, as argued by Hausmann et al. (2005), investment matters for purposes of igniting growth. However, if the country's objective is sustaining growth, then the problem is one of developing institutions. Felipe and Usui (2008) elaborate on the issue and show that, historically, higher growth has been possible in many cases without a high investment-output ratio; and that a higher investment-output ratio does not lead systematically to higher growth.

Likewise, Lewis (2004) has criticized the view that capital accumulation is the key to growth and development, as well as the public debate around the prescription that what poor countries need is more capital. He makes two crucial points: (i) capital does not automatically increase labor productivity; and (ii) what capital does is to increase the capacity for growth. This means that developing countries could increase their performance dramatically without any significant increase in capital. To become rich, however, they need additional capital. The problem in most developing countries lies in the low efficiency with which the existing capital is used. To see this, one can write the growth rate of the capital stock as the product of the investment-output ratio and capital productivity.[44] This means that capital accumulation depends on two factors: one is the amount of investment (as a share of output), and the other one is the productivity with which this investment is used. Lewis seems to reverse the role of capital in development with respect to Hausmann et al. (2005): in the short run, developing countries do not need more capital; what they need is to use more efficiently the capital they have. To achieve this, reform of the rules and regulations governing competition is the key. It is in the long run, on the other hand, that developing countries will need more capital.

Lewis' point is that developing countries' performance could improve substantially by improving the productivity of capital. Lewis insists that "improving the rules and regulations governing competition would improve not only labor productivity *but also capital productivity*" (Lewis 2004, 251; emphasis added).[45] Naturally, in the long run, and in order to become a rich country, developing countries with spare labor capacity (that is, labor surplus), need to build offices and manufacturing plants where these workers can work. That is, countries need to increase the capacity to produce goods and services. In his own words: "Of course, the total capital required to increase capacity depends on the efficiency with which the capital is employed" (Lewis 2004, 250).

---

[44] Algebraically: $\hat{K}=(\Delta K/K)=(I/K)=(I/Y)\times(Y/K)$, where $\hat{K}$ is the growth rate of the capital stock, (I/Y) is the investment share, and (Y/K) denotes capital productivity.

[45] Section 5.4 argues that the empirical evidence shows that capital productivity tends to decline as countries develop.

The increase in private consumption can be a powerful complementary mechanism to achieve full employment. As Kalecki (1944) argued, public and private investment should be carried out only to the extent to which they are considered useful. If the effective demand that they generate fails to provide full employment, then the gap should be filled by increasing consumption and not by undertaking further investment, which most likely will be unproductive. This (that is, promoting consumption) is the advice that some Asian countries (e.g., PRC, Malaysia, Thailand) are receiving today, that is, to shift their growth strategy from investment-driven (and export-driven) to domestic demand-led growth by activating private consumption through, for example, decreases in indirect taxation, opening markets to induce price competition, or by developing the credit card market. As argued above, a number of East and Southeast Asian countries relied on investment for decades and this strategy paid off. Now, the argument goes, it is about time to shift strategy. There are many other countries in the region, however, that still would benefit considerably from an increase in investment (this is a constant issue in countries like India, Pakistan, or Philippines), not for the case of generating effective demand, but to accelerate expansion of productive capacity indispensable for the rapid growth of output.

In practice, governments should pursue a sensible combination of public and private investment, and subsidies to consumption. The private sector should invest in all those activities that it considers profitable;[46] the public sector should invest in all those areas that are needed for the development of the country (and that help the private sector); and the gap to full employment (if there is still any) should be covered by higher consumption. How is the government's spending program to be split? This is a matter of social priorities, and the government will have to decide whether in a given year it builds more schools or provides more milk for children.

Finally, what role can income redistribution (Kalecki's third method) play in the pursuit of full employment? The idea is that when income is redistributed from the higher to the lower income earners total consumption will increase, as the latter group has a higher propensity to consume. One possible policy would be to increase the income tax on the rich (and use it to subsidize private consumption) and simultaneously decrease indirect taxation on necessities consumed by the poor. The problem with this type of policy is that governments have to watch the overall impact on private investment.

---

[46] One option being considered today is the so-called public–private partnership (PPP) as a mechanism to develop physical infrastructure. PPPs act as an alternative to traditional public sector finance—freeing up resources and accelerating investment programs. They have the advantage of reducing the fear of deficits and encouraging private participation.

5.5   Planning and industrial policy

One important implication of the discussion in the previous section is that the strategy of full employment based on stepping up investment requires "planning", a term that, unfortunately, has acquired a bad name (see Easterly 2006), although it is done everywhere. Indeed, most, if not all, medium and long-term term development plans of both developed and developing countries specify the amount of total (public) investment as well as the allocation across sectors.[47] For example, the Ninth Malaysia Plan (2006–10) and the Third Industrial Master Plan (2006–20) contain policies to push Malaysian industry up the value chain and have well defined targets in terms of growth rates and sectors' shares in output. Through the Malaysian Industrial Development Authority (MIDA), the government executes policies and initiatives intended to shape an industrial base to face the future challenges of the country. MIDA assumes the key roles of planning, coordinating and promoting the growth of industries in the manufacturing sector.

A balanced development path requires coherent planning not only of the forthcoming volume of investment, but also of the composition of investment (sectors and types of goods), which must be directed purposefully toward the breaking of bottlenecks in supply. However, given that resources are scarce, perhaps "planners" ought to think, and surely many do, not in terms of balanced growth but in terms of unbalanced growth à la Hirschman (1958), that is, by selecting the projects that make the greatest contribution to development.

Planning does not mean establishing a command economy, or even a developmental state, but the development of a partnership between public and private sectors to coordinate their activities in a way that complement each other (Hausmann and Rodrik 2006). Planning the development of a country is necessary because development is a long-term process. This consists in the introduction of new industries, and in this process there are substantial time lags between the decisions to build new facilities and the output that they produce.

Second, as discussed above, private investment may not go into all areas of the economy. The private sector will direct investment to the areas where it expects its venture will be profitable (and this is how it should be) and not necessarily to where a developing country needs capital the most. This argument applies to private foreign investment as well. Will it go into education and health? What about the objectives of employment and job creation? The government will therefore have to step in. Full employment is the government's responsibility. The private sector alone

---

[47]   And certainly so do the so-called "country strategy programs" prepared by the development institutions that lend to the developing countries.

cannot be responsible for the achievement of full employment simply because, as argued in Section 5.3, it is not its responsibility. Private investors are not driven by concerns for social well-being. What must be accepted with regard to the general level of employment and output is that there is no invisible hand channeling self-interest into some social optimum. Surely growth in a market economy has to be driven by a dynamic private sector. But the role of the government cannot be reduced to that of mere support to private sector activities, especially when achievement of full employment as a means to reduce poverty is at stake. Government has two key roles in a developing economy. First, it has to allow the operation of the free market dynamics whereby the government reduces its interference through deregulation. And second, it has to intervene actively in selected areas, the most important being the creation of physical infrastructure and the provision of a platform to enable the workforce to participate in productive activities.[48]

Third, and related to the previous point, it will be necessary to coordinate with the private sector to avoid mismatches, bottlenecks, and waste of scarce resources.

Fourth, planning is necessary because only when the structure of investment across sectors and types of goods has been determined will the country be able to decide the choice of technique of production—a key issue for economies with considerable labor surpluses. Some sectors of the economy, by their own nature, require capital-intensive techniques. These will absorb large shares of investment but will not absorb too much labor. This is also the case of much foreign investment, as it embodies techniques with relatively high capital-labor ratios. What can developing countries do? A solution could be to favor labor-intensive techniques that absorb the labor surplus in areas such as public investments (infrastructure), housing construction, and agriculture as long as this is permitted by the supply of food surplus (these new workers would not be highly productive though). Another solution is to simultaneously favor capital-intensive techniques in other areas of the economy where this is unavoidable.

But, there is an additional issue that must be taken into account. This is that most likely the sectors that will lead to the largest increase

---

[48] This means that claiming, for example, that the role of government is simply to develop and maintain a private sector; promote a business-friendly environment that addresses market failures, institutional weaknesses, and policy shortcomings; as well as invest in infrastructure and human capital, build institutions, maintain macroeconomic stability, protect property rights, and maintain the rule of law is to recognize openly that the role of government in development is huge. If governments have to do all these things, it is difficult not to acknowledge that they do play a key role. The problem is that governments in many developing countries cannot execute these functions adequately (hence these countries have both weak private sectors and weak governments). This is why reforms of the public sector are necessary in many cases.

in total output are those intensive in capital, while additional demand resulting from the increase in the overall wage bill would be directed to consumer necessities, whose supply is probably not increasing at the same pace. Summing up, to embark upon a large investment program without a coherent plan will mean a great deal of wasted effort as it will surely lead to disproportional (across the different sectors of the economy) and disruptive growth.

As noted above, planning in a modern economy should be understood as the development of a partnership between public and private sectors to coordinate their activities in a complimentary way. This is the essence of modern industrial policy (Hausmann and Rodrik 2006).

Industrial policy has traditionally been understood as any type of selective intervention or government policy that attempts to alter the sector structure of production toward sectors that are expected to offer better prospects for economic growth than without such intervention. Use of this type of intervention has its adherents (those who believe in market failures) and its detractors (those who believe in the efficient working of markets). The latter argue that industrial policy interventions have often degenerated into an exercise in "picking winners", a game played by government officials deciding what activities and sectors to promote and to spend public money on.[49]

In a series of papers, Rodrik (2004 and 2006) has argued in favor of a new type of industrial policy. He acknowledges the existence of generic market failures, but argues "that the location and magnitude of these market failures is highly uncertain" (Rodrik 2004, 3). He argues that information and coordination externalities are more important than technological externalities, for the former weaken the entrepreneurial drive to restructure and diversify low-income economies.

Rodrik argues that industrial policy is not about addressing distortions in the traditional way (that is, by enumerating technological and other externalities and then targeting policy interventions on these market failures), but about eliciting information from the private sector about significant externalities and about the constraints to structural transformation (hence industrial policy also encompasses activities in agriculture and services) and the opportunities available. This requires "strategic collaboration" between the public and private sectors to determine the areas in which the country has a comparative advantage. The reason is that entrepreneurs may lack information about where the comparative advantage of a country lies and governments may not even know what it is that they do not know. And certainly most governments do not have the adequate knowledge to pick winners.

---

[49] The literature evaluating the pros and cons of industrial policy is inconclusive. While some authors argue positively about it (e.g., Amsden 1989), others are critical (e.g., Pack and Sagi 2006).

Moreover, uncertainty arising from lack of communication, that is, from one decision maker having no way of finding out the concurrent decisions and plans made by others, complicates things to the point that, if sufficiently great, it may inhibit investment decisions and arrest growth. In these circumstances, markets alone are likely to undersupply the incentives and demand for new activities necessary to transform the economy. These market failures are more prevalent in developing economies. As Rodrik notes: "The trick for the government is not to pick winners, but to know when it has a loser" (Rodrik 2004, 12). This requires the development of the appropriate institutional arrangements for industrial policy.

Industrial policy should be conceived as a process whereby the state and the private sector jointly arrive at diagnoses about the sources of blockage in new economic activities and propose solutions to them. Industrial and technological upgrading requires purposeful effort in the form of industrial policy, in particular, effective government action and public–private collaboration. But this needs, first, a government that does not take any particular view or stand on the activities to be promoted or the instruments to be deployed. It only requires the government to build the private–public institutional setting from which information on profitable activities and useful instruments of intervention can be extracted. The key issue is not whether to protect, but how to protect and promote industry in order to ensure technical progress leading to higher labor productivity.[50] Second, it needs a private sector that is willing to do its part of the deal, that is, invest.[51]

Understood this way, industrial policy is a very powerful tool for successful industrialization and structural change. Perhaps a market-driven development model could not have, by itself, accelerated transitions between different patterns of specialization and delivered the high growth rates that some Asian countries experienced. This is not because market-based successes were absent. The reason is that theory suggests exactly the opposite, namely, that market forces are unlikely to address efficiently the coordination problems that arise in the transition across production and trade patterns. Indeed, coordination failures are

---

50   Amsden (2000) and Amsden and Hikino (2000) argue that the new rules of the World Trade Organization (WTO) allow countries to promote their industries, including the manufacturing sector, in particular under the umbrella of advancing science and technology (e.g., by setting up technology parks). Subsidies in exchange for monitorable, results-oriented performance standards are acceptable. Countries can, for example, target national champions. The hurdles that developing countries face are of the following nature: (i) informal political pressures by the developed countries in favor of market opening; (ii) countries that make use of WTO rules to promote their industries are subject to "reciprocal control mechanisms"; and (iii) their lack of "vision".

51   This is important in some developing countries, where a well-established elite may not see change with good eyes.

likely to arise in the transition from old to new patterns of production and trade specialization. This situation is characteristic of semi-industrialized countries, in which old comparative advantages in labor-intensive industries are being eroded, and new ones in capital and technology-intensive activities emerge only slowly. This view explains the successes of not only Korea and Taipei,China, but also of Singapore. Young (1992), in a well-known paper, compared the growth record of Singapore and Hong Kong, China, arguing that Singapore's had been based exclusively on capital accumulation (Soviet style according to Krugman 1994). Felipe (2000 and 2008), Felipe and McCombie (2001 and 2003) have discussed this literature, and have argued that its theoretical and empirical problems make the results and implied conclusions far from correct. It is true that at one point Singapore's government pushed the economy into new and more advanced sectors and perhaps the effort was not a complete success, but there is no doubt that without such a push the economy would not have ventured "by itself" into many of the areas in which it is doing well now.[52] As ADB (2007b) documents, Singapore's manufacturing sector is the most technologically advanced (after Japan's) in Asia.

In conclusion, the key to a successful transformation of the economies of many developing countries lies in embedding private initiative in a framework of public action that encourages restructuring, diversification, and technological dynamism beyond what market forces on their own are capable of generating.

5.6   Conclusions

This chapter has argued that in order to achieve inclusive growth, governments must commit effort and resources to the pursuit of full employment. The reason is that the main problem developing countries face is massive unemployment and underemployment. This is the result of the shortage of capital equipment and productive capacity. Why is the pursuit of full employment desirable? The reason is that a full employment economy creates a high level of overall purchasing power. Moreover, a full employment economy has the capacity to deliver great social benefits as it eliminates misery, poverty, and social injustice. Therefore, it is more rational to argue that developing countries cannot afford unemployment and underemployment than to suppose that they cannot afford full employment. Given the importance and relevance of the notion of full employment, governments must be held responsible for their achievement.

---

[52]   An example is the post-1979 rapid rise in real wages, partly encouraged by the Singaporean government in an attempt to stimulate productivity growth.

The chapter has also argued that the main policy to achieve full employment in developing countries is to step up investment. However, in reality, this is not so simple, for the private sector may decide not to collaborate, either because it decides to invest in areas that may be profitable but not relevant to the development of the country; and/or because the public sector may face obstacles to implementing a large program of public investment (e.g., budget deficits may not be politically acceptable).

Finally, the chapter has argued that investment requires planning, and that this should be understood as a partnership between public and private sectors to coordinate their activities in ways that complement each other. Industrial policy should be conceived as a process whereby the state and the private sector jointly arrive at diagnoses about the sources of blockage in new economic activities and propose solutions to them.

References

ADB. 2007a. "Inequality in Asia." In *Key Indicators 2007*. Asian Development Bank, Manila.

_____. 2007b. "Growth Amid Change." In *Asian Development Outlook 2007*. Asian Development Bank, Manila.

Ahya, C., A. Xie, A. Agarwal, D. Yam, and S. Lam. 2004. "India and China: New Tigers of Asia; A Special Economic Analysis." Morgan Stanley Research, New York.

Ahya, C., A. Xie, S. S. Roach, M. Sheth, and D. Yam. 2006. "India and China: New Tigers of Asia, Part II: Special Economic Analysis." Morgan Stanley Research, New York. Available: ibef.org/download/indiaandchina.pdf.

Akerlof, G. A. 1982. "Labor Contracts as Partial Gift Exchange." *Quarterly Journal of Economics* 97:543–69.

Akyüz, Y., and C. Gore. 1996. "The Investment-Profits Nexus in East Asian Industrialization." *World Development* 24:461–70.

Ali, I., and H. H. Son. 2007. Defining and Measuring Inclusive Growth: Application to the Philippines. ERD Working Paper Series No. 98, Economics and Research Department, Asian Development Bank, Manila.

Ali, I., and J. Zhuang. 2007. Inclusive Growth toward a Prosperous Asia: Policy Implications. ERD Working Paper Series No. 97, Economics and Research Department, Asian Development Bank, Manila.

Amsden, A. 1989. *Asia's Next Giant: South Korea and Late Industrialization*. New York: Oxford University Press.

_____. 2000. "Industrialization under WTO Law." United Nations Conference on Trade and Development." Available: unctad-10.org/pdfs/ux_tdxrt1d7.en.pdf.

Amsden, A., and T. Hikino. 2000. "The Bark is Worse than the Bite: New WTO Law and Late Industrialization." *American Academy of Political and Social Science* 570:104–14.

Beveridge, W. H. 1944. *Full Employment in a Free Society*. London: Allen and Unwin.

Blinder, A. 1987. *Hard Heads Soft Hearts*. Reading: Addison-Wesley.

Blomstrom, M., R. E. Lipsey, and M. Zejan. 1996. "Is Fixed Investment the Key to Economic Growth?" *Quarterly Journal of Economics* 111:269–76.

Brown, I. 1997. *Economic Change in South-East Asia, c.1830-1980*. Oxford: Oxford University Press.

Coronel, S. S., Y. T. Chua, L. Rimban, and B. B. Cruz. 2004. *The Rulemakers: How the Wealthy and Well-Born Dominate Congress*. Philippine Center for Investigative Journalism, Manila.

Dew-Becker, I., and R. Gordon. 2005. Where did the Productivity Growth Go? Inflation Dynamics and the Distribution of Income. NBER Working Paper No. 11842, Cambridge, MA.

Deyo, F., ed. 1987. *The Political Economy of the New Asian Industrialism*. Ithaca: Cornell University Press.

Dobb, M. 1959. *Economic Growth and Planning*. New York: Monthly Review Press.

Easterly, W. 2002. *The Elusive Quest for Growth: Economists' Adventures and Misadventures in the Tropics*. Cambridge and London: MIT Press.

_____. 2006. "Planners versus Searchers in Foreign Aid." *Asian Development Review* 23(1):1–35.

Economist, The. 2008. "What's Holding India Back?" 8–14 March. Page 11.

Eisner, R. 1995. "Our NAIRU Limit: The Governing Myth of Economic Policy." *The American Prospect* 21:58–63. Available: prospect.org/cs/articles?article=our_nairu_limit.

_____. 1997. "Full Employment and Inflation: Where We Stand and Where We can Go." US House of Representatives, Committee on Banking and Financial Services, Subcommittee on Domestic and Monetary Policy, Hearing of July 23, 1997. Available: financialservices.house.gov/banking/72397re.htm.

Felipe, J. 2000. "On the Myth and Mystery of Singapore's 'Zero TFP'." *Asian Economic Journal* 14(2):187–209.

_____. 2008. "What Policymakers should Know about Total Factor Productivity." *Malaysian Journal of Economic Studies* 45(1):1–19.

_____. 2009. *Inclusive Growth, Full Employment, and Structural Change Implications and Policies for Developing Asia*. London: Anthem Press.

Felipe, J., and G. Estrada. 2008. "Benchmarking Developing Asia's Manufacturing Sector." *International Journal of Development* 7(2):97–119.

Felipe, J., and R. Hasan, eds. 2006. *Labor Markets in Asia: Issues and Perspectives*. London: Palgrave Macmillan for the Asian Development Bank.

Felipe, J., and J. S. L. McCombie. 2001. "Biased Technical Change, Growth Accounting, and the Conundrum of the East Asian Miracle." *Journal of Comparative Economics* 29(3):542–65.

_____. 2003. "Some Methodological Problems with the Neoclassical Analysis of the East Asian Miracle." *Cambridge Journal of Economics* 27(5):695–721.

_____. 2008. "What can the Labour Demand Function Tell us About Wages and Employment? The Case of the Philippines." In J. Berg, and D. Kucera, eds., *In Defence of Labour Market Institutions: Cultivating Justice in the Developing World*. Houndmills, Basingstoke, Hampshire, New York: Palgrave Macmillan.

_____. 2009. "Are Estimates of Labor Demand Functions Mere Statistical Artefacts?" *International Review of Applied Economics* 23(2):147–68.

Felipe, J., and N. Usui. 2008. Rethinking the Growth Diagnostics Approach: Questions from the Practitioners. ERD Working Paper Series No. 132, Economics and Research Department, Asian Development Bank, Manila.

Felipe, J., E. Laviña, and E. X. Fan. 2008. "The Diverging Patterns of Profitability, Investment and Growth of China and India, 1980–2003." *World Development* 36(5):741–74.

Felipe, J., M-L. Ledesma, M. Lanzafama, and G. Estrada. 2007. Sectoral Engines of Growth in Developing Asia: Stylized Facts and Implications. ERD Working Paper Series No. 107, Economics and Research Department, Asian Development Bank, Manila. Forthcoming in the *Malaysian Journal of Economic Studies*.

Fields, G. 1995. "Income Distribution in Developing Economies: Conceptual, Data, and Policy Issues in Broad-Based Growth." In M. G. Quibria, ed., *Critical Issues in Asian Development*. Hong Kong, China; Oxford; New York: Oxford University Press.

Foley, D., and A. Marquetti. 1999. "Productivity, Employment and Growth in European Integration." *Metroeconomica* 50(3):277–300.

Foley, D., and T. Michl. 1999. *Growth and Distribution*. Cambridge and London: Harvard University Press.

Galbraith, John K. 1996. *The Good Society: The Humane Agenda*. Boston: Houghton Mifflin Co.

Galbraith, James K. 1997. Dangerous Metaphor: The Fiction of the Labor Market. Public Policy Brief No. 36, The Jerome Levy Economics Institute of Bard College, New York.

Hamilton, C. 1986. *Capitalist Industrialization in Korea*. Boulder, CO: Westview Press.

Haque, N. U. 2006. "Beyond Planning and Mercantilism: An Evaluation of Pakistan's Growth Strategy." *The Pakistan Development Review* 45(1):3–23.

Hausmann, R., and D. Rodrik. 2006. "Doomed to Choose: Industrial Policy as Predicament." John F. Kennedy School of Government, Harvard Universtiy. Available: www.ksghome.harvard.edu/~drodrik/doomed.pdf.

Hausmann, R., D. Rodrik, and A. Velasco. 2005. *Growth Diagnostics*. The John F. Kennedy School of Government, Harvard University.

Herrera, E. 2008. "More than Common Economic Indicators." *The Manila Times.* 18 March. Available: manilatimes.net/national/2008/mar/18/yehey/opinion/20080318opi2.html.

Hirschman, A. 1958. *Strategy of Economic Development*. New Haven, CT: Yale University Press.

Kaldor, N. 1970. The Case for Regional Policies. *The Scottish Journal of Political Economy* 17(3):337–48.

Kalecki, M. 1939. *Essays in the Theory of Economic Fluctuations*. London: Allen and Unwin.

_____. 1943 [1971]. "Political Aspects of Full Employment." In M. Kalecki, *Selected Essays on the Dynamics of the Capitalist Economy*. Cambridge, UK: Cambridge University Press.

_____. 1944. "Three Ways to Full Employment." In T. Balogh, ed., *The Economics of Full Employment*. Oxford: Basil Blackwell.

_____. 1966 [1991]. "The Difference between Crucial Economic Problems of Developed and Underdeveloped Non-socialist Economies." In J. Osiatyński, ed., *Collected Works of Michal Kalecki*. Oxford: Clarendon Press.

Keynes, J. M. 1936 [1951]. *The General Theory of Employment, Interest and Money*. London: Macmillan and Co. and St. Martin's Press.

Krugman, P. 1994. "The Myth of Asia's Miracle." *Foreign Affairs* November/December: 62–78.

_____. 1999. *The Accidental Theorist*. London: Penguin Books.

Lau, L. 1990. *Models of Development: A Comparative Study of Economic Growth in South Korea and Taipei,China*. San Francisco: ICS Press.

Lewis, A. W. 1954. "Economic Development with Unlimited Supplies of Labor." *The Manchester School* 22:139–191.

Lewis, W. W. 2004. *The Power of Productivity*. Chicago and London: The University of Chicago Press.

Marquetti, A. 2003. "Analyzing Historical and Regional Patterns of Technical Change from a Classical-Marxian Perspective." *Journal of Economic Behavior and Organization* 52(2):191–200.

McCombie, J. S. L., and A. P. Thirlwall. 1994. *Economic Growth and the Balance of Payments Constraint*. New York: St. Martin's Press.

Minsky, H. P. 1965. "The Role of Employment Policy." In M. S. Gordon, ed., *Poverty in America*. San Francisco: Chandler Publishing Co.

_____.1968. "Effects of Shifts of Aggregate Demand upon Income Distribution." *American Journal of Agricultural Economics* 59(2):328–39.

_____. 1973. "The Strategy of Economic Policy and Income Distribution." *The Annals of the American Academy of Political and Social Science* 409:92–101.

Oulton, N., and M. O'Mahony. 1994. *Productivity and Growth. A Study of British Industry, 1954–1986*. Cambridge: Cambridge University Press.

Pack, H., and K. Sagi. 2006. "Is There a Case for Industrial Policy? A Critical Survey." *World Bank Research Observer* 21:267–97.

Pasha, H. A. 2007. "Inclusive Growth: The Asian Experience." Available: www.pndpunjab.gov.pk/user_files/File/Inclusive_Growth_31%20Aug%20FINAL%20sent.pdf.

Pollin, R. 1998. "The 'Reserve Army of Unemployed' and the 'Natural Rate of Unemployment': Can Marx, Kalecki, Friedman, and Wall Street All be Wrong?" *Review of Radical Political Economics* Summer:1–13.

Prichett, L. 2003. "A Conclusion to Cross-National Growth Research: A Foreword 'To the Countries Themselves.'" In G. McMahon, and L. Squire, eds., *Explaining Growth. A Global Research Project*. Basingstoke: Palgrave Macmillan.

Rajan, R. G., and L. Zingales. 2003. *Saving Capitalism from the Capitalists*. London: Random House Business Books.

Rawls, J. 1971. *Theory of Justice*. Cambridge, MA: Harvard University Press.

Rodriguez, F. 2005. "Comment on Hausmann and Rodrik." Department of Economics and Latin American Studies Program, Wesleyan University, Connecticut.

Rodrik, D. 2004. "Industrial Policy for the Twenty-First Century." John F. Kennedy School of Government, Harvard University. Available: ksghome.harvard.edu/~drodrik/UNIDOSep.pdf.

_____. 2006. "Industrial Development: Stylized facts and Policies." John F. Kennedy School of Government, Harvard University. Available: ksghome.harvard.edu/~drodrik/industrial%20development.pdf.

Roemer, J. E. 2006. Economic Development as Opportunity Equalization. Cowles Foundation Discussion Paper No. 1583, Yale University, New Haven, CT.

Ros, J. 2000. *Development Theory and the Economics of Growth*. Ann Arbor: The University of Michigan Press.

Sen, A. 1999. *Development as Freedom*. New York: Alfred A. Knopf.

Shapiro, C., and J. Stiglitz. 1984. "Equilibrium Unemployment as a Worker Discipline Device." *American Economic Review* 74(3):433 44.

Smith, A. 1776 [2003]. *The Wealth of Nations*. New York: Bantam Classic Edition.

Stiglitz, J., J. A. Ocampo, S. Spiegel, R. Ffrech-Davis, and D. Nayyar. 2006. *Stability with Growth*. Oxford: Oxford University Press.

Tatom, J. A. 2006. "Not all Deficits are Created Equal." *Financial Analysts Journal* 62(3):12–9.

Thirlwall, A. P. 1987. *Keynes and Economic Development*. New York: St. Martin's Press.

Vickrey, W. 1993. "Today's Task for Economists." *The American Economic Review* 83(1):1–10.

_____.1997. "A Trans-Keynesian Manifesto (Thoughts on Assets Based Macroeconomics)." *Journal of Post Keynesian Economics* 19(4):495–510.

Wang, H., and S. Li. 1995. *Industrialization and Economic Reform in China*. Beijing: New World Press.

Young, A. 1992. "A Tale of Two Cities: Factor Accumulation and Technical Change in Hong Kong and Singapore." *Macroeconomics Annual* 1992:13–63.

6

Why is Access to Basic Services Not Inclusive?

Guanghua Wan and Ruth Francisco[1]

6.1   Introduction

Many consider the provision of basic social services, such as schooling and health care, both the ends and means of economic development. Education is commonly viewed as an important dimension of human development in Asia, while a shortage of skilled labor is often cited as a growth constraint in many countries or sectors. Delivery of basic services therefore has attracted considerable attention from national governments, development agencies, nongovernment organizations (NGOs), and the research community.

Despite the greater supply of basic services in developing Asia and beyond, evidence shows that the poor have failed to gain sufficiently from it. This chapter therefore explores the causes of such failures. Section 6.2 provides a brief account of the current state of service delivery in developing countries, with a special focus on Asia. Section 6.3 presents a synthesis of the barriers the poor face in accessing various services, with boxes highlighting good practices in pro-poor service delivery in developing countries. Section 6.4 summarizes and concludes.

6.2   Unequal access to basic services: A brief account

Developing countries and development institutions in the past 2 decades have increased efforts to improve the quality and accessibility of basic social and infrastructure services and to make them more inclusive. But outcomes have been mixed: while some have been successful, others have

[1]   The authors thank Xianbin Yao, Director General, Regional and Sustainable Development Department for initiating this paper and Juzhong Zhuang, Assistant Chief Economist, Economics and Research Department, for constructive comments on an earlier draft.

benefited the rich more than the poor. And in many communities in the developing world, the poor still lack adequate access to basic services (O'Donnell et al. 2007).

6.2.1   Primary education

Because they lack resources to fund even the basic necessities, the poor account for a large part of deficits in school enrollment. Poor children are less likely to start school and more likely to drop out (World Bank 2004a). In India, the poorer half of the rural population accounted for 72% of the deficit in grade 5 completion among 15–19 year-olds (World Bank 2004b). In Bangladesh, Pakistan, and Philippines, the gap in school attendance and the dropout rate between the poorest and richest income quintiles remained high (Table 6.1).

Table 6.1   Proportion of girls and boys attending school: Poorest and richest quintiles (%)

Country (survey year)	Poorest		Richest	
	Boys	Girls	Boys	Girls
Bangladesh (2004)	71	77	90	88
Nepal (2006)	83	78	95	94
Pakistan (2006/07)	49	32	88	88
Philippines (2003)	69	75	90	91

Note: Values reflect primary school children aged 6–10 (5–9 for Pakistan).
Source: Demographic and health surveys, available: www.measuredhs.com, downloaded 17 November 2008.

6.2.2   Health services and public spending on health care

Health services fail to reach the majority of the poor, who suffer the greater burden of poor health as a result. Poor households are 5 times more likely to become sick than rich households (Dalton and Peacock 2005) and are less likely to receive basic health services (Barat et al. 2004, Pillai et al. 2003, Peters et al. 2002, Mahal et al. 2000, Demery 2000, Makinen et al. 2000). Poor children, for instance, are usually less likely to be fully immunized, even in countries with national immunization programs (Yazbeck et al. 2005, Wagstaff 2002).

There are significant gaps in the proportion of facility-based deliveries between the poor and the rich, particularly in South and Southeast Asia. Figure 6.1 indicates that publicly provided maternal and neonatal health services largely benefit the rich although they are intended for the poor. Pregnant women belonging to the poorest quintile in Bangladesh are 8 times less likely to deliver with the help of a skilled birth attendant (SBA) and 9 times less likely to have facility-based delivery than the richest quintile (Koenig et al. 2007). Based on data from 21 countries, Filmer (2003) concluded that there is a big gap favoring the rich in the share of total health expenditures. While 25% of health subsidies benefit the richest income quintile, only 15% benefit the poorest.

Figure 6.1   Births delivered in public and private facilities (%)

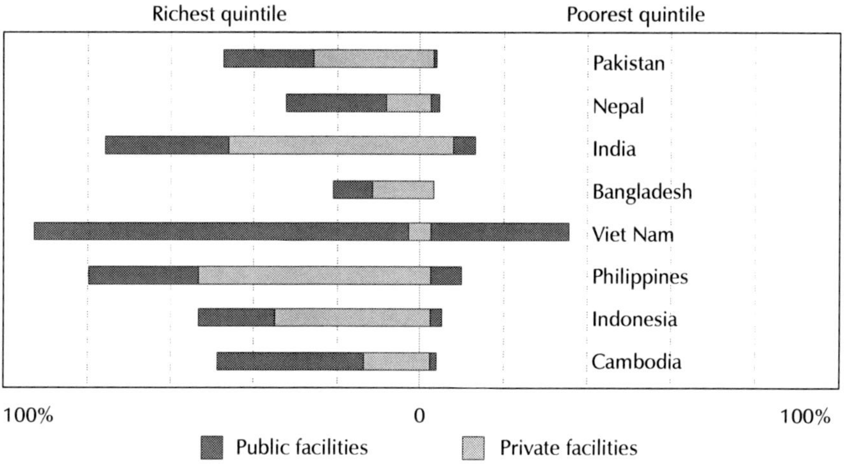

Source: World Bank (2004a).

6.2.3   Water and sanitation

Two-thirds of Asians still lack access to adequate sanitation, the majority of them poor (Bridges 2007). Over 1990–2006, the use of improved sanitation (including flush toilets, pour-out toilets/latrines, ventilated improved pit latrines, pit latrines with slab, and composting toilet) was significantly lower among the poor (WHO/UNICEF 2008). Recent data drawn from Multiple Indicator Surveys and Demographic and Health Surveys (DHS) in 38 developing countries indicate that the poorest quintile is 3 times less likely to use improved sanitation than the richest (Figure 6.2).

In Nepal, while 79% of the richest income quintile had access to improved sanitation, only 10% of the poorest quintile had access (UNICEF 2006). In the Philippines, the number of low-income households with access to sanitation was at least 22% lower than high-income households (DOH 2008a). In Jakarta, Indonesia, there is also a big gap in access to sanitation between low- and high-income households (World Bank 2004a). Needless to say, the gap in access to sanitation between urban and rural residents is significant (Pretus et al. 2008, Table 6.2). In Cambodia, 56% of urban households have access to improved sanitation. This percentage was only 16% in rural areas.

Figure 6.2   Improved sanitation coverage in 38 developing countries by wealth quintile (%)

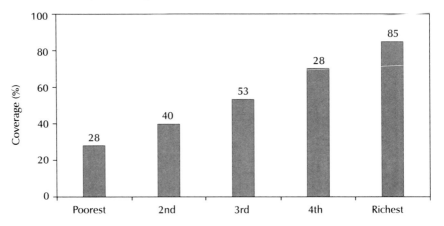

Source: WHO/UNICEF (2008).

Defecation in open spaces such as fields, forests, bushes, and bodies of water suggests a lack of access to sanitation. Due to limited coverage of sewerage systems, the percentage of people using open defecation was notably high in urban (15%) and rural areas (63%) in South Asia (WHO/UNICEF 2008).

Waterborne diseases are common in developing countries because of poor water supply. As of 2000, the coverage of urban water supply in Asia was below 30%. In areas with access to safe water and sanitation, service is below par. In the Philippines, for example, at least one half of water systems operated by local government units did not meet drinking quality standards, and waterborne diseases ranked as the second leading cause of morbidity (DOH 2008b).

The percentage of the South Asian population with access to safe water is low—Bangladesh (74%), Bhutan (62%), and Sri Lanka (79%). There is also inequity in water access. In India, the poor consumed less than 15 liters per capita per day, while the rich consumed up to 300 liters per capita per day (ADB 2006). The situation is similar in Indonesia—more than 30% of the poorest households had no access to safe water. For the richer households, this percentage was less than 10% (World Bank 2004a).

Table 6.2   Proportion of households with access to improved sanitation facilities (%)

Country (survey year)	Urban	Rural
Cambodia (2005)	56	16
India (2005/06)	53	18
Indonesia	65	27
Nepal (2006)	37	20
Pakistan (2006/07)*	76	36
Philippines (2003)*	77	54

Note: Except for Indonesia and the Philippines, data for improved (unshared) sanitation facilities include any flush toilet facility, ventilated improved latrine, and pit latrine with slab. Data for the Philippines cover households with own flush toilet only.

Source: Demographic and health surveys, available: www.measuredhs.com, downloaded 17 November 2008.

6.2.4   Electricity

In South Asia, electricity coverage expanded from around 41% in 2001 to 52% in 2005 (IEA 2002 and 2006), but remained the second lowest among the world's regions. At the same time, the rural-urban difference in coverage is high, with more than 80% of those with no access to electricity in rural communities (Komives et al. 2005, IEA 2006).

6.3   Barriers to service delivery and cases of successful intervention

Generally speaking, the failure of effective service delivery to the poor is driven by a combination of demand- and supply-side factors. On one hand, use of basic services, even when available and adequate, would be low if financial constraints were binding on the demand side. On the other hand, if the quantity or quality of supply is inadequate or uncertain, access would remain limited even if households could afford the services. Demand and supply are also hampered by information and institutional barriers.

6.3.1   Demand factors

The main demand-side barrier to accessing service is affordability. However, as argued below, even when a service is provided free or at low cost, poor households may still be unable or decide not to use it because of other financial considerations.

A. Although water/electricity tariffs are low in most developing Asian countries, connection cost can be high

High connection cost is a major factor explaining why many poor households do not have access to water service and electricity. In some areas, water connection can cost as much as $200, while the tariff can be as low as $0.05 per cubic meter (McIntosh 2007). In the Philippines, the water connection fee represented 25% of annual household income for the poorest quintile (UNDP 2006). In this case, poor households may not be able to afford reliable water supply even if an installment payment option is available. This is why illegal connections are widespread, especially in the poor areas of Manila (Bridges 2007).

The average domestic water tariff in Asia is only $0.18 per cubic meter (ADB 2006). However, such a low tariff means little to the poor who cannot afford the connection fees and have to turn to alternative suppliers that usually charge much higher tariffs than service utilities (ADB 2006). In Manila, while the poor pay $15 a month to get water from intermediaries, connected users pay only $5 (ADB 2006). This clearly indicates a mismatch in the pricing and the institutional structure of water service delivery (Davis et al. 2008). Willingness to pay also varies across communities (Box 6.1). Hence, for the installment option to make an impact in the poorest communities, a water connection subsidy or deferred payment option may also be required. Box 6.2 provides additional insight into Asian cities' efforts to make water services more affordable to the poor.

Box 6.1   Willingness to pay for in-house access to water supply

- *Sri Lanka:* In water project sites, even the poor were willing and able to pay for connection (ADB 2002).
- *Dalian, People's Republic of China:* Affordability of water connection and supply was not an issue, despite large increases in domestic tariff rates (ADB 2002).
- *Hyderabad, India:* Many poor households were willing to invest in water networks, as well as sewerage systems, if provided with financing at market rates (Davis et al. 2008).
- *Philippines:* Of those who used hand pumps and standpipes and without in-house connection, only less than half were willing to pay to get connected. Nonetheless, more households were willing to pay to connect if installment payment was an option (ADB 2002).

Box 6.2   Making water services accessible and affordable
           to the poor

- *Phnom Penh, Cambodia:* More than 80% of residents enjoy a 24-hour
  supply of clean water at only $0.25 per cubic meter ($0.10 below the
  recommended tariff for Asian cities). Despite the low tariff, the Phnom
  Penh Water Supply Authority generates enough revenue to fully cover
  operations and maintenance because of high collection rates.
- *Malé, Maldives:* Residents agreed to pay $5 per cubic meter to operate
  seawater desalination plants and provide 24-hour water supply, at a
  time when the groundwater lens was heavily damaged by pollution. To
  afford the high tariff, Malé residents consume only 34 liters per person
  per day (6 liters below the average consumption in other Asian cities).
- *Kathmandu, Nepal:* City leaders segmented the city into individual water
  supply zones. The tariff was raised one zone at a time as the city's water
  system was upgraded.

Source: ADB (2006).

B. High cost of latrine construction

Lack of financial resources is one major factor preventing the poor
from building their own latrines. Most Nepalese households have to
borrow from private moneylenders for this purpose, with an interest
rate of around 12%–36% (Pretus et al. 2008). Leaving credit availability
aside, loan repayment is a major concern especially for the poor, since
70% of Nepalese households have outstanding loans that need to be
repaid (UNICEF 2006). For a household already burdened with debts,
it requires more than just providing loans with low interest rates or
hardware subsidies (Box 6.3). ADB encountered this problem during
the start-up of the Community-Based Water Supply and Sanitation
Programme in Banskhor, Kapilvastu district in Nepal. Because of the
low uptake of revolving loan funds, the project was forced to distribute
funds on a first-come, first-serve basis (Pretus et al. 2008). In Ramghat
(Surkjet), Nepal, despite having access to construction material
subsidies, households still avail of informal loans to construct latrines.
Informal loans usually do not require collateral but come with excessive
interest rates.

Box 6.3   Financing options for better sanitation

Various models have been adopted to improve sanitation coverage in Nepal. They include one or a combination of hardware subsidies, loans, and support for community awareness. The results indicate the following.

A latrine construction material subsidy is resource-intensive. It does not encourage ownership among recipients and is often unsustainable. An example of fully subsidized project is CARE's Accessing Services for Households.

Minimum subsidies and revolving loans require less program funds and promote ownership, but can be ineffective in reaching the poorest households. Lack of necessary materials may prevent latrine construction and maintenance. Because of these, it can be ineffective in improving sanitation. Examples of nongovernment organizations that provide minimum subsidies include the Rural Reconstruction and Community Forest in Nepal.

Community-led latrine subsidies that raise community awareness and encourage collective action to adopt safe hygiene and healthy behavior can better target program resources and promote sustainable sanitation. Examples of successful community-level programs in Nepal include ADB's Community-Based Water Supply and Sanitation Programme, and Nepal Water for Health's Community-Led Basic Sanitation for All. These programs encouraged households to build latrines through their own initiative by creating community awareness. These programs also provided financial and latrine construction material subsidies to very poor households and revolving loans for low- and middle-income households.

Source: Pretus et al. (2008).

C. Unaffordable education and health services

South Asian public schools charge tuition fees, except in Bangladesh and Sri Lanka. Among Southeast Asian countries, such fees accounted for 80% of total household expenditure on primary education for the poorest quintile in Cambodia, and almost 50% in Thailand (World Bank 2004b). Even in the People's Republic of China (PRC), the figure was 29%.

In health services, relatively few sought basic maternal care in Bangladesh, primarily due to concerns about medical costs (Koenig et al. 2007). On average, only one out of three sought care in a facility, even among women who reported having one or more life-threatening pregnancy complications. In poor households in Cambodia and India, the decision to treat children was deterred mainly by the lack of financial resources (Annear et al. 2008, Pillai et al. 2003).

D. Opportunity costs and out-of-pocket expenses

Even with low or no tuition fees to be paid, children could still be deterred from attending schools because of opportunity costs such as foregone incomes. Attending basic facility-based maternal and child health services also entails opportunity cost.

There are other direct and indirect costs for school attendance and visits to health facilities by poor families, including medicines, laboratory tests, rooms (for in-patients), food, compulsory uniforms, school supplies, transportation, and compulsory/voluntary contributions. Many public schools in South Asia charge textbook fees and require parent-teacher association and other community contributions.

Out-of-pocket expenses remain high, as a proportion of health expenditures, , especially in South Asia (Table 6.3). Medicines accounted for 30%–50% of average total health care expenditures in developing countries (Whitehead et al. 2001). In the Philippines, inability to pay, especially among the poor, severely hampers access to essential medicines (DOH 2008a). Out-of-pocket health expenditure led to indebtedness and impoverishment among the poor in Cambodia (Van Damme et al. 2004) and Viet Nam (Wagstaff and van Doorslaer 2003).

Table 6.3   Out-of-pocket expenditure on health by region, 2006

Region	Out-of-pocket expenditure (% of private expenditure on health)	Births attended by skilled health staff (% of total)
East Asia and Pacific	88	87
Europe and Central Asia	82	95
Latin America and Caribbean	74	88
Middle East and North Africa	90	77
South Asia	94	41
Sub-Saharan Africa	45	45

Source: World Bank, World Development Indicators Online, downloaded 2 November 2008.

6.3.2   Supply factors

Access to services is often absent or limited by poor supply. The availability of teachers, classrooms, desks, and books obviously limits the number of children who can be enrolled in public schools. In Viet Nam, because of limited availability of teachers and classrooms, the majority of children in rural areas attended school with two or more shifts a day, resulting in an average daily class time of only around 3 hours (Glewwe 2004). In rural Kazakhstan, there were only a few functioning sanitation systems and only a few districts had sewerage systems (Bridges 2007). In Indonesia, sewerage systems serve only less than 3% of the urban population. Many of these systems lack maintenance and need repairs. Basic supplies are often scarce in remote rural communities. Construction and maintenance of sanitation facilities cannot be rendered, even with financial subsidies or credit (Pretus et al. 2008). Meanwhile, availability of essential drugs in the Philippines remains limited, especially in the poorer regions, such as the Autonomous Region in Muslim Mindanao and the Cordillera Administrative Region, where the rates for morbidity and mortality from preventable causes are high (DOH 2008b).

A. Quality of service

Greater financial and physical access to basic services may not improve development outcomes if service quality is below par. Quality of health and education services is determined by the level of competency, effort, attitude, regular availability, and attendance of teachers and health professionals; the availability of adequate material inputs (e.g., instructional materials, medical supplies); and the availability of appropriate health and school facilities and infrastructure.

Low-income households, as is evident in New Delhi, for example, usually end up with less competent providers than high-income households (Das and Hammer 2007a). In substandard public health facilities, the poor face inconvenient schedules, long waiting times, and other problems (World Bank 2004b, Serneels et al. 2007). Patients in India receive below par care either because of incompetent doctors or the lack of incentives among competent doctors to do what they know they should (Das and Hammer 2004). The quality of care provided by qualified public doctors in poor communities was extremely low and sometimes even worse than care offered by unqualified private sector doctors (Das and Hammer 2004, 2007a, and 2007b).

In the Philippines, a survey in the province of Compostela Valley, characterized by low use of maternal health services and a high rate of maternal deaths, showed that mothers prefer to have their deliveries assisted by *hilots* or traditional birth attendants (TBAs) than SBAs. This is not only because of financial considerations but also because TBAs are usually more caring than SBAs (UPecon-HPDP 2008) and the quality of professional services has a poor reputation. Low use of maternal health services, in turn, results in more pregnancy complications, as well as maternal and neonatal deaths.

In education, meanwhile, parents may remove children from school if they appear to be learning little. Poor education quality, naturally, leads to poor education outcomes. According to the World Bank (2008), despite its exceptional success in achieving universal primary enrollment and keeping school-age children at school, learning outcomes in Sri Lanka are appalling. Two-thirds of primary school graduates still lack basic language and mathematical skills and only 80% of students finish elementary school.

For water and electricity services, quality indicators include frequency or regularity of service and availability of service personnel when needed. But the service hours of most water systems in Bangladesh, India, and Pakistan are limited: most water systems in Bangladesh provide only up to 4 hours daily. Also, while staffing-connection ratios in these countries are high, utility personnel dedicated to serving the concerns of the poor are often lacking (Bridges 2007, McIntosh 2007). Nearly all of India's 5,161 cities and towns have piped water systems but operational efficiencies are low (Bridges 2007). In Indonesia, many regional, government-owned water enterprises are too small and inefficient (Bridges 2007).

B. Absenteeism

Absenteeism of service professionals affects service quality and quantity. It is a serious problem in developing countries where it is nearly impossible for the poor to "vote with their feet" because substitutes are rarely available and public-private market competition is limited. In the poor rural communities of Rajasthan, India, community health centers were closed 56% of the time during regular opening hours because of absent health professionals (Banerjee et al. 2004). Worse still, facility closures were unannounced and therefore unpredictable. Box 6.4 lists some causes of teacher and health professional absenteeism.

Box 6.4   Causes of absenteeism and lack of motivation among teachers and health professionals in developing Asia

- Job dissatisfaction[1]
- Nonmedical duties[1]
- Poor facility/school infrastructure[2,3]
- Lack of monitoring by and credibility of facility administration[3,1]
- Low salary[1]
- Proximity of residence to the health facility/school and access to road[2,3]
- Rural electrification[2]

Source: [1] Hossain et al. (2007), [2] Chaudhury and Hammer (2004), [3] Kremer et al. (2005).

South Asia, which has the second lowest percentage of trained primary school teachers in the world, has a high rate of absenteeism. In Bangladesh, India, and Indonesia, absenteeism among health professionals is particularly high (Table 6.4). Absenteeism is negatively correlated with the level of local economic development and is higher among rural primary health clinic doctors than those in larger clinics (Chaudhury and Hammer 2004, Banerjee et al. 2004).

Table 6.4   Estimated rate of absenteeism among primary school teachers and health professionals (%)

Country	Rate of absenteeism	
	Teachers	Health professionals
Bangladesh	16	35
India	25	40
Indonesia	19	40

Source: Chaudhury et al. (2006).

Analysis of nationally representative data from Indonesia reveals that absenteeism among teachers harms student performance significantly (Suryadarma et al. 2006). If well-trained teachers are available but absent, student attendance will not translate into better education outcomes. In health services, even if doctors are qualified, partial availability of health services may not translate into good outcomes.

Clearly, absenteeism is a crucial barrier that needs to be overcome, especially in rural communities. An experimental intervention tested recently in rural India (Box 6.5) reduced absenteeism and improved education outcomes.

Box 6.5   Monitoring attendance and financial incentives to reduce absenteeism: Evidence from rural India

Lack of incentives and poor monitoring are the primary reasons for high absenteeism. The impact of salary level on attendance and learning outcomes is weak and limited (Chaudhury et al. 2006, Kremer et al. 2005, World Bank 2004a). Monitoring by head teachers can be ineffective, as an earlier experiment in Kenya showed, since they may have personal motives to falsely report poor performance of staff (Kremer and Chen 2001).

But using digital cameras to monitor teacher attendance reduced absenteeism by 50% in treatment schools—from 36% to 18% (Banerjee and Duflo 2006). A randomized experiment in rural India showed that monitoring observable effort and teacher attendance and providing financial incentives accordingly can reduce absenteeism by 21 percentage points. Furthermore, teachers in treatment schools were more likely to be teaching when present. Consequently, both instruction time and student attendance increased. Also, a 10% reduction in absenteeism translates into 0.10 standard deviation improvement in student test scores (Duflo et al. 2008).

C. Lack of devotion of service professionals

Kremer et al. (2005) report that on average, only half of primary public school teachers in India present at the time of their visit were engaged in classroom activities. Similarly, Chaudhury et al. (2006) find that not all health workers in Bangladesh, India, and Indonesia present during the time of their visit were actually working. Such a lack of devotion is partly related to administrative and non-instructional activities. A survey in rural public schools in Bangladesh revealed that these activities accounted for 19%–55% of total school days (Tietjen et al. 2004).

Despite these problems, some success stories deserve mention. In the Philippines, a randomized field experiment found that national accreditation of doctors and insurance payments could improve quality of care in poor hospital districts (Box 6.6). In Cambodia, the use of a participatory approach and performance-based resource management were found useful to improving quality of education (Box 6.7). Box 6.8 discusses the lessons from the successful rehabilitation of the Phnom Penh Water Supply Authority (PPWSA), from a poor to an outstanding service provider.

Box 6.6   Accreditation and insurance payments to improve quality of care: Lessons from the quality improvement and demonstration study in the Philippines

The Quality Improvement and Demonstration Study tested the effectiveness of two policy interventions in improving quality of care and health care use in 30 hospitals in the rural areas of the Visayas islands. Of these hospitals, 10 served as the control group; another 10 were given bonus payments if they passed a certain quality-of-care index; and the remaining 10 served as "access sites" wherein insurance coverage of patients was expanded. Results indicate that both accreditation from a national insurance program and insurance payments strongly improve quality of care (Quimbo et al. 2008). This finding suggests that financial incentives could indeed motivate service providers to improve quality.

D. Urban-rural gap in the endowment of health personnel

In many developing countries, human resources for health and education services are inadequate and unevenly distributed (Dussault and Franceschini 2006, DOH 2008c, and Chomitz et al. 1998). This is in part because, as occurred in Indonesia, doctors and nurses are usually reluctant to relocate to remote communities, where the poorest are usually concentrated (Chomitz et al. 1998). In the Philippines,

211

efforts to get health workers to take part in public health services after training largely failed as they used different ways to evade the system (Hongoro and McPake 2004).

Box 6.7   Capacity building and performance-based resource management to improve quality of education

The Education Quality Improvement Project in Cambodia demonstrates that:
- A small investment in teacher training can produce a large impact on student performance. A dollar per pupil investment in teacher training help raise average achievement scores by 1% (World Bank 2005).
- Empowering local communities to identify their needs and propose changes and investments can lead to quality improvements in education, especially in post-conflict situations (World Bank 2002).
- Performance-based resource management can further the gains from universal access to education (World Bank 2004b).

Box 6.8   Lessons from water utility reform in Cambodia

From 1993 to 2006, the Phnom Penh Water Supply Authority (PPWSA) successfully (i) reduced the staff-connection ratio from 22 to only 4 staff per 1,000 connections; (ii) increased its production capacity by more than 3 times; (iii) expanded coverage area from 25% to 90%; (iv) increased supply duration from 10 to 24 hours per day; (v) achieved an almost 100% collection rate from only less than 50%; and (vi) achieved full cost recovery from previously heavy subsidies.

Important lessons from PPWSA's experience include the following.
- Water does not have to be provided for free to be accessible to all. Fees for services are important to sustain and expand good quality service. Also, poor households will be considerably better off paying for safe, piped water compared to what they used to buy from private vendors with questionable quality.
- It is possible to transform a deteriorating and poorly performing water utility into an outstanding service provider if it is given sufficient administrative autonomy and strong support by the government.
- A water utility that is fully accountable and independent from political pressures can successfully meet clean water targets through a transparent environment where tariffs can cover costs and service is equitable to all.

PPWSA's success would not have been possible without its investment in building staff capacity and in instilling discipline and teamwork. It appears that its experience can be replicated in other communities with the active involvement of civil society and commitment of governments to make water services more inclusive.

Source: ADB (2007b).

6.3.3 Institutional factors

A. Poor governance and corruption

Aside from the level and composition of public spending,[2] quality of governance—measured by the quality of bureaucracy and the level of corruption—also affects the effectiveness of public spending (Rajkumar and Swaroop 2008). In essence, absenteeism, as discussed earlier, is an indicator of poor governance. It can be viewed as an outcome of poor enforcement of civil service rules (e.g., poor monitoring).

Corruption in various public sectors in South Asia and Southeast Asia is not uncommon (Quah 2003). Davis (2004) documents corruption in water and sanitation service delivery in South Asia, where "rent-seeking" is present in many communities. Field personnel receive informal payments to either speed up water supply and sewer repair work, lower meter readings, or provide and conceal illegal connections. Public water service agencies and politicians receive bribes from "predetermined" construction contractors to undermine competitive public bidding of contracts.

Azfar and Gurgur (2007) find that corruption reduces immunization rates; delays immunization of newborns; increases waiting time in facilities, especially in rural areas where most of the population are dependent on public health services; erodes satisfaction in public health services and education; lowers performance of public schools; and discourages the use of public health facilities. They also find that corruption disproportionately affects the poor more than the wealthy.

Aside from raising income inequality by reducing progressive taxation and making distribution of subsidies regressive (Gupta et al. 2002), corruption can undermine delivery of public services in various ways (Box 6.9). A serious consequence of poor governance and corruption is low revenue generation from water and other utilities despite high connection fees. This is caused by leakage and illegal connections, low tariffs, and poor collection rates (Bridges 2007, McIntosh 2007). Most water systems in Bangladesh, India, Indonesia, Kazakhstan, Pakistan, and Philippines have high levels of non-revenue water. In Bangladesh, non-revenue water is typically around 40%–60% of total supply but can be as high as 70%. In Indonesia it is typically around 30%–50% (Bridges 2007).

---

2   There is consensus in the theoretical and empirical literature that both the level and the composition of public spending matter in achieving better human development outcomes. However, a theory on optimal expenditure composition is still lacking (Paternostro and Rajaram 2007). As such, most empirical assessments rely on practical analytical frameworks and examples of public expenditure levels and composition that yielded better results in the past.

Box 6.9   Corruption harms health care and educational services

Based on cross-country regression analysis, corruption is found to undermine delivery of public services by:
- increasing the price of services and lowering the level of government output and services, including the provision and financing of health care and education (Shleifer and Vishny 1993);
- reducing human capital (Ehrlich and Lui 1999) and national expenditure on education and health (Mauro 1998, Rajkumar and Swaroop 2008); and
- lowering government revenue (Hindricks, Keen, and Muthoo 1999) and reducing the quantity and quality of public services (Bearse, Glomm, and Janeba 2000).

Moreover, the poor quality of public services reduces willingness to pay and discourages use. It also encourages tax evasion.

Source: Gupta et al. (2001).

Low tariffs and poor cost recovery in Bangladesh, Cambodia, Kazakhstan, Pakistan, Philippines, and Samoa undermine the development of the water sector, with revenue covering only 90% of average operating costs (ADB 2006 and 2007a). Thus, it is hard to make services inclusive and sustainable.

B.   The costs of deficient roads and distance from services

Transport expenses and opportunity costs (in travel time) increase with distance. And because of poor roads and lack of transport services, the poor in remote communities are usually disadvantaged in accessing primary education and basic health services. Households that live far from water and electric utilities therefore, are likely to be underserved or unserved.

In Bangladesh and Nepal, distance to a health care facility significantly affects the use of maternal services in rural areas (Jamil et al. 1999, Hotchkiss 2001, Anwar et al. 2005). Pregnant women residing in Bangladeshi villages at least 2 miles from outreach clinics are 20% less likely to receive tetanus toxoid shots[3] than otherwise.

Not unrelated to distance, the physical immobility of pregnant women also often prevents them from receiving tetanus toxoid immunization, as seen in Bangladesh (Jamil et al. 1999). Physical mobility of mothers may be restricted if nobody can stay at home to look after younger children. In Bangladesh, both proximity to outreach clinics and the availability

---

3   This immunization helps reduce the risk of birth complications.

of home visits by reliable health workers have important bearing on the use of child immunization services, especially among poorer households (Jamil et al. 1999).

According to the World Health Organization, 75% of maternal deaths can be prevented through timely access to delivery-related care (WHO 2001). Recognizing the importance of transport and road networks in bringing health services closer to the poor, various transport-related interventions have been pursued, not only in Asia but also in other developing nations (IDS 2007). These interventions include: (i) different financing mechanisms for emergency transport, fuel costs, and drivers (e.g., cost sharing, community saving, and pooled insurance schemes); (ii) training community midwives in home delivery and in emergency management and the setting up of maternity waiting homes; (iii) improvement of rural transport infrastructure; and (iv) improvement of referral networks between and among health centers. However, these interventions have been implemented mostly only on a small scale and rigorous assessments are yet to be made (Campbell and Graham 2006).

In addition to transport and marketing costs, intermediaries serving the poor face higher tariffs per cubic meter (UNDP 2006) because most water utilities adopt a rising block tariff system—a discriminatory pricing strategy wherein the block price increases progressively with the volume of water consumed. In turn, water intermediaries pass on the high tariff to their poor clients who cannot afford high water connection fees. Hence, those living in urban slums pay 5–10 times more per liter of water than wealthy residents (UNDP 2006). Further, rural communities outside formal water networks face the even bigger hurdle of organizing and managing their own water systems.

C. Lack of information and awareness

Lack of information and awareness among the poor is another barrier to effective delivery of available services. Inadequate information among poor households is usually caused by the lack of formal education among households and limited awareness campaigns by public service providers.

Generally speaking, information and education among households influence demand for health care through one or a combination of the following: (i) health education affects behavior and practice, as discussed above; (ii) numeracy and literacy help future parents, especially mothers, recognize symptoms of sickness; and (iii) formal education improves perception and behavior toward facility-based health care (Glewwe 1999).

Lack of information about the danger signs or symptoms of health conditions and risks may delay decisions to seek treatment.

In particular, maternal education is found to be negatively related to such delays in India (Pillai et al. 2003) and positively correlated with the use of health services in Bangladesh (Anwar et al. 2005, Chakraborty et al. 2003). Analysis of data from Bangladesh, Indonesia, Philippines, and three other countries indicate that poor maternal education is strongly associated with delivery by a TBA (Bell et al. 2003). Mothers who did not finish high school are 2–6 times less likely to deliver with a health professional in attendance than those who finished high school. In Bangladesh, children whose mothers did not finish primary education were 70% less likely to be fully immunized (Jamil et al. 1999).

Lack of information about the costs and benefits of safe water affects households' willingness to pay and may lead to poor decision making. According to Bridges (2007), most rural households in Cambodia are unaware of the negative health effects of unsafe water. This, coupled with high connection fees, makes poor households turn to alternative water sources, which may be unsafe and more expensive. In India, lack of information about the government's campaign precluded poor and vulnerable households in remote villages from receiving subsidies (WaterAid 2006).

Lack of information and education are also major barriers of access to sanitation. As indicated by recent community-level financing for sanitation projects in Nepal, lack of awareness and education about sanitation and health practices led to a poor sense of ownership among beneficiaries of latrine subsidies, which meant latrines were not used or were poorly maintained (Pretus et al. 2008). Open defecation, a health hazard, is remarkably high in South Asia, as discussed in Section 6.2. In rural PRC, where there has been significant progress in improving overall access to sanitation, open defecation also remains common. This unhealthy practice can be greatly reduced with more education and awareness campaigns (Bridges 2007).

Box 6.10 cites examples of effective strategies for improving knowledge and awareness and promoting better health practices.

Many South Asian countries have recently adopted strategies to address the weakness of public service delivery and accelerate the progress of human development. Box 6.11 highlights some prospects and challenges in scaling up initiatives to accelerate the progress of service delivery in Asia. Box 6.12 presents some lessons from rural PRC in expanding its water and sanitation services.

D. Multiplicity of basic services

It is important to point out that the availability and quality of one service, or the lack of it, can affect the effectiveness of the delivery of other services in many ways. In Nepal, for instance, social exclusion limited the success of provision and management of emergency funds (IDS 2007). In Bangladesh, trained midwives are not close enough to households, restricting availability.

Box 6.10   Promoting behavior change though information, education, and communication campaigns

- *India:* Sanitation campaigns led to a 30% increase in the adoption and use of latrines in rural communities (Pattanayak et al. 2007).
- *India:* Evidence from a cluster-randomized efficacy trial in rural Uttar Pradesh revealed that community-based mobilization and education that are compatible with the local sociocultural landscape could improve care for newborns and reduce neonatal mortality in poor rural areas (Kumar et al. 2008).
- *Nepal:* The SUMATA "Care, Share and Prepare" initiative, which urged mothers-in-law and husbands to care, share, and prepare for childbirth, demonstrated that the use of communication channels through a participatory approach was highly effective in increasing community awareness about pregnancy complications (JHPIEGO 2004a).
- *Indonesia:* The large-scale media campaigns of the project Suami SIAGA's "alert husband" significantly improved knowledge, attitudes, and practices in childbirth and pregnancy emergencies. Mothers exposed to the campaigns were more likely to seek the assistance of skilled attendants during deliveries, while husbands were more likely to take an active role during pregnancy (JHPIEGO 2004b, Nanda et al. 2005).

Based on survey data from the Philippines, Ghuman et al. (2006) find that the preschool health and nutritional status of children affect primary school enrollment and educational outcomes. On the other hand, parental education, especially maternal education, exerts intergenerational effects on birth spacing and the health-seeking behavior of children. It is not hard to understand that the lack of clean water and electricity can undermine the quality of health services and contribute to the spread of infectious diseases. Lighting is often needed for reading and completing homework. Therefore, the unavailability of electricity may also affect school attendance and learning outcomes.

Box 6.11   Accelerating progress in service delivery:
            Some prospects and challenges

In Dhaka, Bangladesh, devolution of management (including building
capacity) to the community, backed by the strong support of a nongovernment
organization (NGO), successfully expanded water services to cover informal
settlers (Ahmed 2003).

Bangladesh has been relying on its NGOs to provide many of its services
for the poor. Results have been impressive. However, if checks and balances
are not installed, corruption may limit the effectiveness of private contracting
(World Bank 2008).

The devolution of some 2,400 schools in Nepal to communities,
meanwhile, demonstrates positive results in reducing teacher absenteeism.
Devolution was intended to restore the accountability of service providers.
In this setting, school management committees, composed of parents and
influential local citizens, receive and allocate unconditional block grants for
school administration from the government. School management committees
can hire and fire teachers and pay them according to their performance.

Nonetheless, there are limits to how much devolution of services
to communities can achieve. In India, devolution has no effect on teacher
absenteeism (World Bank 2008). A village education committee was tasked to
certify a teacher's attendance before he or she got paid. But most committees
signed off regardless of whether or not the teacher was present.

Box 6.12   Scaling up services for the poor: Lessons from rural
            People's Republic of China

The success of the PRC in expanding its water and sanitation services and
making them more inclusive highlights the importance of the following:
   • strong and determined leadership, both at the national and local levels
   • simple, clear rules to enforce accountability
   • strong coordination between government departments and agencies
   • community participation to avoid failure of project implementation
   • commitment from users to contribute financially and allow the utility to
     recover costs
   • building capacity at all levels for sustainability
   • sharing experience and knowledge to ensure mutual, common
     understanding of goals
   • integration of sanitation and health education with rural water supply

Source: Shuchen et al. (2004).

6.4   Conclusions

Because the delivery of basic services is interrelated, it is important to ensure that the delivery of all services is inclusive. Making services affordable and accessible to all entails more than just providing free services. Identifying the constraints, as discussed in Section 6.3, is an important first step in formulating appropriate strategies or an integrated approach to make services inclusive.

The following summarizes important points for policy makers in order to help improve access to basic services, especially in poor communities. It should be noted that since binding constraints vary across communities, what works for some communities might not work for others. Hence, undertaking baseline case studies to identify country-specific and location-specific barriers is crucial to making service delivery effective and equitable.

6.4.1   Making services available and affordable to the poor

Improving service access involves several elements. For example, more attention is needed to the design of targeting mechanisms that are practical and effective in promoting inclusive delivery and access to basic services.

And since resources are crucial for maintaining and expanding services, a user fee structure that is compatible with the ability and willingness to pay is encouraged. This not only promotes ownership but also increases revenue collection and cost recovery.

To promote sustainability, subsidy programs could be linked with income-generating activities. Also, subsidies should be minimal and integrated with community mobilization and awareness-enhancing activities.

The poor ought to be provided with assistance to reduce their out-of-pocket expenses. Higher insurance support for the poor could be financed by implementing innovative interventions, such as a progressive fee-for-service.

6.4.2   Removing physical barriers to improve access

Reliable road and transport networks are important for the poor and remote communities to afford and have access to health and education services. Farm-to-market roads not only help enhance farming productivity and profitability but also play a significant role in making basic social services accessible. Establishing emergency, community-based transport and communication networks is especially crucial in remote communities where SBAs are scarce, birthing facilities are absent, and rates of maternal and neonatal mortality are high.

6.4.3 Promoting awareness of what and where services can be accessed

Better information and increased awareness raise the willingness of households to pay and access basic services. To this end, various information, education, and communication strategies could be customized to the cultural and demographic landscape of poor communities, such as the true costs and benefits of clean water, good sanitation, and healthy practices and behaviors, as well as the importance of education. In addition, social programs must encourage school enrollment, especially among poor households. Improved education will have a lasting impact on the ability and willingness of future generations to access basic services.

6.4.4 Focusing effort on quality of services

Service quality helps determine willingness to access, willingness to pay, and human development outcomes. In this context, it is important to build the capacity of service workers and professionals so that they are skilled and responsive to the needs of clients. Performance-based incentives are needed to improve effort and attitudes among professionals and their support staff, especially in areas where absenteeism is common, human resources are scarce and unevenly distributed, and development outcomes are poor.

6.4.5 Enhancing governance and addressing corruption

To discourage corruption and achieve better outcomes public-private partnerships should be intensified. In addition, both providers and users of services should assume full or maximum accountability of service provision and use. Government authorities should actively perform their regulatory functions to monitor and evaluate staff performance. This could be assisted by installing reliable and tamper-proof technology-aided tools. Similar tools can be used to monitor electricity and water consumption, helping curb corrupt and illegal practices. It is also useful to assess and communicate client feedback to service providers. Aside from promoting quality improvement, this helps ensure accountability and build clients' confidence in accessing the services.

References

ADB. 2002. Impact Evaluation Study on Water Supply and Sanitation Projects in Selected Developing Member Countries. Asian Development Bank, Manila.

———. 2006. Should Asia's Urban Poor Pay for Water? Water Briefs, Asian Development Bank, Manila.

———. 2007a. *Asian Water Development Outlook 2007*. Asian Development Bank, Manila.

———. 2007b. "Country Water Action: Cambodia Phnom Penh Water Supply Authority: An Exemplary Water Utility in Asia." Asian Development Bank, Manila. Available: www.adb.org/water/actions/CAM/PPWSA.asp.

Ahmed, R. 2003. *NGO Intermediation: A Model for Securing Access to Water for the Urban Poor*. Available: www.wateraid.org.uk/in_depth/in_depth_publications/1503.asp, downloaded 20 November 2008.

Annear, P. L., M. Bigdeli, R. C. Eang, and B. R. Jacobs. 2008. "Providing Access to Health Services for the Poor: Health Equity in Cambodia." In B. Meessen, X. Pei, B. Criel, and G. Bloom, eds., *Health and Social Protection: Experiences from Cambodia, China and Lao PDR*. Studies in Health Services Organisation and Policy No. 23, International Labour Office, Geneva.

Anwar, A. T. M. I., J. Killewo, M. K. Chowdhry, and S. K. Dasgupta. 2005. "Bangladesh: Inequalities in Utilization of Maternal Health Care Services—Evidence from Matlab." In D. R. Gwatkin, A. Wagstaff, and A. S. Yazbeck, eds., *Reaching the Poor with Health Nutrition, and Population Services: What Works, What Doesn't and Why*. World Bank, Washington, DC.

Azfar, O., and T. Gurgur. 2007. "Does Corruption Affect Health and Education Outcomes in the Philippines?" *Economics of Governance* 9(3):197–244.

Banerjee, A., and E. Duflo. 2006. "Addressing Absence." *Journal of Economic Perspectives* 20(1):117–32.

Banerjee A., A. Deaton, and E. Duflo. 2004. "Wealth, Health, and Health Services in Rural Rajasthan." *American Economic Review* 94(2):326–30.

Barat, L. M., N. Palmer, S. Basu, E. Worrall, K. Hanson, and A. Mills. 2004. "Do Malaria Control Interventions Reach the Poor? A View Through the Equity Lens." *The American Journal of Tropical Medicine and Hygiene* 71(2):174–78.

Bearse, P., G. Glomm, and E. Janeba. 2000. "Why Poor Countries Rely Mostly on Redistribution In-kind." *Journal of Public Economics* 75(3):463–81.

Bell, J., S. Curtis, and S. Alayón. 2003. Trends in Delivery Care in Six Countries. DHS Analytical Studies No. 7, ORC Macro and the International Research Partnership for Skilled Attendance for Everyone, Calverton, MD.

Bridges, G. 2007. "Country Papers." In *Asian Water Development Outlook 2007*. Asian Development Bank, Manila.

221

Campbell, O. M., and W. J. Graham. 2006. "Strategies for Reducing Maternal Mortality: Getting on with What Works." *Lancet* 368:1284–99.

Chakraborty, N., M. Islam, R. Chowdhury, W. Bari, and H. Akhter. 2003. "Determinants of the Use of Maternal Health Services in Rural Bangladesh." *Health Promotion International* 18(4):327–37.

Chaudhury, N., and J. S. Hammer. 2004. "Ghost Doctors: Absenteeism in Rural Bangladeshi Health Facilities." *World Bank Economic Review* 18(3):423–41.

Chaudhury, N., J. Hammer, M. Kremer, K. Muralidharan, and F. H. Rogers. 2006. "Missing in Action: Teacher and Health Worker Absence in Developing Countries." *Journal of Economic Perspectives* 20(1):91–116.

Chomitz, K., G. Setiadi, and A. Azwar. 1998. What do Doctors Want? Developing Incentives for Doctors to Serve in Indonesia's Rural and Remote Areas. World Bank Policy Research Working Paper No. 1888, World Bank, Washington, DC.

Dalton, A., and S. Peacock. 2005. Study of the Link between Health and Poverty: Technical Report. World Health Organization, Phnom Penh.

Das, J., and J. Hammer. 2004. Which Doctor? Combining Vignettes and Item Response to Measure Doctor Quality. World Bank Policy Research Working Paper No. 3301, World Bank, Washington, DC.

———. 2007a. "Location, Location, Location: Residence, Wealth, and the Quality of Medical Care in Delhi, India." *Health Affairs* 26(3):338–51.

———. 2007b. "Money for Nothing: The Dire Straits of Medical Practice in Delhi, India." *Journal of Development Economics* 83(1):1–36.

Davis, J. 2004. "Corruption in Public Service Delivery: Experience from South Asia's Water and Sanitation Sector." *World Development* 32(1):53–71.

Davis, J., G. White, S. Damodaron, and R. Thorsten. 2008. "Improving Access to Water Supply and Sanitation in Urban India: Microfinance for Water and Sanitation Infrastructure Development." *Water Science & Technology* 58(4):887–91.

Demery, L. 2000. *Benefit Incidence: A Practitioner's Guide*. World Bank, Washington, DC. Available: http://siteresources.worldbank.org, downloaded 15 February 2009.

DOH. 2008a. "Improve Access of the Poor to Quality and Affordable Essential Drugs." *Health Policy Notes* 1(6):1–6. Department of Health, Manila.

———. 2008b. "Multi-sectoral Action Key to Improving Access to Water and Sanitation Services." *Health Policy Notes* 1(5):1–4. Department of Health, Manila.

———. 2008c. "Ensure Adequate Supply and Equitable Distribution of Competent Human Resources for Health in the Country." *Health Policy Notes* 2(2):1–6. Department of Health, Manila.

Duflo, E., R. Hanna, and R. Stephen. 2008. Monitoring Works: Getting Teachers to Come to School. CEPR Discussion Papers 6682, Centre for Economic Policy Research, London.

Dussault, G., and M. C. Franceschini. 2006. "Not Enough There, Too Many Here: Understanding Geographical Imbalances in the Distribution of the Health Workforce." *Human Resources for Health* 4(12). Available: www. human-resources-health.com/content/4/1/12.

Ehrlich, I., and F. T. Lui. 1999. "Bureaucratic Corruption and Endogenous Economic Growth." *Journal of Political Economy* 107(S6):S270–29.

Filmer, D. 2003. "Determinants of Health and Education Outcomes." Background Note for *World Development Report 2004: Making Services Work for Poor People*. Available: www-wds.worldbank.org, downloaded 15 February 2009.

Ghuman, S., J. R. Behrman, S. Gultiano, and E. M. King. 2006. *Children's Nutrition, School Quality, and Primary School Enrollment in the Philippines*. New York, NY: Population Council.

Glewwe, P. 1999. "Why does Mother's Schooling Raise Child Health in Developing Countries? Evidence from Morocco." *The Journal of Human Resources* 34(1):124–59.

_____. 2004. "An Investigation of the Determinants of School Progress and Academic Achievement in Vietnam." In P. Glewwe, D. Dollar, and N. Agrawal, eds., *Economic Growth, Poverty, and Household Welfare in Vietnam*. World Bank, Washington, DC.

Gupta, S., H. Davoodi, and R. Alonso-Terme. 2002. "Does Corruption Affect Income Inequality and Poverty?" *Economics of Governance* 3(1):23–45.

Gupta, S., H. Davoodi, and E. R. Tiongson. 2001. "Corruption and the Provision of Healthcare and Education Services." In A. K. Jain, ed., *The Political Economy of Corruption*. London: Routledge.

Hindricks, J., M. Keen, and A. Muthoo. 1999. "Corruption, Extortion and Evasion." *Journal of Public Economics* 74:395–430.

Hongoro, C., and B. McPake. 2004. "How to Bridge the Gap in Human Resources for Health." *Lancet* 364:1451–56.

Hossain, N., Rashid-ud-Zaman, N. Banksand, and H. C. Geirbo. 2007. BRAC Research Report: The Incentives and Constraints of Government Doctors in Primary Health Care Facilities in Bangladesh. Research and Evaluation Division, Bangladesh Rural Advancement Committee, Dhaka.

Hotchkiss, D. R. 2001. "Expansion of Rural Health Care and the Use of Maternal Services in Nepal." *Health & Place* 7(1):39–45.

IDS. 2007. *Maternal Health and Transport, Key Issues Guide*. Institute of Development Studies, United Kingdom. Available: www.eldis.org/ go/topics/resource-guides/health/key-issues/maternal-health-and-transport, downloaded 25 November 2008.

IEA. 2002, 2006. *World Energy Outlook*. International Energy Agency, Paris.

Jamil, K., A. Bhuiya, K. Streatfield, and N. Chakrabarty. 1999. "The Immunization Programme in Bangladesh: Impressive Gains in Coverage, but Gaps Remain." *Health Policy and Planning* 14(1):49–58.

JHPIEGO. 2004a. "Building Partnerships to Save Mothers: Nepal's SUMATA Initiative." *Mobilizing for Impact*. August:1–4.

_____. 2004b. "Indonesia's SIAGA Campaign Promotes Shared Responsibility." *Mobilizing for Impact* September:1–4.

Koenig, M. A., K. Jamil, P. K. Streatfield, T. Saha, A. Al-Sabir, S. El Arifeen, K. Hill, and Y. Haque. 2007. "Maternal Health and Care-Seeking Behavior in Bangladesh: Findings from a National Survey." *International Family Planning Perspectives* 33(2):75–82.

Komives, K., V. Foster, J. Halpern, Q. Wodon, R. Abdullah. 2005. Water, Electricity, and the Poor: Who Benefits from Utility Subsidies? World Bank, Washington, DC.

Kremer, M., and D. Chen. 2001. An Interim Report on a Teacher Attendance Incentive Program in Kenya. Harvard University, Cambridge, MA.

Kremer, M., N. Chaudhury, F. Halsey Rogers, K. Muralidharan, and J. Hammer. 2005. "Teacher Absence in India: A Snapshot." *Journal of the European Economic Association* 3(2–3):658–67.

Kumar, V., S. Mohanty, A. Kumar, R. P. Misra, M. Santosham, S. Awasthi, A. H. Baqui, P. Singh, V. Singh, R. C. Ahuja, J. V. Singh, G. K. Malik, S. Ahmed, R. E. Black, M. Bhandari, and G. L. Darmstadt. 2008. "Effect of Community-Based Behaviour Change Management on Neonatal Mortality in Shivgarh, Uttar Pradesh, India: A Cluster-Randomised Controlled Trial." *The Lancet* 372(9644):1151–62.

Mahal, A., J. Singh, F. Afridi, V. Lamba, A. Gumber, and V. Selvaraju. 2000. Who Benefits from Public Spending in India? National Council of Applied Economic Research, New Delhi.

Makinen, M., H. Waters, M. Rauch, N. Almagambetova, R. Bitran, L. Gilson, D. McIntyre, S. Pannarunothai, A. L. Prieto, and G. R. Ubilla. 2000. "Inequalities in Health Care Use and Expenditures: Empirical Data from Eight Developing Countries and Countries in Transition." *Bulletin of the World Health Organization* 78(1):55–65.

Mauro, P. 1998. "Corruption and the Composition of Government Expenditure." *Journal of Public Economics* 69(2):263–79.

McIntosh, A. 2007. "Water Supply and Sanitation Issues in South Asia." Discussion Paper for the *Asian Water Development Outlook 2007*. Asia-Pacific Water Forum, Asian Development Bank, Manila.

Nanda, G., K. Switlick, and E. Lule. 2005. Accelerating Progress towards Achieving the MDG to Improve Maternal Health: A Collection of Promising Approaches. Health, Nutrition and Population (HNP) Discussion Paper, International Bank for Reconstruction and Development and World Bank's Human Development Network, Washington, DC.

O'Donnell, O., E. van Doorslaer, R. P. Rannan-Eliya, A. Somanathan, S. R. Adhikari, D. Harbianto, C. C. Garg, P. Hanvoravongchai, M. N. Huq, A. Karan, G. M. Leung, C. W. Ng, B. R. Pande, K. Tin, K. Tisayaticom, L. Trisnantoro, Y. Zhang, and Y. Zhao. 2007. "The Incidence of Public Spending on Healthcare: Comparative Evidence from Asia." *The World Bank Economic Review* 21(1):93–123.

Paternostro, S., and A. Rajaram. 2007. "How does the Composition of Public Spending Matter?" *Oxford Development Studies* 35(1):47–82.

Pattanayak, S. K., K. Dickinson, J-C. Yang, S. R. Patil, P. Praharaj, and C. Poulos. 2007. Promoting Latrine Use: Midline Findings from a Randomized Evaluation of a Community Mobilization Campaign in Bhadrak, Orissa. Environmental and Natural Resource Economics Working Paper 07–02, Research Triangle Institute, North Carolina.

Peters, D. H., A. S. Yazbeck, R. Sharma, G. Ramana, L. H. Pritchett, and A. Wagstaff. 2002. *Better Health Systems for India's Poor: Findings, Analysis, and Options*. World Bank, Washington, DC.

Pillai, R. K., S. V. Williams, H. A. Glick, D. Polsky, J. A. Berlin, and R. A. Lowe. 2003. "Factors Affecting Decisions to Seek Treatment for Sick Children in Kerala, India." *Social Science & Medicine* 57(5):783–90.

Pretus, L. D., O. Jones, L. Sharma, and R. K. C. Shrestha. 2008. Money Down the Pan? Community Level Models for Financing Sanitation in Rural Nepal: A Sector Review. Asian Development Bank and WaterAid, Nepal.

Quah, J. S. T. 2003. "Causes and Consequences of Corruption in Southeast Asia: A Comparative Analysis of Indonesia, the Philippines and Thailand." *Asian Journal of Public Administration* 25(2):235–66.

Rajkumar, A. S., and V. Swaroop. 2008. "Public Spending and Outcomes: Does Governance Matter?" *Journal of Development Economics* 86(1):96–111.

Quimbo, S. A., J. W. Peabody, R. Shimkhada, K. Woo, and O. Solon. 2008. "Should We Have Confidence if a Physician is Accredited? A Study of the Relative Impacts of Accreditation and Insurance Payments on Quality of Care in the Philippines." *Social Science and Medicine* 67(4):505–10.

Serneels, P. M., M. Lindelow, J. G. Montalvo, and A. Barr. 2007. "For Public Service or Money: Understanding Geographical Imbalances in the Health Workforce." *Health Policy and Planning* 22(3):128–38.

Shleifer, A., and R. W. Vishny. 1993. "Corruption." *The Quarterly Journal of Economics* 108(3):599–617.

Shuchen, M., T. Yong, and L. Jiayi. 2004. "Rural Water Supply and Sanitation in China: Scaling Up Services for the Poor." A case study from *Reducing Poverty, Sustaining Growth: What Works, What Doesn't, and Why*. A Global Exchange for Scaling Up Poverty Reduction Success, Global Learning Process and Conference, 25–27 May, Shanghai.

Suryadarma, D., A. Suryahadi, S. Sumarto, and F. Halsey Rogers. 2006. "Improving Student Performance in Public Primary Schools in Developing Countries: Evidence from Indonesia." *Education Economics* 14(4):401–29.

Tietjen, K., A. Rahman, and S. Spaulding. 2004. *Time to Learn: Teachers' and Students' Use of Time in Government Primary Schools in Bangladesh.* Basic Education and Policy Support Activity. Creative Associates International, Inc., USAID, Washington, DC.

UNDP. 2006. *Human Development Report 2006: Beyond Scarcity: Power, Poverty and the Global Crisis.* New York: Palgrave Macmillan for the United Nations Development Programme.

UNICEF. 2006. *Situation of Children and Women in Nepal.* United Nations Children's Fund, Kathmandu.

UPecon-HPDP. 2008. Family Health Book (FHB) Baseline Surveys. UPecon Foundation, Inc. Health Policy Development Program, University of the Philippines Diliman, Quezon City.

Van Damme, W., L. van Leemput, I. Por, W. Hardeman, and B. Meessen. 2004. "Out-of-pocket Health Expenditure and Debt in Poor Households: Evidence from Cambodia." *Tropical Medicine & International Health* 9(2):273–80.

Wagstaff, A. 2002. "Poverty and Health Sector Inequalities." *Bulletin of the World Health Organization* 80(2):97–105.

Wagstaff, A., and E. van Doorslaer. 2003. "Catastrophe and Impoverishment in Paying for Health Care: With Applications to Vietnam 1993–98." *Health Economics* 12(1):921–33.

WaterAid. 2006. Total Sanitation in South Asia: The Challenges Ahead. WaterAid Discussion Paper, WaterAid, London.

Whitehead, M., G. Dahlgren, and T. Evans. 2001. "Equity and Health Sector Reforms: Can Low-income Countries Escape the Medical Poverty Trap?" *The Lancet* 358(9284):833–36.

WHO. 2001. Maternal Mortality in 1995: Estimates Developed by WHO, UNICEF, UNFPA. World Health Organization, Geneva.

WHO/UNICEF Joint Monitoring Programme for Water Supply and Sanitation. 2008. *Progress on Drinking-Water and Sanitation: Special Focus on Sanitation.* Available: www.who.int/water_sanitation_health/monitoring/jmp2008/en/index.html, downloaded 6 November.

World Bank. 2002. Achieving Education for All in Post-conflict Cambodia. *Education Notes.* Available: www.worldbank.org/education, downloaded 19 November 2008.

_____. 2004a. *World Development Report 2004: Making Services Work for the Poor.* Washington, DC.

_____. 2004b. "School Fees: A Roadblock to Education for All." *Education Notes*. Available: www.worldbank.org/education, downloaded 19 November 2008.

_____. 2005. *Cambodia: Quality Basic Education for All. Human Development Sector Reports*. East Asia and the Pacific Region, Washington, DC. Available: www.worldbank.org, downloaded 19 November 2008.

_____. 2008. Can South Asia End Poverty in a Generation? Available: www. web.worldbank.org, downloaded 19 November 2008.

_____. Various years. World Development Indicators Online. Available: http://devdata. worldbank.org/dataonline/.

Yazbeck, A. S., D. Gwatkin, A. Wagstaff, and J. Qamruddin. 2005. "Why were the Reaching the Poor Studies Undertaken?" In D. R. Gwatkin, A. Wagstaff, and A. S. Yazbeck, eds., *Reaching the Poor with Health Nutrition, and Population Services: What Works, What Doesn't and Why*. World Bank, Washington, DC.

7

Social Protection in Asia

Donghyun Park

7.1 Introduction: The case for social protection in developing Asia

Broadly speaking, social protection refers to society's protection of its individual members from various lifetime risks. Some population groups, in particular the poor, are more vulnerable to such risks than others. Social protection usually takes the form of government programs such as labor market interventions, social insurance, and social safety nets. Among these, the modern cradle-to-grave welfare state throughout developed countries firmly took root in the postwar era.

Until quite recently, conventional wisdom held that poorer countries could not afford social protection and that they should concentrate on achieving rapid economic growth. Such perception was shaped by the Washington Consensus that implied that poverty reduction naturally follows from growth (see, for example, Perry et al. 2006). The experiences of the East Asian miracle economies seemed to vindicate this line of thinking. Decades of uninterrupted economic growth lifted hundreds of millions out of poverty through trickle-down effects.

The devastating Asian financial crisis of 1997/1998, however, shattered the complacent notion that growth and growth alone guarantees poverty reduction, alerting regional governments to the importance of social protection. The economic impact of the crisis was severe and resulted in high unemployment and other social dislocations. In retrospect, a major silver lining of the Asian crisis was that, in its aftermath, governments across Asia began paying more attention and devoting more resources to social protection. Economic growth based on sound macroeconomic policies is necessary for sustained poverty reduction, but it is not sufficient. There is a growing global consensus that sustained poverty reduction requires social protection programs that directly address the needs of society's most vulnerable groups. In Asia, this consensus is bolstered by the painful memories of the social and economic havoc wrought by the region-wide financial crisis.

The definition of economic growth has thus been evolving from a narrow concept based on an increase in gross domestic product (GDP) per capita to a broader concept encompassing the *quality* of growth. A natural consequence of this evolution is the concept of inclusive growth. Social protection is an integral and indeed indispensable ingredient of inclusive growth for two reasons. First, failure to protect those who do not directly benefit from economic growth, such as the chronically poor, is intrinsically inconsistent with inclusive growth. Social protection is a mechanism for ensuring that the marginalized and the vulnerable benefit from and thus participate in growth. Second, social protection can stimulate economic activity and growth by encouraging individuals to take risks. Investment and other productive endeavors typically involve risk-taking, and social protection helps cushion the adverse effects should the rewards fail to materialize.

The case for social protection is part and parcel of a general demand for more inclusive growth. At the same time, a number of specific factors are lending a sense of urgency to the task of strengthening social protection in Asia.

First, Asia is set to experience rapid *population ageing* in the 21st century. A young continent reaping the demographic dividend of a large, youthful workforce is giving way to a graying continent where the ratio of retirees to workers is on the rise. The proportion of the elderly relative to working-age population (Figure 7.1) and total population (Figure 7.2) is increasing. It is evident that the entire region will have a drastically different, much grayer demographic profile by 2050.

As in the industrialized countries, this demographic transition is driven by falling fertility (Figure 7.3) and rising life expectancy (Figure 7.4), driven by a constellation of economic and social factors. For example, throughout Asia improved female education is bringing down births per woman and better medical care is contributing to longer average life spans. Other demographic indicators such as the median age and life expectancy at 60 also point unequivocally toward a graying continent (Table 7.1). Social protection is vital for ensuring that the large numbers of the elderly do not fall victim to old-age poverty, lack of access to health care, and other risks.

Figure 7.1   Ratio of population aged ≥65 to population aged 15−64 (%), 1950−2050

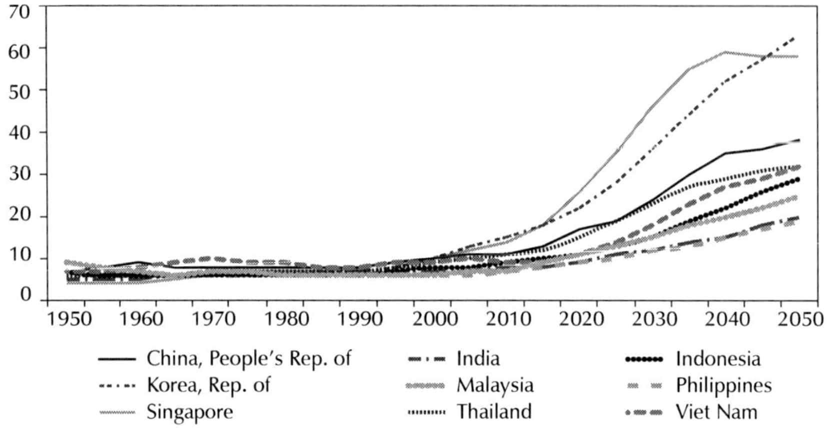

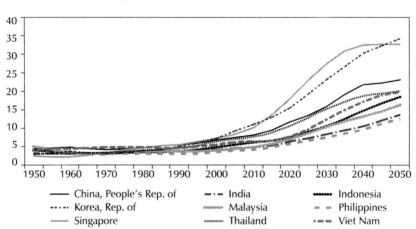

Source: *World Population Prospects: The 2008 Revision,* available: esa.un.org/unpp, downloaded 10 November 2009 (United Nations Secretariat 2008).

Figure 7.2   Ratio of population aged ≥65 to total population (%), 1950−2050

Source: *World Population Prospects: The 2008 Revision,* available: esa.un.org/unpp, downloaded 10 November 2009 (United Nations Secretariat 2008).

Figure 7.3   Fertility rate (number of children per woman),
1950−2050

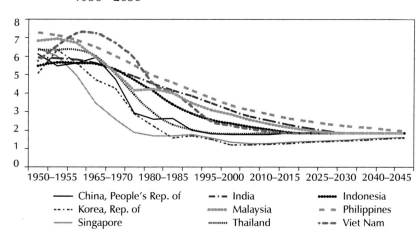

Source: *World Population Prospects: The 2008 Revision*, available: esa.un.org/unpp, downloaded
10 November 2009 (United Nations Secretariat 2008).

Figure 7.4   Life expectancy at birth (years),
1950−2050

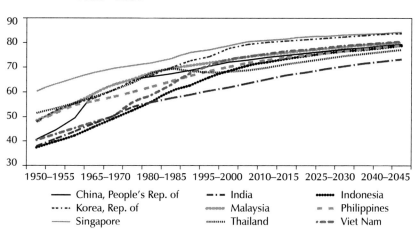

Source: *World Population Prospects: The 2008 Revision*, available: esa.un.org/unpp, downloaded
10 November 2009 (United Nations Secretariat 2008).

231

Table 7.1   Demographic indicators of selected Asian countries

Economy	Total population (millions)		Average annual rate of change of population		Total fertility rate		Median age	
	2007	2050	2005–2010	2045–2050	2005–2010	2045–2050	2005	2050
World	6,671.2	9,191.3	1.17	0.36	2.6	2.0	28.0	38.1
PRC	1,328.6	1,408.8	0.58	-0.32	1.7	1.8	32.5	45.0
India	1,169.0	1,658.2	1.46	0.32	3.1	1.8	22.7	38.6
Indonesia	231.6	296.9	1.16	0.10	2.2	1.8	26.5	41.1
Korea, Rep. of	48.2	42.3	0.33	-0.89	1.2	1.5	35.0	54.9
Malaysia	26.6	39.6	1.69	0.41	2.6	1.8	24.7	39.3
Philippines	87.9	140.5	1.90	0.50	3.2	1.8	21.8	36.3
Singapore	4.4	5.0	1.19	-0.38	1.2	1.6	37.5	53.7
Thailand	63.9	67.4	0.66	-0.27	1.8	1.8	32.6	44.3
Viet Nam	87.4	120.0	1.32	0.21	2.1	1.8	24.9	41.6

Economy	Life expectancy at birth		Life expectancy at 60, 2000–2005		Population aged 60 and above (%)		Population aged 60 and above (millions)	
	2005–2010	2045–2050	Men	Women	2005	2050	2005	2050
World	67.2	75.4	–	–	10.3	21.8	672.8	2,005.7
PRC	73.0	79.3	20	17	11.0	31.1	144.0	437.9
India	64.7	75.6	18	17	7.5	20.2	87.6	334.9
Indonesia	70.7	78.6	18	16	8.3	24.8	18.9	73.6
Korea, Rep. of	78.6	83.5	23	18	13.7	42.2	6.6	17.8
Malaysia	74.2	80.1	19	17	6.7	22.2	1.7	8.8
Philippines	71.7	78.7	19	17	6.0	18.2	5.1	25.5
Singapore	80.0	84.6	23	20	12.3	39.8	0.5	2.0
Thailand	70.6	78.1	20	17	11.3	29.8	7.1	20.1
Viet Nam	74.2	80.3	20	18	7.6	26.1	6.5	31.3

– = data not available, PRC = People's Republic of China.

Source: World Population Prospects: The 2006 Revision and World Urbanization Prospects: The 2005 Revision, available: esa.un.org/unpp, downloaded 10 January 2008 (United Nations Secretariat 2006).

Second, the weakening of informal family-based support mechanisms suggests a bigger role for formal social protection throughout the region. Asians have traditionally relied upon their children to take care of material needs in old age. The family network was in effect Asia's pension system, especially in rural areas where the extended families of three generations often lived together under one roof. More broadly, informal family-based support served as a social protection mechanism in which family members and neighbors helped each other in times of need. However, the far-reaching social changes of the region's economic progress are less conducive to intra-family assistance. Such changes include rapid urbanization (Figure 7.5) and the declining economic importance of agriculture (Figure 7.6). Changing social and cultural norms and values are also contributing to the weakening of traditional family-based support. In short, urbanization, industrialization, and cultural changes are creating a vacuum in Asia's family-based social protection—a vacuum that must be filled by formal social protection.

Figure 7.5   Urban population as share of total population (%), 1950–2050

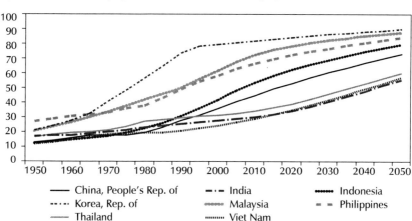

Source: *World Population Prospects: The 2006 Revision and World Urbanization Prospects:* The 2007 Revision, available: esa.un.org/unpp, downloaded 10 November 2009 (United Nations Secretariat 2008).

Third, Asia has reaped enormous benefits from economic globalization through access to foreign markets, capital, and technology (Figure 7.7). However, as in other parts of the world, the competitive pressures unleashed by globalization produce both winners and losers. The very nature of globalization, which accelerates restructuring and reallocation of resources, exacerbates economic insecurity. Effective social protection systems are seen as the best shock absorbers against the structural changes brought about by globalization. In the best-case scenario, a robust social protection system will protect the poor from external shocks and strengthen political support for globalization. More precisely, globalization has made social protection essential for at least three reasons: (i) to cushion the burden of restructuring; (ii) to increase the legitimacy of often painful structural reforms; and (iii) to encourage risk-taking by individuals and firms by providing a floor level of income.

Figure 7.6   Agriculture as share of GDP (%), 1960–2007

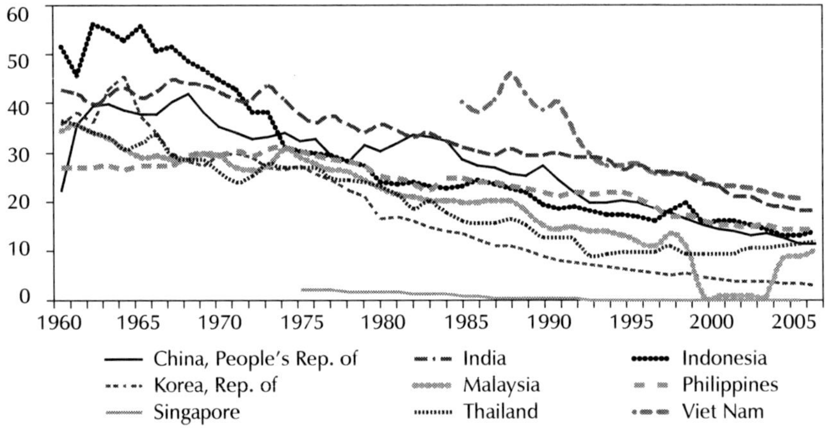

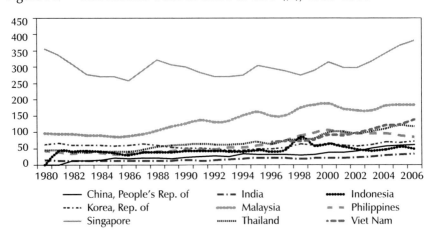

Source: World Bank, World Development Indicators Online, downloaded 10 November 2009.

Figure 7.7   International trade as share of GDP (%), 1980–2006

Source: International Monetary Fund, International Financial Statistics online database, available: www.imfstatistics.org/imf, downloaded 16 May 2008.

Fourth, labor market developments stemming from globalization also strengthen the case for pension reform in the region. By forcing firms and industries to cut labor costs, globalization has brought about greater labor market flexibility. This entails a loss of job security for workers— evident in the rising importance of part-time work. Although beneficial for employers, part-time work generally entails lower pay, more limited benefits, and generally less favorable conditions for workers. Part-time workers often have no coverage or partial coverage under social protection programs. Flexibility also increases labor mobility, which limits the access of workers to social protection, e.g., loss of vested pension rights. Furthermore, the labor markets of Asian countries, especially the poorer countries, are characterized by large numbers of informal sector workers who lack access to even minimum levels of social protection (Figure 7.8). Those workers are not protected by labor regulations and lack pensions, health care, and other benefits.

Figure 7.8   Share of informal sector employment in urban employment (%), various years

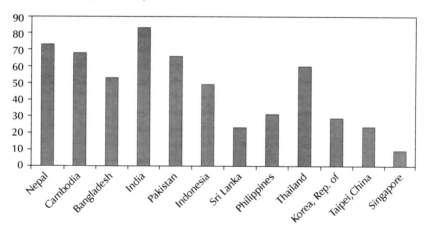

Source: ADB (2005).

Fifth, the demand for good governance is growing throughout Asia. Successful economies such as the Republic of Korea (Korea) and Taipei,China have made the transition from authoritarian political systems to full-fledged multiparty democracies. More generally, regardless of the political system, technological progress is promoting openness, transparency, and accountability in governments. The diffusion of the internet and information technology is limiting the ability of Asian governments to control and manipulate information. The freer flow of information is forcing governments to be more accountable for abuses of power and poor governance. Even in Asian countries with limited political openness the growing demand for good governance is evident in social discontent and unrest. The poor and the vulnerable are finding their voices and asking for government assistance in managing the risks they face. In short, Asians who need social protection the most are beginning to vocally demand it.

7.2   The ABCs of social protection: Basic concepts

As its name implies, social protection refers to the broad set of government policies and programs designed to protect individuals from becoming poor, vulnerable, and marginalized. According to the social protection strategy of the Asian Development Bank (ADB 2003), social protection refers to "the set of policies and programs designed to reduce poverty and vulnerability by promoting efficient labor markets, diminishing people's exposure to risks, and enhancing their capacity to protect themselves against hazards and the interruption/loss of income."

Social safety nets and social security are sometimes used as alternative terms for social protection. However, both are somewhat more restricted and less precise concepts. Social safety nets have an ambiguous meaning, but one narrow definition refers to it as welfare programs and targeted programs for the poor. Social security denotes the existing comprehensive mechanism for social protection in industrialized countries. In the United States, for example, social security programs pay monthly benefits to those whose earnings decline due to retirement, death, or disability, and also help cover medical expenses. Social security is often used interchangeably with pension, even though pension is only one part of social security. Box 7.1 provides a glossary of terms related to social protection.

Social protection policies and programs involve five main types: (i) labor market policies and programs; (ii) social insurance programs; (iii) social assistance; (iv) micro and area-based schemes; and (v) child protection. Labor market policies and programs are designed to facilitate labor adjustments and promote the efficient operation of labor markets. Social insurance programs cushion the risks associated with unemployment, disability, work, injury, and old age. Social assistance and welfare programs protect those with no other means of adequate support. A few countries use means-tested programs to cover a very large portion of the population against risks due to old age, disability, death, or unemployment. An example of micro- and area-based schemes is social funds, which are financed to provide temporary employment in public works in local communities. Child protection activities are designed to help children meet their basic needs such as health and education. The diversity of the specific activities that fall under the five main types of social protection policies and programs suggests that social protection is a fairly comprehensive concept (see Table 7.2).

Box 7.1   Glossary of social protection concepts

Individual risk bearing: In the context of insurance, individual risk bearing means that an individual assumes all the risk, without any sharing of risks with others. For example, in defined contribution pension plans, the individual is responsible for his own investment and longevity risks. Individual risk pooling is to be contrasted with social risk pooling.

Social assistance: Social assistance or welfare programs seek to protect those without any other means of adequate support. Social assistance programs are usually means-tested and designed to cover the poor and marginalized groups that social insurance programs fail to reach. In the context of pension systems, in many countries social assistance-type pensions financed out of general revenues provide minimum pension benefits for the lifetime poor.

Social insurance: A core component of social protection is government-mandated social insurance programs that provide income support, protecting individuals from risks stemming from unemployment, disability, work injury, sickness, maternity, old age, and death. Social insurance thus runs the gamut of insurance programs that protect individuals from the wide range of risks they face. One of those risks is the loss or reduction of income during old age, which is addressed by pension—i.e., old-age insurance.

Social insurance principle: Social insurance is to be contrasted with private insurance. Individuals can voluntarily purchase insurance on their own from the private market. Social insurance, on the other hand, involves mandating everyone to be a member of an insurance program, and thus to pool their risks.

Social protection: Social protection is defined as the set of policies and programs designed to reduce poverty and vulnerability by promoting efficient labor markets, diminishing people's exposure to risks, and enhancing their capacity to protect themselves against risks and loss of income. Social protection involves five major kinds of programs: social insurance programs, social assistance, labor market policies and programs, micro- and area-based

continued.

Box 7.1 *continued*.

schemes, and child protection. Pension systems are often a part of social insurance programs and may also involve some social assistance.

Social risk pooling: Social risk pooling for insurance programs, including pensions, can take one of two forms. First, every member of society may be required to join a mandatory insurance program. In this case, the whole society pools the risks of individual members and bears the risks on their behalf. For example, in government-mandated defined benefit pension plans, investment and longevity risks are shared by all members of society. Second, social risk pooling also occurs when an insurance program is financed out of budgetary revenues since those revenues are derived from the whole society. This type of risk pooling is especially relevant for programs that target the poor.

Social safety net: Social safety net is sometimes used as an alternative term for social protection. However, social safety net sometimes refers only to welfare and targeted programs for the poor.

Social security: Social security is another alternative term for social protection. However, social security is a narrower concept than social protection since it usually denotes the existing mechanism for social protection in industrialized countries. In the United States, for example, social security programs pay monthly benefits to those whose earnings decline due to retirement, death or disability, and also provide help with medical expenses. Social security is often used interchangeably with pension, even though pension is only one part of social security.

The social security programs listed in Table 7.2 can be categorized into four general categories in terms of the benefits they deliver. First, some programs bring direct and tangible benefits to subgroups of the poor and the vulnerable through cash or in-kind transfers. Examples include social assistance payments, scholarships or other educational assistance, health subsidies, food aid, disaster aid, and food for work programs.

Second, some programs, insurance in particular, directly benefit only a limited proportion of the population they cover. For example, the young do not receive benefits even though they make contributions to the pension system.

Third, some programs provide benefits for the community as a whole rather than individual households. Examples include social funds and community-based schemes such as microinsurance.

Fourth, some programs are legal and legislative measures such as child protection laws, which bring less tangible benefits to the poor and the vulnerable.

Table 7.2   Social protection: Components
             and subcomponents

Components	Subcomponents
Labor market programs	Direct employment generation (microenterprise development and public works)
	Labor exchanges and other employment services
	Skills development and training
	Labor legislation (including minimum age, wage levels, health and safety, etc.)
Social insurance programs	Programs to cover the risks associated with unemployment, sickness, maternity, disability, industrial injury, and old age
Social assistance and welfare programs	Welfare and social services targeted at the sick, indigent, orphans, and other vulnerable groups
	Cash/in-kind transfers (e.g., food stamps)
	Temporary subsidies for utilities and staple foods
Micro and area-based schemes (community-based)	Microinsurance schemes, agricultural insurance
	Social funds (usually involving the construction, operation, and maintenance of small-scale physical and social infrastructure)
	Disaster preparedness and management
Child protection	Early child development activities, e.g., basic nutrition, preventative health, and educational programs
	Educational assistance (e.g., school-feeding, scholarships, fee waivers)
	Health assistance (e.g., reduced fees for vulnerable groups)
	Street children initiatives
	Child rights and advocacy/awareness programs against child abuse, child labor etc.
	Youth programs to reduce health risks (especially HIV/AIDS and drugs) and antisocial behavior
	Family allowances (e.g., in-kind or cash transfers to assist families with young children to meet part of their basic needs)

Source: ADB (2008b).

Social risk management is a useful concept for understanding the motivation behind social protection. According to the World Bank (2001), individuals, households, and communities are exposed to risks from a variety of sources. Some of those risks are natural—such as earthquakes—while others are manmade—such as environmental degradation.

The poor suffer disproportionately from risk due to greater exposure to and a lack of capacity to manage it, and consequently become more risk-averse and less productive. While the poor have developed self-protection mechanisms to cope with risks, such as family-based risk pooling and saving during good times, these are often costly and inefficient.

There is thus a compelling rationale for government intervention and social security programs. This is especially true in developing Asia where market-based risk management arrangements are still weak because market institutions are still evolving. Furthermore, informal family- and community-based risk management is declining in Asia due to urbanization and industrialization. Nevertheless, the appropriate social risk management strategy for any country will have to incorporate all three types of arrangements, although the optimal mix will differ across countries.

The broader strategic choice facing Asian countries in the context of social protection can be framed in terms of individual risk bearing versus social risk pooling, representing fundamentally different approaches to managing risks. The two approaches are not mutually exclusive and the choice between the two is one of balance. Social protection entails efficiency costs since it requires contributions and tax payments from workers and firms. These costs are more affordable for industrialized economies than developing Asian economies, for which rapid economic growth remains an urgent priority. In addition to affordability, a society's subjective tradeoff between efficiency and equity also plays a key role in determining the extent of social protection and social risk pooling. The economic, social, and political contexts shaping strategic choices on social protection will differ among Asian countries. Nevertheless, all Asian countries will need to make such choices and their choices will have far-reaching repercussions for their social and economic development for years to come.

Broadly speaking, an optimal social protection system is one that covers as much of the society as possible, delivers adequate yet affordable benefits for the target population, and does both on a financially sound basis. For individuals, society, and the government, the main objectives of any social protection system are to (i) protect against unexpected loss of income and smooth consumption over a person's lifetime, (ii) provide insurance against risks such as sickness and unemployment, (iii) redistribute income from the better-off to the worse-off, and (iv) alleviate both chronic and transient poverty. However, these have to be traded off against economic growth, labor market efficiency and flexibility, and against other needs like health, education, and infrastructure. Individual, fiscal, and societal affordability should be kept in mind when designing social protection systems, and benefits must evolve over time in line with affordability.

Any social protection system must perform five core functions: (i) reliable collection of contributions, taxes and other receipts, including any loan payments (in some social protection programs, a member is permitted to borrow for housing, education or other purposes, but the loan needs to be repaid); (ii) timely and accurate payment of benefits for each of the programs; (iii) securing efficient financial management and productive investment of assets, if any; (iv) maintaining an effective communication network, including development of accurate data and record keeping mechanisms to support collection, payment, and financial activities; and (v) production of financial statements and reports that promote better governance, fiduciary responsibility, transparency, and accountability. In developing Asia, organizational reforms that enable the social protection system to perform the five tasks more professionally and effectively are a prerequisite for broader systemic reform.

At the systemic level, a well-designed social protection system should ideally be: broad-based, that is, *adequate* in both coverage and range of risks covered; *affordable* from individual, business, fiscal, and macroeconomic perspectives; financially sound and *sustainable* over time; *robust* so as to withstand macroeconomic and other shocks; and provide a minimum *safety net* for the poor and the vulnerable. This implies a fairly complex objective function for a social protection system. Societies need to decide through policy makers the relative weights given to adequacy, affordability, sustainability, robustness, and level of safety nets. A classic example of a tradeoff is that between adequacy and financial sustainability. Different societies will make different tradeoffs according to their circumstances; and the same society may opt for different tradeoffs at different stages of its social and economic development.

7.3   The state of social protection in developing Asia

Having reviewed the case for social protection in Asia and its conceptual underpinnings, the chapter can now evaluate its state in the region. Given the breadth and diversity of social protection policies and programs, this is a daunting task in a country, let alone a region. Nevertheless, a study completed by ADB (2008b), *Social Protection Index for Committed Poverty Reduction, Volume 2: Asia*, sets out to do just that.

The study had its origins in an earlier pilot study commissioned by ADB to assess and compare social protection in six Asian countries. The pilot study was motivated by the fact that there had been few attempts to quantify the impact of social protection activities in terms of expenditure, beneficiaries, or impact of the programs, and to assess social protection schemes using a standard methodology. It was later extended to 25 other Asian countries, including Japan, and provides the most comprehensive and systematic analysis of social protection in Asia to date. The inclusion of Japan is useful because it provides an industrialized-country benchmark. The study covers all of Asia's subregions—East Asia, South Asia, Central and West Asia and the Pacific—and most of its countries (see Table 7.3).

Table 7.3   Countries included in the 2008 ADB study

Central and West Asia	South Asia	East Asia	Pacific
Armenia	Bangladesh*	Cambodia	Cook Islands
Azerbaijan	Bhutan	China, People's Rep. of	Fiji Islands
Kazakhstan	India	Indonesia*	Marshall Islands
Kyrgyz Republic	Maldives	Japan	Nauru
Tajikistan	Nepal*	Korea, Rep. of	Papua New Guinea
Uzbekistan	Pakistan*	Lao PDR	Tonga
	Sri Lanka	Malaysia	Tuvalu
		Mongolia*	Vanuatu
		Philippines	
		Viet Nam*	

* Pilot study countries.
Lao PDR = Lao People's Democratic Republic.
Source: ADB (2008b).

The study is based on the construction of an internationally comparable social protection index (SPI) that provides a realistic and acceptable summary of the overall level of social protection activities in a country. The SPI provides a summary measurement tool of the extent to which Asian and Pacific countries provide welfare, labor market, social security, health insurance, microcredit, child protection, and targeted education and health support programs to their citizens, and especially those living below the poverty line. It is designed as a starting point for diagnostic evaluations of national social protection programs to enable the monitoring of changes in social protection provision over time, and to facilitate international comparisons. Conceptually based on the human development index[1], the SPI is derived from four social protection summary indicators (SPSIs):

---

[1]   The Human Development Index, an index combining life expectancy, literacy, and GDP per capita for countries worldwide, is compiled by the United Nations Development Programme.

(i)   social protection expenditure (SPEXP)
(ii) social protection coverage (SPCOV)
(iii) social protection distribution/poverty targeting (SPDIST)
(iv) social protection impact on incomes of the poor (SPIMP).

The ADB study defined social protection as the set of policies and programs that enable vulnerable groups to prevent, reduce, and/or cope with risks, and that: (i) are targeted at vulnerable groups; (ii) involve cash or in-kind transfers; and (iii) are not activities usually associated with other sectors such as rural development, basic infrastructure, health, and education (see Table 7.4).

Table 7.4   Components and subcomponents of social protection included in the 2008 ADB study

Component/subcomponent of social protection	Included/ excluded	Comments
Labor market programs		
Direct employment generation (microenterprise development and public works)	Included	Includes loan-based programs to support small businesses, etc.
Labor exchanges and other employment services	Included	Including retrenchment programs
Skills development and training	Excluded	Unless targeted at particular groups, such as the unemployed or disadvantaged children
Labor legislation (including minimum age, wage levels, health and safety, etc.)	Included	Not amenable to quantification
Social insurance programs		
Programs to cover the risks associated with unemployment, sickness, maternity, disability, industrial injury, and old age	Included	
Health insurance	Included	
Social assistance and welfare programs		
Welfare and social services targeted at the disabled, the indigent, those affected by disasters, and other vulnerable groups	Included	
Cash/in-kind transfers (e.g., food stamps, health cost exemptions, or subsidies)	Included	

continued.

Table 7.4 *continued*.

Component/subcomponent of social protection	Included/ excluded	Comments
Temporary subsidies for utilities, housing, etc.	Included	Only if targeted at particular vulnerable groups; general subsidies are excluded even if their rationale is to assist the poor
Micro and area-based schemes		
Microinsurance/microfinance schemes	Included	Microfinance seen as an important aspect of social protection; mainstream rural credit programs will be excluded
Agricultural insurance	Included	Not very common
Social funds	Excluded	Except where direct transfers to households occur
Disaster preparedness and management	Included	Reconstruction of physical infrastructure is excluded; cash/in-kind grants included; number of beneficiaries not amenable to quantification
Child protection		
Child rights and advocacy/awareness programs against child abuse, child labor, etc.	Included	Not amenable to quantification
Early child development activities	Excluded	Unless directly targeted to particular groups, (e.g., children of single mothers), or involving handouts such as child/maternity benefits
Educational assistance (e.g., school-feeding, scholarships, fee waivers)*	Included	Assistance for upper secondary and tertiary education is excluded
Health assistance* (e.g., health cost reduced fees/subsidized medicines for vulnerable groups)	Included	Will generally be included under social assistance
Family allowances	Included	Transfers through the tax system are excluded
Street children/child worker/orphan initiatives	Included	

* = Basic education and health services are excluded.
Source: ADB (2008b).

Of the four component SPSIs of the SPI, two (SPEXP and SPIMP) relate to expenditures while the other two (SPCOV and SPDIST) relate to coverage. Furthermore, two components (SPEXP and SPCOV) target the general population while the other two (SPIMP and SPDIST) specifically target the poor (see Table 7.5).

Table 7.5   Characteristics of social protection summary indicators

Variable targeting	Expenditure	Coverage
General	SPEXP	SPCOV
Pro-poor	SPIMP	SPDIST

SPCOV = social protection coverage, SPDIST = social protection distribution, SPEXP = social protection expenditure, SPIMP = social protection impact.
Source: ADB (2008b).

Each of the four SPSIs is a ratio of two variables. Computing the numerator requires data on specific variables such as expenditures, beneficiaries, and poverty targeting of the major social protection programs. Computing the denominator requires data on general variables such as GDP and the poor population (see Table 7.6). Finally, the SPI, the overall summary of social protection, is an equally weighted sum of its four component SPSIs.

Table 7.6   Social protection summary indicators: Data requirements

SPSI	Numerator	Denominator
SPEXP	Total expenditure on all social protection programs	Gross domestic product
SPCOV	Beneficiaries of social protection programs targeted at key target groups	Reference populations for key target groups
SPDIST	Number of social protection beneficiaries who are poor	Poor population
SPIMP	Average social protection expenditure for each poor person	Poverty line

SPCOV = social protection coverage, SPDIST = social protection distribution, SPEXP = social protection expenditure, SPIMP = social protection impact, SPSI = social protection summary indicator.
Source: ADB (2008b).

The following discussion looks at the results for each of the four SPSIs. Social protection expenditure (SPEXP) is defined as the ratio of a country's total social protection expenditure to its GDP. The measure indicates the amount of resources a country devotes to social protection programs relative to its economic size. SPEXP values range from a low of 0.3% in Papua New Guinea to a high of 16% in Japan (Figure 7.9). Other Asian countries with high SPEXP values include Korea, a newly industrialized economy, and three Central Asian countries. Japan, and to a lesser extent Korea, have comprehensive social security systems in line with their high incomes. The high SPEXP values of some Central Asian countries are a legacy of the cradle-to-grave welfare states of the Soviet era, and may not be sustainable. Countries with the lowest SPEXP values tend to be low-income. Asia as a whole allocates about 4.8% of its output, on average, to social protection programs. In terms of the composition of SPEXPs, social insurance accounts for the largest share in Asia as a whole as well as in each of the subregions (Table 7.7). With the exception of Japan, Korea, and some Central Asian states, social insurance programs are confined to the public and formal sectors, and thus exclude large segments of the population, including the great majority of the poor.

Figure 7.9   Social protection expenditure as share of GDP (%)

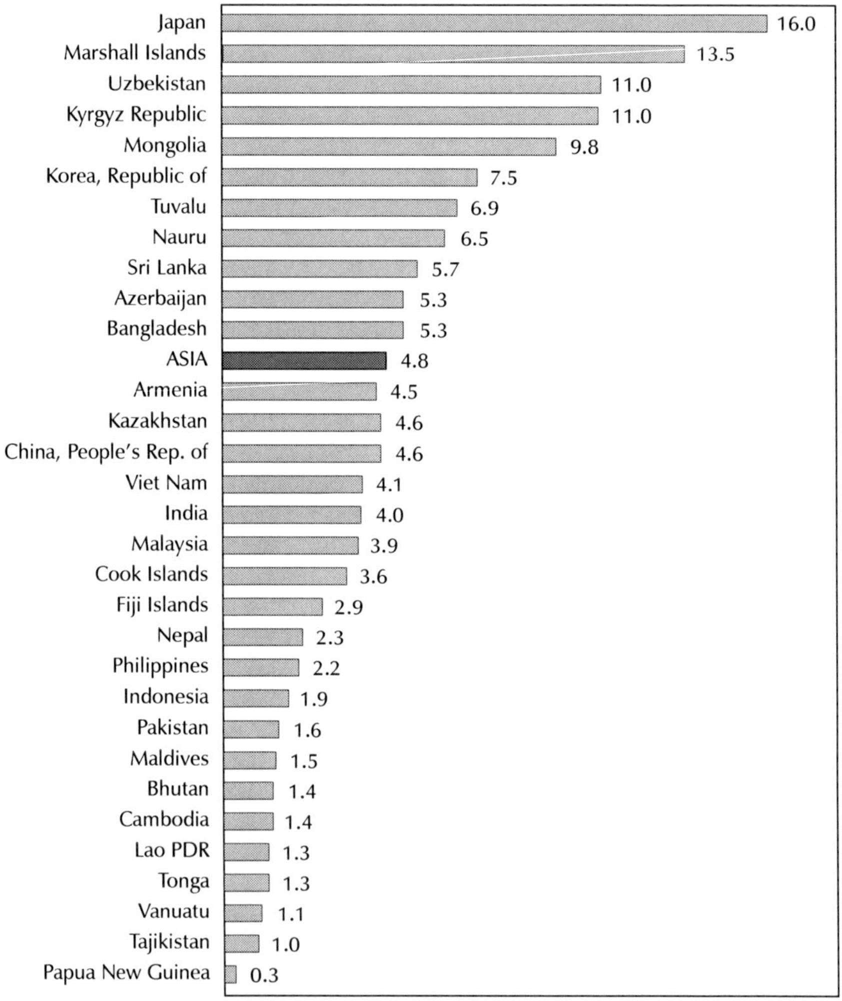

Japan	16.0
Marshall Islands	13.5
Uzbekistan	11.0
Kyrgyz Republic	11.0
Mongolia	9.8
Korea, Republic of	7.5
Tuvalu	6.9
Nauru	6.5
Sri Lanka	5.7
Azerbaijan	5.3
Bangladesh	5.3
ASIA	4.8
Armenia	4.5
Kazakhstan	4.6
China, People's Rep. of	4.6
Viet Nam	4.1
India	4.0
Malaysia	3.9
Cook Islands	3.6
Fiji Islands	2.9
Nepal	2.3
Philippines	2.2
Indonesia	1.9
Pakistan	1.6
Maldives	1.5
Bhutan	1.4
Cambodia	1.4
Lao PDR	1.3
Tonga	1.3
Vanuatu	1.1
Tajikistan	1.0
Papua New Guinea	0.3

Lao PDR = Lao People's Democratic Republic.
Source: ADB (2008b).

Table 7.7   Social protection expenditure by program category (%)

Region	Labor market programs	Social insurance*	Social assistance	MCF	Child protection	All
Central Asia	2	58	24	6	9	100
South Asia	7	44	13	26	9	100
East Asia	6	64	13	13	4	100
Pacific	12	53	20	8	8	100
All Asia	7	55	17	13	7	100

*All social insurance including pensions, health insurance, maternity, and survivors' and disability benefits.
MCF = microcredit finance.
Source: ADB (2008b).

The SPCOV measures the coverage of social protection, i.e., what proportion of the target population actually receives some social protection. SPCOV is *not* obtained by simply summing up the total number of beneficiaries of all social protection programs due to overlap between programs. That is, some people may receive benefits from more than one program. Instead SPCOV is obtained by applying weights to the coverage rate of each of seven target groups—the unemployed, underemployed, elderly, sick, poor, disabled, and children with special needs. Different social protection programs target different groups— e.g., pensions and social assistance targeting the elderly. The coverage ratio varies widely among Asian countries for all seven target groups (Table 7.8). The overall coverage ratio (SPCOV) for Asia as a whole is 0.35 on average (Figure 7.10). Japan, Korea, and the Central Asian states have the highest overall coverage while Papua New Guinea and other Pacific states, along with Pakistan, have the lowest overall coverage.

Table 7.8   Target group coverage ratios (%)

Coverage ratios	Unemployed/ under-employed	Elderly	Sick (health care)	Social assistance (the poor)	MCF (the poor)	Disabled	Poor children
Maximum	100	100	100	100	100	100	100
Minimum	0	1	0	1	0	0	2
Average	31	52	22	54	18	41	62
Median	21	40	7	58	10	22	62
SD	30	38	32	35	22	39	37
Ratio: SD/mean	95	74	142	64	123	96	61

MCF = microcredit finance, SD = standard deviation.
Source: ADB (2008b).

Figure 7.10   Overall social protection coverage

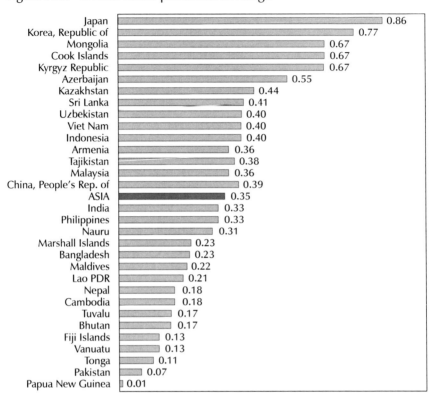

Lao PDR = Lao People's Democratic Republic.
Source: ADB (2008b).

The SPDIST measures the extent to which a country's social protection policies and programs reach the poor. This indicator is based on an overall estimate of the pro-poor targeting of major social protection programs—i.e., poor beneficiaries of social protection programs as a percentage of the poor population. The approach used for SPCOV—the weighted sum of different social protection programs— was not used for SPDIST due to the greater difficulties in choosing appropriate weights. For Asia as a whole, on average, poor beneficiaries of social protection programs account for 56% of the poor population (Figure 7.11). Japan, Korea, and the Central Asian states have the highest poverty targeting rates. Both India and Sri Lanka also score well due to large-scale social assistance programs—the public food distribution system in India and Samurdhi in Sri Lanka. At the other end, Papua New Guinea and other Pacific states, along with Pakistan, have the lowest poverty targeting rates.

Figure 7.11   Social protection distribution/poverty targeting (%)

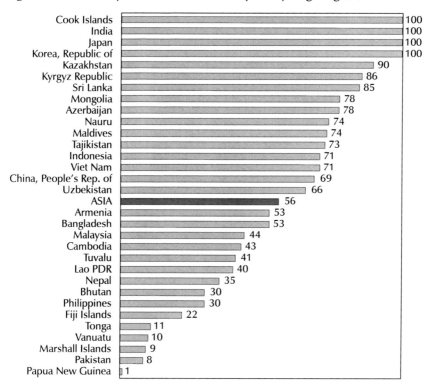

Lao PDR = Lao People's Democratic Republic.
Source: ADB (2008b).

The SPIMP measures the extent to which social protection programs increase the income of the poor. While SPDIST measures the extent to which social protection programs reach the poor, it gives no information about the magnitude of the assistance they provide. SPIMP was designed to address this issue. It is defined as the per capita SPEXP going to the poor as a percentage of the national poverty line. For Asia as a whole, the average SPEXP for each poor person is 23% of the poverty line (Figure 7.12). The income impact of social protection is highest in Japan, Korea, Central Asian states, and People's Republic of China (PRC), and lowest in Papua New Guinea, other Pacific states, Pakistan, and Tajikistan. In the PRC, much of the SPEXP for the poor takes the form of training, health care, and other non-cash programs that do not directly increase income. Furthermore, the expenditures disproportionately benefit the urban population.

Figure 7.12   Impact of social protection on income of the poor (%)

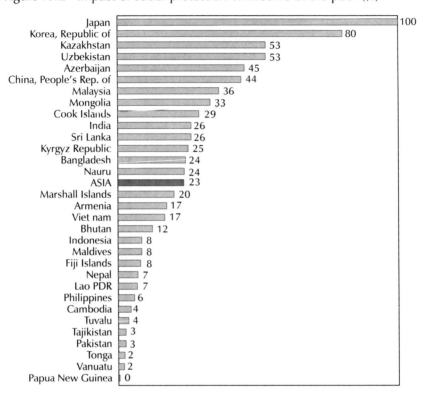

Lao PDR = Lao People's Democratic Republic.
Source: ADB (2008b).

The SPI measures the overall state of social protection and is computed from the four component SPSIs. The SPI is a summary of social protection that assigns equal weights to four aspects of social protection—expenditures, coverage, distribution or poverty targeting, and impact on income of the poor. Transforming the four SPSIs into a single SPI is a straightforward two-step exercise: (i) scale SPEXP using the maximum value of 0.16; and (ii) add the scaled SPEXP value to the values of the three other SPSIs and divide the sum by four. SPI values range from a minimum of 0.01 in Papua New Guinea to a maximum of 0.96 in Japan (Figure 7.13). The countries with the strongest social protection are Japan, Korea, and the Central Asian states, while those with the weakest social protection are Papua New Guinea and other Pacific states, along with Pakistan. For Asia as a whole, the average value of SPI is 0.36. Using Japan's SPI value as the proxy value for the SPI value of industrialized countries, Asia's social protection is currently around 37.5% of that in the industrialized countries.

Figure 7.13   Social protection index: overall summary of social protection

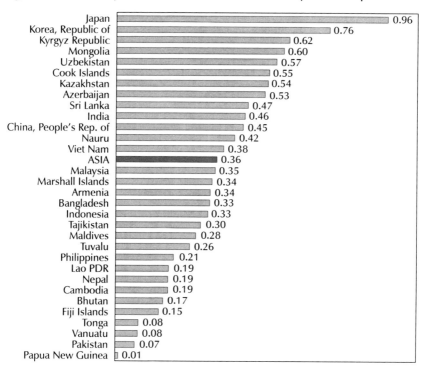

Lao PDR = Lao People's Democratic Republic.
Source: ADB (2008b).

In addition to quantitative estimates, the ADB study also yields some interesting qualitative information about social protection in Asia. This information is a by-product of the analysis of each country's social protection systems, which were a prerequisite for finding the data needed to compute the SPSIs and SPI. Virtually all countries had a formal social insurance system. In the majority of cases, those systems were limited to the government and formal employment sectors. As such, they had little relevance to the informal and rural sectors, which constituted a large segment of the population and contained the majority of the poor. Similarly, almost all countries had traditional social welfare programs that targeted vulnerable groups such as the poor and the elderly. However, the beneficiaries of such programs were limited to the poorest of the poor. Much more prevalent were large-scale targeted social assistance programs involving cash or in-kind (i.e., food) assistance. Many countries also had targeted programs to improve educational attendance, as well as various programs to improve access to health services of the poor. Finally, most countries also had some labor market programs, although these varied considerably in nature and coverage.

7.4   Asian pension systems and pension reform

Having surveyed the current state of social protection in Asia from a broad perspective, it would be useful to take an in-depth look at a single component of social protection. Given the enormous scope and diversity of social protection programs, it is difficult to make meaningful generalizations about the challenges facing those programs. For example, protecting children requires addressing a whole different set of issues than, say, mitigating the effects of unemployment. Therefore, analyzing a single program and identifying the various challenges facing that particular program may give a better feel for what Asian governments need to do to protect the poor and the vulnerable. Furthermore, while it is true that no two social protection programs are identical, diagnosing one particular program, identifying its major shortcomings, and mapping out directions for reform also hold some valuable lessons for strengthening other programs and social protection in general.

The social protection program chosen for a closer look is the pension system. A core component of social protection is government-mandated social insurance programs that, by providing income support, protect individuals from risks stemming from unemployment, disability, work injury, sickness, maternity, old age, and death. Social insurance thus runs the gamut of insurance programs that protect individuals from the wide range of risks they face during their lifetime. One of those risks is the loss or reduction of income during old age, which is addressed by pensions—i.e., old-age insurance. Park (2009) provides an in-depth analysis of where Asian pension systems stand today and what they need to do to improve their performance. Box 7.2 provides a glossary of pension-related terms. Due to the fundamental reshaping of Asia's demographic profile, discussed earlier, old-age income support will be one of the biggest social and economic challenges facing Asia in the 21st century. The weakening of informal, family-based old-age support also provides further rationale for reforming Asia's pension systems.

Broadly speaking, an optimal pension system is one that covers as much of the society as possible, delivers adequate yet affordable retirement benefits for its members, and does both on a financially sound basis. The primary objectives of any pension system are to (i) smooth consumption over a person's lifetime; (ii) provide insurance against longevity risk, inflation risk, investment risk, and other risks; (iii) redistribute income; and (iv) relieve old-age poverty.

Box 7.2   Glossary of pension concepts

Defined benefit: As the name suggests, defined benefit (DB) pension schemes are the polar opposite of defined contribution (DC) schemes. Under DB pension schemes, the benefits to be paid (from contributions by employees, employers, and government where applicable) are defined but contributions are not. The benefits are determined by a fixed formula that involves factors such as total number of years worked. In DB schemes, the scheme sponsor—e.g., employer, government—bears the investment and longevity risk. Contributions may be used directly to finance payments to retirees or instead to purchase assets, but in either case retirement benefits do not depend on the returns on investment of assets.

Defined contribution: Under defined contribution (DC) pension schemes, contributions (by employees, employers, and government where applicable) are defined but retirement benefits are not. Contributions are used to purchase assets, and the size of benefits depends on the rate of return on those assets. If the investment of assets yields high returns, pension benefits will be relatively high. In DC schemes, the member has to bear the investment and longevity risk.

Defined contribution, notional: In a notional defined contribution scheme, a worker's account is set up as a bookkeeping device to keep track of contributions plus imputed interest at a rate determined by the government. However, funds never accumulate in these accounts. Instead, current contributions are used to pay current benefits, and the accounts are notional or empty. When the worker reaches retirement age, the notional accumulation in his/her account is converted into an annuity and paid out of the contributions that younger workers are making at that time.

Financial reserves: Financial reserves arise when the timing of receipts and payments differs due to deliberate policy decisions or demographic factors. The accumulated reserves are subsequently used to pay pension benefits, but they need to be invested in the mean time.

Fully funded: In contrast to a pay-as-you-go (PAYG) scheme, under a fully funded (FF) scheme the contributions of current workers do not finance the benefits of current retirees. Instead those contributions are used to purchase assets and the returns to those assets—i.e., their principal and interest—are used to pay the future benefits of the current workers. Under a FF scheme, unlike a PAYG, workers essentially finance their pension benefits with their own contributions. A broader definition of FF is that the value of a pension scheme's long-term assets equals the value of its long-term liabilities.

Inflation risk: The risk that the real value or purchasing power of pension benefits is eroded due to inflation.

Investment risk: The risk that the investment of a pension scheme's assets may yield poor or even negative returns.

continued.

Box 7.2 *continued*.

Longevity risk: The risk that the resources accumulated for use during retirement may be exhausted before death.

Mandatory versus voluntary: The basis of participation is mandatory for some pension schemes and voluntary for others.

Partially funded and unfunded: Partial funding occurs when long-term assets cover some but not all long-term liabilities. Unfunded means there is no long-term accumulation of assets to cover long-term liabilities.

Pay-as-you-go: Under a PAYG pension scheme, the contributions of current workers are used, directly or indirectly, to finance the benefits of current retirees. Therefore, in a PAYG scheme, the contributions of current workers pay for the benefits of current retirees.

Pension fund: Pension fund refers to the fund designated to disburse post-retirement benefits that members may receive from the pension scheme sponsors. These could be a public or private corporation, nonprofit organization, or government. In general, the term pension is used when the benefits are paid periodically throughout life after retirement. A pension fund usually refers to DB schemes.

Pension system: A country's pension system consists of all the different pension schemes in operation in the country. Under a pension scheme, which provides old-age income support, current workers pay contributions or taxes into the system and current retirees receive benefits or payments from the system. Pension schemes may be mandatory or voluntary, sponsored by the employer or the government, DC or DB, and PAYG or fully funded.

Prefunding: Prefunding refers to accumulating assets to pay for future pension benefits. DC schemes are based on prefunding, but prefunding also occurs in DB schemes that have financial reserves.

Provident fund: A provident fund is essentially a savings scheme that may be voluntary or mandatory. A mandatory scheme is usually called a national provident fund if it is managed by a governmental organization. Usually, a provident fund pays a lump sum of accumulated balances that equal contributions plus interest income minus pre-retirement withdrawals to each member upon his or her retirement. Provident funds are typically DC schemes.

Replacement rate: The basic measure of the adequacy of pension benefits for old-age income support. It is the ratio of post-retirement monthly income to pre-retirement monthly income or the average monthly wage in the economy.

State/national pension scheme versus occupational pension scheme: A state or national pension scheme covers all individuals in a country. An occupational pension scheme only covers the employees of the employer setting up the scheme.

The core functions of pension systems are analogous to the core functions of social protection programs laid out in Section 7.2—e.g., reliable collection of contributions and timely payment of benefits. These are functions that any pension system, regardless of design, must perform effectively. The ideal properties of a well-designed pension system are also analogous to those of a well-designed social protection program, outlined in Section 7.2. Therefore, an optimal pension system should be adequate, affordable, sustainable, robust, and equitable.

Population ageing is an Asia-wide phenomenon but there are significant differences across subregions. In particular, whereas the demographic transition is already well under way in East and Southeast Asia, it is still in its infancy in South Asia. In view of this fact, Park (2008) looks at the pension systems of eight countries in East and Southeast Asia—namely, PRC, Indonesia, Korea, Malaysia, Philippines, Singapore, Thailand, and Viet Nam.

In general, Asian pension systems are relatively new and very much in a state of flux. The oldest systems are those of Malaysia, Philippines, and Singapore, but even those are constantly evolving. The relatively advanced Korean system was created only in 1988 and is still undergoing reforms. Indonesia enacted a law designed to establish a comprehensive social security system in 2004 although it has yet to be fully implemented. Likewise, Thailand and Viet Nam are in the process of revamping their pension systems to extend coverage and improve benefits. The ongoing consolidation of the PRC's pension system from a highly fragmented structure to a two-pillar structure reflects the structural transformation of its economy and society.

One key characteristic of a pension system is the pension age, or the age at which retirees begin to receive their benefits. This ranges from 55 in Indonesia, Malaysia, and Thailand to 65 in Korea and the Philippines (Table 7.9). Pension age is lower for women than men in the PRC and Viet Nam. The difference between life expectancy and pension age is the number of years that a retiree has to depend on pension benefits. The larger this difference, the larger the liabilities of the pension system. The life expectancy-pension age gap ranges from 6.7 years in the Philippines to 19.2 years in Malaysia and 21.2 years for women in Viet Nam. The pension age is expected to rise throughout Asia in response to rising life expectancy.

The pension systems of all eight countries are government-run. However, the basic structure of the pension systems for formal sector workers is far from uniform in the eight countries (Table 7.9). The pension systems of Indonesia, Malaysia, and Singapore are defined contribution (DC) or notional defined contribution while those of Korea, Philippines, Thailand, and Viet Nam are defined benefit (DB). The PRC's pension system combines a DB pillar with another pillar consisting of DC and *notional defined contribution* schemes. The DC systems are generally *prefunded* while DB systems are not. Among the eight countries, ignoring broader social safety nets, only the pension systems of three countries explicitly redistribute income. The Philippines has a minimum pension that pays higher benefits to poor retirees. In the PRC, the redistributive element takes the form of a DB basic pension. In both the PRC and Korea, pension benefits depend partly on average earnings.

Table 7.9   Pension age and basic structure of pension systems, 2007

Country	Pension age (years)	Difference between life expectancy and pension age (years)		Defined benefit or defined contribution	Element of income redistribution
		Male	Female		
China, People's Rep. of	60 (55)	11.3	19.8	Defined benefit, defined contribution, and notional defined contribution	Yes
Indonesia	55	13.7	17.7	Defined contribution	No
Korea, Rep. of	65	10.0	17.2	Defined benefit	Yes
Malaysia	55	17.0	21.7	Defined contribution	No
Philippines	65	4.5	8.9	Defined benefit	Yes
Singapore	62	16.0	19.9	Defined contribution	No
Thailand	55	11.5	20.0	Defined benefit	No
Viet Nam	60 (55)	12.3	21.2	Defined benefit	No

Note: The pension age in parentheses refers to the pension age for women, where different from men. Life expectancy refers to life expectancy at birth.
Source: Park (2009).

The contribution rate for employees and employers differs substantially across countries (Table 7.10). The employee contribution rate ranges from 2% of wages in Indonesia to 20% in Singapore. Total contribution rates are highest in Singapore and Malaysia and lowest in Indonesia and Thailand. The formula for computing pension benefits also varies widely across the five countries with DB pension systems (PRC, Korea, Philippines, Thailand, and Viet Nam).

Table 7.10   Pension contribution rates of employees and employers (%)

Country	Employee	Employer	Total
PRC (defined benefit)	0.00	20.00	20.00
PRC (defined contribution)	8.00	0.00	8.00
Indonesia	2.00	3.70	5.70
Korea	4.50	4.50	9.00
Malaysia	11.00	12.00	23.00
Philippines	3.33	6.07	9.40
Singapore	20.00	14.50	34.50
Thailand	3.00	3.00	6.00
Viet Nam	5.00	10.00	15.00

PRC = People's Republic of China.
Source: Park (2009).

Asian countries face a strategic choice between social risk pooling and individual risk bearing in pension system design. The pension systems of Malaysia and Singapore are unique in the region for their heavy tilt toward individual risk bearing and the relative absence of social risk pooling. Unlike the other countries of the region, the two countries explicitly reject the social insurance principle in old-age income support. Both countries have national provident funds, which are essentially mandatory savings schemes. Relative to Malaysia and Singapore, social risk pooling plays a greater role in the pension systems of the other six countries. However, the six diverge widely in the economic, institutional, and technological capacity needed to apply the social insurance principle. For example, the Korean pension system is part of a comprehensive social security system comparable to those found in welfare states. At the other end, Indonesia is just beginning to lay the foundations of a new social insurance-based social security system. The main pension systems of Korea, Philippines, Thailand, and Viet Nam are all DB systems that protect individual members from investment and longevity risks, as is the PRC's basic pension.

This brief survey of Asian pension systems indicates a great deal of heterogeneity in design and structure. Pension reform requires a diagnosis of the main weaknesses of the pension systems. Those weaknesses impede the ability of pension systems to fulfill their basic objectives such as enabling consumption smoothing and relieving poverty. A diagnosis is essential for identifying the main areas of pension systems that need to be improved and strengthened, and hence for mapping out the strategic directions of reform. Broadly speaking, Asian pension systems suffer from failure in (i) performing the core functions of pension systems as well as (ii) fulfilling the ideal properties of well-designed pension systems such as adequate coverage. Asian pension systems still have some way to go before achieving their main objectives.

With the exception of Korea and Singapore, Asian pension systems suffer from inadequate institutional capacity. The resulting administrative and transaction costs impede the ability of pension systems to perform their core functions to varying degrees in PRC, Indonesia, Malaysia, Philippines, Thailand, and Viet Nam. For example, administrative inefficiency interferes with the ability to reach groups such as rural and informal sector workers. That many Asian pension systems are in a state of flux further adds to high administrative and transaction costs. Compliance cost is a specific transaction cost that hurts Asian pension systems. For example, in the Philippines, which has a superficially comprehensive pension system, widespread noncompliance means a big gap between nominal and effective old-age income support. The lack of institutional capacity can be attributed in large part to the generally weak governance and regulation of Asian pension systems. Strengthening governance and regulation will be essential for improving operational efficiency and transparency.

At one level, Asian pension systems are failing because they fail to effectively perform the five core functions of pension systems due to high transaction costs and lack of strong governance. At another level, they are failing because, to varying degrees, they are not well-designed pension systems, i.e., in terms of adequacy, affordability, robustness, sustainability, and equity. At this level, the biggest failure of Asian pension systems is that they cover only a limited part of the total population. The percentage of population covered by pension systems differs from country to country, but no country has managed to achieve anywhere near universal coverage. The share of the labor force covered by pension systems ranges from 13.2% to 58%, while the coverage rate for working-age population ranges from 10.8% to 40% (Figure 7.14). By way of comparison, in developed countries such as Germany, Japan, and the United States, pension systems typically cover 90% of the labor force and 60–75% of the working-age population. Coverage throughout Asia is much higher for urban, formal sector, and public sector workers than for rural, informal sector, and private sector workers.

Another key performance indicator where Asian countries perform poorly is the replacement rate, or the ratio of retirement income to pre-retirement income. The replacement rate is a widely used measure of the adequacy of pension benefits as a source of post-retirement income. A higher replacement rate enables the pensioner to achieve a higher standard of living. Pension experts generally recommend a replacement rate of between 66% and 75%, adjusted for longevity and inflation risks.

Figure 7.14   Share of labor force and share of population aged 15–64
covered by pension systems (%), 2007

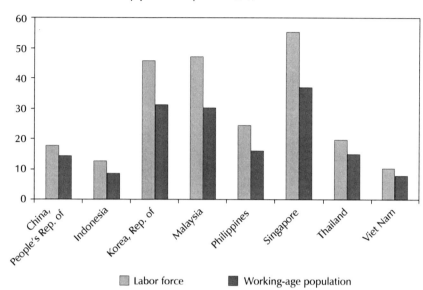

Source: OECD (2008), ADB staff estimates for Malaysia and Singapore.

Two pension modeling studies completed in 2008, one by ADB (2008a) and the other by the OECD (2008), compute the replacement rate for Asian pension systems. According to the ADB study, the replacement rate ranges from 19% in Indonesia to 79% in the Philippines (Figure 7.15). The OECD study finds that the replacement rate ranges from 15% in Indonesia to 77% in the Philippines. Both studies indicate that replacement rates are higher in PRC, Korea, Philippines, and Viet Nam than in Indonesia, Malaysia, Singapore, and Thailand. Among the eight countries, only the Philippines has replacement rates within the recommended range in both studies. This implies that by and large Asian pension systems are not providing an adequate retirement income for retirees.

The PRC's relatively high replacement rate is deceptive in light of its low coverage. If pension benefits are generous but only a small segment of the population receives those benefits, it is unclear whether the pension system is adequate. A useful index that gives a more accurate picture of the adequacy of a country's pension system is the product of multiplying the coverage rate and replacement rate. The proposed index thus incorporates both replacement rate and coverage. The adequacy index is computed on the basis of coverage of the labor force. For the ADB study's replacement rates, the index ranges from 3% in Indonesia

259

to 24% in Korea (Figure 7.16). For the OECD study's replacement rates, the index is between 2% in Indonesia and 22% in Korea. For both sets of replacement rates, the most adequate pension systems seem to be those of Korea, Malaysia, and Philippines, and the least those of Indonesia, Thailand, and Viet Nam.

Figure 7.15   Replacement rate: Ratio of retirement income to pre-retirement income (%), 2007

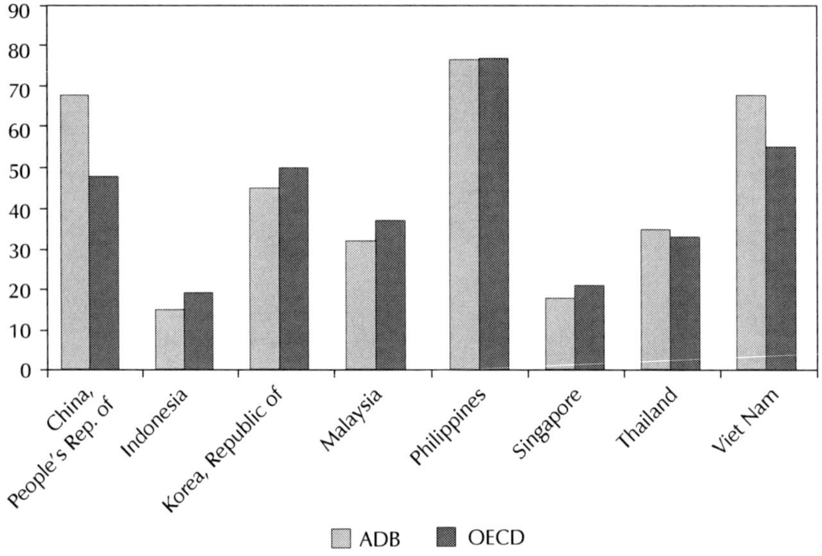

Source: ADB (2008a), OECD (2008).

The adequacy of the Philippine pension system brings the issues of sustainability and affordability to the fore. Generous benefits for much of the population are not sustainable in the long run if the country cannot afford them. In this case, the adequacy of the pension system is more apparent than real. A widely used index of sustainability is implicit pension debt, which can be broadly defined as the present value of future pension promises. In Asian countries with DB pension systems, pension promises are unfunded or only partly funded. Studies by the World Bank found the implicit pension debt of PRC, Korea, and Philippines to be substantially larger than the public debt of those countries (Figure 7.17). Therefore, relatively healthy fiscal positions should not be allowed to obscure fiscal risks arising from large future pension liabilities. Furthermore, in all three countries the relative size of the implicit pension debt is large enough to raise concerns about the pension system's ability to honor its future promises. In Korea, such concerns spurred a reduction of benefits beginning in 2008. The implicit pension debt is much higher in the PRC and the Philippines than in Korea, which suggests that the need for sustainability-enhancing reform is even stronger in those countries.

Figure 7.16 Adequacy index of pension systems, 2007

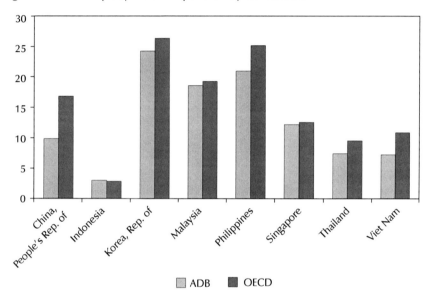

Note: The coverage rate used in the calculation is the coverage rate of the labor force.
Source: ADB (2008a), OECD (2008), ADB staff estimates for the coverage rates of Malaysia and Singapore.

Pension contributions do not seem to significantly distort the incentives of employees to work and employers to hire, even in countries with the highest contribution rates. In this sense, the pension costs are affordable. Given the immaturity of many Asian pension systems, it is too early to tell whether they are robust to adverse shocks. However, the more established pension systems of the region have come through the Asian financial crisis unscathed. Finally, as stated earlier, only the pension systems of PRC, Korea, and Philippines have safety nets designed to protect the elderly poor. However, those safety nets fail to provide enough income for even a minimum standard of living. For example, the basic monthly pension in the Philippines is only ₱300 or less than $7 (as of December 2008), and a recently introduced means-tested benefit for the Korean elderly is only about 5% of the average wage.

Figure 7.17   Ratio of implicit pension debt to GDP and ratio of public debt to GDP in selected countries, 1999/2000

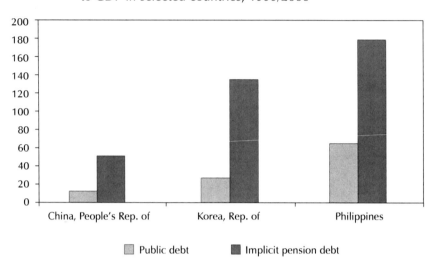

GDP = Gross domestic product.
Source: Holzmann et al. (2004), Sin (2005).

7.5   The way forward

It should be abundantly clear from the preceding analysis that while developing Asia has made a great deal of progress in strengthening its social protection systems, much work remains to be done if the region is to protect the most vulnerable segments of the population from hardship and marginalization. The region's social protection systems fall well below their developed-country counterparts in fulfilling this central mandate, but are comparable to those of other middle-income developing regions such as Latin America.

The three outstanding problems pertain to coverage, adequacy of benefits, and poverty relief. In many developing Asian countries the coverage of social protection programs is largely limited to the formal sector, government workers, and urban areas, which means that millions do not have access to any protection at all. Another common problem, clearly seen in the case of pension systems, is that the level of protection provided by social protection programs is often inadequate.

Yet another region-wide shortcoming is that the programs have generally failed to effectively target those in greatest need of assistance and thus mitigate poverty. On the positive side, all developing Asian countries now have formal social protection systems and are making varying degrees of progress in fortifying them. Furthermore, the fact that some poorer Asian countries have established relatively well-functioning systems indicates that effective social protection is as much a matter of political will and good governance as resources.

At the outset of this chapter, social protection was defined as society's protection of its individual members from the various lifetime risks they face. An alternative but ultimately equivalent definition of social protection is society's provision of security to its members. The single most important determinant of economic security for both the young and the old is the long-term trend rate of economic growth. Sustained economic growth is the ultimate form of social protection, especially in poor developing countries.

It is easy to lose sight of the fact, in light of their remarkable overall economic performance, that the majority of Asian countries still fall into this category (Figures 7.18 and 7.19). By the same token, whether Asia can sustain its economic dynamism is crucial to the economic security of its citizens. The central importance of growth for economic security means that short-term gains in social protection are more apparent than real if they undermine growth and thus long-term economic security.

Figure 7.18   Per capita GDP of selected Asian and industrialized countries ($), 2007

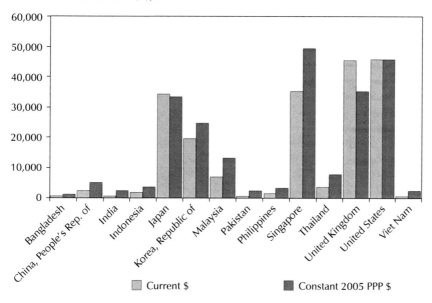

GDP = gross domestic product, PPP = purchasing power parity.
Source: CEIC Data Company Ltd.; International Monetary Fund, World Economic Outlook database, available: www.imf.org/external/pubs/ft/weo/2009/01/weodata/index.aspx, downloaded 16 May 2008.

Figure 7.19   Average annual growth of GDP and per capita GDP (%), 1981–2007

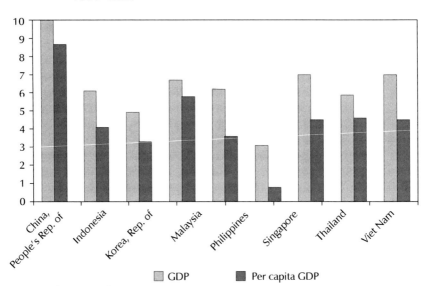

GDP = gross domestic product.
Note: GDP and per capita GDP are measured in constant 2005 purchasing power parity dollars.
Source: International Monetary Fund, World Economic Outlook database, available: www.imf.org/external/
              pubs/ft/weo/2009/01/weodata/index.aspx, downloaded 16 May 2008.

While social protection programs often promote equity, they entail efficiency costs since they are financed by taxes. Those efficiency costs are more affordable for richer societies. The tradeoff between income growth and income distribution is thus more skewed toward growth in developing Asian countries than in the far richer industrialized countries. Full-fledged welfare states that provide comprehensive social security are neither feasible nor desirable for Asia at this stage of its economic development. This is not to say that Asian countries must write off social protection as a luxury for richer countries, which they can only afford in the distant future. To the contrary, as explained earlier, population ageing, weakening of family-based support, globalization, and other factors are increasingly turning social protection into a necessity. However, social protection is not an end in and of itself but a means to promoting economic and social security.

The need to seriously consider the impact of social protection on economic growth has some practical implications for Asian policy makers. For example, the failure to undertake painful but necessary pension reform—e.g., cutting benefits, extending retirement age, and raising contributions—is likely to result in large fiscal liabilities, which, in turn, will jeopardize macroeconomic stability, growth, and security. The upshot is that Asian social protection programs should be designed and implemented in a way that promotes rather than interferes with growth. For example, labor market programs should devote more resources toward skills development and training rather than labor legislation on minimum wage and working conditions. Skills development is a higher priority in developing Asia while labor legislation is a higher priority in industrialized countries. Imposing industrialized-country priorities on Asian social protection may be counterproductive for promoting economic security. For example, labor market legislation that imposes excessive burdens on employers and employees may interfere with labor market flexibility and increase unemployment.

The difference in social protection needs and priorities is not limited to industrialized countries versus developing Asian countries. There is a great deal of heterogeneity among Asian countries themselves in terms of their preferences and constraints. For example, the Central Asian states' strong performance was largely a legacy of the cradle-to-grave welfare state of the Soviet era. Likewise, the relative absence of social risk pooling in the pension systems of Malaysia and Singapore reflects a social preference for individual risk bearing as the primary mechanism for addressing old-age risks. The governments of better-off Asian countries have more fiscal resources available and are generally better equipped than their low-income counterparts to protect their citizens from risks. There are thus no one-size-fits-all solutions. Instead, each country must take into account its own objectives and capacity to guide its reform strategy and process. However, a number of common region-wide themes emerge from the overview of Asian social protection and pension systems. Those themes will help set direction for reforming and strengthening social protection throughout the region.

One common area of reform is to strengthen institutional and administrative capacity to perform the five core functions of social protection systems. Strengthening institutional capacity is the point of departure for social protection reform in Asia, a well-functioning social protection system is simply not possible without adequate capacity. The mundane nature of core functions such as paying benefits on time and developing accurate record keeping systems should not detract from their significance. Therefore, it may be advisable for countries to first devote resources to strengthening their institutional and administrative capacity before implementing ambitious reform programs. Strong governance and regulation are essential for the operational efficiency and transparency of *any* social protection program, and thus also for building up institutional and administrative capacity. Examples of specific measures to promote governance include better accounting, more rigorous financial controls, human resource development, computerization, and greater disclosure to stakeholders. Transparency and accountability will inspire the confidence of the general public and encourage participation in social protection programs.

Another common direction for reform is to separate out social protection programs targeting the entire population from those targeting specific high-risk groups. For example, government-mandated national pension systems are designed to provide adequate old-age income support to the entire population, including the elderly poor. Old-age poverty is especially relevant for Asia where the lifetime poor account for as much as 30% of the labor force in some countries. Unfortunately, even well-run Asian pension systems have been ineffective in fighting old-age poverty. The best way to support the elderly poor may be to establish a *social pension* system that pays a minimum amount for basic sustenance to those who qualify through means-testing. The basic social pension will be financed from general budgetary revenues rather than contributions. A separate social pension system with the explicit objective of poverty relief helps prevent the ad hoc uses of the main pension system's funds. Conversely, a clear-cut separation of general programs from targeted programs will help prevent the diversion of scarce social protection resources to less vulnerable groups, and channel those resources to those who need them most.

Another common theme is that social protection reform requires complementary reform in other areas—fiscal and labor market—to be effective. A social protection system does not exist in a vacuum but within the context of the broader economy and society that defines its objectives and constraints. At a macroeconomic level, fiscal reform and consolidation would give Asian governments the fiscal flexibility to allocate more resources to social protection. At a microeconomic level, fiscal reforms should aim to improve the efficiency with which public services, including social assistance, are delivered.

Another complementary area where reforms are needed is the labor market. In some Asian countries, labor laws and regulations have not been modernized to provide a better balance between creation of new jobs and preservation of old jobs. Much of skills development and training, as well as other social protection programs designed to improve the productivity of high-risk groups, would go to waste in the absence of flexible and well-functioning labor markets. Reforms in other areas would also promote economic security. For example, financial reform that raises the returns to saving would reduce old-age risks for both the poor and the non-poor.

After decades of growth-oriented policies and rapid economic growth, Asia is finally paying more attention to social protection. This shift is not merely due to the fact that Asian countries have become richer and can thus afford to devote more resources to protecting their citizens from various risks. It also reflects a growing recognition that the traditional narrow definition of growth is ultimately harmful for growth. Economic growth in a society where a large segment of the population remains poor, vulnerable, and marginalized cannot possibly be inclusive.

More fundamentally, the social and political constraints to sustaining high growth will eventually become overwhelming in the absence of well-functioning social protection systems. In Asia, population ageing, weakening of family-based support, globalization and other factors are tightening those constraints as never before. In short, the case for strengthening social protection in Asia is as much economic as social.

References

ADB. 2003. *Social Protection: Our Framework Policies and Strategy*. Asian Development Bank, Manila.

_____. 2005. "Labor Markets in Asia: Promoting Full, Productive, and Decent Employment." In *Key Indicators 2005*. Asian Development Bank, Manila.

_____. 2008a. Pension Modeling Study for Eight East Asian Countries. Asian Development Bank, Manila. Processed.

_____. 2008b. *Social Protection Index for Committed Poverty Reduction, Volume 2: Asia*. Asian Development Bank, Manila.

Holzmann, R., R. Palacios, and A. Zviniene. 2004. Implicit Pension Debt: Issues, Measurement and Scope in International Perspective. Social Protection Discussion Paper Series No. 0403, World Bank, Washington, DC.

OECD. 2008. *Pensions at a Glance: Asia/Pacific Edition*. Organisation for Economic Co-operation and Development, Paris.

Park, D. 2009. "Ageing Asia's Looming Pension Crisis." ADB Economics Working Paper No. 165, Asian Development Bank, Manila.

Perry, G., O. S. Arias, J. H. Lopez, W. F. Maloney, and L. Serven. 2006. Poverty Reduction and Growth: Virtuous and Vicious Circles. World Bank Latin American and Caribbean Studies. World Bank, Washington, DC.

Sin, Y. 2005. China Pension Liabilities and Reform Options for Old Age Insurance. Working Paper Series No. 2005-1, World Bank, Washington, DC.

United Nations Secretariat. 2008. *World Population Prospects: The 2008 Revision and World Urbanization Prospects: The 2007 Revision*. Department of Economic and Social Affairs, Population Division, United Nations Secretariat. Available: esa.un.org/unpp.

World Bank. 2001. *Social Protection Sector Strategy: From Safety Net to Springboard*. Washington, DC.

267

8

Governance and Institutional Quality and the Links with Growth and Inequality: How Asia Fares

Juzhong Zhuang, Emmanuel de Dios,
and Anneli Lagman-Martin[1]

8.1   Introduction

Economic growth in developing Asia in recent decades has been nothing short of impressive. For the region as a whole, per capita gross domestic product (GDP) in 2005 purchasing power parity (PPP) terms increased from $1,403 to $3,174 between 1990 and 2005, growing at an annual rate of 5.6%, a pace with few parallels globally and in history. This has led to substantial reductions in extreme poverty: the incidence of poverty measured at $1.25 a day declined from 52% to 27%, and at $2 a day from 79% to 54% (see Chapter 1). However, economic success on such a massive scale has not been uniform across the region. Growth has largely been driven by the People's Republic of China (PRC), India, and several Southeast Asian countries. In many parts of Asia, growth has been slow, increases in per capita income have been limited, and the incidence of extreme poverty remains high. In South Asia in 2005, for example, 43% of the population still lived below the $1.25-a-day poverty line and 76% lived on less than $2 a day. Whether and how lagging economies can catch up with the region's high performers remain a significant development challenge.

Globally, income growth has been effective in reducing absolute poverty, but less so in reducing relative poverty or inequality. In Asia, although spells of growth have raised incomes for all sections of the population in most countries, inequality has also increased, both in income and in non-income dimensions such as access to education and

1   The authors would like to thank Xianbin Yao, Rana Hasan, Ifzal Ali, M. G. Quibria, Guanghua Wan, and Tun Lin for comments on an earlier version of the paper, and Yi Jiang for assistance in data processing. Views expressed in the chapter are entirely those of the authors, not necessarily of the ADB, members of its Board of Directors, or the countries they represent.

health services. This has occurred even in the high-performing economies (see Chapters 2 and 3). As a result, there is a growing realization among policy makers around the region that further progress in achieving broad development goals may be possible only if the character of economic growth itself is changed toward promoting greater inclusiveness. This means not only the sustained generation of new productive opportunities, but also broad access to those opportunities (Ali and Zhuang 2007). The concept of inclusive growth is increasingly being embraced in the region (see Chapter 1).

This chapter looks at the role of governance and institutions in supporting inclusive growth in developing Asia. The essentiality of good governance and institutions has been a key focus in development policy discussions in recent years. While their intrinsic value as ends of development in their own right is now universally accepted and underlies the very notion of inclusiveness, their instrumental value as a means to better growth performance and more equal income distribution is still not well understood—despite the emergence of a considerable, and still growing body of literature (Rodrik 2008). The chapter provides a brief review of this literature, and, in the process, takes a close look at two critical issues that have attracted a great deal of attention: the measurement of governance and institutional quality, and the direction of causality between institutional development and economic development. It then examines how Asia fares in various widely used measures of governance/institutional quality relative to the rest of the world and to what extent certain aspects have been more relevant than others driving the region's recent growth and changing income inequality. Many Asian countries are often considered "outliers" when one looks at the governance/institutions-growth nexus. The chapter investigates to what extent this is the case and its possible explanations, and what these mean for policy formulation in pursuing inclusive growth.

8.2 Governance/institutions vis-à-vis growth and inequality: A literature review

8.2.1 Searching for deep determinants of growth

The current concern in the economics literature over the role of governance and institutions (as well as geography, culture, etc.) can be viewed as part of an ongoing search for the "deep determinants" of economic growth and development. To a large extent, this can be traced to a growing dissatisfaction beginning in the late 1980s with what was until then the pre-eminent "neoclassical" growth model introduced in the 1950s by Solow (1956) and Swan (1956). The standard neoclassical growth model identifies capital accumulation or investment as the central factor in explaining levels of per capita income. Successive attempts to test the neoclassical model empirically, however, turned up ambiguous results at best. This led to a reconsideration of the concept of the "factors of production" to include human capital (Becker 1962) and, in the late 1980s and early 1990s, the development of endogenous growth models to incorporate the level of technology and rate of innovation (Grossman and Helpman 1991).

At a more fundamental level, however, it can be said that all growth models hitherto fail to answer truly *causal* questions. Even if capital accumulation or technological innovation accounts for significant differences in long-run levels of per capita output across countries, the question remains why certain societies succeeded while others failed to take the actions necessary to accomplish such accumulation or innovation. North and Thomas (1973) argue that the factors listed (innovation, economies of scale, education, capital accumulation, etc.) are not causes of growth; they *are* growth. It is in this sense, therefore, that existing growth models have elucidated only the "mechanics" or "correlates" of growth, but have not truly touched on its deep determinants.

Against this background, a new stream of the economics literature has emerged as part of the continued search for deep determinants, known as the new institutional economics (NIE), proceeding primarily from the work of Douglass North (North and Thomas 1976; North 1981, 1990, and 2005). The NIE attempts to extend neoclassical economics by incorporating institutional analysis, focusing on the role of institutions in explaining long-term economic performance. North defines institutions as "rules of the game", that is, the human-devised formal and informal constraints that shape human interactions. Formal institutions refer primarily to constitutions, statutes, and explicit government rules and regulations, codified and enforced by impersonal mechanisms—most importantly, the state with its coercive power and organization. Informal institutions or constraints, on the other hand, include unwritten rules such as traditions, norms and codes of behavior, taboos, and other social mechanisms based on and enforced through interpersonal ties and relations.

Some interpret North's earlier work, based on the history of Western Europe and the United States, as suggesting a unidirectional progression from informal to formal institutions. Aron (2000), for example, writes that North describes a continuum, with unwritten taboos, customs, and traditions at one end, and constitutions and law governing economics and politics at the other; in the absence of formal rules, a dense social network leads to the development of customs, trust, and normative rules that constitute an informal institutional framework; with economic development comes a unidirectional move along the continuum, as increasing specialization and the division of labor associated with more complex societies raise the rate of return to formalizing political, judicial, and economic rules and contracts that facilitate political or economic exchanges.

The NIE's emphasis on impersonal and impartial institutions derives from the central importance of affirming and protecting property rights and contracts, which allows the extension of market exchange, investment, and innovation over wider economic spheres and geographic areas at a reasonably low cost.[2] Predictable contract enforcement and property rights protection are particularly important for transactions beyond simple face-to-face and spot exchanges, which are otherwise fraught with uncertainty and possible opportunism because of the separation in space or time, and, consequently, entail significant transaction costs. For this reason, effective enforcement of rules and sanctions against violation is needed. Only with sanctions would institutions make the actions of individuals predictable (Kasper and Streit 1998).

In the continuum argument, effective sanctions come to support growth only when embodied in the government of a state. The implicit assumption is that only such an extensive organization is capable of internalizing the scale economies inherent in defining rules and has the implicit monopoly of coercive power needed to enforce the rules. Endowing the state with overarching power, on the other hand, creates the opposite problem of possible bias, opportunism, corruption, and usurpation in the discharge of state power by those in leadership positions. Weingast (1993) argues that a government strong enough to protect property and enforce contracts is also strong enough to confiscate the wealth of its citizens. This inherent paradox provides the rationale for accountability and transparency, checks and balances, and wide participation of various organizations as part of the requirements for social order and control.

Thus, according to this framework, accountability, rule of law, political stability, bureaucratic capability, property rights protection and contract enforcement, and control of corruption are mutually reinforcing aspects of growth-enhancing institutions. From this broad theoretical argument follows a hypothesis that societies that fail to establish such formal institutions effectively would be faced with very high costs in market transactions and would be unable to control the "grabbing hand of the state", and, consequently, to support private initiatives, market exchanges and investments, and economic development. The above line of reasoning, however, does not preclude the possibility of a reverse causality. In fact, an alternative view, supported by empirical evidence, predicts that a

---

2   Much of this summarizes the argument in North (1981 and 1990) and North, Wallis, and Weingast (2006) as well as drawing from Greif (2005).

higher level of development will generate the need for and lead to better institutions (Paldam and Gundlach 2008).

Even though North himself drew a distinction between formal and informal institutions, the NIE literature since his original work has focused largely on the role of formal institutions. More recently, however, there has been growing interest in understanding how informal institutions contribute to economic development. Lauth (2005), for instance, looks at how informal and formal institutions interact with each other in a society by distinguishing among three types of relationship: *complementary*, when informal and formal institutions co-exist side by side and mutually reinforce and support each other; *substitutive*, when formal institutions are ineffective and informal institutions play a functionally equivalent role, or vice versa; and *conflicting*, when the two systems of rules are incompatible. Empirical evidence suggests that informal institutions can explain part of the cross-country differences in economic performance (see, for example, Knowles 2005; Knowles and Weatherston 2006; and Easterly, Ritzen, and Woolcock 2006).

The concepts emphasized in the informal institutions literature also feature in the social capital literature.[3] Interest in how social capital is linked with economic development began largely after the seminal work of Coleman (1988) and Putnam (1993). Coleman characterizes social capital as social organization that facilitates the achievement of goals that could not be achieved in its absence or could be achieved only at a higher cost. Putnam defines social capital as features of social organization such as trust, norms, and networks that can improve the efficiency of society. Many different definitions of social capital have emerged since (Durlauf and Fafchamps 2005). Noting that most of these definitions include the notions of trust, cooperative norms, and networks/associations within a society, Knowles (2005) argues that social capital is a notion similar to what North (1990) defines as informal institutions.[4] Rauf (2009) argues that informal institutions are responsible for generating social capital, and social capital captures impacts of informal institutions.

A major hypothesis in the social capital literature is that social capital improves economic performance by reducing transaction costs and encouraging cooperation, a point also made by North with regard to informal institutions. Knowles (2005) summarizes the key channels through which social capital may contribute to economic growth: (i) increasing the number of mutually beneficial trades, (ii) solving collective action problems, (iii) reducing monitoring and transaction costs, and (iv) improving information flows. But the literature also acknowledges cases where social capital

---

3   As well as the culture-economics literature.
4   Knowles (2005) notes that although North (1990) is frequently cited by researchers in both the social capital literature and the NIE literature, neither group of researchers tends to acknowledge the work of the other.

can have negative effects: customs or norms could sometimes *hinder* the introduction of new techniques; social networks and associations may provide benefits for members (insiders) at the expense of non-members (outsiders), and so on. Durlauf and Fafchamps (2005) argue, on the basis of an extensive survey, that while the social capital literature has produced many insights, a number of conceptual and statistical problems exist in the current use of the term "social capital" by social scientists.

8.2.2   From institutions to governance

Alongside these theoretical developments, accumulated experience among international development agencies shows that structural adjustment programs and macroeconomic stabilization plans based on external assistance often failed or have been stymied by intervening political factors. This has led to enquiries into the political environment and the processes that influence policy implementation, beyond the design and content of policy itself. A stream of empirical studies point to how the effectiveness of external assistance depends not only on the nature of the policies pursued, but also on the nature of government (e.g., Burnside and Dollar 2000). On the basis of some empirical observations, for example, Easterly (2006) argues that countries pursuing destructive policies such as high inflation, high black market premiums, and chronically high budget deficits may miss out on growth; but it does not follow that one can create growth simply with macroeconomic stability. The involvement of larger structures in the determination of policy, its implementation, and outcomes is the entry point for "governance".

Governance, according to the Oxford English Dictionary, is the "manner or way of governing". The root—govern—derives from the Greek "κυβερναν"(kyvernan) for "steer", e.g., to steer the "ship of state". More recently, the use of the term gained ground as various researchers and groups used the word with varying connotations. At one end, governance has been used to refer to entire systems of political institutions and traditions; at the other, the phrase "governance issues" has sometimes become a euphemism for corruption. In the economics and development literature, however, the spread of the term governance arose from the need to extend the analysis beyond the design of government policy to political process and behavior.

The current use of the governance concept may be traced to a World Bank study (1989) on Africa that defined governance as "the exercise of political power to manage a nation's affairs". Later, the World Bank (1992) defined governance as "the manner in which power is exercised in the management of a country's economic and social resources for development". The Organisation for Economic Co-operation and Development (OECD), on the other hand, defined governance as "the exercise of authority in government and the political arena". According to this definition, "*Good* public governance helps to strengthen democracy and human rights, promote economic prosperity and social cohesion, reduce poverty, enhance environmental protection and the sustainable use of natural resources, and deepen confidence in government and public administration" (Tarschys 2001, 28).

Huther and Shah (1996) explicitly linked governance to the notion of institutions, defining it as "all aspects of the exercise of authority *through formal and informal institutions* in the management of the resource endowment of a state." This was carried through the work of Kaufmann, Kraay, and Zoido-Lobatón (KKZ 1999) and Kaufmann, Kraay, and Mastruzzi (KKM 2003). KKZ/KKM advanced a working definition of governance: the *traditions and institutions* by which authority in a country is exercised. This led to what is now probably the most widely used set of governance indicators, measuring (i) the process by which those in authority are selected, monitored and replaced; (ii) the capacity of the government to effectively formulate and implement sound policies and provide public services; and (iii) the respect of citizens and the state for the institutions that govern economic and social interactions among them.

It has been suggested that, prior to this, governance as a concept was theoretically weak, since it provided neither typology, nor metric, nor direction of development. For this reason, "good governance" tended to be reduced to a tautological evaluation of outcomes or results rather than an analysis of its organic elements and the means by which it might be achieved. With its explicit reference to institutions, however, the governance idea became associated with the emerging stream of the NIE, lending theoretical support to a concept that had heretofore been primarily developed by practitioners.

8.2.3   Measuring governance/institutional quality

A significant and growing amount of empirical work has sought to substantiate the expected governance/institutions-to-growth nexus described in the previous section. Such empirical work has typically involved cross-country regression exercises linking per capita income growth (as the dependent variable) with measures of governance/institutional quality (as explanatory variables), while controlling for other variables that may also affect per capita income growth. This type of empirical study has, however, often been criticized for its methodological weaknesses. The two most discussed issues are the measurement of governance/institutional quality and the direction of causality between institutional development and economic performance.

Barro (1991), among the first to conduct cross-country regression exercises, used an objective count of instances of political instability such as coups d'etat, political assassinations, and revolutions to proxy the threat to the security of property rights. Subsequent authors such as Mauro (1995) and Knack and Keefer (1995) used indicators drawn from *subjective* expert assessments, particularly those produced by investment consulting firms, such as the Political Risk Services group (which produces the International Country Risk Guide [ICRG]),[5] the Business Environmental Risk Intelligence (BERI), and so on.

At the same time, the growing importance attached to good governance and institutions stimulated empirical research aimed at measuring governance by think tanks, multilateral agencies, and nongovernment organizations (NGOs), leading to the publication of a large number of governance indicators series (see Box 8.1). Among these, the most popular and widely used today are the Worldwide Governance Indicators (WGIs) produced by the World Bank—stemming from the work of KKZ/KKM. The WGIs are based on about 30 opinion/perception-based surveys of various governance measures from investment consulting firms (such as those described above), NGOs, think tanks, governments, and multilateral agencies, and classified into six clusters (KKM 2009):[6]

(i)   *Voice and Accountability,* measured by the extent to which a country's citizens are able to participate in selecting their government, as well as freedom of expression, association, and the press

(ii) *Political Stability and Absence of Violence,* measured by the likelihood that the government will be destabilized by unconstitutional or violent means, including terrorism

(iii) *Government Effectiveness,* measured by the quality of public services, the capacity of the civil service and its independence from political pressures, and the quality of policy formulation

(iv) *Regulatory Quality,* measured by the ability of the government to provide sound policies and regulations that enable and promote private sector development

---

5   As an example, the ICRG rating comprises 22 variables in three subcategories of risk: political, financial, and economic. The political risk index is based on expert assessments of 12 political risk components on numerical scales: government stability (0–12), socioeconomic conditions (0–12), investment profile (0–12), internal conflict (0–12), external conflict (0–12), corruption (0–6), military in politics (0–6), religious tensions (0–6), law and order (0–6), ethnic tension (0–6), democratic accountability (0–6), and bureaucratic quality (0–4). The scores are added to arrive at a total "political risk" rating (1–100), where the higher the score, the lower the risk (see https://www.prsgroup.com/ICRG_Methodology.aspx).

6   The latest WGIs, released in 2009, are based on 35 different data sources from 33 organizations around the world, aggregating the data from hundreds of disaggregated questions and covering 212 countries (KKM 2009).

(v)   *Rule of Law*, measured by the extent to which agents have confidence in and abide by the rules of society, including the quality of property rights, the police, and the courts, as well as the risk of crime

(vi)   *Control of Corruption*, measured by the extent to which public power is exercised for private gain, including both petty and grand forms of corruption, as well as elite "capture" of the state

For each country, the various component indicators in each cluster are rescaled and aggregated, using an unobserved-components method, to yield a value centered at zero and ranging from −2.5 to 2.5, with larger positive values indicating better governance.

Despite their popularity and wide application in empirical studies, subjective and perception-based governance indicators have been subject to various criticisms, with many urging a more circumspect and critical use of these indicators. Owing to their wide following and influence, the WGIs have understandably come in for the closest scrutiny. Kaufmann and Kraay (2008) summarize the major critiques into those related to (i) issues concerning comparability over time and across countries,[7] (ii) biases in expert assessments,[8] (iii) correlated perception errors, (iv) definitional issues,[9] and (v) reliance on "subjective" data.[10] Admitting that measuring governance is difficult, and that all measures of governance are necessarily imprecise, subject to margins of error, and requiring interpretative caution, they acknowledge that there is scope for developing new and better indicators of governance to address some of the noted weaknesses of the existing measures (Kaufmann and Kraay 2008, KKM 2009).

---

[7]   The critiques include (i) unsuitability for cross-country and over-time comparison due to the use of different sets of underlying data sources in different years; (ii) inability to detect changes in a country's governance performance over time due to the construction of each component across countries: any movement of a country's indicator through time reflects only changes in its relative position on the scale of all included countries, regardless of whether the quality of governance *per se* has improved or not; and (iii) substantial margins of error in the aggregate WGIs.

[8]   It has been suggested that the large role of expatriate opinions in the primary sources is likely to color their assessments with the culture of the respondent's home (e.g., Western industrialized) country; or then again organizations responsible for these primary sources may profess strong ideological opinions that permeate the formulation of questions. NGO sources may have a stringent view of the needed accountability and access, while business-oriented organizations and business people themselves may have a bias against most forms of government intervention.

[9]   As an example, the WGI corruption score lumps together and equally weights responses to questions about petty corruption with grand corruption, frequency of acts with amounts stolen, and social consequences.

[10]   Subjective perceptions may not reflect specific objective realities.

Box 8.1 Major indicators of governance and institutional quality

The growing importance attached to good governance and high-quality institutions has stimulated empirical research aimed at measuring governance, leading to the publication of a large number of governance indicators series.

The most popular and widely used today are the *Worldwide Governance Indicators* (WGIs)—first released by the World Bank in 1996. Sometimes referred to as "KK", "KKZ", or "KKM" following the originators' names, these indicators were published every other year between 1996 and 2002, and annually thereafter. Covering over 200 countries, the WGIs compile data from 37 sources, such as cross-country surveys of firms, and expert assessments from commercial risk rating agencies, NGOs and think tanks, and governments and multilateral agencies. The WGIs consist of composite indicators of six key dimensions of governance: (i) voice and accountability, (ii) political stability and absence of violence, (iii) government effectiveness, (iv) regulatory quality, (v) rule of law, and (vi) control of corruption.

Another indicator widely quoted in the media and academic research is the *Global Competitiveness Index* produced by the World Economic Forum with Columbia University, covering 134 countries. First introduced in 2004, this index measures national competitiveness, taking into account macro and micro foundations of national competitiveness. A total of 113 variables are aggregated into a weighted average of 12 pillars, including institutions, infrastructure, macroeconomy, health and primary education, higher education and training, goods market efficiency, labor market efficiency, financial market sophistication, technological readiness, market size, business sophistication, and innovation.

Based on expert assessments, the *World Governance Assessment* of the Overseas Development Institute attempts to establish how the quality of governance varies over time in countries around the world. The pilot phase covered 16 countries, while phase 2 covered 10. Thirty indicators are used for six dimensions of governance—civil society, interest aggregation, government stewardship, policy implementation, economic society, and dispute resolution.

Transparency International's *Corruption Perceptions Index*, first introduced in 1995, measures the perceived levels of public sector corruption for 180 countries. The index is calculated using data from 13 sources from 11 independent institutions, including risk agencies/country analysis.

Used by the United States' Millennium Challenge Corporation and the World Bank in its Country Policy and Institutional Assessment, among others, *the Global Integrity Index* assesses the opposite of corruption: existence and effectiveness of and citizen access to key governance and anti-corruption mechanisms. The index aggregates more than 300 integrity indicators,

continued.

Box 8.1 *continued*.

organized into six main governance categories—civil society, public information and media; elections; government accountability; administration and civil service; oversight and regulation; anti-corruption and rule of law—and subcategories.

Covering 141 countries, the Fraser Institute's *Economic Freedom of the World* index measures the degree to which a nation's policies and institutions are supportive of economic freedom, the cornerstone of which are personal choice, voluntary exchange, freedom to compete, and security of privately owned property. First introduced in 1986, the index aggregates 42 variables gathered from external sources as the International Monetary Fund, World Bank, and World Economic Forum. The index measures the degree of economic freedom in five areas, such as size of government; legal structure and security of property rights; access to sound money; freedom to trade internationally; and regulation of credit, labor and business.

The *Economic Freedom Index*, produced by the Heritage Foundation and The Wall Street Journal, was first introduced in 1995 and now covers 162 countries. The index measures and aggregates 10 individual freedoms which are vital to the development of personal and national prosperity—business freedom, trade freedom, fiscal freedom, government size, monetary freedom, investment freedom, financial freedom, property rights, freedom from corruption, labor freedom—into a simple overall score. The entire series is revised for consistency each time changes in methodology are instituted.

First introduced in 1972, Freedom House's *Freedom in the World Country Ratings* measures the degree of democracy and political freedom in 193 countries and 15 related/disputed territories. Country scores by experts are transformed into indexes of political rights (electoral process, political pluralism and participation, functioning of government) and civil liberties (freedom of expression and belief, associational organizational rights, rule of law, personal autonomy and individual rights), which are then averaged to show an overall freedom rating. Depending on the ratings, nations are classified as "Free", "Partly Free", or "Not Free".

For other indicators, readers can refer to the United Nations Development Programme's user's guide on governance indicators (2007). The guide contains basic information on 35 governance indicator sources, including methodology, example of results, valid/invalid uses, and assumptions.

Source: Arndt and Oman (2006), UNDP (2007), websites of various indexes.

8.2.4   Empirical evidence and the issue of causality

Barro (1991) finds that political instability, proxied by the frequency of coups d'etat, political assassinations, and revolutions, had a significant and negative impact on GDP growth during 1965–1985, after controlling for other variables suggested by the standard growth model. Several subsequent studies using indicators drawn from *subjective* expert assessments confirm Barro's findings. Reestimations of Barro's model explaining growth of per capita GDP show the "rule of law" variable to be particularly potent, suppressing the effects of other governance variables such as corruption and quality of the bureaucracy (Barro and Sala-i-Martin 1995). On the other hand, Mauro (1995) finds bureaucratic quality to be significant in a growth equation, even while corruption is not. Seeking to capture contract enforcement and property rights protection, Knack and Keefer (1995) represent governance as a single 50-point composite index culled from a subset of the ICRG dataset. Regressed against investment ratios, this construct is found to be significantly positive in a Barro-type growth equation using cross-section data—an improvement of one standard deviation raising growth of per capita output by 1.2 percentage points. The World Bank (2007) cites that an improvement in governance measured by KKZ/KKM indicators by one standard deviation raises incomes about three-fold in the long run, and reduces infant mortality by two-thirds.

Apart from the issues related to the measurement of governance/institutional quality discussed above, earlier studies aiming at empirically testing the governance/institutions-growth nexus has been plagued by the problem of "simultaneity". The simultaneity problem became evident in the lack of robustness in results in earlier studies, which were found to be sensitive to sample periods covered, estimation techniques employed, and specific combinations of variables being omitted or included. Aron (2000) concludes her survey by underscoring the simultaneous determination of growth, investment, and institutions and pointing out how studies "often deal inadequately with endogenous institutional measures". This effectively prevents one from distinguishing whether it is primarily better governance scores that caused growth to be high, or the other way around. This is not a trivial matter from the policy viewpoint.

This problem cannot be easily addressed, mainly because too few explicit governance data were available *prior* to the growth periods being investigated. However, a precedent-setting attempt to circumvent this problem was made by Acemoglu, Johnson, and Robinson (2001 and 2002), who used a historical variable—the rates of mortality among (European) colonial settlers during colonial times—to explain growth performance. This "instrumental variable" turned out to be closely related to *current* assessments of governance, particularly the risk of expropriation while, on the other hand, it cannot be disputed that they existed completely *prior* to the occurrence of growth itself. Hence, the condition of prior occurrence to establish the causality can be met. The significant influence of historical settler-mortality in predicting subsequent growth bolsters a narrative in which low mortality encouraged denser European settlement and a greater involvement in the formation of early institutions that respected property rights.[11] These early institutions are posited to have persisted to the present and influenced contemporary economic growth, thus indirectly substantiating the governance-growth nexus.

Subsequently, Rodrik, Subramanian, and Trebbi (2004) show that the Acemoglu, Johnson, and Robinson results were robust even if variables purporting to capture geography and trade policy openness were included. Interestingly, Rodrik, Subramanian, and Trebbi used settler-mortality as an instrument to capture exogenous variations in the KKM composite index. But while the instrumentation of governance variables may seem to resolve the problem of simultaneity, it gives rise to a different problem, namely that of attribution of the impact of the instrumental variable(s), and hence the theoretical interpretation of the causality.

In the original Acemoglu, Johnson, and Robinson articles, "settler-mortality" was a proxy for the "risk of expropriation". The same instrumental variable, on the other hand, was used by Rodrik, Subramanian, and Trebbi to explain the "rule of law". Other authors have interpreted the same variable even more differently. Easterly and Levine (2003), for example, interpret settler-mortality as part of a *geographical* determinant of institutions, together with crops and germs, along the lines suggested by Diamond (1997). Glaeser et al. (2004), in questioning the causal role assigned to institutions, argue that the instrumental variable employed (namely, historical settler-mortality) is actually more closely associated with current measures of human capital than with governance/institutional variables. If the same instrumental variable can be used to "explain" variations in one current institutional or governance aspect, what is the guarantee that it cannot also explain *another* institutional aspect, or perhaps even a *non-institutional* variable heretofore excluded? The use of instrumental variables thus still fails to close the causality debate.

While the foregoing discussions focus on improvement in institutional quality leading to better development performance, an alternative view is that economic development promotes institutional development, and that this direction of causality may be more important than the one from institutional development to economic development. Paldam and Gundlach (2008) empirically test both directions of causality by

---

[11]   Acemoglu, Johnson, and Robinson (2001 and 2002) test a model where simultaneously: (i) current per capita output growth is affected by current risk of expropriation and other factors; and (ii) current risk of expropriation depends on past settler-mortality and still other factors.

focusing on democracy as the macro institution and corruption as the micro institution. They find that, on balance, the prediction of increases in the level of income leading to improvements in institutional quality fits the data better than the one of the opposite direction, although not without exceptions. On the basis of this finding, they caution against the unguarded expectation that institutional reforms in all dimensions will improve economic performance in formulating development policies.

8.2.5   Linking governance/institutions with inequality

The literature on governance and institutions has mostly focused on their relationship with economic growth. More recently, however, there is growing interest in their link with income distribution and inequality. These interests have been dominated by two perspectives. One is how political institutions and democracy are linked with income distribution and inequality, and the other is how corruption is related to inequality. The consensus emerging from the literature appears to be that there is two-way causality in both cases. Political institutions and democracy influence how income and wealth are distributed in society. Income/wealth distribution and inequality also help shape political institutions and how democratic a society is likely to be. Similarly, corruption increases income inequality, while higher levels of income inequality also make corruption more likely.

A.   Political institutions and inequality

For the first relationship, it has long been recognized that income distribution in an economy depends also on political factors. One hypothesis has been that a more egalitarian distribution of political rights in the form of a democracy should be accompanied by a more equal income distribution. The existing evidence, however, does not find any robust relationship between democracy and inequality in cross-country regression exercises. For example, Bollen and Jackman (1985) fail to detect such a relationship; Li, Squire, and Zou (1998) find limited support for a negative relationship between democracy and inequality; and Gradstein, Milanovic, and Ying (2001) find that democracy has a negative but weak effect on inequality.

Gradstein, Milanovic, and Ying argue that a casual inspection of recent events in East Europe as well as in East Asia casts doubt on the idea that any simple relationship between democracy and inequality exists. Despite restrictive political rights in East European countries under communist regimes, income distribution was relatively egalitarian—which they attributed in part to the prevailing political ideology—while democratization of East European countries in the 1990s actually resulted in an increase in income inequality. Similarly, while some East Asian economies such as the Republic of Korea; Singapore; and Taipei,China have been among the economies with the most egalitarian income distribution in the world, their political record was historically far from democratic. Thus, Gradstein, Milanovic, and Ying argue for a consideration of additional factors—such as ideology—when examining income distribution and its relationship to democracy. Their analysis of panel data for 126 countries reveals that ideological factors are important determinants of income inequality. Greater democratization in Judeo-Christian societies is likely to result in a substantial reduction in inequality, but not so much in others (Buddhist/Hindu, Confucian, and Communist). The authors also find that democracy is more likely to reduce inequality in countries with a parliamentary than a presidential system.

Rogowski and MacRae (2004) argue that institutions co-vary with political and economic inequality. Supported by historical case studies from ancient Greece to recent times, they find that changes in economic and military technology, trade, and factor endowments influence the evolution of political institutions toward being more or less democratic. However, where these exogenous changes increase social and economic inequality, countries are likely to adopt less representative political institutions or to do away with democratic institutions altogether. On the other hand, decreasing inequality creates incentives to broaden political participation.

The view that inequality influences institutions is echoed by other authors. Boix (2001) argues that one of the key conditions for a stable democracy is relative equality across individuals in economic and social conditions. His model takes off from the well-known correlation between development and democracy—that democracy prevails when income differences decline and political resources across the population are balanced. Perotti (1996) and Bénabou (1996) argue that inequality could lead to politically unstable institutions as power swings back and forth between redistributive populist factions and oligarchy-protecting conservative factions. It has been argued that initial conditions such as income distribution play a key role in the rise of democratic institutions. With high initial inequality, the ruling elite can suppress democracy and equal rights before the law so as to preserve their privileged position (e.g., Bourguignon and Verdier 2000) or has the power to capture larger rent, thus enriching itself further at the expense of the poor and perpetuating high inequality and slower growth (Gradstein 2007). Acemoglu (2008) develops a model in which the oligarchy blocks democracy to preserve its privileges.

Chong and Gradstein (2007) argue that there is strong empirical support for the mutually reinforcing mechanism between inequality and institutions, but the direction of causality from inequality to institutions is stronger than the reverse causality. They argue that inequality causes weak institutions because the rich and powerful obstruct changes in the institutions to protect their ability to capture rents. Also, weak judicial systems which do not give adequate protection to the poor constrain the ability of the poor to extract rents. They also find that low measures of institutional quality are associated with persistently high or worsening inequality, which leads to persistently poor institutional outcomes.

B. Corruption and inequality

One of the earlier contributions to the corruption-inequality literature is Johnston (1989), claiming that corruption tends to preserve or widen existing income inequalities. Li, Xu, and Zou (2000) find that the relationship between corruption and income inequality exhibits an "inverted-U" shape—high or low corruption levels correspond to low income inequality, while an intermediate level of corruption is associated with high income inequality. They assert that corruption affects inequality through capital market imperfection, government spending, and asset distribution. The World Bank (2000), on the other hand, finds that lower levels of corruption are statistically associated with lower levels of inequality and that corruption hurts the poor through a number of channels, including lower economic growth, more regressive taxes, lower and less effective social spending, disincentives to investment in the human capital of the poor, and unequal distribution of assets. Gyimah-Brempong (2002) adds that the choice of development strategy, through highly subsidized capital and exacerbated by high levels of corruption in most African countries, influences income inequality.

Gupta, Davoodi, and Alonso-Terme (2002) identify a number of mechanisms by which corruption could increase inequality. For example, corruption can lead to tax evasion, defective tax administration, and exemptions that favor the wealthy (and well-connected). This can erode the effective tax base and undermine possibilities for compulsory income/wealth redistribution from rich to poor, thus perpetuating or even increasing inequality. Corruption can also prevent effective targeting of social programs to the truly needy when funds from poverty alleviation programs are siphoned off from poor to powerful/rich individuals. Corruption can hurt human capital formation by lowering tax revenues. Reduced funding for education lowers the ability of the poor to invest in human capital; because the rich can invest in human capital from non-public sources or lobby the government to redirect social spending toward higher education and tertiary health, economic inequality worsens (Mauro 1998; Tanzi and Davoodi 1997; Gupta, Davoodi, and Alonso-Terme 2002). Finally, when corruption changes the rules of the game in favor of the rich and well-connected, it increases uncertainty and risk for the poor and not so well-connected, which discourages investment in their

283

human and/or physical capital, perpetuating inequality (Gupta, Davoodi, and Alonso-Terme 2002).

Begovic (2005), however, argues that these mechanisms are not very convincing, and thus cast doubt on the theoretical explanation of the link between corruption and inequality. For instance, decreasing the effective tax burden can have beneficial effects on growth, not necessarily decreasing inequality, but increasing the poor's prospects of improving their welfare. He also disputes the claim that tax exemptions and evasion only favor the rich and well-connected. On the extent to which corruption-induced poor targeting of social programs really contributes to increasing inequality, Begovic finds it unrealistic to assume that the rich will deliberately undermine social programs by siphoning off rather limited funds, when engaging in other forms of corruption may generate much higher returns. Poor targeting of social programs results in inefficient lowering of inequality, rather than an increase in inequality.

In a comparative study of 129 countries, You and Khagram (2005, 136) argue "that inequality fosters a norm of corruption as acceptable behaviour, that corruption is likely to reinforce or widen existing inequalities, and that vicious circles of inequality-corruption-inequality are thus likely to manifest." They also find that the effect of inequality on corruption is likely to be greater in more democratic countries. Uslaner (2008) argues that the roots of corruption lie in economic and legal inequality, and economic inequality provides a fertile breeding ground for corruption, and, in turn, leads to further inequalities—an inequality trap.

8.2.6 Linking inequality with growth via institutions

The understanding on the role of governance and institutions in economic development can be enhanced by an appreciation of the relationship between inequality and growth. This relationship has been extensively studied, beginning with work spawned by Simon Kuznets' (1955) well-known "inverted-U" hypothesis that economic growth first causes increasing, then decreasing, inequality. It is now generally accepted, however, that this broad characterization of the growth-inequality pattern is not empirically borne out.

A second line of thinking hypothesizes how inequality affects growth. The literature of the 1950s and 1960s was typified by the Kaldorian hypothesis that an unequal income distribution may promote growth based on the higher savings propensities of the rich versus those of the poor (Kaldor 1956). Recent literature, however, has emphasized different mechanisms. Easterly (2007) highlights three. The *first* focuses on human capital: where the distribution of incomes and opportunities is unequal, growth cannot be high because human capital will be denied to the vast majority. The *second* focuses on political economy: in a highly inequitable society, the majority who are poor may favor redistributive policies; whether ultimately successful or not, a social preoccupation with pressures for redistribution will divert social attention and energy away from policies that would otherwise have promoted growth.

The *third* mechanism through which inequality affects growth focuses on institutions. Discussions in the previous section have highlighted the possible two-way causality between political institutions and inequality and that between inequality and corruption. Inequality could also affect growth through its negative impact on "trust", "cooperative norms", and "social cohesion", as these informal institutional mechanisms help reduce transaction costs, promote cooperation, and play a substitutive role when formal institutional arrangements are weak and ineffective (Putnam 1993; Woolcock 1998; Fukuyama 2000; Easterly, Woolcock, and Ritzen 2006). Easterly, Woolcock, and Ritzen (2006) provide empirical evidence that social cohesion, proxied by inequality, endogenously determines institutional quality, which in turn causally determines growth.

8.3 Governance/institutions vis-à-vis growth and inequality: How Asia fares

This section first looks at where Asia and its various subregions stand in the governance and institutional quality ranking vis-à-vis other regions of the world. Despite caveats highlighted earlier, this study uses the WGIs that measure six dimensions including voice and accountability, political stability and absence of violence, government effectiveness, regulatory quality, rule of law, and control of corruption. Governance "surplus" or "deficit" in each of these dimensions for each developing Asian economy is then estimated by comparing its score in a particular indicator with a corresponding international reference line (see Kaufmann 2003, Quibria 2006). Finally, this section looks at whether or not developing Asian economies with governance in surplus in a particular dimension grow faster and have lower income inequality than economies with governance in deficit in the same dimension.

8.3.1 Governance scores

Table 8.1 reports average governance scores calculated from the WGIs for various regions in the world and subregions of Asia in 2008. Each composite indicator for each economy is constructed to yield a value centered at zero and ranging from −2.5 to 2.5, with larger positive values being superior. In calculating regional averages, populations were used as weights.

Table 8.1   Worldwide governance indicators by region/subregion, 2008

Region/Subregion	2008 Governance Indicators					
	Voice and accountability	Political stability	Government effectiveness	Regulatory quality	Rule of law	Control of corruption
Asia	−0.72	−0.78	−0.05	−0.35	−0.27	−0.43
Central and West Asia	−1.12	−1.93	−0.69	−0.74	−0.94	−0.87
East Asia	−1.64	−0.27	0.24	−0.26	−0.30	−0.31
Pacific	0.11	−0.37	−0.75	−0.54	−0.74	−0.57
South Asia	0.29	−1.09	−0.13	−0.41	0.00	−0.36
Southeast Asia	−0.66	−0.83	−0.25	−0.24	−0.53	−0.72
Eastern Europe	0.46	0.20	0.03	0.05	−0.03	−0.35
Former Soviet Union	−0.77	−0.43	−0.43	−0.65	−0.84	−0.89
Latin America and Caribbean	0.17	−0.41	−0.15	0.25	−0.51	−0.17
Middle East and North Africa	−1.21	−0.77	−0.39	−0.63	−0.31	−0.28
OECD	0.95	0.49	1.25	1.10	1.14	1.21
Sub-Saharan Africa	−0.63	−1.05	−0.75	−0.70	−0.83	−0.80

OECD = Organisation for Economic Co-operation and Development.
Note: East Asia excludes Japan, which is lumped with the OECD countries.
Source: Means of each region/subregion are computed from the Worldwide Governance Indicators (http://info.worldbank.org/governance/wgi/index.asp) and weighted by population based on the World Development Indicators Online database.

In 2008, Asia scored lower than the OECD grouping and Eastern Europe in all six dimensions, and lower than Latin America and the Caribbean in all except government effectiveness and rule of law, but higher than sub-Saharan Africa in all except voice and accountability; higher than the former Soviet Union in all except political stability, and higher than the Middle East and North Africa in all except control of corruption and political stability (where Asia is marginally lower). Across the six dimensions of governance, Asia scored relatively high in government effectiveness and rule of law (ranking the third highest after the OECD and Eastern Europe); but relatively low in political stability (ranking the second lowest, before sub-Saharan Africa), and in voice and accountability (ranking the third lowest, before the Middle East and North Africa and the former Soviet Union). Asia's ranking in regulatory quality and control of corruption lies in between.

Table 8.1 shows a great deal of heterogeneity within Asia. Among the five subregions: (i) East Asia ranks the first in political stability, government effectiveness, and control of corruption, second in regulatory quality and rule of law, but last in voice and accountability; (ii) South

Asia ranks first in voice and accountability and rule of law, second in government effectiveness and control of corruption, third in regulatory quality, and second last in political stability; (iii) Southeast Asia ranks first in regulatory quality, third in voice and accountability, political stability, government effectiveness, and rule of law, and second last in control of corruption; (iv) the Pacific ranks second in voice and accountability and political stability, third in control of corruption, second last in regulatory quality and rule of law, and last in government effectiveness; and (v) Central and West Asia ranks second last in voice and accountability and government effectiveness, and last in the other four dimensions.

Figure 8.1 compares governance scores of developing Asian economies in 2008 with those in 1998 to show how these changed during the last decade. The picture is quite mixed. Among the developing Asian economies for which data are available, the score in voice and accountability improved in 10 economies and slipped in 25; in political stability it improved in 16 and slipped in 16; in government effectiveness it improved in 16 and slipped in 18; in regulatory quality it improved in 16 and slipped in 19; in rule of law it improved in 18 and slipped in 15; and in control of corruption it improved in 18 and slipped in 15. The figure shows that, during 1998–2008, the number of economies registering improvement was greater than those registering slippage in the rule of law and control of corruption. In the other four dimensions, the number of economies registering slippage is greater than those registering improvement. In each of the six dimensions, there are a few economies registering no change in the period.

Figure 8.1   Trends in governance indicators: Developing Asia,
1998 and 2008 (ordered by magnitude of improvement)

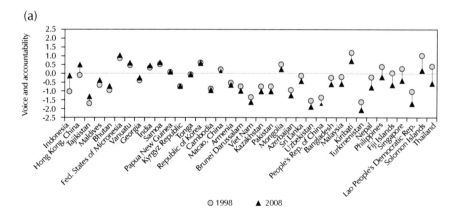

continued.

Figure 8.1 *continued*.

(b)

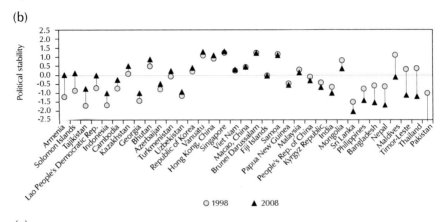

○ 1998   ▲ 2008

(c)

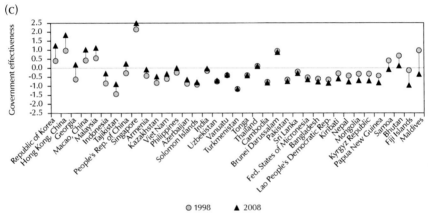

○ 1998   ▲ 2008

(d)

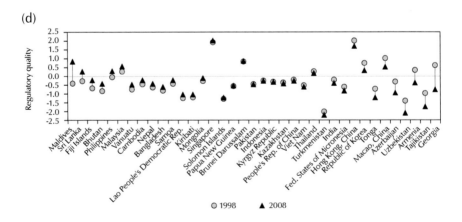

○ 1998   ▲ 2008

continued.

288

Figure 8.1 *continued*.

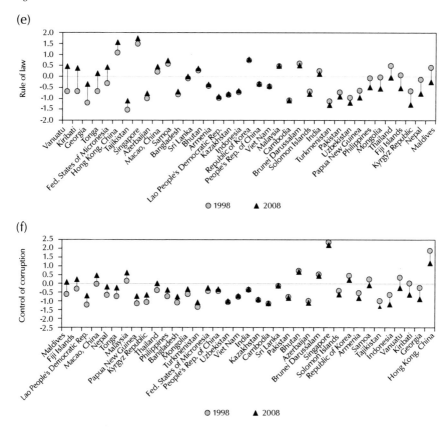

Source: Worldwide Governance Indicators (http://info.worldbank.org/governance/wgi/index.asp).

8.3.2   Governance surplus and deficit

To validate the governance/institution-growth nexus in the context of Asia, Quibria (2006) estimates the governance surplus or deficit for each developing Asian economy. He does this by comparing an aggregated governance measure (calculated from the six governance indicators of the 2002 WGIs) with an international reference measure that is estimated from a regression line—referred to in this chapter as international reference line—generated by regressing the 2002 WGIs' aggregate governance measure against per capita real income using a cross-section of 151 countries. The international reference line indicates the expected level of governance/institutional quality corresponding to each level of income. Therefore, if the actual score of a particular economy lies above the international reference line, the economy is considered as having governance surplus; if it lies below the international reference line, the economy is considered as having a governance deficit.

Quibria argues that if the governance-to-growth relationship exists and is dominant, one should expect the economies with governance surplus to show higher growth than those with deficit. However, he finds that during 1999–2003, economies with governance surplus in fact experienced much lower growth than those with governance deficit. A simple regression of growth performance of 29 developing Asian economies against the aggregate governance measure, after controlling for per capita real GDP, yields a significant coefficient but with the wrong sign.[12] Quibria raises a number of possible reasons for this paradoxical result. One hypothesis is that it may not be the aggregate score on governance, but some of the individual scores that are important for economic growth. This possibility is appealing, particularly in light of the caveat (notably from KKZ/KKM themselves) that these indicators, properly speaking, should not be aggregated into a single measure.

To test this hypothesis, this study first estimates governance surplus or deficit in each of the six dimensions of the WGIs for each developing Asian economy in both 1998 and 2008, following Quibria's approach. The study then investigates how these measures of surplus or deficit are related to the growth performance of these economies during 1998–2008. In particular, the focus is on the relationship between measures of governance surplus or deficit in 1998 and the subsequent growth performance, to avoid the simultaneity problem discussed earlier. The 1998 dataset covers 164–169 economies, including 33–37 developing Asian economies, depending on data availability; while the 2008 dataset covers 166–168 countries, with 36–37 developing Asian economies. Per capita real GDP was measured in purchasing power parity (PPP) terms at constant 2005 international dollars. Six international reference lines are estimated, each corresponding to one of the six governance dimensions.

Figures 8.2 and 8.3 show a positive relationship between the governance score and per capita real GDP for all six dimensions in 1998 and 2008. In 1998, for example, judging from the slope of the fitted regression lines and estimated R-squared, government effectiveness has the highest correlation with per capita real GDP, with a coefficient of 0.6145 and R-squared of 0.6494; followed by rule of law, regulatory quality, control of corruption, political stability, and voice and accountability, which is least correlated with a coefficient of 0.4834 and R-squared of 0.4269. In 2008, the correlation between governance indicators and per capita real income remained more or less the same. Government effectiveness remained the most highly correlated; political stability, and voice and accountability remained the least correlated with the income level. The relatively low

---

[12]   The equation used is GDP growth = a + b (ln GDP per capita) + c (governance) + error.

correlation between voice and accountability and political stability, on one hand, and per capita real income, on the other, can also be seen from the wider scatters of the sample observations in Figures 8.2(a), 8.2(b), 8.3(a), and 8.3(b) than those in the other figures.

Figure 8.2   Governance scores and per capita real income, 1998

(a)

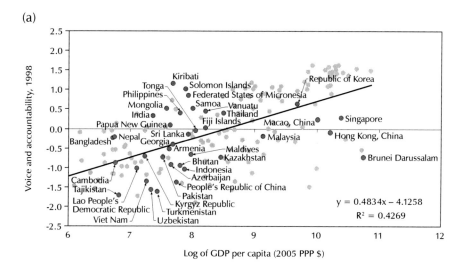

(b)

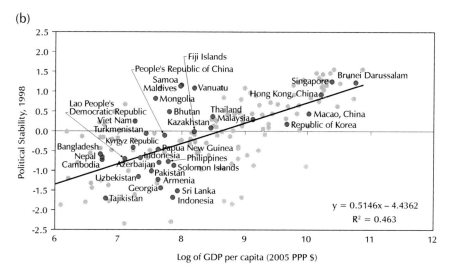

continued.

Figure 8.2 *continued.*

(c)

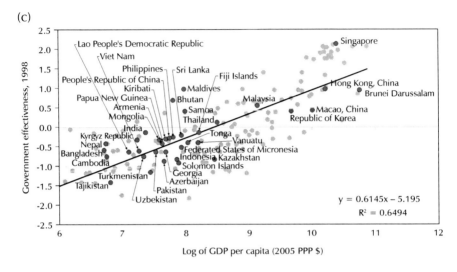

(d)

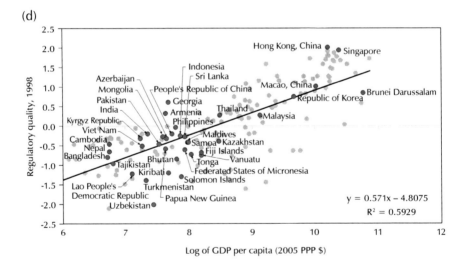

continued.

Figure 8.2 *continued.*

(e)

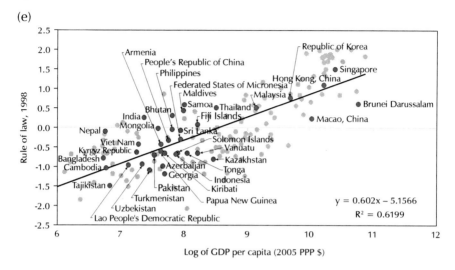

(f)

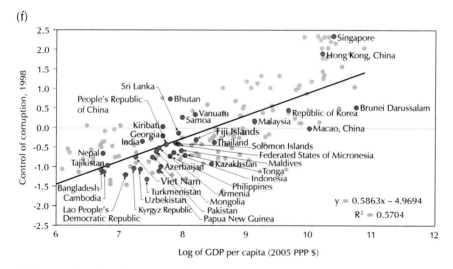

GDP = gross domestic product, PPP = purchasing power parity.
Source: Authors' estimates based on data from the World Bank's Worldwide Governance Indicators
(http://info.worldbank.org/governance/wgi/index.asp) and World Development Indicators
Online.

Figure 8.3   Governance scores and per capita real income, 2008

(a)

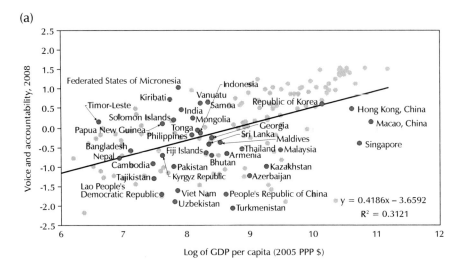

(b)

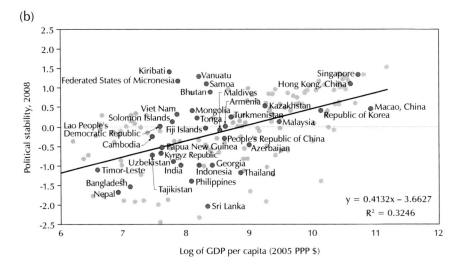

continued.

Figure 8.3 *continued.*

(c)

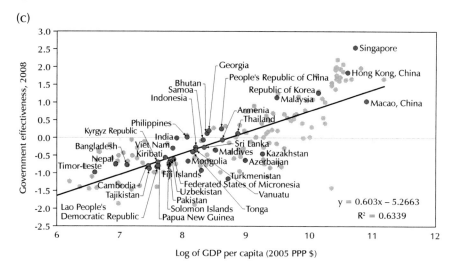

(d)

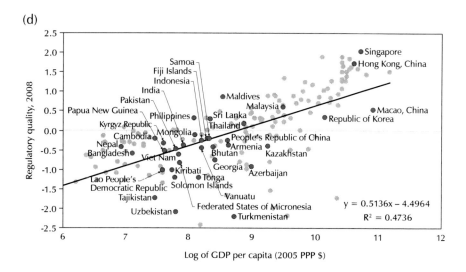

continued.

295

Figure 8.3 *continued*.

(e)

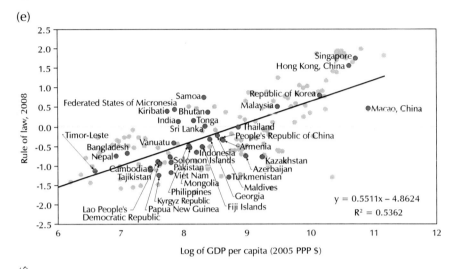

(f)

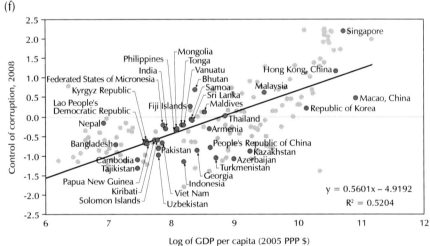

GDP = gross domestic product, PPP = purchasing power parity.
Source: Authors' estimates based on data from the World Bank's Worldwide Governance Indicators (http://info.worldbank.org/governance/wgi/index.asp) and World Development Indicators Online.

Before turning to an examination of how governance surplus or deficit measures relate to growth performance in developing Asia, it is useful to look at how these changed during the last decade.[13] Figure 8.4 compares the percentage of economies with governance in surplus in each of the six

---

13   It should be noted that a change in the surplus or deficit for a particular economy can be due to a change in the economy's governance score or a shift in the international reference line.

Figure 8.4   Percentage of developing Asian economies with governance
surplus, 1998 and 2008

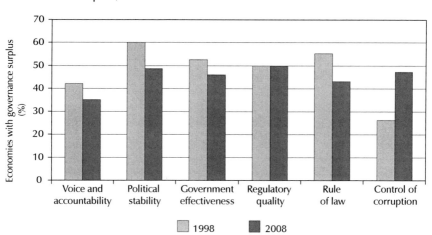

Source: Authors' estimates based on data from the World Bank's Worldwide Governance Indicators
(http://info.worldbank.org/governance/wgi/index.asp) and World Development Indicators
Online.

dimensions for developing Asia as a whole in 1998 with 2008. During
1998–2008, among 36–38 developing Asian economies, the percentage
with surplus declined from 42% to 35% in voice and accountability;
from 60% to 49% in political stability; from 53% to 46% in government
effectiveness; from 55% to 43% in rule of law; remained unchanged in
regulatory quality; but increased from 26% to 47% in control of corruption.
In fact, all five subregions saw the proportion of economies with surplus in
control of corruption increasing during 1998–2008. More detailed results
for the five subregions are as follows:

(i)   In Central and West Asia, none of the economies had a surplus in
voice and accountability in both 1998 and 2008. During 1998–
2008, the proportion of economies with surplus decreased
in government effectiveness, regulatory quality (from 50% to
22%), and rule of law (from 20% to 0%), but increased slightly
in political stability and control of corruption.

(ii)   In East Asia, the proportion of economies with surplus
decreased in all dimensions except government effectiveness
and control of corruption, with the decline particularly
significant in regulatory quality, from 83% to 40%.

(iii)   In the Pacific, the proportion of economies with surplus
remained more or less unchanged in voice and accountability
(89%) and government effectiveness (33%), and increased in
the other three dimensions.

297

(iv)   In South Asia, the proportion of economies with surplus increased significantly in regulatory quality (from 43% to 83%) and control of corruption (from 57% to 100%), but decreased in the other four dimensions.

(v)   In Southeast Asia, the proportion of economies with surplus increased in voice and accountability, government effectiveness, regulatory quality, and control of corruption (from 10% to 38%), but decreased in political stability (from 70% to 50%) and rule of law (from 60% to 38%).

8.3.3   Linking governance/institutions with growth and inequality

Do developing Asian economies with governance in surplus grow faster and have lower income inequality than those with governance in deficit? This section looks at the empirical evidence. First, all developing Asian economies (where data are available) are classified into two groups, one with governance in surplus and the other in deficit on the basis of 1998 data. The respective average annual growth rates of per capita real GDP of the two groups during 1998–2008 are then calculated. For the income inequality measure, the Gini coefficients reported in the 2009 Human Development Report (UNDP 2009) are used. This avoids the simultaneity problem.

A.   Governance/institutions and growth performance

Figure 8.5 shows that, in the case of voice and accountability, there were 16 economies with governance in surplus and 20 economies in deficit in 1998. For the economies in surplus, the average annual growth rate of per capita real income during 1998–2008 was 2.3%,[14] with India growing at the highest rate of 5.6% and Solomon Islands at the lowest, a negative rate of 1.1%. For the 20 economies in deficit in voice and accountability, the average annual growth rate of per capita real income was 6.7%, almost 3 times as high as the economies in surplus, with Azerbaijan growing at the highest rate (14.3%) and Pakistan at the lowest (2.7%). These results appear to suggest that voice and accountability is not a critical driver of growth performance for this particular sample of economies during this particular period.

Among the economies with deficit in voice and accountability, Azerbaijan, Turkmenistan, and Kazakhstan are oil/gas-rich countries. During 1998–2008, the world oil price increased from $11.8 to $95.6 per barrel.[15] This exogenous factor has certainly contributed to these

---

14   Following Quibria (2006), the simple arithmetic average is calculated rather than weighted by the size of population to avoid the results being dominated by a few big economies.

15   Average weekly spot price (free on board) for all countries weighted by estimated export volume,

economies' GDP growth, but may be argued to have nothing to do with their governance or institutional quality. To get rid of the impact of this exogenous factor, the average annual growth rate for the economies in deficit in voice and accountability was recalculated by excluding the three oil/gas-rich economies, as well as Macao, China (Macao) since its growth relied largely on the gambling and associated tourism industry. The average annual per capita GDP growth rate of the economies in deficit in voice and accountability after the four are excluded was 5.6%, which is still more than twice as high as the economies in surplus in this dimension.[16]

This paradoxical result also applies to political stability. Twenty developing Asian economies in 1998 had surplus and 13 had deficit in this indicator. For the economies in surplus, the average annual growth rate of per capita real income was 4.7%, with Turkmenistan growing fastest (13.5%) and Papua New Guinea slowest (−0.2%). In the case of deficit economies, the average annual growth rate was 5.8%, 1.1 percentage points higher than that for surplus economies, with Azerbaijan growing at the highest rate (14.3%) and Solomon Islands at the lowest (−1.1%). After excluding the three oil/gas-rich economies and Macao, the average annual growth rate for the surplus economies was 4.0% and that for the deficit economies was still 0.7 percentage points higher, at 4.7%.

In the case of government effectiveness, regulatory quality, and rule of law, on the other hand, better *initial* governance/institutional quality does *subsequently* lead to better growth performance. Twenty developing Asian economies had surplus in government effectiveness and 16 had deficit in 1998. The average annual growth rate for economies in surplus was 4.5% (none of the three oil/gas-rich economies or Macao was in surplus). For the deficit economies, the average annual growth rate was 5.0% including those rich in oil/gas and Macao, but only 2.9% excluding them. These results show that economies with better government effectiveness grew 1.6 percentage points faster (annually during 1998–2008) than those with weak government capacity if oil/gas-rich economies and Macao are not considered. In the case of regulatory quality, the average annual growth rate for the 19 economies in surplus was 5.8% and that for the 16 economies in deficit was 4.0%, if oil/gas-rich economies and Macao are included; when these economies are excluded, the corresponding figures are 5.0% and 3.0%, respectively. Similarly, in the case of rule of law, the average annual growth rate for the 21 economies in surplus was 4.5% (none of the three oil/gas-rich economies or Macao was in surplus) and that for the 15 in deficit was 5.4%, with oil/gas-rich ones and Macao

---

taken from the Energy Information Administration website (http://www.eia.doe.gov/).

[16] Regressing the annual average per capita GDP growth rate between 1998 and 2008 against the score of voice and accountability in 1998 yields a negative, statistically significant coefficient, with or without controlling for per capita GDP in 1998.

included. Excluding these economies, the average annual growth rate for those in deficit was 3.3%.[17]

Finally, in the case of control of corruption, 10 economies had surplus and 28 had deficit in 1998. The average growth rate during 1998–2008 for the surplus economies was 3.9%, with Georgia the fastest growing (7.6%) and Vanuatu the slowest (0.4%). For the deficit economies, the average annual growth rate was 5.4% when including oil/gas-rich ones and Macao, but 4.0% when these economies are excluded. Thus, the two groups had more or less the same growth performance.[18]

Figure 8.5   Governance surplus/deficit and income growth rate

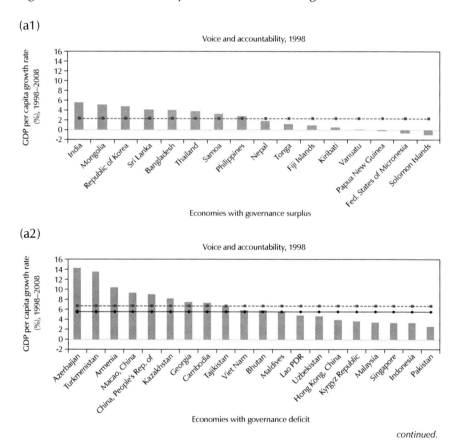

(a1)

(a2)

continued.

continued.

---

17   Regressing the annual average per capita GDP growth rate between 1998 and 2008 against the score of government effectiveness, regulatory quality, or rule of law in 1998 yields a positive, statistically insignificant coefficient, with or without controlling for per capita GDP in 1998.

18   Regressing the annual average per capita GDP growth rate between 1998 and 2008 against the score of control of corruption in 1998 yields a negative, statistically insignificant coefficient, with or without controlling for per capita GDP in 1998.

Figure 8.5 *continued*.

(b1)

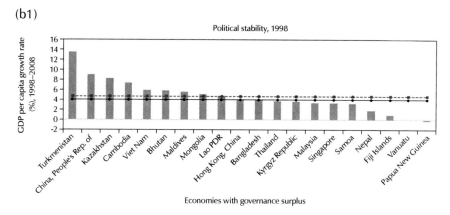

(b2)

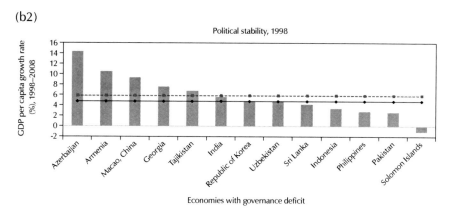

(c1)

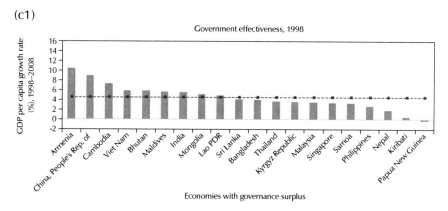

continued.

Figure 8.5 *continued*.

(c2)

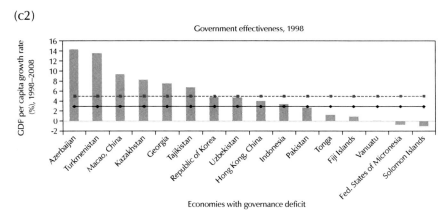

(d1)

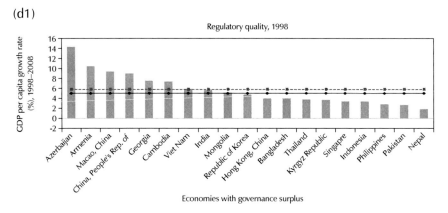

(d2)

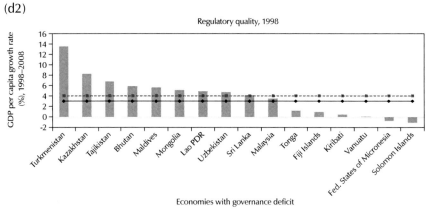

continued.

Figure 8.5 *continued*.

(e1)

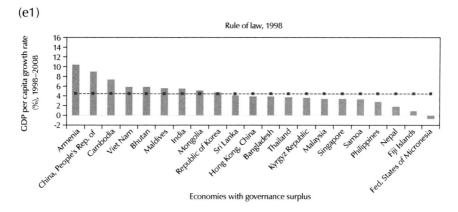

(e2)

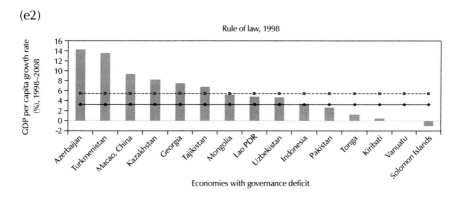

(f1)

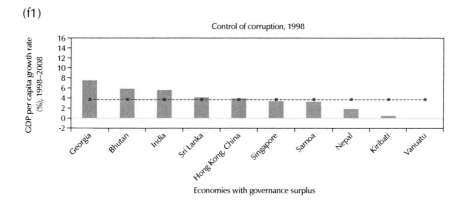

continued.

Figure 8.5 *continued.*

(f2)

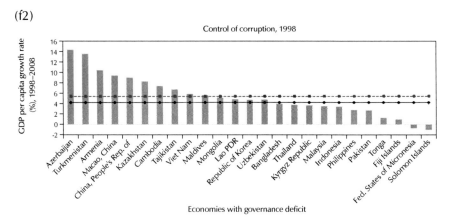

--■-- = average annual growth rate of all economies listed; —◆— = average annual growth rate of all economies listed, excluding oil/gas-rich countries and Macao, China; GDP = gross domestic product; Lao PDR = Lao People's Democratic Republic.

Source: Authors' estimates based on data from the World Bank's Worldwide Governance Indicators (http://info.worldbank.org/governance/wgi/index.asp) and UNDP (2009).

B. Governance/institutions and income inequality

Figure 8.6 shows Gini coefficients of developing Asian economies grouped by whether each of them is in surplus or deficit in each of the six dimensions of the WGIs. The picture here is not as clear-cut as in the case of linking governance quality with growth performance. In the case of voice and accountability, the average value of the Gini coefficients is 40 for economies in surplus and 38 for those in deficit, with no significant difference. This also applies to political stability (40 and 37 for economies in surplus and deficit, respectively), government effectiveness (40 and 37), regulatory quality (38 and 40), and rule of law (40 and 38). The only governance indicator making a relatively significant difference to the Gini coefficient is control of corruption, but with the direction counterintuitive to what is predicted by theory: the average value of the Gini coefficients of the economies with control of corruption in surplus is 43 and while that of the economies in deficit is 37.

Figure 8.6   Governance surplus/deficit and Gini coefficient

(a1)

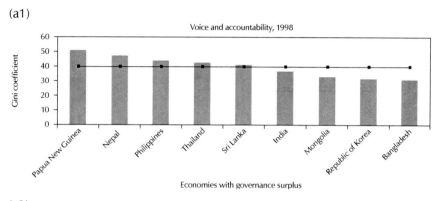

(a2)

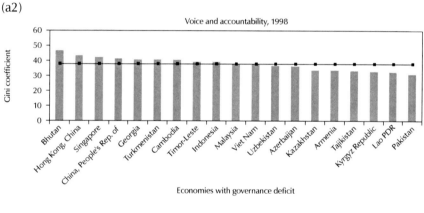

(b1)

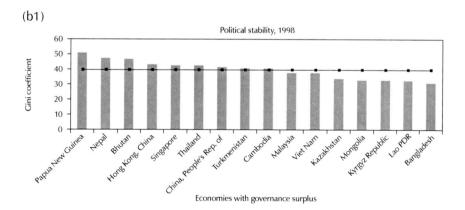

continued.

Figure 8.6 *continued*.

(b2)

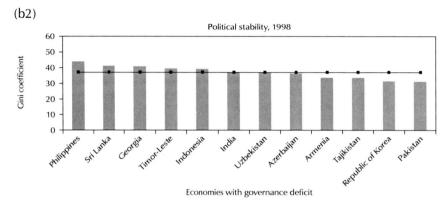

(c1)

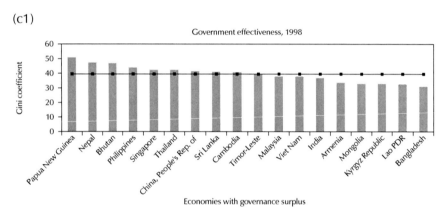

(c2)

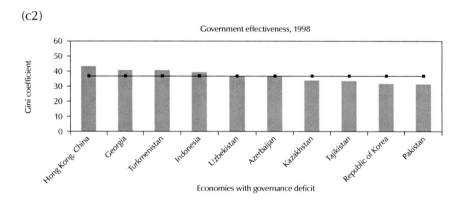

continued.

Figure 8.6 *continued*.

(d1)

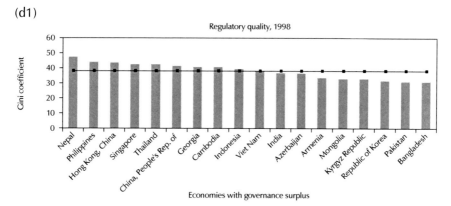

(d2)

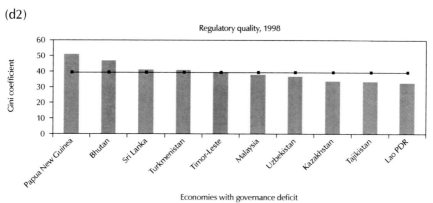

(e1)

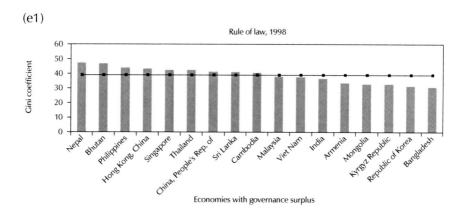

continued.

Figure 8.6 *continued*.

(e2)

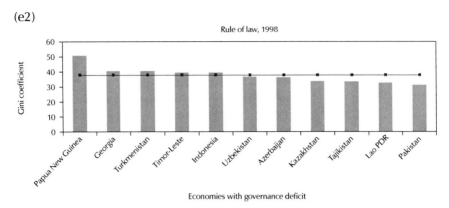

(f1)

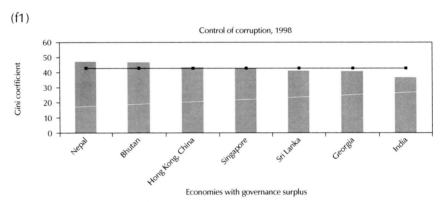

(f2)

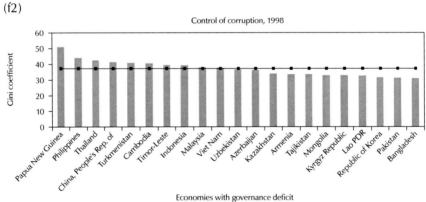

—■— = average value of Gini coefficients of all economies listed, Lao PDR = Lao People's Democratic Republic.

Source: Authors' estimates based on data from the World Bank's Worldwide Governance Indicators (http://info.worldbank.org/governance/wgi/index.asp) and UNDP (2009).

8.3.4   Interpreting the results

The results presented in the previous section support Quibria's (2006) suggestion that, given the multidimensional nature of governance/institutional quality, uncovering its instrumental role may require going beyond its totality to look at specific dimensions. According to the above results, dimensions of governance/institutional quality with a significant power in explaining the cross-country differences in growth performance in developing Asia are government effectiveness, regulatory quality, and rule of law. These results suggest that Asian economies are not "outliers" as far as the relationship between the quality of these governance dimensions and growth performance is concerned. On the other hand, this study fails to detect such a relationship in the cases of voice and accountability, political stability, and control of corruption. How can these paradoxical results be explained?

One explanation may lie in the measurement problems of these governance indicators. As highlighted earlier, these include issues concerning comparability over time and across countries, biases in expert assessments, correlated perception errors, definitional issues, and reliance on "subjective" data. In the case of the indicator for control of corruption, for example, a frequent criticism is that it lumps together and equally weights responses to questions about petty and grand corruption, leading to concerns over whether it can accurately capture overall corruption in a country (KKM 2006).[19] In the case of democracy, which is closely related to voice and accountability, Bardhan (2008) makes a distinction among three aspects related to: (i) some basic minimum civil and political rights enjoyed by citizens, (ii) procedures of accountability in the day-to-day administration under overarching constitutional rules of the game, and (iii) periodic exercises in electoral representativeness. In the case of India, for example, he argues that while its achievement has been impressive in terms of the third aspect over the last half century, its performance is somewhat mixed in terms of the second. He also notes that, except in several states, all these aspects of democracy are weaker at the local village or municipal level than at the federal or state levels in India. It is not clear to what extent the perception-based survey can capture dimensions of governance/institutional quality as complex as voice and accountability.

---

[19]   More recently, Daniel Kaufmann—one of the pioneers of the World Bank's WGIs—argues that corporate capture, in the form of privatization of public policies for the self-interest of those with enormous political and economic power but "without bribes having exchanged hands", which, in his view, is in the realm of corruption, was very important in leading to the global financial crisis (Kaufmann 2008). It is not clear to what extent this type of corruption is captured by the control of corruption indicator in the WGIs.

Apart from the measurement problems associated with governance indicators, recent developments in the literature suggest that there could be other explanations. One is causality between governance/institutional quality and growth performance that is the reverse of what is assumed in the NIE literature, or a causal link from growth to governance/institutional quality that is stronger than the one in the opposite direction. In either case, there may or may not be a correlation between the initial governance/institutional quality and subsequent growth performance. Fukuyama (2008), for example, notes a view arguing that growth produces a propertied middle class, which then presses for rule of law to protect those rights, and subsequently political participation. Paldam and Gundlach (2008) argue that the causality from governance/institutions to growth would predict a divergence of development, whereas from growth to governance/institutions would predict a convergence of institutions to a level that is consistent with the level of development. Their empirical observations support the hypothesis of the convergence of institutions.[20]

Another explanation is the possible context-dependency of the governance/institutions-growth nexus. This means that, even if the direction of causality goes from governance/institutions to growth performance, it is entirely possible that various components of governance/institutional quality as measured by the WGIs are observed to have differing impact on growth performance, depending on a country's history, its stage of development, the length of the time horizon investigated, or other specific circumstances. Fukuyama (2008), for instance, argues that state capacity may be more important than either rule of law or democracy at low levels of per capita GDP. This argument appears to be consistent with the casual observations from Figures 8.2 and 8.3 that data points are scattered more widely in the cases of voice and accountability and political stability, than in the case of government effectiveness, especially when per capita income is low.

More generally, Rodrik (2008) argues that even though the existence of a causal link from governance/institutions to growth performance is now widely accepted, this does not suggest that one can systematically rely upon improved governance to generate growth over the time horizon that policy makers care about (a decade or two). Improved governance in a particular dimension would be effective in generating growth when the poor governance in that dimension is among the most binding development constraints for a country. Acemoglu (2008) argues that

---

[20] They show that 39 ex-colonial African countries became independent during 1956–1960, with the 14 British ex-colonies starting with relatively democratic constitutions, the 17 French ex-colonies adopting less democratic constitutions, and 8 other ex-colonies beginning with democracy levels that were in between; only 8 years after independence, nearly all of the cross-country variation in the level of democracy had vanished, with all political systems converging to almost the same level of autocracy.

while there is relatively strong evidence showing that the broad clusters of institutions—comprising economic, political, and legal aspects—are essential for long-run economic development, scholars must be modest enough to admit that they are only beginning to understand exactly how specific aspects of institutions influence economic outcomes.

A further possible explanation lies in the role of informal institutions. KKZ/KKM's six governance indicators focus largely on formal institutions, whereas the recent theoretical and empirical studies have shown that informal institutions (and social capital) can complement formal institutions or play a substitutive role when formal institutions are weak, and can explain some of the cross-country differences in growth performance (see earlier discussions). There is a large body of literature that attempts to theorize the role of Confucian values in explaining the high growth of many East Asian economies that were seen to have weak hold or slow take-up of Western-style formal institutions, such as the PRC and Viet Nam currently, and Republic of Korea; Malaysia; Taipei,China; and Thailand in the 1970s and 1980s (Roderick 1980, Dore 1987, Peter and Hsiao 1988, Tai 1989, etc.). It has been noted that the basic teachings of Confucianism[21] stress the importance of education for moral development of the individual so the state can be governed by moral virtue (informal institutions and constraints) rather than by the use of coercive laws— formal institutions (Levinson and Christensen 2002, Qin 2008). The workings of informal institutions in some East Asian economies may be seen from a relatively high level of trust among people in these societies, as shown in the results of the recent World Values Survey [22] (Figure 8.7).

One of the questions in the World Values Survey is that "Generally speaking, would you say that most people can be trusted or that you need to be very careful in dealing with people?" Figure 8.7(a) shows that the percentage of the respondents who answered "most people can be trusted" is very high for some of the fast-growing East Asian economies, such as the PRC at 52% and Viet Nam at 51%, compared with around 40% for the United States and 30% for the United Kingdom. Figure 8.7(b) shows a positive relationship between the level of trust and real per capita income on the basis of data covering all sample countries of the World Values Survey. After controlling for the level of income, PRC, Indonesia, Thailand, and Viet Nam are found to have significant surplus in trust.

---

21   Confucian values that are often emphasized include loyalty, filial piety, thrift, hard work, humanity, importance of education, meritocracy, morality, individual sacrifice, social harmony, etc.

22   The World Values Survey is a worldwide network of social scientists studying the impact of changing values and beliefs on social and political life. The database makes it possible to examine cross-level links, such as between public values and economic growth; or between environmental pollution and mass attitudes toward environmental protection; or between political culture and democratic institutions. The fifth wave of the survey covers 2005–2008 and 57 countries and contains over 200 variables (http://www.worldvaluessurvey.org).

Figure 8.7   World values survey on trust among people

(a)

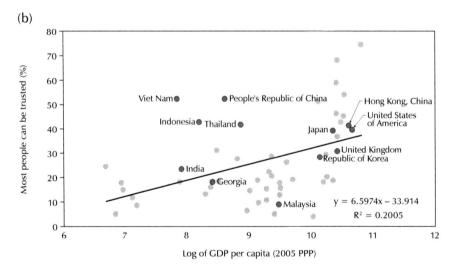

Source: Authors' estimates based on the fifth wave (2005–2008) of the World Values Survey (http://www.worldvaluessurvey.org), downloaded 27 October 2009.

(b)

Source: Authors' estimate based on the World Values Survey (http://www.worldvaluessurvey.org) and World Bank's World Development Indicators Online.

In the case of the governance/institutions-inequality nexus, it is more difficult to interpret the finding of no correlation presented earlier. To begin with, the literature on the relationship between governance/institutions and income inequality is much smaller and newer than that connecting governance/institutions and growth. So, the former is more poorly understood than the latter. In addition, the measurement problems of the governance indicators, discussed earlier, remain relevant. The possible reverse causality could also make it difficult to discern any link between the initial governance/institutional quality and subsequent income inequality. One may argue that it takes much longer for the governance/institutional quality to affect income distribution than for it to affect growth performance.

Further, Chaudhuri and Ravallion (2007) make a distinction between "bad inequality" and "good inequality". Good inequality reflects and reinforces the market-based incentives needed to foster innovation, entrepreneurship, and growth. Bad inequality, on the other hand, is rooted in market failures, coordination failures, governance failures, and social exclusion, and often reflects inequality in opportunity. Improvements in governance and institutional quality are likely to reduce bad, but not necessarily good, inequality.

Similarly, Easterly (2007) makes a distinction between "structural" inequality and "market" inequality. The former reflects such historical events as conquest, colonization, slavery, and land distribution by the state or colonial power; it creates an elite by means of these non-market mechanisms. In his view, structural inequality is unambiguously bad for subsequent development in theory. Market inequality, on the other hand, arises because of uneven success in free markets among different individuals, cities, regions, firms, and industries. Market inequality has ambiguous effects, and cannot be eliminated entirely by improvements in governance and institutions. If rising inequality in many developing Asian economies in recent years reflects to some or a large extent "good inequality" or "market inequality", then it can be argued that it will be less correlated with governance/institutional quality.

8.4   Conclusions

The long-run positive association between governance and institutional quality, on one hand, and growth and level of income, on the other, is strong and incontrovertible, both conceptually and empirically. A two-way causal link between the two is also well-recognized in the literature. That is, while institutions and their implied governance results may well be "supply-side" factors that drive economic growth, they are also attendant products of growth itself—partly because rising incomes and education levels create a "demand" for them. It has become a major task, therefore—and an active field of research—to tease out the relative importance of one or the other direction of causality. A further area of research has been motivated by the fact that the concept of "quality" of governance/institutions is multidimensional. It is therefore quite possible that—and important to find out whether—certain aspects of governance/institutional quality are more relevant or critical than others in determining growth performance for specific countries during specific periods.

At least as much is suggested when a simple classification framework is applied to developing Asia. Under the widely used KKM/KKZ composite governance indicators produced by the World Bank, it is found that developing Asian economies with governance in surplus in the dimensions of government effectiveness, regulatory quality, and rule of law in 1998 grew faster during 1998–2008 by 1.6, 2.0, and 1.2 percentage points per year on average, respectively, relative to the economies with governance in deficit in these dimensions (oil- and gas-rich countries and Macao excluded). These results provide support for a causal link leading from good governance and institutions to superior growth performance, and dispel the notion that developing Asian countries are "outliers" from this relationship.

However, such a causal link cannot be detected in the cases of voice and accountability, political stability, and control of corruption. This provides room for several possible explanations, ranging from the measurement problems associated with governance indicators to reverse causality, the context-specific nature of the governance/institutions-growth nexus, and the role of informal institutions.

There are also convincing arguments for an association between governance/institutional quality, particularly political accountability, democracy and control of corruption, on one hand, and income distribution and inequality, on the other, although this association is empirically much weaker. A two-way causality between the two is widely agreed, with the causal link from lower income inequality to better governance/institutional quality arguably stronger. Applying the same classification framework, it is found that levels of income inequality across economies with governance in surplus are not very different from those with governance in deficit in almost all dimensions. Without further qualification, this seems to suggest that initial levels of governance/institutional quality do not matter much for the subsequent pattern of income distribution in the context of developing Asia. Possible explanations for such results range from an imperfect understanding or specification of the underlying causal relationships; measurement problems associated with governance indicators; and the varying nature of rising inequality in the region.

Compared with other regions in the world, developing Asia scored relatively high in government effectiveness and rule of law, but low in political stability and absence of violence, and voice and accountability, with scores of regulatory quality and control of corruption lying in between, in 2008. Compared with the OECD grouping and Eastern Europe, developing Asia still has a lot to catch up in all governance dimensions. During 1998–2008, however, a large number of developing Asian economies saw their governance scores improving in various dimensions, although a large number of economies also slipped. In the areas of rule of law and control of corruption, more economies improved than slipped. There was also a significant increase in the proportion of economies with surplus in control of corruption (compared with an international reference line), from 26% to 47%. These results suggest that significant improvements in governance do and can occur within a relatively short period of time.

What do all these mean for policy? As stated at the beginning of this chapter, the intrinsic value of good governance and institutions as ends of development in their own right is now universally accepted and underlies the very notion of inclusiveness. Therefore, good governance should be pursued in all dimensions as a basic development goal. To maximize its instrumental value, the current literature points to the need for recognizing the context-specific nature of the linkages between governance and institutional quality, on one hand, and growth and inequality, on the other, and for focusing on the aspects that are most binding and critical to a country's development in a particular period. There is also a need for cautioning against unguarded expectations that any institutional improvement would lead to better growth performance and more equal income distribution in a relatively short period of time. Taken at face value, the empirical findings in this chapter seem to suggest that strengthening government effectiveness, improving regulatory quality and rule of law, and control of corruption could well be used as what Fukuyama (2008) calls potential entry points of development strategies for many countries in the region.

References

Acemoglu, D. 2008. "Oligarchic Versus Democratic Societies." *Journal of the European Economic Association* 6(1):1–44.

Acemoglu, D., S. Johnson, and J. A. Robinson. 2001. "The Colonial Origins of Comparative Development." *American Economic Review* 91(5):1369–401.

_____. 2002. "Reversal of Fortune: Geography and Institutions in the Making of the Modern World Income Distribution." *Quarterly Journal of Economics* 117:1231–94.

Ali, I., and J. Zhuang. 2007. "Inclusive Growth toward a Prosperous Asia: Policy Implications." ERD Working Paper Series No. 97. Economics and Research Department, Asian Development Bank, Manila.

Arndt, C., and C. Oman. 2006. *Uses and Abuses of Governance Indicators.* Development Center Studies, Organisation for Economic Co-operation and Development.

Aron, J. 2000. "Growth and Institutions: A Review of the Evidence." *The World Bank Research Observer* 15(1):99–135.

Bardhan, P. 2008. "Democracy and Distributive Politics in India." In I. Shapiro, P. A. Swenson, and D. Donno, eds., *Divide and Deal: The Politics of Distribution in Democracies*. New York and London: New York University Press.

Barro, R. 1991. "Economic Growth in a Cross-section of Countries." *Quarterly Journal of Economics* 106(2):407–43.

Barro, R., and X. Sala-i-Martín. 1995. *Economic Growth*. New York: McGraw-Hill.

Becker, G. 1962. "Investment in Human Capital: A Theoretical Analysis." *Journal of Political Economy* 70:9–49.

Begovic, B. 2005. Economic Inequality and Corruption. CLDS Working Paper No. 0106, Center for Liberal-Democratic Studies.

Bénabou, R. 1996. Inequality and Growth. CEPR Discussion Paper No. 1450, Center for Economic Policy and Research.

Boix, C. 2001. Democracy and Inequality. Department of Political Science, University of Chicago. Working Paper No. 2001/161. Available: http://www.march.es/ceacs/ingles/publicaciones/working/archivos/2001_161.pdf.

Bollen, K., and R. Jackman. 1985. "Political Democracy and the Size Distribution of Income." *American Sociological Review* 50:438–57.

Bourguignon, F., and T. Verdier. 2000. "Oligarchy, Democracy, Inequality and Growth." *Journal of Development Economics* 62(2):285–313.

Burnside, C., and D. Dollar. 2000. "Aid, Policies, and Growth." *American Economic Review* 90(4):847–68.

Chaudhuri, S., and M. Ravallion. 2007. "Partially Awakened Giants: Uncover Growth in Chin and India." In L. Alan Winters, and S. Yusuf, eds., *Dancing with Giants: China, India, and the Global Economy*. The World Bank, Washington, DC.

Chong, A., and M. Gradstein. 2007. "Institutions and Inequality." *Review of Economics and Statistics* 89(3):456–65.

Coleman, J. 1988. "Social Capital in the Creation of Human Capital." *American Journal of Sociology* Supplement 94:S95–S120.

Diamond, J. 1997. *Guns, Germs, and Steel*. New York: W.W. Norton.

Dore, R. P. 1987. *Taking Japan Seriously: A Confucian Perspective on Leading Economic Issues*. Stanford: Stanford University Press.

Durlauf, S., and M. Fafchamps. 2005. "Social Capital." In S. Durlauf, and P. Aghion, eds., *Handbook of Economic Growth*. Amsterdam: North Holland.

Easterly, W. 2006. *The White Man's Burden*. New York: Penguin Books.

———. 2007. "Inequality does Cause Underdevelopment: Insights from a New Instrument." *Journal of Development Economics* 64:755–76.

Easterly, W., and R. Levine. 2003. "Tropics, Germs, and Crops: How Endowments Influence Economic Development." *Journal of Monetary Economics* 50(1):3–39.

Easterly, W., J. Ritzen, and M. Woolcock. 2006. "Social Cohesion, Institutions, and Growth." *Economics and Politics* 18(2):103–20.

Fukuyama, F. 2000. "Social Capital." In L. Harrison, and S. Huntington, eds., *Culture Matters: How Values Shape Human Progress*. New York: Basic Books.

_____. 2008. "What Do We Know about the Relationship between the Political and Economic Dimensions of Development." In World Bank, *Governance, Growth, and Development Decision-Making—Reflections by: Douglass North, Daron Acemoglu, Francis Fukuyama, Dani Rodrik*. World Bank, Washington, DC.

Glaeser, E., R. LaPorta, F. Lopez-de-Silanes, and A. Shleifer. 2004. "Do Institutions Cause Growth?" *Journal of Economic Growth* 9(3):271–303.

Gradstein, M. 2007. "Inequality, Democracy and the Protection of Property Rights." *Economic Journal* 117:252–69.

Gradstein, M., B. Milanovic, and Y. Ying. 2001. Democracy and Income Inequality: An Empirical Analysis. Policy Research Working Paper No. 2561, World Bank, Washington, DC.

Greif, A. 2005. *Institutions and the Road to the Modern Economy: Lessons from Mediaeval Trade*. Cambridge University Press.

Grossman, G. M., and Helpman, E. 1991. *Innovation and Growth in the Global Economy*. Cambridge, Massachussetts: MIT Press.

Gupta, S., H. Davoodi, and R. Alonso-Terme. 2002. "Does Corruption Affect Income Inequality and Poverty?" *Economics of Governance* 3(1):23–45.

Gyimah-Brempong, K. 2002. Corruption, Economic Growth, and Income Inequality in Africa." *Economics of Governance* 3:183–209.

Huther, J., and A. Shah. 1996. "A Simple Measure of Good Governance." Operations Evaluation Department, World Bank, Washington, DC. Processed.

Johnston, M. 1989. "Corruption, Inequality, and Change." In P. Ward, ed., *Corruption, Development and Inequality*. London and New York: Routledge.

Kaldor, N. 1956. "Alternative Theories of Income Distribution." *Review of Economic Studies* 23:94–100.

Kasper, W., and M. Streit. 1998. *Institutional Economics: Social Order and Public Policy*. Cheltenham: Edward Elgar.

Kaufmann, D. 2003. Governance Redux: The Empirical Challenge. World Bank Institute.

_____. 2008. Presentation by Daniel Kaufmann. Daniel Kaufmann's Farewell Lecture: Governance, Crisis, and the Longer View: Unorthodox Reflections on the New Reality. Available: http://info.worldbank.org/etools/docs/library/245600/DKaufmann%20Farewell%20Event%20Preston%2012%2009%2008.pdf.

Kaufmann, D., and A. Kraay. 2008. Governance Indicators: Where Are We, Where Should We Be Going? World Bank Research Working Paper No. 4370, World Bank, Washington, DC.

Kaufmann, D., A. Kraay, and P. Zoido-Lobatón. 1999. Aggregating Governance Indicators. World Bank Policy Research Working Paper No. 2195, World Bank, Washington, DC.

Kaufmann, D., A. Kraay, and M. Mastruzzi. 2003. Governance Matters III: Governance Indicators for 1996–2002. World Bank Policy Research Working Paper No. 3106, World Bank, Washington, DC.

_____. 2006. "Measuring Corruption: Myths and Realities." *Development Outreach*, September 2006 Issue. World Bank, Washington, DC.

_____. 2009. Governance Matters 2009: Learning from over a Decade of the Worldwide Governance Indicators. The Brookings Institution. Available: http://www.brookings.edu/opinions/2009.

Knack, S., and P. Keefer. 1995. "Institutions and Economic Performance: Cross-country Tests Using Alternative Measures." *Economics and Politics* 7:207–27.

Knowles, S. 2005. "Inequality and Economic Growth: The Empirical Relationship Reconsidered in the Light of Comparable Data." *Journal of Development Studies* 41:135–59.

Knowles, S., and C. R. Weatherston. 2006. Informal Institutions and Cross-country Income Differences. Discussion Paper No. 0604. Department of Economics, University of Otago, Dunedin, New Zealand.

Kuznets, S. 1955. "Economic Growth and Inequality." *American Economic Review* 45(1):1–28.

Lauth, H-J. 2005. The Impact of Informal Institutions on Democratic Performance: Theoretical Reflections and Empirical Findings. Paper prepared for the 2005 Annual Meeting of the American Political Science Association, 1–4 September 2005.

Li, H., L. Squire, and H-F. Zou. 1998. "Explaining International and Intertemporal Variations in Income Inequality." *Economic Journal* 108:26–43.

Li, H., L. C. Xu, and H-F. Zou. 2000. "Corruption, Income Distribution, and Growth." *Economics and Politics* 12(2):954–1985.

Levinson, D., and K. Christensen. 2002. Encyclopedia of Modern Asia. Gale. Available: http://www.gale.cengage.com.

Mauro, P. 1995. "Corruption and Growth." *Quarterly Journal of Economics* 110:681–712.

_____. 1998. "Corruption and the Composition of Government Expenditure." *Journal of Public Economics* 69(2):263–79.

North, D. 1981. *Structure and Change in Economic History*. New York: W.W. Norton.

_____. 1990. *Institutions, Institutional Change, and Economic Performance*. Cambridge University Press.

_____. 2005. *Understanding the Process of Economic Change*. Princeton University Press.

North, D., and R. P. Thomas. 1973. *The Rise of the Western World: A New Economic History*. Cambridge: Cambridge University Press. Available: http://www.economics.uci.edu/~dbell/North.pdf.

North, D., and R. P. Thomas. 1976. *The Rise of the Western World: A New Economic History*. Cambridge University Press.

North, D., J. Wallis, and B. Weingast. 2006. "A Conceptual Framework for Interpreting Recorded Human History." NBER Working Paper No. 12795, National Bureau of Economic Research. Available: http://www.nber.org/papers/w12795.

Paldam, M., and E. Gundlach. 2008. "Two Views on Institutions and Development: The Grand Transition vs. the Primacy of Institutions." *Kyklos* 61(1):65–100.

Perotti, R. 1996. "Growth, Income Distribution, and Democracy: What the Data Say." *Journal of Economic Growth* 1(2):149–87.

Peter, L. B., and H. H. M. Hsiao. 1988. *In Search of an East Asian Development Model*. New Brunswick, NJ: Transaction Books.

Putnam, R. 1993. *Making Democracy Work*. Princeton, NJ: Princeton University Press.

Qin, G. 2008. "The Thinking Way of Confucianism and the Rule of Law." *Journal of Politics and Law* 1(1): 68–75.

Quibria, M. 2006. "Does Governance Matter? Yes, No, or Maybe: Some Evidence from Developing Asia." *Kyklos* 59(1):99–114.

Rauf, M. 2009. "Innovations and Informal Institutions: An Institutionalist Approach to the Role of Social Capital for Innovation." *Journal of Academic Research in Economics* 1:25–34.

Roderick, M. 1980. "The Post-Confucian Challenge." *The Economist*. Feb. 9, 1980.

Rodrik, D. 2008. "Thinking about Governance." In World Bank, *Governance, Growth, and Development Decision-Making—Reflections by: Douglass North, Daron Acemoglu, Francis Fukuyama, Dani Rodrik*. World Bank, Washington, DC.

Rodrik, D., A. Subramanian, and F. Trebbi. 2004. "Institutions Rule: The Primacy of Institutions over Geography and Integration in Economic Development." *Journal of Economic Growth* 9(2):131–65.

Rogowski, R., and D. MacRae. 2004. Inequality and Institutions: What Theory, History, and (Some) Data Tell Us. Paper presented at the annual meeting of the Midwest Political Science Association, Palmer House, Chicago, Illinois, 14 April 2005.

Solow, R. 1956. "A Contribution to the Theory of Economic Growth." *Quarterly Journal of Economics* 70:65–94.

Swan, T. 1956. "Economic Growth and Capital Accumulation." *Economic Record* 32(63):334–61.

Tai, H. C. 1989. *Confucianism and Economic Development: An Oriental Alternative?* Washington, DC: Washington Institute Press.

319

Tanzi, V., and H. Davoodi. 1997. Corruption, Public Investment, and Growth. IMF Working Paper No. 97/139, International Monetary Fund.

Tarschys, D. 2001. "Wealth, Values, Institutions: Trends in Government and Governance." In OECD, *Governance in the 21st Century*. Paris: Organisation for Economic Co-operation and Development.

UNDP. 2007. *Governance Indicators: A Users' Guide*. United Nations Development Programme.

_____. 2009. *Human Development Report 2009—Overcoming Barriers: Human Mobility and Development*. New York: Palgrave Macmillan.

Uslaner, E. M. 2008. *Corruption, Inequality, and the Rule of Law*. Cambridge University Press.

Weingast. B. 1993. "Constitutions as General Structures: The Political Foundations of Secure Markets." *Journal of Institutional and Theoretical Economics* 146(1):286–31.

Woolcock, M. 1998. "Social Capital and Economic Development: Toward a Theoretical Synthesis and Policy Framework." *Theory and Society* 27(2):151–208.

World Bank. 1989. *Sub-Saharan Africa—From Crisis to Sustainable Growth: A Long-term Perspective Study*. Washington, DC.

_____. 1992. *Governance and Development*. Washington, DC.

_____. 2000. *Making Transition Work for Everyone: Poverty and Inequality in Europe and Central Asia*. Washington, DC.

_____. 2007. *A Decade of Measuring the Quality of Governance—Governance Matters 2007: Worldwide Governance Indicators, 1996–2006: Annual Indicators and Underlying Data*. Washington, DC.

_____. Various years. World Development Indicators Online. Available: http://devdata.worldbank.org/dataonline/.

World Values Survey. Various years. Online Data Analysis. Available: http://www.worldvaluessurvey.org.

You, J. S., and S. Khagram. 2005. "A Comparative Study of Inequality and Corruption." *American Sociological Review* 70:136–158.

Part C

Country Studies

9

Growth, Inequality, and the Labor Market: The Philippines

Hyun H. Son[1]

9.1 Introduction

Given rapid population growth and the large increase in labor force participation (LFP), employment growth in the Philippines has been insufficient to lower unemployment and underemployment rates. Productivity growth has been meager and spotty. Labor productivity increased by less than 7% in 1988–2000, far lower than the 30%–50% increase in other Asian countries, such as Indonesia, Republic of Korea, Malaysia, and Thailand. Income generated from employment in the labor market is the main source for most Filipinos, and growth in income therefore depends very much on growth in employment and in labor productivity. Thus, the labor market plays a critical role in determining average income and shaping income distribution among individuals in the Philippines.

This chapter analyzes economic growth and changes in income inequality in the Philippines, with a particular focus on the role of the labor market. A decomposition methodology is proposed to explore the links between growth and income inequality through characteristics such as LFP, employment rate, working hours, and productivity. This helps improve understanding of how the labor market has affected the country's economic growth and changes in income inequality so that the government can formulate labor market policies to enhance growth and reduce inequality.

For data, the analysis uses the Family Income and Expenditure Survey (FIES) and the Labor Force Survey, carried out by the National Statistics Office (NSO various years). Both provide micro unit record data at the household and individual levels. This study uses surveys for three periods: 1997, 2000, and 2003.

[1] This chapter is based on a paper presented at the 45th Annual Meeting of the Philippine Economic Society on 14–16 November 2007, which was subsequently published in 2008 in *The Philippine Review of Economics* XLV(1):69–92 as "The Role of Labor Market in Explaining Growth and Inequality in Income: The Philippines Case." The author thanks Nanak Kakwani and Jane Carangal-San Jose for their valuable and insightful comments and suggestions on the paper.

Section 9.2 explains growth by income components. Section 9.3 investigates the impact of various income components on inequality. Section 9.4 looks at trends in key labor market indicators. Section 9.5 provides a link between growth and labor market characteristics. Section 9.6 examines inequities in key labor market indicators. Section 9.7 explains inequality in labor income. Section 9.8 discusses the issues of education vis-à-vis the labor market, and the last section concludes the chapter.

9.2 Explaining growth by income components

The total per capita income of a household x can be written as the sum of several factor incomes or income components:

$$x = \sum_{j=1}^{k} x_j \qquad (1)$$

where k is the total number of income components and x_j is the per capita income from the jth income component. This analysis considers six income components:

(i)   agricultural wage income
(ii) non-agricultural wage income
(iii) enterprise income (from self-employment)
(iv) domestic remittances
(v)   foreign remittances
(vi) other income (e.g., interest, dividends, pensions, rents, etc.)

Suppose μ is the average per capita income of all households and μ_j is the per capita income from the jth income component, then from equation (1):

$$\mu = \sum_{j=1}^{k} \mu_j \qquad (2)$$

where μ_j/μ is the share of jth income component. This indicator is useful as it indicates from which sources households derive their income. Table 9.1 shows that, in 2003, the non-agricultural wage is the largest source of household income in the Philippines, at about 42%, followed by enterprise income from self-employment at 24%, foreign remittances at 10%, agricultural wage income at 3%, and domestic remittances at less than 3%. During 1997–2003, there was a big increase in the share of foreign remittances, suggesting that this has become an important source of household income. Remittances played an important role as an informal safety net for average households during the Asian financial crisis of 1997/1998. On the other hand, the shares of enterprise income from self-employment and non-agricultural wage income declined by 1 and 2 percentage points, respectively, during the same period.

The story is somewhat different for poor households. First, a major source of income for the poor is enterprise income from self-employment, not from wages. This suggests that poor households are mainly working in the informal sector. The share of this income, however, is falling. In addition, the share of foreign remittances in total income for poor households, at 1.2% in 2003, is far smaller than that for an average Philippine household. Its share of domestic remittances, at 4.7% in 2003, is larger though. These suggest that, while non-poor households rely more on remittances than the poor, they receive remittances mostly from overseas. The poor receive remittances mainly from domestic sources.

Table 9.1   Average annual per capita household income by component

Income component	Per capita income (peso)			Share of total income (%)		
	1997	2000	2003	1997	2000	2003
	All households					
Agricultural wage income	761	775	939	3.2	2.8	3.1
Non-agricultural wage income	10,058	11,597	12,566	42.9	42.6	41.7
Enterprise income	6,097	6,664	7,185	26.0	24.5	23.9
Domestic remittance	502	681	809	2.1	2.5	2.7
Foreign remittance	1,612	2,332	3,009	6.9	8.6	10.0
Other income	4,388	5,149	5,607	18.7	18.9	18.6
Total income	23,418	27,198	30,115	100.0	100.0	100.0
	Poor households					
Agricultural wage income	793	927	1,078	13.9	13.2	13.7
Non-agricultural wage income	1,171	1,548	1,792	20.5	22.1	22.7
Enterprise income	2,393	2,839	3,077	41.9	40.5	39.0
Domestic remittance	259	334	373	4.5	4.8	4.7
Foreign remittance	75	76	97	1.3	1.1	1.2
Other income	1,019	1,287	1,473	17.8	18.4	18.7
Total income	5,710	7,012	7,889	100.0	100.0	100.0

Note: Other income includes interest, dividends, rentals received, and pensions and social security benefits.
Source: Author's calculations based on FIES (NSO various years).

The analysis is next extended to income growth and the relative contribution of each income component. Suppose r is the growth rate of per capita total real income and r_j is the growth rate of the jth income component. Based on equation (2):

$$r = \sum_{j=1}^{k} (\mu_j/\mu)r_j \qquad (3)$$

325

which shows that the growth rate of total income is equal to the weighted average of growth rates of all individual income components, with the weight being the share of each income component in total income. The term $(\mu_j/\mu)r_j$ is thus the contribution of the jth income component to the growth in total income. To calculate per capita real income, the poverty line—which takes into account the differences in the regional cost of living as well as changes in prices over time—is used as the deflator. This involves expressing per capita real income as a percentage of the poverty line where the poverty line is normalized to 100. This is also called per capita welfare in this chapter.

As shown in Table 9.2, per capita total household real income declined during 1997–2003. As would be expected, the fall was particularly large during the crisis period of 1997–2000, when all income components, with the exception of remittances, fell in per capita terms. The fall was more significant for agricultural wage income and enterprise income from self-employment. On the other hand, domestic and foreign remittances grew at annual rates of 3.5% and 6.2%, respectively. These results suggest that the fall in per capita total income could have been much greater in the absence of remittances. This is also indicated by the positive contribution of the growth in remittances to the growth in total household income. All other income components—particularly non-agricultural wage and enterprise income from self-employment—contributed to the shrinkage in total income during the period.

Table 9.2   Per capita welfare, growth rate, and contribution
             to total income growth

Income component	Per capita welfare			Annual growth rate (%)		Contribution to growth in total income (percentage point)	
	1997	2000	2003	1997–2000	2000–2003	1997–2000	2000–2003
All households							
Agricultural wage income	9.9	8.3	9.0	−5.2	2.7	−0.2	0.1
Non-agricultural wage income	113.1	107.0	102.8	−1.8	−1.3	−0.8	−0.5
Enterprise income	72.8	65.1	62.8	−3.5	−1.2	−1.0	−0.3
Domestic remittance	6.0	6.6	6.9	3.5	1.7	0.1	0.0
Foreign remittance	18.1	21.5	24.7	6.2	5.0	0.4	0.4
Other income	50.1	48.2	46.9	−1.3	−0.9	−0.2	−0.2
Total income	270.0	256.8	253.1	−1.6	−0.5	−1.6	−0.5

continued.

Table 9.2 *continued.*

Income component	Per capita welfare			Annual growth rate (%)		Contribution to growth in total income (percentage point)	
	1997	2000	2003	1997–2000	2000–2003	1997–2000	2000–2003
	Poor households						
Agricultural wage income	10.2	9.9	10.2	–1.2	1.1	–0.2	0.2
Non-agricultural wage income	14.1	15.3	15.4	2.8	0.3	0.6	0.1
Enterprise income	30.4	29.2	27.9	–1.4	–1.5	–0.6	–0.6
Domestic remittance	3.3	3.4	3.4	1.6	–0.7	0.1	0.0
Foreign remittance	0.9	0.8	0.8	–5.7	3.2	–0.1	0.0
Other income	12.9	13.3	13.5	1.1	0.4	0.2	0.1
Total income	71.9	71.9	71.2	0.0	–0.3	0.0	–0.3

Note: Per capita welfare is expressed as a percentage of the poverty line where the poverty line is normalized to 100.

Source: Author's calculations based on FIES (NSO various years).

Per capita household income also fell among poor households during 1997–2003, although by much less than did the national average. The fall was largely due to the drop in enterprise income from self-employment. The adverse impact of falling enterprise income on growth of total income was partly offset by growth in non-agricultural wage income among poor households.

To recap, Philippine households derive their income mainly from labor income, with the poor being more reliant on enterprise earnings from self-employment. While remittances buffered income during the crisis years, foreign remittances flowed mostly to the non-poor while the poor tended to rely more on domestic remittances.

9.3   Impact of income components on inequality

A major problem in the Philippines is the regional disparity in living conditions among its 16 distinct regions. Disparity can be very large even within a region, and any analysis of inequality should reflect such variation. Theil's measure of inequality—because it can be decomposed into between- and within-region inequality—is well suited to analyzing inequality in the Philippines (Theil 1967). In this section, the Theil index is used to explain how inequality in total income is impacted by changes in various income components.

Suppose x is per capita total household income, which is a random variable with density function $f(x)$, with mean μ, then Theil's inequality measure can be written as:

$$T = \int_{0}^{\infty} \left[ln(\mu) - ln(x)\right] f(x) dx \tag{4}$$

How does growth in various income components affect inequality? For example, how do foreign remittances affect inequality in per capita total income? If an increase in foreign remittances increases inequality, then remittances are considered anti-poor because they benefit the non-poor proportionally more than the poor. On the other hand, if an increase in foreign remittances reduces inequality, then this income component is considered pro-poor, because it benefits the poor more than the non-poor. From a policy point of view, it is important to know which income components are pro-poor or anti-poor. This can be answered by estimating the elasticity of inequality for various income components.

The elasticity of Theil's inequality measure T in equation (4) with respect to μ_j (mean per capita income from component j) can be written as

$$n_j = \frac{\mu_j}{T} \frac{\partial T}{\partial \mu_j} = \frac{1}{T} \int_{0}^{\infty} \left[\frac{\mu_j}{\mu} - \frac{x_j}{x}\right] f(x) dx \tag{5}$$

which indicates that if μ_j increases by 1%, the inequality measure T will change by n_j%. The sign (positive or negative) of n_j implies whether growth in the jth income component will decrease or increase the inequality of per capita total income. Thus, the jth income component is pro-poor if n_j is negative and anti-poor if it is positive. That $\sum_{j=1}^{k} n_j = 0$ can be easily verified implying that when all income components increase by 1%, total inequality does not change.

Table 9.3 presents the inequality elasticity with respect to various income components. The components that would result in a reduction in inequality are agricultural wage income, enterprise income from self-employment, and domestic remittances. Components that would increase inequality are non-agricultural wage income, foreign remittances, and other income. These have important implications. First, agricultural wage income is pro-poor in the sense that it has contributed to a reduction in inequality. Yet, since its share has been declining over time, the ongoing transformation of the economic structure can be expected to continue to worsen inequality in the future, other things being equal. Second, the share of non-agricultural wage income, from which households derive a major source of livelihood, will continue to increase. Thus, the increasing share of non-agricultural wage income in total household income will be expected to be a major factor contributing to the increase in inequality.

As noted earlier, foreign remittances have contributed significantly to growth in total household income. Overseas remittances go to the non-poor proportionally more than to the poor, and consequently their impact is to increase inequality. But, domestic remittances go to the poor proportionally more than to the non-poor, and thus their impact is to reduce inequality. However, the share of domestic remittances is unlikely to increase sufficiently to have any significant impact on inequality in the near future. Other income—which includes earnings from interest, rents, pensions, dividends, and the like—is always expected to be pro-rich or anti-poor. The share of this type of non-labor income is likely to increase during this era of globalization. Enterprise income from self-employment is pro-poor because a large proportion of the poor are engaged in the informal sector, pursuing enterprise activities despite very low earnings. With economic expansion, the informal sector is likely to shrink and falling enterprise income will become a source of increasing inequality.

Table 9.3   Inequality elasticity of income components

Income component and Theil index	1997	2000	2003
Agricultural wage income	−0.095	−0.099	−0.105
Non-agricultural wage income	0.158	0.163	0.150
Enterprise income	−0.128	−0.143	−0.139
Domestic remittance	−0.024	−0.024	−0.026
Foreign remittance	0.050	0.076	0.099
Other income	0.038	0.026	0.020
Total income	0.000	0.000	0.000
Theil index	0.418	0.413	0.395

Source: Author's calculations based on FIES (NSO various years).

In sum, the analysis suggests that many factors can perpetuate, if not worsen, inequality. Government policies are called for to offset the impact of such factors. An effective policy could be to introduce well-targeted cash transfer programs. A program could be in the form of conditional cash transfers similar to those adopted in many Latin American countries.[2] Such cash transfer programs have been regarded as a leading-edge social policy tool for their ability to target short-run poverty and improve the human capital of the poor. They have also been lauded for their ability to focus on the poor, for making it easier

---

[2]   Well-known conditional cash transfer programs implemented in Latin America include the Progresa (now called Oportunidades) in Mexico, Bolsa Escola and Bolsa Familia in Brazil, Red de Proteccion Social in Nicaragua, Programa de Asistencia Familiar in Honduras, Program for Advancement through Health and Education in Jamaica, and Subsidio Unico Familiar in Chile (Son and Florentino 2008).

to integrate different types of social service (e.g., education, health, and nutrition), and for their cost-effective performance.

9.4   Labor market indicators

As discussed earlier, the average Philippine household derives its major source of income from labor earnings—at more than 70%, as shown in Table 9.1. Thus, the labor market has an enormous impact on both growth and changes in inequality. This section discusses the trends of several key labor market indicators. These are normally defined in terms of individual characteristics, while growth and inequality measures are estimated from household characteristics. A question then arises as to how such different characteristics of households and individuals could be linked.

An initial step is to convert individual labor market indicators into household indicators. This step is a major contribution of this chapter to studies that attempt to link the labor market with growth and inequality. For example, per capita employment in a household is obtained by the total number of employed people in a household divided by the household size. Average per capita employment for the entire sample was calculated as 38.4% in 2003 (Table 9.4). This means that almost two members of a five-member household were on average engaged in some form of employment in the labor market in 2003.

Table 9.4 presents five labor market indicators for households:

   (i)   per capita employment (e)
   (ii)   per capita unemployment (u)
   (iii)   per capita labor force ($l = e+u$)
   (iv)   per capita work hours (h)
   (v)   per capita labor income: nominal (x_l) and real (x_l^*)

Using these indicators, the following definitions can be derived:

   (i)   employment rate $\left(\dfrac{e}{l}\right)$

   (ii)   work hours per employed person $\left(\dfrac{h}{e}\right)$

   (iii)   labor productivity: nominal $\left(\dfrac{x_l}{h}\right)$ and real $\left(\dfrac{x_l^*}{h}\right)$

Per capita labor force for a household is defined as the sum of per capita employment and per capita unemployment; the employment rate in a household is measured by per capita employment divided by per capita labor force; work hours per employed person is obtained by per capita work hours divided by per capita employment.

Table 9.4   Trends in labor market indicators

Labor market indicator	Actual values			Annual growth rate (%)	
	1997	2000	2003	1997–2000	2000–2003
All households					
Per capita employment	0.375	0.373	0.384	–0.1	0.9
Per capita unemployment	0.036	0.048	0.049	10.0	0.7
Per capita labor force	0.410	0.422	0.433	0.9	0.9
Per capita work hours/week	15.3	16.3	16.5	2.0	0.3
Per capita nominal labor income, peso	16,916.0	19,036.0	20,689.0	3.9	2.8
Per capita real labor income, peso	195.8	180.4	174.6	–2.7	–1.1
Employment rate (%)	91.3	88.6	88.6	–1.0	0.0
Work hours per employed	40.9	43.7	42.9	2.2	–0.6
Productivity (nominal), peso/hour	21.2	22.4	24.2	1.9	2.5
Productivity (real), peso/hour	0.25	0.21	0.20	–4.8	–1.4
Poor households					
Per capita employment	0.318	0.317	0.331	–0.1	1.5
Per capita unemployment	0.024	0.031	0.035	8.2	4.4
Per capita labor force	0.342	0.348	0.366	0.6	1.7
Per capita work hours/week	11.0	12.2	12.1	3.7	–0.4
Per capita nominal labor income, peso	4,357.0	5,314.0	5,946.0	6.6	3.7
Per capita real labor income, peso	54.8	54.4	53.5	–0.3	–0.5
Employment rate (%)	93.0	91.2	90.4	–0.7	–0.3
Work hours per employed	34.5	38.6	36.5	3.8	–1.9
Productivity (nominal), peso/hour	7.7	8.4	9.5	2.9	4.1
Productivity (real), peso/hour	0.10	0.09	0.09	–4.0	–0.1

Source: Author's calculations based on FIES and Labor Force Surveys (NSO various years).

In addition, labor productivity is defined as per capita labor earnings divided by per capita work hours. Labor productivity can be expressed in both nominal and real terms. To examine trends in labor productivity, labor earnings should be adjusted for prices. Thus, real productivity is equal to nominal productivity adjusted for prices.

Table 9.4 reveals a number of points that merit emphasis. Per capita employment increased from 0.375 in 1997 to 0.384 in 2003, but this has not been sufficient to lower per capita unemployment given a rise in per capita labor force in the economy. Per capita labor force grew at an annual rate of 0.9% while per capita unemployment jumped by

331

10.0% during the crisis period and increased by slightly less than 1.0% afterward. Thus, the number of jobs available in the labor market has not grown fast enough to absorb the number of new entrants to the labor force. The same can be observed for poor households.

As one would expect, productivity measured in current prices has been increasing. This is due largely to the rise in per capita nominal labor income. However, when per capita nominal labor productivity is adjusted for price changes, the average per capita real labor productivity for the whole economy fell by 4.8% and 1.4% a year during 1997–2000 and 2000–2003, respectively. During the two periods, employed Filipinos worked longer hours but became worse off in terms of their per capita real labor income, thus reducing productivity.

9.5   Linking growth with labor market characteristics

This section attempts to explain how changes in certain labor market characteristics contribute to growth in per capita real labor income. Using the definitions in Section 9.4, the logarithm of average per capita real labor income can be expressed as

$$ln(\bar{x}_l^*) = ln(\bar{l}) + ln\,(\bar{e}/\bar{l}) + ln\,(\bar{h}/\bar{e}) + ln\,(x_l^*/\bar{h}) \tag{6}$$

where the bars on variables indicate the average for all households. For example, $\bar{x}_l^*$ is average per capita real labor income. Taking the first difference in equation (6) yields the growth rate. Thus, the growth rate of per capita real labor income can be expressed as the sum of the contributions by the following four factors:

(i)   average LFP rate (or average per capita labor force)
(ii)   average employment rate
(iii)   average work hours per employed person
(iv)   average real labor productivity

The contributions of these factors are quantified for all households as well as for poor households in Table 9.5. The per capita real labor income declined at an annual rate of 2.73% from 1997 to 2000, stemming from the deep economic crisis in Asia. What factors contributed to this decline? The employment rate contributed to the reduction in the growth rate by 1.02 percentage points. Despite the fall in the employment rate, employed people worked more hours, which contributed to positive income growth of 2.15 percentage points. It appears that during the crisis, people who were employed had to work longer hours because their hourly earnings were falling rapidly. This drop in earnings is reflected by the −4.76 percentage-point contribution of real productivity to growth. Interestingly, the LFP rate increased, contributing 0.89 percentage points to income growth. Normally when the labor market is weak, many workers, particularly women, tend to withdraw from the labor market. The increase in the LFP rate may be explained by the sharp decline in earnings from the labor market.

Table 9.5   Explaining the growth rate in per capita real labor income (percentage point)

	All households		Poor households	
	1997–2000	2000–2003	1997–2000	2000–2003
Labor force participation	0.89	0.92	0.57	1.74
Employment rate	−1.02	0.02	−0.66	−0.27
Work hours per employed	2.15	−0.63	3.79	−1.87
Real productivity	−4.76	−1.42	−3.96	−0.14
Real labor income	−2.73	−1.10	−0.26	−0.53

Source: Author's calculations based on FIES and Labor Force Surveys (NSO various years).

In the post-crisis period, per capita real labor income continued to decline, but at a slower pace. The employment rate improved slightly and at the same time productivity did not decline as sharply as during the crisis. During 2000–2003, more poor people entered the labor force. Despite the increase in the LFP rate among the poor, they were not able to find sufficient employment (as indicated by the negative contribution of the employment rate to the decline in real labor income). They also worked fewer hours, indicating the appalling lack of job opportunities for the poor.

During 1997–2003, growth of per capita labor income in the Philippines was sluggish. Average per capita income continued to decline, albeit much more slowly after the crisis. This drop can be attributed to changes in the labor market, particularly the continuing lack of employment opportunities and persistently low levels of labor productivity.

9.6   Inequalities in the labor market

Section 9.4 indicates the huge impact the labor market can have on inequality in the Philippines. The Theil index can be used to measure inequality in the labor market across households. This index can be calculated for labor market indicators such as the LFP rate, per capita employment, per capita work hours, and per capita labor income. For example, the Theil index for per capita employment is given by

$$T(e) = \int [\ln(\mu_e) - \ln(e)] f(x) dx \tag{7}$$

where μ_e is average per capita employment. $T(e)$ measures inequality in per capita employment across households.

Table 9.6 shows the disparity in key indicators of the Philippine labor market for 1997–2003. Inequality in per capita labor income is much higher than inequality in per capita employment, the LFP rate, and per capita work hours. This suggests that the disparity in per capita employment (and in the LFP rate and work hours) between poor and non-poor households is not very large, while the disparity in per capita labor income can still be substantial. Such a wide gap in earnings between the poor and non-poor could be explained by differences in productivity. Non-poor households have much higher productivity than poor households. Factors that explain productivity differences, however, are complex and are beyond the scope of this chapter.

Table 9.6 also decomposes total inequality in labor market indicators into two components, between-region inequality (reported) and within-region inequality (which can be calculated by subtracting this from 100). As the table shows, between-region inequality can explain 11.54% of total inequality in per capita labor income in 1997. The contribution of between-region inequality to total inequality is much smaller for other indicators such as employment, the LFP rate, and work hours.

Table 9.6   Inequality in labor market indicators (%)

Labor market indicator	Theil index			Change in inequality	
	1997	2000	2003	1997–2000	2000–2003
	Total inequality				
Per capita employment	17.4	17.3	17.2	–0.1	–0.1
LFP rate	15.9	15.4	15.3	–0.5	–0.1
Per capita work hours	31.1	33.3	31.8	2.2	–1.5
Per capita labor income	64.5	65.8	61.3	1.4	–4.5
	Percentage of total inequality explained by between-region inequality				
Per capita employment	1.40	1.72	1.39	0.3	–0.3
LFP rate	1.41	1.62	0.90	0.2	–0.7
Per capita work hours	0.92	0.69	0.43	–0.2	–0.3
Per capita labor income	11.54	10.70	8.75	–0.8	–2.0

LFP = labor force participation.
Source: Author's calculations based on FIES and Labor Force Surveys (NSO various years).

This argues against the misconception that inequality is largely derived from disparity across regions. Instead, inequality can be explained mainly by disparity within each region. As shown in Figure 9.1, inequality in labor income (measured by the Theil index) is particularly high in Western Mindanao and the Ilocos region. Hence, a policy that intends to reduce aggregate inequality should cater to the needs of specific regions.

Figure 9.1   Inequality in labor income within regions, 2003

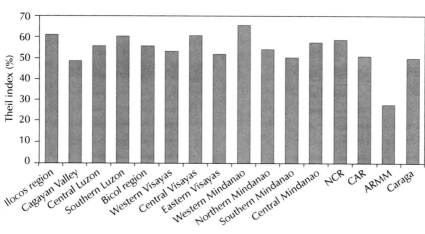

ARMM = Autonomous Region in Muslim Mindanao, CAR = Cordillera Administrative Region, NCR = National Capital Region.
Source: Author's calculations based on FIES and Labor Force Surveys (NSO various years).

9.7   Explaining inequality in labor income

This section examines what accounts for inequality in per capita real labor income based on changes in certain labor market characteristics. Using the definitions in the previous section, the logarithm of per capita labor income can be expressed as

$$ln(x_l) = ln(l) + ln(e/l) \, ln(h/e) + ln(x_l/h) \tag{8}$$

Subtracting equation (8) from equation (6) gives

$$ln(\bar{x}_l) - ln(x_l) = [ln(\bar{l}) - ln(l)] + [ln(\bar{e}/\bar{l}) - ln(e/l)] \\ + [ln(\bar{h}/\bar{e}) - ln(h/e)] + [ln(\bar{x}_l/\bar{h}) - ln(x_l/h)] \tag{9}$$

where $\bar{x}_l$ refers to the average per capita labor income, and the bars on variables indicate the average for all households. Integrating this equation over all households gives

$$T(x_i) = T(l) + [T(e) - T(l)] + [T(h) - T(e)] + [T(x_i) - T(h)] \qquad (10)$$

Equation (10) shows that inequality in per capita labor income is equal to the sum of the contributions of the four labor market characteristics (used in Section 9.5):

(i) $T(l)$ = contribution of the LFP rate
(ii) $T(e) - T(l)$ = contribution of the employment rate
(iii) $T(h) - T(e)$ = contribution of work hours per employed person
(iv) $T(x_i) - T(h)$ = contribution of earnings per hour or labor productivity

Table 9.7 shows the results of the analysis, with the Theil index expressed in percentage terms. The Theil index for per capita labor income in 1997 was 64.5%. The contribution of the LFP rate is significant at 15.9%. This suggests a higher dependency ratio in poor than non-poor households. Compared with average households, poor households may have more children (less than 10 years old) or elderly (more than 65 years old) who do not participate in the labor force.

Table 9.7   Explaining inequality in per capita labor income

	Theil index and its contributing components (%)			Percentage point change	
	1997	2000	2003	1997–2000	2000–2003
Labor force participation rate	15.9	15.4	15.3	–0.49	–0.14
Employment rate	1.5	1.9	1.9	0.41	0.02
Work hours per employed person	13.7	16.0	14.6	2.26	–1.33
Productivity	33.4	32.6	29.5	–0.82	–3.06
Per capita real labor income	64.5	65.8	61.3	1.36	–4.51

Source: Author's calculations based on FIES and Labor Force Surveys (NSO various years).

Inequality in per capita labor income can be reduced significantly by increasing the LFP rate among the poor. The contribution of the employment rate is only 1.5%, which means that the disparity in the employment rate between the poor and non-poor is very small. This suggests that focusing on generating jobs for the poor will not have much impact on inequality. What matters is the quality of jobs. The factor that contributes most to inequality is labor productivity, at 33.4%. The low productivity of the poor can be due to many factors. Most studies (e.g., Hanson 2002, World Bank 2007) emphasize that the poor have low productivity due to a low level of human capital, among other factors. Human capital may be an important factor in causing the productivity difference between the poor and the non-poor. The next section will return to this issue.

During 1997–2000, inequality in per capita real labor income rose 1.36 percentage points, due mainly to changes in inequality in the employment rate and work hours. This suggests that, during the crisis, the employment rate and work hours among poor households fell more sharply than among non-poor households. In the subsequent period (2000–2003), inequality in per capita labor income declined 4.51 percentage points largely because of a fall in the inequality of productivity (−3.06 percentage points). Productivity has become more equal across households. This is consistent with the earlier finding that the fall in real productivity was far smaller among the poor than in the national average. Hence, the gap in productivity between the poor and non-poor narrowed during 2000–2003.

In sum, the findings show that inequality in the Philippine labor market can be attributed largely to within-region disparity, rather than cross-region disparity. Within each region, the inequality in per capita income is significant, caused mainly by inequality in labor productivity. Similar to growth, labor productivity impacts inequality significantly.

9.8   Education and the labor market

The previous sections illustrate the importance of labor income in influencing the pattern and trends of growth and inequality in the Philippines. An analysis of the link between labor income and inequality will be more complete with a review of how the country's education system responds to the needs of the labor market. Due to a lack of information, the current study does not look into the availability and quality of schooling facilities.

Because households make decisions on schooling and the choice to work, it is logical to use a micro approach to look into the relationship between education and labor productivity and earnings. People attend school primarily to improve income prospects and personal well-being. Education is known to lead to higher earnings and to other non-labor market benefits such as better nutrition and health and greater capacity to enjoy leisure (Haveman and Wolfe 1984). In line with the human capital view of education, higher earnings are compensation for increased productivity through education.

A distinctive feature of Philippine development is the achievement of a very high rate of school attendance. Table 9.8 shows per capita employment by education level and gender for all households as well as poor households during 1997–2003. Per capita employed household members with secondary and tertiary education increased during the period, while those with only primary education declined. However, almost 70% of the employed among poor households had acquired only primary education. By gender, the increase in per capita employed household members with secondary and tertiary education is higher for females than for males, particularly among poor households. Consequently, the gender gap in the employment rate at these education levels narrowed somewhat, although it remained high in favor of male members.

Table 9.8   Per capita household employment by education and gender (%)

Education level and gender	Per capita emloyment			Annual growth rate	
	1997	2000	2003	1997–2000	2000–2003
All households					
Primary education	16.5	15.2	15.0	−2.9	−0.3
Male	10.9	9.8	9.9	−3.4	0.4
Female	5.7	5.4	5.1	−2.0	−1.6
Secondary education	12.5	13.1	14.1	1.7	2.5
Male	8.2	8.5	9.1	1.0	2.3
Female	4.3	4.6	5.1	2.9	2.8
Tertiary education	8.5	9.1	9.3	2.3	0.7
Male	4.5	4.8	4.9	1.7	0.8
Female	3.9	4.3	4.4	2.9	0.6
Total	37.5	37.3	38.4	−0.1	0.9
Male	23.6	23.0	23.9	−0.8	1.2
Female	13.9	14.3	14.6	1.0	0.6
Poor households					
Primary education	23.0	21.3	22.6	−2.5	1.9
Male	16.1	14.8	15.7	−2.7	1.8
Female	6.9	6.5	6.9	−2.0	1.9
Secondary education	7.8	9.1	9.3	5.1	0.6
Male	5.2	6.3	6.3	6.2	0.0
Female	2.6	2.8	3.0	3.0	2.0
Tertiary education	1.0	1.3	1.3	9.0	1.0
Male	0.7	0.8	0.8	6.4	−1.2
Female	0.3	0.5	0.5	14.2	4.6
Total	31.8	31.7	33.1	−0.1	1.5
Male	22.0	21.9	22.7	−0.1	1.2
Female	9.8	9.8	10.4	−0.0	2.1

Source: Author's calculations based on FIES and Labor Force Surveys (NSO various years).

A puzzle remains regarding the differences in employability—defined as the probability of being employed with a given level of education—

of males and females by education level. In general, one would expect employability to increase with a higher level of education. Indeed, such pattern is seen in Table 9.9 in all households. For example, in 1997, employability for people with only primary education was 47.8%, rising to 48.9% for those with secondary education, and 56.6% for those with tertiary education. For poor households, however, this pattern is seen only in 2003, but not in 1997 and 2000.[3]

Table 9.9   Employability by education and gender (%)

Education level and gender	1997	2000	2003
		All households	
Primary education	47.8	45.4	34.3
Male	61.5	57.5	43.6
Female	33.6	32.8	24.3
Secondary education	48.9	48.1	49.8
Male	64.0	60.9	63.9
Female	33.6	34.8	35.7
Tertiary education	56.6	54.3	56.8
Male	64.5	61.0	64.1
Female	49.6	48.4	50.4
		Poor households	
Primary education	50.2	47.4	36.0
Male	65.8	62.2	47.2
Female	32.3	30.7	23.4
Secondary education	47.6	47.0	48.1
Male	67.7	65.4	67.9
Female	29.8	29.0	30.0
Tertiary education	43.3	44.0	52.1
Male	67.5	63.2	69.3
Female	24.0	28.5	37.9

Source: Author's calculations based on FIES and Labor Force Surveys (NSO various years).

Table 9.9 also shows the following points. First, employability is far greater for male members of poor households than males of all households at all education levels. This is consistent with the view that poor people cannot afford to be unemployed. Second, women have much lower employability than men, again at all education levels. The male-female gap, however, is much narrower among people with college education. Third, on average, almost 50% of all women with tertiary education were not formally employed, whereas the corresponding figure

---

3   One possible explanation is the "discouraged workers effect", i.e., the experience of an unsuccessful job search increases the propensity to withdraw from the labor force both immediately and in subsequent years.

for poor households was more than 60%–70%, although employability among females with tertiary education belonging to poor households increased during 1997–2003. Fourth, interestingly, employability declined sharply for people with primary education, but increased for those with secondary and tertiary education.

There are two possible explanations for the last point. One is that the demand for labor with secondary and tertiary education increased in the labor market relative to those with primary education. The other is that low-productivity jobs were taken over by the more educated labor force. The finding that labor productivity of educated workers had been on the decline, highlighted in previous sections, appears to support the second explanation. As shown in Table 9.8, per capita employment remained more or less constant during 1997–2003. This implies that employment merely increased in line with population growth. Hence, if there is no improvement in labor productivity, growth in per capita real labor earnings is expected to stagnate. To achieve growth, labor productivity has to increase.

Labor productivity varies by sector and gender. Table 9.10 shows per capita household employment by sector and gender during 1997–2003. The proportion of household members employed in the agricultural sector declined; in the industrial sector, it remained more or less unchanged; in the service sector, it increased. This suggests a structural change wherein the labor force was moving away from agriculture toward the service sector. Overall, about 48% of the employed labor force was in the service sector in 2003. The employment of female household members in the service sector increased notably during the period. This is supported by the claim that the proportion of female college graduates employed in finance, insurance, and real estate has increased over time (Orbeta 2002).

These findings clearly show that the working-age population is increasingly engaged in the service sector. Although the service sector tends to create more jobs, the quality of job matters for earnings in the labor market; for example, while taxi drivers belong to the service sector, so do lawyers and doctors.

9.9   Conclusions

This chapter has analyzed economic growth and income inequality in the Philippines, focusing on the role played by the labor market. From the family income and expenditure surveys and the labor force surveys for 1997, 2000, and 2003, it is found that Philippine households derive their incomes mainly from labor employment, with the poor relying more on earnings from self-employment in the informal sector.

Table 9.10   Per capita household employment by sector and gender (%)

Sector and gender	Per capita employment			Annual growth rate	
	1997	2000	2003	1997–2000	2000–2003
	All households				
Agriculture	14.7	13.8	14.0	−2.2	0.5
Male	10.9	10.4	10.6	−1.6	0.6
Female	3.8	3.4	3.4	−3.8	0.2
Industry	6.3	6.1	6.1	−1.0	0.0
Male	4.5	4.3	4.4	−2.0	0.6
Female	1.8	1.9	1.8	1.3	−1.4
Service	16.4	17.4	18.3	1.9	1.6
Male	8.1	8.3	8.9	0.9	2.2
Female	8.3	9.1	9.4	2.9	1.1
Total	37.5	37.3	38.4	−0.1	0.9
	Poor households				
Agriculture	23.2	21.8	23.1	−2.1	1.9
Male	17.1	16.5	17.2	−1.2	1.5
Female	6.1	5.3	5.9	−4.6	3.4
Industry	3.1	3.4	3.4	3.1	−0.3
Male	2.3	2.4	2.4	1.9	−0.5
Female	0.8	1.0	1.0	6.3	0.2
Service	5.5	6.5	6.7	5.7	0.8
Male	2.6	3.0	3.1	4.8	1.2
Female	2.9	3.5	3.5	6.5	0.4
Total	31.8	31.7	33.1	−0.1	1.5

Source: Author's calculations based on FIES (NSO various years).

Estimates of the inequality elasticity with respect to different income components show that agricultural wage income and earnings from self-employment reduce inequality, while non-agricultural wage income increases it. It is also found that the average per capita real labor income of the households covered by the two surveys declined 2.73% annually from 1997 to 2000 and 1.1% from 2000 to 2003. Decomposing the decline into changes in the LFP rate, employment rate, work hours per employed, and real labor productivity (measured in hourly labor earnings), it is found that the decline in real labor productivity is the most important contributing factor.

To investigate how labor market conditions impact income inequality, inequality in per capita labor income is measured by the Theil index and decomposed into various contributing components. It is found that the inequality in per capita labor income was high and caused largely by differences in labor productivity across individuals, similar to the findings on the determinants of labor income growth. Therefore, to reduce inequality, what matters is not only creating jobs for the poor, but also creating productive or decent job opportunities.

The poor performance of labor productivity in the Philippines is puzzling given the rapid expansion of the size of qualified labor and rising education levels in the labor force in recent years.[4] The study finds that the level of education is an important determinant of employability in the labor market. Employability declined sharply during 1997–2003 for the labor force with only primary education, but increased for those with secondary or tertiary education. This could indicate that more-educated workers were taking low-productivity jobs from less-educated workers and, consequently, wages and labor productivity were falling for the educated and skilled workers. This suggests a mismatch between labor demand and supply in the skill mix.

The study also finds a structural change wherein the labor force was moving away from the agricultural sector toward the service sector. While the share of people employed in agriculture declined, it remained virtually unchanged in industry but increased in the service sector. Within the service sector, the employment of female workers increased significantly during the period. This supports the view that the proportion of female college graduates employed in finance, insurance, and real estate has increased over time.

To accelerate and sustain economic growth, therefore, the government not only needs to support the creation of more productive job opportunities, but also to reckon with the labor mismatch. Expanding the aggregate supply of skills may not be sufficient to address the decline in labor productivity, which in turn has slowed the pace of economic growth. From a policy perspective, going beyond universal coverage in education is imperative because the supply of the right kinds of skills needs to be expanded. For this to happen, employers, individuals, and policy makers need robust, up-to-date information on the real labor market value of different qualifications, to help them navigate through the increasingly complex education system and make optimal investment decisions.

---

[4]   Unfortunately, the quality of education in the Philippines has been falling behind other economies in the region. For example, average scores in mathematics and science are much lower than those in Hong Kong, China; Indonesia; Malaysia; and Thailand (World Bank 2005).

References

Hanson, J. 2002. "Human Capital and Direct Investment in Poor Countries." *Explorations in Economic History* 33(1):86–106.

Haveman, R., and B. Wolfe. 1984. "Schooling and Economic Well-Being: The Role of Nonmarket Effects." *Journal of Human Resources* XIX(3):377–407.

Lin, J. Y., J. Zhuang, M. Tang, and T. Lin. 2008. "Inclusive Growth toward a Harmonious Society in the People's Republic of China: An Overview." *Asian Development Review* 25(1,2):1–14.

NSO. Various years. Family Income and Expenditure Survey. National Statistics Office. Manila. Available: www.census.gov.ph/.

_____. Various years. Labor Force Survey. Manila. Available: www.census.gov.ph/.

Orbeta, A. 2002. "Education, Labor Market and Development: A Review of the Trends and Issues in the Past 25 Years." Paper prepared for the symposium series on perspective papers for the 25th anniversary of the Philippine Institute for Development Studies, Makati City.

Son, H. H., and J. Florentino. 2008. Ex-ante Impact Evaluation of Conditional Cash Transfer Program on School Attendance and Poverty: The Case of the Philippines. ADB Economics Working Paper No. 142, Asian Development Bank, Manila.

Theil, H. 1967. *Economics and Information Theory.* Amsterdam: North-Holland.

World Bank. 2005. *The Philippines: Towards a Better Investment Climate for Growth and Productivity.* Washington, DC.

_____. 2007. *World Development Report 2007: Development and the Next Generation.* Washington, DC.

10

Poverty and Inequality in Nepal: An Empirical Analysis

Yoko Niimi

10.1   Introduction

Nepal made significant progress in reducing poverty between 1995–1996 and 2003–2004, despite political instability. However, poverty incidence remains high—estimated at about 31% in 2003–2004—and inequality also increased during this period. Based on the Gini coefficient, inequality rose from about 34.2 in 1995–1996 to about 41.4 in 2003–2004, the highest in South Asia. Such trends seem to suggest the limited inclusiveness of Nepal's recent economic growth. Given that poverty and inequality are considered among the most significant drivers of recent internal conflicts, it is important that a new growth strategy opens up economic opportunity to excluded groups.

Inclusive growth not only generates economic opportunity, but also ensures equal access. Hence, growth is said to be inclusive when it allows all members of society to participate in, contribute to, and benefit from the growth process on an equal basis, regardless of individual circumstance (Ali and Zhuang 2007). This is a particularly relevant question for Nepal, where exclusion remains an important development hurdle (World Bank and DFID 2006).

This chapter assesses the inclusiveness of Nepal's recent economic growth and examines what factors helped certain groups of households escape poverty between 1995–1996 and 2003–2004. The findings of the analysis will assist policy makers in formulating measures to enhance the inclusiveness of growth and poverty reduction. The empirical analysis is based on data from the Nepal Living Standards Surveys conducted in 1995–1996 (NLSS I) and in 2003–2004 (NLSS II).

The next section provides an overview of recent trends in poverty and inequality to illustrate the inclusiveness of Nepal's recent economic growth. It also assesses the contributions of factors such as differences in education, geographical location, and ethnicity/caste to overall inequality and how these have changed over time. Section 10.3 presents the results of the empirical analysis, followed by concluding remarks.

10.2   Recent trends of poverty and inequality

Nepal's economic growth over the last decade has not been impressive in comparison with other countries in South Asia. Average annual gross domestic product growth during 2001–2006 was about 2.9%, compared with about 6%–7% in the rest of South Asia. Growth was even more disappointing in per capita terms—real per capita income rose only about 0.6% per year during the period. The elasticity of poverty reduction with respect to growth in Nepal is also relatively low by international standards (CBS et al. 2006). While the cross-country elasticity is estimated at about −2 (Ravallion 2001), the elasticity for Nepal was about −0.6 based on per capita expenditure data, implying that every percentage-point increase in per capita expenditure resulted in only a 0.6 percentage-point reduction in the number of poor people (CBS et al. 2006). Such an observation questions how inclusive Nepal's recent economic growth has been. Nevertheless, Nepal has made some good progress in reducing poverty. According to data from NLSS I and II, poverty incidence declined from about 42% in 1995–1996 to about 31% in 2003–2004, a reduction of about 1.4 percentage points per year.

Another way of examining inclusiveness is to look at trends in poverty measures at a more disaggregated level. Nepal is an ethnically diverse country, with more than 59 main ethnic groups, while a deeply embedded Hindu caste system complicates its social structure. It is also geographically diverse, and commonly divided in terms of ecological features (Mountain, Hill, and *Terai* areas), and into five development regions (Eastern, Central, Western, Mid-Western, and Far-Western). Table 10.1 reports changes in poverty headcount ratios for each of these dimensions.

Table 10.1 clearly illustrates the variation in poverty incidence and rate of decline by geography as well as ethnicity/caste. For instance, the poverty headcount ratio was more than halved in urban areas between 1995–1996 and 2003–2004, while it declined only by 20% in rural areas. Hence about 35% of the population in the rural sector was still below the poverty line in 2003–2004. Poverty reduction was particularly significant in urban areas other than Kathmandu. Among rural areas, Rural Eastern Terai and Rural Western Hill observed the greatest reduction in the poverty rate—about 33% and 32%, respectively. On the other hand, the poverty rate increased in Rural Eastern Hill by 19% during this 8-year period. As a result, as many as 43% of the population in 2003–2004 lived in poverty in Rural Eastern Hill, giving it the largest share of the country's poor (about 29%) in that year.

Table 10.1   Poverty headcount ratios in Nepal (%),
              1995–1996 and 2003–2004

	Poverty headcount ratio (%)			Distribution of the poor (%)		
	1995–1996	2003–2004	Change	1995–1996	2003–2004	Change
Urban	21.6	9.6	–56	3.6	4.7	31
Rural	43.3	34.6	–20	96.4	95.3	–1
NLSS regions						
Kathmandu	4.3	3.3	–23	0.3	0.6	100
Other urban	31.6	13.0	–59	3.3	4.1	24
Rural Western Hill	55.0	37.4	–32	32.7	23.6	–28
Rural Eastern Hill	36.1	42.9	19	19.4	29.4	52
Rural Western Terai	46.1	38.1	–17	18.4	18.9	3
Rural Eastern Terai	37.2	24.9	–33	25.9	23.5	–9
Development regions						
Eastern	38.9	29.3	–25	21.0	23.4	11
Central	32.5	27.1	–17	26.9	32.2	20
Western	38.6	27.1	–30	18.7	16.7	–11
Mid-Western	59.9	44.8	–25	18.5	17.7	–4
Far-Western	63.9	41.0	–36	14.8	9.9	–33
Ecological belts						
Mountain	57.0	32.6	–43	10.7	7.5	–30
Hill	40.7	34.5	–15	41.9	47.1	12
Terai	40.3	27.6	–32	47.4	45.4	–4
Ethnicity/caste						
Brahman/Chhetri	34.1	18.4	–46	26.7	15.7	–41
Terai middle caste	28.7	21.3	–26	2.9	1.9	–34
Dalits	57.8	45.5	–21	10.6	10.9	3
Newar	19.3	14.0	–28	2.5	3.4	36
Hill Janajati	48.7	44.0	–10	19.7	27.8	41
Terai Janajati	53.4	35.4	–34	10.4	9.2	–12
Muslims	43.7	41.3	–6	5.7	8.7	53
Other minorities	46.1	31.3	–32	21.4	22.3	4
Nepal	41.8	30.8	–26	100.0	100.0	–

Source: CBS et al. (2006).

On the other hand, the relatively poor areas in the development regions and ecological belts, namely the Far-Western region and Mountain areas, seem to have experienced the greatest decline in poverty. Looking at the variation in the reduction in poverty rates by caste/ethnic group, however, it is apparent that the Brahman/Chhetri, generally considered privileged groups in Nepal, experienced the largest poverty reduction between 1995–1996 and 2003–2004. The disadvantaged groups, namely Dalits, Hill Janajatis, and Muslims saw the least poverty decline. These variations unequivocally indicate the economic exclusion of certain groups in Nepal. It should, however, be noted that although considered privileged, about 18% of the Brahman/Chhetri were still in poverty in 2003–2004. Given their relatively large representation in the total population (about 26%), about 16% of the poor belonged to the Brahman/Chhetri in the same year (Table 10.1). This underscores the fact that people are poor not only because of social exclusion, but also because of other factors that keep certain groups of households in poverty.

A growth incidence curve, which plots the annual growth rate for each percentile of per capita expenditure distribution, also shows that even though per capita expenditure increased for all percentile groups between 1995–1996 and 2003–2004, the growth rate tended to be greater toward the higher end of the expenditure distribution (Figure 10.1). It is, therefore, not surprising to observe an increase in inequality during this period.

Figure 10.1   Growth incidence curve, 1995–1996 and 2003–2004

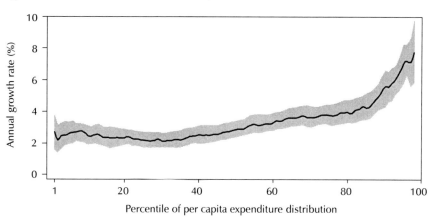

Source: Calculations based on NLSS I and II.

Table 10.2 reports various inequality measures based on per capita expenditure. For instance, the Gini coefficient rose from 34.2 to 41.4 between 1995–1996 and 2003–2004. The increase in inequality is also illustrated by Lorenz curves (Figure 10.2). While inequality worsened in both rural and urban areas, it increased considerably more in the rural sector (Table 10.2).

The first three columns of Table 10.2 provide the generalized entropy index, another inequality measure.[1] Depending on the parameter

---

1   See Box 2.1 in Chapter 2 for a brief description of this index.

used (figures in brackets), the sensitivity of the index to expenditure differences in different parts of the distribution varies. More specifically, lower values of the parameter make the index more sensitive to differences at the lower tail of the distribution; higher values make it more sensitive to differences at the upper end. Comparing the percentage change among the three generalized entropy indexes, the increase in overall inequality is found to be driven by inequality at the upper tail of the per capita expenditure distribution, in both urban and rural areas.

Table 10.2   Inequality in per capita expenditure (%), 1995–1996 and 2003–2004

	GE (0)	GE (1)	GE (2)	Gini coefficient
Nepal				
1995–1996	19.0	21.8	32.7	34.2
2003–2004	27.9	33.7	57.6	41.4
% change	46.8	54.6	76.1	21.1
Urban				
1995–1996	31.9	30.5	37.7	42.6
2003–2004	32.3	32.0	41.0	43.6
% change	1.3	4.9	8.8	2.3
Rural				
1995–1996	15.4	17.0	23.1	30.8
2003–2004	19.9	24.1	42.0	34.9
% change	29.2	41.8	81.8	13.3

GE = generalized entropy index.
Source: Calculations based on NLSS I and II.

Table 10.3 reports the decomposition of inequality by geography, ethnicity/caste, and education level and occupation of the household head for 1995–1996 and 2003–2004. In all dimensions, the share of between-group inequality increased during this period. The biggest increase was observed for the occupation of household head. This seems to reflect a significant increase in skill premiums observed between 1995–1996 and 2003–2004, which resulted in widening wage differentials across different occupations (CBS et al. 2006). Nonetheless, the share of total inequality attributable to between-group inequality was found to be relatively large for geography and the education level of household head, particularly at the low and middle range of the expenditure distribution (i.e., GE[0] and GE[1]), about 24%–25% in the latter period. As for ethnicity/caste, although between-group inequality accounted for a smaller share of total inequality in comparison with other dimensions, it also accounted for a larger share in the low and middle range of the distribution than in the upper range.

Figure 10.2   Lorenz curve on per capita expenditure (%),
1995–1996 and 2003–2004

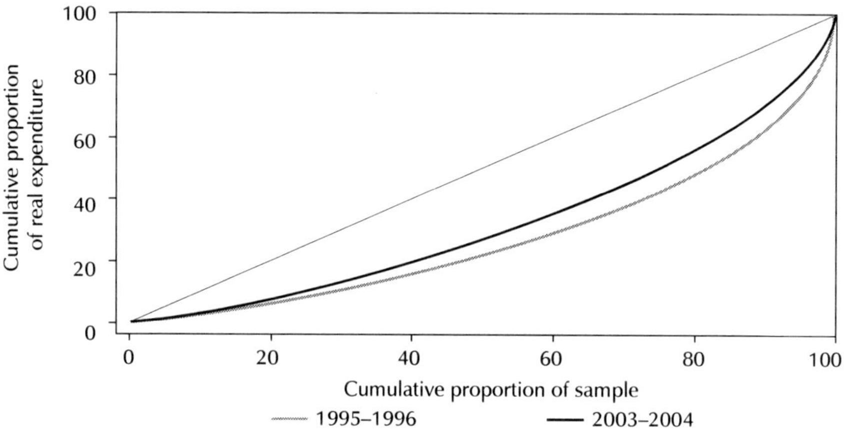

Source: Calculations based on NLSS I and II.

The observations made so far have illustrated the limited inclusiveness of Nepal's recent economic growth, suggesting unequal access to economic opportunity. The importance of equal access to opportunity for all segments of society lies in its intrinsic value as well as its instrumental role. The intrinsic value is based on the belief that equal access to opportunity is a basic human right, and it is unethical and immoral to treat individuals differently in this regard. The instrumental role recognizes that inequality in access to opportunity diminishes growth potential and sustainability, as it leads to inefficient use of human and physical resources, lowers the quality of institutions and policies, erodes social cohesion, and increases social conflict (Ali and Zhuang 2007). Indeed, a recent study shows that the same level of economic growth would have reduced poverty by 13 percentage points more had inequality not worsened between 1995–1996 and 2003–2004 in Nepal (CBS et al. 2006). Given that poverty and inequality are considered among the main causes of the recent conflict in Nepal, it is important that a new growth strategy opens up economic opportunity to excluded groups.

To help policy makers formulate effective measures to enhance the inclusiveness of economic growth and poverty reduction, the rest of the chapter examines the factors that helped certain groups of households escape poverty between 1995–1996 and 2003–2004.

Table 10.3   Decomposition of per capita expenditure inequality (%),
             1995–1996 and 2003–2004

	GE (0)	GE (1)	GE (2)
Geography			
Within-group			
1995–1996	15.9	17.9	27.4
2003–2004	21.2	25.5	47.1
Between-group			
1995–1996	3.1	3.9	5.3
2003–2004	6.7	8.1	10.5
Between-group inequality as percent of overall inequality			
1995–1996	16.2	17.9	16.2
2003–2004	24.1	24.2	18.2
Ethnicity/caste			
Within-group			
1995–1996	16.8	19.5	30.2
2003–2004	23.7	29.2	52.6
Between-group			
1995–1996	2.2	2.3	2.5
2003–2004	4.1	4.5	5.0
Between-group inequality as percent of overall inequality			
1995–1996	11.4	10.5	7.6
2003–2004	14.8	13.3	8.7
Education level of household head			
Within-group			
1995–1996	15.8	18.1	28.1
2003–2004	21.0	25.3	46.4
Between-group			
1995–1996	3.2	3.7	4.6
2003–2004	6.8	8.3	11.2
Between-group inequality as percent of overall inequality			
1995–1996	16.9	17.2	14.0
2003–2004	24.5	24.8	19.4
Occupation of household head			
Within-group			
1995–1996	17.1	19.8	30.5
2003–2004	22.8	27.9	50.9
Between-group			
1995–1996	1.9	2.0	2.2
2003–2004	5.1	5.7	6.7
Between-group inequality as percent of overall inequality			
1995–1996	10.0	9.3	6.7
2003–2004	18.3	17.0	11.7

GE = generalized entropy indexes.
Note: Geography is calculated based on the NLSS regions (see Table 10.1).
Source: Calculations based on NLSS I and II.

350

10.3   Empirical analysis of determinants of poverty dynamics

To identify possible factors behind the observed poverty dynamics, a multnomial logit (MNL) model is applied to the panel component of the NLSS data.[2] Table 10.4 illustrates the changes in poverty status of households during 1995–1996 and 2003–2004.

Table 10.4   Poverty transition matrix (%), 1995–1996 and 2003–2004

		2003–2004		
		Poor	Non-poor	Total
	Poor	18.4	20.4	38.8
1995–1996	Non-poor	13.6	47.6	61.2
	Total	32.0	68.0	100.0

Source: Calculations based on NLSS I and II.

The matrix shows that about 47.6% of households were non-poor in both years and about 20.4% of households escaped poverty during this period. In contrast, about 18.4% of households remained in poverty in both years, while about 13.6% fell into poverty in the latter period. According to Figure 10.3, showing differences in poverty dynamics by region, while a relatively large percentage of households remained in poverty in both years in the Mid-Western and Far-Western regions, the proportion of households that escaped poverty in 2003–2004 was also high compared to other regions. In the case of ethnicity/caste, as expected, a relatively large percentage of the privileged groups— Brahman/Chhetri, Terai middle class, and Newar—were non-poor in both years (Figure 10.4). The percentage of households that moved out of poverty in the latter year was the second smallest for Dalits, after Newar, even though their poverty incidence rate of 57.8% was the highest in 1995–1996 compared to Newar's 19.3% (Table 10.1). These figures clearly indicate that recent economic growth did not uniformly benefit Nepalese households.

10.3.1   Estimation model: Explanatory variables

Based on the MNL model, the present study identifies the factors that helped households escape poverty during 1995–1996 and 2003–2004. Hence the dependent variable is the change in the poverty status of

---

2   See Appendix for a brief description of the data and estimation methodology used.

households, specifically: (1) being poor in both periods (P→P); (2) being non-poor in 1995–1996 and becoming poor in 2003–2004 (NP→P); (3) being poor in 1995–1996 and becoming non-poor in 2003–2004 (P→NP); and (4) being non-poor in both years (NP→NP). The explanatory variables included in the empirical models are listed in Table 10.5. Initial values, i.e., of the year 1995–1996, are used as explanatory variables to avoid endogeneity issues.

Figure 10.3   Poverty dynamics by region (%), 1995–1996 and 2003–2004

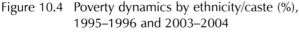

Source: Calculations based on NLSS I and II.

Figure 10.4   Poverty dynamics by ethnicity/caste (%),
                      1995–1996 and 2003–2004

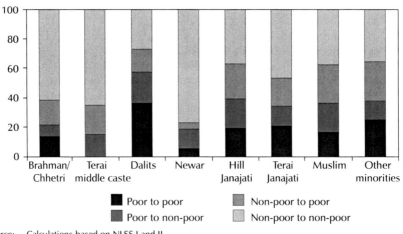

Source: Calculations based on NLSS I and II.

Table 10.5   List of explanatory variables

Explanatory variable	Description	Mean	S.D.
Household head's characteristics			
Age	In years	44.00	14.23
Female	Dummy variable for being female	0.13	
Ethnicity/caste			
Brahman/Chhetri	Dummy variable for being Brahman/Chhetri	0.34	
Terai middle caste	Dummy variable for being Terai middle caste	0.06	
Dalits	Dummy variable for being Dalits	0.09	
Newar	Dummy variable for being Newar	0.07	
Hill Janajati	Dummy variable for being Hill Janajati	0.13	
Terai Janajati	Dummy variable for being Terai Janajati	0.07	
Muslims	Dummy variable for being Muslims	0.04	
Other minorities	Dummy variable for being other minorities	0.20	
Education			
Illiterate	Dummy variable for being illiterate	0.61	
4 or less	Dummy variable for having 4 years or less of schooling	0.15	
5–10	Dummy variable for having 5–10 years of schooling	0.12	
11+	Dummy variable for having 11 years or more of schooling	0.12	
Occupation			
Self-employed agriculture	Dummy variable for being self-employed in agriculture	0.59	
Self-employed/wage: skilled non-agriculture	Dummy variable for being self-employed or a skilled wage worker in non-agriculture	0.11	
Wage agriculture	Dummy variable for being a wage worker in agriculture	0.14	
Wage: unskilled non-agriculture	Dummy variable for being an unskilled wage worker in non-agriculture	0.10	
Out of labor force/ unemployed	Dummy variable for being out of labor force or unemployed	0.06	
Chronically ill	Dummy variable for being chronically ill	0.16	
Household characteristics			
Household size	Total number of household members	5.77	2.66
Share of children aged 0–6	Ratio of number of children aged 0–6 to total household size	0.19	0.18
Access to land			
Own land	Dummy variable for owning any agricultural land	0.86	
Size of irrigated land	Size of irrigated land (hectares)	0.34	1.12
Access to finance			
Loans	Dummy variable for having had loans in the past 12 months	0.64	
Remittances			
No remittances	Dummy variable for not having received any remittances in the past 12 months	0.77	

continued.

Table 10.5 *continued*.

Explanatory variable	Description	Mean	S.D.
Received domestic remittances	Dummy variable for having received domestic remittances in the past 12 months	0.11	
Received international remittances*	Dummy variable for having received international remittances in the past 12 months	0.12	
Remoteness			
Access to paved road	Dummy variable for being able to access paved road within 15 minutes	0.13	
Geography			
Rural	Dummy variable for living in rural areas	0.94	
Development regions			
Eastern	Dummy variable for living in Eastern region	0.27	
Central	Dummy variable for living in Central region	0.34	
Western	Dummy variable for living in Western region	0.22	
Mid-Western	Dummy variable for living in Mid-Western region	0.12	
Far-Western	Dummy variable for living in Far-Western region	0.06	

* If the household received both domestic and international remittances, this variable is 1 for this household.
S.D. = standard deviation.
Source: NLSS I.

A set of household head's characteristics—age, sex, ethnicity, level of education, occupation, and whether he/she suffers from chronic illness—is included in the regression analysis. Given the observed economic exclusion of certain ethnic/caste groups from the descriptive statistics (e.g., Table 10.1 and Figure 10.4), one would expect that some groups had a better chance of moving out of poverty than others, even after controlling for other factors such as educational attainment and access to land. Greater educational attainment, meanwhile, is expected to have increased the probability of escaping poverty. Given the variation in the wage level across different occupations (see Table 10.7), one would expect that each type of occupation affected the household's chance of moving out of poverty differently.

Variables relating to the structure of the household are also included in the analysis, namely the total number of household members and the share of children aged 0–6. Variables that capture the household's access to land, loans, and remittances are also included. In Nepal, land ownership is not just a productive asset, but can also be considered a broader indicator of socioeconomic status. For instance, land titles are thought to be a requirement for obtaining a citizenship certificate or for accessing public services (CBS et al. 2006). Hence households with land are likely to have had a better chance of moving out of poverty. Given the importance of access to irrigation and of land size, a positive coefficient on the size of irrigated land that the household had access to is expected. Accessibility to financial services also generally plays a key role in helping households move out of poverty through, for instance, enabling them to benefit from consumption smoothing and to manage risks. A positive coefficient on access to loans is thus expected. As for remittances, they have become a growing source of income for Nepalese households as a result of the significant increase in both internal and international migration over the last decade. In order to capture the possible effect of remittances on household welfare, a variable that captures whether the household received domestic or international remittances is included.

The last set of variables captures the geographical location and remoteness of the household. Nepal is geographically diverse and a household's location is likely to affect its chance of moving out of poverty. Regional dummy variables are, therefore, included in the regression. Given its geography, remoteness is a difficult issue. Based on NLSS I data, empirical analysis by Fafchams and Shilpi (2008) shows that isolation is associated with a significant reduction in subjective assessments of income and consumption adequacy, even after controlling for consumption expenditures and other factors. One way of tackling remoteness is to improve connectivity by providing adequate infrastructure, particularly roads. Roads do not just ease households' access to basic services such as education and health; they can also enhance access to economic opportunity. Hence, access to paved roads is likely to increase the probability of moving out of poverty.

10.3.2 Empirical results

Table 10.6 reports the estimation results in terms of odds ratios for escaping poverty. As described in the Appendix, an odds ratio in this case is the probability of moving out of poverty relative to remaining poor. A ratio less than 1 implies that the variable reduces the probability of the household escaping poverty, while a ratio greater than 1 implies that the variable increases the probability of the household moving out of poverty. Model 1 is the basic model, which includes variables for the basic characteristics of the household and household head as well as the geographic location of the household (column 1). A number of observations should be noted. If the household head was Dalit, Terai Janajati, or any other ethnic minority, the household had a lesser chance of escaping poverty in comparison with Brahman/Chhetri. Having a higher share of children aged 0–6 also reduced the probability of moving out of poverty. On the other hand, a larger household size, and residing in rural areas and in the Eastern region (relative to urban areas and the Far-Western region, respectively) helped households escape poverty. This seems to

Table 10.6　Odds ratios for escaping poverty

Explanatory variable	Model 1 Coefficient	Model 1 Robust S. E.	Model 2 Coefficient	Model 2 Robust S. E.
Household head's characteristics				
Age	0.988	[0.010]	0.996	[0.011]
Female	1.968*	[0.767]	2.288**	[0.936]
Ethnicity				
(Brahman/Chhetri)				
Terai middle caste	3.118	[2.573]	4.111*	[3.391]
Dalits	0.321***	[0.133]	0.385**	[0.167]
Newar	1.888	[2.205]	2.395	[2.835]
Hill Janajati	0.740	[0.298]	0.878	[0.375]
Terai Janajati	0.424*	[0.205]	0.552	[0.273]
Muslims	2.309	[1.570]	2.619	[1.800]
Other minorities	0.487**	[0.180]	0.573	[0.222]
Education				
(Illiterate)				
4 or less			1.055	[0.398]
5–10			5.989***	[3.796]
11 +			5.043**	[3.692]
Occupation				
(Self-employed agriculture)				
Self-employed/wage-skilled non-agri				
Wage agriculture				
Wage-unskilled non-agri				
Out of labor force/unemployed				
Chronically ill	0.814	[0.289]	0.809	[0.293]
Household characteristics				
Household size	1.135***	[0.051]	1.130***	[0.052]
Share of children aged 0–6	0.062***	[0.045]	0.057***	[0.043]
Access to land				
Own land				
Size of irrigated land (hectares)				
Access to finance				
Loans				
Remittances				
(No remittances)				
Received domestic remittances				
Received international remittances				
Remoteness				
Access to paved road	1.501	[0.687]	1.354	[0.612]
Geography				
Rural	3.855**	[2.410]	4.180**	[2.704]
Development regions				
Eastern	2.335*	[1.057]	1.972	[0.945]
Central	1.288	[0.592]	1.159	[0.550]
Western	1.863	[0.853]	1.650	[0.790]
Mid-Western	1.251	[0.560]	1.120	[0.529]
(Far-Western)				
Numbers of observations		962		962
Pseudo R^2		0.126		0.159

***, **, and * denote statistical significance at the 1%, 5%, and 10% levels, respectively.

S. E. = standard error.

Note:　Those in brackets are reference categories for respective dummy variables.

Source:　Calculations based on NLSS I and II.

Table 10.6 Odds ratios for escaping poverty *(continued)*

Model 3		Model 4		Model 5	
Coefficient	Robust S. E.	Coefficient	Robust S. E.	Coefficient	Robust S. E.
0.996	[0.011]	0.992	[0.011]	0.995	[0.012]
2.577**	[1.113]	3.043***	[1.315]	3.160**	[1.538]
4.229*	[3.527]	4.519*	[3.569]	4.897**	[3.833]
0.358**	[0.164]	0.388**	[0.180]	0.387**	[0.178]
2.494	[2.944]	2.661	[3.054]	2.855	[3.289]
0.869	[0.374]	0.838	[0.364]	0.879	[0.382]
0.543	[0.275]	0.560	[0.299]	0.546	[0.293]
2.441	[1.674]	2.699	[1.837]	2.857	[1.965]
0.538	[0.215]	0.627	[0.254]	0.672	[0.272]
1.063	[0.407]	1.071	[0.404]	1.119	[0.422]
6.046***	[3.821]	5.802***	[3.665]	6.164***	[3.909]
4.711**	[3.422]	3.559*	[2.508]	3.882*	[2.774]
1.674	[0.742]	2.211*	[1.017]	2.178*	[1.003]
1.300	[0.456]	2.032*	[0.795]	2.050*	[0.794]
1.439	[0.680]	2.094	[1.097]	2.113	[1.127]
1.732	[1.143]	2.260	[1.561]	2.460	[1.751]
0.801	[0.297]	0.878	[0.334]	0.879	[0.332]
1.143***	[0.054]	1.117**	[0.061]	1.111*	[0.061]
0.048***	[0.037]	0.049***	[0.039]	0.052***	[0.041]
		2.742**	[1.211]	2.551**	[1.134]
		1.896**	[0.564]	1.936**	[0.557]
				1.258	[0.357]
				2.207*	[1.069]
				0.803	[0.331]
1.329	[0.598]	1.620	[0.764]	1.572	[0.745]
4.839**	[3.137]	3.977**	[2.804]	3.866*	[2.755]
1.994	[0.974]	2.569*	[1.325]	2.551*	[1.333]
1.182	[0.572]	1.489	[0.764]	1.445	[0.755]
1.750	[0.852]	1.960	[0.984]	2.072	[1.061]
1.177	[0.562]	1.260	[0.622]	1.194	[0.604]
	962		962		962
	0.169		0.181		0.189

357

contradict Table 10.1, which reports that the poverty reduction rate was greater for urban than rural households. This can perhaps be explained by the fact that the majority of the poor reside in rural areas and thus a relatively larger number of households became non-poor in rural areas than in urban areas. Most of these results remained robust even when other variables were included in the regressions (see columns 2–5 of Table 10.6).

The results from Model 5 (column 5 of Table 10.6) allow further important observations. First, education is found to be one of the key factors for escaping poverty. In particular, relative to being illiterate, having 5–10 or 11-plus years of schooling seems to have significantly increased the probability of becoming non-poor. However, as Figure 10.5 clearly illustrates, there is a great disparity in education level among the working-age population. Those residing in Kathmandu or in other urban areas, Brahman/Chhetri and Newar, men, and the highest expenditure group tend to have more years of schooling. For instance, individuals aged 15 or above in the highest expenditure quintile have, on average, about 6.3 years of schooling, while those in the lowest expenditure quintile group have only 1.3 years. This can create unequal access to economic opportunity. Ensuring that children, the future labor force, have equal access to education is therefore important to redressing the problem. Despite the progress in school enrollment rates in recent years, particularly primary education, there remains considerable room for making access to education and vocational training more equitable in Nepal.

Figure 10.5   Years of schooling by region, ethnicity/caste, gender, and expenditure quintile for those aged ≥15, 2003–2004

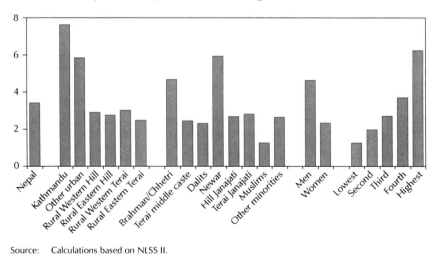

Source: Calculations based on NLSS II.

Second, in the case of occupations (relative to being self-employed in the agricultural sector), being nonfarm self-employed or a skilled wage worker in the non-agricultural sector, or being a wage worker in the agricultural sector was found to have increased the household's chance of escaping poverty. This may be, at least partly, due to the relatively greater increase in wages for these occupations between 1995–1996 and 2003–2004, as noted in Table 10.7.

Table 10.7   Average daily wages (real 1995–1996 rupees), 1995–1996 and 2003–2004

	Agriculture			Unskilled non-agriculture			Skilled non-agriculture		
	1995–1996	2003–2004	Change (%)	1995–1996	2003–2004	Change (%)	1995–1996	2003–2004	Change (%)
Urban	42	58	38	98	92	–6	138	461	234
Rural	44	55	25	79	98	24	81	135	67
NLSS region									
Kathmandu	–	–	–	103	83	–19	173	672	288
Other urban	40	57	43	91	101	11	111	170	53
Rural Western Hill	49	54	10	75	91	21	72	111	54
Rural Eastern Hill	37	54	46	84	90	7	83	137	65
Rural Western Terai	50	63	26	81	94	16	97	126	30
Rural Eastern Terai	42	54	29	75	113	51	80	159	99
Education level (years)									
Illiterate	43	52	21	73	83	14	–	–	–
Less than 5	53	61	15	82	99	21	–	–	–
5–7	44	65	48	94	99	5	–	–	–
8–10	45	63	40	86	108	26	75	113	51
11+	–	–	–	121	142	17	121	426	252
Gender									
Male	48	63	31	84	104	24	102	351	244
Female	39	47	21	59	54	–8	65	126	94
Nepal	44	55	25	81	97	20	94	295	214

– = too few observations. NLSS = Nepal Living Standards Survey.
Source: CBS et al. (2006).

Table 10.7 suggests that there has been a labor market tightening in the agricultural sector, resulting in an increase in agricultural wages between 1995–1996 and 2003–2004. This seems to be the result of greater opportunity for temporary migration, easier commuting to urban centers, and development of the rural nonfarm sector, which may all have lowered the agricultural labor supply in local labor markets (CBS et al. 2006). Nevertheless, while agricultural and unskilled non-agricultural wages increased by about 25% and 20%, respectively between 1995–1996 and 2003–2004, skilled professional wages increased by about 51% for those with 8–10 years of schooling and by about 252% for those with 11 or more years. In other words, despite the increase in agricultural wages, a significant increase in skill premiums has resulted in widening wage differentials across different occupations. This may partly explain why the growth rate of per capita expenditure was found to be greater toward the upper end of the expenditure distribution (Figure 10.1).

Third, access to land was also found to have played an important role in helping households move out of poverty. The regression results suggest that both land ownership and greater access to irrigated land helped households escape poverty. Table 10.8 shows that about 77% of households owned land in Nepal in 2003–2004. A relatively low share of land ownership for those who reside in Kathmandu, those who are Newar, or those in the highest expenditure quintile perhaps reflects that they tend to be less engaged in agricultural activities. When the size of land is taken into account, an unequal distribution of land becomes more visible. While average land holdings declined by about 24% from 1.04 to 0.79 hectares between 1995–1996 and 2003–2004, the reduction was greater among the poorest expenditure quintile group. As a result, the average size of land owned by the poorest expenditure quintile was less than half of that owned by the richest expenditure quintile in 2003–2004. It should, nonetheless, be noted that the relationship between land ownership and poverty is complex and poverty is not limited to marginal and small landholders (Deraniyagala 2005).

Access to irrigated land is even more inequitable. While there was a significant improvement in the share of households with access to irrigation, from 50% to 63% between 1995–1996 and 2003–2004, a greater improvement was observed among wealthier expenditure quintiles (Table 10.8). The proportion of households with access to irrigated land actually remained the same for the poorest quintile. The share of irrigated land in total owned land also increased for all expenditure quintiles, but the increase in the share was again greater for the households at the upper end of the expenditure distribution. Given that rural poverty is increasingly concentrated among small farmers and agricultural laborers (CBS et al. 2006), it is important to improve access to land as well as to irrigation in order to ensure inclusive economic growth.

Table 10.8   Land ownership and access to irrigation, 1995–1996 and 2003–2004

	Land ownership (%)		Average land area* (hectares)		Access to irrigation (%)		Share of irrigated land* (%)	
	1995–96	2003–04	1995–96	2003–04	1995–96	2003–04	1995–96	2003–04
NLSS region								
Kathmandu	20.9	18.8	0.9	0.4	59.1	46.1	50.4	40.9
Other urban	50.0	54.1	1.2	0.8	43.1	63.0	33.1	49.9
Rural Western Hill	94.5	93.5	0.9	0.7	56.8	58.5	24.8	26.2
Rural Eastern Hill	93.3	92.8	0.9	0.8	52.6	59.8	24.7	33.8
Rural Western Terai	89.0	87.4	1.3	0.9	52.6	68.4	43.7	61.3
Rural Eastern Terai	69.2	67.1	1.2	0.9	39.3	68.8	32.4	60.2
Ethnicity/caste								
Brahman/Chhetri	90.6	86.3	1.1	0.8	62.3	74.4	33.3	47.4
Terai middle caste	84.7	86.2	1.2	1.2	31.6	60.7	22.1	45.8
Dalits	81.8	82.9	0.6	0.4	31.2	45.9	18.3	29.6
Newar	71.4	57.3	0.8	0.6	64.1	63.8	40.7	44.5
Hill Janajati	91.6	85.0	0.9	0.7	45.8	47.5	22.0	27.6
Terai Janajati	79.4	79.8	1.6	1.3	60.5	81.7	50.5	71.6
Muslims	61.0	60.4	1.3	0.8	33.3	65.5	22.7	57.1
Other minorities	67.5	62.7	1.1	0.8	38.2	63.6	29.2	50.6
Per capita consumption quintile								
Lowest	82.9	80.7	1.0	0.5	46.9	46.7	20.5	26.5
Second	83.8	79.6	0.9	0.7	47.0	55.5	27.9	35.7
Third	82.3	79.1	0.9	0.7	49.1	62.8	29.9	41.9
Fourth	83.4	82.6	1.1	0.9	50.9	75.0	31.7	54.6
Highest	79.0	64.8	1.2	1.1	56.5	70.4	36.7	54.8
Nepal	82.1	76.8	1.0	0.8	50.4	63.0	29.9	43.6

* Land area and share of irrigated land are means for those who own land.
NLSS = Nepal Living Standards Survey.
Source: Calculations based on NLSS I and II.

Finally, relative to receiving no remittances, domestic remittances had a positive effect on the probability of escaping poverty. There has been a significant increase in both internal and international migration[3] over the last decade. Although Nepal (i.e., within the country) and India are the most common destinations for long-term migrants, there have been new destinations, including Malaysia (which receives the largest number of Nepalese migrants), Qatar, Saudi Arabia, and other Middle Eastern countries.[4] Table 10.9 shows that the outflow rate of migrants was highest in Rural Western Hills and Rural Eastern Terai—about 45% and 24% of men aged 15 and above in 2003–2004, respectively. There is a similar regional variation even when restricting the sample to international migration. Note that these are the only two regions whose share in the country's total poor population declined—by 28% and 9%, respectively—between 1995–1996 and 2003–2004 (Table 10.1). Indeed, Lokshin et al. (2007) find that one-fifth of the poverty reduction during this period can be attributed to work-related migration and remittances. Migration thus seems to offer a new source of employment for Nepalese workers and a potential means for reducing poverty.

These empirical results are broadly consistent with existing studies. Based on data from a household survey conducted in September 2005 by the United Nations' World Food Programme for its vulnerability analysis and mapping, the households identified as vulnerable to food insecurity were found to be poorly educated, possess few productive assets, and have limited access to cash remittances (WFP 2006). Similarly, Bhatta and Sharma (2006) show, using the panel sample of the NLSS datasets, that both human capital and assets such as land and livestock have a significant negative association with both chronic and transient poverty.

In sum, the available empirical evidence suggests that the limited inclusiveness of Nepal's recent economic growth can be explained, at least partly, by the lack of or limited human capital and productive assets in certain segments of the population. One study shows that "discrimination" against disadvantaged groups, measured as lower returns to their human and physical assets, was found to have declined between 1995–1996 and 2003–2004. This implies that the observed increase in inequality has been driven mostly by increasing returns to assets and, to some degree, by faster accumulation of productive assets by relatively more advantaged groups (CBS et al. 2006). Hence improvements in access to social services, infrastructure, and productive assets for disadvantaged groups will be key to enhancing the inclusiveness of growth.

---

3   In the NLSS, long-term migrants are defined as remittance senders who would have lived in the household had they not migrated, i.e., spouse, child, grandchild, parent, or sibling of remittance recipients (92% of all relations) (CBS et al. 2006).

4   Department of Labour and Employment Promotion (2008) cited in Ministry of Finance (2008).

Table 10.9 Migrant workers as share of the population aged ≥15 (%),
1995–1996 and 2003–2004

	Men		Women		All	
	1995–96	2003–04	1995–96	2003–04	1995–96	2003–04
Total Migration						
Nepal	15.9	24.5	1.8	2.2	8.4	12.2
Kathmandu	10.6	7.4	1.9	1.2	6.4	4.2
Other urban	9.6	19.5	2.8	3.9	6.1	11.4
Rural Western Hills	25.6	45.1	2.5	1.5	12.5	19.0
Rural Eastern Hills	9.3	19.8	1.6	2.9	5.3	10.6
Rural Western Terai	12.1	21.6	1.6	1.5	6.6	10.7
Rural Eastern Terai	17.5	24.1	1.4	2.1	9.3	12.1
Migration Abroad*						
Nepal	7.6	14.4	0.3	0.3	3.7	6.6
Kathmandu	1.8	2.5	0.5	0.5	1.1	1.5
Other urban	2.4	9.1	0.4	0.6	1.3	4.7
Rural Western Hill	17.9	33.1	0.5	0.1	8.0	13.3
Rural Eastern Hill	1.7	6.7	0.0	0.2	0.8	3.2
Rural Western Terai	5.8	14.2	0.4	0.3	2.9	6.6
Rural Eastern Terai	6.9	14.5	0.3	0.4	3.6	6.8

* This includes migration to India and other countries.
Source: CBS et al. (2006).

10.4   Conclusions

Despite impressive progress in reducing poverty between 1995–1996 and 2003–2004 in Nepal, the evidence suggests that economic growth was not inclusive. The benefits of growth were not shared equally, with the tendency for relatively well-off households to benefit more than poorer households. For instance, poverty reduction was greater in urban than in rural areas—56% and 20%, respectively—even though the poverty headcount ratio was higher in rural areas. About 35% of the rural population was thus still below the poverty line, compared to only 3% in Kathmandu and 13% in other urban areas in 2003–2004. As a result, there was a sharp increase in inequality between 1995–2006 and 2003–2004.

The chapter also examined, using the panel data from NLSS I and II, what factors helped certain groups of households escape poverty. A multinomial logit model was estimated to analyze the determinants of poverty dynamics. The results suggest that, among other things, educational attainment, land ownership, access to irrigation, occupation in the non-agricultural sector, and receipt of domestic remittances all helped households move out of poverty. On the other hand, being Dalit (the lowest caste) seems to have, even after controlling for other factors, prevented households from doing so.

These findings have important policy implications. To ensure economic growth leads to significant poverty and inequality reduction, growth has to be inclusive. In Nepal, where the inclusiveness of growth was found to be limited, special effort is required to help the poor and the excluded catch up and participate in growth on more equal terms. To ensure that economic opportunity generated by growth is within reach of every segment of society, the government must redress the weak human capabilities of the poor and excluded groups as well as unequal access to productive assets.

Appendix: Data and methodology

Data

The Nepal Living Standards Survey contains two waves of data—the first conducted in 1995–1996 (NLSS I) and the second in 2003–2004 (NLSS II). Both surveys are nationally representative and rich in data for the analysis of poverty and other microeconomic issues. While 3,373 and 4,874 households were surveyed in 1995–1996 and 2003–2004, respectively, 962 households were covered in both surveys constituting a panel dataset. By exploiting the panel component of the sample, it is possible to examine the dynamics of poverty between 1995–1996 and 2003–2004.

It should be noted that the 2003–2004 panel sample does not represent the 2003–2004 population of Nepal. In addition, as in most panel datasets, the panel data from NLSS I and II suffer from the attrition problem. CBS et al. (2006) do point out that the panel failed to follow the most wealthy households in urban areas. Caution should thus be exercised when generalizing the regression results. Nevertheless, comparing the figures reported in Table 10.4 with those in Table 10.1, poverty estimates based on panel data are found to be relatively close to the estimates based on cross-section data. In addition, Bhatta and Sharma (2006) demonstrate that, despite the attrition problem, the panel dataset represents the nation fairly well and their findings provide a sense of assurance.

Methodology

In order to identify possible factors behind the observed poverty dynamics, a multinomial logit model (MNL) is applied to the panel component of the

364

NLSS data. The model analyzes the probability of being in a particular state out of several unordered alternatives. The poverty transition between 1995–1996 and 2003–2004 are examined in terms of (unordered) multiple choices, specifically (1) being poor in both periods (P→P); (2) being non-poor in 1995–1996 and becoming poor in 2003–2004 (NP→P); (3) being poor in 1995–1996 and becoming non-poor in 2003–2004 (P→NP); and (4) being non-poor in both years (NP→NP).

The probability that household i experiences outcome j is expressed as:

$$\text{Prob}\left(Y_i = j\right) = \frac{e^{\beta'_j x_i}}{\sum\limits_{k=1}^{4} e^{\beta'_k x_i}}, j=1,2,3,4 \tag{1}$$

where Y_i is the outcome experienced by household i, x_i is the (n x 1) vector of characteristics for household i, and β_j is the (n x 1) vector of coefficients on x_i applicable to households in state j. The model is identified only up to an additive vector since adding, say, vector m to each β_k leads to the same probabilities of $Y = 1$, $Y = 2$, $Y = 3$, and $Y = 4$. Thus, one β_k must be chosen as the base category and set to zero. All other sets are then estimated in relation to this benchmark. In the analysis, Outcome 1 (the household is poor in both periods) is set to zero, since what is of interest are the factors which helped households escape poverty. The MNL model is most easily interpreted as giving conditional probabilities. By setting Outcome 1 (P→P) as the base category, the coefficients for Outcome 3 (P→NP) indicate the probabilities of moving out of poverty relative to being poor in both years.

The empirical results in this chapter are expressed as an odds ratio—the probability of each outcome relative to the probability of the base category—instead of the MNL coefficients. Setting $Y = 1$ as the base category, the odds ratio for $Y = 3$ for a change in each variable x is given by:

$$\frac{\text{Prob }(Y=3)}{\text{Prob }(Y=1)} = e^{\beta'_3 x} \tag{2}$$

where $e^{\beta'_3 x}$ is the odds ratio for a unit change in variable x. A ratio less than 1 implies that the variable reduces the probability of the household escaping poverty, while a ratio greater than 1 implies that the variable increases the probability of the household moving out of poverty.

References

Ali, I., and J. Zhuang. 2007. Inclusive Growth Toward a Prosperous Asia: Policy Implications. ERD Working Paper No. 97, Economics and Research Department, Asian Development Bank, Manila.

Bhatta, S. D., and S. K. Sharma. 2006. The Determinants and Consequences of Chronic and Transient Poverty in Nepal. CPRC Working Paper No. 66, Chronic Poverty Research Centre, Manchester.

CBS. 1996. *Nepal Living Standards Survey 1995–96.* Central Bureau of Statistics, Kathmandu.

_____. 2004. *Nepal Living Standards Survey 2003–04.* Central Bureau of Statistics, Kathmandu.

CBS, World Bank, DFID, and ADB. 2006. *Resilience Amidst Conflict: An Assessment of Poverty in Nepal, 1995–96 and 2003–04.* Central Bureau of Statistics, World Bank, Department for International Development, and Asian Development Bank, Kathmandu.

Deraniyagala, S. 2005. "The Political Economy of Civil Conflict in Nepal." *Oxford Development Studies* 33(1):47–62.

Fafchamps, M., and F. Shilpi. 2008. Isolation and Subjective Welfare: Evidence from South Asia. Policy Research Working Paper No. 4535, World Bank, Washington, DC.

Lokshin, M., M. Bontch-Osmolovski, and E. Glinskaya. 2007. Work-Related Migration and Poverty Reduction in Nepal. Policy Research Working Paper No. 4231, World Bank, Washington, DC.

Ministry of Finance. 2008. *Economic Survey: Fiscal Year 2007/08.* Ministry of Finance, Kathmandu.

Ravallion, M. 2001. "Growth, Inequality and Poverty: Looking Beyond Averages." *World Development* 29(11):1803–15.

United Nations. 2006. *Nepal: Comprehensive Food Security and Vulnerability Analysis.* United Nations' World Food Programme, Vulnerability and Analysis and Mapping Branch, Kathmandu.

World Bank and DFID. 2006. *Unequal Citizens: Gender, Caste and Ethnic Exclusion in Nepal.* World Bank and Department for International Development, Kathmandu.

11

Decomposing Income Inequality: People's Republic of China, 1990–2005

Tun Lin, Juzhong Zhuang, Damaris Yarcia, and Fen Lin[1]

11.1 Introduction

Rapid growth in the People's Republic of China (PRC), which began as it embarked on economic reforms in the late 1970s, has been accompanied by rising income inequality. During 1985–2006, the country's real per capita gross domestic product grew at an annual average rate of 8.5%. Such strong growth led to an unprecedented reduction in the incidence of poverty, from 32.5% in 1990 to 7.1% in 2005, measured by the $1-a-day international poverty line (Ali and Zhuang 2007). However, the Gini coefficient of per capita income also increased, from about 0.30 in the early 1980s to about 0.45 in 2001 at the national level (Ravallion and Chen 2007).

The literature on income inequality in the PRC is extensive. Researchers have used three types of data: unit-level household survey data, aggregate income data, and grouped household survey data. Due to the absence of consistent data covering the entire PRC, studies based on unit-level data often focus on a particular segment of the population, such as urban households (Cao and Nee 2005, Meng 2004) or rural households (Gustafsson and Li 2002), for isolated years.[2] Aggregate data, often at the provincial level, have been used to investigate the spatial dimension of inequality (Hussain and Zhuang 1994, Kanbur and Zhang 2005).

More recently, attempts have been made to study the PRC's income inequality by extrapolating unit-level data from grouped household income data. Notable examples are Ravallion and Chen (2007) and Chotikapanich et al. (2007). Despite these efforts, the picture of income

---

1   This chapter updates Lin et al. (2008) which used data from 1990 to 2004.
2   Although the National Bureau of Statistics of China (NBSC) has conducted household income and expenditure surveys of urban and rural populations in all the provinces annually since the mid-1980s, NBSC has not released all the unit-level survey data officially.

inequality in the PRC is still incomplete, and many questions remain. For instance, although widening spatial disparity and the urban-rural income gap are often highlighted as key drivers of increases in national inequality, a quantification of their relative contributions using data representative of the entire PRC is still absent.

This chapter investigates income inequality in the PRC using data representing more than 85% of the country's population. It has two specific objectives. The first is to examine the trends of urban, rural, and overall inequality at the national, regional, and provincial levels during 1990–2005. The second is to carry out decomposition analysis to examine and quantify to what extent increasing national inequality was driven by rural inequality, urban inequality, inequality between urban and rural populations, and inequality within and between regions or provinces (including how the relative importance of each of these components has changed over time).

Following Ravallion and Chen (2007) and Chotikapanich et al. (2007), this chapter uses the extrapolated unit-level data from grouped household income data. The grouped data—compiled by the authors from the provincial statistical yearbooks of 23 provinces for 1990, 1995, 2000, and 2005—are disaggregated by province and by rural and urban population. This dataset is the most comprehensive and up-to-date among similar datasets available in the public domain. Chotikapanich et al. (2007) present results based on grouped income data disaggregated only by urban and rural populations, not by province. The grouped data used by Ravallion and Chen (2007), although disaggregated both by province and by rural and urban population, are only up to 2001 and are not available in the public domain.[3] Neither Chotikapanich et al. nor Ravallion and Chen carried out decomposition analysis to quantify the relative contributions of different components of the PRC's overall inequality.

For a country as large as the PRC, to avoid biases, it is important to consider cross-regional differences in the cost of living (COL) when estimating income inequality. This issue has often been overlooked in such studies on the PRC. Both Chotikapanich et al. and Ravallion and Chen tried to eliminate this source of bias by adjusting for urban-rural but not interprovincial COL differences. Ravallion and Chen found that the national Gini coefficient in 2001 would be 0.394 when adjusted for COL differences, compared with 0.447 otherwise. In estimating income inequality, this paper adjusts for both urban-rural and interprovincial COL differences, the latter being derived from a study on province-specific poverty lines (ADB 2001).

---

[3]   The dataset, made available exclusively to the authors by the National Bureau of Statistics of China, is in the form of tabulations of income distribution following a standardized design in which households are ranked by income per person, and all fractiles are population-weighted. See Ravallion and Chen (2007).

In the remainder of the chapter, Section 11.2 discusses the data, Section 11.3 describes the methodology, and Section 11.4 examines income inequality in urban and rural areas as well as at the national, regional, and provincial levels. Section 11.5 presents the results of the decomposition analysis. Section 11.6 summarizes key findings and discusses policy implications.

11.2 Data

This chapter uses the grouped income data of 23 of the PRC's 31 provinces, separated into urban and rural populations. The data are published in the PRC's provincial statistical yearbooks for the years 1990, 1995, 2000, and 2005. The eight provinces not covered are Chongqing, Gansu, Guizhou, Hainan, Jilin, Ningxia, Shandong, and Tibet. Chongqing only gained provincial status in 1997. Data for the other seven provinces are not available either for rural or urban populations, or both. The eight provinces accounted for about 12%–15% of the total PRC population during the study period. Sichuan was also not included in 1995 and 2000 due to the lack of rural population data.

11.2.1 Income and distribution data

The provincial statistical yearbooks provide grouped net income data for rural households and disposable income data for urban households. For rural households, the data are in the form of shares of households corresponding to various ranges of per capita net income in yuan, such as CNY100–200, CNY200–300, and CNY300–500. For urban households, the data are mostly in the form of per capita mean disposable income corresponding to various percentiles of income distribution ($0\text{--}10^{th}$, $10\text{--}20^{th}$, $20\text{--}40^{th}$, $40\text{--}60^{th}$, $60\text{--}80^{th}$, $80\text{--}90^{th}$, and $90\text{--}100^{th}$). In some cases, distributions are presented in quintiles ($0\text{--}20^{th}$, $20\text{--}40^{th}$, $40\text{--}60^{th}$, $60\text{--}80^{th}$, $80\text{--}100^{th}$) or other percentiles. Since the shares and percentiles both refer to households, to estimate distribution of per capita income, the household size of each income group was used as the weight.

Ravallion and Chen (2007) highlighted a number of limitations in the household survey data. One is that the data do not include imputed rents for own-occupied housing. This works toward underestimating income inequality, as richer households tend to live under better housing conditions. Another is that, for rural households, although the net income captures imputed values from consumption of own-farm production, the imputed values may be underestimated in earlier years. This was especially true before the mid-1990s, when public procurement prices rather than local market prices were used in valuation and the former tended to be lower than the latter. This works toward overestimating urban-rural income gaps. A further limitation, which is commonly associated with income as a welfare indicator, is that the data do not reflect imputed values of various public services, such as health, education, water, and sanitation. Since all of these services tend to be better provided in urban than in rural areas, this works toward underestimating urban-rural welfare gaps. These three sources of bias will cancel each other out to some extent, but maybe not completely. Whether the net effect works toward under- or over-estimating income inequality is unclear.

Apart from these limitations, a number of assumptions made in estimating income inequality may also lead to biases. The first is that, for rural households, the highest income range is sometimes defined as "above a certain income level" in the provincial statistical yearbooks, and no upper bound is provided. Datt (1998), in his study of rural inequality in India, assumed that the upper bound is 1.3 times the lower bound when the upper bound is missing for the highest income range. This chapter follows this approach, since after examining cases where both the mean income and income range are presented, this ratio appears applicable to rural PRC. For other income ranges, the midpoint is assumed as the mean income unless the actual mean income is indicated. Second, in a few cases where only expenditure data are available, income data were inferred from the expenditure-income ratio of the next year when both income and expenditure data are available. Third, in a few cases where data on household size are not available, household size was estimated using the following equation:

$$h_{ip} = \alpha_i + \beta_i \overline{h}_p \tag{1}$$

where h_{ip} is average household size of the ith income group in the pth province; $\overline{h}_p$ is mean household size of the pth province, and α_i and β_i are estimated by applying ordinary least squares regression to grouped income data for each income group, separately for urban and rural populations.

Last, for several provinces included in the study, grouped income data are not available in 1990 or 2005. Under such circumstances, the distribution from the nearest year when grouped income data were available was extrapolated. In particular, the income distribution of rural Inner Mongolia in 1990 was extrapolated from 1985; urban Liaoning in 1990, from 1995; rural Shaanxi in 1990, from 1992; rural Shanghai in 1990, from 1992; rural Xinjiang in 1990, from 1992; and urban Xinjiang in 1990, from 1992.

11.2.2   Population data

Due to the lack of consistent rural and urban population data, this chapter follows many other studies (such as Wan 2007), and uses "agricultural population" (*nongye renkou*) and "non-agricultural population" (*fei nongye renkou*) to derive rural and urban per capita income for all the provinces. This is justified by the fact that the sample frames used by the National Bureau of Statistics of China in its household surveys are based on the country's household registration system, which differentiates agricultural from non-agricultural populations.

11.2.3   Province-specific rural and urban cost-of-living data

The provincial statistical yearbooks report nominal incomes. To estimate income inequality—free of biases due to COL differences across provinces as well as between urban and rural areas—this study adjusted nominal incomes by province-specific rural and urban COL indexes. The adjustment involves three steps. The first deflates nominal incomes by province-specific urban and rural consumer price indexes, obtained from provincial statistical yearbooks, taking 1993 as the base year. The effect of this adjustment (temporal price effect) on inequality proved to be small, consistent with earlier studies (see Liu 2006). The second further adjusts both urban and rural incomes by province-specific COL indexes, estimated from province-specific urban poverty lines reported in a study on province-specific poverty lines in the PRC (ADB 2001). In the third step, because province-specific rural poverty lines were not available, the study followed Ravallion, Chen, and Sangraula (2007), which assumed that the urban poverty line was 1.37 times the rural poverty line for all the provinces.

11.3   Methodology

To extrapolate unit-level data from grouped income data, the first step is to estimate a Lorenz curve. To do this, a general quadratic distribution Lorenz curve or a beta distribution Lorenz curve was fitted to province-specific grouped income data for urban and rural populations, respectively.[4] The beta Lorenz curve takes the form:

$$L(p) = p - \theta p^{\gamma}(1-p)^{\delta} \qquad (2)$$

---

[4]   Using a STATA-based version of the World Bank's POVCAL program.

and the general quadratic Lorenz Curve takes the form:

$$L(p) = -\frac{1}{2} [bp + e + (mp^2 + np + e^2)^{\frac{1}{2}}] \tag{3}$$

where $L(p)$ is the share of the bottom p% of the population in income, and $\theta, \gamma, \delta, b, e, m, n$ are parameters to be estimated. Datt (1998) discusses in detail the conceptual issues and procedures underlying this approach.

With the Lorenz curve, unit-level income data can be extrapolated using the following relationship:

$$L'(p) = x/\mu \tag{4}$$

where x is the unit-level income, and μ is the mean per capita income of each province.[5] This states that an individual's income is the product of the slope of the Lorenz curve at the point that the individual represents and the mean income of the population. Therefore, in this study, the derivative of an estimated Lorenz curve with respect to each observation is multiplied by the mean income of each province to extrapolate unit-level income data. Income data are aggregated into national, regional, or provincial data with population as weights. To assess the reliability of the extrapolated unit-level data, the study compares levels of inequality estimated from these data with some of those estimated from actual unit-level data and finds that the results are close. For example, Dai (2005) shows that the Gini coefficient for urban Beijing was 0.16 in 1989, 0.15 in 1991, 0.20 in 1995, and 0.21 in 2000. In this study, the Gini coefficient for urban Beijing was 0.165 in 1990, 0.209 in 1995, and 0.226 in 2000.

To measure income inequality, the Gini coefficient and Theil index are used—the first because of its wide currency and the second because it allows decomposing overall income inequality into contributions by inequalities within and between subgroups of the population. The two measures possess the property of population independence and satisfy the transfer principle. The latter requires that transferring income from a richer to a poorer person, without reversing their ranks in distribution, will lead to a fall in inequality. The expression for the Gini coefficient is:

$$Gini = \frac{-(n+1)}{n} + \frac{2}{n^2\mu} \sum_{i=1}^{n} i \cdot y_i \tag{5}$$

where y_i is income of individual i, μ is the mean income of the population, and n is the number of individuals in the population.

---

[5]   A program developed by the Asian Development Bank was used to generate the synthetic income data.

The Theil index (T) can be computed as:

$$T = \frac{1}{n} \sum_{i=1}^{n} \frac{y_i}{\mu} (ln[\frac{y_i}{\mu}]) \tag{6}$$

where y_i is income of individual i, μ is the population mean income, and n is the number of individuals in the population.

Assuming that a population consists of h subgroups and the Theil index of each subgroup is T_g, the overall inequality of the population measured by the Theil index can then be computed as:

$$T = \sum_{g=1}^{h} s_g T_g + \sum_{g=1}^{h} s_g (ln[\frac{s_g}{p_g}]) \tag{7}$$

where s_g is group g's share of total income and p_g is group g's share of total population. The first summation is the average of Theil indexes of h subgroups weighted by income shares, and gives the component of overall inequality that is due to inequality within subgroups. The second summation is the Theil index calculated on the mean income of each subgroup, hence giving the component of overall inequality that is due to between-group inequality.

Unlike the Gini coefficient, which has a value between 0 (indicating perfect equality) and 1 (indicating perfect inequality), the Theil index only has a lower bound of 0 (indicating perfect equality) but does not have an upper limit. However, it can be shown that the value of the Theil index is 1 for an inequality that is slightly above the equivalent to the frequently cited 80:20 distribution, that is, 80% of the wealth is owned by 20% of the population.

11.4   Empirical results

Using the extrapolated unit-level data, the study is able to estimate income inequality at the national, regional, and provincial levels for 1990–2005. Both nominal income and real income—adjusted by COL differences across provinces and between urban and rural areas—are used in the estimation.

11.4.1   Income inequality: Graphical representations

To show shifts in income distribution during 1990–2005, Figure 11.1 plots the kernel probability density estimates of nominal and COL-adjusted per capita income of the 23 provinces. Income distribution became more and more dispersed over time, suggesting rising inequality. However, there is a big difference between the probability densities of nominal incomes and of COL-adjusted real incomes. After adjusting for COL differences, the changes in the dispersion of income distributions over time became much less significant. This suggests that if COL differences are not adjusted, income inequality will be overestimated. Figure 11.2 plots the kernel probability density estimates of COL-adjusted real income for urban and rural populations. Clearly, changes in dispersion of income distributions over time were more pronounced for urban than for rural populations.

Figure 11.1   Shifts in income distribution: National level

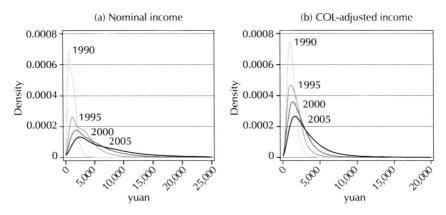

COL = cost of living.
Source: Authors' estimates.

Figure 11.2   Shifts in income distribution: Urban and rural

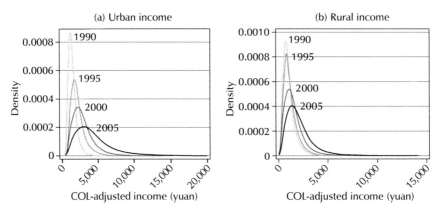

COL = cost of living.
Source: Authors' estimates.

11.4.2 Gini coefficients and Theil indexes

A. National income inequality

Table 11.1 reports national Gini coefficients and Theil indexes of per capita income estimated from the extrapolated unit-level data. In the case of nominal income, the Gini coefficient was 0.345 in 1990 and 0.457 in 2005. In the case of COL-adjusted real incomes, the Gini coefficient was 0.287 in 1990, and increased to 0.388 in 2005. Comparing the results from nominal incomes with those of the COL-adjusted real income, the difference is quite significant. Not allowing for COL differences overestimates the Gini coefficients by about 20%. The trend of the Theil index is similar to that of the Gini coefficient—the Theil index was 0.194 in 1990 and increased to 0.366 in 2005. However, after adjusting for COL differences, the Theil index only increased from 0.135 in 1990 to 0.257 in 2005. COL-adjusted national Gini coefficients and Theil indexes are also plotted in Figure 11.3.

Table 11.1   National income inequality

Year	Theil index		Gini coefficient	
	Nominal	**COL-adjusted**	**Nominal**	**COL-adjusted**
1990	0.194	0.135	0.345	0.287
1995	0.264	0.177	0.397	0.329
2000	0.284	0.199	0.411	0.347
2005	0.366	0.257	0.457	0.388

COL = cost of living.
Source: Authors' estimates.

Figure 11.3   COL-adjusted national Gini coefficient and Theil index

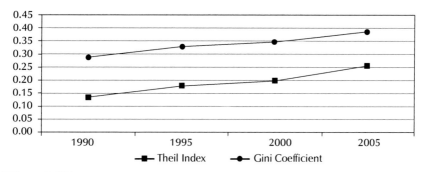

COL = cost of living.
Source: Authors' estimates.

B. Inequality in urban and rural areas

Table 11.2 shows that inequality increased in both urban and rural areas during 1990–2005. Rural inequality was greater than urban inequality in 1990, and the difference was quite significant, whether measured by the Gini coefficient or Theil index, and whether using nominal income or COL-adjusted real income. But the pace of increase of urban inequality was much faster than that of rural inequality, resulting in a convergence between the two: in 2005, they were very close, although rural inequality was still slightly higher than urban inequality.

Table 11.2   Rural and urban income inequality

Year	Theil index		Gini coefficient	
	Rural	Urban	Rural	Urban
Nominal income				
1990	0.161	0.081	0.307	0.220
1995	0.191	0.120	0.334	0.268
2000	0.200	0.148	0.346	0.300
2005	0.206	0.203	0.345	0.345
COL-adjusted real income				
1990	0.141	0.069	0.290	0.205
1995	0.156	0.086	0.305	0.229
2000	0.170	0.116	0.319	0.268
2005	0.180	0.173	0.326	0.322

COL = cost of living.
Source: Authors' estimates.

C. Inequality by region

Looking at inequality by region, the study divided the 23 provinces into three regions:

(i)   Coastal: Beijing, Fujian, Guangdong, Guangxi, Hebei, Jiangsu, Liaoning, Shanghai, Tianjin, and Zhejiang;
(ii)   Central: Anhui, Heilongjiang, Henan, Hubei, Hunan, Inner Mongolia, Jiangxi, and Shanxi; and
(iii)   Western: Qinghai, Shaanxi, Sichuan, Xinjiang, and Yunnan.

Figure 11.4 plots the three regions' Gini coefficients and Theil indexes of per capita income, adjusted by COL differences. In 1990, the coastal and western regions had more or less the same level of inequality, and the central region had the lowest level of inequality, whether measured by the Gini coefficient or Theil index. During 1990–1995, inequality rose for all three regions, with that of the western region rising the fastest. During 1995–2000, inequality continued to rise in all three regions, but there was a notable reduction in the pace, especially in the western and coastal regions. During 2000–2005, however, the pace of increase in inequality accelerated in the coastal region but was reduced in the western region, while inequality in the central region continued to rise at more or less the same pace as in the past 10 years.

Figure 11.4   Inequality by region: Gini coefficient and Theil index
(using COL-adjusted income)

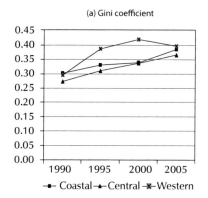
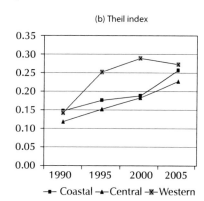

COL = cost of living.
Source: Authors' estimates.

D. Inequality by province

The province-specific unit-level data extrapolated from grouped income data also allow the estimation of inequality by province. Figure 11.5 plots the Gini coefficients and Theil indexes of 23 provinces for 1990, 1995, 2000, and 2005. Xinjiang had the highest level of inequality in all 4 years. Qinghai and Shaanxi were in the top five most unequal provinces in all 4 years.

Figure 11.5   Inequality by province: Gini coefficient
(using COL-adjusted income)

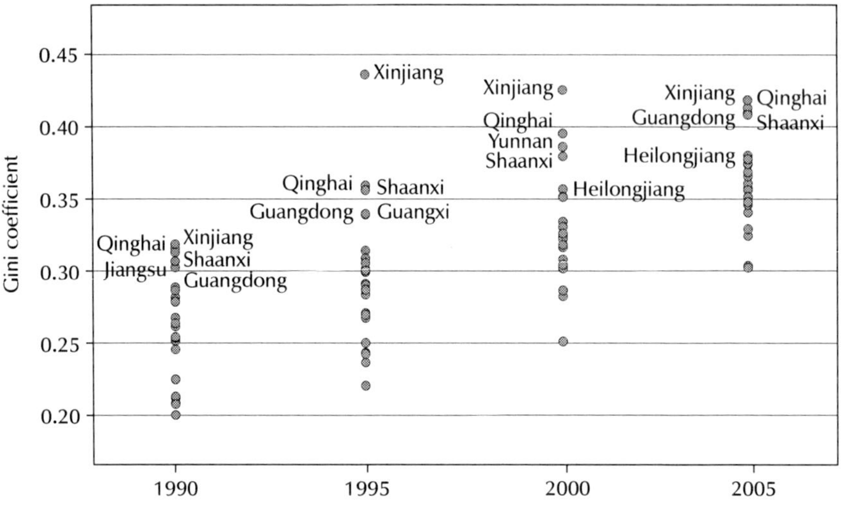

COL = cost of living.
Source: Authors' estimates.

E.   Comparison with other studies

Table 11.3 compares this study's Gini coefficient estimates with those of Ravallion and Chen (2007). In the case of nominal incomes, the estimates are very close to those of Ravallion and Chen (although most were slightly lower), whether looking at national, urban, or rural inequality. For instance, in 1990, estimates of national, urban, and rural inequality are 0.345, 0.307, and 0.220, respectively, compared to 0.349, 0.299, and 0.234 in Ravallion and Chen. For 2000, the estimates are 0.411, 0.346, and 0.300, compared to 0.438, 0.358, and 0.319 in Ravallion and Chen. In the case of COL-adjusted incomes, the estimate of national inequality is only 0.347 in 2000, compared with 0.385 in Ravallion and Chen. This difference is largely because Ravallion and Chen only adjusted for urban-rural COL differences, while here the adjustment of COL differences also covers the interprovincial dimension.

11.4.3   Income inequality: Decomposition

A major advantage of the Theil index as an income inequality measure, compared with others such as the Gini coefficient, is that it allows one to decompose the income inequality of a population into contributions by subgroups. Assessing each subgroup's contribution to overall inequality sheds light on where income inequality comes from, as well as the policies to address it. In the case of inequality in the PRC, the authors have not seen decomposition analysis using unit-level data covering as high as about 85% of the population.

Table 11.3 Comparison with the Gini coefficients reported in other studies

Source	1990	1995	2000	2005
National inequality				
This study (nominal)	0.345	0.397	0.411	0.457
Ravallion and Chen (nominal)	0.349	0.415	0.438	–
This study (COL-adjusted)	0.287	0.329	0.347	0.388
Ravallion and Chen (COL-adjusted)	0.316	0.365	0.385	–
Rural inequality				
This study (nominal)	0.307	0.334	0.346	0.345
Ravallion and Chen (nominal)	0.299	0.340	0.358	–
This study (COL-adjusted)	0.290	0.305	0.319	0.326
Urban inequality				
This study (nominal)	0.220	0.268	0.300	0.345
Ravallion and Chen (nominal)	0.234	0.283	0.319	–
This study (COL-adjusted)	0.205	0.229	0.268	0.322

– = data not available, COL = cost of living.
Source: Ravallion and Chen (2007) and authors' estimates.

A. Inequality within and between regions

A commonly cited cause of rising income inequality in the PRC is the widening income gap between coastal and interior regions. However, the extent to which spatial inequality has contributed to overall income inequality is still not well understood. Efforts to decompose inequality into between-region and within-region inequality often use data in the form of provincial mean income, rather than unit-level income. Such decomposition cannot assess the importance of the spatial dimension in causing the increases in national income inequality. Using the extrapolated unit-level data can answer this question. The results are shown in Figure 11.6.

During 1990–2005, the absolute level of income inequality increased both within and between regions, whether measured in nominal incomes or COL-adjusted real incomes. In terms of relative contributions, however, the picture is mixed. In the case of COL-adjusted real incomes, the contribution of the between-region inequality was less than 1% in 1990, and only increased to 3.8% in 2005; i.e., interregional inequality in the PRC is very insignificant compared with intraregional inequality. This contrasts with the common perception that rising interregional inequality has been a key driver of rising inequality in the PRC during the last 2 decades. Even looking at nominal incomes, the contribution of between-region inequality fluctuated around 10% during 1990–2005. This result is in stark contrast with earlier studies, which concluded that interregional inequality was rising rapidly and accounted for the majority of the PRC's inequality (for example, Wan 2007). Such studies used the provincial mean income data to come up with intraregional inequality, therefore masking the inequality that occurs within each province and understating the magnitude of intraregional inequality and its contribution to overall inequality.

Figure 11.6   Decomposition of inequality by region: Theil index

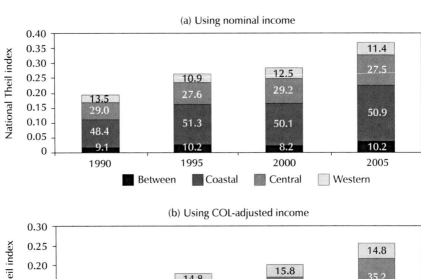

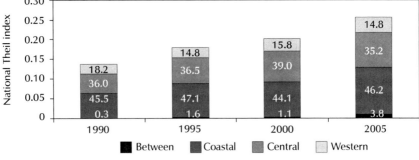

COL = cost of living.
Note: Numbers inside bars add up to 100%.
Source: Authors' estimates.

380

Among the components of intraregional inequality, the contribution of the coastal region increased from 45.5% in 1990 to 46.2% in 2005 using COL-adjusted income; and from 48.4% in 1990 to 50.9% in 2005 using nominal income. However, the contributions of both western and central regions decreased during 1990–2005. In the case of COL-adjusted real income, the contribution of the western region declined from 18.2% in 1990 to 14.8% in 2005, and for the central region from 36.0% to 35.2%.

B. Inequality between and within provinces

Figure 11.7 shows the decomposition of overall inequality into between- and within-province components, in both nominal and real terms. It indicates that the "within" component has been the driving force of rising inequality in the PRC. In the case of nominal incomes, contributions of between- and within-province inequality remained quite stable during 1990–2005, in the range of 21.3%–22.1% and 77.9%–78.7%, respectively, except in 1995 when between-province inequality increased to 26.1% while that of within-province inequality declined to 73.9%. In the case of COL-adjusted real incomes, within-province inequality actually increased, from 86.2% in 1990 to about 87.9% in 2005, while between-province inequality declined from about 13.8% in 1990 to about 12.1% in 2005. Given the relatively small magnitude of the contribution of interprovincial inequality to overall inequality, these results suggest that rising inequality in the PRC during 1990–2005 was largely driven by inequality within each province. The most important drivers of national inequality were Guangdong, Henan, Hunan, Jiangsu, Sichuan, and Zhejiang.

C. Inequality between and within urban and rural sectors

Figure 11.8 shows the components of inequality decomposed by between-urban-rural inequality, within rural inequality, and within-urban inequality. Income inequalities between rural and urban areas and within the urban area were rising fast and together accounted for two-thirds of national inequality in 2005 (adjusting for COL). In the past, rural areas contributed more to total inequality than urban areas and urban-rural disparity, but the trend has reversed over time. In 1990, income inequality within rural areas accounted for 72.2% of national inequality (adjusting for COL), while income inequality within urban areas and between rural and urban areas together accounted for the rest. In 2005, the contribution of within-rural inequality declined to 35.7%; within-urban inequality increased to 33.0%; and between-urban-rural inequality increased to 31.3%.

Figure 11.7   Decomposition of inequality by province: Theil index

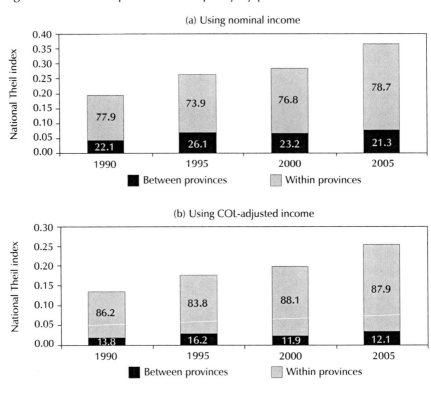

COL = cost of living.
Note: Numbers inside bars add up to 100%.
Source: Authors' estimates.

11.5   Conclusions

This chapter has investigated changes in income inequality in the PRC during 1990–2005 using unit-level data extrapolated from grouped income data of 23 provinces, covering both rural and urban households and representing more than 85% of the population. Key results are summarized as follows.

First, at the national level, the Gini coefficient of per capita nominal income increased from 0.345 in 1990 to 0.457 in 2005. After adjusting for interprovincial and between-urban-rural COL differences, the Gini coefficient increased from 0.287 in 1990 to 0.388 in 2005. These figures suggest that without adjusting for COL differences, the Gini coefficient could be overestimated by almost 20%.

Figure 11.8   Decomposition of inequality by urban and rural area:
Theil index

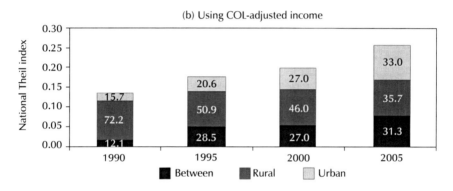

(a) Using nominal income

(b) Using COL-adjusted income

COL = cost of living.
Note: Numbers inside bars add up to 100%.
Source: Authors' estimates.

Second, income inequality increased in both urban and rural areas, but urban inequality increased at a much faster pace. In 2005, urban inequality was more or less equal to rural inequality, with the Gini coefficient of 0.345 for both, using nominal income, and 0.326 and 0.322, respectively, after adjusting for COL differences.

Third, during 1990–2005, income inequality increased in the coastal, central, and western regions; the increase was most pronounced in the western region. During 2000–2005, the increase was largest in the coastal region. In 2005, inequality was the highest in the western region, followed by the coastal region and central region. Across provinces, income distribution was constantly most unequal in Guangdong, Qinghai, Shaanxi, and Xinjiang; and constantly more equal in Beijing, Jiangxi, Shanghai, and Tianjin.

Fourth, from the decomposition analysis, during 1990–2005, rising inequality between urban and rural areas and within urban areas was the major source of rising national inequality. In 1990, after adjusting for COL differences, the between-urban-rural inequality and within-urban inequality accounted for 12.1% and 15.7%, respectively, of national inequality; in 2005, the contribution increased to 31.3% and 33.0%, respectively. While within-rural inequality also increased, the extent of the increase was smaller and, consequently, its contribution to national inequality declined from 72.2% in 1990 to 35.7% in 2005 (after adjusting for COL differences).

Fifth, decomposing national inequality by region, between 1990 and 2005, inequality within the coastal region contributed the most to national inequality, and inequality within the western region increased most rapidly. Compared with intraregional inequality, interregional inequality (i.e., inequality between the coastal, central, and western regions) contributed little to national inequality: 10.2% for nominal incomes and 3.8% after adjusting for COL differences in 2005. This is in sharp contrast to the common perception that rising regional inequality is one of the key drivers of inequality at the national level.

Sixth, decomposing national inequality by province, within-province inequality was the major source of national inequality. After adjusting for COL differences, the contribution of within-province inequality to national inequality increased from 86.2% in 1990 to 87.9% in 2005, while the contribution of between-province inequality declined from 13.8% to 12.1% during the same period. These figures further show that rising regional inequality was not a major driver of rising national inequality in the PRC. It is also found that the biggest contributors to national inequality in 2005 were Guangdong, Henan, Hunan, Jiangsu, Sichuan, and Zhejiang.

These results suggest that the most effective ways of reducing overall inequality in the PRC are to narrow the income gap between urban and rural areas and to reduce income inequality among the urban population. Regional income disparity (between coastal and western regions and among rich and poor provinces) remains large and needs to be reduced; indeed it is very important for poverty reduction because the majority of the poor in the PRC is located in the western region. However, because it is not a major source of inequality, the impact of this reduction on inequality at the national level may be limited.

References

ADB. 2001. Urban Poverty in the PRC. Asian Development Bank Technical Assistance Report, TAR-PRC 33448. Asian Development Bank, Manila.

Ali, I., and J. Zhuang. 2007. Inclusive Growth toward a Prosperous Asia: Policy Implications. ERD Working Paper Series No. 97, Economics and Research Department, Asian Development Bank, Manila.

Cao, Y., and V. Nee. 2005. "Remaking Inequality: Institutional Change and Income Stratification in Urban China." *Journal of the Asia Pacific Economy* 10(4):463–85.

Chotikapanich D., D. S. P. Rao, and K. K. Tang. 2007. "Estimating Income Inequality in China Using Grouped Data and the Generalized Beta Distribution." *Review of Income and Wealth* 53(1):127–47.

Dai, E. 2005. Income Inequality in Urban China: A Case Study of Beijing. Working Paper Series Vol. 2005–04, The International Centre for the Study of East Asian Development, Kitakyushu.

Datt, G. 1998. Computational Tools for Poverty Measurement and Analysis. FCND Discussion Paper No. 50, Food Consumption and Nutrition Division, International Food Policy Research Institute, Washington, DC.

Gustafsson, B., and S. Li. 2002. "Income Inequality Within and Across Countries in Rural China 1988 and 1995." *Journal of Development Economics* 69(1):179–204

Hussain, A., and J. Zhuang. 1994. Evolution of Inter-provincial Inequality in China, 1952–1996. Occasional Paper No. 22, Suntory and Toyota International Centres for Economics and Related Disciplines, London School of Economics, London.

Kanbur, R., and X. Zhang. 2005. "Fifty Years of Regional Inequality in China: A Journey Through Central Planning, Reform and Openness." *Review of Development Economics* 9(1):87–106.

Lin, T., J. Zhuang, D. Yarcia, and F. Lin. 2008. "Income Inequality in the People's Republic of China and Its Decomposition: 1990–2004." *Asian Development Review* 25(1,2):119–36.

Liu, H. 2006. "Changing Regional Rural Inequality in China 1980–2002." *Area* 38(4):377–89.

Meng, X. 2004. "Economic Restructuring and Income Inequality in Urban China." *Review of Income and Wealth* 50(3):357–79.

NBSC. Various years. *Provincial Statistical Yearbook*. National Bureau of Statistics of China, Beijing.

385

Ravallion, M., and S. Chen. 2007. "China's (Uneven) Progress against Poverty." *Journal of Development Economics* 82:1–42.

Ravallion, M., S. Chen, and P. Sangraula. 2007. New Evidence on the Urbanization of Global Poverty. World Bank Policy Research Working Paper 4199, The World Bank, Washington, DC.

Wan, G. 2007. Regional Income Inequality in Rural China, 1985–2002. Research Paper No. 2007/05, World Institute for Development Economics Research, United Nations University, Tokyo.

12

Evolution of Income Mobility: People's Republic of China, 1991–2002

Niny Khor and John Pencavel

12.1 Introduction

Although average income has shown remarkable growth in the People's Republic of China (PRC) in the past few decades, income inequality has also increased noticeably in recent years. This increase has been subject to considerable research and concern.[1] However, perhaps a more pertinent question for households and individuals over the longer run is not so much the disparity of income across households in a given year, but rather the degree of income mobility: would they be perpetually stuck in the lower economic rungs or would they have a reasonable chance to scale the economic ladder? The conventional use of annual income to measure income inequality may provide a misleading indicator of enduring income inequality in societies where there is considerable year-to-year income mobility. Income mobility may mitigate the impact of widening income inequality reflected in annual cross-section data over a longer period.

Studies on income mobility in the PRC are still relatively few. One reason is that income mobility can only be measured when panel data on individuals or households are available. An important aspect of this analysis is to use observations on income to determine the degree to which income inequality in a given year is smoothed through income mobility over time (Gottschalk 1997, Fields 2001). Nee (1996), one of the earlier studies on income mobility in the PRC, provides evidence that income mobility among rural households increased in the latter years of 1978–1989. Khor and Pencavel (2006) find that the increase in income inequality among urban individuals during 1990–1995 was accompanied by a level of income mobility higher than observed in the

---

1 See for example, ADB (2007); Chen and Ravallion (2004); Gustafsson and Li (2001); Khan and Riskin (1998 and 2001); Knight and Song (2003 and 2005); Lin, Zhuang, and Yarcia (2008).

United States. Extending their inquiry to household incomes,[2] Khor and Pencavel (2008 and 2009) find considerable income mobility among households in the PRC during the same time periods, with mobility among rural households lower than among urban households.

This chapter examines income mobility among Chinese households by extending the analysis in Khor and Pencavel (2008 and 2009) to the early 2000s, drawing information on household income surveys carried out under the Chinese Household Income Project (CHIP) in 1996 and 2002 (Riskin, Zhao, and Li 2000). A number of findings emerge from this analysis. First, in the early 1990s, the increase in income inequality in the PRC was accompanied by a level of income mobility comparable to other developing countries in transition, and higher than that found in developed countries such as the United States. By the early 2000s, however, while income inequality increased further, income mobility decreased, implying that the probability of being stuck in a relatively lower income level increased for households. Second, the experiences of urban and rural households in income mobility diverged. In the early 1990s, income mobility was higher among urban households than among rural households. Between the early 1990s and early 2000s, income mobility decreased for both, but the decrease was more pronounced for urban households; by the early 2000s, urban and rural households had more or less the same level of income mobility. Third, the Gini coefficients for 3-year average incomes are between 90% and 95% of the corresponding Gini coefficients for single-year incomes, suggesting that income mobility could mitigate the levels of income inequality.

In the rest of this chapter, Section 12.2 describes data sources and construction of variables. Section 12.3 discusses income inequality and mobility among Chinese urban and rural households. Section 12.4 examines correlates of income mobility. Section 12.5 looks at income inequality from a longer-term perspective, and Section 12.6 concludes.

12.2 Data sources and procedures

12.2.1 Chinese Household Income Project

This chapter draws on information from household income surveys in 1996 and 2002 under the Chinese Household Income Project (Riskin, Zhao, and Li 2000).[3] The 1996 survey covers 7,998 rural households

---

[2] This is especially pertinent given the high degree of intrahousehold risk-sharing in developing countries to mitigate idiosyncratic shocks (see Kochar 1995).

[3] The Chinese Household Income Project is a research effort jointly sponsored by the Institute of Economics, the Chinese Academy of Social Sciences, the Asian Development Bank, and the Ford Foundation, with additional support provided by the East Asian

and 6,931 urban households (CHIP2), while the 2002 survey covers 9,200 rural households and 6,835 urban households (CHIP3). The rural sample was drawn from 19 provinces while the urban sample represents households across 11 provinces. To obtain income observations for the same households over time, in each CHIP survey, respondents were asked to provide income information not only for the current year, but also previous years. The analysis in this chapter makes use of data in 1991, 1993, and 1995 from CHIP2, and 1998, 2000, and 2002 from CHIP3, for both urban and rural households. Altogether, the two datasets provide a description of more than a decade of household incomes during a period of remarkable economic growth (Table 12.1).

Table 12.1   Descriptive statistics for households

		CHIP2			CHIP3	
	Year	Urban	Rural	Year	Urban	Rural
Variables (mean)						
Real total income	1991	11,111.99	5,369.72	1998	15,095.65	7,267.67
Real total income	1993	12,753.95	5,875.79	2000	17,410.56	8,517.55
Real total income	1995	13,743.39	6,326.01	2002	21.299.28	9,426.26
Real per adult-equivalent	1991	4,531.38	1,709.88	1998	6,296.33	2,382.19
Real per adult-equivalent	1993	5,184.61	1,864.84	2000	7,266.57	2,826.57
Real per adult-equivalent	1995	5,600.24	2,002.57	2002	8,911.49	3,122.04
Household size	1995	3.13	4.34	2002	3.00	4.11
Household head characteristics						
Female		33.9%	3.8%		32.6%	0.04%
Age		45.96	44.49		47.99	46.33
Member of Communist Party		34.0%	14.9%		38.7%	0.18%
Minority ethnic group		4.2%	5.7%		3.8%	0.02%
Average years of schooling		10.42	5.44		10.71	7.27

CHIP = Chinese Household Income Project.
Note: Real incomes are expressed in 1995 yuan.
Source: Authors' estimates.

This study uses measures of pre-transfer/pre-tax household income inclusive of cash payments, income in kind, state-financed subsidies, and the consumption of agricultural products by households engaged in agricultural production. The investigation into the effects of changes in how income is defined suggests that the principal findings are robust with respect to alternative definitions. All income variables

Institute, Columbia University. Khan and Riskin (2001) provide a careful analysis of initial findings. Fields and Zhang (2007) suggest that these two datasets, along with the China Health and Nutrition Survey (used in Khor and Pencavel 2008) could be useful in answering income mobility questions.

are measured in real terms in 1995 yuan. A major issue in estimating inequality is the quality of income data, such as measurement errors and outliers, often more prevalent at the two tails of the distribution. Following a common practice to mitigate such measurement errors, the data are thus trimmed by omitting the 0.5% of the lowest and 0.5% of the largest values of income in each sample. This tends to reduce the measures of income inequality. But an assessment of the impact of this trimming procedure reveals inconsequential effects on the inferences about inequality and mobility.[4]

12.2.2 Adjustments for household size and composition

Households have different sizes and compositions, and household income is often not independent of these differences. This is shown by the data in Table 12.2 reporting the average number of children (N^C), the average number of adults (N^A), and the average number of members (N^{A+C}) for each income decile of total household income for rural and urban households, respectively.[5] Overall, rural households are bigger than urban households. For both, size increases with income level. Between 1995 and 2002, however, there was a significant decrease in average household size in both urban and rural areas.

To determine whether the results of the analysis in this chapter are independent of alternative ways of comparing households, in addition to using total household income (y_i) with no adjustments for household size and structure, the study computed per capita household income ($y_i/[N^A_i + N^C_i]$) and per adult-equivalent household income defined as $y_i/(N^A_i + \theta.N^C_i)^v$ where θ is the weight attached to children and v is the scale economy parameter. The implications of alternative values of θ and v were examined and the general results do not change noticeably with respect to different values chosen.[6] The estimation of per adult-equivalent household income is based on values of θ at 0.75 and of v at 0.85. These values imply that, for example, in evaluating the value of a given yuan or dollar of household income, a household consisting of five adults and no children is "equivalent" to a household with two adults and four children.

---

4   Cowell, Litchfield, and Mercader-Prats (1999) provide an analysis and application of the practice of trimming the tails of income distribution data. The deletion of outliers is a standard (though by no means universal) procedure in labor economics. Card, Lemieux, and Riddell (2004) is a recent example that uses the Current Population Survey, as Khor and Pencavel (2009) does.

5   Children are defined as household members younger than 18.

6   The authors examined values of θ between 0.50 and unity and values of v between 0.50 and unity. Per capita household income corresponds to $\theta = v = 1$. The results are not sensitive to the choices of θ and v.

Table 12.2   Household size and composition by income decile:
              Rural and urban, 1995 and 2002

	Income deciles										
	1st	2nd	3rd	4th	5th	6th	7th	8th	9th	10th	Mean
CHIP 1995, rural households											
N^C	1.08	1.11	1.25	1.32	1.38	1.41	1.35	1.34	1.39	1.26	1.29
N^A	2.87	2.76	2.72	2.87	2.96	3.08	3.17	3.20	3.27	3.55	3.05
N^{A+C}	3.95	3.87	3.98	4.19	4.34	4.50	4.53	4.54	4.66	4.82	4.34
CHIP 1995, urban households											
N^C	0.72	0.75	0.79	0.75	0.73	0.72	0.69	0.60	0.56	0.56	0.69
N^A	2.10	2.25	2.25	2.32	2.38	2.40	2.47	2.63	2.75	2.92	2.45
N^{A+C}	2.82	3.00	3.04	3.07	3.11	3.12	3.15	3.23	3.31	3.48	3.13
CHIP 2002, rural households											
N^C	0.91	1.07	1.06	1.06	1.14	1.05	1.12	1.11	1.12	0.99	1.06
N^A	2.68	2.80	2.92	2.93	3.02	3.15	3.12	3.24	3.32	3.46	3.07
N^{A+C}	3.59	3.87	3.98	3.99	4.16	4.20	4.24	4.35	4.44	4.45	4.13
CHIP 2002, urban households											
N^C	0.57	0.56	0.52	0.55	0.54	0.49	0.56	0.52	0.46	0.46	0.52
N^A	2.21	2.31	2.39	2.39	2.45	2.47	2.49	2.56	2.78	2.77	2.48
N^{A+C}	2.78	2.87	2.91	2.94	2.99	2.96	3.06	3.08	3.24	3.23	3.01

CHIP = Chinese Household Income Project.
Source: Authors' estimates.

12.3   Income inequality and mobility among rural and urban households

12.3.1   Annual income inequality

Figure 12.1 shows the kernel probability density estimates of rural and urban household incomes in 1991 and 1995; Figure 12.2 shows those for 1998 and 2002. Several important observations emerge from these figures. First the central tendency of urban incomes is above that of rural incomes across all years.[7] In addition, it is also evident from Figure 12.1

---

[7]   This changes little if familiar differences between urban and rural households are held constant in computing rural-urban income disparity. Thus, holding constant indicators of household size and structure, the age of the household head, whether the household head is a Communist Party member, and whether the household head is an ethnic minority, results in the mean rural household income being 41% of the mean urban household income (see Khor and Pencavel 2006). The densities are estimated using the Epanechnikov kernel with a bandwidth of 0.05. The pattern is qualitatively the same in the United States: the rural household income distribution is to the left of that of the urban household. However, the degree of displacement of the rural relative to the urban income distribution in the United States is considerably less than in the PRC (see Khor and Pencavel 2009).

that the annual income distribution among rural households in the PRC is wider than among urban households in 1991 and 1995. In other words, income inequality among urban households is lower than among rural households for these years. However, for 1998 and 2002, the kernel densities of the distribution of household income in urban areas are not manifestly different from those of rural households (see Figure 12.2). This reflects the fact that rural income distribution did not change very much between 1995 and 2002, while the urban distribution became wider and more unequal.

Figure 12.1 Kernel density estimates of the frequency distribution of household income, 1991 and 1995

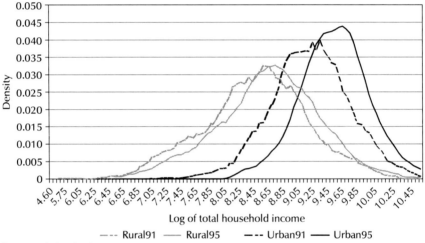

Log of total household income

- - - Rural91 ——— Rural95 — - — Urban91 ——— Urban95

Source: Authors' estimates.

While many studies have documented the rise in income inequality in the PRC in recent years, an interesting trend that emerges from comparing the two rounds of the CHIP data is the difference in the experience of urban and rural households. The visual impression given by the kernel densities is confirmed by the indicators of income inequality in Table 12.3. The lower panels of Table 12.3 indicate that rural income inequality exceeds urban income inequality not only for household income but also for household income adjusted for household size and composition.[8] Although inequality in the PRC as a

---

[8] Using a maximum likelihood method to compute an entire distribution from grouped summary information, Wu and Perloff (2004) calculate Gini coefficients of household income of 0.338 among rural households and 0.221 among urban households in 1995, values that are somewhat lower than those in Table 12.3 but the magnitude of the rural-urban difference is similar to the gap computed in this study. The indicators of income

whole has gone up, in contrast to urban areas, income inequality among rural households actually declined between 1995 and 2002.[9] This pattern does not vary across household income definitions and inequality measurements employed: the Gini coefficient, the ratio of income at the 90th percentile to income at the 10th percentile, the coefficient of variation of incomes, and the standard deviation of the logarithm of incomes. For example, the Gini coefficient for total household income per adult-equivalent of rural households decreased from 0.350 to 0.336, while for urban households it increased from 0.254 to 0.302 (Table 12.3). As a result, the gap in income inequality between urban and rural areas narrowed from the early 1990s to the early 2000s.

Figure 12.2   Kernel density estimates of the frequency distribution of household income, 1998 and 2002

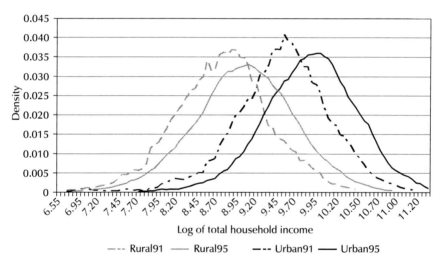

Source: Authors' estimates.

<hr />

inequality in 1995 among rural households in the People's Republic of China in Benjamin, Brandt, and Giles (2005) are slightly lower than those in Table 12.3, for instance, the Gini coefficient for per capita household income of 0.33 versus 0.358.

9   Most studies, on the other hand, find rural inequality in the PRC increasing during the same period. Possible explanations for the differences may include the peculiarities of the sample selection and measurement errors in reported income. However, Khor and Pencavel (2009) performed Monte Carlo simulations drawing independent subsamples from the pooled urban and rural sample of CHIP2, finding robust results on income mobility measures. The source of the decrease in rural inequality for CHIP3 warrants further research.

Table 12.3   Annual household income inequality:
Rural and urban, 1995 and 2002

	Rural households		Urban households	
	1995	2002	1995	2002
Household income				
Gini coefficient	0.354	0.334	0.257	0.303
90th/10th percentile ratio	5.729	4.884	3.203	4.153
Coefficient of variation	0.705	0.658	0.495	0.579
Standard deviation of log income	0.677	0.621	0.464	0.563
Per capita household income				
Gini coefficient	0.358	0.348	0.265	0.311
90th/10th percentile ratio	5.316	5.101	3.389	4.355
Coefficient of variation	0.755	0.716	0.508	0.609
Standard deviation of log income	0.677	0.638	0.480	0.577
Per adult-equivalent household income				
Gini coefficient	0.350	0.336	0.254	0.302
90th/10th percentile ratio	5.200	4.689	3.163	4.146
Coefficient of variation	0.721	0.681	0.485	0.585
Standard deviation of log income	0.665	0.619	0.459	0.560

Source: Authors' estimates.

12.3.2   Indicators of income mobility: Income quintiles

How significant is income mobility among Chinese households? Is there a difference in income mobility between rural households and urban households? A commonly-used method to answer such questions is to construct an income transition matrix. An income transition matrix cross-classifies households into income quintiles from I (the bottom or poorest quintile) to V (the top or richest quintile) in two periods. Each quintile contains the same number of households.[10] Each element of the income transition matrix shows the fraction of households in income quintile j in 1 year that occupies income quintile k in a subsequent year, denoted as p_{jk}.

The two periods examined are 1991 and 1995 using CHIP2 data and 1998 and 2002 using CHIP3 data. The transition matrices, based on per adult-equivalent household income, are presented in Table 12.4 and Table 12.5, with separate panels for urban, rural, and pooled households. A chi-square test of the null hypothesis that the transition matrices are symmetrical cannot be rejected with a high level of confidence.[11]

---

10   To ensure an equal number of households in each quintile, if households at the quintile cutoffs have the same income, they are allocated randomly to the adjacent quintiles.

11   A maximum likelihood test of the symmetry of these transition matrices involves calculating the

According to the top panel of Table 12.4, in rural areas, 61% of those who occupied the poorest fifth of households in 1991 were in the same quintile in 1995, whereas in urban areas, this figure is 48%. These suggest more income mobility in urban than in rural areas. During 1998–2002, however, there was a considerable decrease in quintile movements, especially in urban areas, reversing the initial pattern. While the percentage of rural households in the bottom quintile in 1998 who found themselves remaining in the bottom quintile in 2002 was still 61%, now 68% of urban households in the bottom quintile in 1998 remained there 4 years later.

Table 12.4   Per adult-equivalent household: Income transition matrix, 1991 and 1995

Rural			1995				
			I	II	III	IV	V
	1991	I	0.613	0.213	0.114	0.035	0.024
		II	0.242	0.361	0.236	0.118	0.043
		III	0.090	0.267	0.311	0.235	0.097
		IV	0.037	0.136	0.251	0.338	0.237
		V	0.017	0.022	0.089	0.274	0.599
Urban			1995				
			I	II	III	IV	V
	1991	I	0.478	0.234	0.157	0.101	0.029
		II	0.294	0.256	0.212	0.157	0.081
		III	0.153	0.249	0.263	0.202	0.133
		IV	0.067	0.206	0.229	0.277	0.221
		V	0.007	0.055	0.139	0.263	0.537
Pooled			1995				
			I	II	III	IV	V
	1991	I	0.702	0.242	0.042	0.012	0.002
		II	0.252	0.445	0.208	0.074	0.021
		III	0.040	0.251	0.360	0.244	0.106
		IV	0.005	0.056	0.303	0.379	0.256
		V	0.001	0.006	0.088	0.291	0.614

Summary	Rural	Urban	Pooled
Average quintile move	0.765	0.970	0.600
Immobility ratio	0.444	0.362	0.500
Adjusted immobility ratio	0.835	0.743	0.909

Source: Authors' estimates.

statistic $\Lambda = \sum_{i>j} (p_{ij} - p_{ji})^2 / (p_{ij} + p_{ji})$ which has a chi-square distribution with $q(q-1)/2$ degrees of freedom (with q equal to the number of quantiles). For the transition matrices in Tables 12.5 and 12.6, the symmetry hypothesis cannot be rejected with a very high level of confidence (i.e., calculated p values close to unity). See Bishop, Fienberg, and Holland (1975).

In the case of the richest household quintile, 60% remained in the same rank in 1991 and 1995 among rural households, as compared with 54% among urban households, again suggesting greater income mobility in urban than in rural areas. Between 1998 and 2002, the corresponding figure is 68% for rural households and 74% for urban, another indication that the trends of mobility in urban versus rural areas have reversed. The transition matrices based on per capita household income yield similar inferences.

To facilitate comparisons of income mobility, three summary indicators of income mobility are calculated: (i) the average quintile move; (ii) the fraction who remain in the same quintile, also called the "immobility ratio"; and (iii) an "adjusted immobility ratio", namely, the fraction who remain in the same quintile plus the fraction who move one quintile.[12] The computed values of these three summary indicators of income mobility from 1991 to 1995 and from 1998 to 2002 are reported at the bottom of Table 12.4 and Table 12.5, respectively. From 1991 to 1995, income mobility was higher among urban households than among rural households: the average quintile move is higher, and the immobility ratio and the adjusted immobility ratio are lower for urban households (0.970, 0.362, and 0.743) than for rural households (0.765, 0.444, and 0.835). [13]

---

[12] The average quintile move is defined as $\frac{1}{5}\left\{\sum_{j=1}^{5}\sum_{k=1}^{5}(|j-k|)\,p_{jk}\right\}$. The fraction who remain in the same quintile is defined as $\frac{1}{5}\sum_{j=1}^{5}p_{jj}$. The immobility ratio resembles Shorrocks' (1978) indicator: $(q-T)/(q-1)$ where T is the trace of the matrix and q the number of quantiles (here, 5). As a reference point, if every entry in the transition matrix (that is, if every value for p_{jk}) were one-fifth (sometimes described as "perfect mobility"), the average quintile move would take the value of 1.6, the immobility ratio would be 0.20, and the adjusted immobility ratio would be 0.52. At the other extreme, if the transition matrix were an identity matrix with unit values on the main diagonal and zeros elsewhere (sometimes described as "complete immobility"), the average quintile move would be 0 and the immobility ratio and the adjusted immobility ratio would each be 1. Evidently, the range of values of the average quintile move is from 1.6 to 0, that of the immobility ratio 0.20 to 1, and the adjusted immobility ratio of 0.52 to 1. Higher values of the average quintile move indicate greater mobility and higher values of the immobility ratio and the adjusted immobility ratio indicate less mobility.

[13] In addition to household income, income mobility measures are computed for urban individuals using CHIP3. While the transition matrices are not reported in this chapter, the results show that income mobility for individuals exceeds that of households. For example, average quintile move for urban individuals is 0.688 between 1998 and 2002. During this same period, for urban individuals, the immobility ratio and the adjusted immobility ratio are 0.485 and 0.870 respectively. These measurements show more mobility for individuals regardless of the measures of household income chosen, and suggestive of risk-sharing across households, as earlier surmised. Similar results were found using CHIP2 data (see Khor and Pencavel 2009).

Table 12.5   Per adult-equivalent household: Income transition matrix, 1998 and 2002

Rural		2002				
		I	II	III	IV	V
	I	0.613	0.218	0.098	0.044	0.028
	II	0.230	0.411	0.220	0.096	0.043
1998	III	0.085	0.237	0.375	0.212	0.091
	IV	0.044	0.102	0.236	0.420	0.198
	V	0.028	0.033	0.070	0.227	0.640
Urban		2002				
		I	II	III	IV	V
	I	0.628	0.242	0.080	0.035	0.016
	II	0.258	0.394	0.217	0.091	0.041
1998	III	0.080	0.266	0.349	0.212	0.095
	IV	0.024	0.077	0.287	0.404	0.209
	V	0.011	0.023	0.068	0.259	0.640
Pooled		2002				
		I	II	III	IV	V
	I	0.681	0.228	0.070	0.016	0.005
	II	0.237	0.500	0.203	0.051	0.009
1998	III	0.065	0.225	0.469	0.198	0.042
	IV	0.015	0.041	0.227	0.513	0.204
	V	0.002	0.006	0.030	0.222	0.740

Summary	Rural	Urban	Pooled
Average quintile move	0.717	0.679	0.502
Immobility ratio	0.492	0.483	0.581
Adjusted immobility ratio	0.847	0.873	0.930

Source: Authors' estimates.

From 1998 to 2002, however, concurrent with the increase in income inequality, the level of income mobility for Chinese households decreased. The slowdown in income mobility was particularly marked among urban households, where the percentage of households remaining in the same quintile increased almost a third from 36.2% in the earlier period to 48.3%. These suggest that income distribution was becoming less fluid in more recent years. More strikingly, the urban-rural difference in income mobility is reversed: between 1998 and 2002, the average quintile move was higher for rural than for urban households.

How does income mobility in the PRC compare to other developing countries? Khor and Pencavel (2008) observe that measured income mobility seems to be higher in developing countries than in developed nations: the percentage of those remaining in the same quintile over 5 years is larger than 50% in most developed countries, compared to

397

about 40% in Peru, South Africa, and Viet Nam. In addition, other economies in transition exhibited higher income mobility than the PRC. For example, Hungary and Russia transitioned to a market-based economy at similar times (between 1989 and 1991). In 1994, the annual (one-year) measured average quintile move is 0.572 for Hungary, 0.996 for Russia, and 0.349 for Chinese households between 2001 and 2002.[14]

12.3.3 Indicators of income mobility: Income clusters

The indicators of income mobility discussed in the previous paragraphs are not invariant to the extent of income inequality in a society. In other words, a household experiencing a given increase in income is more likely to cross quintiles in an economy with a narrow income distribution than a household experiencing the same income increase in a society with a wide income distribution. Because the inequality of the annual distribution of income is different in rural areas from that in urban areas, it is useful to consider constructing an income transition matrix defined not on the basis of income quintiles but on alternative classification schemes to ensure that the results are robust. The alternative scheme used here is deviations from median income, or income clusters.

Five income clusters are specified: households with incomes that are (i) less than 0.65 of the median income; (ii) between 0.65 and 0.95 of the median income; (iii) between 0.95 and 1.25 of the median income; (iv) between 1.25 and 1.55 of the median income; and (v) above 1.55 of the median income. Obviously, if the median is the same in the two societies, the income cut-offs will be the same, but they will correspond to different fractions of households when income dispersion is different in the two societies. In a society with a wider income distribution, more households will be in the income cluster of less than 0.65 of the median compared with a society with a narrower income distribution. The results of measuring transitions across income clusters rather than across income quintiles are shown in Table 12.6.

Between 1991 and 1995, there was a tendency for the difference in mobility between rural and urban areas to attenuate. As expected, in rural areas where the income distribution was wider, mobility appears to be greater when measured by movements across income clusters

---

14   The comparison itself might not be very meaningful since the unit of analysis upon which the transition matrices are based varies from country to country, but looking at the trends, year-to-year income mobility in the PRC increased from 1990 to 1994, while it decreased in Russia and Hungary. This increasing trend in income mobility for Chinese individuals and households is evident regardless of whether income mobility is measured using quintiles or deciles.

than measured by movements across income quintiles; and, in urban areas where the annual income distribution is narrower, mobility tends to be less when measured by transitions across income clusters than measured by transitions across income quintiles. However, it remains the case that household income mobility in urban areas exceeded that in rural areas during 1991–1995.

Table 12.6   Summary of income mobility, 1991–1995 and 1998–2002

	Quintiles		Clusters	
	Rural	Urban	Rural	Urban
1991–1995				
Household income				
Average cluster/quintile move	0.748	0.973	0.847	0.906
Immobility ratio	0.455	0.360	0.473	0.371
Adjusted immobility ratio	0.840	0.744	0.802	0.780
Per capita household income				
Average cluster/quintile move	0.757	0.930	0.824	0.886
Immobility ratio	0.442	0.373	0.466	0.384
Adjusted immobility ratio	0.842	0.763	0.813	0.787
Per adult-equivalent household income				
Average cluster/quintile move	0.765	0.970	0.839	0.913
Immobility ratio	0.444	0.362	0.464	0.367
Adjusted immobility ratio	0.835	0.743	0.801	0.777
1998–2002				
Household income				
Average cluster/quintile move	0.709	0.668	0.744	0.704
Immobility ratio	0.499	0.485	0.506	0.492
Adjusted immobility ratio	0.847	0.878	0.837	0.859
Per capita household income				
Average cluster/quintile move	0.693	0.663	0.741	0.691
Immobility ratio	0.502	0.489	0.518	0.498
Adjusted immobility ratio	0.854	0.88	0.838	0.867
Per adult-equivalent household income				
Average cluster/quintile move	0.717	0.679	0.760	0.707
Immobility ratio	0.492	0.483	0.499	0.488
Adjusted immobility ratio	0.847	0.873	0.835	0.862

Source: Authors' estimates.

Between 1998 and 2002, however, income distribution widened for urban households and narrowed slightly in rural areas. As a result, similar to that observed for rural households, mobility for urban households in the period appeared to be greater when measured by movements across income clusters than measured by movements across income quintiles. Perhaps more importantly, these results using income clusters confirm the finding in Section 12.3.2 of a slowdown in income mobility for urban households to the extent that by some measures, income mobility in urban areas in this period was *lower* than in rural areas.

12.3.4 Income mobility: Another robustness test

Another commonly used measure of income mobility is the slope coefficient from a regression of current household income (here, logarithm of *per adult-equivalent income$_{it}$* is used) on lagged household income (logarithm of *per adult-equivalent income$_{it-1}$*).

$$y_{it} = a_t + \beta\, y_{i,t-1} + e_{it} \tag{2}$$

where the error term $e_{it} \sim N(0,1)$. When β is zero, income follows a random walk; a value of unity implies complete immobility of income (current household income is completely predetermined by past income).[15]

Table 12.7 presents these estimated coefficients separately for urban and rural households. The patterns are broadly consistent with earlier observations. Income mobility in urban areas is greater than that in rural areas during 1991–1995, with the slope coefficient of the lagged household income of 0.580 for urban households and 0.716 for rural households. During 1998–2002, the coefficient for urban households increases to 0.737, while that for rural households increases only to 0.745, suggesting a convergence in income mobility between urban and rural households. These results suggest that income mobility declined for both groups, with the decline being more significant for urban households.

Table 12.7   Income mobility: Another robustness test

	$\hat{\beta}^{urban}$	$\hat{\beta}^{rural}$
1991–1995	0.580	0.716
	(0.009)	(0.008)
1998–2002	0.737	0.745
	(0.008)	(0.008)

Note: $\hat{\beta}$ is derived from equation (2).
Source: Authors' estimates.

---

15   Note that here β does not distinguish between upward and downward mobility.

12.4   Correlates of income mobility

The indicators of income mobility in Table 12.6 describe the extent of income mobility across income quintiles over 5 years, but they are silent about those attributes of households associated with upward or downward mobility. Moreover, one might think of income mobility as a property that needs to be measured not simply between one pair of years, but between many pairs of years. Put differently, because there are transitory factors that operate in any given year, the "permanent" probability of upward or downward income mobility is not fully observed using information on only one pair of years. Thus, define π_i as a latent index of permanent income mobility of household i and suppose π_i is a linear function of observed characteristics of household X_i and unobserved factors u_i:

$$\pi_i = \beta X_i + u_i \tag{3}$$

where u_i is assumed to be distributed normally with zero mean and unit variance. This standardized normal assumption will give rise to the estimation of an ordered probit model.

Although permanent income mobility π_i is unobserved, a household's position in the elements of the income transition matrices during 1991–1995 and during 1998–2002 in Tables 12.5 and 12.6 provides information on the permanent mobility of this household. Based on whether a household occupies an element on the diagonal of an income transition matrix or above or below the diagonal, one could define a new variable z_i with the following features: $z_i = 1$ for households occupying a cell below the main diagonal (that is, for households experiencing downward mobility), $z_i = 2$ for households occupying a cell on the main diagonal of the income transition matrix (households experiencing no mobility), and $z_i = 3$ for households in a cell above the main diagonal of the income transition matrix (households experiencing upward mobility).[16] The relation between the observed variable z_i and the latent variable π_i is given as follows:

$$z_i = 1 \ if \ \pi_i \leq 0$$
$$z_i = 2 \ if \ 0 < \pi_i \leq \gamma_1$$
$$z_i = 3 \ if \ \gamma_2 \leq \pi_i$$

where γ_1 and γ_2 are censoring parameters to be estimated jointly with β.

---

[16]   Thus, in the income transition matrix in which each element is defined by $\{j, k\}$ where j denotes the income quintile in the initial year and k the income quintile in the final year, $z_i = 1$ if household i occupies an element where $j > k$, $z_i = 2$ if household i occupies an element where $j = k$, and $z_i = 3$ if household i occupies an element where $j < k$.

The X variables consist of household size and the following characteristics of the head of household: gender, age (entered as a quadratic form), years of schooling, an ethnic minority, and, for the PRC, membership in the Communist Party. The results of the maximum likelihood estimation of the β parameters of equation (3) for the marginal effects are given in Table 12.8.

Table 12.8   Marginal effects from maximum likelihood estimation

	Probability (downward mobility)		Probability (no mobility)		Probability (upward mobility)	
	Rural	**Urban**	**Rural**	**Urban**	**Rural**	**Urban**
CHIP2 (1991–1995)						
Woman = 1	0.010	−0.029**	−0.001	0.001	−0.010	0.027*
	(0.026)	(0.011)	(0.002)	(0.001)	(0.025)	(0.011)
Years of Schooling	−0.0044**	−0.0116**	0.0001	0.0005**	0.0043**	0.0111**
	(0.002)	(0.002)	(0.000)	(0.000)	(0.002)	(0.002)
Minority = 1	0.042*	−0.041**	−0.004	−0.001	−0.038**	0.042*
	(0.023)	(0.024)	(0.003)	(0.002)	(0.019)	(0.026)
Communist = 1	−0.011	−0.048**	0.001	0.001	0.011	0.047**
	(0.014)	(0.011)	(0.002)	(0.001)	(0.014)	(0.011)
Age/10	−0.035	−0.200**	0.001	0.008**	0.034	0.192**
	(0.031)	(0.034)	(0.001)	(0.003)	(0.031)	(0.033)
$(Age)^2/1,000$	0.045	0.199**	−0.001	0.008**	−0.044	−0.190**
	(0.030)	(0.030)	(0.001)	(0.003)	(0.030)	(0.030)
Household size	−0.017**	0.001	0.001*	−0.001	0.017**	−0.001
	(0.004)	(0.006)	(0.001)	(0.001)	(0.004)	(0.006)
CHIP3 (1998–2002)						
Woman = 1	0.029	−0.023**	−0.002	0.000	−0.027	0.022**
	(0.021)	(0.001)	(0.002)	(0.000)	(0.019)	(0.001)
Years of schooling	0.000	−0.009**	0.0001	0.0004**	0.000	0.009**
	(0.002)	(0.001)	(0.0002)	(0.000)	(0.002)	(0.001)
Minority = 1	0.031	−0.047**	−0.002	−0.002	−0.029	0.049*
	(0.032)	(0.021)	(0.004)	(0.003)	(0.028)	(0.026)
Communist = 1	−0.022**	−0.018**	0.000	0.001	0.023**	0.017**
	(0.010)	(0.010)	(0.000)	(0.000)	(0.011)	(0.009)
Age/10	−0.001	0.008**	0.000	−0.0003*	0.001	−0.007**
	(0.003)	(0.003)	(0.000)	(0.000)	(0.003)	(0.003)
$(Age)^2/1,000$	0.003	0.001**	−0.004	0.008*	0.000	0.006**
	(0.004)	(0.000)	(0.005)	(0.003)	(0.000)	(0.003)
Household size	−0.017**	0.009	0.002	0.000	0.011**	−0.001
	(0.004)	(0.006)	(0.003)	(0.000)	(0.004)	(0.006)

CHIP = Chinese Household Income Project.
Note: The standard deviations are in parentheses.

For rural households, it appears that the only significant predictor of income mobility across these two time periods is household size. Each additional member of a rural household lowers the probability of downward mobility by 1.7% across both survey rounds. In the early 1990s, education of the head of household is still associated with lower income mobility: each year of schooling reduces the probability of downward mobility by 0.4%, which is, nonetheless, a much smaller magnitude than the corresponding impact of education for urban households. However, education is no longer a significant deterrent of downward mobility by the second survey round. Between 1998 and 2002, Communist Party membership emerges as a statistically significant predictor of income mobility, lowering the probability of downward income mobility by 2.2%. This effect is in turn stronger than that found for urban households.

The discussion above touches only on downward mobility since, in general, the magnitude of the marginal effect of a given variable on the probability of upward mobility is close to the negative of the effect of the same variable on the probability of downward mobility. This is consistent with the symmetry of the income transition matrices reported earlier. In summary, the marginal effects are not the same for the urban and rural sectors: female-headed households tend to be more upwardly mobile in urban areas than male-headed households, whereas no meaningful gender differences in mobility in rural areas are evident.[17] Ethnic minorities tend to be more downwardly mobile in rural areas than non-minorities but such differences are not apparent in urban areas. While larger households tend to be more upwardly mobile in rural areas, there is no relation between household size and mobility in urban areas. Though the probability of upward income mobility follows an inverted U-shape with respect to age in both rural and urban areas, it reaches a peak at an age for those about 11 years younger in rural than in urban areas. More years of schooling are associated with a greater probability of upward income mobility.

These results highlight the differences in the mobility patterns of rural and urban households. The sharp rural-urban differences in levels of income are exhibited also in rural-urban differences in the factors associated with income mobility. The empirical regularities associated with income mobility among urban households are not the same as the empirical regularities among rural households.

---

[17] Female-headed households in urban areas have a 3% higher probability of upward mobility than male-headed households.

12.5   A long-term perspective on income inequality

What is the relationship between measures of inequality based on income averaged over 3 years and those based on income in a single year? At least for one measure of inequality, namely, the coefficient of variation of incomes, a precise expression may be derived to link these measures. Suppose there are observations on incomes for years r, s, and t. Though it is not difficult to generalize the expression below, suppose the income distribution in each of these 3 years is stationary.[18] Then the coefficient of variation of income averaged over 3 years C may be written as

$$C = C_r * \left(\frac{1}{3}\right)[\, 3 + 2 \, (\rho_{rs} + \rho_{st} + \rho_{rt})]^{\frac{1}{2}} \tag{4}$$

where C_r is the coefficient of variation in income in a single year r and ρ_{jk} is the correlation coefficient between incomes in years j and k. Equation (4) expresses the inequality of income averaged over 3 years as proportional to income inequality in a single year where the factor of proportionality depends on the correlation coefficients in incomes, the values of ρ_{jk}. To understand equation (4), consider limiting cases. Suppose the correlation coefficients ρ_{jk} are all unity, a state of complete income immobility. Then the factor of proportionality is unity and C equals C_r. But as the correlation coefficients fall in value, so C falls relative to C_r. When all values of ρ_{jk} are zero, C is 58% of C_r and it requires negative values of ρ_{jk} to reduce C further as a fraction of C_r.

Table 12.9 presents the values of ρ_{jk} for the PRC. For those correlation coefficients 4 years apart (1991 and 1995), the values are higher among rural households than urban—which is consistent with the earlier result of greater income mobility between 1991 and 1995 in urban areas. For the latter 4 years (1998 and 2002), the correlation coefficients are higher for both rural and urban households, reaffirming the previous findings of a decrease in income mobility.

Using average values for ρ_{jk} in equation (4) leads to the suggestion that the inequality of the averages of 3-year incomes will be lower than the inequality in a single year. Table 12.10 compares measures of inequality in a single year with measures of inequality using incomes averaged over 3 years. For both urban and rural households, the data show a consistent decrease in inequality across various indicators when income is measured over a longer term. For CHIP2, the Gini coefficient for rural households declined from 0.350 in 1995 to 0.332 using longer-term income averages,

---

[18]   Being stationary means it has the same mean and standard deviation. The assumption of a constant standard deviation (σ) is not egregiously at variance with these data. For instance, for total household income, among urban Chinese households, σ for 1993 is 1.10 of σ for 1991, and σ for 1995 is 1.14 of σ for 1991.

while for urban households, it declined from 0.254 to 0.242. For CHIP3, there is a similar decline in income inequality using longer-term income averages. Overall, in line with the conjectures of equation (4), the Gini coefficient for these longer-term averages is between 90% and 95% of the corresponding Gini coefficient for a single year of incomes.

Table 12.9 Correlation coefficients of per adult-equivalent household income for the same households across different years

	CHIP2			CHIP3	
	1993	1995		2000	2002
Rural			Rural		
1991	0.824	0.701	1998	0.851	0.700
1993	1.000	0.765	2000	1.000	0.714
Urban			Urban		
1991	0.877	0.643	1998	0.885	0.729
1993	1.000	0.760	2000	1.000	0.844
Pooled			Pooled		
1991	0.910	0.768	1998	0.919	0.821
1993	1.000	0.846	2000	1.000	0.882

CHIP = Chinese Household Income Project.
Source: Authors' estimates.

Table 12.10 Per adult-equivalent household income inequality using average income

	Rural households		Urban households	
CHIP2	1995	1991, 1993, 1995	1995	1991, 1993, 1995
Gini coefficient	0.350	0.332	0.254	0.242
90th/10th percentile ratio	5.200	4.666	3.163	3.011
Coefficient of variation	0.721	0.669	0.485	0.461
Standard deviation of log income	0.665	0.625	0.459	0.435
CHIP3	2002	1998, 2000, 2002	2002	1998, 2000, 2002
Gini coefficient	0.338	0.306	0.302	0.284
90th/10th percentile ratio	4.898	4.177	4.146	3.811
Coefficient of variation	0.685	0.604	0.585	0.546
Standard deviation of log income	0.621	0.554	0.559	0.524

CHIP = Chinese Household Income Project.
Source: Authors' estimates.

12.6   Conclusions

Annual income data may provide a misleading indicator of enduring income inequality in societies where there is considerable year-to-year income mobility. Using panel data on household incomes, this chapter has looked at changes in the patterns of income mobility in the PRC between the early 1990s and early 2000s, a period when income inequality was rapidly rising. A number of interesting findings emerged from the analysis.

In the early 1990s, income mobility in the PRC was comparable to other developing countries in transition, and higher than that for the United States and several countries belonging to the Organisation for Economic Co-operation and Development. It was also lower among rural households than among urban households.

Between the early 1990s and early 2000s, however, concurrent with rising income inequality, the level of income mobility among Chinese households decreased. The slowdown in income mobility was particularly stark among urban households. The percentage of urban households remaining in the same quintile increased almost a third from 36.2% in the earlier period to 48.3%. For rural households, the percentage of those remaining in the same quintile increased from 44.4% to 49.2%.

Moreover, the acute slowdown in urban income mobility was such that by some measures, the urban-rural difference in income mobility was reversed: between 1998 and 2002, the average quintile move was higher for rural households than for urban households. Furthermore, the adjusted immobility ratio, which measures the percentage of households remaining in the same quintile or nearby, indicates lower income mobility for urban households by the early 2000s.

To put these findings in context, in the early 1990s rural households faced significantly higher income inequality than urban households, while experiencing lower income mobility. The results for the 2000s indicate that this difference between urban and rural households has been reduced significantly. Nonetheless the overall slowing of income mobility implies that the probability of being stuck in a relatively lower level of income has increased for PRC households.

To check the robustness of these findings, this chapter has presented several alternatives for measuring income mobility, apart from indicators calculated using income transition matrices based on income quintiles. It used income clusters constructed using median income as an anchor. Correlations of income over the years where data are available and regressions of current income on lagged income similarly show a higher degree of income mobility in urban than in rural households between 1991 and 1995. This decreased significantly between 1998 and 2002, leading almost to a convergence of measured coefficients for both urban and rural households.

In addition, this chapter has investigated the correlates of income mobility. The results indicate that the factors associated with income mobility of urban households are not the same as those for rural households. Among urban households, several characteristics of the heads of households are found to be positively correlated with upward income mobility, including higher levels of schooling, being a woman, being an ethnic minority, and having Communist Party membership. For rural households, on the other hand, the main correlate associated positively with upward income mobility across years is household size. While the education level of heads of rural households mattered in the 1990s, by the 2000s the only other positive correlate with upward income mobility for rural households was Communist Party membership.

These issues have useful implications for policy. First, policies targeted toward inclusive growth ought to take into account longer-term income. A focus on annual income may overstate the degree of income inequality faced by individuals and households. In addition, means-tested programs ought to take into consideration not just individual income, but also household income. Indeed, the data show that the degree of income mobility is smaller for households than for individuals, indicative of risk-sharing within households. Thirdly, the twin trends of increasing income inequality and decreasing income mobility in the PRC may be exacerbated by recent policies that accentuate and perpetuate the urban-rural divide, such as the privatization of urban public housing.

References

ADB. 2007. "Inequality in Asia." In *Key Indicators 2007*. Asian Development Bank, Manila.

Benjamin, D., L. Brandt, and J. Giles. 2005. "The Evolution of Income Inequality in Rural China." *Economic Development and Cultural Change* 53(4):769–824.

Bishop, Y., S. Fienberg, and P. Holland. 1975. *Discrete Multivariate Analysis: Theory and Practice*. Cambridge, MA: MIT Press.

Card, D., T. Lemieux, and C. Riddell. 2004. "Unionization and Wage Inequality: A Comparative Study of the U.S., the U.K., and Canada." NBER Working Paper No. 9473. National Bureau of Economic Research.

Chen, S., and M. Ravallion. 2004. "China's (Uneven) Progress Against Poverty." World Bank Policy Research Working Paper No. 3408.

Cowell, F., J. Litchfield, and M. Mercader-Prats. 1999. "Income Inequality Comparisons with Dirty Data: The UK and Spain during the 1980s." London School of Economics DARP Working Paper No. 45.

Fields, G. 2001. *Distribution and Development: A New Look at the Developing World*. Cambridge: The MIT Press.

Fields, G., and S. Zhang. 2007. "Income Mobility in China: Main Questions, Existing Evidence, and Proposed Studies." Available: http:// digitalcommons.ilr.cornell.edu/workingpapers/70/, downloaded 15 September 2009.

Gottschalk, P. 1997. "Inequality, Income Growth and Mobility: The Basic Facts." *The Journal of Economic Perspectives* 11(2):21–40.

Gustafsson, B., and S. Li. 2001. "The Anatomy of Rising Earnings Inequality in Urban China." *Journal of Comparative Economics* 29:118–35.

Khan, A., and C. Riskin. 1998. "Income and Inequality in China: Composition, Distribution and Growth of Household Income, 1988 to 1995." *The China Quarterly* 154:221–53.

_____. 2001. *Inequality and Poverty in China in the Age of Globalization*. New York: Oxford University Press.

Khor, N., and J. Pencavel. 2006. "Income Mobility of Individuals in China and the United States." *Economics of Transition* 14(3):417–58.

_____. 2008. "Measuring Income Mobility, Income Inequality, and Social Welfare for Households of the People's Republic of China." ADB Working Paper Series No. 145. Asian Development Bank, Manila.

_____. 2009. "Income Inequality, Income Mobility, and Social Welfare for Urban and Rural Households of China and the United States." *Research in Labor Economics* (forthcoming).

Knight, J., and L. Song. 2003. "Increasing Urban Wage Inequality in China: Extent, Elements and Evaluation." *Economics of Transition* 11(4):597–619.

_____. 2005. *Towards a Labour Market in China*. Oxford: Oxford University Press.

Kochar, A. 1995. "Explaining Household Vulnerability to Idiosyncratic Income Shocks." *The American Economic Review* 85(2):179–64.

Lin, T., J. Zhuang, and D. Yarcia. 2008. "China's Income Inequality at the Provincial Level: Trends, Drivers, and Impacts." Paper presented at the 11th International Convention of the East Asian Economic Association, 15–16 November 2008, Manila.

Nee, V. 1996. " The Emergence of a Market Society: Changing Mechanisms of Stratification in China." *American Journal of Sociology* 100: 908–949.

Riskin, C., R. Zhao, and S. Li. 2000. "Chinese Household Income Project, 1995." [computer file], ICPSR version, Amherst, MA, University of Massachusetts, Political Economy Research Institute [producer], 2000. Inter-university Consortium for Political and Social Research [distributor], Ann Arbor, Michigan, November.

Shorrocks, A. F. 1978. "The Measurement of Mobility." *Econometrica* 46(5):1013–24.

13

Occupational Segregation and Gender Discrimination in Labor Markets: Thailand and Viet Nam

Hyun H. Son[1]

13.1 Introduction

There is a deeply unequal sharing of the burdens of life between women and men in most parts of the world. While gender inequality can take many different forms,[2] this chapter focuses on gender inequality in earnings in the labor market—an important dimension of promoting broad-based or inclusive growth (Behrman and Zhang 1995)—in the context of Thailand and Viet Nam.

The gender pay gap is universal, but its size varies by country. This chapter analyzes the disparity in terms of three factors: individual characteristics, occupational segregation, and gender discrimination in the labor market. Of the many studies that have attempted to explain such earnings disparity, Oaxaca (1973) pioneered a decomposition methodology that explains the male-female wage gap by two components: one shows the difference due to observable male and female characteristics and the other captures the difference in the earnings' generating function, and is sometimes interpreted as a measure of discrimination. Other prominent studies[3] on the gender

---

1   This chapter derives from Son (2007). The author would like to acknowledge helpful and insightful comments from Professors Nanak Kakwani and Jacques Silber on an earlier draft, as well as Juzhong Zhuang and Jane Carangal-San Jose for their suggestions and comments.

2   Sen (2001) argues that gender inequality is not a homogeneous phenomenon, but a collection of disparate and interlinked problems. He discusses different types of disparity, including mortality inequality, natality inequality, basic facility inequality, special opportunity inequality, professional inequality, and household inequality.

3   There are also studies by Blinder (1973) and Deutsch and Silber (2007) in this area. While Blinder takes a framework of analysis similar to Oaxaca, Deutsch and Silber provide an extension of Oaxaca's approach. The method proposed by Deutsch and Silber is based on two techniques: (i) the breakdown of inequality by population subgroups; and (ii) Mincerian earnings functions to derive a decomposition of wage disparity into differences in human capital, differences in rates of return, and differences in unobservable characteristics.

differential in earnings include: Cotton (1988), which analyzed costs and benefits of discrimination; Neumark (1988), which proposed an alternative procedure from a particular Beckerian discrimination model; and Oaxaca and Ransom (1988 and 1994), which proposed a procedure to estimate the nondiscriminatory wage structure in analyzing union/non-union wage differentials.

This chapter proposes a decomposition methodology to explain the welfare disparity between male and female workers in terms of occupational segregation by gender, discrimination within occupations, and inequality in earnings. Based on Atkinson's welfare function, the proposed decomposition method takes into account the sensitivity of inequality within each occupational group as well as between male and female workers.[4] This enables the investigation of the extent of gender disparity in welfare and earnings between the not-so-poor and the ultra-poor.

This chapter also proposes an approach to adjusting per capita earnings by a host of personal and job characteristics, which are generally considered major controlling factors in determining individual earnings in the labor market. These factors include, among others, years of education, weekly hours worked, work experience, race, and geographical location. This adjustment differs from a Mincerian type of earnings regression. Moreover, this chapter isolates the net impact of each controlling factor on segregation, discrimination, and inequality in earnings, using the so-called Shapley decomposition method (Shapley 1953), which looks at all possible elimination sequences.

Section 13.2 delineates a welfare measure that captures gender disparity in earnings. Section 13.3 derives a new decomposition methodology that explains gender welfare disparity in terms of segregation, discrimination, and inequality in earnings. Section 13.4 describes a new method to adjust welfare by a host of personal and job characteristics. Section 13.5 looks into capturing the net impact of personal and job characteristics on gender welfare disparity. Section 13.6 is devoted to empirical analysis of labor markets in Thailand and Viet Nam. Section 13.7 concludes.

13.2   Social welfare

To derive a welfare measure, it is assumed that social welfare is the sum of individual utilities that are functions of their respective incomes, and that every individual has the same utility function. The social welfare function based on these assumptions will be additive, separable, and symmetric.

---

[4]   Although Atkinson's welfare function is used to derive an inequality component for this study, other welfare functions and hence other inequality measures may also be used.

Suppose x is the labor market earnings of an individual. It is assumed that x is a random variable with probability density function $f(x)$. If $u(x)$ is the individual utility function, which is increasing in x, i.e., $u'(x) > 0$, and concave, i.e., $u''(x) < 0$, then the average welfare of society is defined as:

$$W = \int_0^\infty u(x)f(x)\,dx \tag{1}$$

Atkinson (1970) proposed a welfare measure that is invariant with respect to any positive linear transformation of individual utilities. It is derived from the concept of the equally distributed equivalent level of income x^* which, if received by every individual, would result in the same level of social welfare as the present distribution, that is,

$$u(x^*) = \int_0^\infty u(x)f(x)\,dx \tag{2}$$

where x^* is the per person welfare measure of society and is a measure of social welfare in terms of income.

The inequality measure proposed by Atkinson is:

$$A = 1 - \frac{x^*}{\mu} \tag{3}$$

where μ, given by:

$$\mu = \int_0^\infty xf(x)\,dx \tag{4}$$

is the mean income of the society. Using equation (3), social welfare x^* can be written as:

$$x^* = \mu\,(1-A) \tag{5}$$

which shows that social welfare depends on two factors: mean income and inequality in the society.

If the inequality measure A is to be scale-independent, the utility function must be homothetic. A class of homothetic utility functions is given by:

$$u(x) = \alpha + \beta \frac{x^{1-\varepsilon}}{1-\varepsilon} \qquad\qquad \varepsilon \neq 1$$

$$= \alpha + \beta \ln(x) \qquad\qquad \varepsilon = 1 \tag{6}$$

where $\beta > 0$ and α and β are any two constants. Note that ε is a measure of the degree of inequality aversion. As ε rises, greater weight is given to transfers at the lower end of the income distribution and less weight to transfers at the top. If $\varepsilon = 0$, it reflects an inequality-neutral attitude, in which case social welfare is measured by the mean income of society. The larger the value of ε, the greater is the concern of the society about inequality. When ε approaches infinity, the society becomes most concerned about the poorest person. In this case, social welfare is measured by the income of the poorest person in society. Thus, ε is a measure of society's concern about inequality, which is generally not estimated from the data. This study assumes two alternative values of ε, 1 and 2.

Substituting (6) into (2) gives the average welfare level of society as:

$$x^* = \left[\int_0^\infty x^{1-\varepsilon} f(x)\, dx \right]^{\frac{1}{(1-\varepsilon)}} \qquad \varepsilon \neq 1$$

$$= \exp \left[\int_0^\infty \ln(x) f(x)\, dx \right] \qquad \varepsilon = 1 \qquad (7)$$

where exp stands for exponential. Note that the social welfare measure x^* is invariant to any positive linear transformation of the utility function. The social welfare measure x^* can be defined for males as:

$$x_m^* = \left[\int_0^\infty x^{1-\varepsilon} f_m(x)\, dx \right]^{\frac{1}{(1-\varepsilon)}} \qquad \varepsilon \neq 1$$

$$= \exp \left[\int_0^\infty \ln(x) f_m(x)\, dx \right] \qquad \varepsilon = 1 \qquad (8)$$

where $f_m(x)$ is the density function for males. Similarly, the social welfare function for females can be defined as:

$$x_f^* = \left[\int_0^\infty x^{1-\varepsilon} f_f(x)\, dx \right]^{\frac{1}{(1-\varepsilon)}} \qquad \varepsilon \neq 1$$

$$= \exp \left[\int_0^\infty \ln(x) f_f(x)\, dx \right] \qquad \varepsilon = 1 \qquad (9)$$

where $f_f(x)$ is the density function for females.

Substituting x^* into equation (3) gives Atkinson's measure of inequality for different values of the aversion parameter ε. Thus, Atkinson's inequality measure among males and females can be written as:

$$A_m = 1 - \frac{x_m^*}{\mu_m}$$

and

$$A_f = 1 - \frac{x_f^*}{\mu_f} \qquad (10)$$

where μ_m and μ_f are the mean earnings of male and female workers, respectively.

13.3 Decomposition methodology: Segregation, discrimination, and inequality

This study defines an index of welfare disparity between males and females as:

$$\pi = 100 \times \left[ln\ (x_m^*) - ln\ (x_f^*) \right] \tag{11}$$

which is the welfare of male workers over female workers, expressed as a percentage. If, for instance, $\pi = 110$, male workers enjoy 10% greater welfare compared to female workers. Combining equation (10) and equation (11):

$$\pi = 100 \times \left[ln\ (\mu_m) - ln\ (\mu_f) \right] + 100 \times \left[ln\ (1-A_m) - ln\ (1-A_f) \right] \tag{12}$$

where the first term in equation (12) measures the disparity in the mean earnings of males and females and the second term measures the disparity that is caused by the difference in inequality in earnings between males and females. If the second term is positive (negative), this implies that inequality in earnings is greater (less) within the female group than within the male group.

The first term in equation (12) can be further decomposed into two components: occupational segregation and labor market discrimination (within occupation). Suppose there are k mutually exclusive occupations or industries in an economy. The ith occupation has F_i female labor force and M_i male labor force such that $\sum_{i=1}^{k} F_i = F$ and $\sum_{i=1}^{k} M_i = M$, where F and M are the total number of female and male workers in the economy, respectively.

Let $\delta_{fi} = F_i/F$ and $\delta_{mi} = M_i/M$, where δ_{fi} and δ_{mi} refer to the proportion of female and male workers in occupation i. Then, $\sum_{i=1}^{k} \delta_{fi} = 1$ and $\sum_{i=1}^{k} \delta_{mi} = 1$ must always hold. The mean male and female earnings can be written as:

$$\mu_m = \sum_{i=1}^{k} \delta_{mi} \mu_{mi} \tag{13}$$

and

$$\mu_f = \sum_{i=1}^{k} \delta_{fi} \mu_{fi} \tag{14}$$

where μ_{mi} is the mean earnings of males in the ith occupation and similarly, μ_{fi} is the mean earnings of females in the ith occupation. The difference between μ_{mi} and μ_{fi} indicates the gender discrimination in the ith occupation, whereas the difference between δ_{mi} and δ_{fi} captures the gender segregation in the ith occupation. The discrimination and segregation over all occupations can be aggregated to obtain overall measures of discrimination and segregation in the labor market. This is done by using the Shapley decomposition method, as follows:

$$100\times\left[\ln(\mu_m)-\ln(\mu_f)\right]=100\times\left[\ln\left(\sum_{i=1}^{k}\delta_{fi}\mu_{mi}\right)-\ln\left(\sum_{i=1}^{k}\delta_{fi}\mu_{fi}\right)+\ln\left(\sum_{i=1}^{k}\delta_{mi}\mu_{mi}\right)-\ln\left(\sum_{i=1}^{k}\delta_{mi}\mu_{fi}\right)\right]$$

$$+100\times\left[\ln\left(\sum_{i=1}^{k}\delta_{mi}\mu_{fi}\right)-\ln\left(\sum_{i=1}^{k}\delta_{fi}\mu_{fi}\right)+\ln\left(\sum_{i=1}^{k}\delta_{mi}\mu_{mi}\right)-\ln\left(\sum_{i=1}^{k}\delta_{fi}\mu_{mi}\right)\right]$$

$$\tag{15}$$

where the first term in the right-hand side measures the contribution of differences in the mean earnings of males and females in different occupations to the total disparity in the mean earnings. This term is an overall measure of discrimination in the labor market.[5] On the other hand, the second term in the right-hand side measures the contribution of differences in the proportion of male and female workers in different occupations, which is an overall measure of occupational segregation by gender. Thus, combining (12) and (15) gives

$$\pi = D + S + A \tag{16}$$

which shows that the welfare disparity between male and female workers can be written as the sum of three components:

(i) Discrimination in the labor market (D), which is measured by the first term in the right-hand side of equation (15). $D = 0$ if the mean earnings of male and female workers are equal in every occupation from i to k.

(ii) Segregation in the labor market (S), which is measured by the second term in the right-hand side of equation (15). $S = 0$ if the proportion of male workers is equal to that of females for every occupation from i to k.

(iii) Difference in inequality of earnings between male and female groups (A), which is measured by the second term in the

---

5 In comparing the Blinder-Oaxaca (B-O) approach and this study's approach to understand this discrimination component, earnings may be assumed to depend on (i) individual characteristics (often labeled human capital variables), (ii) rates of return on these human capital characteristics (often labeled discrimination component), and (iii) unobservable factors. The B-O approach gets rid of (iii) by working only with the means of the two groups so that the gender earnings differential depends only on (i) and (ii). This study's approach gets rid of (i) by proposing a new method that equalizes all the individual characteristics.

right-hand side of equation (12). $A = 0$ if inequality of earnings among males (A_m) is equal to inequality of earnings among females (A_f).

13.4 Adjusting welfare by individual characteristics

Males and females possess different attributes in education, age, geographical location, ethnicity, and so forth. These attributes affect welfare disparity and its components in various ways, and it is important to control them before measuring the true magnitude of male-female earnings disparity. While this can be generally achieved by a regression model, this chapter proposes an alternative methodology to adjust individual earnings by the various attributes of male and female workers. This methodology is delineated as follows.

Let X be a $n \times 1$ vector of earnings for both males and females. Suppose there are four attributes that largely determine individual earnings: educational level (E); years of work experience (G); geographical location (regions/provinces and urban/rural areas, R); and ethnic group (W). The vector X will change as one eliminates the differences in earnings due to these four attributes. The following illustrates adjustments with respect to education only.

Suppose there are e_k educational groups in the population and μ_j^e is the mean earnings of all individuals in the jth education group, where j varies from 1 to e_k. Each education group has different mean earnings. Thus, the idea here is to construct a new vector of earnings, which eliminates the difference in the mean earnings attributed to education, as follows:

$$\overline{X}(E) = \frac{X\mu}{\mu_j^e} \tag{17}$$

If the vector $\overline{X}(E)$ is partitioned into e_k educational groups, the mean earnings of each partitioned educational group will have the same mean equal to μ. The disparity index π and its components using the vector $\overline{X}(E)$ can then be calculated. Thus, $\pi(\overline{X}[E])$ will be the male-female welfare disparity index when the variation in earnings due to education is controlled. This methodology can be used for controlling any number of attributes.

This study has controlled for three attributes in the cases of Thailand and Viet Nam, namely education, work experience, and geographical location. Thus, $\pi(\overline{X}[E,G,R])$ is the male-female disparity index when the three attributes are simultaneously controlled. Any male-female disparities that remain after controlling for these three attributes signify the unexplained factors.

It should be noted that due to complex interactions among different attributes, $\pi(\overline{X}[E,G,R])$ will not be equal to the sum of $\pi(\overline{X}[E])$, $\pi(\overline{X}[G])$, and $\pi(\overline{X}[R])$.

13.5 Net effect of individual characteristics on gender welfare disparity

This section discusses a methodology to separate or isolate the impact of individual attributes on the male-female disparity index. The methodology provides answers to questions such as: What is the impact of education on occupational segregation by gender? How does education affect labor market discrimination against or in favor of females? Is discrimination against females different between rural and urban areas? Does ethnicity increase or decrease segregation and discrimination?

Given that $\pi(X)$ is the male-female disparity index (before controlling for a host of personal and job characteristics), and $\pi(\overline{X}[E])$ is the disparity index when the earnings differences due to education are eliminated, $\pi(X) - \pi(\overline{X}[E])$ should measure the impact of education on male-female disparity. Similarly, one can capture the effects of other attributes such as work experience and geographical location. These are the total effects of each attribute. The major difficulty with this methodology stems from the fact that individual attributes interact with one another. This requires separating and isolating the net effect of individual attributes on the total male-female earnings disparity.

The total effect of all three attributes can be written as:

$$\pi(X) - \pi(\overline{X}[E,G,R]) = \theta(E) + \theta(G) + \theta(R) \qquad (18)$$

where $\theta(E)$ is the net effect of education which, as discussed earlier, is not equal to the total effect of education given by $\pi(X) - \pi(\overline{X}[E])$. To compute the net effects requires taking into account all possible interactions, using the Shapley decomposition method.

13.6 Empirical analysis

13.6.1 Data description

This study uses the "employment" module from the 2002 Viet Nam Living Standards Survey (VLSS) and the 2004 labor force surveys for Thailand. The data selected are wage and salary earners aged 15–65, both male and female. From this process, the total sample size was 566,833 workers for

Thailand and 39,555 for Viet Nam. The working population was divided into 28 occupations for Thailand and 58 for Viet Nam. In addition, wage or salary is defined to include monetary wage earned from employment and fringe benefits such as holiday allowance, social subsidies (e.g., sick leave, maternity leave, etc.), business trip allowances, and other benefits.

13.6.2   Results: Decomposition analysis

The methodology developed in Section 13.3—to explain the disparity in welfare between male and female workers in terms of the three components of occupational segregation, gender discrimination, and inequality in earnings—is applied to data for the two countries, and the results are presented in Table 13.1.

Table 13.1   Decomposition of total disparity in welfare between male and female workers

Aversion parameter	Total disparity	Segregation	Discrimination	Inequality
		Unadjusted		
Thailand				
$\varepsilon = 1$	8.29	−7.24	13.53	2.00
$\varepsilon = 2$	11.34	−7.24	13.53	5.06
Viet Nam				
$\varepsilon = 1$	17.90	−1.93	14.36	5.47
$\varepsilon = 2$	33.80	−1.93	14.36	21.37
	Adjusted for education, work experience, and geographical location			
Thailand				
$\varepsilon = 1$	15.20	3.42	12.16	−0.38
$\varepsilon = 2$	14.78	3.42	12.16	−0.80
Viet Nam				
$\varepsilon = 1$	16.84	0.82	13.62	2.39
$\varepsilon = 2$	29.88	0.82	13.62	15.44

ε = inequality aversion parameter.
Source: Author's calculations.

Viet Nam shows a far greater disparity in welfare between male and female workers than Thailand. For instance, the average welfare of males is 17.90% higher than that of females in Viet Nam, and 8.29% higher in Thailand. This result holds for the value of the inequality aversion parameter (discussed in Section 13.2) equal to unity. Gender welfare disparity tends to increase with the value of the inequality aversion parameter. In the case of Viet Nam, the disparity escalates by almost two-fold when the aversion parameter changes from 1 to 2. This suggests, moreover, that gender welfare disparity is far greater among the ultra-poor compared to the not-so-poor in the labor market.

Using the proposed decomposition methodology, discrimination appears to be the dominant factor explaining welfare disparity. As expected, the discrimination component leads to a widening gap between male and female welfare. These findings are true for both countries.

In terms of occupational segregation by gender, a reduction in the gender disparity of earnings is observed for the two countries. In particular, the impact of the segregation component on total welfare disparity is far greater in Thailand than in Viet Nam. More importantly, the strong effect of segregation in Thailand tends to offset the impact of discrimination on the gender welfare gap.

Segregation is related to the extent to which it is possible to distinguish between male- and female-intensive occupations. Accordingly, the degree of segregation, which depends upon the shape of the distribution across occupations based on the gender ratio, is examined. The gender ratio here is defined as the difference between the proportion of male workers and of female workers engaged in each of the 28 occupations for Thailand and 58 for Viet Nam (see Appendix Tables A13.1 and A13.2).

In Thailand, female workers are largely in clerical and service occupations, or professions such as education, life science, and health; male workers are heavily employed in the extraction and building trades, as drivers and in mobile-plant operations. Appendix Table A13.1 also suggests that elementary jobs (e.g., crafts and related trade, machine assembly, sales and services) as well as teaching appear to be particularly female-intensive in Thailand. However, these occupations differ substantially in monthly wage. For instance, the monthly wage for a female worker in the crafts and related trading occupation is 1,777 baht, far below the average monthly wage of 3,774 baht. By contrast, the monthly wage for a teaching associate job is 6,920 baht.

Moreover, Appendix Table A13.1 clearly depicts that quite a significant proportion of females are working in relatively high-paying professions in Thailand such as teaching, life science, and health. This finding explains why occupational segregation by gender contributes to a fall in total disparity in welfare between males and females in Thailand. In Viet Nam, female workers tend to concentrate in industries such as fur, leather, textiles, and education and training.

The gender welfare disparity can also be explained by the difference in inequality in earnings between males and females. In Table 13.1, the decomposition results show that for both countries the inequality component results in an increase in total disparity in welfare between males and females. This implies that welfare inequality among female workers is greater than among male workers. This claim is substantiated by the results in Table 13.2, which presents inequality of welfare using

Atkinson's measure.[6] What is interesting is that after adjusting for a host of personal and job characteristics, inequality remains higher among female workers than male workers in Viet Nam. In Thailand, the earnings disparity between males and females declines when attributes such as education, work experience, and geographical location are considered. This is also reflected in the decomposition results in Table 13.1: for Thailand, inequality reduces gender welfare disparity after adjusting for the three attributes.

Table 13.1 also indicates that gender welfare disparity does not decline dramatically after controlling for the three attributes. While the disparity declines after the adjustment in Viet Nam, it widens in Thailand. This suggests that the gender welfare gap cannot be fully explained, even after taking into account differences in personal and job characteristics across occupations.

Table 13.2   Welfare inequality based on Atkinson's measure

Aversion parameter	Total	Males	Females
		Unadjusted	
Thailand			
$\varepsilon = 1$	36.82	36.24	37.50
$\varepsilon = 2$	54.02	52.90	55.22
Viet Nam			
$\varepsilon = 1$	37.76	36.38	39.76
$\varepsilon = 2$	67.62	64.42	71.26
	Adjusted for education, work experience, and geographical location		
Thailand			
$\varepsilon = 1$	17.02	16.90	16.59
$\varepsilon = 2$	29.96	29.80	29.24
Viet Nam			
$\varepsilon = 1$	30.81	30.04	31.69
$\varepsilon = 2$	60.24	57.36	63.46

ε = inequality aversion parameter.
Source: Author's calculations.

13.6.3   Results: Net effects of individual attributes based on the Shapley decomposition method

This section discusses the empirical results of the proposed methodology to separate the impact of individual attributes on male-female disparity in welfare (see Section 13.5).

[6]   See also Appendix Tables A13.3 and A13.4 showing the decomposition results for all possible adjustments.

Table 13.3 shows that the net effects of education, work experience, and regions and urban/rural areas can explain 6.92% of the welfare disparity between male and female workers in Thailand. While all three attributes appear to play a significant role in explaining the disparity, education is the major contributor to reducing gender disparity, suggesting that Thailand's female workers are more educated. A greater proportion of female workers is found to have been educated at the university level (Appendix Figure A13.1). Among the ultra-poor in the labor market, the average level of education also appears to be higher among females than among males (see Table 13.3). Moreover, the results indicate that work experience increases gender disparity in welfare, while location reduces it. These suggest that female workers in Thailand tend to have less years of work experience than male workers, and that females are more likely to live in richer regions such as Bangkok and the central region.

Table 13.3   Thailand: Contribution of individual attributes to total disparity (%)

Contribution by	Total disparity	Segregation	Discrimination	Inequality
Education				
$\varepsilon = 1$	−7.04	−10.63	−0.44	4.04
$\varepsilon = 2$	−2.23	−10.63	−0.44	8.85
Work experience				
$\varepsilon = 1$	4.05	0.25	5.44	−1.63
$\varepsilon = 2$	1.89	0.25	5.44	−3.79
Geographical location				
$\varepsilon = 1$	−3.93	−0.28	−3.62	−0.03
$\varepsilon = 2$	−3.11	−0.28	−3.62	0.79
Total				
$\varepsilon = 1$	−6.92	−10.66	1.37	2.38
$\varepsilon = 2$	−3.44	−10.66	1.37	5.85

ε = inequality aversion parameter.
Source: Author's calculations.

Education plays a critical role in explaining segregation and earnings inequality in Thailand. The results in Table 13.3 indicate that education reduces segregation and increases the difference in inequality in earnings between male and female workers. In explaining discrimination, location and work experience are shown to be important contributors. While location contributes to a reduction in discrimination against female workers, work experience increases discrimination. More importantly, the results suggest that in Thailand, work experience is more important than education and location in reducing discrimination and thus in closing the male-female earnings gap. Women are more likely to have worked part-time rather than full-time. As women have increased their labor force participation over time, their accumulated work experience has also grown.

Based on data on work experience in the Panel Survey of Income Dynamics (PSID) in Thailand, Blau and Kahn (1997) showed that changes in accumulated work experience have been far larger than those in education, resulting in a much larger share of the decline in male-female wages. A number of recent studies have explored the contribution of gender differences in actual work experience and labor force interruptions to the gender earnings gap (Light and Ureta 1995, Kim and Polachek 1994). These studies confirm that differences between men and women in labor market participation are important causes of the gender pay gap.

As in Thailand, education is a major contributor to total gender disparity in welfare in Viet Nam (Table 13.4). Education reduces total gender disparity by 1.84%, suggesting that a greater proportion of female wage earners are concentrated at higher educational levels such as junior college diploma and masters (Appendix Figure A13.2). Given the concern with the ultra-poor, the net contribution of education to total gender disparity in welfare increases to 2.12%. This suggests that among the ultra-poor, female workers have a lower level of education than their counterparts. In Viet Nam, over 25% of female workers have no formal education, compared to slightly over 20% of male workers. (Appendix Figure A13.2).

Table 13.4   Viet Nam: Contribution of individual attributes to total disparity (%)

Contribution by	Total disparity	Segregation	Discrimination	Inequality
Education				
ε = 1	−1.84	−3.80	−1.17	3.13
ε = 2	2.12	−3.80	−1.17	7.09
Work experience				
ε = 1	2.92	1.03	1.89	−0.01
ε = 2	1.74	1.03	1.89	−1.19
Geographical location				
ε = 1	−0.01	0.03	0.01	−0.05
ε = 2	0.07	0.03	0.01	0.03
Total				
ε = 1	1.07	−2.74	0.74	3.08
ε = 2	3.92	−2.74	0.74	5.93

ε = inequality aversion parameter.
Source: Author's calculations.

Similar to Thailand, work experience can significantly impact total gender disparity in welfare in Viet Nam. Work experience increases gender disparity by 2.92% and 1.74% for the aversion parameters equal to 1 and 2, respectively. This implies that female wage earners have less work experience than males. It is also found that whereas female workers are concentrated in the younger age cohort (15–30), male workers are clustered at 30–65.

Overall, the gender disparity in welfare of 1.07% in Viet Nam is accounted for by education, work experience, and geographical location. Disparity is largely explained by years of work experience, which is less for female workers. The net effects of the three attributes on the gender welfare gap increased sharply to 3.92% in the case of the ultra-poor. But the gender welfare gap is mainly due to education in this case. Moreover, in Viet Nam, occupational segregation by gender reduces welfare disparity between males and females, while both gender discrimination and earnings inequality increase the disparity. In explaining segregation, discrimination, and inequality, two attributes—education and experience—stand out as main contributors.

The above findings suggest that factors such as hours of work, education, work experience, and location cannot fully capture the gender disparity in earnings and welfare. There are other factors that could account for the gap in male-female earnings and welfare.

First, measures of the nature and type of job-related tasks have a significant relationship to the gender pay gap (Hersch 1991, Macpherson and Hirsch 1995). Chauvin and Ash (1994) find that among white collar professional workers, much of the gender pay gap is associated with differences in the share of base versus contingent pay on the jobs in which women and men are engaged. Similarly, although industries (e.g., cultivation, heavy industry, construction) can be classified as labor-intensive, the intensity of labor in heavy industry and construction is far greater than in cultivation. This explains why women barely work in heavy industry and construction, and are mostly employed in the agricultural sector.

Second, employer preference may also account for the gender pay gap. In economic downturns, more women than men are likely to be laid off as redundant workers (Croll 1998). Faced with the pressure of product and market competition, enterprises may prefer to recruit or retain males rather than shoulder the fringe benefits or costs associated with the reproductive time of females. For instance, industries (e.g., airlines, garment, and other manufacturing) in Viet Nam have a regulation forbidding the birth of a child in the first 2 years of employment (Long et al. 2000).

Third, cultural factors can play a role in explaining the gender pay gap. Hersch and Stratton (1997) examined whether the greater time and energy that women devote to housework may influence their productivity in the labor market, as well as their preferences for particular types of employment. They found that hours devoted to housework have a negative effect on hourly wage rates even when individual fixed effects are controlled for. This result is broadly consistent with Becker's (1985) theory that a share of the male-female wage differential is due to productivity differences that arise from the fact that women bear greater household responsibilities than men do.

In a similar context, a recent study by Brewer and Paull (2006) shows that the hourly pay of women relative to men in Britain tends to take a U shape over women's working lifetime: the gender pay gap widens up to a certain age and then improves. The supporting argument for this is that women make choices to sacrifice their careers when they have children, reducing their lifetime earnings. Gender differences in the formal labor market stem from the division of parental duties, with mothers primarily responsible for child care. Further research on this issue is clearly needed after taking into account the female's domestic work outside her labor in the market.

Finally, the unexplained gender pay gap may be because men and women make different educational and career choices. At school, boys and girls study different subjects, and boys' chosen subjects often lead to more lucrative careers. Later, men and women specialize in different degrees and work in different professions. As a result, the average hourly pay for a female at the start of her working life is likely to be lower than that of a male, even though she may be more qualified.

13.7   Conclusions

This chapter has proposed a new decomposition methodology to explain the welfare disparity between male and female workers in terms of three components: segregation, discrimination, and inequality. While segregation captures occupational segregation by gender, discrimination measures the earnings differential between males and females within an occupation. The inequality component shows the difference in inequality in earnings between male and female workers. If this component is positive (negative), the earnings inequality is greater (smaller) among females than males.

When the proposed decomposition methodology is applied to Thailand and Viet Nam, the results suggest that the gender disparity in welfare is largely accounted for by labor market discrimination against female workers. Relative to discrimination, the other two components— occupational segregation and earnings inequality—play a smaller role in explaining the gender welfare gap. Regarding segregation and earnings inequality, both countries tend to have a similar pattern: females are mainly in sales and services or professions in teaching and clerical work, whereas males are highly represented in heavy industry and construction and machine operation, with earnings among females more unequal compared to males.

Even taking into account individual characteristics such as hours of work, education, work experience, and location, discrimination still dominates over the other two components. This is consistently true for both Thailand and Viet Nam. Surprisingly, when differences in education, work experience, and location are controlled for, there is not much change in the gender welfare disparity for Viet Nam. In contrast, the gender welfare gap opens up markedly in Thailand after accounting for education, work experience, and location. On this account, the unexplained gender gap could be due largely to other reasons, including cultural factors, employer's preference, and nature and type of job-related tasks.

This chapter has also proposed a new approach to adjusting earnings by a host of personal and job characteristics. Per capita earnings are adjusted by hours of work, education, work experience, and location (regions/provinces and urban/rural areas). Although only three attributes were used as controlling factors (which are considered the key factors in discussions of gender differences in earnings), the proposed method can be applied to any number of other variables of interest.

Furthermore, the study has attempted to isolate the net impact of each of these individual characteristics on segregation, discrimination, and earnings inequality. In this process, the findings suggest that schooling and work experience play key roles in determining segregation, discrimination, and earnings inequality. The empirical results show that education tends to reduce segregation and discrimination, but can increase inequality in earnings between male and female workers. Overall, education reduces gender disparity in welfare for the two countries. This indicates that female workers have higher levels of education than their male counterparts. Among the ultra-poor, a higher level of education was also observed among female workers in Thailand, which was not the case for Viet Nam. As for work experience, it had a strong net effect on segregation, discrimination, and earnings inequality. This was true for both countries. This finding, thus, suggests that in Thailand and Viet Nam, women have worked fewer years than men.

The findings present a number of policy implications. To narrow gender gaps—apart from instituting anti-gender discrimination measures— governments can gear resources toward providing affordable child care to reduce the opportunity costs of working and raising women's productivity as formal workers. Governments can also pursue programs that enhance girls' subject choices and improve career advice at school to encourage girls to pursue fields such as mathematics and science.

424

Appendix: Data tables and figures

Table A13.1 Thailand: Male- and female-dominated occupations (%)

Occupational groups	Total	Male	Female	Difference
Male-dominated occupations				
Legislators and senior officials	0.59	0.95	0.10	0.84
Corporate managers	1.32	1.67	0.85	0.82
General managers	0.65	0.79	0.46	0.33
Physical, math, and engineering science professionals	0.70	1.00	0.30	0.71
Physical and engineering science associate professionals	2.71	3.18	2.06	1.12
Market-oriented skilled agricultural and fishery workers	6.18	6.69	5.49	1.20
Extraction and building trades workers	7.33	12.00	1.08	10.91
Metal, machinery, and related trades workers	5.40	9.22	0.28	8.94
Stationary-plant and related operators	1.13	1.53	0.60	0.93
Drivers and mobile-plant operators	5.46	9.45	0.12	9.33
Laborers in mining, construction, manufacturing, and transport	7.25	7.67	6.68	0.99
Female-dominated occupations				
Life science and health professionals	1.19	0.61	1.97	−1.36
Teaching professionals	3.40	2.28	4.90	−2.62
Other professionals	1.35	1.12	1.66	−0.54
Life science and health associate professionals	0.54	0.36	0.79	−0.42
Teaching associate professionals	0.21	0.10	0.36	−0.25
Other associate professionals	4.20	3.03	5.75	−2.73
Office clerks	5.72	3.75	8.33	−4.58
Customer services clerks	1.26	0.83	1.85	−1.02
Personal and protective services workers	5.71	4.98	6.68	−1.70
Model, sales persons, and demonstrators	4.96	3.58	6.79	−3.21
Subsistence agricultural and fishery workers	0.03	0.02	0.03	−0.01
Precision, handicraft, printing, and related trade workers	1.77	1.53	2.08	−0.55
Other craft and related trades workers	5.72	3.24	9.03	−5.79
Machine operators and assemblers	9.40	6.44	13.40	−6.96
Sales and services elementary occupations	8.10	6.39	10.47	−4.07
Agricultural, fishery, and related laborers	7.57	7.44	7.74	−0.30
Armed forces	0.15	0.15	0.16	0.01
Total	100.00	100.00	100.00	

Note: Difference represents the difference between the proportion of male workers and the proportion of female workers working in each occupational group.

425

Table A13.2   Viet Nam: Male- and female-dominated occupations (%)

Industry	Total	Male	Female	Difference
Male-dominated occupations				
Forestry workers	0.38	0.46	0.25	0.22
Aquaculture	3.06	4.11	1.27	2.84
Laborers in coal mining	0.49	0.57	0.37	0.19
Laborers in oil and gas drilling	0.07	0.09	0.03	0.05
Metal mining workers	0.08	0.10	0.05	0.05
Mining for rocks and stones	0.86	1.18	0.32	0.87
Tobacco products	0.06	0.07	0.03	0.04
Other nonmetal mineral production	1.94	2.06	1.75	0.31
Metal production and products	0.28	0.37	0.12	0.25
Metal products (e.g., tools, boiler, etc.)	1.27	1.76	0.43	1.33
Other equipment and machinery	0.20	0.24	0.14	0.11
Motor vehicles and spare parts	0.09	0.09	0.08	0.01
Other transportation equipment	0.45	0.60	0.19	0.40
Furniture production	2.12	2.74	1.07	1.67
Recycling and reprocessing	0.07	0.07	0.07	0.00
Electricity production and distribution	0.59	0.81	0.22	0.59
Extract, clean, and distribute water	0.17	0.20	0.12	0.08
Construction	11.93	17.50	2.44	15.06
Vehicle sales, maintenance, and repair	0.84	1.15	0.32	0.83
Wholesale and agent sales	1.13	1.21	1.01	0.20
Road, railroad, and pipeline transport	2.31	3.44	0.39	3.05
Water transport	0.49	0.70	0.15	0.55
Airline transport	0.06	0.08	0.03	0.05
Services in transport	1.13	1.49	0.51	0.98
Real estate	0.10	0.12	0.06	0.06
Rental of equipment and computer-related activities	0.09	0.11	0.06	0.05
Other business activities	0.57	0.63	0.45	0.19
Government administration and national defense	4.63	5.87	2.55	3.32
Communist party, professional associations	0.95	1.13	0.64	0.48
Female-dominated industries				
Wood processing and production	1.81	1.67	2.05	−0.38
Paper and paper products	0.39	0.32	0.52	−0.20
Printing and publishing	0.34	0.29	0.42	−0.13
Coke, crude oil, uranium processing	0.05	0.04	0.05	−0.00
Chemicals and chemical products	0.47	0.46	0.49	−0.03

continued.

Table A13.2 *continued.*

Industry	Total	Male	Female	Difference
Plastic and rubber production	0.51	0.37	0.73	–0.36
Office and computer equipment production	0.06	0.06	0.07	–0.01
Other electronic, electric equipment	0.27	0.26	0.30	–0.05
Communication equipment	0.12	0.08	0.17	–0.09
Medical and laboratory equipment	0.07	0.02	0.15	–0.12
Retail sales workers	2.85	2.33	3.74	–1.41
Workers in hotel and restaurant	1.63	0.88	2.93	–2.05
Post and telecommunications	0.46	0.41	0.53	–0.12
Financial intermediary	0.23	0.18	0.31	–0.13
Insurance and pensions	0.19	0.15	0.27	–0.12
Assistance in finance	0.29	0.21	0.41	–0.20
Science and technology activities	0.25	0.22	0.30	–0.08
Education and training	6.50	3.17	12.15	–8.99
Social relief (hospital, clinic, etc.)	1.48	1.00	2.30	–1.30
Culture and sports	0.51	0.51	0.52	–0.02
Public sanitation	0.43	0.39	0.49	–0.10
Other services (ironing, laundry, etc.)	0.74	0.60	0.96	–0.36
Personal services	1.51	0.69	2.89	–2.20
Total	100.00	100.00	100.00	0.00

Note: Difference is obtained by subtracting the proportion of female workers from the proportion of male workers in each occupational group.

Table A13.3 Thailand: Decomposition of total disparity in welfare (%)

Aversion parameter	Total disparity	Segregation	Discrimination	Inequality
Unadjusted				
$\varepsilon = 1$	8.29	–7.24	13.53	2.0
$\varepsilon = 2$	11.34	–7.24	13.53	5.1
Adjusted for education				
$\varepsilon = 1$	18.24	3.53	16.01	–1.3
$\varepsilon = 2$	17.36	3.53	16.01	–2.2
Adjusted for work experience				
$\varepsilon = 1$	5.84	–7.32	8.78	4.4
$\varepsilon = 2$	12.74	–7.32	8.78	11.3
Adjusted for location				
$\varepsilon = 1$	13.81	–7.00	18.48	2.3
$\varepsilon = 2$	15.79	–7.00	18.48	4.3

continued.

Table A13.3 *continued.*

Aversion parameter	Total disparity	Segregation	Discrimination	Inequality
Adjusted for education and work experience				
$\varepsilon = 1$	12.77	3.12	9.95	−0.3
$\varepsilon = 2$	12.60	3.12	9.95	−0.5
Adjusted for education and location				
$\varepsilon = 1$	20.76	3.85	18.36	−1.5
$\varepsilon = 2$	19.55	3.85	18.36	−2.7
Adjusted for work experience and location				
$\varepsilon = 1$	10.99	−7.06	13.83	4.2
$\varepsilon = 2$	15.93	−7.06	13.83	9.2
Adjusted for education, work experience, and location				
$\varepsilon = 1$	15.20	3.42	12.16	−0.4
$\varepsilon = 2$	14.78	3.42	12.16	−0.8

Note: Location refers to regions and urban/rural areas.
Source: Author's calculations.

Table A13.4   Viet Nam: Decomposition of total disparity in welfare (%)

Aversion parameter	Total disparity	Segregation	Discrimination	Inequality
Unadjusted				
$\varepsilon = 1$	17.90	−1.93	14.36	5.5
$\varepsilon = 2$	33.80	−1.93	14.36	21.4
Adjusted for education				
$\varepsilon = 1$	19.39	1.92	15.26	2.2
$\varepsilon = 2$	31.82	1.92	15.26	14.6
Adjusted for work experience				
$\varepsilon = 1$	14.63	−2.89	12.15	5.4
$\varepsilon = 2$	32.23	−2.89	12.15	23.0
Adjusted for location				
$\varepsilon = 1$	17.91	−1.97	14.37	5.5
$\varepsilon = 2$	33.68	−1.97	14.37	21.3
Adjusted for education and work experience				
$\varepsilon = 1$	16.83	0.83	13.66	2.3
$\varepsilon = 2$	29.90	0.83	13.66	15.4

continued.

Table A13.4 *continued.*

Aversion parameter	Total disparity	Segregation	Discrimination	Inequality
Adjusted for education and location				
$\varepsilon = 1$	19.40	1.93	15.21	2.3
$\varepsilon = 2$	31.79	1.93	15.21	14.7
Adjusted for work experience and location				
$\varepsilon = 1$	14.64	−2.94	12.18	5.4
$\varepsilon = 2$	32.14	−2.94	12.18	22.9
Adjusted for education, work experience, and location				
$\varepsilon = 1$	16.84	0.82	13.62	2.4
$\varepsilon = 2$	29.88	0.82	13.62	15.4

Note: Location refers to provinces and urban/rural areas.
Source: Author's calculations.

Figure A13.1 Thailand: Percentage of male and female workers by education level

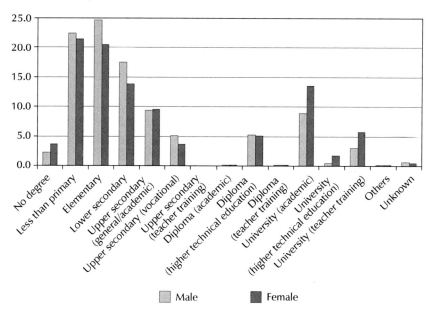

Figure A13.2 Viet Nam: Percentage of male and female workers by education level

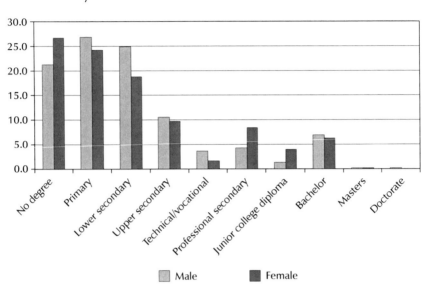

References

Atkinson, A. B. 1970. "On the Measurement of Inequality." *Journal of Economic Theory* 2:244–63.

Becker, G. S. 1985. "Human Capital, Efforts and the Sexual Division of Labor." *Journal of Labor Economics* 3(1, Suppl.):S33–58.

Behrman, J. R., and Z. Zhang. 1995. "Gender Issues and Employment in Asia." *Asian Development Review* 13(2):1–49.

Blau, F. D., and L. M. Kahn. 1997. "Swimming Upstream: Trends in the Gender Wage Differential in the 1980s." *Journal of Labor Economics* 15(1):1–42.

Blinder, A. S. 1973. "Wage Discrimination: Reduced Form and Structural Estimates." *Journal of Human Resources* 8:436–55.

Brewer, M., and G. Paull. 2006. Newborns and New Schools: Critical Times in Women's Employment. DWP Research Report No. 308, Department for Work and Pensions, Institute for Fiscal Studies.

Chauvin, K. W., and R. A. Ash. 1994. "Gender Earnings Differentials in Total Pay, Base Pay and Contingent Pay." *Industrial and Labor Relations Review* 47(4):634–49.

Cotton, J. 1988. "On the Decomposition of Wage Differentials." *Review of Economics and Statistics* 70:236–43.

Croll, E. J. 1998. *Gender and Transition in China and Vietnam.* Swedish International Development Agency, Stockholm.

Deutsch, J., and J. Silber. 2007. "Earnings Functions and the Measurement of the Determinants of Wage Dispersion: Extending Oaxaca's Approach." FEDEA Working Paper No. 2007–19, Fundación de Estudios de Economía Aplicada.

Hersch, J. 1991. "Male-Female Differences in Hourly Wage: The Role of Human Capital, Working Conditions and Housework." *Industrial and Labor Relations Review* 44(4):746–59.

Hersch, J., and L. S. Stratton. 1997. "Housework, Fixed Effects and Wages of Married Workers." *Journal of Human Resources* 32(2):285–307.

Kim, M. K., and S. W. Polachek. 1994. "Panel Estimates of Male–Female Earnings Functions." *Journal of Human Resources* 29(2):406–28.

Light, A., and M. Ureta. 1995. "Early Career Work Experience and Gender Wage Differentials." *Journal of Labor Economics* 13(1):121–54.

Long, L. D., L. N. Hung, A. Truitt, L. P. Mai, and D. N. Anh. 2000. Changing Gender Relations in Vietnam's Post *Doi Moi* Era. Working Paper No. 14, World Bank, Washington, D.C.

Macpherson, D. A., and B. T. Hirsch. 1995. "Wages and Gender Composition: Why do Women's Jobs Pay Less?" *Journal of Labor Economics* 13(3):426–71.

Neumark, D. 1988. "Employer's Discriminatory Behavior and the Estimation of Wage Discrimination." *Journal of Human Resources* 23:279–95.

Oaxaca, R. 1973. "Male-Female Wage Differentials in Urban Labor Markets." *International Economic Review* 9:693–709.

Oaxaca, R., and M. Ransom. 1988. "Searching for the Effect of Unionism on the Wages of Union and Nonunion Workers." *Journal of Labor Research* 9:139–48.

_____. 1994. "On Discrimination and the Decomposition of Wage Differentials." *Journal of Econometrics* 61:5–21.

Sen, A. 2001. "Many Faces of Gender Inequality." *Frontline* 18(22). Available: http://www.hinduonnet.com/fline/fl1822/18220040.htm.

Son, H. H. 2007. Occupational Segregation and Gender Discrimination in Labor Markets: Thailand and Vietnam. ERD Working Paper Series No. 108, Economics and Research Department, Asian Development Bank.

Shapley, L. 1953. "A Value for n-person Games." In H. W. Kuhn, and A. W. Tucker, eds., *Contributions to the Theory of Games,* Vol. 2. Princeton, NJ: Princeton University Press.

14

Inclusiveness through Food Security: The Philippines' National Food Program

Shikha Jha and Aashish Mehta[1]

14.1   Introduction

Hunger has risen in the Philippines during the last 5 years of stable economic growth. The Social Weather Stations' (SWS) hunger index clearly indicates sharply deteriorating food security beginning in 2003 (Figure 14.1). This has occurred despite the country's longest spell of uninterrupted growth in per capita real gross domestic product (GDP) since the 1980s (Figure 14.2). Household consumption per capita (not shown) also trended upward over the same period, although not as fast. This chapter examines the performance of the Philippines' main food security agency—the National Food Authority (NFA)—to understand why hunger has risen despite income growth and significant public expenditure on food security programs, and what might be done about it.

Figure 14.1   Self-reported hunger

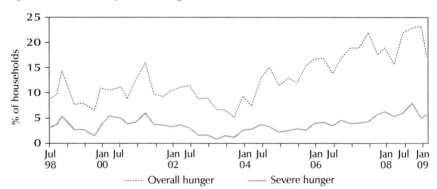

Note: Severely hungry households report involuntarily going without food "often" in the last 3 months. Overall hunger reflects involuntarily going without food at least once in the last 3 months.

Source: Social Weather Stations, available: www.sws.org.ph/, downloaded 27 May 2009.

---

1   The authors thank Pilipinas F. Quising for superb research assistance. The usual disclaimer applies.

Figure 14.2   Per capita real gross domestic product

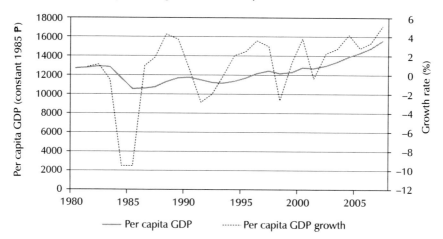

GDP = gross domestic product.
Source: World Bank, World Development Indicators Online, downloaded 27 May 2009.

Why did hunger increase even as average income and consumption grew? In a related work, Mehta and Jha (2009) show that the data are inconsistent with: (i) explanations based on deteriorating income distribution (the income distribution actually improved slightly while hunger and per capita GDP rose); (ii) explanations based on declining per capita rice production and imports (these increased as well); and (iii) those attaching causality to rising average rice prices (food prices rose slower than the GDP deflator). Rather, Figure 14.3 suggests that hunger occured because food prices rose rapidly in the poorest parts of the country.

This chapter focuses primarily on rice, a staple food in the Philippines. The correlation between poverty rates and increases in rice prices from 2003 to 2007 is 0.67. The poor depend much more on rice than the rich; the fraction of rice purchased (rather than consumed out of home production) is extremely high, and the urban poor are especially dependent on rice purchases (Table 14.1). It is natural to think, therefore, that rising rice prices in regions with deeper poverty are an important contributor to the rise in hunger.

In this context, the operations of the NFA have become increasingly important. This chapter argues that the effectiveness of the agency is hobbled by conflicting and poorly defined objectives. It reviews literature that argues that: (i) the NFA, which has a legal monopoly on the import of rice, imports too little rice to meet demand at world prices; (ii) these import restrictions induce crop choices that exacerbate soil erosion and introduce long-term reductions in productivity that can increase poverty;

(iii) the NFA's domestic procurement programs—given their miniscule size—scarcely alter farm-gate prices; and (iv) the cost per dollar of subsidy delivered to poor consumers is extremely high. The chapter also analyzes household survey data that show that much of the subsidized rice the NFA distributes is consumed by non-poor households. It also cites evidence that households report consuming less than half of the total amount of rice the NFA claims to have distributed in 2006.

Figure 14.3   Rice price change (2002–2007) versus poverty rate (2006), by region

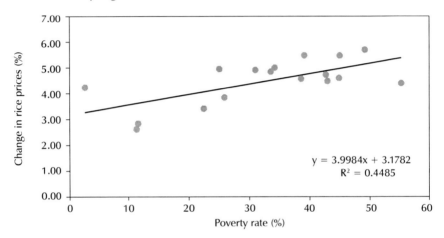

Source: Regional poverty rates calculated from FIES (NSO 2006). Rice price inflation measures the annualized percent increase in the retail price of well-milled rice, as reported by the Bureau of Agricultural Statistics' CountryStat Database, available: http://countrystat.bas.gov.ph/, downloaded 30 May 2009.

Table 14.1   Importance of rice for different economic classes, 2006

Quintile	Mean total household per capita expenditure (peso)			Share of rice in total food expenditure (%)			Share of purchased rice in total rice consumed (%)		
	Both	Rural	Urban	Both	Rural	Urban	Both	Rural	Urban
1	9,495	9,393	9,943	33.5	33.5	33.6	87.2	85.7	93.4
2	15,646	15,552	15,846	28.6	29.7	26.3	88.0	85.1	94.1
3	23,613	23,266	23,962	22.7	25.0	20.4	89.5	83.9	95.1
4	37,316	36,618	37,668	17.1	20.2	15.6	91.6	83.8	95.6
5	87,461	77,467	89,819	11.5	14.9	10.7	92.7	83.4	94.9

Source: Authors' calculations from FIES (NSO 2006).

The chapter argues that institutional reforms at the NFA are prerequisites for tackling food security. These include a clarification of its objectives and the rationale for its monopoly on rice imports, better targeting, and greater transparency.

An overarching theme is that the very limited efforts to target rice to the poor are not sustainable or appropriate. The evidence provided on the causes of hunger implies a polarization in households' ability to buy food, and has made the targeting of food subsidies an issue of paramount importance. Hunger that is highly prevalent, but localized within the populace, calls for localized policy interventions, not blanket attempts to control staple prices, especially given that the Philippines has prioritized fiscal prudence in its attempts to reduce its debt burden.

14.2 The global food price crisis and rice prices in the Philippines

In percentage terms, retail rice prices for the nation as a whole rose 24% from 2002 to 2007. From 2007 to 2008 alone, they rose a further 31%, while the percentage of households reporting involuntary hunger during the 3 months prior to the SWS survey rose to 23.7%. Rice imports of 1.79 million metric tons were worth only $494 million in 2007, but rice imports in 2008 cost the government about $1.5 billion, mainly because of a price surge in the middle of the year (Reno 2009).

In 2008, global prices of oil and food swung wildly. Both have moved in tandem during this decade (Figure 14.4). In particular, the correlations of rice, wheat, and maize prices with crude oil prices were 0.83, 0.80, and 0.80, respectively, between January 2003 and May 2009. High fuel prices increase transport and production costs, add to inflation, and reduce real incomes. However, demand for food, due to its low income elasticity, does not fall proportionately. Thus, the effects of higher fuel prices on food production costs outweigh the effects of reduced food demand. This puts upward pressure on food prices and causes them to move in concert with fuel prices (World Bank 2009). Increased demand for food crops to manufacture biofuels has also contributed to higher food prices and a stronger correlation between food and fuel prices (Rosegrant 2008). A number of other forces may have been responsible for the steep hike in food prices: rising incomes, rapidly expanding direct demand for food and indirect demand for feed, urbanization, production shocks and lagging productivity in agriculture, declining global food stocks, trade restrictions, a weaker United States dollar, and speculative activities.[2]

---

[2] See, for example, ADB 2008, Timmer 2008, Farm Foundation 2008, IFPRI 2007, Mitchell 2008, Trostle 2008.

Figure 14.4   International commodity prices

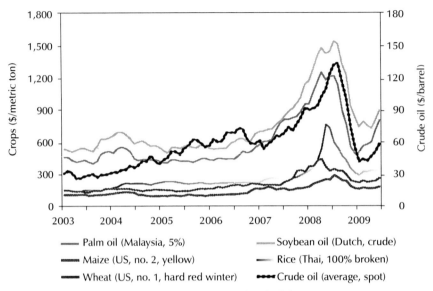

Source: World Bank, Commodity Price Data (Pink Sheet), downloaded 8 June 2009.

As most of the major factors listed above reversed course in the latter half of 2008, food prices eased. The decline has been attributed to a better supply response, falling oil prices, and a slowdown in global growth. Indeed, global cereal production reached a record high in 2008, and was sufficient to satisfy the expected increase in demand in 2009 while allowing for a moderate replenishment of world stocks (FAO 2008). While it may therefore appear that the spike was only temporary, that the bubble has burst, and that price corrections are now in motion, the Food and Agriculture Organization notes that food prices remain high in developing countries and continue to increase in several countries, affecting the food security of many vulnerable populations. In the coming years, demand will continue to grow, but limited productivity growth and pressure on exhaustible resources such as fossil fuels and water will exert upward pressure on prices. FAO-OECD (2008) and OXAN (2009) projected the prices of cereals and oilseeds to remain 10%–35% higher in real terms in 2008–2017 than in 1998–2007. This is expected to be supported by renewed economic growth, particularly in emerging markets; higher demand for biofuels; increased scarcity of agricultural inputs such as fertilizer, water, and land; and higher production and transport costs.

Such a renewal of the upward trend in food prices will influence food security in developing countries and will call for policies to address the challenge, which will be particularly severe in the food-importing nations of South Asia and Southeast Asia. These regions account for more than 60% of the world's poor, a majority of whom (75%) reside in rural areas and depend on agriculture for their income, but are still large buyers of food (e.g., see Table 14.1). Food prices therefore have significant implications for their food security. While medium- to long-term measures are important for sustained high agricultural growth, developing countries need to be prepared to shield the poor from possible short-run price shocks through well-targeted, reliable, and efficient food-based safety nets. This deepens the motivation for examining the readiness and effectiveness of the Philippines' rice subsidy policy.

14.3 The NFA rice program

As Table 14.1 shows, most Filipinos, especially urban dwellers, buy a significant share of their rice, with limited reliance on home-grown rice or payment in kind. The NFA seeks to support this activity and to achieve food security through multiple objectives. To keep food affordable for consumers, it sells rice through accredited retailers at a mandated, below-market price. The retailers receive a fixed margin on the sale. The NFA also offers price support to farmers through its procurement of *palay* (unmilled rice). It also attempts to stabilize prices, which it attempts to do by holding buffer stocks equivalent to 30 days of consumption in addition to 15 days of emergency holdings. To stabilize prices and supplies over time, the NFA buys *palay* during peak harvest and sells rice from its stock during the lean season to retailers. It also carries out processing activities, dispersal of *palay* and milled rice to strategic locations, and distribution to various marketing outlets. The NFA procures less than 1% of local rice production at a fixed price. As a government board, it has a legal monopoly on the import of rice.[3] Between 1998 and 2004, its imports averaged about 13% of domestic production (Senate Economic Planning Office 2006). Over 95% of the subsidized rice distributed to consumers is imported. The NFA's volume of sales and the consumer price subsidy were increased significantly in 2008 in view of escalating rice prices (Figure 14.5). The import bill for rice in the first half of 2008 was $858 million, almost 4 times that in 2007.

Funding for the NFA comes from various sources, including budgetary subsidies, domestic and foreign borrowing (against government guarantees), and official development assistance to the Philippine government, such as food aid. The NFA is the largest recipient of government subsidy, accounting for 10% of budgeted

---

3   In response to the food-price crisis in 2008, the government lifted the import ban on rice and corn by private traders.

support to all government corporations for 2009 (see www.dbm.gov. ph/BESF09/ E1. pdf). It is also exempt from the payment of taxes, and duties and fees, and from import restrictions. Yet it was also the largest loss-making government corporation as of 2007.

Figure 14.5   NFA sales and consumer price subsidy

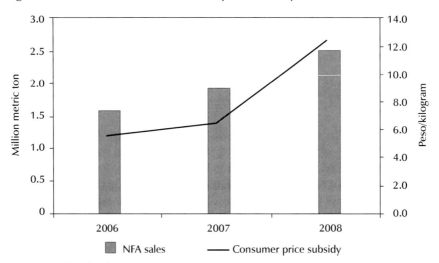

NFA = National Food Authority.
Source: Authors' calculations with basic data from *Budget of Expenditures and Sources of Financing* (DBM various years).

The Senate Economic Planning Office (2006) has raised concern about the financial position of the NFA. Its liability-to-assets ratio exceeds 1 and is among the highest of all government corporations. To support domestic producers, the NFA's average procurement price is 9% higher than the market price. To support consumers, it sells rice 18% cheaper than non-NFA ordinary rice. Its official gross margins are negative as its sales revenues are not enough to cover even its variable operating costs. Moreover, anecdotal evidence points to pilferage and diversion of rice stocks, misrepresentation of cheaply bought NFA rice as better-milled and processed varieties, and overpricing. Acknowledging such governance issues, the NFA established a Corporate Governance Committee in 2006 to strengthen, among other things, its internal transparency and accountability.[4]

---

4   Sound design principles and sustained reform of the institutional framework within which such programs operate, including transparency, expenditure controls, and decentralization, can substantially improve program governance, as shown by the example of Nepal's food-for-work program (Meagher et al. 1999).

A number of studies examining the NFA's programs have shown that it suffers from several weaknesses, including poor targeting, governance problems, and conflicting objectives. Some of these findings are reviewed below, and gaps in the literature this chapter helps to fill are highlighted.

UNESCAP (2000) finds that the design of NFA programs entails inherent losses that are covered by budgetary allocation and debt creation. It estimates the cost per dollar of subsidy delivered to the poor, finding these numbers high. These calculations are revisited using recent data and empirical estimates of the leakage of rice to the non-poor and the proportion of rice that does not appear to reach consumers. Moreover, the UNESCAP study suggests that the regional distribution of the subsidy is not related to the regional incidence of poverty. This suggestion is re-examined carefully.

Roumasset (2000) notes that faced with the goal of maintaining multiple prices, NFA interventions did not stabilize prices. Moreover, they raised consumer and producer prices above the free-trade level at substantial efficiency and financial costs. While consumers paid 75% more in the market than they would have under free trade, farmers received only half of this difference in terms of higher prices. The price distortions created negative protection for consumers that outweighed the positive protection for producers, resulting in deadweight loss or economic waste.[5] These results are reinforced by Yao et al. (2007) who examine the effectiveness of the program over 21 years from 1983 to 2003. They find that while domestic prices were more stable than world prices during 1996–2003, they were almost twice as high. Moreover, farmers in some regions benefited, but consumers in others paid higher prices. Given its small procurement operations, the program had a limited impact on prices. It should be stressed that these results concern prices on the regular rice market, not the price of the NFA-subsidized rice. Results from Section 14.1 suggest that rising local rice prices explain the rise in hunger, underscoring the importance of eliminating distorting policies that raise rice prices.

Based on a survey, the World Bank (2001) finds that in aggregate a much higher percentage of the poor purchased NFA rice than the non-poor. This result was driven by targeting through inferior quality rice, sold particularly to poor households and in rural areas. The purchase of NFA rice by the non-poor in the World Bank survey was explained, in part, by its use for domestic helpers and pets. While the poor were more likely to participate, the percentage of NFA rice that was sold to the non-poor was found to be higher than the percentage sold to the poor, implying

---

5   A related criticism, albeit one that does not directly affect the NFA's ability to promote food security, is that the relatively high protection rates offered to crops, such as rice and especially corn, induce more planting of these crops and greater soil erosion. Coxhead (2000) demonstrates this using a general equilibrium model.

weak targeting of resources through the general subsidy. The extremes of misallocation are evident in the fact that the island of Mindanao, one of the poorest parts of the country, had the lowest subsidized rice availability. Also, the constituent regions of Mindanao experienced some of the highest price increases, thereby accounting for much of the positive association between poverty and price increases noted in Section 14.1.

According to Balisacan et al. (2000), inferior quality rice need not have a low nutritional content, so self-targeting is helpful. However, he argues, the subsidy can be better targeted through food stamps and rural food-for-work programs. Other alternatives include geographical targeting, screening and imposition of penalties for leakage, and undercoverage. The findings in Section 14.1 reinforce the importance of geographical targeting; Section 14.6 will examine whether or not leakage is higher in poorer regions.

This brief review of the literature on the NFA highlights its large administrative costs, corruption, inefficient implementation, and leakage. The universal nature of the NFA subsidies is particularly costly. These are familiar themes in the wider literature on food security. For example, Rogers and Coates (2002) estimate that the leakage to the non-poor population from untargeted food subsidies and food ration programs in Brazil, Egypt, India, and Pakistan are as high as 50%–80%. In contrast, self-targeting food programs using inferior foods have a lower leakage rate of 10%–20%. Empirical evidence gathered by Coady (2004) also shows that universal food subsidies are usually accompanied by high leakage to the non-poor and economic inefficiencies resulting from distorted consumer and producer prices. It shows that such leakage due to weak targeting costs governments on average $3.3 to transfer $1 to the poor. This suggests universal subsidies should be used only as a stop-gap policy until targeting of subsidies can improve their cost effectiveness.

14.4   Costs of the NFA program

To consider the economic viability of its rice operations, the NFA's net cost is calculated as the difference between its costs (of local procurement and imports, administrative, and other operating costs) and revenue from subsidized sales. For 2008, this cost is estimated at ₱68.6 billion (Table 14.2) or 0.9% of GDP. The total consumer price subsidy delivered is computed as the product of the estimated quantity of NFA rice sold times the difference between retail market and NFA prices. Because the estimated quantity of subsidized NFA rice sold to the poor is assumed to be equal to the officially reported amount supplied by the NFA, the baseline figures in Table 14.2 implicitly assume zero pilferage and no leakage of subsidized rice to the non-poor.

440

Comparing the cost of the NFA with the accrual of subsidy to consumers gives a cost–benefit ratio of between 1.5 and 2.2 in 2006–2008 (Table 14.2). This means that to transfer $1 of subsidy to consumers in 2008, it cost the NFA $2.2. Assuming that 54% of the subsidy is not delivered (see Section 14.5 for justification), because the rice is diverted to the regular market, the cost–benefit ratio doubles to $3.3–$4.8. Assuming that in addition to this missing rice, 48% of the subsidy is given to the non-poor (a figure measured in Section 14.6), then the cost per dollar of subsidy delivered to the poor rises to some $6.3–$9.3. These figures are comparable with those of UNESCAP (2000), which estimates the cost of transferring $1 in rice subsidy (to consumers without any leakage and no missing rice) at $1.27 and $2.10 in 1997 and 1998, respectively; and $2.54 and $4.20 (with 50% leakage but no missing rice).

Table 14.2   Rice subsidy: Cost–benefit calculations

Measure	Unit	2006	2007	2008
Effective NFA program cost	Million peso	16,428	18,602	68,582
Maintenance and other operating expenses	Million peso	6,417	1,610	4,209
Less: Net profit (loss) from sales	Million peso	(10,010)	(16,991)	(64,372)
Consumer price subsidy = Retail price of rice – NFA rice retail price	Peso/kilogram	5.56	6.47	12.38
Imputed volume of NFA sales	Metric ton	1,566	1,911	2,504
Total consumer subsidy	Million peso	8,704	12,364	31,005
Cost–benefit ratio = NFA cost/consumer subsidy		1.89	1.50	2.21
Assuming 48% leakage		3.63	2.88	4.25
Assuming 54% missing rice		4.11	3.26	4.80
Assuming 48% leakage and 54% missing rice		7.90	6.27	9.24

NFA = National Food Authority.
Note: Gross sales and cost of sales not only cover rice but are a close approximation as the bulk of NFA sales relates to rice. Cost of sales includes procurement of *palay*, conversion from *palay* to milled rice, transport, and import. Maintenance and other operating expenses exclude personal services.
Source of basic data: *Budget of Expenditures and Sources of Financing* (DBM various years).

With people living close to the poverty line, it is normatively a bit extreme to remove from consideration all benefits accruing from rice consumed by the non-poor. However, even without such leakage, the costs of the program are extremely high. While UNESCAP estimates the annual cost of the program from data derived from the NFA's balance sheet position, this chapter's data are drawn from operational reports on sales and operating costs.

Official data for 2003–2004 show that almost 60% of NFA rice was distributed in Metro Manila and other regions in Luzon, and that Mindanao and Metro Manila each received about 25% of the total (Senate Economic Planning Office 2006). These data are at variance with the World Bank's (2001) field surveys, which found that Mindanao was underserved. The discrepancy between these figures is consistent with the disappearance of NFA rice, as explored further later.

14.5   Who benefits from NFA subsidies?

To get a deeper insight into the distribution of subsidies, the 2006 Family Income and Expenditure Survey (FIES) of the National Statistics Office is used, which provides disaggregated household consumption expenditure data for NFA rice. FIES is a nationwide survey of households conducted every 3 years. It provides information on household sources of income in cash and in kind and their levels of consumption by expenditure item. Related information such as family size; number of employed family members; occupation, age, and educational attainment of household head; and housing characteristics are also included. The results of the survey are used to estimate the standards of living and disparities in income of Filipino families, as well as their consumption and spending patterns.

Using a stratified sampling scheme based on the 2000 Census of Population and Housing, the survey is conducted on two occasions using the same questionnaire. The first interview is usually conducted in July of the reference year to gather data for January–June. The second interview is done in January of the following year, to account for the last 6 months (July–December). The concept of "average week" consumption is used for all food items, including NFA rice. The FIES explicitly asks consumers how much NFA rice they consume. For expenditures on fuel, light, and water; transportation and communication; household operations; and personal care and effects, the reference period is the "past month." For all other expenditure groups and for the sources of income, the "past 6 months" is used as reference period. All these are done to minimize memory bias and to capture the seasonality of income and expenditure patterns. Annual data are estimated by combining the results of the first and the second visit. Estimates of income and expenditure in kind are based on prevailing market prices. In the case of NFA rice consumption and total rice consumption, the data are collected on a 6-month recall basis.

The first and perhaps most important point to note about rice distributed by the NFA is that much of it does not appear in the FIES. In a related work, Mehta and Jha (2009) demonstrate that under conservative assumptions, 54% of the rice that the NFA reports distributing does not appear in the FIES. They also examine the data carefully and argue that this finding cannot plausibly be explained away by a variety of measurement errors: (i) the FIES is extremely carefully designed to provide accurate estimates of variables at the national and regional levels and provides a good estimate of general rice consumed (that is, an estimate that coincides roughly with the national disappearance data); (ii) the NFA is very particular in ensuring that its retailers and distributors prominently identify NFA rice as such, and since NFA rice is substantially cheaper than regular rice, it is unlikely that households are unaware that they are consuming NFA rice; and (iii) one of the two FIESs takes place in July during the period of peak NFA rice consumption so the result cannot be explained by seasonal recall bias. It should be emphasized that the following description of who benefits from NFA subsidy programs refers only to those who received the portion of NFA rice whose distribution is captured in the FIES.

FIES data show that the NFA rice subsidy is progressive (Table 14.3). This is consistent with the observation that the relative dependence on the NFA for rice purchases is higher for the poor (Table 14.4). The data also reveal that among the families that buy NFA rice, 52% are poor compared to the national headcount ratio of 26%. An average poor household buying NFA rice has six family members sharing an annual income of ₱59,000. This translates into ₱27 (at 2006 exchange rates) or merely $0.53 per day per capita.

Table 14.3   Distribution of consumer subsidies, 2006

Expenditure quintile (%)	Mean per capita expenditure (peso)	Per capita NFA rice consumption (kg)	Price subsidy (peso/kg)	Per capita subsidy (peso)	Per capita subsidy (% of mean expenditure)
	1	2	3	4 = 2 X 3	5 = 4 /1
0–20	9,495	14.2	5.6	79.1	0.83
20–40	15,646	9.4	5.6	52.2	0.33
40–60	23,613	5.4	5.6	30.0	0.13
60–80	37,316	3.2	5.6	17.8	0.05
80–100	87,461	1.4	5.6	7.6	0.01

NFA = National Food Authority.
Note: Column (2) is obtained by dividing mean NFA rice expenditure by NFA retail price.
Source: Authors' calculations from FIES (NSO 2006).

Table 14.4   Mean rice expenditure, 2006

Expenditure quintile (%)	Share of NFA rice in total rice expenditure (%)	Total rice expenditure (peso)
0–20	12.3	12,063
20–40	6.0	12,424
40–60	3.2	11,931
60–80	1.9	11,124
80–100	0.7	9,853

NFA = National Food Authority.
Source: Authors' calculations from FIES (NSO 2006).

One interesting fact is that while NFA rice subsidies are officially universally available with unlimited purchase, they are used by only about 16% of the population. The FIES data indicate that of the 12 million households in the country, only about 2 million purchase NFA rice.

Table 14.5 provides a first-cut approach to understanding how much of the benefits of the NFA subsidies accrue to the poor. It shows that rural poverty is almost 4 times as high as urban poverty, and that the population is roughly evenly split between urban and rural areas. It follows that if NFA rice were targeted to the poor, regardless of their location, its beneficiaries would be split 80–20 in favor of rural households. Plainly, urban households, which comprise one-third (rather than one-fifth) of the program's beneficiaries, are slightly favored relative to this scenario.

Table 14.5   Rural-urban distribution of poor, non-poor, and NFA recipients (%), 2006

	Non-poor	Poor	Total	Share of population	Share of NFA recipients
Urban	89.0	11.0	100	49.6	32.6
Rural	58.6	41.4	100	50.4	67.4
Total	73.7	26.3	100	100.0	100.0

NFA = National Food Authority.
Source: Authors' calculations from FIES (NSO 2006).

14.6   Access by the poor and leakage to the non-poor

The performance of food-based safety net programs has not always been satisfactory, often reflecting high administrative costs, corruption, and leakage to the non-poor. Several factors could make food-based programs successful. Analyzing the experience of safety net programs in a number of countries, Subbarao et al. (1997) list the following elements of a good design to successfully and efficiently reach the poor:

    (i)   low program cost as a percent of total budget to ensure sustainability

    (ii)   low transaction costs of participation for the poor

    (iii)   balancing the cost of fine-tuned targeting with the risk of leakage to the non-poor

    (iv)   targeting to ensure sustainable, efficient, and non-distorting subsidies

    (v)   modest size of transfer to minimize costs associated with responses to perverse incentives created by the subsidy and

    (vi)   especially designed delivery mechanisms for poor women, children, or indigenous groups.

How does the NFA's rice distribution program fare against each of these criteria? First, as seen from Table 14.2, ignoring leakage to the non-poor and pilferage, the NFA program cost as share of GDP had been low until the abrupt rise in 2008. The 2008 import price increase has put tremendous pressure on the program budget, implying the need for extreme fiscal probity. Second, participation costs for the poor are high due to a lack of stores in their neighborhoods (World Bank 2001). Third, to reduce leakage, the government is currently running a redesigned pilot program for geographical targeting of low-priced, better-quality rice in the poorest *barangays* through the use of passbooks and a specified quota of 2 kilograms of rice per person per week.[6] On incentive costs and delivery mechanisms, while some studies (e.g., Balisacan et al. 2000 and World Bank 2001) noted a lack of targeting and alleged missing rice (NFA rice that is observed in official disappearance data but is not accounted for in the FIES), this chapter systematically analyzes these issues using the latest household-level data.

This section enumerates various indicators of program access among the poor as proxies for some of the above design parameters, including the two types of targeting errors:

Type-I Error (error of exclusion): the fraction of the poor excluded
Type-II Error (error of inclusion): the fraction of beneficiaries who are non-poor

---

6   The *barangay* is the smallest political/administrative unit into which cities and municipalities in the Philippines are divided.

Let:

T = sample size
T_a = number of people having access to NFA rice
P = number of people below the poverty line
P_a = number of poor having access to NFA rice

Therefore:

Overall access = T_a/T
Poverty headcount ratio (HCR) = P/T
Percent of poor who are beneficiaries = P_a/P
Percent of beneficiaries who are poor = P_a/T_a
Undercoverage = $1 - P_a/P$ (Type-I error)
Leakage to the non-poor = $1 - P_a/T_a$ (Type-II error)
Pro-poor bias = $(P_a/P) / (T_a/T) - 1$

The poverty line is defined as the minimum income required for a family/individual to meet basic food and non-food requirements. In 2006, the annual per capita poverty threshold was ₱15,057. The HCR is given by the ratio P/T and equaled 0.26 in 2006 but varied widely geographically, ranging from 0.11 for urban areas to 0.41 for rural areas (see Table 14.5). Since NFA rice is universally available, both the poor and the non-poor are eligible to buy it.

Overall access measures the share of the population that uses the program. The indicator P_a/P determines how many of the poor access it. Its complement $1 - P_a/P$ therefore gives the share of the poor who are excluded (Type-I error). On the other hand, P_a/T_a calculates the share of the poor among those who use the program. Its complement $1 - P_a/T_a$ likewise determines the share of unintended (non-poor) beneficiaries who are included among the users (Type-II error).

Table 14.6 presents a summary of the indicators of access to NFA rice. The results show that only 25% of the poor benefit from the program while 75% remain uncovered. At the same time, 48% of the beneficiaries are non-poor. This implies that Type-I error (75%) is much larger than Type-II error (48%). Reducing the former would improve the coverage of the poor even though leakage would occur. Lowering the latter would reduce the leakage to the unintended population, but a large fraction of the poor would continue to remain outside the safety net. Minimizing a "loss function" consisting of a weighted average of the two errors with a higher weight for Type-I error is likely to be an appropriate policy objective, reducing exclusion more than inclusion.

Table 14.6   Access to NFA rice by residence, 2006

Indicator	Formula	Total	Urban	Rural
Headcount ratio	P/T	0.26	0.11	0.41
Overall access	T_a/T	0.12	0.08	0.17
Ratio of poor having access to NFA rice to total poor	P_a/P	0.25	0.24	0.25
Undercoverage	$1-P_a/P$	0.75	0.76	0.75
Ratio of poor among beneficiaries	P_a/T_a	0.52	0.32	0.61
Leakage to the non-poor	$1-P_a/T_a$	0.48	0.68	0.39
Pro-poor bias	$(P_a/P) / (T_a/T)-1$	0.96	1.95	0.47

Source: Authors' calculations.

The pro-poor bias ($[P_a/P] / [T_a/T]-1$) is a measure of "fairness" in universal targeting. It equals ($[P_a/T_a] / [P/T]-1$,) which is based on the ratio of the share of poor among all users to the share of poor in the entire population (HCR). If this ratio = 1, pro-poor bias is zero, implying a fair share to the poor. If the ratio is less than 1, the poor get less than their fair share and vice versa. The household survey data show the pro-poor bias to be positive. It is a healthy 0.96 (= [0.52/0.26]−1) on average, implying the poor are overrepresented among NFA users by a factor of 1.96, but with wide variation. Pro-poor bias is low in rural areas (0.47) and high in urban areas (1.95). It should be emphasized that these figures reflect only the fairness of participation on the extensive margin.

The aggregate measures do not fully reflect the variation by area of residence, especially in the case of leakage to the non-poor. The distribution between the poor with access to the program and those without it is similar in urban and rural areas, implying similar levels of Type-I error. But there is a stark difference in these areas in Type-II error. The high leakage of 68% to the urban non-poor relative to a lower 39% to the rural non-poor may arise from a number of favorable factors in towns and cities such as higher availability of more accredited retailers, larger supply of subsidized rice, better awareness, and lower opportunity cost of sending employees to buy NFA rice.

The wide differences between rural and urban areas indicate geographic variation in access to the program. Table 14.7 further disaggregates the measures of access by region while Figure 14.6 plots regional measures of access, pro-poor bias, and Type-I and Type-II error against the regional poverty headcount ratio. They demonstrate, consistent with the NFA's operating procedure of targeting more food-insecure regions, that total access increases with the poverty headcount ratio. Undercoverage appears to be slightly reduced in poorer regions

Table 14.7   Access to NFA rice by region, 2006

Region	Headcount ratio	Overall access	Ratio of poor having access to NFA rice to total poor	Under-coverage	Ratio of poor among beneficiaries	Leakage to the non-poor	Pro-poor bias
	P/T	T_a/T	P_a/P	$1-P_a/P$	P_a/T_a	$1-P_a/T_a$	$(P_a/P)/(T_a/T)-1$
NCR	0.03	0.06	0.21	0.79	0.10	0.90	2.72
CAR	0.25	0.20	0.28	0.72	0.35	0.65	0.39
I – Ilocos	0.22	0.10	0.21	0.79	0.48	0.52	1.12
II – Cagayan Valley	0.26	0.08	0.10	0.90	0.35	0.65	0.36
III – Central Luzon	0.12	0.04	0.13	0.87	0.36	0.64	2.07
IVA – CALABARZON	0.11	0.04	0.12	0.88	0.33	0.67	1.96
IVB – MIMAROPA	0.43	0.23	0.29	0.71	0.55	0.45	0.28
V – Bicol	0.43	0.47	0.54	0.46	0.49	0.51	0.15
VI – Western Visayas	0.34	0.03	0.05	0.95	0.61	0.39	0.83
VII – Central Visayas	0.34	0.12	0.17	0.83	0.49	0.51	0.42
VIII – Eastern Visayas	0.45	0.21	0.33	0.67	0.69	0.31	0.54
IX – Zamboanga Peninsula	0.49	0.16	0.22	0.78	0.70	0.30	0.41
X – Northern Mindanao	0.39	0.18	0.29	0.71	0.63	0.37	0.63
XI – Davao	0.31	0.18	0.32	0.68	0.54	0.46	0.73
XII – SOCSARGEN	0.39	0.14	0.22	0.78	0.64	0.36	0.63
XIII – Caraga	0.45	0.19	0.32	0.68	0.74	0.26	0.64
ARMM	0.55	0.22	0.26	0.74	0.68	0.32	0.22

ARMM = Autonomous Region in Muslim Mindanao; CALABARZON = Cavite, Laguna, Batangas, Rizal, Quezon; CAR = Cordillera Administrative Region; CARAGA = Agusan del Norte, Agusan del Sur, Surigao del Norte, Surigao del Sur; MIMAROPA = Marinduque, Occidental Mindoro, Oriental Mindoro, Romblon; SOCSARGEN = South Cotabato, North Cotabato, Sarangani, Sultan Kudarat.

Source: Authors' calculations.

as a result. Leakage to the non-poor is also lower in poorer regions. However, this finding is unsurprising, because the fraction of all households that is non-poor is also lower in poorer regions, and the simple leakage measure $(1-P_a/T_a)$ does not take this into account. In fact, when the level of non-leakage (P_a/T_a) is compared to the fraction of the population that is poor (yielding a normalized measure of non-leakage or pro-poor bias), pro-poor bias is lower in poorer regions. In summation then, the procedure of targeting rice to poorer regions does successfully improve coverage in poorer regions, but comes at a cost; it reduces the accuracy with which the subsidy is targeted. The result should probably be considered cautionary when considering a massive expansion of the program, as undertaken in 2008.

Figure 14.6   Regional access to NFA rice by level of poverty, 2006

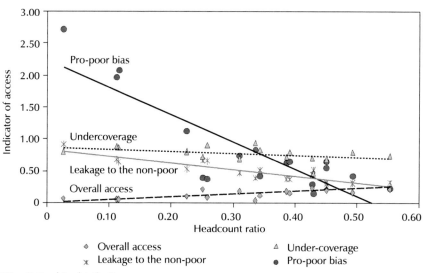

NFA = National Food Authority.
Source: Table 14.7.

Finally, the limited good news—that total access increases slightly with the poverty headcount ratio—contrasts with the findings of Section 14.1, which showed that high-poverty regions nevertheless saw more rapid rice price increases. Mehta and Jha (2009) show that NFA rice consumption per capita (which takes into account not just access, but the amounts consumed) is totally uncorrelated with poverty rates across provinces. They also show that the fraction of rice that goes missing is lower in poorer regions. In this context, still greater geographical targeting of subsidies to poor regions would be helpful.

14.7 Conclusions

The incidence of hunger rose rapidly in the Philippines beginning in 2003, despite rapidly rising per capita GDP, consumption, rice production, rice consumption, and rice imports. Growing hunger is also not explained by rising average food prices nor by a precipitous income shock. Rather, it is explained by rapidly rising *local* food prices, particularly those of rice, in the poorest regions of the country.[7]

In this context, the NFA rice subsidy program is an important safety net, and receives massive subsidies. The NFA endeavors to satisfy multiple, often conflicting, objectives to achieve food security, including price supports to consumers and producers and stabilization of market prices. Its key feature is an untargeted transfer of subsidized rice to households across the country. The volume of NFA sales and the depth of the consumer price subsidy were significantly increased in 2008 in view of escalating rice prices, raising the NFA cost to 0.9% of GDP.[8]

This chapter has analyzed crucial economic aspects of the program —including its cost effectiveness, reach to and support for the poor, and targeting effectiveness—by making use of the latest household consumption expenditure survey data.

The subsidy to consumers is progressive across economic classes, with poorer households more likely to participate. Furthermore, the percentage of the population having access to NFA rice is higher in regions with greater poverty. About 52% of the program's users are poor, and the average per capita income of its poor beneficiaries is merely $0.53 per day.

While the NFA rice program is universal with unlimited purchase, it is used by only about 16% of the population, partly because of limited supplies, and partly because of high participation costs, especially for the poor. The targeting effectiveness of the program is low, as reflected in high exclusion and inclusion errors. The results show that only 25% of the poor benefit from the program, while 75% are excluded. At the same time, 48% of the beneficiaries are non-poor. This leakage is particularly high in urban areas where 68% of the participants are non-poor, against 39% in rural areas. This implies a serious misallocation of resources in favor of towns and cities.

The chapter has also found that more than half of the rice distributed in 2006 according to official figures does not appear in the household surveys. While part of this discrepancy might arise from

---

[7] The reasons for faster price increases in poor regions (e.g., being cut off from more prosperous areas or due to lack of supplies or low production) need to be uncovered by future research. Whatever secular forces gave rise to this problem, the NFA was unable to counteract them.

[8] Based on official figures reported in www.gmanews.tv/story/124368/Tax-subsidies-for-NFA-rice-imports-to-hit-P39B.

450

measurement error, the rest probably owes to pilferage, damage in storage, and loss in transit. Moreover, even assuming no pilferage or leakage, transferring $1 of subsidy to consumers costs the NFA around $2. Assuming that 54% of the rice did not reach consumers and that 48% of the amount reaching consumers went to the non-poor, then the cost per dollar of subsidy reaching the poor works out to around $8. Certainly, that overstates the normative consequences of leakage to the non-poor, many of whom are close to the poverty line, but a cost of even $4 per $1 of subsidy appears rather high for a country seeking to pay down its national debt.

The NFA rice program can better reach the poor if its inclusion and exclusion errors are reduced, its access and availability to the poor improved, and the quality of governance bolstered. In today's times of volatile food prices, strengthening food-based safety nets to more effectively and efficiently include the poor in the growth process has become more important than ever.

References

ADB. 2008. Special Report: Food Prices and Inflation in Developing Asia: Is Poverty Reduction Coming to an End? Economics and Research Department, Asian Development Bank, Manila.

Balisacan, A. M., R. G. Edillon, A. B. Brillantes, and D. C. Canlas. 2000. "Approaches to Targeting the Poor." Report prepared for NEDA in support of the UNDP-Assisted Project on Strengthening Institutional Mechanisms for Convergence of Poverty Alleviation Efforts, National Economic Development Authority, Manila.

Coady, D. P. 2004. Designing and Evaluating Social Safety Nets: Theory, Evidence, and Policy Conclusions. Food Consumption and Nutrition Division Discussion Paper No. 172, International Food Policy Research Institute, Washington, DC.

Coxhead, I. 2000. "Consequences of a Food Security Strategy for Economic Welfare, Income Distribution and Land Degradation: The Philippine Case." *World Development* 28(1):111–28.

DBM. Various years. *Budget of Expenditures and Sources of Financing.* Department of Budget and Management, Manila.

Farm Foundation. 2008. The 30-year Challenge: Agriculture's Role in Feeding and Fueling a Growing World. Issue Report No. 45719, Oak Brook, IL.

FAO. 2008. Crop Prospects and Food Situation No. 5. Food and Agriculture Organization, Rome. Available: www.fao.org/docrep/011/ai476e/ ai476e00.HTM.

FAO-OECD. 2008. *Agricultural Outlook 2008–2017*. Food and Agriculture Organization, Rome. Available: www.fao.org/es/esc/common/ecg/550/en/AgOut2017E.pdf?bcsi_scan_D4A612CF62FE9576=0&bcsi_scan_filename=AgOut2017E.pdf.

IFPRI. 2007. The World Food Situation: New Driving Forces and Required Actions. Food Policy Report, International Food Policy Research Institute, Washington, DC.

Meagher, P., K. Upadhyaya, and B. Wilkinson. 1999. Combating Rural Public Works Corruption: Food-for-Work Programs in Nepal. World Bank, Washington, DC. Processed.

Mehta, A., and S. Jha. 2009. Governance and Hunger: A Case Study from the Philippines. University of California-Santa Barbara Center Global Studies Working Paper No. 07, California.

Mitchell, D. 2008. A Note on Rising Food Prices. Policy Research Working Paper No. 4682, World Bank, Washington, DC.

NSO. 2006. *Family Income and Expenditure Survey 2006*. National Statistics Office, Manila.

OXAN. 2009. "Food Price Volatility is Still Likely." January 8. Oxford Analytica, England. Available: www.oxan.com/display.aspx?ItemID=DB147878.

Reno, A. R. 2009. "NFA Rice Procurement Highest since 1979." Available: business.inquirer.net/money/breakingnews/view/20090108–182057/NFA-rice-procurement-highest-since-1979.

Rogers, B. L., and J. Coates. 2002. Food Based Safety Nets and Related Programs. Social Protection Discussion Paper Series No. 225, World Bank Institute, Washington, DC.

Rosegrant, M. 2008. Biofuels and Grain Prices: Impacts and Policy Responses. International Food Policy Research Institute, Washington, DC. Available: www.ifpri.org/pubs/testimony/rosegrant20080507.pdf.

Roumasset, J. 2000. Black-hole Security. Working Paper No. 00–5, University of Hawaii, Manoa. Paper prepared for PRAEO meetings of the International Western Economic Association, Sydney.

Senate Economic Planning Office. 2006. *A Profile of Selected Philippine Government-Owned and Controlled Corporations*. Manila.

Subbarao, K., A. Bonnerjee, J. Braithwaite, S. Carvalho, K. Ezemenari, C. Graham, and A. Thompson. 1997. "Safety Net Programs and Poverty Reduction: Lessons from Cross-Country Experience." In *Directions in Development*. World Bank, Washington, DC.

Timmer, P. 2008. Causes of High Food Prices. ADB Economics Working Paper No. 128, Economics and Research Department, Asian Development Bank, Manila.

Trostle, R. 2008. Global Agricultural Supply and Demand: Factors Contributing to the Recent Increase in Food Commodity Prices. Economic Research Service Report WRS-0801, US Department of Agriculture, Washington, DC.

UNESCAP. 2000. *Social Safety Nets in the Philippines: Analysis and Prospects.* United Nations Economic and Social Commission for Asia and the Pacific, Bangkok.

World Bank. 2001. Philippines: Filipino Report Card on Pro-Poor Services. Report No. 22181-PH, Washington, DC.

_____. 2009. *Global Economic Prospects: Commodities at the Crossroads.* Washington, DC.

_____. Various years. Commodity Price Data (Pink Sheet). Available: econ. worldbank.org/WBSITE/EXTERNAL/EXTDEC/EXTDECPROSPECTS/ 0,contentMDK:21148472~menuPK:476941~pagePK:64165401~piPK: 64165026~theSitePK:476883,00.html.

Yao, R. T., G. E. Shively, and W. A. Masters. 2007. "How Successful are Government Interventions in Food Markets? Insights from the Philippines Rice Market." *Philippine Journal of Development* 34(1):35–59.

Index

G

H

Lightning Source UK Ltd.
Milton Keynes UK
UKOW050604170911

178794UK00001B/44/P